ABORTION

POLITICS, MORALITY AND THE CONSTITUTION

A Critical Study of ROE v. WADE and DOE v. BOLTON and a Basis for Change

Stephen M. Krason

Foreword by Senator John P. East

UNIVERSITY
PRESS OF
AMERICA

LANHAM • NEW YORK • LONDON

University Press of America,™ Inc.

4720 Boston Way
Lanham, MD 20706

3 Henrietta Street
London WC2E 8LU England

Library of Congress Cataloging in Publication Data

Krason, Stephen M.
Abortion : politics, morality, and the Constitution.

Includes index.
1. Abortion—Law and legislation—United States.
I. Title.
KF3771.K73 1984 344.73'0419 84-15192
ISBN 0-8191-4036-8 (alk. paper) 347.304419
ISBN 0-8191-4037-6 (pbk. : alk. paper)

All University Press of America books are produced on acid-free paper which exceeds the minimum standards set by the National Historical Publications and Records Commission.

DEDICATION

This book is dedicated to Frank E. Isaac, who first motivated my interest in politics and thus made my graduate and legal education, and ultimately this book, possible; and Dr. Richard H. Cox, my mentor, whose teaching and help enabled me to understand and accept the truths upon which my perspective in this book is based.

Copyright Permissions

Permission has been granted to use the quotations from the following: *Abortion and Social Justice* copyright © 1972 by Thomas W. Hilgers; *Democracy in America,* copyright © 1966 by Harper & Row; *The Morality of Abortion: Legal and Historical Perspectives*, copyright © 1970 by the Fellows of Harvard College; "Abortion and the Constitution: The Need for a Life-Protective Amendment," copyright © 1975 by California Law Review Inc.; "An American Tragedy: The Supreme Court on Abortion," copyright © 1973 by Fordham Law Review; *New Perspectives on Human Abortion*, copyright © 1981 by University Publications of America, Inc.; "The Phoenix of Abortional Freedom: Is a Penumbral or Ninth-Amendment Right About to Arise from the Nineteenth-Century Legislative Ashes of a Fourteenth-Century Common-Law Liberty," copyright © 1971 by New York Law School; *The Politics of Aristotle*, copyright © 1972 by Oxford University Press; "The Supreme Court on Abortion: The Socio-Political Impact of Judicial Activism," copyright © 1979 by John S. Putka; "Law and the Enforcement of Morals in Early America," copyright © 1971 by David H. Flaherty; *Privacy in Colonial New England*, copyright © 1972 by the Rectors and Visitors of the University of Virginia; "DeGeneratione Animalium," copyright © 1912, by Oxford University Press; "De Anima," copyright © 1931 by Oxford University Press; *The Abolition of Man*, copyright © 1947 by Macmillan Publishing Co.; "Abortion and Inalienable Rights in Classical Liberalism," copyright © 1975 by the University of Notre Dame; "Genetics, Politics, and the Image of Man," copyright © 1978 by the Human Life Foundation, Inc. (Reprinted from *The Human Life Review*, 150 East 35th St., New York, NY 10016. Subscription $15 per year); *John Locke's Two Treatises on Government* (Peter Laslett, ed.), copyright © 1963 by Cambridge University Press, publisher; *Abraham Lincoln and American Political*

COPYRIGHT PERMISSIONS

Acknowledgements

There are many whom I wish to thank for giving me assistance and advice in my research and writing of this book, which was originally my Ph.D. dissertation. First of all, I wish to thank my Ph.D. dissertation advisor, Dr. Richard H. Cox. I owe him a great debt of gratitude, not only for his assistance on the dissertation, but over the entire course of my graduate school career. I also thank the other members of my dissertation committee, Dr. Richard B. Friedman, Dr. Stephen C. Halpern, and Prof. W. Howard Mann. Prof. Mann's influence during my law school career is reflected especially in my analysis and proposal in Appendix A.

I thank the Christopher Baldy Center for Law and Social Policy at the State University of New York at Buffalo for providing funding to permit me to work full-time on the dissertation, and the Political Science Department of the same university for various types of assistance while I was doing my research. I also thank Mr. John F. Lulves, Jr. and the Intercollegiate Studies Institute, Inc. for their kind assistance.

I want to especially acknowledge two valued friends, Robert Wise and Timothy Hubbard, who provided me with much needed materials, ideas, advice and, in Tim's case, transportation while doing my research. They are deeply appreciated friends.

My gratitude goes to Mr. Edward Golden and Mrs. Helen Greene who kindly granted me interviews.

Many individuals and organizations supplied materials and information, answered specific inquiries, and/or gave suggestions. Among them are: James Likoudis, Dr. Raphael T. Waters, Dr. John D. McLaughlin, Planned Parenthood of Buffalo and especially Mrs. Jane Holland of its volunteer staff, Mrs. J. C. Willke and Greater Cincinnati Right to Life, Dr. and Mrs. Thomas A. O'Connor, the National Right to Life Committee, Gail P. Quinn of the National Conference of Catholic Bishops' Respect Life Program, Dr. Norman C. Thomas, Dr. Daniel Novak, Prof. Norman Dorsen, Dr. Paul M. Dowling, James Gaston, Stuart Gudowitz, Mr. and Mrs. Paul Likoudis, Michael C. Schwartz of the Catholic League for Religious and Civil Rights, Rev. James X. O'Reilly, Minnesota Citizens Concerned for Life, American Psychiatric Association, American College of Obstetricians and Gynecologists, New York State Right to Life Committee, and Eric D. Smith.

I must offer my warmest thanks to Mrs. Judie Brown, President of American Life Lobby, Catholics United for the Faith, the Buffalo Regional Right to Life Committee, Inc., Mrs. Ann O'Donnell, Howard Lee Cheek, Jr., and many other individuals, organizations, and institutions, too numerous to name, who helped me promote the book or responded to my appeals to insure a sufficient number of pre-publication orders to permit this book to go to press.

I must thank Mrs. Elizabeth Atkins, who did an outstanding job in the typing of the book manuscript and Gregory Wolfe for typesetting the chapter and section titles. More thanks than I can ever express must go to Mrs. Mary Ann Sanscrainte for her undeserved gift of typing the manuscript of the doctoral dissertation that the book is based on. Such generosity is almost without parallel, and proves that God will help us if we trust Him.

Lastly, but in no way least, I wish to thank my beloved wife Therese, a devoted fighter for life, for her assistance in doing the Index and in proofreading and preparing the manuscript for publication under the pressures of a fast-approaching deadline, and generally for her considerable help, support, and advice--and for her constant and unconditional love.

S.M.K.
May 31, 1984

Table of Contents

Table of Figures

Foreword

A decade after the United States Supreme Court tried to settle the abortion issue, it is plainly evident that it did not. When it legalized abortion, the Court failed socially. It failed medically. It failed legally. And it failed politically. Because of these failures, the movement to reverse *Roe v. Wade*, and to establish the constitutional right to life of unborn children remains alive and determined.

The *Roe* ruling failed socially because it struck at the heart of society's traditional reverence for the sanctity of all human life. By declaring that the unborn child is not a "person" under the Constitution, the Supreme Court divorced the concept of personhood from that of humanness. In spite of the decree, many Americans passionately continue to hold that all humans, regardless of their degree of biological development, are persons who have the most basic right to live. These "right-to-lifers" are a sociological phenomenon because they constitute a rare social activist group--one that does not have its own self-interest at stake.

The Court's medical failure lies in its putting the medical profession at war with itself. At a time when the development of fetal monitoring and intrauterine treatment techniques are enabling doctors to consider the fetus a patient, others in the profession work to perfect abortion methods so that no unwanted child will emerge from the womb alive. Whether the doctor will heal or kill the unborn child in a given case is solely the mother's choice, which reduces the physician to a mere technician.

Perhaps more ominous, *Roe v. Wade* gave rise to the "wrongful life" theory of legal action, which is enjoying increasing acceptance in Federal and state courts. This development gives the parents of a handicapped child the right to sue the doctor who attended the pregnancy when they can show that he should have discovered the defect so that an abortion could have been obtained. The resulting pressures on physicians encourage infanticide as doctors seek to avoid potential financial liability for children whom they "negligently" caused to be born alive.

That the threat of legalized infanticide against handicapped newborn children might be a real one was demonstrated convincingly by the famous "Baby Doe" case at Bloomington, Indiana in April 1982. The Down's syndrome baby boy's death by starvation, at his parents' request and with the approval of the Indiana Supreme Court, called public attention to a practice that is widely believed to occur hundreds, perhaps even thousands of times every year in the United States. Widespread revulsion at "Baby Doe's" starvation death led the Reagan Administration's Department of Health and Human Services to promulgate a tough anti-infanticide regulation. The "Baby Doe Rule" was challenged in Federal court by the American Academy of Pediatrics. With "Baby Doe's" death, then, the battle over infanticide was joined.

Roe is a legal failure because it engendered the nearly universal scorn of constitutional scholars from across the ideological spectrum. U.S. Solicitor General Rex Lee was charitable when, in his 1982 brief for the Supreme Court on three pending abortion cases, he told the Court that the *Roe* right to an abortion was constructed on a foundation of constitutional shadows. There is no support whatever for the notion that the framers of the Fourteenth Amendment even remotely considered abortion, much less intended to guarantee access to it, yet that part of the Constitution is where the Court claimed that the right to abort is grounded.

The *Roe v. Wade* decision failed politically because it was extreme. With it, the Court struck down the abortion laws of all 50 states. Before *Roe*, those few states that permitted elective abortions at all allowed them only early in pregnancy. After *Roe*, each was required to permit abortion on demand through the second trimester of pregnancy. *Roe* requires states to allow an abortion, even after the point at which the fetus becomes viable outside the womb, when the mother's life or health would be endangered by a live birth. In *Roe*'s companion case, *Doe v. Bolton*, the Court defined health so broadly as to include threats to emotional well-being.

Such a sweeping frustration of the legislatively expressed will of the people of every state was bound to produce a fierce political reaction, and did. Since 1973, the abortion issue has remained one of the most hotly debated and controversial items on the agenda of the Congress. Though Congress has not acted to reverse *Roe*, it has voted repeatedly to restrict severely the Federal funding of abortions.

While the popular view of the Senate's June 1983 defeat of a constitutional amendment to reverse the Supreme Court's abortion decisions is that it was a humiliating loss for the cause, in reality the vote underscored the political weakness of *Roe v. Wade*. The fact that the Senate vote took place at all is progress for the opponents of *Roe*. Prior to 1982, when the Senate Committee on the Judiciary first voted to overturn *Roe*, no anti-*Roe* measure had been cleared for action on the floor of either House of Congress. Before the Senate vote, neither body had considered such an amendment.

Counting leading anti-*Roe* Senator Jesse Helms, who abstained on principle because the proposal was not strong enough, 50 U.S. Senators now are on record as favoring a constitutional amendment to reverse *Roe v. Wade*. Regardless of the tactical wisdom of forcing a vote on an amendment that was well short of the 67 votes that the Constitution requires for passage, the Senate vote served the useful purpose of demonstrating that *Roe* is so constitutionally and intellectually flawed that it has failed to generate a political consensus behind it. Ultimately, in fact, politics may pave the way for *Roe*'s final undoing by the Court itself.

What are the chances that the Court itself might reverse the controversial *Roe v. Wade* decision? There are signs of genuine hope for that prospect in the Supreme Court's June 1983 reaffirmation of *Roe* in its *Akron* decision.*

---

* *City of Akron v. Akron Center for Reproductive Health*, 103 S.Ct. 2481 (1983).

One sign of hope came from the *Akron* dissent of the newest Justice, Sandra D. O'Connor. Though previous dissenters to Supreme Court abortion rulings have confined themselves to attacking *Roe*'s constitutional weakness, Justice O'Connor's critique of the *Akron* decision took a new tack. Justice O'Connor exposed the internal inconsistency of *Roe*'s abortion regulatory framework. *Roe v. Wade*, she argued, bore the seeds of its own destruction.

Under *Roe*, the absolute right to an abortion theoretically exists only so long as it remains statistically safer for the mother's health than normal childbirth. The countervailing power of the states to protect the life of the unborn child is tied to viability. As Justice O'Connor noted, medical science will continue to enhance the safety of abortions that are performed ever later in pregnancy. Simultaneously, technological advances will enable doctors to save the lives of ever more prematurely born infants. Thus, asserted Justice O'Connor, the regulatory scheme of *Roe* is on a collision course with itself. It cannot survive.

The other principal sign of hope in the Court's 1983 reaffirmation of the 1973 *Roe v. Wade* ruling has to do with that body's membership. With the addition of Justice O'Connor, the anti-*Roe* minority on the Court has grown to three of the five Justices who will be required in order to reverse the abortion decisions. The average age of that minority is 59. It includes the two youngest Justices.

The six-man, pro-*Roe* majority on the Court, by contrast, is edging towards retirement. The average age of these Justices is 73. It is very likely that President Reagan, whose opposition to *Roe v. Wade* is well-known, would receive the opportunity to appoint at least two more members of the Court by the end of a second term in 1989. In fact, such vacancies could occur by the end of the President's first term in January 1985.

Under attack after the close of its first decade as constitutionally shallow, intellectually flawed, and politically vulnerable, *Roe v. Wade* may not endure through its second. Those observers who assert that its recent confirmation by the Supreme Court, coupled with the setback for its opponents in the Senate, spell the end of the threat to *Roe* are mistaken. It continues to stand on shaky ground. Eventually, *Roe v. Wade* will fall.

Stephen M. Krason's searching and scholarly critique of the Supreme Court's abortion privacy doctrine, as enunciated in *Roe v. Wade* and *Doe v. Bolton* in 1973, is a significant contribution to the case for its reversal. He brings to his work the multi-faceted analytical perspective of one who is trained professionally in the fields of law, political science, and theology. Those lawyers who someday will work on the Supreme Court case that becomes the vehicle by which *Roe v. Wade* is reversed will find Dr. Krason's book to be a very useful tool.

Dr. Krason's extensive survey of the legal, political, and philosophical literature on the abortion question will make his book valuable to others in the anti-abortion cause as well. For victory in the Supreme Court cannot be depended upon as the only hope to end abortion on demand in America. The battle must be fought on many fronts. Dr. Krason's book will help the legislative lobbyists who push for pro-life legislation. It will help the political activists who fight for pro-life candidates in elections at many levels of government. And it will aid those who channel their pro-life energies into educating the public. But perhaps most important, it will serve as one more bit of evidence that the will to resist the worst decision in the history of the Supreme Court has not abated.

The Honorable John P. East
Chairman

Steven R. Valentine
Counsel

Subcommittee on Separation of Powers
Committee on the Judiciary
United States Senate

Washington, D.C.
September 30, 1983.

Introduction

Once or twice a century, an issue comes along which shakes a nation to its foundations. It requires us to put to ourselves, as individuals and as a people, questions that many would just as soon avoid: What do we really believe in? What principles take precedence for us? What do we want our way of life to be like? Slavery was such an issue in the last century; abortion is today.

Abortion and slavery are also alike in that they are different from most other national issues in that they allow little room for compromise. There is no in-between position or neutrality about abortion. If one says that he is "personally opposed" to abortion, but will not make a judgment for others, or even if one is silent about it, he implicitly takes a position and gets to the heart of the public issue of abortion, which is whether our political society should tolerate its practice. In another sense, abortion is *unlike* slavery and virtually every other political issue. This is because it concerns the most profound of human questions and experiences: life and death, duties to others, sex, marriage and family. It is also something which has the potential, in this era when it is so widespread, of touching each of our lives in some way.

In 1973, the U. S. Supreme Court sought to resolve this issue in a way which would virtually close off all future attempts for political resolution and supposedly usher it off the public agenda. The Court had tried to do that with slavery too, in *Dred Scott v. Sandford*. Men often do not know history or do not learn from it, however. This was so with the Justices who comprised the majority in the abortion cases, *Roe v. Wade* and *Doe v. Bolton*. Any objective observer of the American scene in the years since then will acknowledge that abortion hardly has vanished from the public forum. If anything, the decisions ignited an even more intense controversy and shifted it from the state level to the national level. The abortion issue is thus a timely and important subject for any student of American politics.

A thorough study of the abortion question, which I have attempted in this book, must be at once general and specific. It must be general because there are many dimensions to the question: moral, constitutional, medical, biological, political, social, philosophical, and historical. It must be specific because to understand abortion in present-day America we must know what the Supreme Court said in its opinions which created our national policy on the subject. In this book, I examine the specific, the *Wade* and *Bolton* opinions and the briefs submitted to the Court in these cases, and move from them to the general since within their pages these various dimensions all appear. I am critically studying the policy that *exists*: how it developed, the reasons used to justify it, the broader thinking which motivated it. Thus, I focus my attention on the pro-abortion briefs and views. I confine my attention -- except for scattered references -- to the two main decisions by the Court. These deal with the primary question of whether abortion should be legal and set down the basic policy. The decisions that followed merely clarified or extended this basic policy (by, for example, determining whether spousal or parental consent should be required for abortion) or deal with subsidiary issues (such as whether the government should pay for abortions for poor women).

I cover all of the dimensions of the problem mentioned, to some degree. I look at the points brought up in the opinions and the briefs and question them, respond to them, and inquire into their accuracy. In doing this, I consider, where necessary, other materials and the effect of the policy in the years since its adoption. I examine, in particular depth, the broader issues of constitutional law and political philosophy indicated in the opinions and briefs. I also examine the efforts of the movement to change the restrictive anti-abortion laws which culminated in the *Wade* and *Bolton* decisions.

A comprehensive critique of these decisions and the pro-abortion position makes up the bulk of this book and leads up to my attempt to show how the American political order should deal with abortion in the final Chapter.

I am concerned about justice and I agree with Aristotle and the other classical political philosophers that it is the central political question. Notice, however, that I do not say that I want to show how a *just* political order should deal with abortion, but how the *American* political order should. I am proposing an alternative to the Supreme Court's "solution." It is true that it is the alternative which, I believe, is dictated by justice and by the truth -- meaning that it is based on a true assessment of the nature of and justifications for abortion, the requirements of our Constitution, and the nature of life in the womb -- but is also compatible with our traditions and the character of our political order and the realities of political life today. Our political order was intended by its Founders to be concerned about justice, but its primary preoccupation was to be the protection of the natural rights of individuals. Most provisions of the Bill of Rights, as well as the way the political order has typically proceeded when it has sought to protect these natural rights, make it seem that liberty is the foremost, if not the most basic, one. America is linked to the political philosophy of classical antiquity, but it is a state founded on the principles of the "new political science" as formulated by the early modern political thinkers. Thus, although I turn to the classics to propose a resolution of the abortion issue, I acknowledge that this can only be done within the context of our American political tradition.

The solution I put forth in the final Chapter will be said by many to be unconstitutional, politically unrealistic, or not in accord with America's political traditions. They will make such criticisms because they will approach the subject with a contemporary political perspective. This, however, is *not* the perspective that was present at America's Founding. The fact is that the Framers of our Constitution and their contemporaries and the political thinkers that they relied upon did *not* believe liberty to be absolute or government to be barred from legislating to promote virtue or to regulate what are commonly called matters of "personal morality." I am asking America to return to her roots in resolving the abortion issue. This does not mean that I do not give current thought and prejudices about liberty their due. On the contrary, it will be seen that I place a premium on political prudence. I accept the need to deal carefully with this issue and face the limitations imposed by political realities, but I favor no accommodation with these contemporaries on the level of principle -- as regards either their flawed notions about the American political order or the application of these to abortion.

Abortion is often said to be a religious issue, and it *is* in the sense that most religious traditions have some moral teaching about it. It is *not* a religious issue, however, if by "religious" one means that a public resolution of the question is impossible without reference to religious doctrine (with the result that the only possible solution is for government to let it be a matter of "individual choice"). I agree that, in our type of political order, neither abortion not any other political issue should be decided on the basis of sectarian religious principles. I agree with Claremont political science professor Harry V. Jaffa's following statement about the undesirability of using Thomistic thought -- which is primarily found in the Catholic tradition -- as a basis for our social science (and, it follows implicitly, for our social policy):

> ...our social science, if it is to be of any use, must be addressed to Moslems and Jews as well as to Christians, to Buddhists and Hindus as well as to believers in the Bible; it must finally, be addressed "not only to those who enjoy the blessings and consolations of revealed religion, but also to those who face the mysteries of human destiny alone."[1]

While America's religious differences are not as great as

the entire world's (to which Jaffa refers), our nation *is* pluralistic. Most of us share the Judeo-Christian tradition, but within this there are, of course, diverse beliefs. The response of the contemporary liberal on an issue like abortion has been like that mentioned above. He calls upon our political order to embrace in large part, moral relativism as its official philosophy. Its law and policy should forbid only those actions which an overwhelming consensus agrees is wrong or which clearly harm the state or the "public interest" (as defined by liberals) or do physical or mental harm to individuals. There is usually no concern with what is right or wrong or what is best for man according to his nature and his end as man.

As an alternative, Jaffa proposes classical thought and, in particular, Aristotle. He does this, partly, for the same reason I stated above as my preference for the classics: because of their concern for justice as the rightful end of politics. It is more broadly, however, because they recognize the existence of a natural moral order of which man is part and which defines his true nature. This moral order determines what are the proper ends of his existence. Man's end -- the happiness which comes from leading a virtuous life -- is inseparable from justice. This is because justice, the end of politics, is possible only when men individually are trying to achieve their rightful end.

This book, as probably is apparent already, takes a strong position on the abortion issue. This position is not the result of pre-determined bias or sectarian belief, however. It was formed only after much serious consideration of the facts about unborn life and the harms from abortion and of the nature of rights and the role of law in our political order. It should further be noted that I came to my conclusion that abortion should not be legal after previously thinking the opposite.

I have written this book in the hope that it will motivate other people similarly to think more deeply about the abortion issue and to consider aspects that they may not have considered before. Perhaps people who vaguely think that our present policy of virtual abortion-on-demand is undesirable, but are not yet able to say they oppose legalized abortion, will find here -- if they approach this question with an openness to the truth -- the facts and arguments that will convince them.

This book also has other purposes. First, I hope it can serve as a sourcebook for persons in the anti-abortion movement -- scholars, lawyers, and laymen alike -- and can be a place for them to turn for new arguments to justify anti-abortion legislation. Second, I hope that sympathetic legislators will find it to be a valuable tool to use in the shaping of a new public policy on abortion. Finally, I have written this for those students and scholars of political philosophy who, like Jaffa, are concerned about our positive law concurring with the natural moral order, but who fear the use of religious doctrines to accomplish this on an issue like abortion. I hope that I have provided them with a reasonable line of argument which will accomplish their objective and yet allay their fears.

Abortion is primarily a moral question. What should become apparent from the pages that follow, however, is that it is also a pressing political question for America. It is not political just in the sense that it is an issue in campaigns or that probably it will have to be resolved in the end by the political branches of the government, but also because it represents a clash of drastically different political philosophies. On this level, it can have far-reaching implications -- it can indeed shake our nation to its foundations. Pro-abortionism, like a number of other public movements and ideologies in recent times -- some of which have focused on matters closely related to it -- holds an implicit view of politics which challenges that of our Founding Fathers. This is seen in its eagerness to ignore certain points which they regarded as essential for a republic to survive: political liberty as opposed to individual license; the need for a virtuous and self-restrained citizenry; the right of our popular institutions to make our public policy; and the existence of at least a limited notion of public morality. Under the onslaught of thinking such as this, the common understanding about the nature of our political order has been transformed. The question may now be: Can our republic, our liberal democracy, continue as it has been when the conditions for its existence and the philosophy behind it have been altered? Abortion, then, is an issue that all Americans must confront and decide about.

Chapter One

The Backdrop for the Supreme Court's Decisions: The Emergence of the Pro-Abortion Consensus and the Movement Opposing It

Introduction

The effort to legalize abortion culminating in the 1973 Supreme Court decisions at first involved only a tiny number of persons from primarily the medical and legal communities. It began with a few books, conferences, and proposals that gained little public notice. It grew into a massive national political movement that turned abortion into a major political issue, and influenced legislatures and courts to change a legal standard that had prevailed for most of history.

This historical review of the social, political, and legal dimensions of the abortion battle before 1973 is important because without it we cannot understand how the Supreme Court decisions came about. It is almost certain that the determined push to change the abortion laws and the shaping of a new national consensus, at least among the most influential elements in American political society, were responsible for the decisions. Before the 1960s, the matter of abortion was hardly discussed and little was written about it. As we shall see, there was little agitation to change the laws and virtually no claims that abortion was a legal right. Professor John T. Noonan, Jr. of the law school at the University of California at Berkeley and a scholar of the abortion issue writes that "[p]olitically, the subject was untouchable before the 1960s. No one in a public forum sought to challenge the accepted limits."[1] Obviously, much had changed within less than a decade and a half.

Although I shall begin by speaking about the issue before the 1960s, the focus of my historical survey shall be the 1962 to 1972 period. I have selected this time frame because it takes us from the start of the public debate over liberalizing the abortion laws[2] at the time of the unveiling of the American Law Institute's (ALI) model reform statute and the thalidomide scare of 1962 to the eve of the announcement of the *Wade* and *Bolton* decisions.

The Abortion Issue Before the 1960s

Prior to the 1960s, the push for legal abortion had not galvanized into an identifiable movement. There were no groups officially seeking to change the laws or devoted exclusively to a concern with abortion and there appears to have been no political activity. The only activity consisted of two professional conferences (in 1942 and 1954) and a small number of books on the subject. It was mostly physicians and, to a lesser extend, lawyers who were involved.

The groundwork for the contemporary pro-abortion movement was laid by Dr. Abraham Rongy in his 1933 book *Abortion: Legal or Illegal?*[3] In this polemical work, he focused on two themes which have become familiar in pro-abortion rhetoric: that abortion statutes were an inappropriate intrusion of Christian -- specifically, Catholic -- morality into the law and that they were undesirable because of the allegedly widespread violations of them by physicians.[4] His book was sponsored by the National Committee on Maternal Health, a private group composed of certain elements in the American birth control movement.[5] This movement usually took pains to sharply distinguish between contraception and abortion.

What is said later in this Chapter about Margaret Sanger, however, raises questions about how strong its opposition to abortion really was.

In 1936, the first comprehensive study of the abortion problem was published: Dr. Frederick J. Taussig's *Abortion Spontaneous and Induced*.[6] The book dealt with the medical, historical, anthropological, economic, theological, ethical, and legal aspects of abortion. It also examined legal abortion in the Soviet Union. It was not solely a reference work, however, as it contained the author's recommendations for the regulation of abortion, assailed the existing laws as "certainly antiquated,"[7] and expressed the hope that it "may prove of some value in stimulating thought and furnishing data that may serve as a basis for a program of revision."[8] He also repeated Rongy's theme that the "unjust" laws were turning physicians into lawbreakers.[9]

In 1942, a conference on all aspects of abortion was held under the auspices of the National Committee on Maternal Health. Its proceedings were published as a book enditled *The Abortion Problem*.[10] According to its chairman, Dr. Howard C. Taylor, Jr., the conference concluded that the law could do little to remedy a supposedly acute abortion problem. Public opinion, and particularly medical opinion, had to be changed and sex education and contraceptive information had to be made more widely available.[11] This conference thus first put forth the position, frequently heard in pro-abortion argumentation today, that if contraception were only more widely available and people better "educated" about sex, the "need" for abortion would disappear.[12]

Another conference was organized by the Planned Parenthood Federation of America (PPFA) held in New York City in 1954. Unlike the 1942 conference, it excluded a consideration of spontaneous abortion and focused only on induced. An edited version of the proceedings of the conference was published as a book in 1958 under the title of *Abortion in the United States*, edited by Dr. Mary Steichen Calderone, the Medical Director of PPFA and later head of the Sex Information and Education Council of the United States (SIECUS).[13]

The "Statement" at the back of the book summarizing the conference and spelling out its recommendations appears in retrospect as a blueprint for action for the pro-legalized abortion movement. It echoes the 1942 conference and the books mentioned above when it states that maintaining laws "that do not receive public sanction and observance is of questionable service to our society."[14] It likewise views the increased availability of contraception and sex education as a way to reduce the number of abortions while saying the restrictive laws prevent this. Two points are made which will be emphasized by the abortion movement in the years ahead: the laws must be changed to cut down on illegal abortions and the laws are unfair because they make abortions available to the educated and affluent but not to the underprivileged. An insight into the thought behind the conference is seen in its recommendations for sex education and new laws. It calls for a "realistic" sex education, as well as "higher standards of sexual conduct" and "a greater sense of responsibility toward pregnancy." It also says that it seeks statutes which "recognize the mounting approval of phychiatric, humanitarian, and eugenic indications for the legal termination of pregnancy" (the later common pro-abortion euphemism for the procedure was already being used) and which "give to physicians the latitude to include these indications in their recommendations for therapeutic abortion."[15]

Most remarkable, in light of what I shall go on to say about the push for legalized abortion in the 1960s, is the closing paragraph of the "Statement." It calls upon the resource organizations for the drafting of model legislation -- the National Conference of Commissioners on Uniform State Laws, the American Law Institute (ALI), and the Council of State Governments -- to propose new (liberalized) statutes and upon "professional organizations in the various fields of medicine, law, religion, sociology, and education" to "recognize the present importance and ramifications of the abortion problem." It hopes that they might then "by developing a body of informed opinion within their own ranks, be instrumental in developing a body of informed opinion among the citizens of this country, so that solutions... would be approached...in the most enlightened and democratic manner possible."[16] Many of these organizations eventually heeded the conference's call.

Three important books also came out in the 1950s: Dr. Harold Rosen's anthology *Therapeutic Abortion* in 1954[17] (revised and reprinted as *Abortion in America* in 1967), Glanville Williams' *The Sanctity of Life and the Criminal Law* in 1957,[18] and Dr. Alfred Kinsey's *Pregnancy, Birth and Abortion* in 1958.[19] All were directed essentially at professional audiences.

Rosen's book grew out of a panel at the 1952 meeting of the American Psychiatric Association. Most of its chapters deal with facets of the psychiatric questions surrounding abortion. It demonstrates the early involvement of psychiatrists in the issue.

The Kinsey study supplied some of the first allegedly "hard facts" on the abortion problem in America, including the frequency of abortions and information about the characteristics of women who get them and about whether illegal abortions were mostly performed by physicians. His data possibly provided useful information for the pro-abortionists to build their case in the years ahead.

I was informed that the Williams book was very influential in shaping the legal and philosophical thinking on abortion[20] and a glance at it shows that it sets out some of the major arguments which became the standard fare of abortion advocates within the next decade. One is the "tragedy" of the "unwanted" child. It viewed abortion as a "humanitarian" means of eliminating the "appalling cruelty" committed against "unwanted" children.[21] Another, echoing Rongy, is that laws against abortion are inappropriate because they are based on religious beliefs. This is no longer valid because "abortion is no longer thought to be wrong." Further, he indicates that he believes that since abortion is relatively safe when done by a skilled physician the laws cannot be justified on medical grounds.[22] He explains what the relationship between the state and the medical community should be on this issue:

> If abortion is no longer thought to be wrong, it is not permissible to turn around and attempt to justify the abortion laws on medical grounds, even if the operation is regarded as medically undesirable, because it is not for the legislature to pronounce upon this. Had such an attitude been adopted in the days before Pasteur, the law might logically have forbidden all surgical operations, which killed as often as they cured; but fortunately

> medicine was left to do its best and to improve its methods. The invocation of medicine to justify the abortion laws is to use the name of science to forbid scientific progress.[23]

This view, as we shall see, was eventually to translate itself into the Supreme Court's decree that the abortion decision should be left to "the medical judgment of the pregnant woman's attending physician."[24]

Williams also made the argument which was to become the chief cry of feminists: that abortion laws interfere with a woman's right to control her own body.[25] He dismissed the argument that legal change would cause sexual restraint to break down, and insisted that the law should not "punish" a woman for illicit sexual intercourse. His statement that this could not justify the sweeping nature of the restrictions on abortion because most are performed on married women will later be seen in the main pro-abortion brief in the *Wade* case (See Chapter Four).

Williams also explicitly endorses the ideology behind the pro-abortion position and the *Wade* and *Bolton* opinions: modern relativism. He claims that "[in] utilitarian philosophy [which he implies is what Western society adheres to], the welfare of every member of society must be considered, even when he is breaking the law. Punishment is an evil that can be justified... only when the evil of punishment...is less than the evil...from the want of penal restraint"[26] and that "legal inquisition into conduct is not justified on moral or religious grounds if no sufficient social purpose is to be served."[27]

Thus, the philosophical and tactical groundwork for the pro-legalized abortion movement had been laid before the 1960s. The only thing needed now was a catalyst to galvanize it into a political force, convince important professional organizations to endorse legal change, and, most importantly, to shift public opinion enough to make serious public debate about it possible. This came in the form of the thalidomide scare of 1962.

The Shaping of the Consensus for Legalization, 1962-1972

The Significant Role of Organized Groups

The involvement of private organizations, many of which were nationwide, prominent, and influential, in the abortion issue -- mostly as advocates for changing the laws -- began in 1962.

It was not their activity alone which built up pressure for changing the laws. Pro-change organizations were joined by important organs of the press and, later on, by groups and legislators working actively in legislatures to enact new laws. Books and academic articles were written and conferences held which promoted the cause of new laws. I am inclined to believe, however, that the public statements and position papers of prominent groups, especially medical and religious ones, may have been the most convincing influence on legislators. The political parties could not provide a guide for a matter like abortion, so organized groups were the ones looked to. The groups which had been most outspoken on abortion -- at least until the years just before 1973, when feminist groups emerged -- were medical and religious ones. Also, legislators turned to these particular types of groups because in the popular thinking -- when a person did not look more deeply into it -- abortion appeared to be a medical and religious issue. Later, it also appeared to be an issue of "women's rights." These groups may have been more influential than even the most respected organs of the press, such as *The New York Times*. This is because, in the mind of the legislator, the specialized knowledge and expertise of members of these groups would likely weigh heavier than what would seem to be merely the political preferences of editorialists.

The same analysis does not apply to Justices of the Supreme Court. Their role and frame of reference is different, even if, in essence, they often engage in the same sort of activity. Nevertheless, organized groups may have had an important part in shaping their thinking also. As I will show in the next Chapter, medical views and disagreements among religious groups on abortion were important factors in the making of their decisions in *Wade* and *Bolton*. The possible influence of organized groups is suggested further by the substantial number of them, including many prominent ones, which either joined the appellants' briefs or filed *amicus curiae* briefs in the cases, calling for the Court to strike down the anti-abortion statutes. These groups have a wide range of purposes. Some are concerned with health, such as the American College of Obstetricians and Gynecologists (ACOG), the American Public Health Association (APHA), the American Psychiatric Association (APA), the New York Academy of Medicine, and the Planned Parenthood Federation of America (PPFA) (though there could be arguments raised about whether it is appropriate to call the latter a "health" organization). There were religious groups, such as the United Church of Christ, the American Jewish Congress, the New York State Council of Churches, and the Unitarian Universalist Association. There were womens' organizations, such as the National Organization for Women (NOW), the American Association of University Women (AAUW), and the Professional Women's Caucus. There were legal groups, or groups which touch the law and some other area of concern, such as the American Civil Liberties Union (ACLU), the National Legal Program on Health Problems of the Poor, and New Women Lawyers.[28] There were also organizations concerned specifically with the abortion or population questions, such as the National Abortion Action Coalition, the California Committee to Legalize Abortion, and Zero Population Growth, Inc. Organizations also filed briefs urging affirmance of the laws, but their numbers were dwarfed by those wanting their invalidation.[29]

Alexis de Tocqueville is generally thought of as one of the most astute and insightful commentators ever on the American political order, and his monumental *Democracy in America* reveals the role played by independent associations in a democracy. Modern political scientists have followed Tocqueville in emphasizing the importance of group activity in American politics.[30] Tocqueville explains why groups or associations assume the importance they do in a democracy:

> Aristocratic communities always contain, amongst a multitude of persons who by them-

> selves are powerless, a small number of powerful and wealthy citizens, each of whom can achieve great undertakings singlehanded. In aristocratic societies men do not need to combine in order to act, because they are strongly held together. Amongst democratic nations, on the contrary, all the citizens are independent and feeble; they can do hardly anything by themselves, and none of them can oblige his fellow-men to lend him their assistance. They all, therefore, fall into a state of incapacity, if they do not learn voluntarily to help each other.[31]

Tocqueville also writes about associations in the U. S. being formed "to resist enemies which are exclusively of a moral nature" and gives the example of temperance.[32] As we shall see, the activity on the abortion question -- both for and against the restrictive laws -- for the most part falls into this category.[33]

Tocqueville's assessment of how associations come together and operate also seems pertinent to the abortion campaign in the U.S. He says that an association consists simply in the "public assent which a number of individuals give to certain doctrines, and in the engagement which they contract to promote the spread of those doctrines by their exertions."[34] All the organizations that filed briefs and/or took public positions on abortion fit this description. Most of the pro-legalized abortion associations were standing organizations, set up for purposes broader than advocacy of this one issue. One of their primary activities, however, is to promote public policies which they believe will help them carry out these purposes. Most of the "anti"-groups -- the Catholic Church would be a notable exception -- were organized to promote, almost exclusively, their position on abortion and closely related issues.

Finally, we should take note of one other point made by Tocqueville:

> Nothing, in my opinion, is more deserving of our attention than the intellectual and moral associations of America. The political and industrial associations of that country strike us forcibly; but the others elude our

> observation, or if we discover them, we understand them imperfectly, because we have hardly ever seen anything of the kind. It must, however, be acknowledged that they are as necessary to the American people as the former, and perhaps more so.[35]

The abortion issue -- particularly the pro-abortion position -- is a clear contemporary example of what Tocqueville says about the importance of "intellectual and moral associations" in American life. Virtually all of the organizations on both sides were either "intellectual" ones -- i.e., organizations of professionals who have had to meet fairly high academic criteria and who provide an important service to the public -- or "moral" ones -- i.e., those seeking to promote an established set of moral doctrines (e.g., churches or church organizations) and those set up to promote a position on this one specific issue or a related group of issues (e.g., the various anti-abortion and feminist groups). The former -- at least as judged from the groups active in the abortion issue -- are organized in part to promote their pecuniary ends. They also seek to promote matters in the specific areas of their concern which will benefit others or the public at large (e.g., good medical service so as to insure good public health). The latter are exclusively seeking to promote in society and through public policy particular philosophical or moral positions. Any pecuniary benefit to them redounds only indirectly and, perhaps, unintentionally.

Year-by-Year Events

1962

In the early 1960s in Europe, babies with deformed or underdeveloped limbs were being born to mothers who had taken the tranquilizer thalidomide, which was manufactured and used primarily in Europe, during early stages of their pregnancies. The effects of this drug are discussed more fully in Chapter Six. This tragedy reached the U.S. in the summer of 1962 when a Phoenix, Arizona housewife and television personality, who had recently become pregnant, began taking thalidomide pills that had been prescribed for her husband when on a trip to Europe. After reading in the local newspaper about what thalidomide had done in Europe, Mrs. Sherri Finkbine went to her doctor. He told her that her chances of having a deformed baby were great and recommended a "therapeutic" abortion. He arranged it for her by approaching the local three-doctor medical board which had to approve the requests for such abortions.[36] Mrs. Finkbine, saying that she wanted to help other women avoid her predicament, called the local newspapers to ask them to run an article on thalidomide without revealing her name. The newspaper agreed, but instead of the low-keyed article simply warning about the drug which she expected, it ran a front-page story which shouted in bold headlines: **"Drug Causing Deformed Infants May Cost Woman Her Baby Here."**

The story quickly went out on the wire services and attracted international attention. The doctors, fearing widespread publicity and criminal prosecution, cancelled her scheduled abortion and petitioned the Arizona Supreme Court for a declaratory judgment about whether what they regarded as the "vague" state abortion statute would permit them to proceed. The case was dismissed, but Mrs. Finkbine's name became public as a result of the action and she quickly became the center of controversy as passions were raised both for and against her. Unable to get a legal abortion anywhere in the U.S., she went to Sweden.[37]

The New York Times followed the development of the story from the time it broke to the abortion in Sweden, but it focused most of its attention on the problem of the dangers of marketed drugs to the public.[38] It did not concern itself much with the abortion law. *Time* and *Newsweek*, on the other hand, strongly emphasized the plight of the Finkbines in light of the restrictive law and prominently quoted Mrs. Finkbine as saying how terrible it would be to let a child live deformed. This was the only context in which the unborn child's welfare was discussed in any of the publications. Both also ran pictures of a visibly anguished Mrs. Finkbine giving a motherly embrace to her young son.[39] *Time* and *Newsweek* seem to have intended to create sympathy for what they saw as an upright young couple victimized by an unfair law.

The Finkbine case also stirred a conflict among religious leaders. The Bishop of the Episcopal Church in Arizona and a prominent local Baptist pastor said the abortion was justified. A local rabbi called it "'a merciful act of justice.'" Rabbi Israel Margolies of New York City, an early religious spokesman against the restrictive laws, also defended it. Catholic and Fundamentalist Protestant clergy in the Phoenix area condemned it.[40] In that same year, a national religious body for the first time called for a liberalization of abortion laws, albeit indirectly. The United Presbyterian Church voted at its national meeting to "urge churchgoers to work for uniform laws defining and regulating therapeutic abortion." As would be the case with the statements of other religious organizations in the years to come, the Church apparently treated abortion as a matter of sexual morality instead of one involving the ethics of taking human life. It was considered along with other resolutions calling for legal or public policy changes on matters involving sexual morality.[41] In its statement, the Church also urged that abortion be permitted in cases where there are "'strict medical indications,'" but disapproved abortion "'as a means of family planning.'"[42]

The United Presbyterian Church action could not have been prompted by the Finkbine episode because it took place a couple of months before it. It could have been influenced by the other major event involving the abortion laws that year: the promulgation of the model abortion statute by the American Law Institute. The ALI is an organization of judges, lawyers, and law professors which drafts model legislation. Its "Proposed Official Draft" of the statute came out a few weeks before the Church's meeting. Its final draft came out in the month the Finkbine story hit the press. It provided that a licensed physician be permitted to perform an abortion if he believed that there was a "substantial risk" that continuing the pregnancy would "gravely impair" the physical or mental health of the mother, or that the pregnancy resulted from rape, incest, or other felonious intercourse (intercourse with a girl below 16 was to be deemed "felonious"). It also required that abortions be performed in a licensed hospital, except in emergencies.[43] Statutes like the ALI model became the objective of liberalization efforts until the end of the 1960s.

The abortion question was also given mass exposure earlier in 1962 when a popular network television drama, "The Defenders," ran an episode highlighting it. It concerned a physician who is prosecuted for performing abortions. At his trial he is portrayed as a decent man whose desire was purely to help young women in need whose plight is created by the restrictive laws. Critic Jack Gould, reviewing the program in *The New York Times*, wrote that it deliberately created sympathy for the abortionist, never challenged his intellectual and moral position or explored the question of the unborn child's humanity, and amounted to "an appeal for revision of the law."[44]

Thus, in 1962, the abortion issue first exploded upon the public. The effort of influential national organizations and the press and media to promote legal change began to take shape.

1963

Some of the earliest serious efforts to change the laws were made during this year. The Kansas State Senate passed a "reform" bill, but a committee in the House of Representatives killed it. Efforts to pass a reform bill in Minnesota also failed. A bill was also stopped in a legislative committee in California.[45]

1964

Mass attention was again focused on the abortion question in 1964 when the possibility was raised of fetal deformity in pregnant women who contracted German measles during the U.S. epidemic of that year. (In Chapter Six it is shown that the chances of this occurring are actually quite small.) Nevertheless, it caused questioning about hospital abortion practices, socio-economic inequalities affecting access to abortion (which became one of the main pro-abortion themes in later years), and the purpose and effectiveness of the laws.[46]

In 1964, the prestigious New York Academy of Medicine called for an ALI-type statute for New York and argued squarely that the restrictive law had to be changed because most of the medical profession and public did not agree with it. It contended that "'permissive medical practices based on sound medical judgment should be recognized, not forbidden by law.'"[47]

1964 also saw the creation of the Association for the Study of Abortion, probably the first national organization in the U.S. concerning itself exclusively with the abortion problem. Dr. Bernard Nathanson, a pro-abortion advocate turned staunch anti-abortionist calls it "an immaculately respectable and strictly academic" group, which included physicians, lawyers, sociologists, and clergymen.[48] It aimed its efforts, which were mostly educational, primarily at a professional audience.[49] While it was to remain non-political, its first President, Dr. Robert E. Hall of Columbia University's College of Physicians and Surgeons, called upon obstetricians, the professionals most immediately concerned with abortion, to lead the battle for legal reform.[50]

1965

The push for liberalization noticeably stepped up in 1965. Another religious group, the National Federation of Temple Sisterhoods, a Reform Jewish group, called for a liberalization of laws governing both abortion and homosexuality. Along with its male counterpart, the Union of American Hebrew Congregations, it also backed readily available birth control and divorce law revision.[51] Again, a religious group linked abortion to other changed positions on sexual morality.

1965 also saw the first major organizations taking a stand for a complete repeal of the laws. The New York Civil Liberties Union (the New York State affiliate of the ACLU) proposed repealing that state's penal code provision which banned abortion except when the mother's life is endangered, and penalizing a person for committing it only when he is not a duly licensed physician.[52] The NYCLU thus became the earliest promoter of the position finally accepted by the Supreme Court. The parent organization, the ACLU, took the same position that year. It became the first national organization "to assert the right of all women to obtain abortions."[53]

Abortion also received prominent exposure in the scholarly legal literature in 1965 for the first time. Most of an issue of the *Western Reserve Law Review* (now *Case Western Reserve Law Review*) was devoted to exploring the legal, medical, and religious aspects of abortion.[54] I shall speak about one of the articles in it, by Dr. Kenneth J. Ryan, later. A number of the essays called for reform or outright repeal, a few spoke in a neutral -- but basically approving tone -- about the more liberal laws in European countries, and only two -- by Catholic and Orthodox Jewish clergymen -- argued strongly against abortion. (One of the clergymen, Father Robert F. Drinan, S.J., later took the position that abortion restrictions should be taken out of the law entirely.)[55] While one cannot easily assess the impact of this set of essays, it is likely that they established within at least a part of the legal community a certain view of the facts and nudged it in the direction of reform.

Within the medical community, the first serious attempt was made to move the American Medical Association (AMA) in the direction of supporting reform. In a report cleared by the AMA's board of trustees in November 1965, the organization's Committee on Human Reproduction urged the enactment of ALI-type statutes.[56] The AMA's House of Delegates took no action, but it was still a significant step for an organization that had taken a firm anti-abortion stand since 1859.

In New York State, a survey pushed by Dr. Hall and conducted by professors of obstetrics and gynecology from the State's medical schools showed that 87 percent of New York obstetricians supported an ALI-type statute.[57] A leading state physician, Dr. Carl Goldmark, Jr., president of the New York County Medical Society, spoke out for it.[58] Dr. Kenneth R. Niswander of the State University of New York at Buffalo Medical School presented further evidence of the changed medical opinion by making public a Buffalo study showing that physicians were increasingly stretching the law to authorize abortions.[59]

Finally, the campaign for liberalization was taken up by the press in 1965. *The New York Times* editorialized on the subject three times that year. In each of these, the *Times* argued that compassion required that the laws be changed. In one, the New York State law was called "barbarous";[60] another was written under the headline **"The Cruel Abortion Law"**;[61] and the other referred to "the high cost in human misery" being caused by the present law.[62] The emotional appeal of America's most influential newspaper and the perspective it presented for understanding the abortion issue no doubt helped shape the thinking on the subject of many of its readers.

The editorial of February 13, 1965 gives us an insight into the thinking behind the *Times'* position, as well as the points it believed were important to stress to establish its argument. Most noteworthy is its unwillingness to acknowledge the presence of a moral issue. It suggested that the law should be changed simply because the opinion of 87 percent of New York obstetricians in the survey mentioned above favored it. It claimed that "imperative human needs" made change necessary, but it did not say what they were or explain how it was not just human *wants* which were involved. It talks about abortion being an issue on which "many emotions and values" conflict and claimed not to be able to see how the "moral law" should be construed as requiring that "monstrously deformed fetuses" be brought into the world. The words and notions expressed suggest that the *Times'* moral position rested not on a firm belief in the existence of right and wrong, but on the relativistic view of morality as being determined by the individual. As we shall see, it exaggerated the severity of the problem of the thalidomide defects by saying that the babies "struggle through birth...to lead a short, pitiful, institutionalized existence that can hardly be called life." It thus also accepted a "quality of life" criterion for existence and sought to make a judgment for another person, based on a dubious notion of compassion, that non-existence is better for him than life with some defect. Ironically, the *Times* believed that a law which stops the taking of life, as opposed to one which permits it, was "barbarous."[63]

This *Times* editorial, along with the two others of 1965, clearly put forth the central pro-abortion rallying cry of recent years: that the laws wreaked great havoc on women's physical and mental health. It apparently did not, however, supply proof for this. The *Times*, as it was to frequently do in this controversy, placed the Catholic Church squarely at the center of efforts to obstruct reform. It also argued that there must be "latitude for expert medical judgment" in deciding when a pregnancy threatens a woman's health which the law did not then allow.[64]

In its April 7, 1965 editorial, the *Times* commented upon another media effort to apparently portray abortion reform in a positive light, a CBS-TV documentary which the editorial said emphasized "[t]he bitterly cruel choices forced upon individual women and on the medical profession by overly restrictive law." With its shrill cry that the laws forced women into the dangerous "underworld" of illegal abortion and its citation of figures which wildly exaggerated the numbers of illegal abortions and maternal deaths resulting from them (see Chapter Six), The *Times'* December 8, 1965 editorial gave considerable credence to the main argument of the pro-abortionists.[65]

The *Times'* -- and the early pro-abortion movement's -- argument for legalization in the hard cases (along ALI lines, essentially)[66] was, of course, a position which disregards act-based morality (i.e., it viewed the wrongness of abortion not as resulting from the nature of the act but from the circumstances under which it is done). Once this was asserted, there was no logical obstacle to the seeking of total legalization. Indeed, in its December 8 editorial the *Times* termed the ALI proposal as simply "[a] starter toward abortion law reform."[67]

Thus, 1965 ended with the push for reform beginning to gather momentum in major organizations, the professional and academic communities, and the press. In 1966, that momentum would begin to seem like a juggernaut which would propel the pro-abortion movement toward its first legislative successes in 1967.

1966

In 1966, the medical community continued to assert its views for liberalization. The Association for the Study of Abortion publicized a poll it conducted which showed "[t]he nation's psychiatrists...overwhelmingly in favor" of liberalization. It also emphasized that 90 percent of New York State psychiatrists had this view.[68] Also, the New York Obstetrical Society endorsed the ALI approach,[69] and the New York Medical Society held its first-ever public meeting late in the year to promote reform.[70]

Religious groups in New York State also began to speak up for reform. The New York State Council of

Churches, the State's largest interdenominational Protestant organization, urged the legislature to pass an ALI-type bill. It was joined by the Protestant Council of Churches of New York City and the Episcopal Diocese of New York. The latter's resolution called the then-existing New York law "'unduly restrictive and uncharitable.'"[71]

The Liberal Party of New York also endorsed abortion reform in 1966.[72]

The pressure was thus building up for legal change in New York State in this year, but the bill in the legislature failed to get out of committee.

In the nation's largest state, California, an organization called the Society for Humane Abortion, which devoted itself primarily to educating the public on what it viewed as the inadequacies of present laws, held a conference on abortion and human rights in San Francisco in January 1966. The organization was especially active in the media and on college campuses in California.[73] The controversial late Episcopal Auxiliary Bishop of California, James A. Pike, also called for the change of laws on abortion and those involving other sexual practices.[74]

On the national level, other major organizations joined the chorus for reform. The American Lutheran Church adopted a statement on "Sexual Integrity in Modern Society" at its biennial convention which included the assertion that there are "'times and circumstances when interruption of a pregnancy may be necessary for therapeutic reasons.'"[75] A panel of physicians at the annual clinical meeting of ACOG gave support to reform roughly along ALI lines.[76] The American Medical Women's Association also passed a resolution calling for liberalization and in it emphasized the claim that 10,000 women died each year from criminal abortions.[77]

1966 also produced two books of note on abortion: Lawrence Lader's *Abortion* and David Lowe's posthumously published *Abortion and the Law*.[78] Lader's book is an oft-cited early work which even the *Wade* opinion made reference to. It is a somewhat useful sourcebook on the early history of the abortion reform effort in the 1960s, but is also polemical. It is likely that it had some impact in stimulating the push for complete repeal which Lader was an early advocate of and later sought to accomplish by organizing The National Association for the Repeal of Abortion Laws (NARAL). It was also probably somewhat influential in getting the abortion issue framed as a women's issue. The Lowe book made its appeal for legal change by presenting arguments from eminent medical authorities and a number of anonymous sad case histories of women who sought out criminal abortionists.

1967

This year can rightfully be called the turning point. Except for a slight, quiet modification in Mississippi's statute in 1966, it was during this year that states began to change their laws. The clamor from professional organizations and the press also heightened and, most revealing of the changed situation, groups began to loosely form to defend the unborn child and fight the liberalization efforts. (The history of the anti-abortion movement is traced later in this Chapter.)

The states which acted in 1967 -- California, Colorado, and North Carolina -- adopted some form of the ALI proposal. It is interesting to note that the new California law was signed by then-Governor Ronald Reagan, who is usually associated with an anti-abortion position. He said that he signed the bill, which permitted abortion when the woman's physical or mental health was threatened or she had conceived as a result of rape or incest, because he believed it justified to take a life to save another life. He refused to accept a provision which would have also permitted it for eugenic reasons.[79]

Meanwhile, the medical community appeared to have moved firmly behind liberalization by 1967. Early in the year, a survey was released by the magazine *Modern Medicine* which showed that 86.9 percent of physicians overall, 83.7 percent of obstetrician-gynecologists, and 94.6 percent of psychiatrists favored liberalization.[80] 90.6 percent of New York State physicians were for liberalization.[81] I shall return to this survey later on.

The late Dr. Alan F. Guttmacher, the well-known obstetrician and birth control authority and long-time president of PPFA, also spoke out for reform although his organization remained officially silent.[82] In 1967, he also edited a frequently cited anthology which was entitled *The Case for Legalized Abortion Now*, in which he made it clear that his sentiments were for repeal even though prudence dictated that only reform currently should be pushed for.[83] Even while PPFA made no open endorsement of legalized abortion, stirrings in that direction occurred at the conference of the International Planned Parenthood Federation (IPPF), with which it is affiliated. A group of physicians reported to the conference on the results of a worldwide survey commissioned by IPPF on abortion, specifically mentioned the situation in the U.S., and urged more liberal abortion laws throughout the world.[84]

In May of 1967, the Medical Committee for Human Rights, a liberal medical group formed originally to assist civil rights efforts in the South, called for "'the immediate reform of archaic laws concerning induced abortion and...that these reforms must be based upon consideration of health in the broadest definition, rather than upon political and religious factors.'"[85]

Finally, in June 1967, the A.M.A.'s House of Delegates departed from the organization's policy of over 100 years and endorsed ALI-type legislation. This action signalled that the medical profession was *officially* -- as segments of it had been *in fact* for some time -- in the pro-abortion camp.

Medical and scientific experts were not unanimous in this position -- or perhaps even certain if it was based on a proper understanding of the question -- in 1967. This can be seen from the conclusions of the International Conference on Abortion held that year in Washington, D.C. under the joint sponsorship of Howard Divinity School and the Joseph P. Kennedy, Jr. Foundation. While the participants at the Conference -- well-known physicians, geneticists, biochemists, and other scientists -- had diverse views on what the law on abortion should be, they held, almost unanimously (one dissent out of sixty participants) that they "'could find no point in time between the union of sperm and egg, or at least the blastocyst stage, and the birth of the infant at which we [they] could say that this was not a human life.'"[86] The Conference was one of the few major efforts made at that point to focus some attention on the question of the unborn child's humanity, instead of just the woman's putative welfare.

Conflict brewed on the religious front over abortion in 1967. In New York City, the Protestant Council of the City of New York and three Jewish organizations -- the New York Federation of Reform Synagogues, the Association of Reform Rabbis, and the New York Metropolitan Region of the United Synagogue of America (Conservative) -- issued a statement in February which attacked the Catholic Church for maintaining a "harsh and unbending posture" on the State's abortion law.[87] The statement was issued in response to a pastoral letter from New York's eight Roman Catholic Bishops which urged their people to "'do all in your power to prevent direct attack upon the lives of unborn children'" and called on the Bishops to respect the "'differences'" among denominations if "'ecumenism is to have any real meaning.'" The Catholic Bishops were not alone among religious groups in opposing liberalization, however. The *Times* article reporting this also stated that a number of Orthodox Jewish rabbis had spoken out against it.[88]

Also in New York that year, the Clergy Consultation Service on Abortion was formed to provide assistance to women in obtaining abortions in states or countries where they were legal and to give advice on such alternatives as keeping the child or putting him up for adoption.[89] The clergymen said that they were undertaking this because "'women today are forced by ignorance, misinformation and desperation into courses of action that require humane concern on the part of religious leaders'" and pledged also to work for liberalization of the State's law. In another example of a situation and motive instead of act-based view of morality which can be understood, in light of what shall be said in Chapter Three, as turning the Hippocratic Oath on its head, the clergymen said the following:

> "When a doctor performs...an abortion motivated by compassion and concern for the patient, and not simply for monetary gain we do not regard him as a criminal but as living by the highest standards of religion and of the Hippocratic Oath."[90]

The Episcopal Dioceses of New York City and Albany also endorsed the reform bill in the state legislature.[91]

On the national level, the American Baptist Convention urged its congregations to support the ALI proposal minus the deformity provision.[92] The General Convention of the Episcopal Church in the U.S. endorsed the basic ALI model.[93]

Pressure from religious groups for abortion reform thus intensified in 1967, especially in New York where it also boiled over into interdenominational controversy.

In the national press, *Time* magazine ran a "Time Essay" -- which stated an editorial position -- on October 13, 1967 which strongly endorsed the reform effort. This piece sought to impress upon its readers a number of the common pro-abortion positions. It presented the usual caricature of the illegal abortionist as a "defrocked doctor" or "bungling amateur," gave the impression that many disastrous attempts at self-abortion are made, tried to justify reform statutes as just a *de jure* acceptance of what hospitals were already doing *de facto*, and put forth the view that this was just another "sex-law issue" involving private conduct that the public had no legitimate interest in.[94] It also spent a good bit of time discussing the Catholic prominence in this issue and the opposition of other religious denominations to it. It made some questionable or flatly untruthful assertions -- as we shall see in Chapter Six -- about the numbers of illegal abortions, the safety of legal abortions, the accuracy of Eastern European abortion data, and the connection between abortion and contraception (i.e., that more easily available contraception means less abortion). It sided with the growing feminist sentiments on the subject by contending that men do not understand the female abortion experience (and thus implied that male law-makers cannot legitimately legislate for women on this). It also foreshadowed later pro-abortion rhetoric by equating the restriction of abortion with Prohibition.[95] It explicitly rejected "moral absolutes" -- i.e., act-based morality -- and called for a law based on "each concrete situation" (but did not make clear which circumstances, if any, would merit prohibiting abortion). The moral questions about destroying the unborn child were raised, but quickly dismissed. The essay also presented a certain notion of progress as linked up with science. It saw the "central problem" as being that abortion was regulated by the criminal law instead of "medical knowledge" and believed that "conscience" (translated: freedom) and "intelligence" translated: modern science) should be permitted to govern, instead of "archaic and hypocrital concepts and statutes" (translated: morality and law based on it).[96]

1968

In 1968, amidst a backdrop of social and political turmoil in the nation as a whole, the abortion reform movement reached a fever pitch. It was also during this year that the emphasis began to shift from reform to repeal.

Medical and health organizations began to call for repeal. In May, the executive board of ACOG, in effect, endorsed this by saying that abortion should be permitted if the woman's "'total environment, actual or foreseeable'" warrants it.[97] In November, the American Public Health Association (APHA) spoke out for repeal.[98] Also in November, PPFA reversed its long-standing policy and endorsed abortion as a family planning measure and called for the repeal of existing laws.[99] I shall speak further about PPFA's switch later.

Among religious organizations, the Unitarian Universalist Association went on record for repeal,[100] as did the American Baptist Convention in the first twelve weeks of pregnancy.[101]

In New York State, Governor Rockefeller's commission on abortion issued its report urging passage of a slightly liberalized version of the ALI Bill, which was attacked as "'inadequate'" by another religious group, the Clergy Consultation Service on Abortion.[102] Rockefeller endorsed the commission's report, but the legislature again did not enact any kind of reform bill. Meanwhile, the *Times* coupled its efforts with the governor, reform advocates in the legislature, and the various prominent groups and individuals seeking to change the State's law. In two editorials early in the year, it squarely pointed to New York's Catholic heirarchy as the force resisting reform, emphasized that modern notions of "justice" required reform,[103] and stated flatly that "[a]bortion is a medical and legal, not a religious or political, matter."[104]

Elsewhere, Maryland and Georgia adopted ALI statutes. The Georgia statute was, of course, the one successfully challenged in *Doe v. Bolton*.

1968 also saw a major academic conference on abortion at Hot Springs, Virginia. The timing, sponsorship, and participants at the conference lead one to think it was convened to build more momentum for the pro-abortion cause. The conference, which included participants from a number of countries, was sponsored by the pro-abortion Association for the Study of Abortion. There were a few anti-abortion speakers, but most were pro-abortion and many were prominent in the reform movement. At this conference, the matter of making a constitutional challenge to the abortion laws in the courts was discussed at length.[105] According to *The New York Times*, the "nearly unanimous" consensus of the conference was the following: "[a[bolish all existing abortion laws and leave the rights of childbirth up to each woman on the advice of her doctor."[106]

The pro-abortionists also got an unexpected boost from the federal government in 1968 when the Presidential Advisory Council on the Status of Women, headed by former U.S. Senator Maurine Neuberger of Oregon, issued a report calling for the repeal of all abortion laws.[107]

Also in 1968, two important publications appeared. The first was Professor Cyril Means' long, influential article on the history of the New York State abortion law in the *New York Law Forum*, discussed in Chapter Three.[108] The other was Russell Shaw's *Abortion on Trial*, which was anti-abortion.[109]

1969

This year can also be seen as a critical one in the drive to legalize abortion. This is because it was then that the first major court decisions were handed down striking abortion statutes and the pro-abortion movement, probably on the basis of these decisions, set out plans to divert at least some of their efforts to the courts. In September 1969, the California Supreme Court, in *People v. Belous*,[110] declared the provision of the State's original abortion statute that the operation could be performed if it were "necessary to preserve her [the mother's] life" unconstitutionally vague. In November, federal district judge Gerhard A. Gesell likewise struck down the District of Columbia's abortion statute in *U.S. v. Vuitch*[111] because he said its provision which permitted abortions "for the preservation of the mother's life or health" was unconstitutionally vague.

After the *Belous* decision, the James Madison Constitutional Law Institute, which was on the appellants' Supreme Court brief in *Wade*, the ACLU and the Association for the Study of Abortion filed a suit challenging the then restrictive New York statute.[112] Immediately after the *Vuitch* ruling, the James Madison Institute announced that an anonymous donor had given it $60,000 to bring similar suits in other states. The ACLU said it was cooperating with the Institute and also stated that it planned to challenge statutes in four states in different parts of the country on its own.[113]

1969 also saw reform laws passed in Arkansas, Delaware, Kansas, New Mexico, and Oregon.

On the medical front, the push for legalization received a further boost from the psychiatric fraternity. The Group for Advancement of Psychiatry published a book called *The Right to Abortion: A Psychiatric View* which recommended that "abortion, when performed by a licensed physician, be entirely removed from the domain of criminal law."[114] In December 1969, the Board of Trustees of the American Psychiatric Association also adopted this policy.[115] *Modern Medicine* also released the results of another poll it took which showed that nearly 63 percent of American physicians favored making abortion available "to any woman capable of giving legal consent upon her own request to a competent physician." Fifty-one percent believed it should be "without qualification."[116] (Surveys on abortion are often of questionable reliability because responses vary according to how the questions are worded.[117] Be that as it may, the upshot of this survey is that a clear majority -- 51 percent -- of physicians in the U.S. favored abortion on demand.)

Feminists also began to gain attention on this issue in 1969. The Congress to Unite Women, a coalition of feminist groups, called for new programs for women and sweeping legal changes, including the repeal of abortion laws.[118] On November 15, 1969, feminists staged a small demonstration at the HEW Building in Washington, D.C. as a spin-off of the anti-war demonstration going on in the city. They clamored for the Department of Health, Education, and Welfare to provide free "walk-in" abortion clinics for all women.[119] At the AMA convention in New York City, women pickets surrounded the building, demanding that doctors sign a petition for repeal.[120]

Also in 1969 a conference was convened in Chicago to organize the National Association for the Repeal of Abortion Laws (NARAL), the first national group set up exclusively to seek *repeal* of abortion laws.[121] Nathanson chronicles its early history in his book *Aborting America*. He explains how it, by design, sought to promote the idea that abortion was strictly a woman's issue and to portray the Catholic hierarchy as *the* enemy of repeal. He indicates that the NARAL organizers planned to single out the hierarchy even if it had not involved itself in the political battle.[122] As we shall see, it did, particularly in New York.

By 1969, in addition to the associations previously mentioned, the following major national organizations advocated reform or repeal: the Methodist Church, the Reformed Church in America, Americans for Democratic Action, the Citizens' Committee for Children, the Federation of Jewish Philanthropies, the Federation of Protestant Welfare Agencies, the Social Service Employees Union, the National Board of the Young Women's Christian Association (YWCA), the American Ethical Union, and the State Communities Aid Association.[123]

1969 also saw more books dealing in whole or in part with abortion. On the pro-abortion side were Guttmacher's *Birth Control and Love*[124] and Nancy Howell Lee's *The Search for an Abortionist*.[125] On the anti-abortion side were Charles E. Rice's *The Vanishing Right to Live*[126] and David Granfield's *The Abortion Decision*.[127] This was also the time when feminist books calling abortion a woman's right began to appear. In 1969, there was also a conference in San Francisco sponsored by the pro-abortion California Committee on Therapeutic Abortion. The papers delivered were compiled into a book, *Abortion and the Unwanted Child*.[128]

Let us turn to the situation in New York State in 1969. By this time, such state organizations as the Association of the Bar of the City of New York, the Physicians' Forum, the New York Chapter of the American

Humanist Association, the Metropolitan Council of the American Jewish Congress, the New York Chapter of the American Jewish Committee, the New York Conference of the United Church of Christ, the Metropolitan Republican Club, and the New York Young Democratic Club had endorsed reform or repeal of the state's abortion statute.[129]

A number of organizations threw their weight behind repeal of the statute for the first time in 1969. Among religious ones, these included the New York State Council of Churches, the New York City Council of Churches, the Presbytery of New York City, and the Episcopal Diocese of New York.[130]

The New York State Liberal Party shifted from its former position to repeal.[131] The New York State Bar Association's public health committee also implicitly endorsed repeal by cautioning the legislature against "'accepting any reform bill which fails to meet existing evils and which is so dissolved in ambiguities as to make *bona fide* compliance with its provisions on the part of doctors and hospitals almost impossible.'"[132]

The Correctional Association of New York joined the chorus for repeal, but the Medical Society of New York, while still favoring reform, would only go so far as to support enactment of the proposal made by the Governor's Commission the year before.[133]

In New York State the feminist movement also began to assert itself publicly and dramatically in the pro-abortion movement. Since changing the law was first brought up in the legislature, such feminists as Mrs. Mary Lindsey (the former New York City Mayor's wife), Gloria Steinem, Betty Friedan, and Bella Abzug had lobbied for it and influenced the mostly male legislators with the claim that they had no right to legislate for women on a "woman's issue" like this.[134] The *New Yorker* reported that a hearing held in New York City by some state legislators on the proposed reform bill (the Blumenthal bill) was noisily disrupted by a small number of feminists who, claiming that any abortion laws violate the right of a woman to control her body, wanted total repeal. It also mentioned that the rejuvenated feminist movement, which had some ideological differences, was united in seeing abortion as a fundamental right of women and that various feminist groups, from the supposedly moderate National Organization for Women (NOW) -- which had supported legalized abortion since its second national conference in 1967, a year after its founding -- to a radical collective called "Women's Liberation" was speaking out for the Cook (repeal) bill.[135] When this bill finally passed in 1970, Governor Rockefeller gave credit to "'[w]omen's liberation'" for playing an "'important part'" in its passage.[136]

The push for legal change in New York in 1969 was prompted also by the *Times* and the report of a Joint Legislative Committee. The latter endorsed a version of the ALI model.[137] The *Times* ran three editorials in May 1969.[138] It endorsed the Joint Committee's recommendations. It also again pointed to the Catholic hierarchy as the obstructionists. It gave the strong impression that the sentiment of both pertinent professional organizations and the general public was overwhelmingly on the side of change. (The public's views will be considered shortly.)[139] It used a raid on an illegal abortion mill in the Bronx, which resulted in several college students being held, to dramatize the "plight" created for persons by the present law.[140]

Despite all this pressure, the legislature defeated the reform bill after a debate marked by a dramatic speech by a handicapped legislator. Assemblyman Martin Ginsberg, who was crippled by polio at thirteen months, was credited with shifting the Assembly against the bill, which contained the provision permitting the abortion of malformed unborn children, after mentioning a number of famous persons who overcame handicaps to achieve greatness and saying that "[i]f we are prepared to say that a life should not come into this world malformed or abnormal, then tomorrow we should be prepared to say that a life already in this world which becomes malformed or abnormal should not be permitted to live." Before the speech there were six more votes in the Assembly than needed for the bill's passage. After it, fourteen legislators pledged to support the bill defected and it lost.[141] The *Times* editorialized that it "was beaten by an emotional, irrelevant plea by one legislator, thereby condemning children yet unborn to untold human suffering."[142] (The following year, under pressure from constituents, Ginsberg switched and voted for the even more permissive Cook bill.)[143] We can see that by the start of the 1970s the pro-abortion position was supported and actively promoted -- in varying degrees -- by a wide range of groups. It had the active support of important elements of the American press and, as began to be apparent, the courts. It had formed itself into a political movement and had begun to score significant legislative and legal victories. It was also moving rapidly toward a consensus calling for the outright repeal of abortion statutes. In 1970, it was to score its greatest victory prior to the *Wade* and *Bolton* decisions: the legalization of abortion in New York. The importance of organized groups in all this can be seen in the fact that in its report on changing the New York law, the Joint Legislative Committee referred to above included an appendix listing all the groups that advocated change. It made no reference to surveys or other expressions of the views of the general public.

1970

Before turning to the New York repeal, let me mention these national developments in 1970. On the religious front, the American Lutheran Church reaffirmed its stand in support of legalized abortion for "'therapeutic reasons,'" but declined to go further.[144] The Presbyterian Church in the U.S. called for repeal.[145] Two top leaders of Orthodox Judaism in the U.S., the rabbi-presidents of the Union of Orthodox Jewish Congregations of America and the Rabbinical Council of America, prompted by the new New York law, spoke out against legal abortion.[146]

The Women's Strike for Equality made free abortion on demand a chief demand of a nationwide demonstration it held.[147]

Most dramatic, however, was the A.M.A.'s decision to change its policy and support abortion on demand, with only the stipulations that a licensed doctor perform the operation in a properly accredited hospital after consulting two other physicians.[148] As we shall see, the Supreme Court discussed this policy change in the *Wade* opinion and it is likely that it was an important influence on the Court.

More court decisions struck down abortion statutes,[149] but courts also began to sustain them against constitutional attack.[150] Besides New York, Hawaii passed a repeal law and Alaska, South Carolina, and

Virginia, passed reform laws. In Washington, the legislature passed a repeal provision which the voters approved in a referendum. This was the only state in which the citizens directly voted to change the law on abortion.[151] There was some suggestion in 1970, however, that the counterattack against the reform/repeal push was beginning. I shall trace this in my Section on the early history of the anti-abortion movement. It was seen partly in the fact that the first major scholarly books making wholesale, well-documented attacks on legalized abortion began to appear, such as Germain Grisez's *Abortion: the Myths, the Realities, and the Arguments* and John T. Noonan, Jr.'s anthology *The Morality of Abortion: Legal and Historical Perspectives.*[152] Daniel Callahan, of the Institute of Society, Ethics and the Life Sciences (Hastings Center), argued for respecting the dignity of unborn human life in *Abortion: Law, Choice, and Morality*, even while supporting moderately permissive laws.[153] I believe that the pro-abortion side gathered much momentum from the fact that it had for a long time produced most of the books on abortion. These unanswered tomes helped to frame the issues and establish a certain version of the facts about abortion in the minds particularly of the educated and influential groups in society.

I shall not go into a history of the passage of the Cook or Cook-Lichter repeal bill in New York. This is detailed in Lawrence Lader's *Abortion II: Making the Revolution* and Nathanson's *Aborting America*. I shall just state that, as Lader points out, a coalition of groups was responsible for bringing about the change. He emphasizes, as Governor Rockefeller did, the important role that women's groups and women individually played in this.[154] Both Edward Golden and Mrs. Helen Greene, two early New York State anti-abortion activists and later presidents of the New York State Right-to-Life Committee, agreed that feminist groups were an important force.[155] Golden singled out NOW, Lader's group NARAL, and the New York State Council of Churches as particularly influential.[156] Both saw the "woman issue" as pivotal, Golden stating that he believed that many votes were cast by legislators solely because of the view that women had long been treated as inferior and this was the way of atoning for it. He added that another issue which was influential was the religious one. The anti-abortion position was seen by many as a Catholic one and an appeal was made by groups like the New York State

Council of Churches that "separation of church and state" demanded that the bill be passed. He thought the Council quite influential in the 1970 legislative battle, but Mrs. Greene believed that the Protestant and Jewish groups and also the medical groups had influence mostly in the sense that they did not support the anti-abortion position.[157]

To be sure, legislators did not just allow the positions of organized groups to influence them. Lader makes reference to the substantial outpouring of opinions that legislators received from their constituents. He explains, however, that many of these demonstrations of constituent support were due to the efforts of organized groups.[158]

The influence of *The New York Times* must also be considered. In the weeks before the legislature's action, the *Times'* editorials, in effect, endorsed repeal (where previously they had supported only reform).[159] In one, it sounded supportive of the notion that a woman has a "right" to abortion.[160] It should also be emphasized that the Cook-Lichter bill passed by just one vote in the Assembly -- a dramatic last-minute change by a legislator who had previously voted "nay."[161]

1971-1972

The battle lines were now drawn and repeal was the objective of the pro-abortion movement. The momentum had drifted, however. The New York victory was the peak of the pro-abortionists' political strength. Only one more state -- Florida in 1972 -- liberalized the law by legislative means. (It did so along A.L.I. lines after the Florida Supreme Court struck down its old statute).[162] Also, in 1972 legalization proposals were overwhelmingly defeated in non-binding referenda in two states. The change may have been due to the anti-abortion movement. The pro-abortion strategy was now more of a judicial one. Even the judicial results were mixed, however. State statutes were declared unconstitutional in Connecticut,[163] Illinois,[164] Kansas,[165] New Jersey,[166] and, as mentioned, Florida.[167] Statutes were upheld in Kentucky,[168] North Carolina (which had a liberalized statute),[169] Utah,[170] Mississippi,[171] South Dakota,[172] and Indiana.[173]

Also, the U.S. Supreme Court handed down its decision in the *Vuitch* case in 1971.[174] It reversed Judge Gesell's decision striking down the D.C. abortion statute, saying, per Justice Black, that the statute was not unconstitutionally vague because it permitted abortion if the woman's "health" were threatened and interpreted "health" to include mental health.[175]

On the national scene, a few additional groups added their voices to the pro-abortion cause. Most notable of these was the American Bar Association, which in 1972 called for abortion on demand during the first twenty weeks of pregnancy.[176] The National Association of Social Workers took a pro-legalization position in 1971.[177] Among religious organizations, the United Church of Christ in 1971 and the United Methodist Church and the United Presbyterian Church in the U.S.A. (Northern) in 1972 called for repeal.[178] The Southern Baptist Convention announced its support for ALI-type laws in 1971.[179] Meanwhile, other religious groups joined the Catholic Church (which I shall speak about later) in opposing changing the laws, such as (once again) the Rabbinical Council of America[180] and the National Baptist Church, the largest black church in the U.S.[181]

Nationally, feminist organizations were increasingly active. The Women's National Abortion Action Coalition conducted a march on Washington, D.C. in November 1971.[182] Strong, although then unsuccessful, efforts were made in 1972 to get the National Women's Political Caucus to take a pro-abortion position.[183]

One fact of interest has come out since the *Wade* and *Bolton* decisions. One of the sources of funding for the pro-abortion movement before 1973 was the Playboy Foundation, an adjunct of *Playboy* magazine. The Foundation financially aided such pro-abortion groups as NARAL, the Clergy Consultation Service, and the Women's National Abortion Coalition.[184]

In 1971, eminent pro-abortionists from different fields gathered in Los Angeles for a conference entitled "Therapeutic Abortion: A Symposium on Implementation." The proceedings of this conference are reported on by an anti-abortion leader. Father Paul Marx, O.S.B., in a fascinating little book, *The Death Peddlers: War on the Unborn.*[185] Another important anti-abortion book came out in 1972, *Abortion and Social Justice*, a comprehensive anthology edited by Thomas W. Hilgers, M.D. and Dennis J. Horan.[186] On the pro-abortion side, there was the feminist tract *Abortion Rap*, by Diane Schulder and Florynce Kennedy,[187] and Professor Means' second long, significant article in the *New York Law Forum*, which will be discussed in Chapter Three.[188]

In New York State, the anti-abortion movement gained greater and greater strength. It did not succeed in getting the 1970 law changed in 1971 but, in a dramatic reversal, did get the legislature to vote to repeal it in 1972. Governor Rockefeller vetoed the repeal bill, however. It was, nevertheless, an impressive show of strength for the young movement. A number of groups fought to save the 1970 statute. They included some different ones from 1970. NARAL was there.[189] *Newsweek* pointed to the resumed activity of feminist groups and Protestant and Jewish clergymen, particularly the New York State Council of Churches.[190] Both the *Times* and Golden pointed to the role of Planned Parenthood,[191] which appears to have not been active as an organization in the 1970 battle. Golden and Mrs. Greene had different views about which group was the primary force behind the 1972 anti-repeal efforts. Mrs. Greene thought the ACLU, but Golden called Planned Parenthood the "catalyst."[192] The Catholic Church was active, but mostly by making public statements for repeal.[193] The repeal effort may have been aided by the making public of a letter from President Nixon to Terrence Cardinal Cooke supporting the effort.[194]

I shall state some conclusions about this rise of organization support for legalized abortion and its relationship to the Supreme Court decisions shortly.

The Divergence of Opinion: The Professional/Educated Class and the General Public

I have shown how over a ten year period -- bringing us to just before the Supreme Court's decisions -- an amazingly broad consensus on legalized abortion developed among a large number of important organizations with diverse purposes. We shall see from looking at public opinion polls in this Subsection that these organizations' official positions were probably representative of their members' views. Most of what I shall consider here, however, shall focus on the question of whether their positions were in accord with those of the general public.

It is a general belief that the better educated and more affluent become members of groups, such as those which pushed for legalized abortion. Further, within all sorts of large organizations -- most of the ones referred to are large -- small leadership groups and professional staffs are the most active and quickly become dominant. These persons -- particularly the staffers -- are usually highly educated or have some professional expertise. If not affluent, they at least come from middle class or better backgrounds.[195] Actually, the educated and affluent would seem to be especially well represented in some of the groups because of their very nature (e.g., medical groups, legal groups). Because of this, it is valid to examine the views on abortion of the college-educated and affluent groups in American society, reflected through major opinion surveys and to roughly equate them with the views of the members of the various groups. I shall thus be comparing the views of the best educated and most affluent with those of the general public. There is, to my knowledge, no information -- or at least none that I would be able to have access to -- that could permit me to say conclusively that the groups represented the views of most of their members on abortion. I shall assume this to be true, again, because the representative mechanisms within most of these groups are such that they would generally result in this being the case and because, as we shall see, the position of the better educated and more affluent is basically in accord with that of the groups. (In saying this, however, I am not overlooking the fact that the rank-and-file organizations are often motivated to shape their positions on issues by their leaders.)

MEDICAL OPINION

In 1967, according to the two surveys published by *Modern Medicine* mentioned earlier, 86.9 percent of American physicians favored "liberalizing the laws."[196]

In 1969, 63 percent favored abortion being, in effect, a matter between a woman and her doctor and 51 percent favored that this be "without qualification" (i.e., favored repeal of the laws). As far as specialities are concerned, as far back as 1965, a survey of U.S. psychiatrists showed that "86 to 90 percent...[of those] who replied" favored liberalization and nearly a quarter (23.5 percent) wanted repeal.[197] The 1967 *Modern Medicine* survey revealed, as mentioned, that 94.6 percent of psychiatrists favored liberalization. In the 1969 survey, nearly 80 percent of psychiatrists were for abortion being for the woman and her physician to decide. Almost 72 percent of these wanted no qualifications or repeal.[198] These surveys have led sociologist William Brennan to conclude that "psychiatry has proven to be the field of medical specialization most susceptible to pro-abortion sentiment."[199]

As to obstetrician-gynocologists, 83.7 percent in the 1967 survey favored liberalization. In 1969, 41 percent wanted repeal and almost 51 percent repeal or liberalization.[200] In an ACOG/APHA survey in 1967, 78.6 percent of the heads of obstetrics departments of 372 U.S. and Canadian hospitals were found to favor liberalization or repeal.[201]

I have also already stated that by 1970 the three major pertinent medical associations -- the A.M.A., A.P.A., and ACOG -- were for repeal.[202] Medical opinion was thus by then overwhelmingly for at least liberalization and predominately for repeal.[203]

One might ask why psychiatrists were so overwhelmingly in favor of the loosening of anti-abortion laws and why they were in the forefront among medical specialists in pushing for this. I could find no study which specifically sought to answer this question. A few authors pointed to facts which suggest at least a partial answer, however. For one thing, psychiatrists felt uncomfortable assuming the responsibility for giving what were, in effect, dispensations from the restrictive laws.[204] They were called upon to do this both under the statutes which forbade virtually all abortion and the liberalized ALI-type statutes, which resulted in psychiatric or mental health reasons being the ones for which abortion was primarily sought. Many psychiatrists believed that they, in some sense, were doing the "dirty work" of the legal system.[205] A frequent theme sounded by advocates of legal change, which would seem particularly applicable to psychiatrists, was that the physician risked placing himself in legal jeopardy every time he prescribed an abortion because the laws were unclear.

This was probably a gross overstatement, but many perceived it to be the case. Psychiatrists, I assume, were made further uncomfortable by the fact that, when faced with a patient who sought abortion, they became point men in the struggle to deal with the cross-pressures of the pro- and anti-abortion attitudes generally, as well as with sharply conflicting views in their own profession about whether an abortion is more likely to improve or damage a woman's mental health.[206] Moreover, psychiatrists, being human, were no doubt unhappy at having to be, for the most part, the ones that had to deal with panic- and conflict-stricken women and face personal disapproval or rebuke from them if they could find no basis for granting their abortion requests. Often, too, as experts have written, the psychiatrist would feel manipulated by women who would exaggerate their symptoms in order to justify an abortion.[207]

Literally, as Betty Sarvis and Hyman Rodman state in *The Abortion Controversy*, "the [p]sychiatrist in particular...[was] often caught up in the eye of the storm"[208] on the abortion question and, in dealing with abortion-seeking patients, "has so much of his personal and professional esteem caught up in the process that he finds it painful to deal with it objectively."[209]

The latter suggests another possible reason why psychiatrists wanted the abortion laws changed. They are supposed to be scientists and so are expected to be coldly objective and "value-free." This is emphasized to them in both of the types of sciences that their profession spans: medical science and social science (i.e., psychology). They did not want to deal with a matter which requires them to weigh considerations of morality.

Also, since they are unique among physicians in that they employ the theories of modern psychology, it follows that they have digested and are influenced by those theories -- and the theories of contemporary social science generally -- more than the others. This is reflected in their greater support for changing the abortion laws because one of the prevailing notions of social science is an extreme conception of individual freedom and rights, grounded (as explained in Chapter Eight) in little more than the whims or desires of the individual.

The following, then, may have been the reasons why psychiatrists pushed initially for the liberalized ALI-type statutes: a belief that more freedom had to be granted the woman, an exaggerated sense of pity for the woman, and a concern that they were clearly acting illegally in prescribing abortions. The personal dilemmas that they faced in working with patients and dealing with the disagreements within their profession may well have been the factors most responsible for their becoming dissatisfied with the liberalized statutes and deciding to push for complete legalization.

Some of these same reasons might be given to explain the significant role that obstetrician-gynocologists also played in the pro-abortion campaign. They were not so directly influenced by contemporary social science as psychiatrists, but were also "in the eye of the storm" in that they had to face confused, agitated pregnant women -- even though they usually did not bear the burden psychiatrists did of having to decide if there were a justification for their abortions, since by this time it was acknowledged that there were virtually no physical health indications for abortion.

THE DIVISIONS OF OPINION IN THE GENERAL PUBLIC

What were the opinions on abortion of the rest of the public, including those who were members of the educated and most affluent classes and those who were not? "Educated" here means those who have at least graduated from a four-year college or university, and "affluence" shall be measured by where on the income scale people appear. I shall list pertinent figures from Gallup Polls taken between 1962 and 1972, and suggest what they say on the question. It must be understood that the poll figures to which I had access for 1962, 1965, and 1968 do not break the results down by income category. They *do* break them down by educational level, but only for white non-Catholic men and women.

The results are thus an incomplete picture of opinion according to these socio-economic groupings for these years, although they represent the views of a clear majority of the population. As such, they probably also adequately represent the views of the socio-economic groupings from which most of the members of the organizations in question were drawn.

The percentages for 1962, 1965, and 1968 are as follows:[210]

1) Those who said they "disapproved" of legalizing abortion "to preserve the mother's health":

EDUCATIONAL LEVEL	1962	1965	May 1968	Dec. 1968
College*	5	4.5	1.5	2.5
High School**	9	10.0	9.0	8.0
Grade School***	15	18.0	9.5	14.5

* Denotes those who have a four-year college or university degree or above.
** Denotes those who have a high school diploma.
*** Denotes those who have a grade school education or less.

The same meanings of these terms are applied throughout.

2) Those who said they "disapproved" of legalizing abortion "if the child might be deformed":

EDUCATIONAL LEVEL	1962	1965	May 1968	Dec. 1968
College	17.0	19.5	14.5	12.0
High School	21.0	25.5	22.5	20.0
Grade School	27.5	30.5	17.0	25.0

3) Those who said they "disapproved" of legalizing abortion "if the parents cannot afford another child":

EDUCATIONAL LEVEL	1962	1965	May 1968	Dec. 1968
College	69.5	65.0	61.5	54.5
High School	74.0	75.0	73.0	69.0
Grade School	67.5	67.5	70.0	72.5

4) Those who said they "disapproved" of legalizing abortion "if no more children are desired":

EDUCATIONAL LEVEL	1962	1965	May 1968	Dec. 1968
College	-	-	76.0	72.5
High School	-	-	88.5	83.0
Grade School	-	-	85.5	80.0

In 1969, the Gallup Poll asked the following question: "Would you favor or oppose a law which would permit a woman to go to a doctor to end a pregnancy at any time during the first three months?"[211]

	FAVOR	OPPOSE	NO OPINION
EDUCATIONAL LEVEL			
College	58.0	34.0	8.0
High School	37.0	53.0	10.0
Grade School	31.0	57.0	12.0
INCOME LEVEL			
$15,000 and over	54.0	37.0	9.0
$10,000-$14,999	44.0	45.0	11.0
$ 7,000-$ 9,999	43.0	47.0	10.0
$ 5,000-$ 6,999	34.0	60.0	6.0
$ 3,000-$ 4,999	31.0	56.0	13.0
Under $3,000	33.0	55.0	12.0

(These figures include all religious and racial groups, as do those for 1972.)

In 1972, the Gallup Poll asked this question: "As you may have heard, in the last few years a number of states have liberalized their abortion laws. Do you agree or disagree with the following statement regarding abortion: 'The decision to have an abortion should be made solely by the woman and her physician.'"

	AGREE	DISAGREE	NO OPINION
EDUCATIONAL LEVEL			
College	74.5	22.0	4.0
High School	65.0	30.0	5.0
Grade School	47.0	45.0	8.0
INCOME LEVEL			
$15,000 and over	74.0	24.0	2.0
$10,000-$14,999	68.0	27.0	5.0
$ 7,000-$ 9,999	71.0	26.0	3.0
$ 5,000-$ 6,999	55.0	40.0	5.0
Under $5,000	53.0	38.0	9.0

It is obvious that the variance in responses is produced by different wording of the questions when we consider the surveys done by Gallup, the National Opinion Research Center (NORC), and demographer Judith Blake in 1972 and 1973. Keeping in mind the Gallup Poll just mentioned, let us look at the results of the following question which was also asked by Gallup in 1972 and 1973: "Do you think abortion operations should or should not be legal where the parents simply have all the children they want although there would be no major health or financial problems involved in having another child?" The overall result was that 67 percent "disapproved," 27 percent "approved," and 6 percent had "no opinion in 1972, and 68 percent "approved," 27 percent "disapproved," and 5 percent had "no opinion" in 1973. NORC, meanwhile, asked the following: Please tell me whether you think it should be possible for a pregnant woman to obtain a legal abortion if she is married and does not want any more children?" In 1972, 57 percent "disapproved," 38 percent "approved," and 5 percent had "no opinion." In 1973, 51 percent "disapproved", 46 percent "approved," and 3 percent had "no opinion."[212] In January 1973, during the week after the *Wade* and *Bolton* decisions were announced, Professor Blake commissioned the following two survey questions:

> "1. Some states have laws that say abortion cannot be performed after a woman has been pregnant a certain period of time. Do you think there should be some such time limit or do you think there should be no legal restriction concerning the time when abortion can be performed?"

and

> "2. [If there should be a limit] Taking into account that a woman may not know she is pregnant until three or four weeks after conception, after what month of pregnancy do you think it should be illegal to perform an abortion?"

Fifty-one percent said that abortion should be limited to the first three months, while 16.5 percent said that they were against all abortion. Only 27.5 percent would have permitted it after the third month.[213]

Keeping in mind that these polls only roughly approximate public opinion, let me draw some conclusions. Those with a college education or better consistently are less "disapproving" (more in favor of) legalized abortion for almost every reason than are those of less education and the gap seems to widen over the period of the surveys. As far as income level is concerned, we can say that support for legalized abortion increases progressively, with only a few deviations, as one goes up the income scale. Legalization is most approved by those in the highest income category ($15,000 and over).

The best educated and most affluent groups were more supportive of liberalization and/or legalization than were others. Also, the comparison of the physician surveys with the Gallup Polls suggests that physicians were more supportive of liberalization/legalization than the most affluent and educated groups overall.

To be sure, the Gallup Polls through 1968 show that most of the public would probably have supported the ALI-type statutes which were at that time the focal point of reform efforts. To the extent that most groups were still promoting this type of reform, at least until 1968, they were pursuing an objective that most of the public agreed with. It seems clear, however, that most of the public never supported the pro-legalization (i.e., abortion on demand) position that most groups went to after 1968 and that the Court decreed as the law of the land in 1973.

The following cautious conclusion can thus be made: the Supreme Court's decisions were not wanted by most citizens.[214] It was primarily the best educated and most affluent groups in American political society --

prominent among which were physicians -- whose views accorded with those of the Court. While it is impossible to know for sure what influenced the thinking of each of the seven Justices in the majority in *Wade* and *Bolton*, it is reasonable to say -- especially in light of how weak the constitutional basis of the decisions is -- that the Court's decisions were an acceptance of the opinion of the affluent, educated strata of American political society. Since these are the people who are most typically the members of the organizations I mentioned -- except the religious groups, although in many of these they are the ones who are the most involved in policymaking -- we can infer that these organizations *did* represent the views of most of their members. We can also say that by looking at the evolution of the pro-abortion movement by focusing on these organizations, we can get a good understanding of how legal change was brought about. It was these organizations, representing the most articulate and influential segment of American political society, which forged a new consensus and perhaps led the way for more permissive views on abortion among the rest of the public -- although not as permissive as theirs.

Noonan, William A. Stanmeyer, and the late Joseph O'Meara, all law professors, wrote that in *Wade* and *Bolton* the Supreme Court responded to the wishes of an articulate, activist minority.[215] This Subsection supports their assertions. The Court perhaps "followed the election returns," as the expression goes, but they were the returns from only a small segment of the public: the educated, affluent classes and the influential organizations they belong to which claimed a special knowledge about and interest in abortion. I am not, of course, suggesting that the criterion for Supreme Court decision-making should be whether a majority of the population will be in agreement. I am saying that it also cannot be the will of a particular *minority*, which is the criterion, but rather what is dictated by our fundamental law, which is contained in the Constitution and its common law and natural law background.

Why the Pro-Abortion Consensus Emerged and Was Successful

An important question that must be asked is why,

after almost universal condemnation of abortion throughout the history of America and of Judeo-Christian civilization generally, a substantial consensus developed for its legalization in all cases among the most influential strata in our society and in some cases among the rest of the public? Why did it happen even as greater biological insights were making it more certain that the unborn child is alive from fertilization? The common themes struck by the organizations in their statements for liberalization and/or legalization and editorials from the press give an explanation for this.

One theme that is sounded often in the statements and writings is simply that the abortion laws were outmoded and that a new thinking, which accords with the supposedly greater enlightenment of contemporary man, must be allowed to shape the laws. On the one hand, this is just a reflection of the "new is better" ethos which frequently appears in modern thinking. On the other -- as I will discuss in Chapter Eight -- it is a strong statement of confidence in modern science and of the ability of people to use it to the best ends. The argument runs like this: modern science has made it possible to accomplish certain things that could not be accomplished before (e.g., medically safe abortions), so we should allow the decision about using this new technology to be made solely by the "scientific expert" (in abortion, the physician) and the person seeking the "benefit" of it (the pregnant woman in abortion). This is a solution most in accordance with the "right" notion of human freedom, which recognizes that the individual, with proper advisement, always can make the best choice for himself.

A second theme, seen particularly in the editorials, which had a great effect, was that the laws were "cruel" and "uncompassionate." This judgment is made because the laws required the woman to bear a difficult and inconvenient (whether great or slight) burden. It is a point filled with irony and exaggeration. It is ironic because, especially when used later in the debate after the objective had become repealed, it completely ignores the fact that the woman's pregnancy is the result of an act of sexual intercourse which she -- except in the case of forcible rape -- took part in voluntarily. The laws are not responsible for her pregnancy, she is. It is exaggerated because to call the condition of pregnancy -- whether wanted or unwanted --

"cruel" is a distortion of a common term. With modern medicine, pregnancy is not physically onerous for most women and the psychological problems -- which in a mentally healthy woman will probably not be serious, as we shall see -- can be overcome with the proper help. To refer to pregnancy with the same term that one might use to refer to genocide is ludicrous. The exaggeration is heightened by the fact that the editorials, etc. seem not to have sought out information about the true likelihood of the threat to the woman's health by pregnancy which, if real, might lend an amount of credence to the claim of "cruelty." As I shall show in Chapter Six, however, there is not really much of a threat.

Third, the "quality of life" theme comes through clearly. It is seen particularly in statements such as ACOG's of 1968 which called for expanding the grounds for legalized abortion to take into account the woman's "'total environment, actual or foreseeable.'" Statements made by the United Methodist and United Presbyterian Churches in 1972 -- the texts of which I am making specific reference to for the first time -- point to abortion as justified when the physical, emotional, social, or economic welfare of the woman or her family may be adversely affected.[216] It was also seen in the arguments for legalized abortion to prevent the birth of deformed or "unwanted" children.

The "quality of life" advocated here is essentially a condition of life in which the individual woman or couple will be able to pursue the things which give the greatest amount of personal satisfaction, free from undesired or unpleasant responsibilities. A large part of this is material satisfaction. A second aspect of this "quality of life" argument is the notion of getting as much "control" over one's life as possible, insuring that "burdensome" problems do not crop up. There is also a society-wide dimension to this. Society should use the technological means at its disposal to insure that there is as "perfect" and as "productive" a population as possible -- according to a definition of these terms that society, or part of it has established. They are a financial and emotional burden to their families and society. Moreover, many do not look nice and just are not like the rest of us.

A fourth theme present is the situational, as opposed to the act-based, notion of morality. This will become clearer after I consider, in Chapter Eight, the relativism and utilitarian ethic reflected in the pro-abortion position.

A fifth theme is connected to the fourth. It is the notion which took hold in the latter part of the pro-abortion crusade that the abortion decision should be left, essentially, to the individual woman. How this point is connected to the one above is seen most clearly in the way this is expressed in the statements of some of the religious groups mentioned. They said that the decision should be left entirely to the woman, in accordance with her own conscience.[217] It is not even made clear if there are norms that the conscience is to be shaped by. This suggests that morality is something which is not objective or, if it is, the objective order cannot be known by the individual. Thus, all that we can expect are subjective judgments made in accordance with what the individual's conscience says. This is particularly striking when one considers that the moral issue involved is one of human life.

A final theme is the attempt, particularly by the press and some religious groups, to paint the anti-abortion position as a Catholic position, and to view the controversy as a sectarian struggle. There was little effort by the press even to explore the non-religious reasons why abortion should *not* be legal and widely available.

In light of the above and all that has been said about the history of the pro-abortion movement, then, let us see why the consensus emerged.

First, one can point to the "sexual revolution." Although building up and creeping into parts of American society for some time, the general hostility to moral restraints and authority (leveled especially at the primary shapers of morality in the American people, the churches) throughout the 1950s and 1960s caused that revolution to become widespread. The abortion laws were clearly an impediment to the realization of the objective of the "sexual revolution": maximum sexual freedom and opportunity for sexual "self-expression" as the individual desires, so long as he does not "hurt" anyone else. Abortion was a logical outgrowth of the contraceptive ethic which made this revolution possible (i.e., the consequences of sexual freedom could be avoided). Why the obvious difference between contraception and abortion -- that a new life is destroyed in abortion but not in contraception -- did not enable people to distinguish the two, one can only speculate about.[218] Instead of making this distinction which would have made abortion unacceptable, most tried to explain away the biological and commonsensical arguments about the unborn child's humanity. Perhaps the prevalence of violence and weakening of respect for human life seen elsewhere in American society at that time -- e.g., the bloody riots in the cities, the soaring crime rate, and the way the U.S. was conducting the Vietnam War -- were important factors. No doubt the great affluence of many Americans and a general belief that technology will solve everything made many morally numb. It is not surprising that the younger generation became unwilling to assume burdens -- such as unwanted pregnancies -- that scientific know-how and money could make it possible to avoid.

A second reason was the increasing secularization of religion in America. Many denominations embraced the sexual revolution and relativistic sexual morality. Many churches not only did not teach the wrongness of abortion, but actually promoted legal changes to make it more available. It is reasonable to believe that the liberal churches had a big impact on convincing legislators and judges to change the law. They also probably were responsible for shifting public opinion more in support of legal change.[219]

A third reason, also relating to religion, was latent anti-Catholicism in America. The "Catholic issue" was deliberately stirred up by NARAL and possibly influenced some New York State legislators. Writers such as Noonan, Grisez, and Father Andrew Greeley have also shown examples of how pro-abortionists have made appeals to anti-Catholic prejudices.[220]

A fourth reason was the rise of contemporary feminism. This feminism arose out of the liberal and radical social activism of the 1960s.[221] A major component of it was the insistence that the woman has an absolute right to control her body and that abortion laws interfered with this right. The assertion of this supposed right by feminists late in the 1960s may have been the main force behind the pro-abortion movement's shift from liberalization to legalization. The feminist movement was able to influence public policymakers with their demands for legalized abortion among other things partly because, in the wake of the Negro civil rights movement, there was an extreme sympathy with any group that could make a case for being "oppressed."

A fifth reason was the changes in liberalism that occurred in the 1960s. In the Kennedy and Johnson years, liberalism was clearly ascendant. Even in the more conservative Nixon years, a liberal public policy-making consensus was still prevalent in Congress and, to some degree, in the federal bureaucracy. (This was especially the case on policy questions relating to sex and the family.)[222] Liberalism, influenced by new psychological and scientific ideas about sexuality and prodded by the New Left, took an increasingly extreme view of human freedom and for the first time advocated the elimination of old legal restraints on sexual behavior. Professor James Hitchcock of St. Louis University writes that New Deal liberalism had avoided bringing moral questions into the political realm in order to preserve its coalition. The "new liberalism," however, brought them to the forefront and embraced the positions which opposed the "old" morality. He claims this is an outgrowth of the secularism liberals had long espoused quietly, but which became rampant and open in the 1960s.[223] Actually, the perspective from which the liberal advocacy of legalized abortion comes can be traced to broader aspects of modern liberal thought, as I will show in Chapter Eight.

The sixth reason, which one person I contacted emphasized to me,[224] was the common notion that we were facing a population crisis which demanded drastic action to control. (I explore this question in Chapter Six.)

The final reason for the emergence of the consensus and its ultimate success was the widespread ignorance of so many of the biological facts about the unborn child and the general facts about the nature of the criminal abortion problem (for example, I pointed to how widely accepted were dubious figures about the number if illegal abortions and resulting maternal deaths). Mrs. Greene emphasized that ignorance made it difficult to get people concerned about the abortion problem. I believe that this ignorance was particularly apparent among public policymakers.

An Examination of One Prominent Group in the New Consensus: Planned Parenthood Federation of America

One of the organizations comprising the pro-legalized abortion consensus to which I have referred is the Planned Parenthood Federation of America (also known as Planned Parenthood/World Population). I have selected PPFA for these reasons: information about it was readily accessible to me from its local office; in the 1970s, it became the leading organization in the pro-abortion movement; it has a long history and there is a substantial amount written about it and its most famous leaders, so one can trace the roots of its position on abortion; and the history of its stand on abortion is interesting.

Late in 1968, PPFA came out for legalized abortion. There is some dispute about the organization's thinking on this subject prior to that time. A number of anti-abortion authors have quoted a PPFA pamphlet that was used in the early 1960s to try to underscore the extent to which the organization allegedly changed its position on the subject.[225] The pamphlet seems to demonstrate disapproval of abortion by the organization and maintains a clear belief that human life begins at fertilization. The pertinent passage in the pamphlet is among answers to what it says are commonly asked questions about birth control. One of the questions is "Is it [birth control] abortion?" The answer given is as follows:

> "Definitely not. An abortion kills the life of a baby after it has begun. It is dangerous to your [the mother's] life and health. It may make you sterile so that when you want a child you cannot have it. Birth control merely postpones the beginning of life."[226]

There is dispute about whether this statement actually was intended to reflect a PPFA position on abortion. Its prominence in the pamphlet, however -- one would certainly think that PPFA would have edited it out if the organization were sympathetic to abortion, in light of the fact that the pamphlet was widely used for several years -- and other facts that I shall now consider make one believe that the organization definitely had held abortion in low repute, at least publicly, before 1968.

Let us go back to Margaret Sanger, the primary founder of the American birth control movement of which PPFA has been a part.[227] Mrs. Sanger always spoke out against abortion and promoted contraception as an alternative to it.[228] (More on this shortly.) Most patients seeking abortions at birth control clinics run by PPFA and its predecessors were rejected absolutely. Sometimes, however, abortions for medical reasons were arranged by clinic workers, even though they were illegal.[229]

On the international level, Planned Parenthood officials often spoke out against abortion. At the Third International Conference on Planned Parenthood in Bombay in 1952, the president of the Japan Birth Control League, Kan Majima, said that legalized abortion in Japan was only an emergency measure and "'could be done away with when more logical and humanitarian concepts are widely accepted.'" Also at that Conference, Hans Harnsen, president of the West German Committee on Planned Parenthood, denounced the acceptance of abortion as a means of birth control.[230] At the 1967 IPPF Santiago Conference, the "Rapporteur's Summary" of the discussions on abortion concluded that abortion "'cannot be recommended as a method of family planning.'"[231]

There were other indications of the unpopularity of abortion within PPFA. In a 1954 publication, "The Facts Speak for Planned Parenthood," PPFA made reference to the "350,000 to 1,250,000 or more illegal abortions" annually in the U.S. and said that it "substitutes conception control" for "these desperate acts."[232] In 1964, its president, Dr. Guttmacher who, as I mentioned, was an advocate of legal change, said of the PPFA Executive Committee: "'I think I would have a tough time in getting them to take a stand on a liberalization of abortion laws.'"[233] In March 1965, PPFA wrote the following in *Cosmopolitan* magazine:

> "'The methods by which population was curbed in other times were drastic -- abortion,

> infanticide, starvation and other forms of death. No one wants to return to these methods.'"[234]

There may have been some disagreement within PPFA's ranks about the adoption of its pro-legalization position. This was possibly manifested in the vote by its affiliates in 1971 on setting its priorities for a five-year period. The great majority of affiliates -- 67 percent -- accepted its placement at a priority level of 3 on a scale from 1 to 10 by the Executive Committee of PPFA.* Fifty-eight percent accepted the Board's decision to give PPFA efforts to promote legalized abortion as a public policy a priority of 6. Only 23.6 percent wanted abortion generally to be a higher priority and 36.7 percent wanted the public policy efforts to be emphasized more. A small, but noticeable, minority wanted a lesser emphasis in both cases, 9.4 percent -- 20 of 212 affiliates -- in the former category and 5.1 percent -- 11 of 212 -- in the latter. Disagreement with PPFA's pro-abortion position can most likely be discerned among these latter affiliates (particularly the 5.1 percent wanting to lower the already-low priority given to pro-abortion public policy efforts). It can also be seen possibly in the fact that "public policy" -- i.e., the promotion and support of efforts to legalize abortion -- was given a priority of 6 by the Executive Committee in the first place and ratified by a full 58 percent of affiliates (123). This means that 63.1 percent of affiliates (134 of 212) wanted public policy efforts to be a fairly low PPFA priority.[235]

The apparent change in Dr. Guttmacher's stated position on the matter of when human life begins perhaps parallels PPFA's change in thinking, except that it came earlier. In 1961 he had written the following about the union of sperm and egg: "Fertilization, then, has taken place; a baby has been conceived."[236] In 1968, he wrote this: "My feeling is that the fetus, particularly during its early intrauterine life, is merely a group of specialized cells that do not differ materially from other cells."[237] He could not have changed his position because of any new biological revelations.

---

*1 was the highest priority; 10 the lowest

Even though PPFA did not have an explicit position on abortion before 1968, the evidence indicates that its general view was one of disapproval, and it did not promote abortion or include it, even in legal ways, among its services.

Noonan writes that the "birth controllers" like PPFA were influenced to push for legalized abortion in the late 1960s for a number of reasons, most of which are identical to the reasons for the emergence of the pro-abortion consensus generally: the "new" sexual morality; the fact that "zero population growth" advocates, calling for more drastic means to solve the supposed overpopulation problem, got the upper hand over the old-line birth controllers; and the serious questions which arose about the safety of the birth control pill, the "magic solution" of a few years before.[238]

According to Golden, PPFA apparently was not actively involved in the 1970 repeal effort in New York, and this appears to be confirmed by what Nathanson says. Golden, as already mentioned, believed that it was the "catalyst" behind the pro-abortion groups in 1972 who were seeking to keep the repeal law in effect.[239]

Although PPFA is now at the forefront of the pro-abortion movement, it apparently did not play a significant role in the early reform/repeal effort in the U.S. generally. Nathanson, in fact, writes that abortion rights advocates such as those in NARAL wanted PPFA to get involved in their movement and, after PPFA endorsed the repeal of anti-abortion laws in 1968, believed that it "was dragging its feet inexcusably" in not doing so.[240] Possibly PPFA held back because its tax-exempt status forbade lobbying (the law has since been changed to permit some lobbying by tax-exempt organizations) and it wanted to protect its federal funding, which had begun only recently.

PPFA's pro-legalization position could have been anticipated, to some degree. It had sponsored the 1954 conference which produced conclusions sympathetic to changing the laws. Among the organizers of the 1968 Hot Springs, Virginia conference were such prominent PPFA figures as Guttmacher, Harriet Pilpel, Esq., and Dr. Louis M. Hellman, and PPFA consultant Dr. Christopher Tietze. Further, both Guttmacher and Pilpel had been active for some time in abortion reform efforts.

It has even been said that, contrary to popular belief, Margaret Sanger, despite often stating the contrary, really favored the liberty of abortion. In her book about the history of the birth control movement in America, Linda Gordon, who is clearly sympathetic to Sanger, the movement, legalized abortion, and the feminist notion of contraception and abortion as something necessary for women's liberation, writes how Sanger, in her 1914 pamphlet *The Woman Rebel*, did "something she was never to do at any later time." She defended abortion as a woman's right, even while saying that birth control would make abortion unnecessary.[241] Elasah Drogin, who is *not* supportive of Sanger or her views, writes that Sanger was motivated by sex theorist Havelock Ellis, her one-time protégé and lover, to change her pro-abortion thinking, for strategic reasons. She would be more likely to further her birth control cause if she did this.[242]

Further, PPFA repeated in its pro-abortion statements themes from its pro-contraception efforts. The jump from one to the other may have been logical for the organization (again, for some reason the fact of fertilization having occurred in the one case and not in the other was not considered an important difference).

In upcoming chapters, the following points will be emphasized in the PPFA briefs in *Wade* and *Bolton*: the unavailability of contraception to many and contraceptive failure; the problems of allowing unwanted children to come into the world; the fundamentality of the right to choose whether or not to bear a child; and the problem of overpopulation. We see all or most of these same arguments raised by Planned Parenthood in its briefs in the two major Supreme Court cases on contraception, *Griswold v. Connecticut*[243] and *Eisenstadt v. Baird*.[244] In the brief for the appellants in *Griswold*, the executive director and medical director of the Planned Parenthood League of Connecticut (PPFA's Connecticut affiliate), all of these arguments, or closely related ones, were put forth.[245] In PPFA's *amicus curiae* brief in *Eisenstadt*, all except overpopulation appears. There is a long section entitled "The Nature and Scope of the Problems Presented by Extra-marital Pregnancy" which recounts many of the same arguments about the problems of adolescent pregnancy for mother and baby, the difficulties of teen-age motherhood, illegitimacy, and "unwantedness" that appear in PPFA's brief in *Wade* and *Bolton*.[246] Since *Wade* and *Bolton* were on the Court's docket for the first time in the same term that *Eisenstadt* was decided, and the same two PPFA attorneys, Harriet Pilpel and Nancy Wechsler, were on both briefs, the similarity of the arguments is not surprising. This similarity, however, does demonstrate how the attorneys and the organization they represented viewed both abortion and contraception in the same perspective.

The "unwantedness" theme is an old one with PPFA. Indeed, PPFA's motto over the years has been "Every Child a Wanted Child."[247] In a 1954 publication, "The Facts Speak for Planned Parenthood," there appears the following statement: "...it is the birthright of every child everywhere to be brought into the world by choice instead of by chance -- to be a wanted child."[248] This objective of "wantedness" appears to have been so deeply ingrained in the PPFA perspective -- so essential to the creation of the good society -- that it had to be achieved no matter what. When it was seen that contraception was not enough to achieve it, abortion -- the means of accomplishing this which PPFA had previously scorned -- had to be turned to. The flaw in the PPFA perspective permitting this is the fact that it, in essence, assigned worth -- which is determined by whether a child is "wanted" or not -- almost totally according to the parent, or parents' point of view. The truth, of course, is that *every* child has an intrinsic worth. This "wantedness" notion is thus based on a moral relativism built around individual desires which was simply transferred to one activity -- abortion -- from another -- contraception.

Two other points can be seen in this 1954 publication -- which is aimed strictly at promoting birth control -- which emerged later in the abortion debate. Both appear in the context of the discussion about "unwantedness" and one, in fact, closely related to this point. The first is the concern about enhancing the "quality of life." This notion comes through in the following two passages:

> We have gone far with public health programs all over the world to cut death rates ... Unless the eminently desirable "death control" programs are matched with equally effective birth control programs we shall be multiplying

> the numbers of the half-alive. Eventually the dilemma will be solved by famines, pestilence, war...[249]

and

> Planned Parenthood operates in an important and neglected field of preventive medicine that can do much to prevent and reduce many of the social and health ills that weaken family life and threaten the world today.[250]

We see the willingness to attribute social and other problems -- i.e., the things which lower our quality of life -- to the bringing of "unwanted" and "unfit" children into the world.

The second point, seen in the following passage, is that "unwanted" children typically become a burden on society:

> Every dependent child reared by the government, which is to say the taxpayer, costs about $18,000. A great many dependent children are unwanted children whose parents could not cope with them. Unwanted children are likely to be sick children -- emotionally and physically. They are a fruitful source of neurotics, alcoholics, delinquents and criminals...[251]

These two points are both seen in a 1939 publication of the Birth Control Federation of America, PPFA's predecessor. The Federation published a speech presented by Dr. Haven Emerson of Columbia's College of Physicians and Surgeons under the title of "What May Health Departments Do to Further Improve the Quality of Life? -- the Whether or Not and When of Pregnancy." Dr. Emerson was promoting the development within public health departments of reproduction and family planning programs. He said concern should be "with the constructive use of our knowledge of human biology for *better quality* of population, and for greater safety of mother and child."[252] He spoke of health departments undertaking these programs "in the interest of better quality and sufficient sum of human reproduction."[253] While it is true that one of his purposes in the speech was to provide some social rationale that would justify the involvement of *public* health departments in this area, he did not seem at all reluctant to view it as something which rightfully could be directed for social objectives. He referred to the activity he was proposing as "biological guidance in human reproduction for social ends."[254]

A further aspect of the Planned Parenthood perspective is seen in the above passages. That is that human wrongdoing and weakness are not to be overcome by change occurring within the individual -- by developing virtue in the child so he will act responsibly and morally, and in the parents so they will change their attitude toward a child they did not want -- but rather by preventing him from being born in the first place.

Even though an appeal made to the individual parents -- which I am sure is sincere -- that childbearing should be a matter for *their* choice and desires, there is a concern that this be done for *society*. Our "quality of life" *as a society* -- which becomes a kind of moral imperative -- will be enhanced only when we eliminate the very *possibility* that "undesirable" persons will become part of it. It is, then, a social good which is to be furthered, even while it is presented in the context of individual rights (of the parents) and the preventing of individual hardship (for the "unwanted" child). This is why it can seriously be claimed that a new child should be destroyed by abortion for his own good.[255]

All of the problems mentioned in the passages above from the PPFA literature and the briefs are to be solved before they are allowed to manifest themselves by means of the effective contraception and safe abortion which science has made possible. One might say that they can be "cut off at the pass" by scientific progress. Moreover, there is in what I have discussed here a near-obesssion with gaining complete control over the circumstances of life. We shall observe this also in the *Wade* and *Bolton* briefs. Whether such complete control is achieved and the human condition is so markedly improved through science as PPFA and other advocates of contraception and abortion think, or whether the results may actually be quite the opposite, shall be considered in Chapter Eight.

The Emergence of the Anti-Abortion Movement

David B. Truman writes the following:

> Any mutual interest...any shared attitude, is a potential group. A disturbance in established relationships and expectations anywhere in the society may produce new patterns of interaction aimed at restricting or eliminating the disburbance. Sometimes it may be this possibility that alone gives the potential group a minimum of influence in the political process.[256]

The successes achieved by the pro-abortion movement in the latter part of the 1960s -- i.e., the "disturbance" of the established legal situation brought about by its efforts -- can be said to have brought people together into the anti-abortion movement as a reaction against it. In this Section, we will see the history of the anti-abortion movement, to just after the *Wade* and *Bolton* decisions were handed down. This will roughly parallel the period of the rise of the pro-abortion consensus, giving particular focus to New York State. New York State is singled out for these reasons: it was the state where the anti-abortion movement appears to have begun and where it gained its greatest level of organization and strength before 1973; it was also where the most intense battle over legalized abortion occurred before 1973; and information about the early movement, as well as the controversy, there was readily accessible in *The New York Times* and from prominent persons active in it. Just, how as a reaction to the pro-abortion movement, the anti-abortion movement got its start and what role it played in the *Wade* and *Bolton* cases will be the focus of this Section. Most of the history of the anti-abortion movement occurred *after* 1973.[257]

The Movement's Beginnings: New York State

The anti-abortion movement in the U.S. dates at

least to 1963. Law professors Robert Byrn and Charles E. Rice, whose writings on abortion I shall be referring to, were among the organizers of a small, informal group in the New York City area, Metropolitan Right to Life.[258]

The statewide anti-abortion movement dates to 1966. Mr. Edward Golden and Mrs. Helen Greene were among the earliest participants, and Mrs. Greene explained its origins.

The first anti-abortion efforts on the state level in New York began after the Catholic Physicians Guild, a lay group, was alerted in 1966 to the reform bills in the state legislature. The Catholic bishops of the state became involved in 1966 by making statements to alert people in their dioceses.[259] (We will see later more about the Catholic Church's role in the anti-abortion movement.) In the earliest years, anti-abortionists gathered mostly in each others' homes.[260] The first statewide meeting did not take place until 1970 in Loudonville.[261] Writing in the *National Right to Life News* several years ago, Mr. Golden spoke about the nature of the early anti-abortion efforts: "The Right to Life movement in its genesis was mostly a letter writing operation run by individuals who encouraged concerned citizens to contact their state legislators and express their fear of loosening the laws controlling the practice of abortion."[262] Mrs. Greene told me that in those early years people were very reluctant to get involved. They did not even want to write letters to legislators because they did not know what to say to them. Whenever they actually met their representatives their typical reaction was to feel "honored" that they were face to face with an important person.[263]

Mrs. Greene said that the typical reaction of people, both Catholic and non-Catholic, was one of disbelief that the abortion laws would ever be changed. As already noted, she believed that the major early obstacle was simply peoples' ignorance about abortion and the biological facts about the unborn child. People thought it improper to talk about anything relating to pregnancy and childbirth. The anti-abortion movement was engaged in educational activity in different parts of the state from 1966 on. Much of it at first was directed toward women's groups. In 1969, they began to speak in schools.[264]

The Movement's Beginnings: Other States

Elsewhere in the country, anti-abortion groups were also getting started. Mrs. Barbara Willke, who with her husband Dr. John C. Willke have become a major international speaking team against abortion, explained that groups started spontaneously in individual states as people tried to respond to the reform efforts in their legislatures. The Willkes, after many years' activity in the field of sex and family life education, became involved in anti-abortion efforts at the urging of their two college-age daughters. They helped to organize both Cincinnati Right to Life and the Ohio Right to Life Society.[265] They later wrote the *Handbook on Abortion* which has come out in three editions since 1971, and satisfied a crucial need by supplying rank-and-file members of the anti-abortion movement with a handy compilation of information to refute the usual pro-abortion arguments. It has since become the most widely read book in the world presenting the anti-abortion case, and has been translated into eight languages.[266]

In Colorado, where the first liberalized law was passed, Mrs. Mary Rita Urbish, a housewife and political neophyte, organized the anti-abortion movement. Her efforts were probably typical of the earliest anti-abortion efforts in most states. She testified at the legislative hearings on the 1967 bill. Frustrated by what was happening, she organized a "Mother's March" of a couple hundred women at the State Capitol, gathered signatures with her friends on petitions against the bill, and engineered a heavy mail, telegram, and telephone effort to get the governor not to sign the bill. She was unsuccessful, but shortly afterwards helped organize the group that was eventually to become the Colorado Right to Life Committee. Her anti-abortion efforts also prompted her to become involved in politics for the first time, serving as a delegate to county and state Democratic conventions, and as campaign manager for an anti-abortion legislative candidate.[267]

In Minnesota, one of the nation's most effective anti-abortion organizations, Minnesota Citizens Concerned for Life (MCCL), got started in 1967. (A national organization, American Citizens Concerned for Life, was later formed as a spin-off from MCCL.) The story of its origins was typical. In that year a bill to liberalize the state's abortion law was introduced in the legislature. The people who appeared at the Capitol to argue against the law, realizing that the battle against abortion would be a long one, believed that a formal organization was needed and set up MCCL. In 1969, intensive lobbying by the rapidly growing organization defeated an effort to pass an abortion on demand bill. In 1971, MCCL became involved in the judicial arena by filing an *amicus curiae* brief for a case in the state courts challenging the constitutionality of the Minnesota abortion statute.[268] It also joined in a brief before the Supreme Court in *Wade* and *Bolton*.

By the time of *Wade* and *Bolton* in 1973, MCCL already had 10,000 members and succeeded in getting the Minnesota legislature to pass a resolution in the same year calling upon Congress to enact a constitutional amendment to overturn the decisions.[269]

MCCL has been active both in educational and legislative efforts. Its latter efforts have been much broader than those of most anti-abortion groups. It has backed legislation for the following purposes: to stop child abuse, to require school children to receive German measles vaccinations, to provide tax benefits for adoptive parents, and to provide insurance coverage for unwed mothers, among other things.[270] It has thus clearly adopted a perspective which has sought not only to legally prohibit abortion, but also to eliminate, by means of social welfare legislation and other types of legal prohibitions, the kinds of conditions which often spawn it and make it an easier choice for women.

The Movement's Emergence as a Political Force: New York State

The difference between what happened in 1970 and in 1972 in New York State is the story of a state anti-abortion movement which came into its own. The movement was still diffuse and organization was limited in 1970. Large numbers of people had not yet come into it, and only a few people -- amateurs -- were lobbying in Albany. In a 1972 article in *The New York Times Magazine*,

Golden was quoted as follows: "'The people who had been conducting the campaign in favor of abortion had done their work in the corridors of the Legislature, and we hadn't. We'd been conducting an education campaign, counting on that to win the issue, but now we knew we'd have to roll up our sleeves and really become political.'"[271] The same article said that until 1970, "most of the formal opposition to legal abortion [in New York State] had been mounted primarily within the Catholic Church." It gave the example of a few state legislators who had been denounced by their parish priests for their stand on abortion.[272] Mrs. Greene told me that up to that time the Church was the only force in the state that had consistently opposed liberalization and/or legalization. She said, however, that the Church hierarchy was reluctant to push too hard. They would just make public statements. Catholic groups were used to get the message out, but no lobbying was done on behalf of the Church. The New York State Catholic Conference *did* lobby for the 1972 bill.[273]

After the 1970 vote, New York State Right to Life became a more cohesive group, plunging into the political thicket. It helped to upset a number of pro-legalization legislators. Efforts were made to keep the anti-abortion movement visible in Albany almost every legislative day -- e.g., by picketing or visits to legislators -- and to keep constant pressure on legislators. A bill to repeal the repeal law was barely kept from getting out of committee in 1971 and the legislature actually did vote for its repeal in 1972. It was known by Right to Life that Governor Rockefeller would veto the 1972 repeal, but it still decided to make an all-out effort in the Legislature, because it believed that a successful legislative vote would give the anti-abortion movement around the country a moral boost.[279] Just a few weeks before the 1972 vote, the anti-abortion movement in New York State showed its strength by assembling 10,000 persons for a demonstration in New York City. The rally was sponsored by the Knights of Columbus, a Catholic lay organization, and took place on a day designated by New York City's Cardinal Cooke as "Right to Life Sunday," but was joined in by persons of other faiths as well.[275]

Its incredible electoral victories, and success in bringing about the total repeal of the 1970 act, led Fred C. Shapiro, the writer of *The New York Times*

Magazine article previously mentioned, to say that New York State Right to Life was "considered the strongest of all the state [anti-abortion] movements."[276]

The Movement on the National Level

According to Shapiro, the National Right to Life Committee was founded in 1968 by Juan Ryan, a New Jersey attorney.[277] Ryan was one of the attorneys on the Committee's brief in *Wade* and *Bolton*. Golden confirmed that the national organization was formed in 1968. A meeting was organized in Washington by the United States Catholic Conference (USCC) -- the bureaucratic arm of the U.S. Catholic Bishops -- of the leaders of the anti-abortion movements in about a dozen states, the most prominent of which were New York, California, Illinois, Pennsylvania, and Colorado.[278]

The first national meeting of the anti-abortion movement took place in 1969 at Berea College outside of Chicago, and was attended by Golden. Many of the people who came could not believe how strong the movement to permit legal abortion had become in states like New York and California. The early guiding lights of the national movement were physicians, such as Herbert Ratner (Illinois) and Fred Mecklenburg (Minnesota); but attorneys such as Dennis J. Horan (Illinois) and John E. Archibold (Colorado) were there, too. That first meeting saw a trading of ideas and suggestions about how to carry on the campaign. A cohesive organization would emerge later.[279]

In 1970, there was another national meeting in Minneapolis. At a 1973 meeting in Detroit, the national movement was finally formally organized into the National Right to Life Committee (NRLC). By this time, of course, the term "right to life" had stuck. Mrs. Greene said it originated with a Denver attorney.[280] A national organization was needed to share and circulate important information that anti-abortionists in various states needed to effectively carry on their fight, and simply to give support to each other.[281] Most in the movement were political neophytes, and at these first national meetings there were workshops on lobbying, how to use the media, and fund-raising. The NRLC was the only national organization for a time. New organizations were started as a result of disagreement over strategy and personality conflicts. Although a number of national groups now exist, most anti-abortion activists are card-carrying members of the NRLC.[282]

Other Early Political and Legal Efforts

Although its organization on the national level was limited at this point, the anti-abortion movement registered successes in many states. *Time* attributed to it the thwarting of liberalized abortion laws in such states as Minnesota, Iowa, Missouri, Ohio, the Dakotas, Indiana, Kentucky, and Massachusetts.[283] *The New York Times* reported that a survey of legislators backing successful reform bills in various states showed them to believe that if the anti-abortion movement had been around earlier, their bills would not have been enacted.[284]

The organized anti-abortion movement also worked in the courts to counter the increased efforts there after 1969 by pro-abortion adversaries. In New York State, Professor Byrn and another attorney, Larry Washburn, spearheaded an effort to get the state Court of Appeals, New York's highest court, to rule the 1970 statute unconstitutional, and Byrn himself was appointed guardian *ad litem* for the class of unborn children in order to carry on the suit. It was unsuccessful.[285] In Illinois, the anti-abortion movement lost an effort to stop a federal court from declaring that state's restrictive statute unconstitutional, but succeeded in getting a stay of the ruling from the U.S. Supreme Court.[286] In *Wade* and *Bolton*, the NRLC's *amicus curiae* brief was its first legal effort.[287] The other anti-abortion organizations that joined in briefs were LIFE (League for Infants, Fetuses, and the Elderly), Americans United for Life (AUL), Women for the Unborn, Women Concerned for the Unborn Child, Celebrate Life, and (as mentioned) MCCL. In 1975, the Americans United for Life Legal Defense Fund was organized to insure that the anti-abortion movement would be able to sustain a long-term litigation effort on abortion and other life issues.[288]

The People in the Movement

What types of people became involved in the early anti-abortion movement? In contrast to the people identified with pro-abortion sentiments -- professionals, the educated, etc., -- it was primarily "ordinary people," according to Mrs. Greene. She said that in New York State, at first, not many physicians were active, but a few lawyers were. Professor Byrn was the central legal figure. After the passage of the 1970 law, some very zealous people became involved and caused the movement some embarrassment in the legislature.[289] It seems that on the national level, more professionals were involved from the very start.

At the beginning in New York State, virtually all the people involved in the anti-abortion movement were Catholics. However, more people from other faiths also joined shortly.[290] The greater participation of Catholics at the start is probably due to the fact that that Church's doctrinal opposition to abortion was more sweeping than other churches' and put forth more emphatically to its adherents. The extent to which non-Catholics were involved by 1971 is seen in a *Time* magazine article which reported that the anti-abortion movement was "a mixed bag...[c]onservative Roman Catholics teamed up with a sizable number of liberals. Also included, the Salvation Army and the Mormons, Greek Orthodoxy and Orthodox Jewry, hard-shell fundamentalists and hard-nosed minority of liberal Protestant ethicists." It pointed out that one state's organization was headed by an agnostic of Jewish background, another's by a Methodist, and that a noted politically liberal Episcopal clergyman was also a leader in the movement.[291]

Afterword on the Anti-Abortion Movement

The early development of the anti-abortion movement thus seems to have followed closely the following pattern which Tocqueville mentioned:

> When an opinion is represented by a society, it necessarily assumes a more exact and explicit form. It numbers its partisans and compromises their welfare in its cause: they, on the other hand, become acquainted with each other, and their zeal is increased by their number. An association unites the efforts of minds which have a tendency to diverge in one single channel, and urges them vigorously towards one single end which it points out.[292]

Golden said that this passage described the anti-abortion movement well.[293] It would not, of course, have been adequate to describe the efforts of most of the organizations which supported abortion reform or repeal -- except perhaps for those which were set up exclusively for that purpose, none of which I am examining in this Chapter -- because they were established groups whose primary concerns were broader or focused on other matters.

A study of the history of the anti-abortion movement after 1973 would no doubt show that it increased its numbers of activists, became better organized, and functioned more professionally. (It has not become more cohesive, however. It has been beset by internal squabbling growing out of differences of strategy and disagreements with leadership. It has generally been amazingly united in its unwillingness to compromise on its ultimate objectives, but has often been split -- as seen in the controversy over the so-called Hatch "Federalism" Amendment -- over whether to accept interim compromise solutions.)[294] The movement has tended to follow the general pattern of organizations, becoming more bureaucratic and hierarchical with time though it has not gone too far in that direction. The National Right to Life Committee -- which is the largest organization -- is not rigidly organized from the top down. It has state and local chapters affiliated with it, which are largely independent. The agreement on ultimate objectives means that deviations down the line on fundamentals are unlikely, although state and local boards are known to break with the national board on specific strategies and policies. Moreover, the fact that state and local groups often jealously guard their turf, the substantial absence of a network of bureaucratic rewards and punishments, and the largely volunteer nature of the movement have probably also been important factors in limiting bureaucratization. While the movement has become somewhat more organized and professional, it has also witnessed greater expressions of mass support, as with the annual March for Life in Washington, D.C. which began in 1974.

Immediately after the *Wade* and *Bolton* decisions, the anti-abortion movement, as might be expected, was demoralized. It soon put the pieces together and came to realize that it had to shift its orientation and strategy. It had to consider what could be done within the decisions (e.g., regarding parental and spousal consent). It also had to focus its attention more on the national level and made a constitutional amendment its primary political goal. John S. Putka wrote that the decisions "did much to galvanize the pro-life movement from one which merely issued dire warnings about the future into one which had something very real in the present to fight against."[295]

The Role of the Catholic Church in the Early Anti-Abortion Struggle

The Catholic Church was assailed by the press and other religious groups as being the main obstacle to legal change, and NARAL specifically intended to aim its guns at the Catholic hierarchy. Pro-abortion activists have long claimed -- almost invariably without producing proof -- that the Catholic Church is behind the anti-abortion movement and is funding it. Though organs of the Church did help in the initial organization of the movement, at least in New York State, and the hierarchy made public statements and engaged in some lobbying, it never did so strictly on behalf of the

Right to Life organization. It has also provided facilities, such as meeting places and phones, for the movement.[296] Nevertheless, though many of its people are Catholics, the movement is not a Catholic one, it is not sponsored by the Church even though its aims are supported by it, and it is not funded by it. The Shapiro article reveals how there was some sentiment for setting the movement up along denominational lines at the start -- e.g., the adherents of various faiths in their own groups, without formal sponsorship or attachment to their religious bodies and united by an "umbrella-type" right to life organization -- but the idea was rejected and most of its groups are nondenominational.[297] It was very careful not to get too close to the Catholic Church.[298]

As for funding, both Golden and Mrs. Greene claim that the New York and national organizations never received any funds from the Church or any other religious groups.[299] In its early years, money often came out of the participants' own pockets. Some did things like selling craft items they made to raise funds. Mail appeals began in the early 1970s, as did the "Save a Baby" raffle in New York State.[300] The New York State Right to Life Committee did not have many expenses at the beginning, since it was run largely from Golden's kitchen table. The New York, Minnesota, Michigan, and Ohio organizations provided whatever financial impetus the NRLC needed then.[301] Later on, it became strong enough to make direct mail appeals and is supported partly by funds raised by its state and local affiliates.

Putka said that he was told flatly by the bishop who formerly headed the National Conference of Catholic Bishops (NCCB) that it does not fund the movement, except for the organization it runs, the National Committee for a Human Life Amendment. Individual bishops are free to determine the nature and kind of support they wish to give the movement within their own dioceses.[302] In the NCCB's *Pastoral Plan for Pro-Life Activities* in 1975, it sought to emphasize that it regarded the political strategies then underway in the movement as helpful, but that the movement was not "'operated, controlled or financed by the Church.'"[303]

Since the late 1960s, the U.S. bishops have issued a number of statements expressing principles about the respect for unborn human life. They have tried to emphasize that their position is not a "unique religious conviction," but comes from the entire "'Judeo-Christian heritage of concern for the person'" and is shared "'by specialists in the fields of medicine, law and the social sciences.'"[304] They have also referred to the U.S. Bill of Rights and the U.N. Declaration on the Rights of the Child as supporting their position on the right to life. In March 1974, four U.S. cardinals testified before a Senate Judiciary Committee sub-committee in support of a constitutional amendment.[305]

In summary, the Catholic Church has supported the anti-abortion movement in different ways, but the support has been prudent and very little of it financial. Anyone with the least knowledge of the movement knows that it is not controlled by the Church.

Finally, one cannot help but be impressed by the contradictory nature of the pro-abortion movement's rebuke of the Catholic Church's involvement -- such as it is -- in the issue. Many religious denominations and organizations aided the campaign to change the laws, and were welcomed as the Religious Coalition for Abortion Rights, the first interdenominational religious group to be organized specifically to promote abortion "rights," was later welcomed.

Conclusions

The emergence of the anti-abortion movement had a definite effect on the direction of the political struggle over abortion. Mrs. Greene has said that prior to the Court's decisions, the movement believed it had succeeded in stopping further "erosion" of the legal protection for the unborn. It was not confident that it could actually reverse the legal changes which had already occurred.[306] Clearly, it had checked the reform trend in state legislatures. Its success in getting the repeal law revoked by the New York State legislature suggests, however, that it might well have been able to repeal reform laws elsewhere.

Second, the anti-abortion movement is an example

of a new force in politics emerging specifically to counter substantial legislative changes being brought about by other groups.

Third, the support the anti-abortion movement attracted and the extent of its success in such a short time demonstrated a greal deal of discontent within the body politic with the rapid legal change that occurred in this area. It also demonstrates the volatility of the issue. Minds and votes can be changed quickly as a result of new information, and the exertion of political pressure. It suggests that care must be taken when predicting the outcome of the abortion controversy in America.

Fourth, the source of the surprising success of the anti-abortion movement in its earliest years, and since, probably rests from its uncompromising views and the willingness of the people in its ranks to persevere on the abortion issue. Many anti-abortionists are willing to cast their vote for or against a candidate on the basis of this one issue alone.[307]

Chapter Summary and Conclusions

The pro-abortion movement gained success largely because its adherents were in the most influential and articulate social classes, and it carried out its efforts primarily through some of the most prestigious and influential private organizations in America. It is a striking confirmation of the influence of what Tocqueville called "the intellectual and moral associations." The medical community was especially important in both setting the stage for and giving momentum to the pro-abortion drive. The appeal of the pro-abortion movement displayed a strong willingness, at least until the feminists became a prominent part of it, to defer to this community on even the moral question involved.

The pro-abortionists also had the political and social sentiment of the times -- particularly, again, of the influentials -- on their side. They came along at a time thus conducive to changing a long-standing public policy. The liberalization of abortion laws and then their abolition is a saga of what happens when the beliefs of the highest socio-economic groups -- beliefs not shared by the public at large -- are transformed into public policy through the determined efforts of organizations they control. The speed of their success shows that this was an issue whose aspects had been insufficiently considered by policymakers asked to make a judgment. Too often the latter accepted the terms with which the pro-abortionists framed the issue, and relied on their own beliefs and biases in making a decision.

The early development of anti-abortion groups is an illustration of Tocqueville's view on how associations come into existence. The emergence of this movement, and its quick successes, was even more stunning than the pro-abortion movement's. It started out as much more of a grassroots effort than the pro-abortion movement, and this probably continues to be so. At the beginning and ever since, it has proven to be most effective in the arena where popular opinion and numbers make the most difference, the legislative, and less effective where they do not, the judicial.

Chapter Two

The *Roe v. Wade* and *Doe v. Bolton* Opinions: Structuring, Language, and the Knowledge Relied Upon

Survey of the *Roe v. Wade* and *Doe v. Bolton* Opinions

The *Roe v. Wade* and *Doe v. Bolton* cases* were decided by a 7 to 2 vote, although only four Justices joined in the Opinions of the Court. Three wrote concurring opinions, which means they joined the decision but not necessarily all of the reasoning stated in the Court's opinion, and, of course, two dissented. The *Wade* case came to the Supreme Court on appeal from a

---

*The two cases were decided together and the decisions handed down the same day, January 22, 1973. When I refer to the "Court's" opinions in these cases, I mean the plurality opinions written by Justice Blackmun and joined by Justices Brennan, Marshall, and Powell. Similarly, when I refer to "the Court's" opinion in other cases mentioned throughout this book, I mean the opinion of a plurality or majority of the Court which is reported as the "Opinion of the Court."

decision of a three-judge federal district court for the Northern District of Texas (Dallas) in 1970.[1] *Bolton* was appealed from the decision of a three-judge federal district court for the Northern District of Georgia (Atlanta) in 1970.[2] I proceed now to examine each of the opinions of the Supreme Court Justices in the cases. In the Subsections in the opinions for the Court in *Wade* and *Bolton*, I examine each part of the opinions as they were divided up by the Court.

The *Wade* Case

THE OPINION OF THE COURT

Introductory Paragraphs - The Court's opinion began with a few statements about the statutes being challenged, the nature of the abortion question, and the Court's role in dealing with it. It says that the Texas statute was typical of those in force in "many States for approximately a century." The Georgia statute, however, was a "modern" one, reflective of "new thinking about an old issue."[3] It states that it is aware of "the sensitive and emotional nature of the abortion controversy" and that one's view about the subject is shaped by one's "philosophy," experiences, religious training, "the moral standards one establishes and seeks to observe" and so on. It also contends that the Court's task is "to resolve the issue by constitutional measurement, free of emotion and of predilection."[4]

Part I - The Court reviewed the provisions of the Texas abortion statute and similar statutes in other states, which made abortion a crime unless performed for the purpose of saving the mother's life.

Part II - The claims of each of the plaintiffs were briefly reviewed and the disposition of the lower federal court is stated. That court declared the statute unconstitutional under the Ninth and Fourteenth Amendments. It granted a declaratory judgment, but refused an injunction.[5]

Part III - This is a very short section which merely stated that the Supreme Court has granted *certiori* because of the denial of injunctive relief under 28 U.S. Code, Section 1253, Volume 28 U.S. Code, Section 1253.

Part IV - This section discusses justiciability, standing, and abstention. "Jane Roe" was a pregnant, single, woman at the time the action was filed.[6] Thus, the Court stated that there was a valid case or controversy. The Court waived the normal requirement that the case or controversy continue until the time of its review of the case because the nature of pregnancy would not otherwise permit appellate review. The action by the plaintiff-intervenor, Dr. James Hubert Hallford, was dismissed because he was at the time a defendant in a pending state court case for violating the statute and, as such, could not challenge it in federal court. The other plaintiffs, "John and Mary Doe," a married couple, challenged the statute because "Mary" had a "'neural-chemical' disorder" and was advised by her physician to avoid pregnancy and discontinue birth control pills. Since she was not then pregnant and the harm to her was only "speculative," the Court dismissed their complaint.[7]

Part V - This was a brief statement of the plaintiff's basic argument on the merits. The plaintiff claimed that the statute violated the woman's liberty under either the Ninth or Fourteenth Amendments or in the Bill of Rights and its penumbras generally.

Part VI - This section contained an historical review of the attitudes and legal constraints on abortion, focusing on the following: ancient attitudes, a consideration of the Hippocratic Oath's condemnation of abortion, English common law, statutory law in England and America, the changing of the American Medical Association's position on abortion, and the positions of two other pertinent organizations, the American Bar Association and the American Public Health Association.*

Ancient Attitudes - The Court stated that in ancient Greece and Rome, abortion was widely practiced and the law offered little protection to the unborn child.

The Hippocratic Oath - The Court contended that the Oath, with its firm mandate to the physician not to per-

---

*The division of Part VI which follows was actually made by the Court in the *Wade* opinion. The divisions of the other Parts which I make do not appear in the opinion, but have been put in by me to make it easier for the reader to follow.

form abortion, is not broadly representative of ancient thinking, but rather of only one school of ancient philosophy, the Pythagorean. It became the "'nucleus of all medical ethics'" only after the rise of Christianity.[8]

The Common Law - The common law on abortion was discussed. The Court stated that at common law, abortion both before and after quickening (i.e., when the mother first feels the child moving in her womb) was "never established as a common law crime."[9] It singles out Edward Coke as being responsible for much of the supposedly erroneous view about what the common law held about abortion.

The English Statutory Law - The Court stated that it was only in the early nineteenth century that England, by statute, made abortion a crime. It surveyed English statutory development since then.

The American Law - The Court stated that it was also in the nineteenth century when abortion was first outlawed in the United States. The usual provisions of state statutes were mentioned.

The Position of the American Medical Association (AMA) - The opinion traced the development of this position for almost 125 years. It pointed out that the AMA adopted resolutions in 1859 which attacked abortion as an "'unwarranted destruction of human life'" and in 1871 which contended that it should be "'unlawful and unprofessional for any physician to induce abortion or premature labor, without the concurrent opinion of at least one respectable consulting physician, and then always with a view to the safety of the child.'"[10]

The court mentioned how this position was maintained until 1967 when the AMA endorsed the idea of changing abortion statutes to make them similar to the Georgia one. In 1970, the AMA adopted resolutions which went even further. It referred to abortion simply as a "'medical procedure'" which, if performed by a physician, does not violate the AMA Principles of Medical Ethics so long as it is done "'in accordance with good medical practice'" and does not violate the law.[11]

The Position of the American Public Health Association and of the American Bar Association - The Court pointed to the fact that both of these organizations recently had endorsed legalized abortion.

More of the specific points the Court included in this section of the opinion are found in Chapter Three.

Part VII - The Court here made a judgment about the purpose of the nineteenth century state anti-abortion statutes, which is important to its further legal analysis. It says that three reasons are generally put forward for the statutes: to discourage illicit sexual conduct, to protect prenatal life, and to protect the woman. It concludes, seemingly relying on the research of Professor Cyril Means of New York Law School (whom it footnotes), that the woman's health was the *sole* purpose. I shall mention more of the specifics stated in this section in Chapter Three.

Part VIII - In this Section, the Court analyzed the right of privacy, which it claimed protects the woman's abortion decision.

The Basis for the Right of Privacy - The Court claimed its previous decisions establish the existence of this right, even though it is not mentioned anywhere in the Constitution. The Court agreed with the appellant's contention, stated above, about the parts of the Constitution from which this right can be inferred. It particularly pointed to the cases which have declared that there is a right of privacy within marital and familial relationships.

Why the Right Applies to Abortion - The Court believed that the right of privacy applied to abortion because of the injuries a woman can suffer by carrying a pregnancy to term. The Court made this connection by talking about the right being "broad enough to encompass a woman's decision whether or not to terminate her pregnancy." Then it said that "the detriment that the State would impose upon the pregnant woman by denying this choice [to have an abortion altogether] is apparent."[12] The possible injuries to the woman that it mentioned are the harm to physical and mental health caused by child-rearing, the problems of bringing an unwanted child into a family unable to care for it, and the stigma of unwed motherhood. The Court also cited several lower court decisions which dealt with this question which agreed that the right of privacy is broad enough to cover the abortion decision.

The Limitation of the Right - The Court insisted that this privacy right is not absolute. It denied "the claim asserted by some *amici* that one has an unlimited right to do with one's body as one pleases" by saying "[t]he Court has refused to recognize an unlimited right of this kind in the past." The right of privacy, it goes on to say, "is not unqualified and must be considered against important state interests in regulation."[13]

Part IX - The Court turned to two vital questions in its legal analysis: the legal personhood of the unborn child and the question of when life begins. The Court stated how pivotal the personhood question is to its legal analysis: "If...personhood is established, the appellant's case, of course, collapses, for the fetus' right to life would then be guaranteed specifically by the [Fourteenth] Amendment."[14]

The Personhood of the Unborn Child - The Court proceeded to argue that the various usages of the term "person" in the Constitution have no application to unborn children. These usages include the Qualifications for Representatives and Senators, the Apportionment Clause, the Migration and Importation provision, and the Emolument Clause in Article I, the Electors provisions and the qualifications for President in Article II, the Extradition provisions and the superseded Fugitive Slave Clause in Article IV, and the Fifth, Twelfth, Fourteenth, and Twenty-second Amendments. This and its conclusion that abortion practices were freer before the enactment of the nineteenth century statutes, lead the Court to hold that the Fourteenth Amendment was not intended to protect the unborn as persons. It mentioned several lower court decisions which concluded likewise.

The Question of When Life Begins - The Court addressed Texas' contention that it was justified in protecting the fetus because human life begins at conception. The Court said it "need not resolve the difficult question of when life begins" and then never faced this issue squarely. It was unwilling to do this because neither academic disciplines -- the Court mentions medicine, philosophy, and theology -- nor religious groups have been able to agree about it. The Court specifically mentioned that while the notion of life beginning at conception is "the official belief of the Catholic Church," the "predominant" view of the Jewish faith and of "a large segment of the Protestant community" is that life does not begin until birth.[15]

The Court in Part IX also emphasized the importance of "viability," the point at which the fetus becomes potentially able to live outside the mother's womb with artificial aid. It says that this point is usually placed at about seven months (twenty-eight weeks), although it may occur as early as twenty-four weeks.

Other Areas of the Law - The Court briefly considers how such areas of the law as torts, property, and inheritence have treated prenatal life. It concluded that interests the law has viewed unborn children as possessing were contingent upon their actually being born alive. Thus, said the Court, the law has never treated them as persons "in the whole sense."[16]

Part X - In this section the Court set out its precise holding.

The Interest of the Woman v. the Interest of the Unborn Child - The Court said that Texas may not override the rights of the pregnant woman to have an abortion by "adopting one theory of life." It acknowledged that the state does have an "important and legitimate" interest both in protecting the woman's health and the "potentiality of human life." The state's interest "grows in substantiality" as the woman approaches term. In order to structure its holding on the basis of this "substantiality" notion, the Court divided pregnancy into three trimesters. It also made the substance of the state's legal regulation of abortion contingent upon which of the two interests above it is trying to promote, as explained below.[17]

The state's interest in maternal health becomes "'compelling'" at the end of the first trimester. This, the Court said, is based on the "now-established medical fact" that maternal mortality from abortion "may be less" than such mortality from childbirth. Thus, at that point the state may regulate abortion "to the extent that the regulation reasonably relates to the preservation and protection of maternal health" (such as requiring that the person performing the abortion meet certain qualifications).[18] Prior to this, the Court said the physician, in consultation with his patient, is free to determine that the pregnancy should be terminated.[19]

The Court's viability analysis, mentioned above, became important when it determined what state regulation would be permitted in order to protect its interest in the "potential life" of the fetus. It claimed this interest becomes "'compelling'" at viability. After this point (roughly the end of the second trimester), the state may prohibit abortion except when it is necessary to preserve "the life and health of the mother."[20]

The decision, then, allows abortion (for any reason) up to the third trimester of pregnancy upon the joint decision of the woman and her attending physician. It is questionable whether the greater authority of the state to restrict third trimester abortions amounts to a significant restriction of this right, as we shall see shortly when I discuss the *Bolton* decision.

Part XI - This section summarized and restated the holding. It also specified that the state may proscribe abortions by non-physicians.[21] It also made two noteworthy statements that its decision meets "the demands of the present day" and "the abortion decision...is inherently, and primarily, a medical decision."[22]

Part XII - The Court closed its opinion by stating that it will withhold judgment about whether the District Court should have granted an injunction because it assumed, now that the statute has been declared unconstitutional, that the Texas authorities would refrain from further prosecutions.

*JUSTICE STEWART'S CONCURRING OPINION**

Justice Stewart's concurring opinion emphasized the need to view "liberty," as protected by the Fourteenth Amendment, as being much more inclusive than just the specific guarantees spelled out in the Constitution and the Bill of Rights. Relying on several previous Supreme Court decisions, he says that it has been made clear that the "liberty" protected by the Fourteenth Amendment includes "freedom of personal choice in matters of marriage and family life."[23] He contended that

---

*All concurring opinions, while published with one or the other of the Court's opinions (I have listed them under the respective one), are to be understood as applying to the Court's decisions in *both* cases.

the right of the individual "to be free from unwarranted governmental intrusion into...the decision whether to bear or beget a child" -- which was set out in its *Eisenstadt v. Baird*[24] decision which struck down a Massachusetts statute forbidding the dispensing of contraceptives to unmarried persons -- "necessarily includes the right of a woman to decide whether or not to terminate her pregnancy.[25] He thus believed that the same liberty which permits the individual, whether married or not, to use contraceptives also permits abortion. He contended that "it is difficult to imagine a more complete abridgment of a constitutional freedom" than that caused by the Texas statute.[26]

JUSTICE REHNQUIST'S DISSENTING OPINION

Justice Rehnquist first took the Court to task for deciding a "hypothetical lawsuit" since the record did not indicate whether the plaintiff (in *Wade*) was pregnant, which, he said, is required for her to have standing.[27] He then said that the Court's detailed explication of specific restrictions on the state's power to draft abortion statutes "partakes more of judicial legislation than it does of a determination of the intent of the drafters of the Fourteenth Amendment."[28] He contended that the fact that so many states had anti-abortion statutes at the time of the Fourteenth Amendment's enactment indicates that its drafters did not intend it to forbid them. He says also that the fact that a debate rages over abortion indicates that the "right" the Court claimed exists is not "so universally accepted" as to be fundamental.[29]

The *Bolton* Case

THE OPINION OF THE COURT

Part I - The Court here stated the provisions of the Georgia statute under challenge. It was a "modern" statute, enacted only a few years before and based on the model proposed by the American Law Institute (ALI). The Georgia statute permitted abortion when, in a physician's "best clinical judgment," the pregnancy would endanger the woman's life or "seriously and permanently injure her health," the child would "very likely" be born with "a grave, permanent, and irremediable mental or physical defect," or the pregnancy resulted from forcible or statutory rape. The statute also required that the physician's judgment be concurred in by at least two other physicians, the abortion be performed in a hospital accredited by the state and the Joint Commission on Accreditation of Hospitals (JCAH), that advance approval be given for the procedure by the hospital's abortion committee; and that the woman be a Georgia resident.[30]

Part II - Justiciability and standing are discussed. The plaintiffs were "Mary Doe" and twenty-three other individuals, including physicians, nurses, clergymen, and social workers. Two corporations, Planned Parenthood Association of Atlanta and Georgia Citizens for Hospital Abortion joined as plaintiffs. "Doe" was a poor, married, pregnant woman at the time the case was filed. Her application for an abortion was denied because she did not meet any of the statute's criteria. She claimed in the suit that her privacy and liberty were denied her under the First, Fourth, Fifth, Ninth, and Fourteenth Amendments. The District Court agreed, granted a declaratory judgment, and invalidated the restriction of legalized abortion to the specific reasons mentioned. It did not strike down the other limitations above and denied injunctive relief. The Supreme Court stated that it took the case on direct appeal under Volume 28, U.S. Code, Section 1253.

Part III - The Court here stated that both "Doe" and the physician-appellants are able to maintain this action. It refused to decide about the status of the other appellants.

Part IV - The Court stated the appellants' claims and passed judgment on the statute.

The Specific Allegations of the Appellants - The Court recounted these allegations:

1) Georgia could not claim to be concerned primarily about the unborn child because the statute placed greater emphasis on the woman's rights;

2) the statute did not adequately protect

the woman because it did not permit abortion in other circumstances in which physical and emotional damage could result to her:

3) the statute, after the District Court's decision, was left unconstitutionally vague because it was not made clear when the physician could lawfully carry out an abortion as "necessary";

4) the above procedural requirements of the statute both violated the woman's right of privacy and the physician's right of due process and right to practice his profession;

5) the residency requirement violated the right to travel; and

6) the statute violated equal protection because it discriminated against the poor.

The Court's Holdings - The Court set aside the vagueness argument because it had previously ruled, in *U.S. v. Vuitch*,[31] that the term "health" is not vague since it is permitted to bear on psychological as well as physical well-being. Then the Court made a key point, the consideration of which, is essential to understanding the full scope of the *Wade and Bolton* decisions:

> ...medical judgment may be exercised in light of all factors -- physical, emotional, psychological, familial, and the woman's age -- relevant to the well-being of the patient. All these factors may relate to health.[32]

This means that abortion, for all practical purposes, is made legal until the point of birth, subject to the physician's agreeing to perform it.[33]

The Court decided as follows on the procedural requirements: it struck down the hospital accreditation requirements because the state did not show why abortions must be confined to such facilities (this opened the way for the legalization of abortion clinics); it judged the hospital abortion committee to be an infringement on the rights to give and receive medical care, and invalidated this provision; it also found the two-physician concurrence repugnant, because the attending physician's judgment "should be sufficient";[34] it ruled the residency requirement an infringement of the Privileges and Immunities Clause of the Constitution because it did not permit all persons to have access to medical care in the state; and it avoided the equal protection argument because its holding already invalidated the statute.

Part V - In this short section, the Court summarized its holdings and announced that it was withholding injunctive relief for the same reason as in *Wade*.

The overall holding of the *Bolton* case is that even the more limited restrictions on abortion found in a statute like Georgia's are unconstitutional.

CHIEF JUSTICE BURGER'S CONCURRING OPINION

Chief Justice Burger concurred because the Texas and Georgia statutes "impermissibly limit the performance of abortions necessary to protect the health of pregnant women, using the term health in its broadest medical context."[35] He apparently did not see the decision as creating the sweeping liberty which subsequently became apparent, and which the above indicates was indeed intended by the Court. We can see this when he says: "Plainly, the Court today rejects any claim that the Constitution requires abortion on demand."[36]

JUSTICE DOUGLAS' CONCURRING OPINION

Justice Douglas' concurrence insisted that the Court should have gone further in laying down a constitutionally-protected right of privacy. He contended that there are certain "customary, traditional, and time-honored rights, amenities, privileges, and immunities" that are included among those intended to be respected by the Ninth Amendment and which are also within the meaning of the term "liberty" in the Fourteenth Amendment.[37] I go into Justice Douglas' catalogue of these later in this Chapter. His basis for granting constitutional protection to the woman's abortion decision seems to be a long series of Supreme Court precedents which establishes that "liberty" -- echoing Stewart -- has a meaning much broader than just bodily restraint on compulsion. The cases are too numerous to repeat here from Douglas' opinion, except to say that they range from First Amendment cases, to cases involving the rights of criminal suspects, to cases involving substantive due process.[38]

Abortion statutes, Douglas said, violate a woman's right to liberty because "childbirth may deprive...[her] of her preferred lifestyle and force upon her a radically different and undesired future."[39] Even the permissive Georgia statute is unacceptable because it "'limits the number of reasons for which an abortion may be sought.'"[40]

Douglas, like Stewart, saw the liberty permitting abortion as being the same as that permitting contraception. Like the Court's opinion, he found it unnecessary to face the question of when life begins, but agreed with the appellants that the Georgia statute cannot really be furthering this aim because of all the circumstances in which it permits abortion.

JUSTICE WHITE'S DISSENTING OPINION

In his short dissent which was joined by Justice Rehnquist, Justice White accused the Court of fashioning a new right which is virtually without foundation in the Constitution. He said abortion is a matter that should be left to the political processes for resolution, and left the reader with an oft-quoted phrase to describe the decisions. He called them "an exercise of raw judicial power."[41]

JUSTICE REHNQUIST'S DISSENTING OPINION

In his second dissent (only one paragraph long), Justice Rehnquist criticized the Court for using the "compelling state interest" standard as the means of determining the constitutionality of the abortion laws.

Commentary on the Opinions

The *Wade* Case

THE OPINION OF THE COURT

THE STRUCTURING OF THE OPINION AND THE ORDER OF ARGUMENT

Introductory Paragraphs - These provide a clue to the kind of evidence and knowledge the Court turned to. The Court spoke of the Georgia statute as re-flect[ing] the influences of recent attitudinal change, of advancing medical knowledge and techniques."[42] The Court was heavily influenced by these same factors in its decisions. The Court provided an early indication of the view it later expressed when it spoke about peoples' philosophy, experiences, and moral standards being tied up in the abortion issue. It did not give serious consideration to the view that unchanging standards of right and wrong are determinative in this matter.

Parts I to V - These dealt with procedural questions and recounted the appellants' arguments. They are placed here because these are the first matters that must be considered before a court can move on to the merits in any case.

Part VI - In this section the Court dealt mostly with history. It is logical that it should come at the beginning of the portion of the opinion addressing the merits because the Court believed it necessary to establish that earlier attitudes toward abortion were more liberal, and it was a liberty at common law. By doing this, it led into Part VII, which showed why this "liberty" was curtailed by statute in the nineteenth century and put to rest one of the important constitutional/legal questions involved. It made easier the acceptance of the Court's position that abortion should be treated primarily as a medical problem. Presenting the pro-legalization positions of the A.M.A., A.P.H.A., and A.B.A. at this point demonstrated support for this view. It gave additional legitimacy to the Court's eventual holding, since these were the most potent concerned organizations. The Court used Part VI to fill out one part of the foundation for its holding. It used the next three sections to fill out the rest.

Part VII - This section bolstered the Court's claim that abortion should be treated as a medical problem by showing that the purpose of the nineteenth century statutes was exclusively medical. The Court progressed from earlier history to this period to solidify its historical claim that there is no basis to prohibit abortion. By the end of this Section, the Court had led us essentially to this proposition: if abortion was historically a legal liberty, and if the medical purpose which motivated the nineteenth century statutes is no longer valid, then there is no reason to have such statutes now. The court relied so heavily on another discipline -- medicine -- up to this point, and framed the issue so squarely as a medical one, that it buttressed its later assertion that we cannot know when life begins because other disciplines, including medicine, are divided about it.[43]

This section concluded one identifiable portion of the opinion. The Court tried to cut out any historical basis for its critics to object to its holding. It built up substantial momentum for itself, and then moved from an analysis of the distant past to one of the recent past and present. Believing it adequately demonstrated a liberty of abortion at common law, it now established the basis for that liberty within the unique confines of the written Constitution which permitted its applicability to the present.

Part VIII - The Court cited its previous decisions, which show that there is a right of privacy, the right to which it believes is in question here. Then, it moved to the next logical step to show how this right applies to abortion. It did this, without adequate explanation, by claiming certain harms can occur to the woman if she is not permitted to have an abortion. It relied here on undocumented medical and psychological evidence. The next step was to seek legal support for this judgment, so that its conclusions could have a legal basis, which it attained by citing lower court opinions applying the privacy right to abortion. Another part of the logical sequence in enunciating a right was the spelling out of limitations on the right.

The Court did this by stating, as noted, that the right does not permit a person to do with his body anything he pleases.

The Court used this section to complete its argument about the right of women to abortion. Moving on, in what is a logical sequence for a legal case, it responded to the counter-arguments. Up to now it tried to establish the general principle, showing why it applies to the specific matter. It stated a limitation of the general principle (i.e., the right of reproductive pricacy). Now it must go on to delineate the limitation of the right in the specific case (i.e., the limits on abortion).

Part IX - Here the Court responded to the counter-arguments. It said the unborn child is: 1) not a "person" under the Constitution;[44] 2) not "alive" from conception for certain, because it is unclear when life begins; and 3) not a full legal "person" in other areas of the law.

Part X - With the counter-arguments answered by the Court, it moved to the next logical point: stating its specific holding, which it did in this section.

Part XI - It is also logical that a section of summary of the full opinion be placed near the end, which it did here. The Court also added some concluding remarks about the reasons for and significance of the decision.

Part XII - This final section, as is customary in legal opinions, spelled out the precise legal remedies.

The overall ordering of the opinion, then, accords with the way that an opinion is usually set up. A logical pattern is seen of building the argument, dealing with counter-arguments, coming to conclusions, etc. The following is a diagram of the opinion:

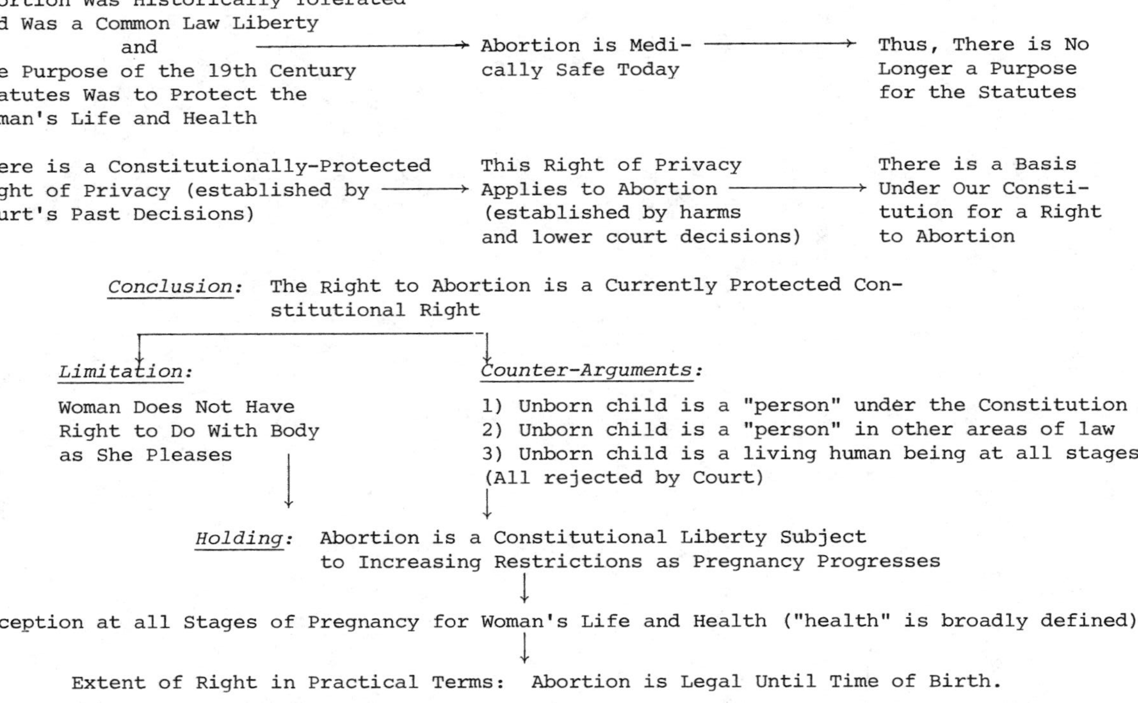
FIGURE 1
Abortion Was Historically Tolerated and Was a Common Law Liberty
and
The Purpose of the 19th Century Statutes Was to Protect the Woman's Life and Health
Abortion is Medically Safe Today
Thus, There is No Longer a Purpose for the Statutes
There is a Constitutionally-Protected Right of Privacy (established by Court's Past Decisions)
This Right of Privacy Applies to Abortion (established by harms and lower court decisions)
There is a Basis Under Our Constitution for a Right to Abortion
Conclusion: The Right to Abortion is a Currently Protected Constitutional Right
Limitation:
Woman Does Not Have Right to Do With Body as She Pleases
Counter-Arguments:
1) Unborn child is a "person" under the Constitution
2) Unborn child is a "person" in other areas of law
3) Unborn child is a living human being at all stages
(All rejected by Court)
Holding: Abortion is a Constitutional Liberty Subject to Increasing Restrictions as Pregnancy Progresses
Exception at all Stages of Pregnancy for Woman's Life and Health ("health" is broadly defined)
Extent of Right in Practical Terms: Abortion is Legal Until Time of Birth.

THE FRAMING OF THE ISSUE AND THE BASIS FOR THE DECISION

The Court framed the issue in *Wade* as one which hinges on constitutional law and legal history. In the final anaylsis, however, the issue was put forth as a medical one. Even if there was a right to abortion at common law, the Court was willing to accept a statutory prohibition if -- and only if -- abortion was not medically safe for the woman.

In constitutional terms, the case is framed in terms of the right of privacy. I believe, however, this is only on the surface. It is the *medical* question which is more fundamental. The application of the right of privacy to abortion is quite problematic. Not only is the use of the right to protect primarily "personal, marital, familial, and sexual" matters a substantial deviation from its earlier applications (see Chapter Five), but the Court's readiness to identify abortion with contraception, child-rearing and so on is questionable.[45] Also, the Court did not make clear how the right of privacy (which is based on little more than its previous decisions) and the right to abortion (which is contained in it) are so "'fundamental'" as to require a "'*compelling* state interest'" to restrict them.[46]

The basis for the decision is the evidence -- historical, legal, and medical -- which the Court applied to the framing of the issue. This included evidence about such matters as whether abortion was a common law liberty, the original purpose of the statutes, the original meaning of the term "person" in the Constitution, and the present-day safety of abortion. In Chapters Three and Six I show that this evidence was incomplete or incorrect. This means that the holding in *Wade* is the result of evidentiary error. The more fundamental evidentiary error of the Court, however, was its failure even to examine the biological evidence about when life begins and the unborn child's humanity on its own merits, instead of simply dismissing the issue as unresolvable because of disagreement within other disciplines. The Court admits that personhood is the decisive question, and if it could have been established, it would have had to change its decision entirely.

THE LENGTH AND DETAIL OF THE PARTS

How important the various parts of the opinion are can be seen by considering their length and detail. The longest section of the opinion is Part IV, which covers most of the history and the various organizations' positions. When coupled with Part III, also historical insofar as it examines the purpose of nineteenth century statutes, more than twenty-two pages are taken up. This emphasizes the importance that the Court placed on history -- especially legal history -- and medical knowledge and opinion. This is further stressed in the subsections on legal history and the changing position of the A.M.A., which contain the greatest detail and the longest footnotes and citations. The Court obviously wanted to have these parts of the opinion well documented.

Part IX, while not exceptionally long, involves some detail and touches on several points. This demonstrates the significance of the "personhood" question for the Court, as it acknowledges. It mentioned a number of specific constitutional provisions which it argued could not have a "pre-natal application," and cited a number of lower court decisions -- and one Supreme Court decision -- for support. It also looked at contemporary religious views on abortion, the status of the unborn in other areas of the law, and the question of life's beginning. Obviously, the Court believed it must address all these points about the child's humanity and does so, even though its discussion and consideration of facts is inadequate.

Thus, the longest and most detailed sections present the Court's most important arguments.

THE KNOWLEDGE DEFERRED TO

The Court deferred to different types of knowledge in the various sections of the opinion.

Part VI - In this first substantive section of the opinion, the Court attempted to establish the existence of an ancient and common law liberty of abortion by appealing to historical works, case precedents, legal treatises and commentaries of the past (such as those of Henry de Bracton and Edward Coke), and contemporary commentators.

Part VII - In determining in this section what the purpose of the nineteenth century statutes was, the Court deferred to lower court decisions, recent and past, and to the contemporary legal commentary of Professor Cyril Means. It also relied on articles in medical and related journals to establish the safety of abortion.*

Part VIII - In this section about the right of privacy, the Court relied on some of its past decisions to establish the existence of the right. It relied on lower federal and state Court decisions to extend the right to abortion. It also seemed to rely on modern psychology, medicine, and social science to establish the existence of the harms it says will befall women. These are the pertinent disciplines, in the absence of specific citations, because of the Court's language. It spoke of "psychological harm" and the woman's "mental and physical health." It referred to "a distressful life and future" for the woman and the "distress" to a family caused by an unwanted child. These are terms that either explicitly refer to psychological concerns or are associated with psychology. Sociological considerations are seen affecting the Court by its talk about a family being "unable, psychologically and otherwise" to take care of an "unwanted" child. The "otherwise" probably refers to sociological factors. Arguments supporting abortion often refer to sociological factors such as insufficient family income to raise a child, the husband and wife having their careers disrupted by a child, and the time and attention a child demands. The Court also said "the additional difficulties and continuing stigma of unwed motherhood may be involved." This sounds like a sociologist's assessment of prevailing social attitudes. Medicine was relied on when the Court mentioned that "[s]pecific and direct harm medically diagnosable even in early pregnancy may be involved."[47]

Part IX - Just as this section made a number of

---

*When I speak about the Court and the concurring Justices deferring to medical knowledge, I mean the views of those in the medical community which the Court chose to accept (i.e., those advocating legalized abortion). My discussions in Chapters Six and Seven establish that this was not the soundest medical knowledge.

different types of arguments, so it relied on different areas of knowledge. It relied on legal and constitutional materials: specific constitutional provisions, the transcript of the oral reargument in the case,[48] a number of lower federal and state court decisions, and one of its own decisions. These were all on the subject of personhood. It relied on a couple of medical reference books when speaking about fetal development and, without citations, clearly deferred to the disciplines of medicine, philosophy, and theology on the question of when life begins. From what I have said, we can judge that this is the most crucial example of deference.

The Court cited four commentators and one *amicus* brief when discussing contemporary religious views on abortion. A serious question can be raised as to whether the Court had access to complete information on this subject. One of the two writers it cited about Catholic views took a position on abortion not in accord with the Church's. Another writer it cited, Lawrence Lader, is a well-known pro-abortion polemicist and activist. (See Chapter One) It claimed that "a large segment of the Protestant community, insofar as ...can be ascertained" believes that life does not begin until live birth and that "organized [Protestant] groups that have taken a formal position on the abortion issue have generally regarded abortion as a matter for the conscience of the individual and her family."[49] To back up these assertions, it cited the *amicus* brief of the American Ethical Union, et. al., the positions of the National Council of Churches, and other Protestant denominations as they appear in Lader's 1966 book (pp. 99-101). Upon turning to this *amicus* brief, however, one finds that of the ten organizations joining it only four of them were Protestant. Of these four, only one was an actual denomination, the United Church of Christ. The other Protestant organizations --the American Friends Service Committee, the Board of Christian Social Concerns of the United Methodist Church, and the Episcopal Diocese of New York -- are just organizations within or parts of denominations. They are also known, along with the National Council of Churches, as being the most liberal and socially activist elements of American Protestantism. The brief gives no evidence to back up the position that most Protestants believe that life does not begin until birth. Only two of the positions cited in the Lader book are from American

Protestant denominations. The others are from overseas denominations or individuals, and none say that abortion should be left to the woman's conscience; most refer to the situations in which abortion is held to be morally permissible. As I showed in Chapter One, however, the Court is correct in what it says about this conscience point, even though its sources are inadequate. As with the *amicus* brief, none of Lader's citations said anything about Protestants not believing that life begins until live birth.

The Court also stated, with reference to the beginning of life, that there is "new embryological data that purport [sic] to indicate that conception is a 'process' over time." It added that the idea that life beginning at conception is rendered problematical by a number of medical advances.[50] It supported these assertions by citing a number of *non-medical* sources -- law review articles and a couple of books --, only one of which is written by a person identified as having medical training (a psychiatrist) and which give few citations to medical sources. The Court presented no evidence demonstrating that it examined any medical sources itself.

Finally the Court relied on legal commentators and law review articles for its argument that unborn children "have never been recognized in the law as persons in the whole sense."[51] As I show in Chapter Three, however, the Court's information here is incomplete or confused.

Part X - In this last substantive section of the opinion, the Court relied on medical knowledge almost exclusively even though it gave virtually no specific citations. It made its crucial three trimester division of pregnancy and claimed that the "viability" of the unborn child (i.e., the point at which he is able to live outside of the womb) is the "'compelling'" point after which the state has an "important and legitimate interest in potential life."[52] It is because of the medical understanding, previously cited, about the safety of abortion in the first trimester that the Court decreed that restrictions be the least then. Thus medicine is the major source of the Court's specific restrictions on abortion legislation.

In summary, it is evident that in the most important sections of the *Wade* opinion, the conclusions of the Court are shaped by an interweaving of medical and constitutional/legal knowledge. Again, in the final analysis, the medical is probably the most important.

JUSTICE STEWART'S CONCURRING OPINION

THE STRUCTURING OF THE OPINION AND THE ORDER OF ARGUMENT

Justice Stewart's opinion emphasized the violation of liberty, as guaranteed by the Fourteenth Amendment, by anti-abortion statutes. First, in setting the groundwork for his claim that the notion of "liberty" goes beyond the freedoms stated in the Bill of Rights, he endorsed the reestablishment of the doctrine of substantive due process in *Griswold v. Connecticut*,[53] the case that the appellants and some *amici* argued was the precedent for striking down the statutes. By accepting this doctrine, he gave a constitutional basis for both the broad notion of liberty and the right to abortion within it. He then gave specific grounds for this view of liberty: various Supreme Court precedents and memorable quotes from two famous late Justices, the first John M. Harlan and Felix Frankfurter. Frankfurter's quote provides additional legitimacy for Stewart's broad noion of liberty by giving a reason for it: this notion must necessarily change as society changes.

With his argument for a broad notion of liberty in place, Stewart moved to the next logical point: showing why it includes the right to abortion. He pointed to Supreme Court precedents which "make clear that freedom of personal choice in matters of marriage and family life" -- he did not mention a right of privacy, which is how his view differs from the Court's -- is protected by the Fourteenth Amendment. This right is made to specifically apply in cases like *Wade* by the *Eisenstadt v. Baird* decision,[54] which made the right one of the *individual* instead of the married couple or family unit. He made what on its surface is a logical conclusion: if the string of cases which have asserted a broad view of liberty (i.e., substantive due process) have protected such rights as that of parents to send their children to a non-public school[55] or the right to teach a foreign language,[56] the right to abortion must also be included. This is because pregnancy and childrearing "are of a far greater degree of significance and

and personal intimacy" than these.[57] (I say that this is logical "on its surface" because a consideration of the nature of abortion, which Stewart, the Court and all the other concurring opinions avoided, would show that it is something entirely different than the other activities protected as "liberties.")

Stewart, in the typical final point of a legal argument, considered the state's interest in protecting the woman's health and protecting "the potential future human life within her."[58] He said these are "legitimate objectives" but dismissed them quickly by saying that Texas' proscription of abortion is too "broad [of an] abridgment of personal liberty."[59] No consideration of the unborn child's humanity or his protection as a "person" under the Constitution was given. Apparently he was satisfied with the Court's inadequate treatment of these.

Justice Stewart's opinion, then, moves in a logical sequence from general to specific, carefully building from one point to another. It is a fairly well constructed legal opinion. A diagram of the opinion would look like the following:

FIGURE 2

SUBSTANTIVE DUE PROCESS ACCEPTED ⟶ BROAD NOTION OF LIBERTY
(reestablished by *Griswold v. Connecticut*)

↓

INCLUDES "FREEDOM OF PERSONAL CHOICE IN MARITAL AND FAMILY MATTERS"

↓ ↓

MADE A RIGHT OF THE INDIVIDUAL IN *EISENSTADT v. BAIRD*

STANDARD OF PERSONAL INTIMACY USED (if activities involving lesser degrees of intimacy to the individual are constitutionally protected, then those involving a greater degree must be protected)

↓ ↓

CONCLUSION:

ABORTION IS A PROTECTED LIBERTY OF THE INDIVIDUAL

THE FRAMING OF THE ISSUE AND THE PROPOSED BASIS FOR THE DECISION

Justice Stewart framed the issue in the following way: If the statutes are a serious infringement on the woman's liberty, they cannot be allowed to stand. The decision results from his conclusion, based on something like commensensical evidence about the degree of intimacy of the matters involved, that such an infringement *does* occur.

THE LENGTH AND DETAIL OF THE POINTS

The point establishing the "broadness" of the notion of liberty is the longest section. It is also supported by the most case citations. The next longest and most tightly argued is the section which concludes that "freedom of personal choice" extends to marital and familial affairs. Very little discussion is spent justifying the inclusion of abortion in this category. This is curious in light of the difference between abortion and the other activities mentioned. It also reveals the implicit view that once "liberty" is established so broadly, the Court is free to include within it whatever it believes changing times demand. (Stewart emphasized this need to respond to changes by his quote from Frankfurter.) The fact that Stewart hardly mentioned the possibility of the unborn child's humanity suggests that he either considered it an unimportant factor or, as stated, was satisfied with the Court's inadequate treatment of it.

THE KNOWLEDGE DEFERRED TO

The only explicit source Stewart deferred to is constitutional precedents. He implicitly deferred to medical views about the safety of abortion when he accepted the Court's view that abortion can be prohibited to protect the woman only later in pregnancy. He also joined the Court in deferring to medicine and the other disciplines it mentioned by his unwillingness to consider when life begins.

JUSTICE REHNQUIST'S DISSENTING OPINION

THE STRUCTURING OF THE OPINION AND THE ORDER OF ARGUMENT

Justice Rehnquist set his opinion up in three parts. The first dealt with procedural matters, the second (longest) with substantive matters, and the third with points concerning the Court's disposition of the case. This is the customary ordering of a judicial opinion. Rehnquist said that for procedural reasons, the Court should have never heard the suit, but since it did, he dissented on the merits as well. There is little significance in this ordering, except that it permitted Rehnquist to argue his points in an orderly manner, and cover each type of his objections.

THE ARGUMENT AS TO HOW THE ISSUE SHOULD BE FRAMED AND THE CASE DECIDED

Rehnquist rejected both the Court's and Stewart's formulation or framing of the issue. He said it is inappropriate to ask if either the right of privacy or liberty, in absolute terms, is violated. The abortion operation, he claimed, is not a private matter, and the Constitution does not protect liberty *per se* from infringement, but only the denial of liberty without due process of law. He believed that the proper issue to consider is whether the right to abortion "'is so rooted in the traditions and conscience of our people as to be ranked as fundamental'" and whether the Drafters of the Fourteenth Amendment intended to include it in their notion of liberty.[60] His answer to both questions is a clear "no." The states, said Rehnquist, have the power to pass anti-abortion statutes.

THE LENGTH AND DETAIL OF THE PARTS

Clearly, the weightiest part of the opinion is the one dealing with the merits, Part II. It is also the one in which Rehnquist presented long lists of the states which had anti-abortion statutes when the Fourteenth Amendment was adopted and those which still retained those statutes. The fact that he spent so much time on the merits indicates his finding of a serious weakness in the Court's views. He gave so much information about the background of state statutes that it underscores his view that the key issue is the intention of the Drafters of the Fourteenth Amendment. He believed this is best demonstrated by this background.

THE KNOWLEDGE DEFERRED TO

Rehnquist relied almost exclusively on historical information and Supreme Court precedents. It is curious that he seemed to share the view of the Justices in the majority by considering it unimportant when life begins. The question for the Court to consider for Rehnquist was not whether abortion should be legal, but whether it should be left to state legislatures to decide. Thus, he did not have to consider anything more than historical and legal background.

The *Bolton* Case

THE OPINION OF THE COURT

THE STRUCTURING OF THE OPINION AND THE ORDER OF ARGUMENT

The *Bolton* opinion has five sections, only one of which deals with substantive questions. The first section summarized the provisions of the Georgia statute; the second and third dealt with procedural matters; the fourth, divided into parts, is addressed to the merits; and the fifth summarized the opinion. It is a well constructed judicial opinion.

The division of Part IV is according to the arguments the appellants made against the statute. The court considered one point at a time, rendering aspects of its holding as it went along. There seems to be no particular ordering. The appellants' arguments which were rejected -- which were the more generalized and more outlandish of their arguments -- are at *both* the beginning and the end. The arguments which were accepted and pertain to specific provisions of the statute are in the middle. The Court moved from one argument to another, presenting its holding and reasoning. It used the early part of the section to make its one crucial addendum to the *Wade* decision: the meaning of the "health" exception which legitimizes abortion up to birth. This point is not essential to the arguments in this section -- although it *is* an important point in itself -- and was probably inserted here because this is where the Court dealt with the merits and addressed questions of the rights of physicians and patients.

There seems to be no particular significance to the ordering of the sections of this opinion. The Court could deal with the points in a shot-gun fashion because they were all subsidiary points, not requiring the substantial explanation the main ones in *Wade* did. What *may* be significant, however, is the way the Court took up various provisions of the statute. It did not take them up in the order they appear in the statute, but rather considered the ones that expressly restricted physicians first. (The first argument dealt with the appellants' general claim the statute did not protect women adequately; but this does not concern a specific provision.) This ordering possibly reflected the importance the Court placed on protecting the physician's rights. This interpretation seemed plausible in light of the laudatory words the Court had for the medical profession in this section and in the *Wade* opinion. (See above.)

THE FRAMING OF THE ISSUES AND THE BASIS FOR THE VARIOUS HOLDINGS

When passing on the procedural parts of the statute, the Court seemed to frame the issue in terms of an infringement on the freedom of physician and patient. The emphasis was more on the physician, than on the woman, as was the case in *Wade*. In disposing of two of the other arguments of the appellants -- the statute's not adequately protecting the woman and the statute's alleged vagueness -- the Court framed the issue in medical terms, adding to the strong emphasis overall that it gave to medical considerations in the *Bolton* opinion. In the former argument, it said the state should be allowed to adjust the purpose of its legislation from (supposedly) just protection of the woman in the last century to both this and protecting the child, since this was done "in light of...advanced knowledge."[61] The Court dismissed the vagueness point because its *Vuitch* decision had established that the exception for "health" was not vague if it included psychological as well as physical well-being.

The Court formulated the challenge to the residency provision as a privileges and immunities question. It decided this point with reference to a strictly constitutional point, but did so out of a medical consideration (i.e., that the right of persons to receive health care in Georgia should not depend on residency). The Court dismissed the equal protection point without any discussion because it became irrelevant after its holdings on the other issues.

In formulating the issue, physician and patient rights were of overriding importance. All of the holdings above that go against the state are based on the evidence. The Court indicated that the state does not provide a sufficient line of reasoning or evidence showing why any of the provisions in question are justified. What is implicit here is the overall medical basis for the decision. *That is, the Court struck down the provisions because the state did not show that the restrictions were needed to better safeguard the health of the woman.*

THE LENGTH AND DETAIL OF THE PARTS

Section IV, which deals with the merits, is longer than the other parts combined. The main purpose of the opinion is to set out the Court's reasoning for its holding. Because of the nature of the statutory provisions, and the emphasis the Court placed on protecting the medical profession, the longest explanations were directed toward showing why the physician should not be restricted by the statute's provisions.

THE KNOWLEDGE DEFERRED TO

Virtually all the specific citations in the opinion were to legal materials, mostly past Supreme Court decisions. As mentioned above, however, medical knowledge (or the lack of its submission by the state to back up its position) and the Court's sense of the medical profession's need were decisive on the various points.

CHIEF JUSTICE BURGER'S CONCURRING OPINION

Little can be said about the structure or ordering of this opinion, which is just over one page long. Burger did not make it clear if he formulated the issue in *Wade* or *Bolton* as one of the right of privacy or liberty, but his reference to just the Fourteenth Amendment (without any reference to the Ninth Amendment) and the statutes "impermissibly limit[ing]" abortions suggests that it is liberty.[62] He did not seem to believe that liberty is infringed by the anti-abortion statutes *per se*, but by the *excessive* restrictions on abortion contained in them, as I said in my summarization of his opinion. It is to this point that he devotes the most attention in his short statement.

Despite stating he is "somewhat troubled that the Court has taken notice of various scientific and medical data in reaching its conclusion," Burger relied primarily on medical knowledge to shape his view about the extent to which the law may restrict abortions. He would permit abortion when required to protect the woman's health "in its broadest medical context."[63] His citation of *Vuitch* suggests that he understood this to mean physical and mental health. He was clearly mistaken -- and one wonders how he could have so grossly misread the *Wade* decision -- when he said the Court did not permit abortion on demand.

JUSTICE DOUGLAS' CONCURRING OPINION

THE STRUCTURING OF THE OPINION AND THE ORDER OF ARGUMENT

Douglas' opinion is in three parts. The parts somewhat parallelled the structuring of the Court's two opinions and the Stewart opinion. Part I sets out Douglas' basic constitutional analysis of the statutes. It showed the basis of the right of privacy and explained why it applies to abortion. Part II clarified specific points relating to the legal analysis. It explained why the woman's health demands that the right to abortion be as broad as the Court declared, it addressed the question of permissible restrictions on the right, and considered -- and dismissed -- the possibility that the unborn child may be fully human. Part III dealt with another specific aspect of the legal analysis: that relating to the rights of physician and patient. He linked this up with both the rights of privacy and liberty, which are the basic part of his legal analysis in Part I. His opinion, then, proceeded logically from general to specific. He made his argument as to why abortion is a legal right, then spelled out certain specifics more precisely, dealt with objections, and finally explored one important aspect of his analysis.

Turning to Douglas' legal analysis in Part I, we see a distinct structuring of the argument. Douglas first showed that there is a right of privacy, and claimed it is found within the Ninth Amendment but it is federally enforceable by the liberty clause of the Fourteenth Amendment. Within this general right are a number of specific rights applying to various activities. These are catalogued below. He said, in effect, that the right to abortion is included within these specific rights, although he did not specify which ones. He indicated it is the harms that can occur to the woman as a result of unwanted pregnancy that permit this right to come into play as a means of protecting these other specific rights. This led him to the conclusion that abortion statutes like Texas' are unconstitutional. Then, in Part III, he made yet another specific application of the right of privacy -- to the physician-patient relationship -- which required the striking down of the restrictions of the Georgia statute. His ordering of this analysis is in fairly good form for a judicial opinion. This is a diagram of the analysis:

FIGURE 3

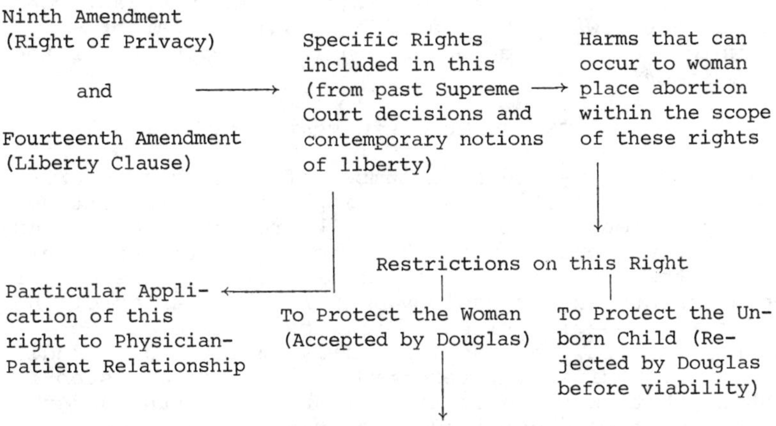

THE FRAMING OF THE ISSUE AND THE PROPOSED BASIS FOR THE DECISION

Douglas' formulation of the issue is very similar to the Court's. The only differences are his recognition that the Ninth Amendment does not establish any federal rights and so his decision rests essentially on the Fourteenth Amendment and his understanding of the right of privacy as broader and more encompassing than the Court's. Like the Court, he wanted to strike down the restrictions in *Bolton* largely because of concern about the rights of physicians and patients, but, unlike the Court, he considered the physician-patient relationship as constitutionally-protected.

The basis for the decision according to Douglas should be the liberty interest of the woman and her attending physician. The basis for the breadth of the decision is what Douglas saw as the medical understanding of how the health of the woman is involved, and of the presence of life in the unborn child.

THE LENGTH AND DETAIL OF THE PARTS

The longest section of the opinion, and also the one with the most points and the greatest number of citations (primarily to Supreme Court precedents), is Part I. Douglas used the opinion to put forth a sweeping theory of the right of privacy -- an important concern of his toward the end of his judicial career -- for which he laid the foundation in his opinion for the Court in *Griswold*.

THE KNOWLEDGE DEFERRED TO

Douglas relied on a number of sources of knowledge, some explicitly and some implicitly. In setting out his various specific rights, he referred to numerous Supreme Court precedents. But the real influence over him, whether he was aware of it or not, was contemporary social theory and psychology. In his discussion of the need for a sweeping right of privacy because of the woman's "health," he was implicitly influenced by medicine. He specifically referred to medicine as establishing that abortion is safer than childbirth, and thus it could not be prohibited to protect women. Curiously, he relied on a *legal* source, former Supreme Court Justice Tom Clark, instead of a biological or medical one, to "prove" that the unborn child is not a human life. A long quote from Clark was used to this effect in Part II, and again in Part III he returned to Clark to support his view that "[w]hen life is present is...basically a question for medical experts."[64] This contradiction, as well as the fact that Douglas never even discussed the evidence amassed by these medical experts, leaves one thinking that this is a question he would have preferred to avoid.

To turn to the point made earlier about psychology and social theory, let me first quote Douglas' cataloging of rights which are supposedly protected by the liberty clause of the Fourteenth Amendment. One is struck by the fact that these rights are found nowhere in the Constitution and the language of these rights is quite different from that used in the Constitution. These are the rights he mentions:

> First is the autonomous control over the development and expression of one's intellect, interests, tastes, and personality. Second is freedom of choice in the basic decisions of one's life respecting marriage, divorce, procreation, contraception, and the education and upbringing of children. Third is the freedom to care for one's health and person, freedom from bodily restraint or compulsion, freedom to walk, stroll, or loaf.[65]

The first of the rights above is full of words that come from psychology: "interests," "tastes," and "personality." These are qualities of the individual with which much of modern psychology concerns itself. "Development" and "expression" are the aspects of these qualities which psychology studies. There is no language in the Constitution that is similar to this. It is often said nowadays -- even by legal scholars -- that the First Amendment protects "freedom of expression," but the language of that Amendment says nothing about "expression." It talks of "freedom of speech." The rights which Douglas mentioned in this first group sound like hackneyed versions of rights which sometimes find their way into popular speech and social science articles.

Similarly, the second group of rights Douglas

mentioned are not suggested by the words of the Constitution. Some of them are, however, rights which were part of the common law tradition (e.g., marriage, procreation, the education and upbringing of children) and, as the Court subsequently held, were understood to be protected by the Constitution. Others (e.g., contraception) were fashioned by the Court. Both contraception and divorce -- the Court has never held the latter to be a constitutionally-protected right -- have long been promoted by certain social reformers who rely on social science, medical science, and psychology to buttress their view.

The third group of rights is a hodge-podge of traditional legal rights (e.g., freedom from bodily restraint or compulsion), rights which are implicitly understood as being included in any notion of liberty (e.g., to care for one's health and person), and vulgarized notions of freedom which do not rise to the status of a legal right (e.g., loafing). This latter "right" also sounds like something which would pop up in a work of contemporary social theory in which at attempt is made to eliminate almost entirely the idea that the individual has obligations to the community if he believes these would interfere with his freedom.

Since it is from this scheme of rights, influenced by modern social and psychological theories, that the right to abortion is derived, it follows that this right itself is based, in Douglas' formulation, on such theories.

JUSTICE WHITE'S DISSENTING OPINION

Justice White, as mentioned, believed the decisions were incorrect because they did not have a constitutional basis. He believed that the "language or history of the Constitution" should have been the reference point, and medical knowledge should have been relied upon to the extent of fashioning an exception for the woman's life and health.[66]

Many of the opinions, particularly the Court's, were structured and ordered to achieve certain purposes. The fact that some points were discussed at greater length and in more detail indicates their greater importance. Many different areas of knowledge are relied on, and the medical -- meaning the view of some in the medical community -- may be the most important to the Court.

An Analysis of the Use of Language in the Opinions

The Importance of Language for the Pro-Abortion Position

Writers have emphasized the importance of language and rhetoric in the abortion debate. In this Section, I shall consider the significance of the language used in the opinions.

The use of euphemisms to describe the unborn child is characteristic of pro-abortion rhetoric. Pro-abortionists usually call the unborn child a "fetus," "conceptus," or "product of conception." These terms are, for them, a kind of psychological warfare to make him seem like a thing and abortion a kind of abstraction. Many would argue that the term "fetus" is not biased in a pro-abortion direction, but is neutral. This is not so because, first, it is biologically inaccurate and, second, it has become morally charged in the abortion debate. The unborn child is not a "fetus" throughout his pre-natal existence. "Fetus" is but one of several stages of intrauterine development, and does not begin until almost the third month of pregnancy (see Chapter Seven). Due to the very fact that the term has been used by pro-abortionists to depersonalize the unborn child, it cannot be said to be neutral. Its use in the abortion debate has indicated that a moral judgment has been made about the humanity and value of the unborn child. As syndicated columnist Joseph Sobran has argued, the word "fetus" should be used only among people who agree on its moral meaning. Otherwise, it "work[s] in favor of him who would deny the humanity of the unborn child, simply by putting the burden of proof on him who asserts that humanity." It permits the battle to be fought on the pro-abortionists' terms.

David Mall, a scholar of rhetoric, says that the notion of progress and the scientific view connected with it have figured prominently in the abortion debate. He writes that "'[p]rogress' and words associated with it become rhetorical trump cards" in this debate. Writing before the *Wade* and *Bolton* decisions, he said that pro-abortionists saw their efforts as being directed to the "'reform' of the abortion laws." And such laws "are characterized as 'archaic', 'outmoded,' 'Nineteenth-Century anachronisms.'"[68] We saw evidence of this in Chapter One.

Mall also says that scientific terminology is significant to pro-abortionists. He agrees that it helps to "dehumanize" the unborn child. Besides describing the unborn child by one of the euphemisms above, the pro-abortion advocate calls abortion "a crime without a victim." The "procedures and implements of science" used in abortion add further scientific appeal to the activity because they make it seem efficient. Efficiency is, of course, a major objective of applied science. Thus, for the pro-abortionist, "'amniocentesis' becomes a dependable method for detecting fetal defects and 'vacuum aspirator' one of the more efficient methods for eliminating them." Often, he says, abortion is referred to as "'therapeutic.'"[69] It is one more scientific remedy for a bad condition.

Mall also points to the use of language to stress the extreme statement of freedom which characterizes the pro-abortion position. Such words as "reproductive autonomy" and "compulsory pregnancy" appear frequently.[70]

Richard Neuhaus, who would agree with contemporary liberals on many issues, departs their company on abortion and explains the importance of language to make this activity palatable. He says that the pro-abortion movement "has successfully escalated convenience to 'right'" and "every effort is made to 'desacralize' the process of birth." He gives the example of one abortion counseling service which instructs its counselors to avoid terms having "excessive emotional significance for the client." Some of the specifics mentioned include referring to the "problem" instead of the pregnancy, the "growth" or "embryo" instead of the "unborn child," and the fact that the pregnancy was "interrupted" or "terminated" instead of the child being "killed."[71]

The Court's Opinions

Such substitution of terms is seen to some degree in the Court's opinions. First, there is the pro-abortionists' use of the language of "progress" that Mall points to. For example, the Court in *Wade* made reference to "a trend toward liberalization of abortion statutes" in recent years. In order to provide support for this it mentioned the states which had modified their laws and approvingly cited a law review article by former Supreme Court Justice Tom Clark which describes these states as having "'led the way.'"[72] Later in the opinion, the Court in a footnote quoted what it calls "an enlightening Prefatory Note" from the model abortion legislation proposed in 1971 by the Conference of Commissioners on Uniform State Laws, in which the terms "liberal" and "liberalization" are used to describe state statutory changes which made abortion easier to obtain.[73]

There are other suggestions of this notion of progress reflected in the opinions. For example, in Justice Douglas' concurring opinion, he says that the "vicissitudes of life produce pregnancies which may be unwanted...or which in the full setting of the case may create such suffering, dislocations, misery, or tragedy as to make an early abortion the only *civilized step* to take."[74] It seems that Douglas regarded letting a woman have an abortion as "progress" because it makes society more civilized.

When the *Wade* opinion mentioned the "continuing stigma of unwed motherhood" as being one of the harms a woman may face when prevented from getting an abortion, the Court also was making a statement about "progress."[75] It is as if the Court implied some nasty attitude from the Dark Ages still lingers, and society has not yet "progressed" as far as it should have.

Another suggestion of this same view is found in the Court's opinion in *Bolton*, where it talked about how understanding the typical physician is of the pregnant woman's situation. The court implied that the physician "is aware of human frailty, so-called 'error.'"[76] The "so-called" gives the impression of a hostility to traditional sexual morality, as if it stands in the way of "progress" toward better understanding the plight of the woman with an unwanted pregnancy.

The Court shares the modern faith in the inevitability of progress. It admitted the disciplines it mentioned cannot arrive at any consensus about when life begins "at this point in the development of man's knowledge."[77] The Court believes that knowledge will at some time be forthcoming to answer this question.

There is also a tendency in the opinions to depersonalize the unborn child, in the manner described by the commentators above. While the Court used the term "unborn" on a few occasions, the overwhelming number of its and the concurring Justices' references to the unborn child are as a "fetus," "potential human life," "potential life," or, once, "developing young in the human uterus." At one place in the *Bolton* opinion, it referred to the unborn child as a "product."[78] It might be argued that the Justices were just using common medical terminology here. I believe, however, that their unwillingness to consider the biological evidence of the unborn child's humanity and their obvious eagerness -- which will become even more apparent after examining the Court's incorrect and incomplete consideration of history in Chapter Three -- to enunciate this new right makes this unlikely.

The Court and the concurring Justices in a number of places utilized the pro-abortionist language of "termination" of a pregnancy, in a further effort to push aside the possibility of the unborn child's humanity.

In its *Bolton* opinion, the Court gave the impression of seeing abortion as primarily a medical procedure, with the moral element removed. The Court referred to the physician as exercising merely his "best clinical"[79] or his "medical judgment."[80] Abortion is also spoken of as part of the "woman's right to receive medical care."[81] The fact that the Court will let a physician advise a woman about having an abortion, with reference only to the same medical criteria and on the basis of the same professional expertise that he advises patients about any other operation, strongly indicates the Court's willingness to push the moral element aside. The Court's cataloging of the harms that legalized abortion will supposedly eliminate and Justices Stewart and Douglas' contentions that abortion will prevent a woman's life from being unfortunately altered add to this conception of abortion as being, in Mall's words, "therapeutic" in nature. It is just another problem for a scientific expert -- the physician -- to solve.

There are other examples of the pro-abortion rhetoric of "freedom" in the opinions that Mall cites frequently. There is mention of "a woman's decision whether or not to terminate her pregnancy" and of her being permitted to exercise her "choice."[82] Justice Stewart spoke of "the right of a woman to decide"[83] and Justice Douglas referred to "autonomous control" and "freedom of choice in the basic decisions of one's life," which include whether to have an abortion.[84] These are the kinds of words and phrases which typically appear in pro-abortion literature, as I shall show more fully later.

Some of the Court's other language in *Wade* and *Bolton* suggests the thought which is behind the opinions, which I shall deal with at more length in Chapter Eight. The Court claimed that it arrived at its decision after balancing the interests of the woman and the potential life within her. This activity of weighing both sides and then deciding which overrides the other is typical of the way courts make decisions today. The language the Supreme Court used in the opinions is the language connected with this activity: "interests," "obligation," "balancing," and "'compelling' point." The "State's important and legitimate interest in potential life" is said to reach the "'compelling' point ...at viability."[85] This means the matter is relative for the Court; there is no universally applicable rule to be applied. The state's interest is determined by the circumstances (i.e., the point in the woman's pregnancy and the likely effects of abortion on women's health). The Court limits its function to the weighing of mutually relative and compromisable interests. This view and language represents an unwillingness to acknowledge the existence of truth, which would mean that certain "interests" would have to be judged better than others and would have to hold sway regardless of changing circumstances.

Another author tells us about the prevailing conception of law evidenced in the abortion opinions.

Writing about the view of law typically transmitted to students in today's law schools, Dean Roger C. Cramton of Cornell University Law School says the following:

> Basic attitudes toward law are affected if everything is perceived merely as a matter of degree, with all distinctions drawn more or less arbitrarily for purposes of convenience. Matters of degree tend to displace polarities that involve basic differences of kind. The very metaphor of "drawing a line," a phrase often on the law professor's lips, suggests a deep arbitrariness of law -- an arbitrariness beyond the rule of genuine reason...[86]

The Court's language in *Wade* reflects such a "line drawing" attitude. Since the Court admitted that it could not resolve the question of when life begins, its acceptance of the viability standard is arbitrary. The discussion of the "interest" of the woman and that of the state in protecting the unborn child and the different weight given to each of these at different points in the pregnancy -- as opposed to assigning, say, a definite, unchangeable value on the unborn life -- reflects an understanding of the question in terms of degrees, according to Cramton's view. The "balancing" activity that the Court engages in by its nature renders the law uncertain -- as Cramton indicates -- because it brings a different result in each case.

By its holding that the state cannot protect life before viability, the Court implicitly adopted "one theory of life" -- the very thing it forbade Texas from doing.[87] This is curious in light of the fact that the very use of the term "theory" suggests that the Court believed that when life begins is not a settled matter -- or perhaps cannot really be determined. This use of wording makes one wonder if the Court simply selected the position most in agreement with its view on abortion.[88]

The Court's endorsement of an arbitrary view about life is seen further by its saying that at viability, the unborn child has "the capability of meaningful life."[89] It is difficult for one to think of a word more indefinite and open to different interpretations than "meaningful."[90]

The entire discussion provoked by the Cramton quote shows the Court's treatment of viability was not, at least in the result, a reconciliation of various scientific views about life, nor is an attempt to base a legal decision upon such a reconciliation legitimate. It was, rather, an attempt to engage in the kind of arbitrary "line drawing" that Cramton speaks about. It can rightfully be called "arbitrary" because the Court did not present any basis for it in biological or other knowledge.

Somewhat related to the above, and underscoring the Court's relativistic thinking, is some other language that it used. One example is the way it used "dogma" and "doctrine" when referring to the teachings of the ancient Pythagoreans and the Roman Catholic Church. The Court tried to show how relying on the Hippocratic Oath as a basis for condemning abortion -- Hippocrates was a Pythagorean -- is not valid because their view was not widely shared in the ancient world, but was merely adhered to by them as "a matter of dogma."[91] The Oath's opposition to abortion does not establish that medicine historically believed that a human being was destroyed in abortion; it merely "echoes Pythagorean doctrines" about life beginning at conception.[92] The impression the Court leaves is that "dogmas" and "doctrines" condemning abortion represent only the beliefs of particular religions and other groups, and cannot possibly claim to be truthful or a guide to formulating the law.

Similarly, the Court passed off the Catholic Church's opposition to abortion as simply "official belief."[93] Nothing is said about a possible non-dogmatic basis for that opposition. The Court -- intentionally or unintentionally -- also implied that this belief is changeable (and thus emphasizes that it, like any other belief, is relative and cannot make a claim of truthfulness).

Conclusion

What can be concluded is that the *Wade* and *Bolton* opinions appear to reflect, at least to some degree, the rhetoric of the pro-abortion movement. The use of language presents abortion primarily as a medical and "therapeutic" procedure, makes the unborn child other than human, gives a "progressive" cast to the pro-abortion position, and adopts the pro-abortion thinking about the freedom and rights of the woman. It also reflects the essential arbitrariness and relativism of modern-day legal thought.

Chapter Conclusion

What I have shown in this Chapter is that the Court's, and some of the other, opinions are carefully structured in order to build up a strong argument and lay down premises from which the conclusions follow logically. The greater importance of different points and sections is indicated, generally, by their greater length and more detailed arguments. I have also shown that many areas of knowledge were relied on by the Justices in order to formulate these conclusions and that medical knowledge, broadly understood to include biology and psychology, seems to be the most important. Finally, I have explained how the language used in the Court's and the concurring opinions is adopted from the pro-abortion movement and reflects the perspective of that movement. That movement has used particular language to make this perspective more acceptable.

Chapter Three

The Supreme Court's Understanding of History, The Legal Background, and the Constitutional Provisions

In this Chapter, I examine the Supreme Court's understanding of the history of abortion, the status of abortion at common law, its status in nineteenth century American law and the purpose of the criminal statutes enacted against it at that time, the way the unborn child has been treated in other areas of the law, and the probable view of the Constitution and the Fourteenth Amendment about the unborn child. I shall also make some observations about the Court's understanding of the right of privacy, which shall serve as a backdrop for my in-depth treatment of this supposed right in Chapter Five. I argue in the present Chapter that the Court made serious errors in all these areas. Since these matters comprise such a large part of the *Wade* opinion, it is necessary that I discuss them, even though -- as will be apparent -- they have been treated at length by other authors.

The Court's Understanding of Ancient History and the Hippocratic Oath

Ancient Political Societies

The part of the *Wade* opinion dealing with ancient attitudes about abortion was not intended to provide a rationale for the Court's decision. The Court simply used it as part of its historical analysis to show that "restrictive criminal abortion laws...are of relatively recent vintage."[1] The Court said the following about abortion in the ancient world:

> We are told that at the time of the Persian Empire abortifacients were known and that criminal abortions were severely punished. We are also told, however, that abortion was practiced in Greek times as well as in the Roman Era, and that "it was resorted to without scruple." The Ephesian, Soranos, often described as the greatest of the ancient gynecologists, appears to have been generally opposed to Rome's prevailing free-abortion practices. He found it necessary to think first of the life of the mother, and he resorted to abortion when, upon this standard, he felt the procedure advisable. Greek and Roman law afforded little protection to the unborn. If abortion was prosecuted in some places, it seems to have been based on a concept of a violation of the father's right to his offspring. Ancient religion did not bar abortion.[2]

Let me consider the accuracy of the Court's statements on history in the above passage and, in particular, of the general view it puts forth that abortion was both legally and morally acceptable in the ancient world.

Dr. Harold O. J. Brown, a professor at Trinity Evangelical Divinity School, has argued that the Court was wrong about this conclusion. He says the following:

> ...even in pagan antiquity, abortion, although widely practiced, was by no means universally approved, and was indeed explicitly condemned as immoral, dangerous, and harmful to the general welfare, by the most important pre-Mosaic law codes and by some of the most celebrated thinkers, philosophers, and moralists of pagan Greece and Rome.[3]

The amount of documented material about abortion in the pre-Christian era is scanty, partly because it was then a dangerous procedure and also because infanticide was so widely practiced as to make it an unnecessary alternative.[4] The Court, citing Arturo Castiglioni's mammoth volume on the history of medicine, correctly stated that abortion was condemned by the ancient Persians. (We shall see shortly that it fails to mention another important fact mentioned by Castiglioni about abortion in the ancient world.) The Persians, however, were not the only ancient people who opposed and punished abortion, nor were they the first.

The earliest known laws on abortion were contained in the Code of Hammurabi in Babylon, which was promulgated in 1727 or 1728 B.C.[5] These laws apparently dealt only with a person's unintentional but culpable causing of a woman to miscarry. They required a financial penalty to the perpetrator, but if the woman also died, and she was a noblewoman, the perpetrator's daughter would also have to be put to death.[6]

The next-known ancient laws on abortion were those of the Assyrian King Tiglath-Pileser I, who in the twelfth century B.C. codified laws which had accumulated from the fifteenth to twelfth centuries B.C.[7] Unlike the Code of Hammurabi, that of Tiglath-Pileser punished the woman who caused herself to miscarry with death. Penalties are also prescribed for accessories to her act, but the part of the surviving text of the code relating to this is defective.[8]

Another ancient civilization that proscribed abortion was the Hittites, even though, as Eugene Quay put it, "[t]heir sexual morality was notoriously low."[9] Their laws in the second century B.C. condoned some sexual deviations, but the prohibition against abortion applied to all persons, means used, and circumstances. They prescribed financial penalties.[10]

There have been no codes of law discovered from the ancient Egyptian civilization. An indication of its view of abortion, however, can be seen in a fourteenth century B.C. religious hymn to the Sun-god Aton which is thought to have been composed by the pharaoh, Amenhotep IV. The hymn talks of Aton "[g]iving life to the son in the body of his mother" and of his being "[n]urse (even) in the womb."[11] Also, a prominent historian of embryology has written that there is no evidence that the Egyptians of this period believed the unborn child not to be alive until birth.[12]

This suggests, admittedly without conclusiveness, that the ancient Egyptians, at least in the period indicated, exhibited a respect for unborn life which would seem incompatible with abortion.

The ancient condemnation of abortion was not limited to Near Eastern civilizations. Quay, a lawyer who reviewed the history of abortion in a law review article in the early 1960s, writes that abortion was opposed in ancient Indian religious writings, such as the Vedas and the Vinayas of the Buddhists. This condemnation was repeated in one of the ancient Indian legal codes that has been discovered, the Code of Manu. This dates from A.D. 100, but the laws it brings together go back hundreds of years before that.[13]

Another ancient people who opposed abortion were the Jews. There were two traditions regarding abortion among the Jews of the pre-Christian and early Christian periods. The first was based on the Hebrew text of that part of the Book of Exodus called the book of the covenant (the Palestinian tradition); the other was based on the Septuagint version of the same text. The Exodus text mentions explicitly only abortion caused by a third party; it says nothing about abortion caused by the mother herself. In this sense, however, it is no different from the Babylonian and Hittite Codes of which I have spoken (these and the Assyrian code apparently influenced the early Jewish legal code).[14] The Palestinian tradition, which was the earlier of the two, did not consider the unborn child a human being in the complete sense until birth. Nonetheless, abortion or dismemberment of the unborn child was permitted *only* when necessary to save the mother's life. The fact that the child was considered part of the mother until birth was not appealed to by the ancient Jews in order to justify free-wheeling abortion practices, or a right by the mother to end her pregnancy. It was referred to mostly to settle questions of property ownership and, since this understanding of the status of the unborn was applied also on the sub-human level, to determine the ownership of an embryo carried by a newly purchased female animal.[15]

Father John Connery, S.J., a professor of theology at Loyola University in Chicago, explains why the ancient Jews could not have accepted easily available abortion:

> The attitude of the Jews toward barrenness as a curse, the regard for fertility as one of God's greatest blessings, the mandate to increase and multiply, the hope of the Jewish maiden that she might bear the Messiah, all militated against any easy attitude toward self-induced abortion, or even any deliberate attitude. And there is no positive evidence of such an attitude.[16]

The later of the ancient Jewish traditions, based on the Septuagint version of Exodus, seemed to consider the unborn child a complete human being from the time he is formed, not from birth. (It thus was similar to the Aristotelian position, as we shall see shortly.) Anyone who caused a woman to have a miscarriage of a formed unborn child (again, there was no mention of self-abortion) was to experience the death penalty. Causing abortion before formation led to a less severe penalty to be decided upon by the woman's husband.[17]

My brief survey of attitudes about abortion in these civilizations suggests two points of disagreement with the Court's interpretation: first, that, at least outside of the Greco-Roman world, ancient peoples did not accept abortion as a moral good which was to go without rebuke and some legislated against it, and, second, ancient religions cannot be said to have uniformly refused to condemn abortion.

Now, consider what the Court said about Greek and Roman abortion practices. The Court cited a number of sources which said abortion was practiced in these civilizations[18] and another which said "it was resorted to without scruple."[19] It mentioned another source which disputes this latter claim.[20] It thus seemed to leave this particular point unresolved. The evidence is that abortion was *not* practiced without scruple. Some of the most eminent physicians, philosophers, and moral spokesmen of Greece and Rome opposed abortion. The law was also not silent about it.

Soranus spoke out against abortion. The Court was fairly accurate in what it said about him above; he opposed abortion except when necessary to save the mother's life. He said that "it is the task of medicine to maintain and save what nature has engendered."[21]

Seneca, while defending infanticide, indicates that he has a sense of the wrongfulness of abortion by writing in praise of his mother for not having had an abortion, like so many others.[22]

The poet Ovid viewed abortion as unnatural and impious. He wrote that "'the first one who thought of detaching from her womb the fetus forming in it deserved to die by her own weapons.'"[23]

The first century Stoic Musonius Rufus referred to abortion as a "danger to the commonwealth" and expressed approval of the laws against it -- despite the fact that the Stoics generally believed that life did not begin until birth.[24]

The Court indicated that Plato and Aristotle were among the Greek thinkers (a majority, according to the Court) who "commended abortion."[25] A closer look at the works of these two great philosophers that were cited by the Court indicated that its conclusion is quite problematical. The Court cited Plato's *Republic*, Book V, 461C. In this passage, Socrates is speaking to Glaucon about how the relations between the sexes must be ordered so as to insure that the best men and women will be the guardians, or highest caste, in the best city. The best men must be brought together with the best women in order to produce the best children (i.e., those most capable of being guardians). He says that only those who are within certain age limits will bear children for the city. In the following passage, which the Court cites, Socrates speaks of the coming together of men and women who are beyond these age limits:

> "...as soon as the women and the men pass the age of begetting, we shall leave the men free to consort with any they will, except with daughter or mother, and daughters' children, and those of an earlier generation than the mother; and the women free except for son or father or those above and below as before. However, with all this allowance, we must warn them to be as careful as possible not to bring any of these conceptions into the light, not even one; but if a child is born, if one forces its way through, they must dispose of it on the understanding that there is no food or nurture for such a one."[26]

The Court's understanding of Plato can be critiqued both with regard to its interpretation of this particular passage and to the position of Plato as determined from *The Republic* generally. Let me address the former first.

Professor Noonan has concurred with the Court's interpretation of this passage as indicating that Plato endorsed abortion. He says that Plato proposes it as a solution to maintain an optimum population level in the ideal city.[27] I believe that it is unclear whether Socrates refers specifically to abortion here. The passage can be read as an endorsement of the regulation of child-rearing generally, but perhaps not specifically abortion. The last part suggests that Socrates is endorsing infanticide, not abortion.[28] Moreover, there is a slim possibility that Socrates may be referring to neither abortion nor infanticide in this passage. He talks of bringing "such conceptions into the light." Just before this passage, in 461A-B he speaks of a child being placed among the population of the city after having been born of parents who were past their prime for child-bearing. Since this will weaken the stock of people in the city, the child will be excluded from receiving holy rites and being prayed over like other children. Socrates says that such a child "was begotten in darkness with incontinence to the common danger."[29] In 461C, then, Socrates may simply be instructing that the child born in the circumstance described should experience the same "darkness" -- denial of being brought into the "light" of social acceptability -- as the one in the circumstance in 461A-B. The reference may thereby be to the attitudes that others should have toward such a child, not to whether he should be permitted to live. Also, the last part, which seems to be the most clear reference to infanticide, may merely be contending that such a child must be banished from or adopted out of the city.

Early in 460C, Socrates says that any children of couples within the childbearing limits "who may be born defective, they [nurses who take charge of children after they are born] will put away as is proper in some mysterious, unknown place."[30] This passage, I believe, is further support for what I said above. Socrates says that defective children will be hidden from the city; he does not say that they will be killed or exposed. If he is not proposing infanticide for defective children -- which was a common practice in the ancient Greek world -- he is unlikely to be doing so for normal, healthy children just because their parents are outside the permitted age limits for child-bearing.

Now, let us consider problems with the Court's interpretation beyond the particular passage cited. First, it will be noticed that I referred above to Socrates having said this or that, *not* Plato. The Court made the error of believing that Socrates is automatically a mouthpiece for Plato and that *everything* he says, without considering the manner and context in which it is stated and its relationship to the larger work, is to be taken at face value. Plato's thought, however, is not so directly spelled out. Since he uses the dialogic mode, we can attribute a particular position to him only after close examination of the work, in which we have gained an understanding of the general point the speaker addresses and the overall argument of the work, and after we have considered the circumstances in which the speaker speaks, his likely purpose in saying what he does, and the statements made by the characters he is speaking with. Even then, we may still not be entirely certain that such and such a point really represents *his* thought.

Secondly, we can see that Socrates' view, when taken in the context of the overall point he is discussing with Glaucon and the entire work, appears in a quite different light than it would otherwise. First of all, we must realize that what Socrates prescribes for his city in *The Republic* cannot be taken as a guide or recommendation for conducting one's life or establishing laws or moral norms for a real political regime. He is, after all, talking only about a "city in speech." He never suggests that it be a guide for a program of political action.[31] Moreover, to get back to Professor Noonan's point, even if he *were* advocating abortion or infanticide it would not be for the sake of bestowing a new liberty on parents, but rather to bring about a desired objective of the city.

About Socrates' entire advocacy of community of women and children and free sexual "cavorting," Plato scholar Allan Bloom of the University of Chicago says that "[g]iven that there will be many erotic improprieties in this city...it seems that Socrates' approach to the matter is quite light-hearted."[32] In other words, Socrates is not putting these things forward as serious political proposals. The city that he constructs is, rather, symbolic. It is symbolic of both the social and personal conditions that philosophy needs in order to thrive. The family represents the conventions and "prejudices" of the community which stand in the way of the philosopher seeking the truth. Such "prejudices" -- in Socrates' time when philosophy was just emerging and even in our time -- force philosophy to remain a private, hidden activity. What Socrates attempts to do is to create a political regime in which this will no longer have to be so.

The family also represents a source of "prejudice" for the individual which prevents him from leading the true philosophic life. The everyday concerns of family life and the emotional commitment a man has to his family deflect him from establishing a set of beliefs which are the most conducive to the pursuit of truth and devotion to the common good.

More basically, the message Socrates tries to convey is that the body obstructs the pursuits of the mind which, of course, must be uppermost for the philosopher. In order to gratify, and even to preserve, the body, a man must develop a certain way of life. This demands a certain set of beliefs respecting the things that Socrates says are to be used for this purpose: private property, the family, the civil order, and even the gods. The beliefs about these are merely conventional; they are not expressive of nature and so make philosophy, which seeks to uncover the truths of nature, a difficult enterprise. Socrates' own life demonstrated philosophy's need for a "city in speech" like the one he describes. As Bloom puts it, only in such a city "will no obloquy be attached to Socrates' deplorable neglect of his family and his indifference to the labor necessary to make a comfortable living."[33]

Socrates' comic or "light-hearted" treatment of serious matters such as the family and sexual propriety, according to Bloom, is also tied up with the need of the philosopher to unshackle himself from convention and "prejudice." The philosopher must be able to reverse the usual roles of treating the tragic seriously and the comic lightly because he must oppose shame. In Socrates' mind, shame is an outgrowth of convention and, as such, stands between men and the truth.[34]

I have made this digression simply to show that one cannot understand from just a surface consideration what is said in a Platonic dialogue. The Court's quick judgment about the passage it cites leaves much to be desired.[35]

The other place in Plato's works that some point to as indicating an endorsement of abortion is Book V of *The Laws*. The passage in question is the following:

> There are many ways of regulating numbers; for they in whom generation is affluent may be made to refrain,[36] and, on the other hand, special care may be taken to increase the number of births by reward and stigmas, or we may meet the evil by the elder men giving advice and administering rebuke to the younger -- in this way the object may be attained. And if after all there be very great difficulty ...and we are at our wits' end, there is still the old device...of sending out a colony...[37]

Abortion as an alternative for controlling population is not mentioned in this passage and, in fact, as a last resort solution, Plato proposes *not* abortion but colonization. The only place that one could possibly infer a reference to abortion is when he speaks of persons being "made to refrain." This, however, could refer to prohibiting intercourse or cohabitation, compulsory contraception, compulsory sterilization, or compulsory abortion. The fact that infanticide was a more common practice than abortion among the Greeks would argue against the likelihood that he is referring to abortion. It is further unlikely because in light of the context of the passage, Plato could only be referring to *compulsory* abortion and I have uncovered no evidence of this in ancient Greece. (The quote of Aristotle below suggests that compulsory infanticide may have been a practice, however.)

The section of Aristotle to which Plato refers opposes abortion as a means of controlling the population, which is the subject of Plato's attention in the passage from *The Laws*. This would seem to argue against the position that Plato is advocating abortion here. I take this position in spite of the fact that in the passage in his writings being referred to, which I shall turn to next, Aristotle justifies the taking of life before a certain stage of the pregnancy.

It is a part of this section (Book VII, 1335.25) that the Court cites to supposedly establish that Aristotle also "commended abortion." The following is the passage which includes the one which the Court cites:

> The question arises whether children should always be reared or may sometimes be exposed to die. There should certainly be a law to prevent the rearing of deformed children. On the other hand, there should also be a law, in all states where the system of social habits is opposed to unrestricted increase, to prevent the exposure of children to death *merely* in order to keep the population down. The proper thing to do is to limit the size of each family, and if children are then conceived in excess of the limit so fixed, to have miscarriage induced before sense and life have begun in the embryo. (Whether it is right or wrong to induce a miscarriage will thus depend on whether sense and life are still to come, or have already begun.)[38] (Emphasis Aristotle's)

The following points are seen in the above passage. The first is that Aristotle proposes abortion as an alternative to infanticide to regulate population.

The second is that abortion is proposed only for the purpose of aiding what Aristotle believes to be an important objective of the state; it is not seen as a liberty to be exercised as the mother wishes. Thirdly, Aristotle permits abortion only up to the point when sensation in the unborn child begins. It was at this point -- forty days for the male and ninety days for the female -- that Aristotle believed, on the basis of the biology of his day, that life begins. Finally, by the phrase "if children are conceived in excess of the limit so fixed," he seems to indicate the preferred means of keeping the population down is not abortion, but preventing conception in some way. Aristotle thus can hardly be said to be advocating easily available abortion -- the position that the Court took in *Wade* and *Bolton* -- but rather, as one commentator put it, makes his proposal in the above passage "with remarkable caution."[39]

The fact that Aristotle is expressing support for infanticide would seem to indicate, however, that he favors abortion. We must note that he supports infanticide only in the case of deformity. He is very prudent about it. One may be led to think that if he favored infanticide in such a case, he surely would have favored abortion, if one had been able to know in his time what the condition of the child was before birth. I take this up further in Chapter Nine.

The Court is also not correct in its belief that, by and large, the ancient Greeks and Romans did not believe abortion to be a subject to be addressed by their laws. Sparta did not permit abortion. Lycurgus, the ancient Spartan law-giver, and his eminent Athenian contemporary, Solon, both prohibited abortion.[40] In making its assertions about the supposed legality and moral acceptability of abortion in Greece and Rome, the Court cited a contrary view attributed to the late historian of medicine Arturo Castiglioni, but dismissed it. Castiglioni tells us that Roman law actually did punish abortion, at least from the time of Augustus (31 B.C.-14 A.D.). He says the following:

> The law against abortion was...strict. Thus the *Lex Cornelia* prescribed that whoever gave an aphrodisiac beverage or caused an abortion should be punished with deportation and the loss of his goods. If the patient should die

> as a result of these practices, the guilty party was condemned to death.[41]

The later pagan emperors, Septimius Severus (193-211 A.D.) and Antonius Caracalla (211-217 A.D.) both punished abortion with banishment.[42]

This passage makes it clear that abortion in ancient Rome was looked upon as worthy of punishment, not only because of harm to the mother. Noonan, however, agrees with the Court that the reason it was punished was not because of a desire to protect the unborn child -- the embryo was regarded as part of the mother-- but apparently for the father's benefit. He also says that it was punished in order to restrain the "bad example" of giving magical potions (abortifacients) which *could* cause death to the recipient.[43] Harold O. J. Brown says that the rationale of the Roman laws may have gone beyond this. Even though infanticide was so common, the Greeks and Romans may have shared the understanding possibly reflected in the other ancient laws: abortion is undesirable because interfering with the course of nature (as occurs when pregnancy is interrupted) is wrong.[44] The fact that abortion appears to have been reproved, although not prohibited, even by the original laws of Rome suggests that the Romans may have been influenced by the thinking of these earlier civilizations.[45]

In short, although the extent to which abortion was prohibited and punished in the ancient world is uncertain and the reasons for the legislation that existed against it unclear, the Court was incorrect in suggesting that, all in all, it was not morally reproved or the subject of legislation.

The Hippocratic Oath

The other aspect of ancient attitudes that the Court addressed concerned the Hippocratic Oath. The Oath, which bears the name of the eminent ancient Greek physician Hippocrates, who lived in the fifth and fourth centuries B.C., contains a strong condemnation of abortion. The pertinent passage is as follows:

> I will neither give a deadly drug to anyone if asked for it, nor will I make a suggestion to this effect. Similarly I will not give to a woman an abortive remedy.[46]

In its discussion of the Oath, the Court relied primarily on the conclusions of the late Ludwig Edelstein in his 1943 monograph *The Hippocratic Oath*. The Court, citing Edelstein, said that the Oath was unable to stop the practice of abortion in Hippocrates' time because it "was not uncontested" even then, and actually reflected the "dogma" of the Pythagorean school of philosophers to which Hippocrates belonged. The Pythagoreans believed that life begins at the moment of conception. The Oath thus represented "only a small segment of Greek opinion" and "was not accepted by all ancient physicians."[47] The Court, for example, quoted Edelstein as saying that Galen, another eminent ancient Greek physician and other ancient medical writers "'give evidence of the violation of almost every one of its injunctions.'"[48] The Court, relying on Edelstein, says that the Oath took hold finally because of the rise of Christianity, which agreed with the Pythagorean ethic.[49] The Court used this explanation to try to discredit the Oath as the binding standard of medical conduct which would enjoin physicians from performing abortions.

Harold O. J. Brown, however, has criticized the Court's interpretation of the Edelstein monograph. Brown states that Edelstein does not seek to question the validity of the Oath as merely reflecting the ethic of a minority, but rather to show how an ethic which came to enjoy universal acceptance originated.[50]

Brown says that the Court was correct in asserting that Edelstein believed that the Oath gained support because it coincided with the convictions of Christianity, which was becoming the dominant religion in the later Roman Empire. It was incorrect, however, in suggesting that Edelstein believed it does not represent universally valid and unchanging principles, merely because it was originally espoused by a small minority, the Pythagoreans.[51] This interpretation by the Court is perhaps a reflection of its underlying philosophical position in these decisions -- as will be discussed in Chapter Eight -- that universal truths are essentially unknowable. This was the Court's position, whether it was aware of it or not.

It is apparently because the Court was not willing to attribute unchanging validity to the Hippocratic ethic -- to see it as anything more than a reflection of dominant opinion -- that Brown goes on to state the following:

> The unspoken implication of the Court's argument seems to be that the Hippocratic Oath need not be taken seriously as an expression of medical ethics because, at the outset, it was the view of a minority, the Pythagoreans, and later, when it came to enjoy majority acceptance, this only took place because the majority by that time had embraced Christianity.[52]

Brown points out that Edelstein does not say, as the Court does, that the Oath was accepted because of the new dominance of Christianity. He states, rather, that the Oath became universally accepted because of the fact that monotheism, whether "'in its purely religious or its more secularized form,'" became the accepted creed. He says that "'[n]ot only Jews and Christians, but the Arabs, the medieval doctors, men of the Renaissance, scholars of the Enlightenment and scientists of the nineteenth century embraced the ideals of the Oath.'"[53] The latter three groups did not endorse the Christian conception of God and man's relationship to Him. Brown is led to conclude that the Court's rejection of the Oath is really a rejection not just of the Judeo-Christian ethical tradition, but of that of Western civilization as a whole.[54]

There is one other point: the Oath was not followed in ancient times because of the moral weakness and decadence which often prevailed. The Oath was held up as an enlightened standard to provide men with moral direction in the midst of this. We are made aware of this by Galen. The Court, as mentioned, cited Galen, who lived in the second century A.D., only to show that the Oath was not much adhered to in his time. It failed to mention that Galen was a fervent follower of Hippocrates, who he believed should be "'venerate[d] equally with the gods.'"[55] Galen called medicine a "'philanthropic art,' and envisaged Hippocrates as its hero."[56] He viewed the low state of affairs to which medicine and life in his time had fallen as being caused by the mass of physicians and "philosophers." He battled them unceasingly, and believed that they were not motivated by a love of truth, but by greed and lust and a desire for political power. He said that while they pretended to admire Hippocrates, they refused to follow him.[57]

Similarly, another ancient physician, the Roman Scribonius Largus, stood out in his time as one who, in the words of one historian of medicine, "proclaim[ed] the sanctity of human life" and "possessed a noble conception of the duties of the medical profession." He was apparently one of the few practitioners of his age who honored the Hippocratic Oath.[58] He is looked back on as a beacon of hope in the mad and morally decadent era of Nero (54-68 A.D.).

The Court's Understanding of Abortion at Common Law

Now, let us consider the Court's position about abortion at common law. I mentioned in Chapter Two that the Court stated that abortion, whether before or after quickening, was never a crime at common law. The Court appeared to rely primarily on the scholarly work of Professor Cyril Means of New York Law School in coming to this conclusion. Means' study of abortion at common law and in earlier American law has been strongly criticized by some scholars. I shall consider these criticisms in this Section and elsewhere in this Chapter.

Professor Means relies on three early English cases to establish his position that abortion was a liberty at common law. The first is a 1327 case which he denominates *The Twinslayer's Case*. The full text of the case, which is quite brief, reads as follows:

> Writ issued to the Sheriff of Glousestershire to apprehend one D. who, according to the testimony of Sir G[eoffrey] Scrop[e the Chief Justice of the King's Bench], is supposed to have beaten a woman in an advanced stage of pregnancy who was carrying twins, whereupon directly afterwards one twin died and she was delivered of the

> other, who was baptized John by name, and two days afterwards, through the injury he had sustained, the child died: and the indictment was returned before Sir. G. Scrop[e], and D. came and pled Not Guilty, and for the reason that the Justices were unwilling to adjudge this thing a felony the accused was released to mainpernors, and then the argument was adjourned sine die. [T]hus the writ issued, as before stated, and Sir. G. Scrop[e] rehearsed the entire case and how he [D.] came and pled.
>
> Herle: to the sheriff: Produce the body, etc. And the sheriff returned the writ to the bailiff of the franchise of such place, who said, that the same fellow was taken by the Mayor of Bristol, but of the cause of this arrest we are wholly ignorant.[59]

One critic of Professor Means' interpretation of this case, Professor Robert A. Destro, of the Law School at The Catholic University of America, writes the following about what the Court actually did in the case:

> From a critical examination of the case report several things appear. First, the writ issued to bring D. into court appears to have been one of homicide, a fact which may be inferred from D.'s release to mainpernors prior to the adjournment of the argument "sine die." Since the writ of mainprise was the early common law equivalent of bail in homicide cases, it is clear that D. was neither acquitted nor released in the reported proceedings, but was held to answer the charge at a later date. Second, it is clear that D. was not acquitted in the course of the reported proceedings; only the argument was adjourned. No mention is made of the writ's being dismissed. Third, it appears that after D. had been released Herle, the Chief Justice of the Common Bench, demanded his presence to answer the charge. But D. was unavailable to answer in the proceedings at York since he had been arrested in Bristol on another charge. Thus, Professor Means' uncritical reliance upon the statement that the judges were un-recalled to answer the charges. Since another of the original uses of the writ of

> mainprise upon which D. had been released was to procure release prior to trial when there was some doubt as to whether or not the killing was felonious, D.'s recall to answer the charges lends support to the proposition that the judges had indeed characterized D.'s actions as a crime.[60]

Another critic of Means, Professor Robert M. Byrn of Fordham University Law School, makes a few additional points. He says that Scrope, the Chief Justice of the King's Bench, appears to be reporting the prior action of the King's Bench to another judicial body. This is suggested by the fact that Herle, who was Chief Justice of the Common Bench but not a member of the King's Bench, is mentioned. The only plausible explanation for his name appearing, according to Byrn, is that the case subsequently went from the King's Bench to the King's Council. The Council, among its other functions, provided assistance and consultation for justices experiencing difficulty in deciding a case. The justices of the realm, such as Herle, served as *ex officio* members on the Council.[61]

He finishes his explanation as follows:

> It is most probable that in 1327 the justices of King's Bench consulted the Council for assistance in deciding a case of first impression, as they attempted to interpret and apply Bracton and Fleta [eminent common law commentators who I shall speak of shortly]. The need to resort to the Council would explain the adjournment sine die and the admission of defendant to bail at the original proceedings before King's Bench. However, since the arrest of the defendant on another charge precluded further proceedings, the Council's instruction was not forthcoming and no final disposition was made of the case. It is authority for nothing except the unwillingness of the court to let the abortionist go unpunished and the justices' puzzlement over how properly to deal with him. Subsequent history would suggest that the justices' dilemma was rooted in problems of proof. Had the abortionist's act really been the cause of the stillbirth? Had the two-day-old twin died from the abortion or some other cause?[62]

The next case Means relies on is one he calls *The Abortionist's Case* (1348). Its short text is as follows:

> One was indicted for killing a child in the womb of its mother, and the opinion was that he shall not be arrested on this indictment since no baptismal name was in the indictment, and also it is difficult to know whether he killed the child or not, etc.[63]

Professor Byrn says that the court did not dismiss the indictment in this case because abortion was not a crime at common law, as Means says. If that were the case, Byrn says, there either would have been no indictment in the first place or else the indictment would have been dismissed expressly on that ground. Rather, Byrn infers that abortion was indeed a criminal offense, but the indictment had to be dismissed for a defect in pleading because there was no baptismal name and an impossibility of proof as to the cause of the child's death.[64]

Means contends that his interpretation of these cases is reinforced by the sixteenth century legal commentator Sir William Stanford, whose discussion of them he quotes at length.[65] Means says that Stanford's analysis is "'definitive.'"[66] Destro, however, argues that Stanford, in his treatise, "was more concerned with the difficulty-of-proof problem inherent in the abortion cases which occasionally came before the courts of England than he was with propounding a theory that abortion was not a secular crime at common law."[67] This is seen, according to Destro, in his disagreement with Bracton (whose views I shall consider shortly) on the question of whether abortion is homicide. Stanford said it could not be because the fact of the child being *in rerum natura* (in existence) at the time he was killed could not be substantiated in abortion.[68]

Byrn and Destro both mention the difficulty-of-proof problem in securing prosecutions. One of the anti-abortion briefs in the cases informed the Court that this -- and not a supposed common law liberty of abortion, as contended by Means -- was the reason for the paucity of prosecutions for abortion at common law. The Court, however, chose to believe Means' interpretation of history.[69] Moreover, there is yet another reason why there were such few prosecutions. This is simply that religious and moral restraints were strong enough in these times that women seldom had abortions.

Before I discuss the third case, I must record what prominent early common law commentators said about abortion, because they are important for considering this case.

The Supreme Court referred to the writings of the following commentators: Henry de Bracton, "Fleta," Sir Edmund Coke, and Sir William Blackstone. As the Court acknowledged, Bracton, writing in the thirteenth century before either of the two cases above were decided, regarded abortion (as mentioned above) as homicide "if the foetus is already formed or quickened, especially if it is quickened."[70] Fleta, writing a century later (apparently also before the cases), concurs. He regards not only the abortionist or the one who gives the woman poison to procure abortion as guilty of homicide, but also the woman herself. He even seems to regard contraception as homicide, saying that he is guilty who has "given or accepted poison with the intention of preventing procreation or conception."[71] As Byrn indicates above, the courts of England in the late Medieval period regarded these two as good sources of the common law on abortion.

In the seventeenth century, Edward Coke wrote the following famous passage in his *Third Institute:*

> If a woman be quick with childe, and by a Potion or otherwise killeth it in her wombe; or if a man beat her, whereby the childe dieth in her body, and she is delivered of a dead childe, this is a great misprision, and no murder: but if the childe be born alive, and dieth of the Potion, battery, or other cause, this is murder: for in the Law it is accounted a reasonable creature; *in rerum natura*, when it is born alive. And the Book in IE. 3 [*The Twinslayer's Case*] was never holden for law. And 3 Ass. p. 2 [*The Abortionist's Case*] is but a repetion of that case. And so horrible an offence should not go unpunished.[72]

The important term in this passage is "misprision." Contemporary commentators have translated this to mean "misdemeanor." The *Oxford English Dictionary* translates it as it applies to law as follows: "a wrong action or omission, specifically a misdemeanour or failure of duty on the part of a public official."[73] The *OED* refers to Blackstone's *Commentaries IV* in 1759 as defining misprisions as "generally understood to be all such high offenses as are under the degree of capital, but nearly bordering thereon."[74] The impression we are left with, particularly in light of the fact that Coke emphasized that abortion was a *great* misprision, is that the translation of "misdemeanor" in its current sense hardly expresses the gravity of the offense in Coke's mind. It was possibly an offense which could be equated to some felonies today which are not punished with death.

Blackstone accepted Coke's understanding of the common law of abortion in his *Commentaries*. He treats abortion in Book I of his *Commentaries*, which is entitled "On the Rights of Persons." Including it in this book suggests that Blackstone regarded abortion as an offense against the unborn child. Thus, his concern was at least partly with the protection of the child and not just the mother. The context of the passage written about the crime of abortion indicates, more specifically, that he believed the unborn child to be endowed with a legally protected right to life, which is included within a broader right of personal security:

> I. The right of personal security consists in a person's legal and uninterrupted enjoyment of his life, his limbs, his body, his health, and his reputation.
>
> > 1. Life is the immediate gift of God, a right inherent by nature in every individual; and it begins in contemplation of law as soon as an infant is able to stir in the mother's womb. For if a woman is quick with child, and by a potion or otherwise, killeth it in her womb; or if anyone beat her, whereby the child dieth in her body, and she is delivered of a dead child; this, though not murder, was by ancient law homicide or manslaughter. But the modern law doth not look upon this offense in quite so atrocious a light, but merely as a heinous misdemesnor. [Citing Coke on this

latter point.][75]

The right of personal security is for Blackstone, an "absolute" right. He believes that the absolute rights of personal security, personal liberty, and private property are natural rights -- as indicated above-- and the "'first and primary end'" of human laws is to maintain and regulate them. These absolute rights are in contrast to "relative" rights which Blackstone says are secondary and largely artificial rights which attach to individuals as part of their legally established relationships with other individuals (e.g., master and servant) and are consequent to civil society.[76]

James Fitzjames Stephen's account of the history of English criminal law tells us that even before the time of Bracton -- indeed, before the Norman Conquest -- abortion was a crime. Before the Conquest, it was apparently regarded as an ecclesiastical offense only.[77] We can see from what Stephen says about English law of that time that this fact does not make it any less of a crime in the law of the realm:

> Probably the clergy were never more powerful in any time or country then they were in England before the Norman conquest. Civil and ecclesiastical legislation went hand in hand. Nearly every set of secular laws enacted by any of the early English kings was coupled with an ecclesiastical code, or contained ecclesiastical provisions: The bishop and the earl sat side by side in every county court.
>
> At the Norman conquest a great change was introduced into this state of things...one authentic monument of William's juris'prudence'...was the law by which he separated the spiritual from the temporal courts... There is not a word in it which suggests that any other authority was needed for the enactment than his own will, though he recites the advice of the ecclesiastical authorities.[78]

What we must conclude from these commentators and from glancing at early English legal history is that abortion was not a common law liberty and, indeed, appears to have long been regarded as a punishable offense, for the most part less than homicide, under English criminal law. Both the Court and Means mention the earliest commentator, Bracton, and the Court mentions Fleta. Neither seem to regard what they say as important, even though each is seeking an answer to the question of whether there was a common law liberty of abortion. Neither discusses what Blackstone says about the unborn child's right to life or right of personal security. The Court seems to completely accept Means' rationale for dismissing Coke's views. I shall discuss this next in relation to the third of the important cases which Means believes shapes the common law of abortion.

The text of the third case, *Sim's Case*, decided in 1601, is as follows:

> Trespasse and assault was brought against one Sims by the Husband and the Wife for beating of the woman, Cook, the case is such, as appears by examination. A man beats a woman which is great with child, and after the child is born living, but hath signes, and bruises in his body, received by the said batterie, and after dyed thereof, I say that this is murder. Fenner & Popham, absentibus caeteris, clearly of the same opinion, and the difference is where the child is born dead, and where it is born living, for if it be dead born it is no murder, for non constat, whether the child were living at the time of the batterie or not, or if the batterie was the cause of the death, but when it is born living, and the wounds appear in his body, and then he dye, the Batteror shall be arraigned of murder, for now it may be proved whether these wounds were the cause of the death or not, and for that if it be found, he shall be condemned.[79]

This case is not out-of-line with what has been said about the two previous cases and my conclusion above about the status of abortion at common law. The court states that the killing of the child in the womb is not to be treated as murder (this is not a case of voluntary abortion) and the difficulty-of-proof problem is again seen as pivotal. The court is unable to indict --specifically for murder; nothing is said about not permitting indictment for a lesser offense -- unless the child is born alive with wounds and later dies.

Means sees other significance in the case. Actually, he says that "[i]t is difficult to ascertain whether this was a decision or not."[80] Coke was the Attorney General at the time of this case, and Means believes, apparently, that it may be Coke and not the Queen's Bench which is speaking. Means -- and, following him, the Supreme Court in *Wade* -- accuse Coke of inventing a crime of abortion in defiance of the two earlier cases.[81] This, he says, is further seen in the quote above from Coke's *Third Institute*.[82] He contends that later in that *Institute*, Coke contradicts his position about abortion being "a great misprision" by the fact that he is unable to enumerate it in his list of the various miscellaneous offenses below the degree of felony which the common law then recognized.[83]

On the basis of what I have said up to now, Means' conclusion is disputable. Coke followed Bracton and Fleta in considering abortion a criminal offense. Actually, as Byrn emphasizes, he deviated from them not in assigning criminality to abortion for the first time, but in treating it as a lesser offense than they did.[84]

Means claims that Coke distorted the law on abortion because of a particular motive:

> Coke obviously felt strongly about abortion after quickening...and in the privacy of his study he faced a painful dilemma.
>
> If he acknowledged the ancient and exclusive ecclesiastical jurisdiction to try and punish laymen for this offense, then, according to his well-known view, those courts could impose only spiritual penalties...for such offense. Coke knew perfectly well that the laypeople of his time, who had seen so much religious upheaval, were no longer cowed, as their medieval ancestors had been, by the threat of purely spiritual penalties. Those who were bent on having abortions after quickening would go ahead and procure them, and thumb their noses at such threats [and thus be free to commit what Coke regarded

> as a terrible crime]...
>
> If Coke had held that the ecclesiastical courts retained jurisdiction of the offense, but that they could impose really effective punishments for it (fine and imprisonment), his concession would have contradicted those numerous writs of prohibition he had issued, whilst still a sitting judge, to ecclesiastical courts where they had tried to fine and imprison laypeople.
>
> If on the other hand, he claimed the existence of the eccleiastical jurisdiction over abortion after quickening, such as had always existed, he either had to let it go unpunished, even by spiritual penalties, or assert a common-law jurisdiction over this offense. He chose the latter expedient.[85]

Means tries to buttress this argument by citing a legal commentator who wrote just after Coke's time, Sir Matthew Hale. Hale said that abortion after quickening, whether voluntary or caused by an assault on the woman, "is not murder nor manslaughter by the law of *England*, because it is not yet *in rerum natura*, tho it be a great crime..."[86] Means says that while one might think that the latter phrase supports Coke's position that abortion was "a great misprision" at common law, actually Hale is referring only to the fact that it was an ecclesiastical offense. This, he contends, is seen by referring to the "Proemium" of Hale's book, where he says the following: "Crimes that are punishable by the laws of *England* for their matter are of two kinds. 1. *Ecclesiastical*. 2. Temporal."[87]

We can immediately raise objections to Means' argument against Coke. John S. Putka, in his unpublished Ph.D. dissertation on *Wade* and *Bolton*, points out that, historically, Means is on shaky ground:

> ...the ecclesiastical courts prosecuted some crimes that were also considered civil crimes. Some forms of murder, for example. The two kinds of courts were not mutually exclusive: prosecution in one did not necessarily imply that the offense in question was not regarded as an offense by the other; it was essentially a matter of lines of jurisdiction.

> ...[Further], [d]uring the English Reformation... King Henry VIII formally severed England's relationship with the papacy by having the British Parliament pass the Act of Supremacy, thereby establishing the Crown as the only foundation of all law in England, be it civil or be it ecclesiastical. Thus, the distinction which Professor Means takes great care to emphasize simply ceases to exist..."[88]

As I pointed out above, even before this formal consolidation of civil and ecclesiastical law under the aegis of the King they had long worked hand in hand and the civil codes were joined with or contained provisions from the ecclesiastical codes.

Secondly, Means produces nothing from Hale which reinforces his position. Simply referring to Hale's "Proemium" which says nothing more than that there were two types of criminal law in England does not prove that he regarded the law against abortion as being an ecclesiastical one. He says no such thing anywhere.

Further, as Putka argues, Means tries to analyze the legal situation in seventeenth century England from the perspective of late twentieth century American constitutional law. He sees the existence of a kind of strict "wall of separation," to use the popular contemporary phrase, between church and state. This simply was not the case. As Putka says above, both ecclesiastical and temporal law derived their authority from the Crown.[89]

Further evidence of the fact that abortion was not a common law liberty is provided by lawyers Dennis J. Horan and Thomas J. Marzen. They point out that prior to the nineteenth century, it was midwives and not physicians who for the most part aided women in reproductive and birth matters. From very early in American history the laws which governed midwifery prohibited abortion. They point to the example of an ordinance passed by the Common Council of New York City in 1716 which required licensing of midwives and expressly forbade their aiding women to procure abortions.[90] This fact directly refutes Professor Means' assertion that prior to 1830 only the common law regulated abortion in New York State.[91] Moreover, there was no reference to quickening in the ordinance,[92] suggesting that abortion was prohibited at all stages of pregnancy. Horan and Marzen thus argue that "on its face, the law was clearly directed *toward protection of prenatal life, not preservation of maternal health.*"[93] They also state that the law was based on English midwife licensing legislation, which similarly forbade abortion. The English legislation differed from the American, however, in that it was administered by ecclesiastical, instead of civil, authorities.[94]

Professor Means states that "only if in 1791 elective abortion was a common law liberty, can it be a ninth-amendment right today."[95] The Court gave itself a bit more leeway than this, saying that the right of privacy which includes the right to abortion is found *either* in the Ninth Amendment or in the liberty clause of the Fourteenth Amendment. I shall consider whether the Fourteenth Amendment can validly be considered the basis for such a liberty shortly. The claim that it is based on the Ninth Amendment can be defeated just on the basis of what I have already said about the common law on abortion. These additional observations, however, are in order.

A number of commentators on the Ninth Amendment have contended that one of the unenumerated rights which it protects is that of privacy.[96] No commentator, however, in the years before the pro-abortion movement gained momentum suggested that this right might include the right to abortion. (The validity of this application of the right will be explored later in this Chapter and in Chapter Five.)

Knowlton H. Kelsey, an Indiana lawyer, wrote what was probably the earliest law review commentary on the Ninth Amendment in 1936.[97] He makes some observations about it and our constitutional liberties generally which are significant for my point:

> The Colonists had argued, petitioned and contended, and finally waged war, not for philosophical perfection of any utilitarian doctrine of rights, but for the rights of Englishmen. These rights were best expressed by and most familiar to the colonists in Blackstone's Commentaries...[98]

He criticizes the specific promoters of this

utilitarian doctrine of rights and explains the meaning of the Ninth Amendment as follows:

> It would not seem improbably that the natural and inherent rights of Englishmen listed by Blackstone and fought for in the War of Independence, are more exact statements of the rights set out in the Constitution and referred to under the Ninth Amendment, than any theoretical or philosophic classification by Bentham, Austin or any other critic, on whose opposition to the teaching of Blackstone the more modern school of jurisprudence seems based.[99]

What were these fundamental rights of Englishmen? Blackstone classifies them under three basic headings: (I) Personal Security; (II) Personal Liberty; and (II) Private Property. He also states certain subordinate rights which follow from these.[100] I mentioned above that one of the subordinate rights under the heading of "Personal Security" is the right to life and that this, for Blackstone, extended to the unborn child. (I should point out that Blackstone was a major legal influence on the American colonists.)[101]

It is necessary to explain why Blackstonian thought is different from the utilitarian thought to which Kelsey refers, particularly when Blackstone's basic definition of law makes him sound like a positivist.[102] He says that law is "'the will of one man, or of one or more assemblies of men, to whom the supreme authority is entrusted...'"[103] The late political science professor Herbert J. Storing, of the University of Virginia, wrote that when there appeared to be some conflict between them, Blackstone believed that the "presumption is always in favor of the law of civil society, not the law of nature."[104] Nevertheless, Blackstone was not essentially a positivist; he had a notion of a higher law or natural rights. This was seen simply in his acceptance of the Lockean notion of natural rights. He believed that there are natural, absolute rights, which, as mentioned earlier, fall under the headings of the rights of personal security, personal liberty, and private property.[105]

Other statements of Blackstone's dispute the claim he was simply a positivist. First, as Storing states, Blackstone ultimately appeals to "'the law of nature'" or "'the God of battles'" as the foundation of law and the best means of limiting political authority.[106] Blackstone makes other references that suggest a notion of basic or natural law. He says there are "'*fundamental principles of law*; which, though legislators may depart from, yet judges are bound to observe.'"[107] He also says that "'even the laws themselves, whether made with or without consent, if they regulate and constrain our conduct in matters of mere indifference, without any *good end* in view, are regulations destructive of liberty.'"[108] Storing says that this "good end in view" is Blackstone's notion of "genuine civil liberty," which the latter defines as "'no other than natural liberty so far restrained by human laws (and no farther) as is necessary and expedient for the *general advantage of the publick*.'"[109] The last emphasized expression suggests a notion of a common good, which is generally connected with an understanding of higher law.

If Blackstone's notions of rights were indeed the basis for our Ninth Amendment, not only does this Amendment *not* include a right to abortion, but it specifically includes the right to life of the unborn child. There could thus be no basis at all under the Ninth mendment for the Court to come to the conclusion it did in *Wade*.

The reference to a "utilitarian doctrine of rights" in the first passage from Kelsey above is also significant. In Chapter Eight I show that the *Wade* and *Bolton* decisions are an example of a positivistic and utilitarian jurisprudence grounded in the will of the individual. I will return to the point that Kelsey makes, that such utilitarianism does not accord with our constitutional traditions.

The Court's use of the Ninth Amendment in *Wade* illustrates one of the points about the new "rights" thinking to be discussed in Chapter Eight. This is, since our rights are not based in God or nature, they must come from the state. The Court rejected the Blackstonian, natural law-based right to life of the unborn child inherent in the Ninth Amendment and manufactured a right to abortion for the mother it claimed is contained in the Ninth Amendment. It showed no natural law basis for this right, however. What the

Court actually did was to substitute its own thinking for the mandate of the natural law. *It is because of the Court's believing itself free to do this that Professors Byrn, Destro, and Rice claim that the* Wade *and* Bolton *decisions were an arbitrary denial by the state of the fundamental right of an entire class of persons.*[110]

Professor Means' -- and the Supreme Court's -- understanding of the status of abortion at common law is very doubtful. There is very little basis for asserting a common law liberty of abortion.

One final point should be made. Throughout the history of the common law, the presence of life in the unborn child was always the criterion used to determine whether abortion should be condemned. The only reason that up to the nineteenth century quickening or some other designated point of animation was believed decisive was because it was erroneously thought no life was present until then.[111] When better knowledge was acquired in the nineteenth century, laws began to be enacted prohibiting abortion at every stage of pregnancy.

The Nineteenth Century English and American Law on Abortion

The nineteenth century appears to have been an important turning point in the law regarding abortion. In both England and America, the first statutes were enacted forbidding and criminally punishing abortion. The law was probably responding to greater biological understanding of the unborn child, beginning with the discovery of the ovum in 1827. It was then learned how conception occurs, and people began to appreciate for the first time that the unborn child is a separate, distinct, and living being from that point on.

The English Statutes

The Supreme Court informed us that the first English abortion statute, Lord Ellenborough's Act[112] was enacted in 1803. It made the abortion of an unborn child after quickening a capital offense and for the first time clearly made pre-quickening abortion a punishable act (it made it less than a capital offense). There appears to be no record of a Parliamentary debate on the bill; there is only a brief reference to Lord Ellenborough's introduction of the bill on March 28, 1803, in which the rationale for its provisions is explained. Thus, we do not know precisely what prompted the statute.

Means and Byrn offer conflicting possible explanations for the Act. Means says that it resulted from an indictment by English authorities in 1802 for attempted abortion. (Apparently, according to Means, the child did not die.) The authorities believed that this was an indictable offense, but took care to spell out in the indictment the harm and discomfort caused the woman because, Means says, they believed that this was an indispensable element of the offense.[113] He thus uses this case as further putative evidence that abortion was not a crime at common law unless, *possibly*, the woman was injured. It was made a crime only with the passage of Lord Ellenborough's Act. The purpose of that Act, however, was only to make sure that the woman was protected.

Byrn takes the view that, while the purpose of the pre-quickening part of the statute is not really known, it may well reflect a growing concern about the unborn child. This, he says, may have followed from the publication in the very year of the statute of Thomas Percival's influential work, *Medical Ethics*, which condemned all abortions except therapeutic ones, and argued that even "the first spark of life" was inviolable.[114] As we shall see shortly, the Court, citing Means, attributed this same purpose to the nineteenth century American abortion statutes and made this an important consideration in its constitutional analysis in the *Wade* opinion.

The Court mentioned four other British abortion statutes which followed that of 1803 during the century and a half before the "liberalizing reforms" of the 1967 English abortion law.[115] These were in the 1828 general revision of the criminal law, in which the provisions were essentially unchanged; in 1837, when the distinction between abortion before and after quickening was removed along with the death penalty; 1861 when there was a new enactment but the 1837 treatment of quickening remained the same; and in 1929, when the stated purpose was to protect "'the life of a child capable of being born alive'" and punished willful abortion as a felony unless done "'in good faith'" to save the mother's life.[116] The Parliamentary debates on these bills either do not exist or (since the abortion provisions were often part of a more comprehensive bill) do not address the subject of abortion, so we cannot gain further insights into them by looking at these.[117]

The American Statutes: Enactment and Purpose

Let us now turn our attention to the nineteenth century American law. The Supreme Court made two assertions about it which are very important to its constitutional analysis. The first is that it was "not until after the War Between the States that legislation [on abortion] began generally to replace the common law."[118] The other is its clear acceptance, as mentioned in Chapter Two, of the view that the purpose of nineteenth century statutes was solely to protect the woman.[119] It cited Means and a number of state cases to support this. It sought to provide further backing for this by saying that the woman herself could not be prosecuted under any of the statutes.

Both of these assertions are subject to question. In a footnote following the former, the Court instructed us to see Eugene Quay's article, cited earlier in this Chapter, for a discussion of the early statutes. Quay includes an appendix of all the statutes on abortion passed by the states and territories of the United

States before 1960. We must note that in this appendix, Quay shows that a full thirty-one of the eventual fifty states had statutes punishing abortion *before* the Civil War. The trend of legislation seems to have accelerated noticeably after the 1827 discovery mentioned above.[120] This suggests that lawmakers were influenced by this to afford greater legal protection to the unborn child.

As mentioned above, the Court relied on Means' research in making the second assertion.[121] The Court considered two other possible purposes for the statutes -- to discourage illicit sexual conduct and to protect the unborn child -- but dismissed them both. While it did not cite Means on this precise point, it followed him in rejecting the first of these because none of the original statutes distinguished between married and unmarried mothers in prohibiting abortion.[122] This conclusion, however, cannot necessarily be inferred. The statutes may have omitted this distinction because it may have been rare for married women to get abortions and so it was not thought necessary to address this; or the legislators may not have thought of this at all; or they may have wanted to include married women out of a belief that the statutes would deter adulterous relationships. Moreover, even though they may have wanted to use the statutes to discourage illicit sexual relations, they may not have wanted to exempt married women from them because of the simultaneous objective of protecting unborn life.

The Court seemed to be convinced of Means' position on the basis of its understanding of the medical history of the time and a couple of state court cases it claimed attributed to the statutes the purpose of protecting the woman. It said the following about the medical history:

> When most criminal abortion laws were first enacted, the procedure was a hazardous one for the woman. This was particularly true prior to the development of antisepsis... Abortion mortality was high...standard modern techniques such as dilation and curettage were not nearly so safe as they are today.[123]

The cases the Court pointed to which it claimed support its position are these: *State v. Murphy*,[124] an 1858 New Jersey case; *Smith v. State*,[125] an 1851 Maine case, and *In re Vince*,[126] a 1949 New Jersey case. The latter two were said by the Court to establish this purpose because they held a woman could not be prosecuted for the abortion. It also mentioned a few Texas cases -- since the *Wade* case came from Texas -- which also held this.[127]

Let us first determine whether the Court was correct about the *Murphy* case. The following passage from it is instructive:

> At the common law, the procuring of an abortion, or the attempt to procure an abortion, by the mother herself, or by another with her consent, was not indictable, unless the woman were quick with child. The act was purged of its criminality, as far as it affected the mother, by her consent. It was an offence only against the life of the child...the mischief designed to be remedied by the statute was the supposed defect in the common law...that the procuring of an abortion, or an attempt to procure an abortion, with the assent of the woman, was not an indictable offence, as it affected her, but only as it affected the life of the *foetus*. The design of abortions, so much as to guard the health and life of the mother against the consequences of such attempts.[128]

The Supreme Court was indeed correct in stating that the case stands for the proposition that the statute's purpose was to protect the mother, but, contrary to the implication of the Court in saying this, it did not exclude the fact that in punishing abortion the State was also motivated by a concern for the unborn child. The passage mentioned the statute just sought to provide an additional reason for the state to punish abortion besides the one under the common law; and it closed a loophole in the common law which prevented it from doing so. The case thus establishes two things which the Court said is not so: that abortion was a crime at common law and that the state legislature that enacted the statute did not seek to prohibit abortion *only* to protect the woman.

The *Smith* opinion states just the opposite of what the Supreme Court said it does. The Maine court quotes

Coke (see the passage above), then states the following:

> In both these instances [when a woman induces her own abortion or miscarries after being beaten] the acts may be those of the mother herself and they are criminal only as they are intended to affect injuriously, and do so affect the unborn child. If, before the mother had become sensible of its motion in the womb, it was not a crime, if afterwards, when it was considered by the common law, that the child had a separate and independent existence, it was held highly criminal.[129]

The above quote makes it clear that the woman could be guilty of a crime for causing self-abortion. The interesting thing is that this quote comes from the very same page of the opinion that the Court referred to as establishing the opposite! What's more, the Maine court goes on to say, indirectly, that the statute did not change the woman's liability for prosecution. According to that court, the statute provided that "every person" who had the intent to cause the abortion of an unborn child, whether quick or not (the statute thus eliminated the quickening distinction), and succeeded in the attempt to do so would be subject to punishment.[130]

Further, there is nothing in the opinion which suggests that the court understood the Maine statute to exclude as one of its purposes the protection of the unborn child. In fact, its repeated assertion that the statute required the intent to destroy the child suggests that it thought quite the opposite. It also referred to the death of the woman which occurred in the case as having occurred "without [the defendant's] intending to kill; and that [that]...death was not in the *execution of that unlawful design*, but was collateral or beside the same."[131] The "unlawful design," the court makes clear, is "to cause the miscarriage" of the unborn child.[132] This language seems to suggest that the statute was directed toward protecting the child. It is by performing the act of aborting the child that the law is violated.

The Court's interpretation of the *In re Vince* case is also incorrect. The *Vince* court held that the New Jersey statute could not be interpreted to permit prosecution of the woman for conspiracy or solicitation to commit abortion because it did not specifically address this.[133] It did say, however, that the statute provided "that a woman who performs an abortion upon herself or consents to its performance upon her by others is chargeable criminally...if the child were quick."[134] The court said that the specific circumstances of this case would not have made the prosecution of the woman for this possible.[135] Thus, she was compelled to testify about the abortion since there was no possibility of self-incrimination. The court, then, as in the above cases, said the opposite of what the Supreme Court in *Wade* claimed it did.

Moreover, two other decisions expressly held that the New Jersey statute did indeed have as one of its purposes to protect the life of the unborn child. These decisions were *State v. Gedlicke*[136] in 1881 and *State v. Siciliano*[137] in 1956.

It is true that the Texas cases the Court cited do establish its point about the woman not being prosecutable. The explanation given by the courts in these cases for this -- that the woman is regarded as the victim in abortion -- would seem to buttress the Supreme Court's point that this fact of non-prosecutability indicated that the nineteenth century statutes were indeed designed to protect the woman. The cases do not say, however, that the woman was seen as the *only* victim or that the law was not also concerned with the child. Nor did they permit a prosecution of the abortionist only when the woman was injured or killed by the operation, which would seem to be likely if she were the law's only concern. Similarly, the fact that abortion was established as a separate offense, instead of being prosecuted as an assault and battery against the woman, suggests that the unborn child must also have been the subject of concern.

Professor Byrn gives us some further reasons for the law's historically not prosecuting the woman as either a principal or an accomplice:

> ...abortion was viewed as an assault upon the woman because she "was not deemed able to assent to an unlawful act against herself"...[Also] [p]ragmatically, conviction of the abortionist frequently depended upon

> the testimony of the aborted woman (especially if a subjective element like quickening were at issue). The woman could hardly be expected to testify if her testimony incriminated her. The omission to incriminate the woman is no more than a statutory grant of immunity.[138]

There were other state court decisions which expressly stated that the protection of the unborn child was at least one of the purposes of the nineteenth century statutes. Professor John D. Gorby of the John Marshall Law School in Chicago mentions eleven such decisions.[139]

Now, let us consider the matter of the medical history. In making its assertion in the passage quoted above that the abortion procedure was "hazardous" for the woman when most of the statutes were enacted, the Court cited only one source: C. Haagensen and W. Lloyd's *A Hundred Years of Medicine*, published in 1943. It makes specific reference to page 19. Page 19 is in a three-page chapter entitled "18th Century Surgery and its Limitations." This page and chapter make no specific reference at all to abortion and the entire book does not contain any references to the abortion operation, even in its chapter on obstetrics and gynecology.[140] The page that the Court referred to contains the following passage, which apparently is what it believed is referring to abortion:

> ...surgery was limited to minor procedures on the surface of the body, and to opening abcesses and amputating limbs that had to be dealt with. The surgeons dared not invade the great cavities of the body, the chest, the head and the abdomen.[141]

Two things must be pointed out. The first is, of course, that the chapter refers to the *eighteenth* century. It cannot be used as a source for arguing that abortion statutes enacted in the nineteenth century -- by which time medicine had progressed further -- were prompted by a contemporaneous concern about the surgical hazards of abortion for the woman.[142] The second is that the Court was incorrect in assuming that most abortions in the nineteenth century were performed by cutting or surgical procedures, as they are today. "Drugs, the human finger, and the water douche were among accepted methods of inducing abortion, and even inducing abortion by puncturing membranes was not considered dangerous to the mother, although it was risky for the child."[143]

The last phrase may seem somewhat confusing. Why should there have been a concern for the child, one might ask, when we know that the purpose of abortion is to destroy the child? The answer is -- and this might provide even further evidence that the nineteenth century statutes were not unconcerned about the unborn child -- that many abortions were performed to save the life of the child at late stages in pregnancy.[144] This was done because some women were unable to deliver their children because the babies' heads were too large to pass through their pelvic structure. For a long time the only alternatives were to perform a Caesarean section, which was then usually fatal to the mother, an embryotomy, in which the child was cut up inside the womb and removed in pieces, or a craniotomy, in which the child's head was crushed (and he died) to permit passage through the birth canal. Physicians soon realized, however, that when they delivered infants who were premature at seven or eight months they were often able to fit through the pelvic openings of their mothers even when they would probably not be able to at nine months. Physicians thus began the practice of inducing premature labor -- i.e., causing abortions -- of women with diminished pelvic openings to save both them and their babies.[145]

Putka writes that medical authorities in the nineteenth century did not regard abortion to be "hazardous," as the Court says:

> Medical authorities in the 19th century, before the adoption of the Fourteenth Amendment, agreed for the most part that induced abortion was a "trifling operation," which was "perfectly safe" for the mother, and surely being of no more danger to her life and health than "an accouchement at term [birth]." At the beginning of the 19th century the induced abortion procedure was highly regarded because of its safety, and most major obstetrics texts devoted an entire chapter to it.[146]

Even Professor Means was not willing to go as far as the Court in saying that "[a]bortion mortality was high." He says the following:

> "Prior to the inauguration of anticeptic surgery it is likely that the maternal death rate from abortions remained at a constant figure, declining thereafter gradually, as a result of the spread of that technique, and more recently with the aid of sulfa drugs and antibiotics, to a figure perhaps one fiftieth of what it had been before Lister."[147]

He adds in a footnote to this that there are "[n]o statistics for the incidence of maternal mortality due to abortion before and after Lister" and that his above statement is "'inferential, and based on a probable parallelism between the incidences of maternal mortality due to childbirth and maternal mortality due to abortion.'"[148]

Thus, the Court's understanding of the medical dangers of abortion to the woman at the time the statutes were enacted is open to question, and its misunderstanding of the state cases makes very doubtful the claim that the statutes' purpose was exclusively to protect the woman. The Court seems to imply that if this was the original purpose of the statutes *and* if medical advances have ceased making it necessary for the law to protect the woman *and* if abortion was not a crime at common law before the statutes, then, somehow, the statutes must now (in 1973) be unconstitutional. It will be considered later whether the Court has the authority to declare statutes unconstitutional merely because it *perceives* them as no longer fulfilling the function for which they were originally designed. The point here is that, even if we were to concede that the Court has such authority, its understanding of the function of these particular statutes was apparently inaccurate.

The Status of the Unborn Child in Other Areas of the Law

The Supreme Court's View

As shown in Chapter Two, the Supreme Court contended that "the unborn have never been recognized in the law as persons in the whole sense."[149] The Court made the following specific assertions:

> In areas other than criminal abortion, the law has been reluctant to endorse any theory that life, as we recognize it, begins before live birth or to accord legal rights to the unborn except when the rights are contingent upon live birth. For example, the traditional rule of tort law denied recovery for prenatal injuries even though the child was born alive. That rule has been changed in almost every jurisdiction. In most States, recovery is said to be permitted only if the fetus was viable, or at least quick, when the injuries were sustained, though few courts have squarely so held. In a recent development, generally opposed by the commentators, some States permit the parents of a stillborn child to maintain an action for wrongful death because of prenatal injuries. Such an action, however, would appear to be consistent with the view that the fetus, at most, represents only the potentiality of life. Similarly, unborn children have been recognized as acquiring rights or interests by way of inheritance or other devolution of property, and have been represented by guardians *ad litem*. Perfection of the interests involved, again, has generally been contingent upon live birth.[150]

Tort Law

An examination of the law in other areas raises questions about the Court's assertions. Let us consider the law of torts first. Professor Noonan and the late Berkeley law professor David W. Louisell write about the status of the unborn child in this area of the law in the 1970 book *The Morality of Abortion: Legal and Historical Perspectives*, mentioned in Chapter One. (The Court cited this book in *Wade*, but not at the point of its discussion about the present topic.) They say that before World War II most American courts denied recovery in tort to a child that had negligently suffered injuries while *in utero*, but that this changed after the War.[151] The earliest cases permitting recovery required that the unborn child have reached the stage of viability at the time of the injuries in order to maintain the action. Since then, however, courts have increasingly rejected viability as a criterion and have permitted recovery irrespective of the time of injury if causation is established. By the time Noonan and Louisell wrote, a few courts had decided that parents, or survivors, can maintain an action where the child is stillborn. In these latter cases, the unborn child "is held to be a 'person' who can be the subject of an action for damages for his death."[152]

An article which surveyed the entire development of the status of the unborn child in many areas of the law appeared as a "note" in Volume 46 of the *Notre Dame Lawyer* in 1971. The article was cited once by the Court in *Wade*, but only when it served its purposes. I shall rely on this article repeatedly in the remainder of this Section in order to show the inaccuracies of the Court's assertions. (Professor Byrn says that this article "analyzed at length" the "unequivocal status of the unborn child as a legal person" in the law.)[153]

The article points to the cases in tort law which were instrumental in changing the law which traditionally denied recovery to the unborn child. The case which perhaps began the erosion of the old rule was *Allaire v. St. Luke's Hospital*. This decision, while following the rule, produced a noteworthy dissenting opinion by Judge Boggs in which he said that medical science had shown that although the unborn child was within the woman's body, it was not just a part of it and the law had to take this fact into account.[154] The traditional rule fell in the landmark decision of *Bonbrest v. Kotz* in 1946,[155] a federal court case in the District of the District of Columbia. The *Bonbrest* court said the following:

> As to a viable child being "part" of its mother...it is not a "part" of the mother in the sense of a constituent element -- as that term is generally understood... Indeed, apart from viability, a non-viable foetus is not part of its mother.[156]

This court thus rejected any lingering notion that the unborn child, at any stage of its development, was a part of his mother's body. The court added that "[t]he law is presumed to keep pace with the sciences and medical science certainly has made progress since 1884."[157] (This was the date of the seminal *Dietrich v. Northampton* decision, which enunciated what I have referred to as the "traditional rule.") *Bonbrest* established the new rule that recovery for the child had to be permitted *at least* at viability and it opened the floodgates. Almost every other jurisdiction that had previously addressed the question and denied recovery reversed itself to permit it. By the time the Supreme Court first considered *Wade* and *Bolton*, twenty-nine states and the District of Columbia permitted recovery.[158] The Court was thus correct in stating that by 1973 most states permitted this, but incorrect in saying that "few courts have squarely so held this." All thirty jurisdictions which by 1973 permitted recovery did so because courts "squarely held" that it was permitted. (Some of these cases involved recovery for the unborn child's injuries, others for his death. There was no indication, however, that the latter would not have also permitted recovery just for injuries and, in fact, were generally premised on the fact that the child's parents or estate ought to be permitted to recover for his death if he could have recovered simply if he had been injured.)

The Supreme Court's statement in the passage from *Wade* just quoted claiming the unborn child could not recover damages unless "viable, or at least quick," is also inaccurate. The note article to which I have been referring mentions that at least nine jurisdictions had clearly rejected the viability requirement by 1973. I examined all of the thirty-two cases from the thirty jurisdictions alluded to which are listed in the article as having announced rules permitting recovery by the unborn. Of these, only nine jurisdictions expressly required viability (by 1973, two of these decided to no longer require it), five expressly stated that the question of whether a non-viable child could recover was not being reached because it was not at issue in the respective case (three of these later held -- prior to 1973 -- that viability was not required), and the remainder either did not mention whether viability was required, implied it was not, or left the matter unclear. (By 1973, two of these had held it was not required.)[159]

The Court, as quoted, says that the legal rights of the unborn child have depended on his ultimately being born alive. This has traditionally been true in tort law. The Court, however, pointed to a trend going against this when it mentioned some courts had begun to allow his parents to bring wrongful death actions upon his demise. Sixteen states had permitted these by the time *Wade* and *Bolton* came to the Court.[160] The Court's conclusion, however, that these actions vindicate the parents' interest, and thus demonstrate only the potentiality of the child's life is a misinterpretation. It is true that wrongful death actions are primarily for the benefit of the deceased's survivors or estate as compensation for the loss of the decedent's support or services.[161] As such, they *do* vindicate an interest of the parents. Nevertheless, a wrongful death action presumes that a *person* existed in the first place; thus the fact that the trend in courts before 1973 permitting them signifies just the *opposite* of what the Court says: unborn children are indeed persons. Professors Louisell and Noonan, in the last sentence of the above mentioned quote, say precisely this. The note article to which I have been referring agrees, saying that such actions by the courts *signal a recognition of the "personality of the unborn child."*[162]

Property Law

Similarly, in the law of property, which the Court makes reference to, the unborn child has rights which "are as old as the common law itself."[163] Blackstone wrote that he is capable of having a legacy or a guardian assigned to him, to have an estate limited to his use, and to take afterwards by such limitation.[164] Starting in the late eighteenth century -- after more of the biological facts of life before birth became known -- the unborn child was held to be within the category of a devise to "children" living at the time of a life tenant's decease and "born" during a testator's lifetime.[165] The unborn child was also considered to be a "life in being" for the purposes of the Rule Against Perpetuities,[166] whether or not it was to benefit the unborn child.[167]

According to Louisell and Noonan, the American courts reached the same results. An unborn child could take under a will leaving property to those "living" at a testator's decease and as a tenant in common with his mother.[168] He could begin to share in the proceeds of a trust from the date of his father's death rather than of his subsequent birth.[169]

A decision often cited to provide a summary of the state of American property law with regard to the unborn child is *In re Holthausen's Will*, decided by the New York courts in 1941. It says the following:

> It has been the uniform and unvarying decision of all common law courts in respect of estate matters for at least the past two hundred years that a child *en ventre sa mere* [in his mother's womb] is "born" and "alive" for all purposes for his benefit.[170]

The trust case alluded to above is an example of a case where live birth was not required for the rights to accrue to the child. The rule of live birth, which the Supreme Court says had "generally" been required, is explained by Louisell and Noonan as not indicating at all that the law judged the unborn not to be "persons in the whole sense." They say that almost inevitably a lawsuit which is commenced on behalf of an unborn child while he is still in gestation will not have been adjudicated until he is successfully born or will have been miscarried or been stillborn. Where a lawsuit is based on accrual of property prior to his birth, but is commenced after it, he will be before the court when the opinion is written. They conclude that under such circumstances "it is understandable, but really gratuitous and superfluous, for the court to observe that the child must be born alive." Such an observation is merely dictum and does not necessarily require a different result when these circumstances do not occur.[171]

Another example of a "property interest" which the courts have held attaches to the unborn child is Social Security survivor's benefits. In 1969, the U.S. Court of Appeals for the Fifth Circuit held that a child conceived a short time before her father's death had the right to receive benefits from his earnings. The court held that the unborn child met the legal requirement of "living with" the father at the time of his death.[172]

Child Support Laws

Finally, there were decisions prior to *Wade* and *Bolton* which held that an unborn child was entitled to support payments from his father in the same way that he would be after birth. In a 1936 decision, *Metzger v. People*,[173] the Colorado Supreme Court affirmed an order requiring a man to contribute thirty percent of his salary to the support of his unborn child.[174] In *Kyne v. Kyne*,[175] a 1940 decision, a California appeals court ruled that an unborn child has a right to have a guardian, to bring suit, to have his father's paternity declared, and to receive support from his father.[176]

We can conclude from this Section, then, that the Court's conclusion about the status of the unborn child in other areas of the law, like its understanding of history and the purpose of the criminal abortion statutes, display definite inaccuracies.[177]

The Court's Conclusion about the Status of the Unborn Child under the Constitution and the Fourteenth Amendment

In Chapter Two, we saw how essential the question of whether the fetus is a "person" under the Fourteenth Amendment was to the Supreme Court. It concluded, of course, that he is not a person. It also claimed that the right of privacy, which it says may be found in the Fourteenth Amendment's guarantee of personal liberty, is "broad enough to encompass a woman's decision whether or not to terminate her pregnancy." Much of what I have already said disputes whether there was a liberty of abortion in the Anglo-American tradition, but the points I make in this Section -- while focusing mostly on the "personhood" question -- can be viewed as also addressing this matter. Serious questions arise about the Court's interpretation of this term as used in the Constitution and in the Fourteenth Amendment, and whether the meaning of the term "liberty" in that Amendment could have been intended by its drafters to include a right to abortion.

The Meaning of "Fetus" and "Person"

What was the common understanding of the terms "person" and "fetus" at the time of the framing of the Constitution and the drafting of the Fourteenth Amendment? Putka speaks at length on this point and concludes that both the men at the Constitutional Convention and those in the Thirty-ninth Congress which passed the Amendment -- both groups of which we assume attached the same meaning to words as they had in common usage in their day -- understood the fetus to be a "person" protected by the Constitution. This is because, to put it in syllogistic terms, since a "fetus" was understood to be a "child" and a "child" is a "person," then a "fetus" would have to be judged a "person." Putka examined numerous dictionaries used in both time periods and the following are representative definitions. At the time of the Framing, a "person" was defined to be "[a]n individual, a man, a woman; one, any one, one's self";[178] at the time of the Fourteenth, "a man, woman, or child, a body."[179] In the first period, a "child" was defined as "[a]n infant, a very young person; a son or daughter; the descendant of a man however remote; one that is in some respect or other like an infant or young person";[180] in the second as "an infant, or person, in its tenderest years; the offspring of a person; the descendant of a man of any age."[181] A "foetus," in the former, was "a child in the womb perfectly formed,"[182] in the latter, the "[f]oetus, signifies the child in the womb, after it is perfectly formed."[183] A fetus, then, was understood in both periods to be a child. The definitions of "foetus" coincide with the understanding prevalent at each time about the unborn child's life beginning at that point in the pregnancy when it moved -- quickening -- by which time it was believed it would have to be fully formed. (The discovery of the ovum, which I mentioned earlier, had not taken place yet when the Constitutional Convention met. It had by the time of the passage of the Fourteenth Amendment, and the efforts to further restrict abortion were well under way. The latter period's definition is from 1848, just when the new knowledge about the unborn child was being more widely disseminated and the anti-abortion efforts were gaining momentum)

The View About the Unborn Child in Early America

There is no record of what the men at the Constitutional Convention thought about abortion or if they, or the members of the First Congress which proposed the first ten amendments (many men who had been at the Convention also sat in the First Congress), viewed the Constitution as protecting the unborn. We can *surmise* that they did so view it, however. Blackstone, who I pointed out held that the unborn child has a right to life, was a great influence on the Framers and their contemporaries.[184]

The other indication we have of the Framers'

thinking -- indirect, to be sure -- concerns something that Thomas Jefferson wrote. In 1822, the State of Louisiana commissioned Edward Livingston, a distinguished international jurist and later U.S. Senator from that state, to draft a model penal code for the state. The code, which became a well-known reference source around the country, contained a provision which prohibited all abortions "except for the purpose of saving the life of the mother." It explained that this prohibition was necessary because "'[t]he destruction of human life, in its inchoate state, does not come within the definition of homicide. It therefore requires a special provision.'"[185] Jefferson wrote Livingston that the code "'will certainly arrange your name with the sages of antiquity.'"[186] Jefferson, of course, was not actually one of the Framers since he was not at the Constitutional Convention. Nor was he in the First Congress. Nevertheless, he was one of the most prominent political figures of the early Republic. Also, since the code became so popular, his views may be taken to be fairly representative of those of the informed public of his time. We must assume that Jefferson's adulation was for the entire code, including its anti-abortion provision, since there is no record of his specifically taking exception to this provision.

The Constitutional Provisions

The Court, as mentioned in Chapter Two, stated that the provisions in the body of the Constitution which use the term "person" could not possibly be referring to the unborn. Let us look at each of the provisions mentioned to see the difficulty the Court created for itself in saying this. The first two references are to the Article I qualifications for holding office as U.S. Representatives and Senators. A representative must be at least age twenty-five, a citizen for seven years, and an inhabitant of the state electing him (*Art.I, Sec.2, Cl.2)*. A senator must be at least age thirty, a citizen for nine years, and an inhabitant of the state he is chosen from (*Art.I, Sec.3, Cl.3*). While it is true that both of these provisions exclude an unborn child, they also exclude a twenty-year-old. Yet, I do not believe that the Court would thereby interpret the provision as negating the legal personhood of a twenty-year-old and permitting or requiring a state to not protect his right to life. The same essential point must be made about the Court's singling out the Constitution's use of the term "person" when referring to the qualifications for becoming President (*Art.II, Sec.1, Cl.5; the Twelfth Amendment; the Twenty-second Amendment*). Just because someone has not been born in the U.S., resided in the nation for fourteen years, and attained the age of thirty-five does not mean he is not a person. These provisions clearly do nothing more than restrict eligibility for the respective offices to a particular group of persons.

If the Court's references to the Emolument Clause (*Art.I, Sec.9, Cl.8*) and the Electors provisions (*Art.II, Sec.1, Cl.2 and the superseded Cl.3*) are to be taken as an indication of who are "persons," then children after birth would likely be excluded because they are unlikely to be -- and in fact would probably be statutorily barred from -- "holding any Office of Profit or Trust"[187] under the United States. Would the Court vote to remove the protection of their right to life under the Constitution?

The Extradition provisions (*Art.IV, Sec.2, Cl.2*) also would exclude some children from being considered "persons." This is because the common law's presumption that a child below seven (the age of reason) is incapable of committing a crime means that he could not be "charged in any State with Treason, Felony, or other Crime" to be subject to the Extradition provisions.

The Court is correct that the Fugitive Slave Clause (*Art.IV, Sec.2, Cl.3*) and the Migration and Importation provision (*Art.I, Sec.9, Cl.1*) -- which pertains to the slave trade -- do not apply to the unborn. Ironically, these provisions were wiped out of the Constitution by the Thirteenth and Fourteenth Amendments because they excluded from legal personhood an entire class of persons (i.e., blacks who were descended from slaves).

As for the Apportionment Clause (*Art.I, Sec.2, Cl.3*), it is true that unborn children are not to be counted as part of the population for the purpose of apportioning the House of Representatives. It is also true that the Clause excludes Indians not taxed as "persons" and considers a black slave as three-fifths of a "person." Would the Court have voted to treat Indians and blacks as not "persons in the whole sense" on the basis of this provision?

Moreover, the fact that unborn children were not to be counted for this purpose has a practical basis. How could a count be accurate when the biological knowledge of the late eighteenth century made it impossible to predict if a woman would not bear twins or triplets instead of a single baby. Actually, because of the high infant mortality rate then, it was very uncertain if a child would even be born alive. Also, it was not yet known that the child from conception is a separate, distinct human organism.

Were the Fourteenth Amendment Protections Intended to Extend to the Unborn Child?

Now, let us see what the possible intentions of the Drafters of the Fourteenth Amendment were. As with the Framers of the Constitution, I have not been able to find any direct statements made by the members of the Thirty-ninth Congress on the matter of abortion, or how they viewed unborn children. Nevertheless, a good insight can be gleaned by inference from other actions that they took and the circumstances of the time.

First, Justice Rehnquist stated in his dissenting opinion that "[b]y the time of the adoption of the Fourteenth Amendment in 1868, there were at least 36 laws enacted by state or territorial legislatures limiting abortion."[188] He concluded from this that "the drafters did not intend to withdraw from the States the power to legislate with respect to this matter."[189] Further, only five of the states which ratified the Fourteenth Amendment did not have criminal abortion statutes on the books.[190] Professor Joseph P. Witherspoon of the University of Texas Law School, who has extensively researched the question of the intention of the Drafters on abortion, says the following:

> ...the conjunction of state ratification of these Amendments [the Thirteenth, Fourteenth, and Fifteenth] with state adoption or modification [i.e., to make them more restrictive] of anti-abortion statutes designed to protect unborn children constitutes a contemporaneous legislative construction by states of the meaning of the Amendments they ratified. That construction can only be that unborn children are human beings and persons under the Constitution. Any other view of their action would be out of line with the history of the period.[191]

What were some highlights of this history that Professor Witherspoon alludes to? The first attempt to get Congress to legislate on abortion came in 1831 when Edward Livingston, referred to above, introduced his well-respected model penal code as a proposed comprehensive U.S. criminal code after his election to the Senate. This proposed code included a section on abortion like the one mentioned above.[192] The code was not enacted, but Congressional action on the subject of abortion had not ended.

Dr. Horatio R. Storer of Boston was appointed head of the American Medical Association's Committee on Criminal Abortion in 1857. Two years later, in 1859, the Committee made the following recommendations which were adopted as resolutions by the AMA's national meeting:

> condemn(ed) the procuring of abortion, at every period of gestation, except as necessary for preserving the life of either mother or child [I have explained the seeming anomaly of the latter] [and]
>
> request[ed] the zealous cooperation of the various State medical societies in pressing this subject upon the legislatures of their respective States.[193]

Witherspoon attributes the passage of tougher anti-abortion statutes in several states to the efforts of physicians like Storer. He also attributes to it the passage of Congressional legislation. This legislation came in the period of the passage of the Civil War Amendments and must certainly be looked to as evidence of how the Drafters believed those amendments affected the unborn. If it does not make it entirely certain that they regarded the unborn child as a person, it makes it quite clear that they did not intend the amendments to remove from the states the authority to pass criminal abortion statutes.

Witherspoon pointed to a number of pieces of such Congressional legislation in his House testimony. The first was the District of Columbia Divorce Act of 1860. This act provided that the offspring of a second and bigamous marriage "born or *begotten* before the commencement of the suit (for divorce), shall be deemed to be the legitimate issue [offspring] of the parent, who, at the time of the marriage, was capable of contracting."[194] The emphasis on "begotten" is mine; it demonstrates clearly the intent of Congress to extend legal rights to the unborn. The fact that the statute uses the words "born" and "begotten" together to indicate no difference of legal rights because of status of birth arguably suggests that Congress understood the unborn child to be a person. The point that this clearly illustrates is the same as that of the Section above about the unborn child in other areas of the law: it does not make any sense for the child to have been given secondary legal rights if he does not already have the primary one, the right to life.

The second piece of legislation cited by Witherspoon is the assimilative crimes provision enacted on April 5, 1866.[195] This legislation made applicable the criminal law of a state to any area which the state had ceded to and placed under the exclusive jurisdiction of the United States government where an offense specified by that State's criminal law was not prohibited under federal law. Witherspoon explains that "[t]his provision clearly adopted as federal law state laws prohibiting abortion including those adopted or amended in the period between 1850 and 1875, most of which...were designed under the Storer guidelines to provide protection for the lives of unborn children." The meaning of this was that the Texas anti-abortion law of 1856 -- which was struck down in *Wade* -- was adopted as federal law applicable to U.S. military installations located in that state.[196]

The most direct piece of federal legislation relating to abortion in this period was enacted by Congress in 1873, five years after the Fourteenth Amendment was proposed. On March 3, 1873, it enacted "An Act for the Suppression of Trade in, and Circulation of...Articles of Immoral Use." The purpose of this statute, according to Witherspoon, was to reach an area of abortion that was left uncovered by most of the state statutes followed within federal jurisdictions under the 1866 assimilative provision. It prohibited the selling, lending, or giving away "of any article...for causing unlawful abortion" as defined by the criminal law of the state in which the federal enclave was located.[197]

The 1873 statute, Witherspoon explains, was illustrative of a direct Congressional condemnation of abortion for this further reason: it recognized the illegality of abortion in the District of Columbia, over whose criminal law Congress had full authority. The District came under the 1866 act because it was a territory ceded to and placed under the exclusive jurisdiction of the federal government. Congress thus adopted the criminal law of Maryland (the state which ceded the territory to the United States which became the District) in any areas of the criminal law which it had not specifically made federal offenses. This included the Maryland abortion law which was patterned after the Storer Committee recommendation mentioned above.[198]

The fact that Storer's recommendations so markedly influenced legislation in this period implies that the members of Congress may have been squarely motivated by the belief that the unborn child is a person to be protected by the law like any other person. Storer, who was also a lawyer, wrote a book with Franklin F. Heard in 1868 under AMA auspices entitled, *Criminal Abortion: Its Nature, Its Evidence & Its Law* in which the following statement appeared:

> Physicians have now arrived at the unanimous opinion, that the foetus in utero is alive from the very moment of conception...(T)he wilful killing of a human being, at any stage of its existence is murder...(A)bortion is, in reality, a crime against the infant, its mother, the family circle, and society...[199]

Professor Noonan has pointed to another fairly direct endorsement of restrictive abortion laws -- and thus the principle of protecting the unborn child -- by the Drafters of the Fourteenth Amendment. In the 1860s the federal territories of Arizona, Colorado, Idaho, Montana, and Nevada all made it a crime to abort "a woman then big with child." Such territorial legislation was subject to Congressional approval. Many of the same Congressmen and Senators who voted to propose the Fourteenth Amendment voted to approve these statutes.[200]

Witherspoon provides the following additional evidence from the statements of important Drafters of the Fourteenth of their intent to protect the unborn. We should recall in considering this that the popular dictionary definition of "child" amd thus "person" at this time included the unborn. He mentions this quote from Congressman John A. Bingham of Ohio, one of the most prominent and frequently cited of the Drafters:

> [The] Constitution...proclaimed that all men in respect of life and liberty and property were equal before the law, and that no person, no human being, no member of the family of man shall...be deprived of his life, or his liberty, or his property, but by the law of the land...[201]

Witherspoon says that they viewed children as having "certain rights which are as unalienable as those of adults"[202] and that the parents of children have a right to control them only with a view to caring for them during their minority when they cannot fend for themselves and to obtain during that time service in return from their children. Because they possessed such inalienable rights, the Drafters affirmed that the Thirteenth and Fourteenth Amendments included their protection.[203] He says that the Drafters often referred to their concern for unborn children and generations yet to come in their debates and statements.[204]

As I will show in Chapter Nine, the state can prohibit abortion irrespective of whether it determines the unborn child to be fully a "person." What we can conclude from this Section, however, is that the Framers of the Constitution and, even more clearly, the Drafters of the Fourteenth Amendment, believed the law could prohibit abortion and, indeed, that constitutional protection extended to unborn children, because they believed them to be biological persons. We cannot be *certain* from the evidence that they regarded them as persons, although the inferences are strong. (Witherspoon argues that the Court did not even concern itself with the Draftees' intent in *Wade* and *Bolton*.)[205]

In Chapter Seven it will be seen how we cannot be *certain* the unborn child is a human being, although the evidence is overwhelming. As President Ronald Reagan has said about the subject, however, "where there is doubt as to the question of life or death, the benefit of the doubt should be given to life."[206] Translated into legal terms, this means that whatever doubt there is about whether the unborn child is entitled to constitutional protection must be resolved in his favor. We should follow Justice Bradley's admonition in his opinion for the Court in *Boyd v. U.S.*[207] (a decision which the *Wade* Court cited in another context):

> ...illegitimate and unconstitutional practices get their first footing in...[this] way, namely: by silent approaches and silent deviations from legal modes of procedure. This can only be obviated by adhering to the rule that constitutional provisions for the security of person and property should be liberally construed.[208]

Finally, the Court stated that the State of Texas conceded in oral reargument that "no case could be cited that holds that a fetus is a person within the meaning of the Fourteenth Amendment."[209]

Actually, there is such a case and, since the Court cited it as one which upheld a state abortion statute (Ohio's), it should have been familiar with it. The opinion in this case, *Steinberg v. Ohio* (1970),[210] says the following:

> Rights [referring specifically to the right of privacy], the provision of which is only implied or deduced, must inevitably fall [when] in conflict with the express provisions of the Fifth and Fourteenth Amendments that no person shall be deprived of life without due process of law. The difference between this case and *Griswold* [discussed in Section VI] is clearly apparent, for here there is an embryo or fetus incapable of protecting itself. There [in *Griswold*], the only two lives were those of two competent adults.[211]

The Court's Application of the Right of Privacy

The *Wade* opinion reveals how exclusively the Court relies on its past decisions to affirm the existence of the right of privacy (since privacy is not mentioned in the Constitution), on then-recent lower court abortion decisions, and some of its past privacy decisions in determining how the right to abortion was included within it.

Several of the decisions the Court cited as establishing a right of privacy, pertain to matters which are in no way connected with abortion and, of the ones which are in the same realm, only one, *Eisenstadt v. Baird*,[212] comes close to being on point. Even that one, as I shall argue, concerns an activity -- contraception -- which is *qualitatively* different from abortion.

Of the decisions completely unrelated to abortion, one pertained to a court-ordered medical examination in a negligence trial,[213] two to searches and/or seizures,[214] two to telephone taps,[215] and one to the possession of obscene materials within the confines of one's home.[216] Of the other "related" cases -- related only in the sense that they pertained to matters involving marriage, the family, and sex and reproduction --, two concerned the right of parents to direct the education of their children,[217] one a compulsory sterilization statute directed at repeat felons,[218] another a prohibition against minors selling goods in public places even with parental consent,[219] another a statute prohibiting interracial marriage,[220] and two others prohibitions against the use and/or dispensing of contraceptives.[221]

Of these, the two contraceptive decisions and the sterilization decision are the only ones that seem applicable, since they alone involve state interference with the reproductive activity of persons as do the abortion cases. The sterilization decision is not a good precedent, however, because it pertained only to a very limited group of persons (those convicted three times of a felony) and it involved a state statute which mandated activity to interfere with individual reproduction, whereas anti-abortion statutes involved state prohibition of an individual decision regarding the reproductive activity.

Anti-contraceptive statutes are like anti-abortion statutes on this latter point. Contraception -- except for those forms of it that actually constitute the termination of the new life after sperm and ovum have joined (e.g., the IUD, certain types of birth control pills) -- is, however, a different activity by its nature than abortion. This is explained simply by one of the lower court decisions which the Supreme Court referred to in *Wade:*

> ...contraception which is dealt with in *Griswold* is concerned with preventing the creation of a new and independent life...
>
> It seems clear, however, that the legal conclusions in *Griswold* as to the rights of individuals to determine without governmental interference whether or not to enter into the processes of procreation cannot be extended to cover those situations wherein, voluntarily or involuntarily, the preliminaries have ended, and a new life has begun.[222]

The late Dean Joseph O'Meara of Notre Dame Law School gives us another reason why, at least as far as the right of privacy is concerned, abortion is different from contraception:

> There is nothing private about an in-hospital abortion -- a fact which Mr. Justice Blackmun seems not to understand. The admissions office must be told that the patient (the woman to be aborted) is entering the hospital for surgery, and the name of the surgeon must be given. In no time at all the surgeons who perform abortions will become known. So the admissions office will know. And, of course, everybody in the operating room will know. Every surgical procedure -- even a routine tonsillectomy -- involves risks. To guard against the risks common to all operations and those peculiar to abortions, all the nurses on the surgical service must be told. Anything else would render the hospital, and perhaps the

> surgeon, liable for damages in case of untoward circumstances. And, of course, those who keep the patients' records will know. Thus, a very considerable number of hospital personnel will know -- will have to know.[223]

I might add that even an early abortion done in an out-patient clinic is not private, in any true sense of the word. Such clinics are operated as public businesses, often advertise, and must meet certain minimal state requirements. The woman must be attended to by a number of persons on the clinic's staff and records are kept. It is in no way the solitary activity that using contraceptives in one's bedroom or bathroom is.

There is another reason why the *Griswold v. Connecticut* case is not a good parallel to *Wade* and *Bolton*, as far as the right of privacy is concerned. The Connecticut statute in question was struck down specifically because it "operate[d] directly on an intimate relation of husband and wife and their physician's role in one aspect of that relation," and the "very idea is repulsive to the notions of privacy surrounding the marriage relationship."[224] *Wade* and *Bolton* clearly were not premised on a notion of *marital* privacy, but of *individual* privacy since they legalized abortion for women whether they are married or not. Noonan's claim that *Eisenstadt v. Baird* -- which held anti-contraceptive statutes to be unconstitutional even if they apply only to non-married persons -- is the only real precedent for *Wade* and *Bolton* is correct.[225] As indicated in Chapter Two, both Justice Stewart and Justice Douglas emphasized the importance of *Eisenstadt's* asserting the existence of a right of individual, as opposed to marital, privacy.

However, from the reasons given by Professor O'Meara and the lower court case quoted above, even *Eisenstadt* is not a good precedent for the abortion decisions.

An additional point about one of the privacy decisions that the Court refers to, *Union Pacific Railway Company v. Botsford*, which was the first decision in which the Court expressly recognized the existence of a right of privacy under the Constitution. It is ironic that the Court, along with many pro-abortion writers, cited this as a precedent in fashioning a woman's supposed right to destroy her unborn child. The case concerned the issue of whether a trial court could order a woman suing a railroad company for negligence because of injuries she suffered to submit to a surgical examination. In affirming the trial court's judgment that it had no legal authority to make such an order, the Supreme Court discussed how the common law treated the question. It said that the only time such an order was permitted -- allowing intrusion into the privacy of one's person -- was in the case of a writ *de ventre inspiciendo*. It explained the purpose of such a writ as follows:

> ...to ascertain whether a woman convicted of a capital crime was quick with child... in order to guard against the taking of the life of an unborn child for the crime of the mother.[226]

The significance of this case, then, according to Professor Gorby, is that even though it "may stand for the notion that there is a common law right to privacy,"[227] it points out that "the common law not only acknowledged a right to life in the fetus but also recognized precedence of this right over the common law right of privacy."[228]

The Status of the Unborn Child's Right to Life When in Conflict with Other Rights

It is interesting to see how the courts, before *Wade* and *Bolton*, treated the right to life of the unborn child when it came into conflict with other rights. Most of these cases have involved the mother's right to refuse blood transfusions -- usually on religious grounds -- when she is carrying an unborn child. (Generally, the law has respected a person's right to refuse a blood transfusion for religious reasons, even if it means his death.) As we shall see, these cases establish that the unborn child is protected under the common law *parens patriae* doctrine.[229]

Three New Jersey decisions and one federal appeals court decision in the District of Columbia illustrate this point clearly. The first two are blood transfusion cases. The first, *Hoerner v. Bertinato* (1961)[230] involved a situation where parents of an unborn child refused to consent to allow that child to have a blood transfusion upon birth, even though physicians said it would be essential to save his life. The court held that the parents were neglectful of the child under the state child welfare statute and awarded temporary custody of the child, immediately after his birth, to the county welfare department to insure that the transfusion be given. In the second, *Raleigh Fitkin-Paul Morgan Memorial Hospital v. Anderson* (1964),[231] the court ordered a blood transfusion for a pregnant woman who had refused it and who, along with her unborn child, would have died without it. The court made it clear that its decision was based on a concern about protecting the child's, not the mother's life. The D.C. federal case, *Application of the President and Directors of Georgetown College, Inc.* (1964),[232] had similar circumstances as *Anderson* and the court came to the same conclusion. The well-known judge, J. Skelly Wright, wrote the opinion. The significant point about these decisions is that they held, in effect, that the unborn child's right to life takes precedence over even one of the most fundamental rights expressly protected by our Constitution -- what some have included as a "preferred right,"[233] -- freedom of religion.[234] *It would seem that these courts indeed regarded the right to life as the preeminent right.*

In the other case, *Gleitman v. Cosgrove* (1967),[235] the New Jersey Supreme Court faced directly the question of whether any condition of disability of the child or economic inconvenience of the parents could override the child's right to life. The parents of an infant, "on his behalf," brought suit for malpractice against a physician who failed to inform them that their child could be born with birth defects after the mother contracted rubella during pregnancy. The baby boy was born with serious sight, hearing, and speech defects. The parents claimed that if they had been so told the mother would have had an abortion. The court held that the parents were barred from recovery in these circumstances and used some strong and forthright language in its opinion:

> It is basic to the human condition to seek life and hold on to it however heavily burdened. If Jeffrey [the child] could have been asked as to whether his life should be snuffed out before his full term of gestation could run its course, our felt intuition of human nature tells us he would almost surely choose life with defects as against no life at all...
>
> The right to life is inalienable in our society. A court cannot say what defects should prevent an embryo from being allowed life such that denial of the opportunity to terminate the existence of a defective child in embryo can support a cause for action...
>
> ...The sanctity of the single human life is the decisive factor in this suit in tort... We are not talking here about the breeding of prize cattle. It may have been easier for the mother and less expensive for the father to have terminated the life of their child while he was an embryo, but these alleged detriments cannot stand against the preciousness of a single human life to support a remedy in tort...
>
> Though we sympathize with the unfortunate situation in which these parents find themselves, we firmly believe the right of their child to live is greater than and precludes their right not to endure emotional and financial injury.[236]

My simple conclusion for this Chapter is that the Court's assertions in the areas considered were incorrect. The importance of many of these assertions to the holdings in *Wade* and *Bolton* means that they were incorrect also.

Chapter Four

The Arguments and the Evidence Presented to the Supreme Court, Part I: Fundamental Rights, Legal Arguments, and the Significance of the Structuring of the *Wade* Appellants' Brief

Introduction

In this chapter a study of the briefs filed with the Court in the *Wade* and *Bolton* cases is undertaken. Between this Chapter and Chapters Six and Seven, all the key points made by the pro-legalization briefs to the Court will be presented and evaluated. These represent virtually the entire set of arguments put forth in the drive to legalize abortion. There are two reasons why so much attention is given to the briefs. First, they are the source of the most direct, immediate attempt to influence the Justices on abortion, as well as their greatest source of information about it. As such, they give the best insight into how the Justices' positions were developed. Second, the briefs probably are some of the best statements of the pro-abortion position. They present the pro-abortion arguments in a logical, comprehensive, and lucid manner. This could only be expected; they were drawn up by skilled lawyers who knew the stakes were high. The achievement of the objectives of the pro-abortion movement rested on the making of a strong case to the Court.

A total of twenty-five briefs were filed by both the parties and *amici curiae* on both sides of the issue in the *Wade* and *Bolton* cases. Only selected, key pro-abortion briefs are examined in Chapters Four, Six and Seven. I consider primarily the pro-abortion briefs in this book because their position is the one largely adopted by the Court.

In this Chapter, we shall see what the selected briefs say on the following points: the nature of the rights asserted and their bases; the notions of personal freedom, morality, and the marital state expressed; the understanding of equal protection put forth; and whether the anti-abortion statutes were unconstitutionally vague and overbroad.

Let us begin the Chapter by considering the significance of the structuring and ordering of the arguments in the *Wade* appellants' brief (hereinafter referred to simply as the "*Wade* brief"). This brief was selected because it is the longest and most comprehensive (in that it deals in detail with virtually every facet of the pro-abortion position) and presents the clearest statement of a philosophy of individual rights and of the nature of man *vis-à-vis* society of any of the pro-abortion briefs.[1] I also consider these other briefs on a few points by way of comparison with the *Wade* brief (and the supplemental brief of the *Wade* appellants): that submitted by the appellants in *Bolton* (plus their supplemental brief), that of the Planned Parenthood Federation of America/American Association of Planned Parenthood Physicians (PPFA) (plus its supplemental brief), and that of the American College of Obstetricians and Gynecologists (ACOG). My entire discussion of the equal protection claim is built around the brief filed by the National Legal Program on Health Problems of the Poor (NLPHPP).[2]

The Structuring of the *Wade* Appellants' Brief

I shall begin this Chapter with a consideration of the structuring of the main brief in the cases, that of the appellants in *Wade*, to determine the impression created in the reader's mind by the particular ordering and to thus understand why it may have been chosen by the appellants' lawyers. It is reasonable to start out with the notion that the structuring of the briefs is important because, after all, the *Wade* case was major constitutional litigation and one of the lawyers, Professor Norman Dorsen, was a seasoned constitutional specialist. We can expect that he would have known the most effective way to draft a brief for the Supreme Court. Moreover,we can expect that any lawyer worth his salt would set out his arguments in a brief in the most logical and patterned way possible, and that there would be some point to the pattern.

The following is the "Index" -- table of contents -- of the *Wade* brief which appears at the beginning of it:

Citation to Opinion Below

Jurisdiction

Statutes Involved

Questions Presented

Statements of the Case

I. Facts Regarding Appellants Which Gave Rise to Actions

A. Jane Roe
B. Mary and John Doe
C. James H. Hallford

II. Decision by the District Court

III. Impact of the Denial of Injunctive Relief Relevant Background and Medical Facts

Relevant Background and Medical Facts

I. The Medical Nature of Abortion

A. Spontaneous and Induced Rejection of Pregnancy
B. Frequency of Medically Induced Abortion in the United States and Texas
C. Medical Safety Aspects of Induced Abortion in Surgical Practice

1. Induced Abortion in 19th Century Medicine
2. Induced Abortion in Contemporary Surgery

II. Legal and Medical Standards of Practice Regarding Induced Abortion in Texas and the United States

A. Induced Abortion at Common Law
B. Legislative History of the Texas Abortion Law
C. Contemporary Legislation on Induced Abortion
D. Contemporary Standards of Medical Practice Regarding Induced Abortion

1. National Medical Organizations
2. The Texas Medical Association

III. Relationship Between Contraception and the Medical Procedure of Induced Abortion

A. Lack of Public Access to Information and Medical Services for Family Limitation by Use of Contraceptives
B. Ineffectiveness of Contraceptives Due to Significant Degree of Failure in Method and Use

Summary of Argument

After presenting the legal questions at issue in the case, the *Wade* brief makes its "Statement of the Case," in which the essential facts are briefly presented and an explanation given as to why the plaintiffs filed the actions pursuant to them. This is the format for the opening part of the typical brief in any court. What appears is a short statement of the harms that the specific appellants are alleging. These are restated in the brief's argument section with reference to more general classes of persons (e.g., pregnant women generally and physicians generally). (It should be pointed out that the *Wade* and *Bolton* cases were filed as class actions on behalf of all pregnant women.)[3]

The harms alleged by appellant Jane Roe were

"economic hardship" and "social stigma" which would result from having an illegitimate child and "emotional trauma" due to not being able to get a legal abortion in Texas. Appellant James Hallford, M.D., who the Supreme Court ruled did not have standing, alleged government intrusion into his rights as a physician. The brief also contended that the appellants were harmed because the lower court had not granted injunctive relief and the Dallas County district attorney was proceeding with prosecutions under the statute.

The purpose of this section of the brief is simply to introduce the Court to points of the case which will be further developed later. It also aims to create, in the minds of the Justices, an initial sense of the alleged injustice done to the appellants and to spark sympathy for their plight. It should not seem strange that I would suggest the latter, despite the fact that one might think that the nation's top jurists are a group of dispassionate people devoted only to rationally determining legal principles. (One need only call to mind the statement made by Chief Justice Hughes to Justice Douglas when the latter assumed his seat on the court.[4])

The next important part of the brief which follows is a lengthy one which involves a host of medical arguments and relevant medical background. This is divided into several sections, which I shall consider since they go into many facets of the medical case for legalized abortion. This medical information is presented before any of the specific legal arguments are. In fact, it takes up nearly a fifth of the pages of the brief. As I shall explain, I believe that both of these facts are significant.

The first aspect that the medical arguments take up is the "medical nature of abortion."[5] This section attempts to show the insignificance of the embryo and the fetus both biologically and legally. Since these points are considered at length in Chapter Seven, all that needs to be said about them at this point is that they extol the value of spontaneous abortion for man and build their argument about the human embryo around his small size and his shape and appearance. The legal points mentioned relate only to the legal obligations of the physician if the child is prematurely born before a certain point in the pregnancy (i.e., the mother miscarries). It is stated that the physician does not have the same legal obligations as he does later in the pregnancy. The obvious purpose of this section is to defeat the state's position that the abortion statutes are aimed at protecting human life because the unborn child is shown, supposedly, not to be human.

The next section is a discussion of illegal abortion. Statistics are presented which appear to show a great number of illegal abortions in the U.S. each year. This section seems to be used to create the sense of a problem of great magnitude and a corresponding sense of the need for a major response. It gives the impression that Texas women were having abortions even though it is against the law, but are sustaining hardships by having to go out of state for them.

After this, the brief goes into the matter of the safety of the abortion operation to the woman. It recalls the nineteenth century when most of the statutes were enacted, then it discusses abortion in the present day. Like the *Wade* opinion, the brief concludes, inferentially, that abortion had to be a risky procedure in the nineteenth century because most surgery was risky. Also like the Court, it cites the Lloyd and Haagensen book on medical history to back this up. The point Putka makes about this book, however, is -- as mentioned -- that abortion in the nineteenth century was generally not done by surgery, and so the dangers of surgery the brief recites are not, for the most part, applicable to it. Similarly, the statistics it presents on maternal mortality at or after childbirth in the nineteenth century do not apply just, or even mostly, to deaths caused by birth itself. The brief states that the high rates of maternal mortality were due mostly to the spreading of infection by physicians. It is questionable whether the mortality rate can even be said to be high or to be generally characteristic of the time. The figures cited are 11.4 percent for women attended by physicians and 2.7 percent for those attended by midwives and these were only from one clinic -- in Vienna! So, both the dangers of surgery in the nineteenth century and the maternal mortality rates stated are inapplicable to abortion. Nothing is actually said about nineteenth century abortion.

At the end of this section, the brief nonetheless concludes that abortion was hazardous to the woman in the nineteenth century -- stating incorrectly that it was a surgical procedure -- and that because of this, "the [Texas] legislature obviously deemed, that a woman risk childbirth, than death on the operating table."[6] This judgment about legislative intent is also made inferentially and there is no evidence that the brief-writers made any effort to look for records of legislative debates or other documents that could have confirmed this.

This section of the brief appears to demonstrate that the purpose of the nineteenth century statutes was to protect the woman and, as seen in the facts it presents, to explain why this is so. It does not cite Professor Means, but follows his line of argument on this, and draws the same conclusion about the purpose of the statutes.

The next section of the brief, which claims to demonstrate the relative safety of present-day abortion procedures, is logically placed after the above section. By doing this, it leaves a strong impression with the reader that the original purpose of the statutes can no longer be considered medically valid. It uses many statistics and medical authorities to back up its claim about abortion safety.

What the brief has done up to this point is to show why, medically, the purpose of the Texas statute had to be what it claims. It proceeds to give legal evidence for its conclusion, and cites the *Murphy* case, discussed in Chapter Three, and a legislative document pertaining to the 1829 New York abortion statute. The brief cites four Texas cases, only one of which was among those cited by the Court. These cases did not state the purpose of the Texas statute; they, like the ones cited by the Court, merely held that the woman can be neither a principal nor an accomplice to the crime of abortion. Also, the brief, as indicated above, makes no reference to Texas legislative documents. The brief-writers apparently believed that all the nineteenth century statutes must have had the same purpose, so the purpose of any can be proved by reference to information about any other one. The brief-writers do not seem to be concerned about the logical error in making this judgment, and the possible factual errors that result from it.

The brief then returns to the contemporary period by making an appeal to scientific expertise. It points out that three major medical organizations, the American Medical Association, the American College of Obstetricians and Gynecologists, and the Texas Medical Association had called for abortion to be strictly a matter between the woman and her physician. In turning to these organizations at this point, the brief reinforces its claims that the nineteenth century statutes no longer have a medical rationale and that contemporary abortion procedures are safe. There is nothing specific in this section of the brief which addresses these points, but this is the strong suggestion that is conveyed by its being placed after the previous sections.

The following section turns then to the relationship between abortion and contraception. It argues simply that abortion is needed because contraceptives are not entirely reliable and many do not know about them or cannot afford them. There is, then a progression in the brief, which makes its argument seem logical. It first purports to show that abortion was once hazardous for women and that this was the reason it was legislated against. Then it claims that it is no longer hazardous, citing medical organizations to back this up (and implicitly suggesting that because of this it should no longer be illegal). Finally, the brief indicates that abortion is actually desirable (in order to achieve the objective of birth control, which is assumed by the brief to be a good thing because it does not even seek to justify it). The section on the medical organizations is an effective transition. The briefs motivate us to believe that its claims about the safety of abortion must be correct, since the major medical organizations support it. Seeing this support, we can then more easily accept the claim that abortion is desirable and needed.

The first part of the brief concludes with a summary of the argument so far presented, and introduces the legal and constitutional arguments that will be made. It also introduces certain words and catch phrases that will be brought up later, such as "autonomy" and the physician's right "to administer medical care according to the highest professional standards." Finally, it begins to explain why the desired legal remedies are needed to correct the harms identified. It thus builds the bridge between the harms and the legal remedies.

The first part of the brief, then, is directed mostly to presenting the medical arguments for abortion and to showing why, in light of medicine the historical purpose of the statutes is no longer valid. It also presents a short preliminary argument, which sets the stage for its later discussion about why the embryo/fetus is not human. The presentation of these arguments before any legal ones reveals the brief-writers' confidence that the Court will be influenced by extra-legal considerations. The fact that these are the kinds of considerations which are normally weighed by legislators in shaping statutes suggests that the brief-writers *expect the Court to be willing to legislate, if it is convinced of the desirability of doing so.*

Placing these arguments first also builds the foundation on which the state's arguments and alleged interests -- which pertain to such matters as the woman's health and the humanity of the unborn child -- can be shown later to be without sufficient merit.

I shall not go into the second part of the brief since it deals with only the technical legal points in the case on such matters as whether there is a case or controversy, the propriety under existing rules of granting injunctive relief, the propriety of judicial action in the absence of a pending prosecution, and the validity of the Supreme Court's taking these appeals under existing procedural rules.

The third and final part of the brief spells out various rights which it claims are violated by the anti-abortion statutes, argues why each of these rights exists (most are not traditional legal rights), and cites legal authorities to back itself up. Then it considers each of the interests the state claimed and shows by further analysis why none are valid. Then, finally, it issues its secondary legal arguments of overbreadth and vagueness.

This final part begins with an introduction acknowledging the difficulty the appellants face in establishing the existence of the rights it asserts, since none appear in the Constitution or its amendments. It explains its way out of this, however, by saying that these rights "meet constitutional standards arising from several sources and expressed in decisions of this Court."[7] It thus, albeit vaguely, sets out a justification for making the kind of constitutional claims it does. This introduction, then, is the logical and necessary starting point for its discussion of rights.

By far, the most elaborate of the discussions on individual rights in the brief centers on the right of privacy. It is at this point in the brief, that the structuring and ordering of arguments is most crucial, because this is the central right claimed. The fact that the Court made it the cornerstone of its decision shows that the brief-writers accurately anticipated the argument that would have the most appeal for it -- if not in deciding the case, then as one premise for the decision. The brief deftly constructs both a right to personal privacy (out of a previously enunciated narrower right of marital privacy in *Griswold*) and a right to abortion as part of both privacy rights. The argument follows logically if one makes certain assumptions about the purpose of contraception and about the nature of the privacy right which is to be protected.

The brief, however, never comes to grip with two fundamental questions which, if allowed to intervene, would cause its privacy argument to collapse: Are abortion and contraception not, by their nature, different? and, Does not the marital relationship give rise to rights and obligations, such as the right of privacy, which do not belong to the individual *qua* individual?

The fact that the brief-writers did not believe it necessary to address these problems illustrates their talent for anticipating the Court. Indeed, even before *Wade* and *Bolton* were handed down, their judgment was shown to be correct on the second of these questions in the Court's decision in *Eisenstadt*.

The brief's progression from the assertion of rights and explanation of their violation (its primary legal arguments) -- interspersed with statements of harms which it seems to see as bringing the privacy rights into play -- to answering the state's claims, to, finally, its secondary legal arguments is an understandably logical ordering for any legal brief. This final part is the heart of the brief since it turns to the essential points that its legal claim is based on and applies the medical points made earlier to its legal arguments.

The Rights Asserted, Their Basis, and the Thought Behind Them

The briefs claim that the following rights were infringed upon by the abortion statutes: the right of privacy (as it extends to the right to bear children and the right to control one's body), the right of a person to seek and receive medical and health care, and the right of a physician to be free from state interference in the practice of his profession. The Court based its decision on the right of privacy. Even though it did not discuss the rights of the physician in the opinions, the Court expressed its clear support for his interests.

The Right of Privacy

The *Wade* brief develops its argument on the right of privacy in the following manner: first, it discusses the "sanctity" of the marital relationship and the family, and states that in order to insure this sanctity the Court had to enunciate the right of marital privacy in *Griswold*. Then it explains how *Griswold* held that the right to have children implied by the right of marital privacy also included the right *not* to have children (more specifically, the right to use contraceptives), and claims that in order for this choice about having children to be fully preserved within marriage, a right to abortion is said to be necessary because contraceptives sometimes fail. Finally, the brief moves out of the realm of marital privacy and asserts that privacy is a right attaching not just to the marriage state but, more fundamentally, to the *individual* and so the right to abortion exists without regard to marital status.

The *Wade* brief goes to all ends to emphasize

the sanctity of marriage. It says that "[t]he importance of the institution of marriage and the family has long been recognized by...[the] Court."[8] It quotes one Supreme Court opinion as saying that marriage is "'the foundation of the family and of society, without which there would be neither civilization nor progress'"[9] and another which called marriage and procreation "'fundamental to the very existence and survival of the race.'"[10] It says that it was the "[r]ecognition of the sanctity of the marital relationship [that]... resulted in recognition of a right of marital privacy" in *Griswold*.[11]

The brief relies exclusively on past Supreme Court decisions as the basis for its assertion of the right of marital privacy. It admits that the Constitution "does not specifically enumerate a 'right to seek abortion,' or a 'right of privacy'" and recites a litany of decisions which had held various activities to be within the ambit of family rights.[12] These include, in addition to the right of a married couple to use contraceptives in *Griswold*, the right to a marriage partner of one's choosing even if he or she is of a different race;[13] the right to control the education of one's children;[14] and the right not to be involuntarily sterilized.[15]

The Court, it will be recalled, cited these and other cases in its discussion of the right of privacy. The brief mentions only cases involving privacy in the realm of sex, marriage, and procreation and in the related realm of intrusions into one's physical person. It also presents a lengthy quote from a lower court decision, *Doe v. Scott*,[16] which emphasizes this very understanding of the right of privacy. The opinion, on the other hand, cited cases involving a privacy right in other areas as well. We may be able to conclude from this that the brief wants to single these realms out for special constitutional protection. (The other briefs I am considering seem to do likewise.) The Court, however, does not indicate in the opinion that it accepts this analysis; it merely states that the "guarantee of personal privacy" has "some extension" to the realm of marriage, family, and procreation.[17]

The argument in *Wade* involves a leap at three points, the extent of which the brief does not seem to be aware. The first leap -- made also by the *Griswold*

Court -- is from the earlier family privacy cases involving the rights to have offspring, and to control the education of those offspring, to the right *not* to have offspring at all. The second leap is from the right to use contraceptives as attendent to the right of marital privacy to the right to use them whether one is married or not (the leap from the *Griswold* to *Eisenstadt* case which I alluded to earlier). The third leap is from a right to use contraceptives to a right to abortion (i.e., the right to stop the biological development of offspring to the right to eliminate the offspring once developed). The *Griswold* to *Eisenstadt* leap cannot be made as logically as the *Wade* appellants seem to believe.

Since the brief is seeking to establish a general right to abortion for all women, instead of just married ones, it does not stop with the claim that the right to marital privacy permits abortion. It sets out to establish the existence of the "[r]elated [r]ights" to *personal* privacy and physical integrity.[18] It again relies squarely on previous Supreme Court decisions to establish the existence of this right -- nothing else. It indicates that it believes this right guarantees protection for an extreme conception of individual freedom when it says that the Court has extended "significant constitutional protection to the citizen's *sovereignty* over his or her own physical person."[19] The brief cites a number of Supreme Court decisions -- beginning with *Botsford* -- which it says established this right of personal privacy. It also refers to a number of lower court decisions which held the right to abortion is contained within this right of privacy. (The *Wade* opinion also cited most of these cases and asserted that the basis for the right of privacy is its past decisions. It relied, in part, on the decisions of lower courts in holding that this right includes the right to abortion.)

In their initial brief, the *Wade* appellants do not refer to the *Eisenstadt* decision because it had not yet been handed down.[20] They do refer to the federal appeals court's decision in *Eisenstadt*, which the Supreme Court later concurred with. They discuss the Supreme Court's *Eisenstadt* opinion at the very beginning of the argument section of their supplemental brief. All quote the statement about the individual nature of the right of privacy in reproductive matters which I mentioned was cited by Justices Stewart and Douglas in their concurring opinions. Indeed, one of the reasons the supplemental brief was filed was probably because they wanted to make specific reference to the Supreme Court's *Eisenstadt* decision.

Like the *Wade* opinion, the *Wade* brief seems to couple the rights of marital and personal privacy to alleged harms that will occur if abortion is denied (that is, it implies that the privacy rights come into operation because these harms accrue). We see these harms presented in the following two passages, one of which refers to the harms that could occur to a married couple if abortion is not permitted and the other to women generally (I shall comment about these passages shortly):

> The number and spacing of children obviously have a profound impact upon the marital union. Certainly the members of this Court know from personal experience the emotional and financial expenditures parenthood demands. For those couples who are less fortunate financially and especially for those who are struggling to provide the necessities of life, additional financial responsibilities can be economically disastrous. For families who require two incomes for economic survival, the pregnancy can be ruinous since the wife will generally have to resign her job. In many other situations, such as where husband and wife are working to put themselves through school, pregnancy at a particular time can present a crisis.[21]

and

> ...[a woman] must also forego further education or a career and often must endure economic and social hardships. Under the present law of Texas, she is given no other choice. Continued pregnancy is compulsory...[22]

Let us consider whether the brief's position respects the sanctity of marriage which it so strongly proclaims or whether, in the final analysis, it undermines it. The first thing to ask is why the marital relationship is treated as something "sacred," to use the term the brief quotes Justice Douglas in *Griswold* as using to describe it.[23] I believe that by briefly considering some major statements about it from both within and outside of the Judeo-Christian tradition, we can see that the reasons pertain to the fact that it involves a special kind of union and from it comes new life, to be held in reverence.

We can see the sanctity of marriage and respect for offspring first proclaimed in the Judeo-Christian tradition in the Book of Genesis in the Old Testament. Genesis 2:24 says that "a man shall leave father and mother, and shall cleave to his wife: and they shall be two in one flesh."[24] Genesis 9:1 mentions God's admonition to Noah and his sons after the flood: "And he said to them: Increase and multiply and fill the earth."[25]

In the New Testament, Jesus, despite seeming to commend the renunciation of marriage to at least some of his followers, carries on this tradition of great reverence for marriage. He even intensifies it by insisting on its indissolubility -- the Jewish law permitted a man to discharge his wife, although there was disagreement about under what circumstances it was justified -- in Chapter 10 of Mark's Gospel.[26] The value that Jesus placed on children -- which also went well beyond that of the Jewish custom of His time -- is seen in His specifically promising salvation to them (see Mark 10:14) and His famous statement in Chapter 18 of Matthew's Gospel that "unless you be converted and be as little children, you shall not enter into the kingdom of heaven."[27]

C. S. Lewis discusses the sanctity marriage has been held in by the non-Judeo-Christian traditions and the reverence and duties they have viewed as being owed to children and posterity. The former is seen in the almost universal condemnation of adultery. For example, mentioned on the ancient Babylonian List of Sins was "'Has he approached his neighbour's wife?'" and the Old Norse pagan work *Volospa* says "'I saw in Nastrond [Hell] ...beguilers of others' wives.'" He mentions the following examples of the latter: The Hindu book *Janet*, where it says that "'[c]hildren, the old, the poor, etc. should be considered as lords of the atmosphere'"; the pagan Greek Stoic Epictetus' mentioning on his List of Duties "'To marry and to beget children'"; the pagan Roman philosopher Juvenal's saying that "'[g]reat reverence is owed to a child'"; the statement in the ancient Chinese Analects that "'[t]he Master said, Respect the young'"; and the American Indian Redskin's saying in his account of the Battle of Wounded Knee that "'[t]he killing of the women and more especially of the young boys and girls...is the saddest part.'"[28]

Marriage, both within and outside of the Judeo-Christian tradition is thus seen as sacred for these reasons: it is a surrendering of individuality and the forming of a union within which love is exchanged in a selfless way, and it brings forth and sees to the nurturing of new life, which is the most miraculous act that humans take part in. For Jews and Christians, it has an even greater depth of sanctity because they acknowledge that it is God who has ordained this institution and blessed the union of the respective couple.

The brief's arguments make it clear that the appellants stand *in opposition* to these two basic reasons for the sacredness of marriage. It is in opposition to the great respect for the *union* created in marriage because it premises its claim for a right to abortion, in the end, on a right of *individual* privacy. The right of marital privacy is only a convenient base, set down by the Supreme Court in *Griswold*, on which to erect this broader right. It also supersedes the right of marital privacy in the brief's argument -- and the *Wade* opinion -- by the very fact that access to abortion is not sought to be limited to married women.

This primary emphasis on the individual over the marital union is seen in the language of the brief. One example of this is the reference to the "sovereignty" over one's person. The brief also claims that "one is entitled to personal autonomy."[29] The term "autonomy" implies an extreme freedom, a total independence of the individual from constraints, even those which are imposed by marriage.[30] The preeminence of the individual is also seen in the following quote which the brief takes from the *Botsford* case:

> "No right is more sacred, [n]or is more carefully guarded...than the right of every individual to the possession and control of his own person..."[31]

The *Botsford* quote conveniently serves the appellants' purpose, but it really did not signify support for the position taken. I discussed this case in Chapter Three and we saw that it pertained to an arm of the state ordering a direct intrusion into the domain of an individual's body -- a surgical examination -- and not a state attempt to stop the individual from making such an intrusion for the sake of protecting another, as in abortion. The case was affirming a common law principle; it is not a precedent for attacking another common law principle, that the individual is not permitted to inflict damage on his own body. The brief, like the *Wade* opinion, fails to note the significance of the common law rule in *Botsford* for the unborn child -- as I explained it in Chapter Three -- just as it does not mention the Court's paramount concern for the unborn child in another decision which it cites to back up its right of privacy claim -- also referred to in Chapter Three -- the *Georgetown College* case.

The brief's disdain for the other pillar of marital sacredness, the respect for the life of offspring -- is seen in the simple fact that it calls for the legalization of abortion. The depth of this disregard for the life of offspring is strongly suggested by the language of the right of privacy section of the brief. The brief's sense of the burdensomeness of pregnancy and parenting is seen by the two passages quoted above. We can particularly take note of the comments that pregnancy "can be ruinous" and "can present a crisis."[32] It further claims that prohibiting abortion "has a maximum destructive impact upon the marriage relationship" and that, for a woman, "there are numerous more subtle but no less drastic impacts."[33] It speaks of "the inhumane severity of laws which impose continued pregnancy and compulsory parenthood" and laments the burden to the woman of "an unwanted pregnancy...and for society, a possible obligation of support."[34] Most revealing, however, is the claim that during pregnancy a woman is "an incubator."[35]

What is also revealed is the appellants' view of the kinds of things in life which they view as the most important. The material things -- economic well-being, a successful career, and the educational accomplishment which make these possible -- are seen as preeminent, even over the life of a newly-conceived child. A utilitarian ethic is asserted in the brief in the same way as in the *Wade* opinion. The individual woman is permitted to choose abortion for whatever material or personal considerations she decides are more important than the child.

The extent to which the brief deemphasizes respect for the life of offspring is seen in its unwillingness to face the crucial question of the difference between contraception and abortion. It looks upon abortion as, in effect, a back-up form of contraception. It does not believe it makes a substantial leap from the right to use contraceptives asserted in *Griswold* and *Eisenstadt* to the right to abortion. There is a lack of understanding about the difference between the nature of things. That is, quite simply, that when a man and woman possess a sperm and ovum, respectively, they have the potentiality of creating a new, separate biological organism *if* certain activity occurs: sexual intercourse, then fertilization of the ovum. Before these happen, there is no new organism. After they happen, there is. There is perhaps a confusion about the meaning of potential and actual.

In any event, in making its jump between the two, at least as far as legal rights are concerned, the brief cites the article by former Supreme Court Justice Tom C. Clark. This article, "Religion, Morality, and Abortion: A Constitutional Appraisal," in Volume 2 of *Loyola University (of Los Angeles) Law Review* (1969), appears to have been quite influential. It was not only cited by the Court in the *Wade* opinion, but also by every one of the pro-abortion briefs I considered. Apparently, the opinion of a former Justice of the Court was viewed as deserving important consideration. The following quote from the article appears in the briefs:

> "[A]bortion falls within that sensitive area of privacy -- the marital relation. One of the basic values of this privacy is birth control, as evidenced by the *Griswold* decision. *Griswold's* act was to prevent formation of the fetus. This, the Court found, was constitutionally protected. If an individual may prevent conception, why can he not nullify that conception when prevention has failed?"[36]

It should be pointed out that Clark, in his article, hardly addresses the essential biological and philosophical questions about the nature of unborn human life. In order for one to reasonably equate abortion and contraception, it would seem that he would have to satisfactorily resolve these first. As it is, Clark does not even mention biological matters and speaks only briefly about philosophy, and then only in connection with religious arguments and the views of a few theologians, social scientists, and medical experts, which are barely gone into.

To sum up, the *Wade* brief's arguments assert the preeminence of the individual over the marital relationship in fashioning the right of privacy. The result of this and the whole enterprise of legalizing abortion -- in spite of the claims of concern about its sanctity -- is to *undermine* marriage. This occurs because the brief is, in effect, assailing the preeminent status of the notion of marriage being a union and the great value that is placed on the offspring that issue from the marital union.

The Right to Health Care

The next right asserted by the briefs is the right to seek and receive health care. This right is discussed by the *Wade* appellants, PPFA, and ACOG. The latter two briefs believe that the right is found in the Ninth and/or Fourteenth Amendments. The *Wade* brief makes no statement about specific constitutional provisions, but finds the right in cases, legislative statements, and the Constitution of the World Health Organization (WHO).

While the PPFA and ACOG briefs say that the right comes from the amendments mentioned, they do not explain how their wording or legislative history supports such a claim. What they do instead is to cite Supreme Court decisions which they claim recognized such a right. The *Wade* brief does this even while admitting that "this Court has not expressly delineated a right to seek health care."[37] Let me briefly consider these cases.

The *Wade* brief cites a number of decisions, PPFA's just two, and ACOG's only one. The primary point that the briefs seek to make in citing these decisions is, of course, that there is such a thing as a right to seek and receive health care. The secondary point it seeks to make, by implication, is that the notion of "health care" includes abortion services. Of all the cases cited on this point, however, only one involves abortion. The one case which is commonly cited by all three briefs is *Jacobson v. Massachusetts* (1904).[38] In this decision, whose treatment by the *Wade* brief I discuss below, the Supreme Court held that a state may enact a statute, pursuant to its police power, which required its inhabitants to be vaccinated against smallpox. A number of other decisions are mentioned by the *Wade* brief. A number of these were lower federal court decisions which held that incarcerated prisoners have the right to file civil rights actions against their jailors for refusing them needed medical treatment.[39] Another held that custodial patients also have a constitutional right to such treatment.[40] Another recognized a right to the protection of health against environmental pollution.[41] Another held that a hospital's refusal to perform a sterilization for non-medical reasons violated individual rights,[42] but the brief gives no indication that this decision stated that any right to *health care* was involved. Another is the *Griswold* decision.

Two observations must be made about these decisions. First, they do not establish the existence of any generalized right of health care because they -- except for *Jacobson* -- are district court opinions which are not binding precedents even for other federal or state judges in the same district. As to *Jacobson*, the *Wade* brief claims that it, in a most indirect way, afforded protection to a constitutional right to health care. The ACOG brief also comes to this conclusion, apparently on the basis of the following quote from the opinion: "'We [the Court] are not to be understood as holding that...the judiciary would not be competent to interfere and protect the health and life of the individual concerned.'"[43]

The former came to its conclusion on *Jacobson* by arguing that since the state could restrict individual freedom in that case through a "compelling interest," under normal circumstances he would retain his "fundamental right" to care for his health.[44] The problem with this interpretation, to begin with, is that the opinion does not say anything about such a fundamental right existing. (The *Wade* brief also does not make reference to the quote cited in the ACOG brief -- stated above -- which, in any case, does not say anything about "rights.") Secondly, the issue in the *Jacobson* case is not whether the state can restrict his freedom by legislating to protect the health of the general public. What was generally in question is the same thing that was in question in *Wade* and *Bolton*: whether the state can use its police power in a particular manner. The brief uses a case which permitted a state to use its police power to restrict individual freedom *to justify a restriction of the police power for the sake of individual freedom.*

Further, in trying to establish that *Jacobson* signified that only a "compelling interest" of the state could be used to restrict a person's liberty, it overstates the point of the quote it takes from the case:

> "...It is not, therefore, true that the power of the public to *guard itself against imminent* danger depends in every case involving the control of one's own body upon his willingness to submit to reasonable regulations established by the constituted authorities, under the sanction of the state for the purpose of protecting the public effectively against such danger."[45] [The brief states that the emphasis is its own.]

This quote is used to endorse the state's power to limit individual rights; it is not a statement that the individual's rights *vis-à-vis* the state are as broad as the brief infers. The brief attaches a significance to the phrase it emphasizes which may not be there. This passage refers only to the circumstances presented to it. It is not saying the state can act to restrict individual freedom for the public good only when there is a serious imminent danger. The opinion has nothing about any "compelling interest" standard. Its endorsement of the notion contained in the Massachusetts constitution that the "'common good'" of that Commonwealth is to be determined primarily by its legislature through its police power[46] and its statement that "[t]he safety and health of...[its] people...are matters that do not ordinarily concern the National Government...[but]... depend, primarily, upon such action as the State in its wisdom may take"[47] suggest that it does not take such a limited view of state power and expansive view of individual liberty as the brief-writers believe.

The ACOG brief uses the quote it takes from *Jacobson* to make the point that the state may not "infringe upon the constitutionally protected right of its pregnant citizens to the medical treatment they require to maintain their good health."[48] The brief uses the decision to assert an expansive right to health care even though the *Jacobson* Court determined the state's action can be limited only on those (probably few) occasions when it could present a serious and certain threat to the individual's life or health. The brief is not limiting its demand for legalized abortion only to those situations. (As I show in Chapter Six, there are few cases when there are such indications for abortion.)

This last point leads to a consideration of the precedents for the secondary purpose I indicated (i.e., that health care includes abortion services). Only one of these decisions, *U.S. v. Vuitch*, involved abortion. *Griswold* was another, and yet another involved sterilization. It has been seen, however, why contraception is not really comparable to abortion and sterilization is not comparable to it for the same reason. As far as *Vuitch* is concerned, it not only does not state there is a constitutionally protected right to health, but it does not claim anywhere that abortion is to be equated with all other health care services.

The *Wade* brief further tries to emphasize the view that abortion is just like any other health care service in discussing the rights of the physician. The upshot of this section of the brief is that physicians are denied their rights because they are not permitted "to make medically sound judgments" in this area like they are in others.[49] In fact, the brief tries to make us believe that this is the only area that might concern them professionally in which their freedom is restricted. It says that physicians can "take any other drastic action they believe is indicated."[50] Abortion is seen in this, and the ACOG and PPFA briefs which also address the question of the physician's rights, as merely a medical procedure.

Lumping abortion with other health care services

is a judgment the brief apparently makes on the basis that "[*a*]*mici* medical organizations recognize the acceptability of abortion."[51] This takes us ultimately to questions of the medical indications for abortion and the nature of the child *in utero*, which I shall explore in Chapter Six. For now, these observations can be made. First, the brief's willingness to make this judgment simply on the basis of what these organizations say without any apparent inquiry into how they came to this conclusion -- as we can judge by the fact that there is no discussion of the point -- indicates an eagerness to accept, unquestioningly, the thinking of experts. And second, just on the basis of common sense, it seems difficult to think of abortion as a simple "health care" problem. This is because when we talk about restoring ourselves to health, we are usually referring to the overcoming of some disease. Pregnancy can in no sense be considered a "disease" and, in fact, has never been so considered by medical science. This seems to argue against treating abortion as just another health care matter.

Questions can also be raised about the legitimacy of the *Wade* brief's claim that legislative action and the WHO Constitution can be relied upon to assert the existence of a "fundamental" right to health care.[52] The legislative action it points to is the Comprehensive Health Planning Act of 1966. The quote from this Congressional enactment the brief cites does not say anything about a "right" to health care. It only affirms that "'our national purpose depends on promoting and assuring the highest level of health attainable for every person.'"[53] In any event, statutes have seldom been used by the Court to establish the existence of fundamental rights within the Constitution.[54] The same objection can be made about the WHO Constitution. Such international documents are often used by international or domestic tribunals to discern points of international law, but it is not customary for American courts to use them as a basis for interpreting our Constitution.

As a final observation on this right to health care, let me quote the other passage from the *Wade* brief which gives us an insight into an aspect of the thought behind it:

> The existence of other types of state statutes, not under constitutional attack, which

> affect matters of personal health does not negate the right asserted here. In contrast to laws which intrude upon the protection of personal health, statutes which prescribe working conditions have an indirect, positive impact on the person's *well-being.*[55]

This quote reflects the contemporary liberal view about the role of government *vis-à-vis* the individual. It expresses the view that government social and economic regulatory legislation is acceptable, even if it restricts the freedom of some individuals or institutions -- because it purportedly benefits other individuals. (Indeed, it may even restrict the latter's freedom -- e.g., to make a contract respecting wages and the conditions of his employment -- but this is seen as acceptable so long as it is for his benefit.) The argument being made by the brief in support of legalized abortion makes clear its support for the other dimension of the liberal view of government versus the individual. On questions of personal -- such as sexual -- activities, the government has little or no authority to infringe upon individual freedom. *There is thus a truncated view of individual freedom, and of the relationship between government and the individual.*

The quote expresses another view as well. It is saying that government legislation designed to improve the individual's material condition -- that is to bolster his bodily "well-being" -- is permissible, but legislation, such as that prohibiting abortion, which seeks to make him follow certain norms of personal morality is not. The only "well-being" which the brief seems to acknowledge as important relates to the physical; there is no concern expressed about the individual's moral and spiritual well-being. In fact, what it seeks to do is profoundly hostile to this. This materialistic position accords with the preeminent emphasis on material concerns in the section of the brief dealing with the right of privacy. This view raises serious doubt about the brief's implication that it stands in the tradition of the Framers, which is stated in a quote it takes from Justice Brandeis:

> "They [the Framers] recognized the significance of *man's spiritual nature*, of his feelings and of his intellect. They knew that only a part of the pain, pleasure and

> satisfaction of life are to be found in material things."[56]

The *Wade* brief contends that since the rights to marital and individual privacy and to seek medical care are "fundamental," the state can act to restrict them only when its interests are "compelling." It says that the Texas statute is invalid because it does not further any of these compelling state interests: promoting the public health, regulating private sexual conduct, and protecting human life. I shall critically examine the arguments the brief makes on these points in Chapter Six.

The Equal Protection Question

The opinions give no evidence the Court was influenced by arguments presented to it that the abortion statutes deprived the poor and non-white of their equal protection rights. Nevertheless, it is worth considering them briefly because these arguments have been made so often by those in the pro-abortion movement in the years prior to *Wade* and *Bolton*, and also in the years since then on the question of public funding of abortions for poor women. The equal protection argument is also worth considering because it gives an insight into the understanding of equality of the pro-abortionist.

The argument that the statutes discriminated against the poor and non-white is made in the *amicus curiae* briefs in both *Wade* and *Bolton* of the National Legal Program on Health Problems of the Poor (NLPHPP) on the basis of numerous studies and sets of statistics presented. These purportedly show that abortions were much more accessible to the affluent before *Wade* and *Bolton*, as shown by the fact that they had many more of them. The studies, which I shall not go into for reasons of space, show that therapeutic abortions -- particularly for psychiatric reasons -- were easier for affluent women than the poor to get. The reason for this, the brief and the studies it cites conclude, is that the affluent have better hospital facilities available to them. The poor generally have to rely on municipal hospitals which, as one of the authorities the briefs cites states without explanation, "'follow the letter of the law of the abortion statute much more exactly than voluntary hospitals, and also the private patients [apparently referring to those in public hospitals] are generally treated by a more lenient interpretation of the law than service patients.'"[57] The result, according to another authority quoted, "'is the creation of a double standard for private and indigent patients'" which is termed "'[p]erhaps the greatest injustice resulting from our present policies.'"[58]

The brief explains that, even though the statutes on their face do not deprive one group of equal protection and may not really have that intent, they are still unconstitutional because its "practical effect" is to deny equal protection for the reasons stated above.[59] It quotes the famous 1886 Supreme Court opinion in *Yick Wo v. Hopkins* as follows:

> "Though the law itself be fair on its face and impartial in appearance, yet, if it is applied and administered by public authority with an evil eye and an unequal hand, so as practically to make unjust and illegal discriminations between persons in similar circumstances, material to their rights, the denial of equal justice is still within the prohibition of the constitution."[60]

While its briefs in *Wade* and *Bolton* are roughly identical, NLPHPP singles out the Georgia statute for special comment because its provisions, mentioned before in Chapter Two, of restricting the performance of abortions to hospitals accredited by the Joint Commission on Accreditation of Hospitals (JCAH) and of requiring approval by additional physicians and a hospital committee allegedly aided in discrimination against the poor and non-white. It claims the former had this effect because most Georgia counties did not have JCAH-accredited hospitals, and that the latter did because it represented an unconstitutional delegation of state power to private individuals who then exercise it to the poor's disadvantage.

First, let us consider the matter of protecting the poor. As one prominent constitutional law textbook tells us, "[t]he Court has *stated* on several occasions that 'lines drawn on the basis of wealth or property... render a classification highly suspect and thereby demand a more exacting judicial scrutiny'...but no decision has held that explicit discriminations against poor people are 'suspect.'"[61] ("Suspect classifications" are government actions which treat certain groups in a manner different from other groups. The Court has generally held that classifications such as these, as they respect certain types of groups, be given "strict scrutiny" by it under the equal protection clause.) One prominent case in which the Court came closest to granting special protection under this clause was *Harper v. Virginia Board of Elections* (1966), which invalidated a state poll tax. Another lesser known case was *Turner v. Fouche* (1969)[62] in which the Court declared unconstitutional a "real property ownership" requirement for school board members. In *Harper*, the Court stated the following:

> Wealth, like race, creed, or color, is not germane to one's ability to participate intelligently in the electoral process. Lines drawn on the basis of wealth or property, like those of race, are traditionally disfavored.[63]

The Court in this quote seems to lump economic status quite squarely in with race and color, the areas in which it has provided the strictest equal protection review for a generation. This is not the Court's rule in this area, however. The normal rule is seen in such decisions as *James v. Valtierra* (1971),[64] which upheld an article of the California constitution which prohibited the construction of low-rent public housing projects without the approval of local voters in a referendum, and *San Antonio Independent School District v. Rodriguez*, (1973),[65] which held that Texas' practice of financing school districts on the basis of local property taxes was not unconstitutional even though it resulted in sizable fund differences between affluent and poor districts. Justice Powell's majority opinion stated that "this Court has never heretofore held that wealth discrimination alone provides an adequate basis for invoking strict scrutiny..."[66]

We can see that what the brief calls for is a decision that goes well beyond the Court's doctrine on equal protection in that it seeks to have laws struck down which not only allegedly place an unfair burden on the poor, but do this not because of any direct state action but because of the private decisions of hospital authorities and individual physicians.

This leads to my next point: the brief, in effect, is asking the Court to declare unconstitutional actions performed by private parties, not governmental officials or entities. This is so, because it contends that abortion statutes have a discriminatory effect, even though their content is not discriminatory. The fact that the action complained of is not done by the state, but by private parties, means that according to long-standing Supreme Court doctrine it is not touched by the Constitution. This doctrine originated with the *Civil Rights Cases* in 1883[67] where the Court held that under the Fourteenth Amendment, which includes the equal protection clause, "it is state action of a particular character that is prohibited. Individual invasion of individual rights is not the subject matter of the amendment."[68]

Legal scholars William B. Lockhart, Yale Kamisar, and Jesse H. Choper tell us that "[t]he basic doctrine of the *Civil Rights Cases*...has remained undisturbed. But the question of what constitutes 'state action' had generated significant controversy."[69] While the Georgia statute might have been subject to such an attack on the grounds that it delegates decision-making authority to private physicians and hospitals and thus vests them with a measure of state authority -- it should be remembered that the Georgia statute was an abortion "reform" statute --, it is difficult to make this claim about the Texas statute and others like it which gave very little medical discretion since they permitted abortion only when the woman's life was endangered. Even the Georgia statute could not be judged so readily to be similar to the areas of private endeavor which have been held to be "state action," such as a political party's primary elections,[70] the activities carried out on land leased by a state to a private party,[71] and restrictive covenants in the conveyancing of privately-owned real estate.[72] It is doubtful that abortions performed by private physicians in private facilities can be denominated "state action" just because state law regulates or forbids it any more than state regulations on a physician's prescribing diet pills make him an agent of the state or the regulation of labor unions under the Taft-Hartley Act makes them federal instrumentalities.

The brief ties the alleged equal protection violation to an unconstitutional delegation of state power. In light of this, it was unreasonable for the brief-writers to expect that the Court would somehow grant there was state action and accept the equal protection claim. The Court would probably just invalidate the statute on the grounds that it represents an unconstitutional delegation of power to private persons.[73] (This, of course, would have satisfied the brief-writers because they would still get the statute invalidated. The point is, however, that the invalidation would have nothing to do with equal protection, which is the primary claim of the brief.) Nevertheless, the alleged equal protection violation, as explained above, comes about so indirectly and unintentionally as to make such a claim very weak.

Yick Wo is also an inappropriate precedent for the brief to cite. First of all, the ordinance in *Yick Wo* involved something like a licensing procedure which was, as the quote above states, "'administered by [a] public authority'" in an on-going manner. There was thus regular and direct state involvement, unlike in the present case. On the second point, let me begin by quoting *Yick Wo:*

> ...[the] facts shown establish an administration directed so exclusively against a particular class of persons as to warrant and require the conclusion that, whatever may have been the intent of the ordinances adopted, they are applied...with a mind so unequal and oppressive as to amount to a practical denial by the State of [equal protection].[74]

This quote shows that the ordinance there was applied with the intention of achieving a discriminatory result, even though its provisions, on paper, were not discriminatory. The abortion statutes, as we can discern from the points stated by the brief (mentioned above), are not only devoid of discriminatory language, but also are not applied with a discriminatory intent. The discrimination allegedly occurs only as an unintended result of private action.

My other observations concern the view of economic equality and the relationship between rich and poor that is taken by the NLPHPP brief. First, much of the argument in the brief -- and this is particularly seen in the points about the lack of access of the poor to private and JCAH-accredited "better" hospitals -- is about one important social benefit, health care, not being equally available to rich and poor. This is a position that might be asserted by a group advocating comprehensive national health insurance or socialized medicine. It is not grounded in any traditional constitutional law understanding of equal protection, that is, of equal treatment under existing laws. Rather, it is a call for the kind of economic equality and redistribution of the fruits of society that would characterize the thinking of a modern-day welfare state planner. The fact that this appears in a legal brief suggests that the brief-writers are ready to have such a notion of equality decreed into existence by the judiciary *even though it is typically able to come about only by legislative action.*

Second, the brief displays a sense of inter-class hostility that one would ordinarily associate with Marxism. For one thing, much of the argument, with its statistics and studies and the like, seems to portray the poor as victims. They are seen as victims of an oppressive society which has little concern for their interests. This is also suggested by the following language of the brief in *Bolton:*

> "Reform" legislation such as that in issue here is far from a complete answer to this problem...[Then, quoting one writer], it must be recognized that moderate reform is essentially middle-class reform. It benefits those who are sufficiently well-educated, well-connected and well-financed to take advantage of the liberalized law.[75]

This quote makes the affluent out to be selfish and eager to shape the law for their own interests. (It thus implies a more general view of law as made without reference to any natural norms of right and wrong, reflective only of what dominant interests seek.) There is more than a hint of contempt for those who are better-off.

Ironically, the brief also is degrading to the poor -- the very people it claims to be protecting. This is seen in its claim that because the affluent have ready access to abortions, the poor should also. The poor have not resolved the problem of "unwanted" pregnancies in the way that the affluent have, so the brief concludes that there must be something wrong. The brief-writers are analyzing the problems of the poor from the perspective of the affluent. The brief tells us that "[u]nwanted births were in general more than twice as high for families with incomes of less than $3,000 as for those with incomes of over $10,000" and that "this differential was 'particularly marked among Negroes.'"[76] It says that "[o]ne explanation for this "high level of unwanted births among the poor and non-white is surely the fact that they do not have equal access to abortions."[77]

The point made by these statements is degrading for two reasons. First, the brief does not even consider the possibility that poor and black women do not want to have abortions when many affluent women would because they find them morally objectionable and/or have religious scruples against them. The poor and black are not recognized as free moral agents; the entire issue is viewed as nothing more than a question of "access." Indeed, the brief actually *discounts* the possibility of the poor having moral objections by saying, without citing a source, that "[t]here is nothing demonstrable in the differences of skin color or economic condition which suggests...the poor and non-whites have a substantially different moral attitude on abortion."[78] Perhaps there is nothing in one's skin color or economic condition that suggests that he may have a particular view on abortion, but there may be something in his cultural background or religious and moral training. Indeed, the evidence strongly suggests that the poor and non-white are opposed to legalized abortion in larger numbers than whites and those who are more affluent.[79]

Second, the above statements could be understood as an implication that the poor and non-white are less sexually responsible than other groups. The possibility again is not considered that the poor and non-white may be deterred from abortion by their morality and so have more "unwanted" pregnancies.[80] (The term "unwanted" is not defined anywhere. As I shall show in Chapter Six it is a very broad term and most pregnancies may, in some sense, be "unwanted.") The brief-writers, in effect, appoint themselves to analyze and provide a solution for the "plight" of the poor and put them down in the process.

One is led to wonder, in light of other statements in the brief, if the brief's concern is primarily the establishment of the legal right to abortion, rather than the vindication of the rights of the poor. Since the brief never raises questions about morals and nature, it ignores the possibility that what is really being asked for is that the poor be given an equal protection right to do what is wrong and unnatural. It seems to advocate an equal protection right to break the law since the thrust of its statistical argument focuses, in effect, on how the affluent have succeeded in getting around the law. Since it wraps its abortion claims in a right of equal health care for the poor, it presents abortion as just another health care matter. In fact, it even seems to portray abortion as a positive good, referring to it as a "benefit" which the state may not "preclude enjoyment of...to...the poor and non-white."[81] As the quote I cited above mentions, the brief may also be more concerned about wiping out that old boogyman the "double standard" -- a major concern in much literature advocating legalized abortion and changed sexual morality -- than in the poor.

The Overbreadth and Vagueness Arguments

It was also argued that the abortion statutes were drafted in language which was too vague to allow the physician performing the abortion to know if he was acting illegally or not, and was overly broad, so that it might be used to prohibit indisputably legal activities. Although a number of the briefs raise these arguments, I shall again focus exclusively on the *Wade* brief where they -- especially the vagueness argument -- are the most comprehensively developed.

Overbreadth

The "overbreadth" argument was made in the *Wade* brief in connection with one of the state's possible interests -- which the brief argues is invalid -- in having an anti-abortion statute: to regulate private sexual conduct. (The other possible state interests, which were also rejected, are the interest in the woman's health and the interest in protecting unborn human life. I shall consider what the brief says about these in Chapter Six.) The first point the brief makes is that the statute, if used for the purpose of discouraging illicit sexual conduct, is overbroad because it applies to both married and unmarried couples.

The second point the brief makes is that if the state wants to stop illicit sexual activity, it already has laws against adultery and fornication. The brief says that to make pregnancy the "penalty" for such activity would be to attribute a "monstrous intention" to the Texas legislature.[82]

Finally, the brief says the following:

> No evidence exists that limited access to abortion curtails promiscuity, nor is it conceivable that such a correlation could exist. The widespread availability of contraception would seem to be a more significant factor.[83]

As an authority for this statement, the brief cites an article by Kenneth J. Ryan, M.D. entitled "Humane Abortion Laws and the Health Needs of Society" which appeared in Volume 17 of *Western Reserve Law Review* (1965) and is also cited by a couple of other briefs.

The brief also says that to use abortion laws to regulate private sexual conduct is "beyond the competence of the state." It cites *Griswold* and *Eisenstadt* in supporting this -- neither of which, of course, involved abortion laws -- and also refers the reader to the *amicus curiae* brief of New Women Lawyers, et al (hereinafter NWL).[84]

In its brief, NWL says that the state has no compelling interest in prohibiting premarital sexual intercourse for the following reasons. First, it implicitly argues that the "community standard" must be appealed to on this point and that that standard is "at present a changing one." Second, there are two "communities" involved in this question -- men and women -- and the latter, who "at best have an indirect voice in the determination of these laws" are the ones who "must suffer from them." The brief argues that instead of helping to preserve the moral fabric of the community, the laws actually "undermine" it because they "force countless women to flagrantly violate the law each year" by getting criminal abortions. Finally, the brief says that even if the maintenance of a "particular standard of morality" were a valid reason for the statutes, they would still be unconstitutional because they place all of... [their] weight and burden on only one sex and are thus an "invidious discrimination."[85]

Let me now critique each of these points -- in both the *Wade* and NWL briefs -- and comment upon the thought reflected in them. The first point about the abortion statute not distinguishing between married and unmarried women was discussed by the *Wade* opinion in a slightly different context, as mentioned in Chapter Three. It claimed the distinction was not made by the nineteenth century statutes, and this was proof for the argument that the discouragement of illicit sexual activity could not have been one of their purposes. There are three responses which can be made to this. First the legislators who enacted the Texas statute in the last century may not have thought to exempt married women because they obtained few abortions. Thus the statute, as written, would still act primarily to deter sexual activity by unmarried women. Secondly, the legislators may not have wanted to exempt married women because including them might have a deterrent effect on adulterous relationships. And thirdly, they also may not have wanted to exempt married women because their simultaneous purpose was to protect unborn life from being aborted by either a married or unmarried mother.

The brief's argument that the state employed its adultery and fornication statutes is ironic, because we are given good reason to believe that the appellants would not favor statutes like these either. A strong sense of this is conveyed by the following: the references to the individual's "sovereignty" and "autonomy"; the fact, as pointed out above, that the brief gives special emphasis to the right of personal privacy affecting matters of sex, procreation, and family; and also its citation of the New Women Lawyers brief on this point, which implies that the law cannot be used to enforce moral norms on matters such as sexuality.[86] Further evidence is seen in the fact that one organization that had a hand in preparing the appellants' case, the American Civil Liberties Union (ACLU), has, through its state affiliates, challenged the constitutionality of state adultery and fornication statutes in court.[87]

The *Wade* brief's statement about the "penalty" of pregnancy being a "monstrous intention" of the legislation is not only a further expression of the notion that pregnancy and child-bearing are terrible burdens, but arguably demonstrates a lack of understanding about nature. The brief seems to view pregnancy as a consequence of illicit sexual activity only because human law determines it should be. Actually it is not the law which makes the woman pregnant; the law only requires her not to destroy the child in her womb and carry him until birth. The brief does not consider what most people's common sense tells them: that pregnancy is the probable result of intercourse, and if a woman does not want to face the risk of becoming pregnant, she should not engage in it. In a sense, then, the possibility of pregnancy is nature's "deterrent" to non-marital sexual activity. I would not call it a "punishment," but rather just nature's way of making us assume the responsibility for our actions.

Now, let us turn to the brief's point about promiscuity and abortion laws, and its reference to Dr. Ryan. When we turn to the page in Ryan's article cited by the brief, we see him assert that there is no connection between such laws and the amount of promiscuity. He cites no studies or statistics to support this. Interestingly, he also claims there is no connection between promiscuity and the availability of contraception, while the brief concedes there may be such a connection.[89] The appellants' admission of this, while arguing for both the right to use contraceptives and the right to abortion as part of the right of privacy, makes it apparent that the spread of promiscuity is not a major concern of theirs.

The statements of the NWL brief about the unfairness of the abortion statutes to women and their undesirability in women's eyes are open to question. The brief says that the "two community" perspective that it takes is one in which it normally would not consider legislation.[90] (The implication is that the usual way it views men and women is as one homogeneous community, presumably with differences muted and legislation thus treating each alike. This latter point is borne out by the fact that laws placing all of their "weight and burden on only one sex" are "invidious discrimination." This would seem to preclude protective legislation for women in the workplace and, for that matter, rape laws.) The fact that it believes it justified to adopt such a perspective here suggests that the brief-writers will practice gender discrimination when it suits their purpose.

As mentioned, the NWL brief contends that women are victimized by these statutes since they were passed by male legislatures, which women had little influence over. This states a political philosophy which goes well beyond just the abortion question. It implicitly calls into question the very nature of representative government. What the brief says, in effect, is that a political official cannot possibly represent constituents unless he is of the same gender as them (and presumably the same race, ethnic group, religion, and whatever else). Not only is this contrary to a basic assumption of representative government, but is typically not borne out by our experience. We see examples every day of public officials whose positions are influenced by aroused citizens.

Secondly, the claim that "the community of women does not supoort these [abortion] laws" is simply not borne out by the facts. Demographer Judith Blake, mentioned earlier, has shown convincingly that American women are seriously divided on the issue of abortion and that a higher percentage of women than men have consistently opposed permissive abortion laws.[91]

The notion of the community's "moral fabric" which is put forth in the NWL brief is drastically at odds with the understanding that most of us have of this term. What we understand by it -- and what would be behind the state's thinking if it were justifying its abortion statute on these grounds -- is the shared moral principles of the community, which are guides for individual behavior and are not of man's making. If these moral principles are undercut or if most people violate them, the community will be morally weakened. The view presented by the brief identifies "moral fabric" with simply the positive law of the state. In this Hobbesian scheme, if the state's laws are violated -- regardless of the moral content of those laws -- the "moral fabric" is weakened. There is no mention of morality or moral norms. The brief merely seeks to change a law which prohibits a certain activity -- without any discussion of the moral worth of that activity -- so that the law, and hence the "moral fabric," are not undermined. We are left doubting whether law for the brief-writers is grounded in anything more than human preferences and desires. Indeed, all the briefs that I have considered make no attempt to base their arguments in a clearly enunciated scheme of morality or even in a discernible philosophy of natural rights.

Let us now consider whether there was any grounds to make the overbreadth argument in light of the rules on overbreadth laid down by the Supreme Court. Let us turn to what one constitutional expert, Professor Laurence H. Tribe of Harvard Law School, has said about this (on the basis of Court decisions):

> A plausible challenge to a law as *void for overbreadth* can be made only when (1) the protected activity is a significant part of the law's target, and (2) there exists no satisfactory way of severing the law's constitutionality from its unconstitutional applications so as to excise the latter clearly in a single step from the law's reach. ...Implicit in overbreadth analysis is the notion that a law should not be voided on its face unless its deterrence of protected activities is substantial.[92]

Most of the section of the *Wade* brief dealing with overbreadth addresses points other than the question of whether the statute infringes on constitutionally-protected activity. The point that *does* go to this directly concerns the failure of the statute to distinguish married from unmarried women. As we can judge from Tribe's statement, however, the issue of overbreadth really does not arise. This is because the "protected activity" which the brief is concerned about is licit -- i.e., marital -- sexual intercourse. An abortion statute in no way infringes upon this marital right. It simply prohibits the destruction of the baby resulting from such union.

Perhaps, it could be claimed that the statute was overbroad because it "deters" married couples from having sexual intercourse because they know that they cannot have abortions if pregnancies result. It is doubtful that even this claim holds water because, first, referring back to Tribe, it is unlikely that anyone could prove that the existence of an abortion statute actually is a "substantial" deterrent to married couples engaging in sexual intercourse. We had abortion statutes for over a hundred years and one would be hard-pressed to find examples of this kind of complaint against them issuing from married couples. Secondly, the "protected activity" of marital sexual intercourse was not a "significant part" of the statutes' concern. Any effect of the statutes on marital intercourse would be purely accidental and incidental. Thirdly, the brief bases its overbreadth claim on the Court's finding that the contraception statute in *Griswold*, because it intruded on the marital relationship, was overbroad. Again, however, the brief fails to make the crucial distinction between contraception and abortion. *Griswold* simply cannot be so readily used as a precedent for *Wade* and *Bolton* because they involve activities which are by their very nature different. Curiously, the brief believes that abortion and contraception statutes can be equated on this point even while it also acknowledges, on the very question of affecting the amount of sexual conduct, that (as mentioned above) contraception is more important than abortion. On one hand, it tells us that abortion statutes are a deterrent to marital sex, while on the other it insists that they are not a deterrent to pre-marital or extra-marital sex, but it gives us no rationale for this distinction.

What must be concluded from this is that the *Wade* brief has a very dubious basis for asserting an overbreadth claim against the Texas statute.

Vagueness

The vagueness argument was similarly weak. The *Wade* brief quotes an opinion of the Court as presenting the usual test of whether a statute is unconstitutionally vague:

> "...a statute which either forbids or requires the doing of an act in terms so vague that men of common intelligence must necessarily guess at its meaning and differs as to its application, violates the first essential of due process."[93]

The argument that the brief presents to support its vagueness point has little to do with vagueness, as thus defined. This section of the brief instead presents the same type of argument that the NLPHPP brief presented for equal protection. It tells how abortion practices before 1973 differed widely among hospitals and cites numerous authorities to back this up. It also cites authorities to try to emphasize its contention that abortion procedures deserve to be treated like any other health care matter and that the notion of "health" must be broadly understood. It tries to show that many more factors go into determining the state of a person's health than just physical ones. Psychiatric and sociological factors are also important. We realize, as we think back to the *Bolton* definition of "health" as involving "physical, emotional, psychological, and familial" factors and "the woman's age," that the Court accepted this view. The "vagueness" argument in the brief, in short, is mostly directed toward providing the rationale for the earlier claim that the physician's right to administer health care is violated by the statute.

The brief mentions the *Vuitch* case, which upheld the District of Columbia abortion statute from a challenge on vagueness grounds. It contends that *Vuitch* is not controlling, however, because the statute there was federal, not state, and the wording was different.[94]

The weakness -- and, indeed, irrelevance -- of

the vagueness argument in the *Wade* case can be seen simply by turning to the wording of the Texas statute. The pertinent sections were the following:

> (Article 1191). If any person shall designedly administer to a pregnant woman or knowingly procure to be administered with her consent any drug or medicine, or shall use towards her any violence or means whatever externally or internally applied, and thereby procure an abortion, he shall be confined in the penitentiary not less than two nor more than five years; if it be done without her consent, the punishment shall be doubled. By "abortion" is meant that the life of the fetus or embryo shall be destroyed in the woman's womb or that a premature birth thereof be caused.
>
> (Article 1192). Whoever furnishes the means for procuring an abortion knowing the purpose intended is guilty as an accomplice.
>
> (Article 1193). If the means used shall fail to procure an abortion, the offender is nevertheless guilty of an attempt to procure abortion, provided it be shown that such means were calculated to produce that result, and shall be fined not less than one hundred nor more than one thousand dollars.
>
> (Article 1194). If the death of the mother is occasioned by an abortion so procured or by an attempt to effect the same it is murder.
>
> (Article 1196). Nothing in this chapter applies to an abortion procured or attempted by medical advice for the purpose of saving the life of the mother.[95]

The brief's argument makes it clear that it is focusing on Article 1196. As we think back to the Court's definition of vagueness stated above, we can judge that a reasonable person would view the claim as not having merit. When the statute talks about "saving the life of the mother," almost anyone would understand this to mean preventing her death. The statute, then clearly tells physicians that abortion is permitted only to actually save a woman's life. The brief, with its attempt to argue that a broad understanding of "health" should be permitted to justify abortion, redefines the term "life" to mean, in effect, "quality of life." Abortion should be permitted whenever it is necessary to maintain -- in someone's (probably the pro-abortionists') sense of the term -- the quality of life of the woman. The statute is vague, then, only because the appellants and some other medical authorities want to assign a new definition to its phraseology.

As far as the brief's claims about *Vuitch* are concerned, the fact that the statutes in the two cases were from different levels of government is not pertinent. Now that most of the limitations of the Bill of Rights have been held to apply to the states, the only areas in which the legislation of the two levels would be held to a different standard of judicial review would be those in which the national government had greater authority to act or had preempted the subject matter in question. No such issue of federalism was involved in these abortion cases, however. The fact that one involved a federal statute and the other a state is irrelevant.

It is true the *Vuitch* statute had different wording than the one in *Wade*. This fact, however, would likely work *against* a vagueness claim in *Wade* rather than for it. This is because the former permitted abortions when the woman's health, instead of only her life, were threatened and the term "health" clearly leaves much more room for confusion and misinterpretation than "life." The appellants, then, were seeking to have the statute in *Wade* struck down for vagueness even though the Court had turned aside such a challenge to a more nebulously-worded statute in *Vuitch*.

The Court apparently did not accept the appellants' overbreadth and vagueness claims in *Wade*. More accurately, it did not address these points, and the arguments lack validity in light of established constitutional doctrine. Why, then, were points such as these made in the brief? Perhaps, they reflect the unfortunate and opportunistic tendency of too many lawyers involved in constitutional litigation to simply throw at a court any argument that might *conceivably* wash. They may also reflect a desire to alter language -- even obvious terms such as these -- in order to achieve the desired social and legal change. The redefinition of a term like "life," the misunderstanding of a common word such as "vague," and the willingness to substantially expand a legal notion like overbreadth in the *Wade* brief give further evidence of an attempt to reshape our beliefs by changing language.

Conclusions

My first conclusion concerns the notion of liberty presented. The notion of liberty is an expansive one, going well beyond the traditional notion of liberty as being actual physical restraint or incarceration. It views the individual as being free to engage in activities which were long considered within the authority of the state to regulate or prohibit under its police power. The philosophy presented is one of extreme individualism, of complete individual autonomy over an area of human endeavor which involves profound physical, moral, and philosophical considerations. There is a fundamental tension between not only the individual and the state but also the individual and more basic social institutions, such as the family. In all of these spheres, individual autonomy and prerogatives are seen as paramount.

The basis for the general notion of liberty and for the specific liberty asserted is primarily judicial decisions, i.e., positive law. There is no appeal to natural rights notions (as we shall see in a later Chapter), which were the foundation of the Declaration of Independence and the Constitution, the basic documents of our Republic. The appeal made to positive law also seems oblivious to the problem of whether law can justly and effectively function without acknowledging moral norms that have to underlie it.

The second conclusion concerns the notion of equality. We see expressed in the briefs the contemporary view of equality: the desire for an equality of liberty. There is a call in the NLPHPP brief for a drastic expansion of equal protection beyond previous Supreme Court decisions to achieve an equality of liberty for all to share in something which will make life more materially comfortable for them, regardless of the moral problems it creates. It is not an equality of political rights, but an equality of cultural liberties that some groups in society believe desirable and seek to extend to everyone. It is an equal right to pursue the "lifestyle" that they deem acceptable.

One also concludes from the briefs that an attempt was made to influence the Court about the need for abortion by changing the common meaning of language. This is seen particularly in the effort to make abortion into just another health care service by altering the meaning of such words as "life" and "well being." One sees also that the writers of the *Wade* brief structured it carefully, in order to create certain impressions in the minds of the Justices and lead them to certain conclusions.

Chapter Five

Unenumerated Rights and the Right of Privacy in the American Constitutional Tradition

As we saw, one of the main decisions the Supreme Court cited as a precedent for the right of privacy was *Griswold v. Connecticut*. *Griswold* can be seen as the genesis of the contemporary right of privacy since it was the first decision to apply this right to matters involving sex, reproduction, and the family. Although *Griswold* really is not a valid precedent for abortion, it is clear that without it there would not have been a *Wade* and *Bolton*.

Griswold and *Wade/Bolton* raise the questions about whether our early political thinking, from which the Bill of Rights emerged, held that there are rights which are not enumerated and, if so, if the Court has the authority to enunciate them. The latter has been the source of much contention on the Court since its beginning. I shall discuss both this continuing judicial debate and the thinking about this in the early days of our Republic in order to fit these decisions into a larger historical framework.

Next, I shall turn to the question of whether the right of privacy has a basis in the constitutional and political thought of the Framers' time. I shall examine the English legal background, the colonial experience, and the statements and documents of the early Republic. Finally, I shall trace the development of the right of privacy in modern Anglo-American law to determine whether it could have been logically construed to apply to contraception and abortion.

The *Griswold v. Connecticut* Opinions

The Opinion of the Court in *Griswold* was written by Justice Douglas, although it was joined by only one other Justice. Justices Goldberg, Harlan, and White wrote separate concurring opinions. Justices Black and Stewart wrote dissenting opinions. I shall discuss only the Douglas, Goldberg, and Black opinions because they contain the key substantive arguments.

The case came to the Court as an appeal of a conviction of two persons connected with a Connecticut birth control clinic for giving married persons information and medical advice on contraception and prescribing contraceptive materials for them. The state's statute made it a crime for any person, married or unmarried, to use contraceptives, or for any person to "assist, abet, counsel, cause, hire or command" their use by another. Even though no married couples were prosecuted for use, the Court permitted the convicted "abettors" to raise the former's rights in order to challenge the use section of the statute. It struck down the statute as a violation of the right of marital privacy.

Douglas saw the case as involving the freedom of association between husband and wife. He acknowledged that this right is not mentioned in the Constitution or the Bill of Rights, but claimed that it is protected nevertheless by a "penumbra" of the First Amendment. This penumbra he said, protects privacy from governmental intrusion. He thus linked privacy partially to the freedom of association, citing one case, *NAACP v. Alabama*, in which he claimed the Court acted to protect the "'freedom to associate and privacy in one's associations.'"[1]

Douglas said there are other specific guarantees

of the Bill of Rights, which create "zones" protecting the penumbral right of privacy. He mentioned the Third Amendment, which affords a protection of the privacy of one's home from having soldiers quartered there without his consent; the Fourth Amendment, which protects persons from unreasonable searches and seizures; the Fifth Amendment, which protects an individual's privacy by permitting him to refuse to testify against himself; and the Ninth Amendment, which, of course, guarantees that other rights not enumerated in the Constitution are still to be respected.

When Douglas discussed freedom of association immediately after discussing the relationships between husband and wife, and married couple and physician, he suggested that the right involved in *Griswold* is grounded in the penumbras of the First Amendment. He did not really specify, however, which specific amendment's penumbras are the basis for it. He said that the case "concerns a relationship [marriage] which lies within the zone of privacy created by *several* fundamental constitutional guarantees."[2] In his last paragraph, he says that "[w]e deal with a right of privacy older than the Bill of Rights..."[3] His suggestion is that the rights attendant to marriage predated the Constitution and so were understood as being protected by it, even though it does not specifically mention them. Douglas thus stated the constitutional perspective underlying his opinion: there are rights which, while not spelled out in the body of the Constitution or its amendments, are fundamental to a democratic people and must be protected.

Justice Goldberg's concurring opinion -- joined by Chief Justice Warren and Justice Brennan -- contended that the right of marital privacy is protected by the Ninth Amendment, and is also based on the previous decisions of the Court. He saw it included in the Constitution's "concept of liberty"[4] and applied to the states through the Fourteenth Amendment. He quoted James Madison and Justice Joseph Story who said the sum total of individual rights were not *just* those spelled out in the first eight amendments. Thus, the Court can act to protect other rights. He says that in doing this, the Justices "are not left at large to decide cases in light of their personal and private notions."[5] He says that they must use as their reference point the "'fundamental principles of liberty and justice which lie at the base of all our civil and political institutions.'"[6] He concludes that the right of privacy is such a fundamental right.

The importance of Goldberg's opinion, then, is that it asserts the right of *personal*, as opposed to *marital*, privacy is fundamental. He quotes Justice Brandeis' dissenting opinion in *Olmstead v. U.S.*, also quoted in the *Wade* brief, which asserts the essentiality of this right:

> "The protection guaranteed by the [Fourth and Fifth] Amendments is much broader in scope. The makers of our Constitution... conferred, as against the Government, the right to be let alone -- the most comprehensive of rights and the right most valued by civilized men."[7]

That Goldberg spoke of the right of personal privacy does not necessarily negate what I said previously about *Griswold* not being a precedent for the *Wade* decision, because it related strictly to *marital* privacy. It must be remembered that Goldberg wrote only for himself and two other Justices, not for a majority of the Court. *A concurring opinion does not stand as a precedent to base future decisions upon.* Moreover, Goldberg shifted gears at the end of the opinion by stating he speaks of "the right of privacy in the marital relation."[8] He also made clear that he would not extend this right to other sexual matters when he says that the constitutionality of adultery and fornication statutes is "beyond doubt."[9]

Goldberg's basis for asserting that the right of marital privacy is fundamental rests on previous decisions of the Court, which granted special constitutional protection for the realm of the family and the activity of child-rearing. He also considered the reason why the law has characteristically sought to protect the home. It is not just because of long-existing property rights, but mostly because it is the center of family life. Finally, he appealed to tradition and said that the family relation is "as old and as fundamental as our entire civilization."[10]

Let me make these observations about the Court's and Goldberg's opinions. First, Goldberg's claim about the limitation of the Justices' discretion by "fundamental principles" and the like is really not much of a limitation. This is because it is too vague and general. It does not provide any guide as to what are the unenumerated rights guaranteed to the people. Goldberg nowhere gave any idea of how these rights are to be identified. Second, Goldberg did not tell us why the right to use contraceptives is to be judged a fundamental right. Indeed, he did not tell us precisely what is meant by a "fundamental right." Third, his explanation that the denial of the use of contraceptives to married persons must be considered an infringement on family rights because the opposite, a law requiring compulsory birth control, would clearly be unconstitutional, is unsatisfactory. He did not explain why the two types of prohibitions are as closely related as he claimed. The *Wade* and *Bolton* decisions demonstrate the ineffectiveness of the requirement of appealing to "fundamental principles" as a check on the Court.

The point that must be noted about both the Douglas and Goldberg opinions is that while each tried to establish the truth of the notion that there are fundamental rights not enumerated in the Constitution and amendments, and the existence of one particular fundamental right, both do it by appealing primarily to past Supreme Court decisions. That is, they appeal to positive law in order to show the existence of something like natural rights, instead of stating a particular theory of natural rights or trying to demonstrate, by philosophical reasoning, an appeal to specific elements of our democratic tradition or history. They did not even try commonsensical arguments about why these rights are inherent in the nature of man or a democratic order.

Black's argument reflects a position he long advocated: the *only* rights are those which are expressly spelled out in the Bill of Rights, and in order to declare a statute or governmental action unconstitutional, the Court must make reference to a particular constitutional provision. He believed that using the Goldberg formula of appealing to "natural justice" or "civilized standards of conduct" would result in the Justices making decisions about constitutionality only according to their own discretion or whim. He said that such a notion gives the Court "awesome veto powers over lawmaking."[11] He insisted the Ninth Amendment was not intended to broaden the Court's or the national government's powers, but "to assure the people that the Constitution in all its provisions was intended to limit the Federal Government to the powers granted expressly or by necessary implication."[12] Black did not say he did not believe there is something called "natural justice" or whatever; he merely believed that it is "mysterious and uncertain"[13] -- that such notions are "regulated by no fixed standard"[14] -- and that Justices of the Supreme Court are not competent to discern it.

An Historical Survey of the On-going Constitutional Debate About Whether the Supreme Court Can Make Decisions on the Basis of Unenumerated Rights, "Natural Justice," Etc.

The debate between Douglas and Goldberg on one side and Black on the other in *Griswold* continued a two-hundred-year-old controversy on the Supreme Court.

The first major clash about this on the Court occurred in the 1798 case of *Calder v. Bull.*[15] Justice Samuel Chase claimed the courts have the authority to declare legislative enactments, either of state legislatures or Congress, void even though they violate no express constitutional provision. He stated his position as follows:

> I cannot subscribe to the omnipotence of a state Legislature, or that it is absolute and without control; although its authority should not be expressly restrained by the constitution, or fundamental law, of the state...There are acts which the federal, or state, Legislature cannot do, without exceeding their authority. *There are certain vital principles in our free Republican governments,*

> which will determine and overrule an apparent and flagrant abuse of legislative power...[16]

Justice Chase, of course, addressed himself more to the question of limiting legislative power without reference to express constitutional provisions than to enunciating rights not expressly spelled out. We are, however, talking about two facets of the same problem. When the Court in *Griswold* enunciated a right to use contraceptives it was correspondingly denying to the legislatures an area in which to continue making law. The issue remains the same when framed in either way: Can the Supreme Court make decisions, particularly as they relate to the relationship between government and the individual, without being able to premise them on express constitutional provisions? Chase thought the answer is "yes," and that the powers of government and the substance of individual rights must be in accordance with the basic principles of republican government, whether spelled out in the Constitution or not. This is because he understood, implicitly, that that purpose of the Constitution is to preserve these principles.

Justice James Iredell argued against Chase. Like Black, he did not say he did not believe there are principles of "natural justice," but simply that -- because these principles "are regulated by no fixed standard" -- courts cannot base decisions upon them. He was concerned that Chase's notion will lead to judges acting on their own discretion. (He spoke of them believing "in their judgment" and "in the[ir] opinion" that a law contravenes natural justice.) He contended that since all American constitutions carefully delineated the parameters of legislative power, the law courts must strictly follow them -- and not go beyond them -- when declaring an act void.[17]

In the *Slaughter-House Cases* (1872), both the majority and the dissenters recognized there are unenumerated rights which are included under the privilege and immunities clause of the Fourteenth Amendment, but disagreed about how extensively the Court should protect them. The Court's (majority) opinion said the following:

> Now what are "privileges and immunities" in the sense of the Constitution? They are undoubtedly *the personal and civil rights which*

> *usage, tradition, the habits of society, written law, and the common sentiments of people have recognized as forming the basis of the institutions of the country.*[18]

Included among these "personal and civil rights" are the right to acquire and possess property and to pursue and obtain happiness and safety. They are subject, however, to legal restraints for "the general good of the whole."[19] In this case, the "general good" allowed a state legislature to permit only certain slaughter-houses to be in business.

The dissenters, Justices Stephen J. Field and Joseph P. Bradley, said the following in support of the notion of unenumerated rights. These are Field's words referring to the Civil Rights Act of 1868: "[t]he privileges and immunities designated are *those which of right belong to the citizens of all free governments."* These include the right in question in the case, that of pursuing lawful employment.[20] Bradley concurred this right is protected and says: "...even if the Constitution were silent, *the fundamental privileges and immunities of citizens*...would be no less real and no less inviolable than they are now."[21]

This case is like *Calder* and *Griswold* in that neither side denied there are principles of natural justice -- in fact, both contend there are --, but unlike them in that none of the Justices are expressly unwilling to have the Court defend them. The majority simply showed a *reluctance* to do so.

In *Lochner v. New York* (1905),[22] the acceptance of unenumerated rights by the Court was implicit in its opinion -- scholars subsequently came to refer to this as "substantive due process" -- and Justice John M. Harlan's (the first Justice John M. Harlan) dissent was critical of it in the same way as Black. The Court appealed to some notion of natural justice when it said that in cases that come before the Court involving social and economic regulatory legislation -- *Lochner* concerned a New York statute regulating employment conditions in bakeries -- the following question must be asked: "Is this a fair, reasonable and appropriate exercise of the police power of the State, or is it an unreasonable, unnecessary and arbitrary interference with the right of the individual to his personal liberty or to enter into contracts in relation to labor...?"[23] It is clear that there is an appeal to unenumerated rights, because the right to make labor contracts does not appear in the Constitution, and the notion of "personal liberty" is, by its nature, vague.

Justice Harlan wrote the following in his dissenting opinion, and was joined by Justices Day and Edward D. White:

> [W]hat are the conditions under which the judiciary may declare such [social and economic] regulations to be in excess of legislative authority and void?...the State is not amenable to the judiciary...unless such enactments are *plainly, palpably, beyond all question,* inconsistent with the constitution of the United States.[24]

In other words, Harlan said there can be disagreement among men about what the notions of "fair, reasonable, and appropriate" mean, so the Court must stick with the express provisions of the Constitution.

The debate between Harlan and the others on the Court is seen again in two late nineteenth and early twentieth century cases which involved the question of whether certain provisions of the Bill of Rights applied to the states. Harlan was on the opposite side in these, however. In *Hurtado v. California* (1884),[25] the Court stated there are principles of "liberty and justice, lying at the foundation of our civil and political institutions" which, whether enumerated or not, cannot be violated by government.[26] The Court said, however, that these do not include the right to a grand jury indictment in a capital case.[27]

Harlan disagreed with this conclusion, saying the Court had failed to take note of an important unenumerated right. He says the following:

> This [the Court's] line of argument, it seems to me would lead to results which are inconsistent with *the vital principles of republican government.*[28]...there is no foundation for the opinion that, under *Magna Carta* or at common law, the right to a trial by jury in a capital case was deemed of any greater value...

> than was the right not to answer, in a capital case, upon a mere information...[29]

In the other case, *Twining v. New Jersey* (1908),[30] the question was whether the Fifth Amendment guarantee of the right to be exempt from compulsory self-incrimination applies to the states under the due process clause of the Fourteenth Amendment. The Court examined the history of this right in English law and its status in the law of the states at the time of the ratification of the Fifth Amendment and, giving an indication that the notion of natural justice is one of its considerations, said:

> This survey does not tend to show that it was then in this country the universal or even general belief that the privilege ranked among *the fundamental or inalienable rights of mankind;* and...it affirmatively shows that the privilege was not conceived to be inherent in due process of law...[31]

The essence of Harlan's dissent was that the Court was simply incorrect in its contention that the right against self-incrimination was not historically fundamental to Anglo-American law. Again, the disagreement was not about whether there are unenumerated rights, but about whether this particular right is among them.

The issue of government restricting the supposed right to make labor contracts came up again in *Adkins v. Children's Hospital* (1923).[32] The Court again appealed to an unenumerated right which it claimed was implied by the Fifth Amendment, and the same objection as Black stated in *Griswold* was raised by one of the dissenters, Justice Oliver Wendell Holmes, Jr.: that permitting the Court to decide a case by making such an appeal to unenumerated rights can result in unchecked discretion on the part of the Justices. Stating how the Court had previously expanded the "innocuous generality" of the liberty to follow ordinary callings into the "dogma" of liberty of contract, which is not mentioned in the Constitution, Holmes contended that this was "merely an example of doing what you want to do, embodied in the word liberty."[33] The Court, he argued, was doing the same thing here and he admonished it to remember that "[t]he criterion of constitutionality is not whether we believe the [particular] law to be for the public good."[34]

Betts v. Brady (1942)[35] was the first of a series of cases leading up to *Griswold* which pitted Black against others on the Court on this issue. He took the opposite position that he took in *Griswold*. As in *Hurtado* and *Twining*, both sides agreed that the notion of natural justice should be taken into account by courts, but disagreed about whether it was applicable in this case. The issue in the case was whether a person's due process rights were violated because he was not given legal counsel when accused of a serious, but non-capital, crime and unable to pay for counsel himself. The Court held that they were not and said the following:

> ...the Fourteenth Amendment prohibits the conviction and incarceration of one whose trial is offensive to *the common and fundamental ideas of fairness and right*, and while want of counsel in a particular case may result in a conviction lacking in such fundamental fairness, we cannot say that the Amendment embodies an inexorable command that no trial for any offense, or in any court, can be fairly conducted and justice accorded a defendant who is not represented by counsel.[36]

It went on to say this:

> That which may, in one setting, constitute a denial of *fundamental fairness, shocking to the universal sense of justice*, may, in other circumstances, and in light of other considerations, fall short of such denial.[37]

Black strongly challenged the Court in his dissenting opinion, which was joined by Justices Douglas and Murphy:

> Denial to the poor of the request for counsel in proceedings based on charges of serious crime has long been regarded as shocking to the *"universal sense of justice" throughout this country*...Any other practice seems to me to defeat the promise of our democratic society to provide equal justice under the law.[38]

Black did not express his later concern that such broad standards as these might give too much discretion to Justices.

In the 1947 case of *Adamson v. California*,[39] Justice Black firmly lined up on the other side of the issue. He put forth for the first time his argument that the Court must rely strictly on enumerated rights and cannot decide cases with reference to a "natural-law-due-process formula." He proposed that what the Court should do instead was to apply the entire Bill of Rights to the states. (This has been called "nationalizing" the Bill of Rights.) He proposed this alternative so the Justices do not "roam at large in the broad expanses of policy and morals and to trespass, all too freely, on the legislative domain of the States as well as the Federal Government."[40]

Justice Felix Frankfurter's concurring opinion defended the Court's authority to appeal to "natural law" principles. (The Court did not find such principles violated, however, by the state law in question which permitted the prosecution to comment to the jury about an accused's failure to testify at his trial. It said that this did not violate self-incrimination.) He said the following:

> If all that is meant is that due process contains within itself certain minimal standards which are "of *the very essence of a scheme of ordered liberty*"..., putting upon this Court the duty of applying these standards from time to time, then we have merely arrived at the insight which our predecessors long ago expressed.
>
> Judicial review of that guaranty of the Fourteenth Amendment [due process] inescapably imposes upon this Court an exercise of judgment upon the whole course of the proceedings in order to ascertain whether they offend those *canons of decency and fairness which express the notions of justice of English-speaking peoples* even toward those charged with the most heinous offenses.[41]

The conflict of constitutional views between Justices Frankfurter and Black continued in the 1952 case of *Rochin v. California*.[42] This case was an appeal on due process grounds of a conviction for narcotics possession. The police had forced their way into the petitioner's house and then into his bedroom where he was with his wife and he quickly swallowed two pills that had been on a night stand next to the bed. After failing to recover the pills themselves, the police took him to a hospital where they forced him to submit to having his stomach pumped. The pills that were thus retrieved were used as the evidence to convict him. The Supreme Court reversed the conviction.

Justice Frankfurter, writing for the Court, said that the due process clause "'inescapably imposes upon this Court an exercise of judgment upon the whole course of the proceedings [resulting in a conviction] in order to ascertain whether they offend *those canons of decency and fairness which express the notions of justice of English-speaking peoples* even toward those charged with the most heinous offenses.'"[43] He goes on to phrase this somewhat differently: "Due process of law is a summarized constitutional guarantee of respect for those personal immunities which...are '*so rooted in the traditions and conscience of our people as to be ranked as fundamental...*' or are '*implicit in the concept of ordered liberty.*'"[44] He further contends that "[c]oerced confessions [like the one here] offend *the community's sense of fair play and decency.*"[45]

Justice Black's *Rochin* concurrence again stressed the fact that there are no settled, readily intelligible natural law norms. He criticized the Court's resort to "nebulous standards."[46] He again insisted that the best guarantee of individual liberty is "faithful adherence to the specific guarantees in the Bill of Rights" and suggested that the Court's view of due process will give it "unlimited power to invalidate laws."[47]

We can see, then, that the argument about whether the Court can make decisions on the basis of unenumerated rights that are only vaguely implied by the Constitution had a long history before *Griswold*. Pursuant to the above survey of it, we can make these conclusions and observations. The Justices of the Court have not disputed the existence of unenumerated rights or notions of natural law, "fundamental fairness," etc. The disagreement has arisen over whether the Court can go ahead and enunciate such rights or notions and make decisions pursuant to them when it cannot clearly infer them from the Constitution's words and provisions. The major danger of this, according to the many dissenting Justices I have considered, is that, if this prerogative is acknowledged, Justices will use it to make decisions according to their own whim and policy preferences. When we consider the fact that in cases like *Lochner* and *Adkins* the Court was unable to give any basis for the "right" it claimed to be protecting and the Justices who have defended the appeal to natural justice have been unable to clearly enunciate how to go about deciding what its principles are, we can see that this danger is a valid one.

There is another point that is observed in decisions like *Lochner*, *Adkins*, and *Griswold*. That is that while the Court explicitly appeals to "the notions of justice of English-speaking peoples," "personal immunities...'rooted in the traditions and consciences of our people,'" "fundamental principles of liberty and justice which lie at the base of all our civil and political institutions," and "a right of privacy older than the Bill of Rights," it perhaps really responds to contemporary views about what activities are to be protected as "rights." Generally, these views are those of an elite opinion-shaping group in the political society, as I showed in Chapter One. In Chapter Eight, we will see how the notion of "rights" it relies on is drastically different from that which underlies the political thought of our Framers. In *Lochner* and *Adkins*, it responded to *laissez-faire*-oriented business interests seeking to stave off government regulation. In *Griswold*, it responded to the medical profession, "progressive" religious leaders, the burgeoning population control and "family planning" fraternity, and upper and upper middle class opinion generally, which had largely accepted the moral liceity of contraception. It is true that it did not use words in any of these opinions which indicate that it uses contemporary public or elite opinion as its guide in enumerating rights. Commentators, however, have overwhelmingly considered this an accurate interpretation of the string of "substantive due process" cases that *Lochner* and *Adkins* are part of.[48] The main brief in *Griswold* was so sure that this would be an influential point with the Court that it went to much length to show how widely contemporary opinion accepted contraception and how the medical profession particularly had come to see it as an important and necessary part of health care.[49] By the time of *Wade* and *Bolton*, as I have shown, the Court had little reluctance in openly relying heavily on one part of the elite opinion of America, the medical profession.

The Thinking About Unenumerated Rights in the Early American Republic

In this Section, I shall look briefly at the views expressed in the political discourse of the early United States about the existence of unenumerated rights. We will look into the debate over a written Bill of Rights that took place between the Federalists and the Anti-Federalists during the ratification struggles over the Constitution and in the First Congress, which finally proposed it.

I shall then consider briefly the question of what the role of the Supreme Court should be if the existence of unenumerated rights is admitted. About this, I shall look to two important documents of early American history, Federalist 78 and the Court's opinion in *Marbury v. Madison.*[50]

Did the Bill of Rights Enumerate All Individual Rights?

Storing surveyed the major points in the debate on the Bill of Rights. Although the evidence is by no means certain, the Anti-Federalists are a good source to turn to because they were the primary agitators for a written Bill of Rights and their view finally prevailed. If even *they* believed that there remained rights which had not been enumerated, it is clear that this would have been a widely shared view in the early Republic. This part of the inquiry is begun by considering the major arguments that the Anti-Federalists put forth for enactment of a Bill of Rights in order to see if the idea of unenumerated rights fits into them.

The first reason the Anti-Federalists stated was that rights, once spelled out, could not be interpreted and distinguished out of existence by the government, and that people could use the statement of rights as a forceful argument against the government if it tried to intrude upon them. As one Anti-Federalist said, "'a declaration of those inherent and political rights ought to be made in a BILL OF RIGHTS, that the people may never lose their liberties by construction.'"[51]

The second reason was stated by "Brutus" (Robert Yates):

> "The powers, rights, and authority, granted to the general government by this constitution, are as complete, with respect to every object to which they extend, as that of any state government -- It reaches to every thing which concerns human happiness -- Life, liberty, and property, are under its control. There is the same reason, therefore, that the exercise of power, in this case, should be restrained within proper limits, as in that of the state governments."[52]

In other words, the federal government has certain powers within its sphere, just as the states do within theirs, so it, like them, must have those powers limited *vis-à-vis* individuals by a Bill of Rights. This is especially so because the federal government was given the broad power to enact all laws "necessary and proper" to carry out its specifically delegated powers.[53]

Thirdly, the existence of state bills of rights was not enough to constrain the federal government because the Constitution "is an original compact" and "'is not dependent on any other book for an explanation... All the defenses of it...so far as they are drawn from the state constitutions, or from maxims of the common law, are foreign to the purpose.'"[54]

Another argument was that while, on the level of logical argument, the contention that no limitations need be made on governmental power over those activities may be true, this may not protect the people on the real-life level. Nor could the Federalist argument -- made forcefully by Hamilton in Federalist 84 -- that a Bill of Rights would actually be dangerous because it would imply that the government actually has these powers be accepted. As one Anti-Federalist said: "'This is indeed a distinction of which the votaries of scholastic philosophy might be proud -- but in the political world, where reason is not cultivated independently of act and experience, such futile distinctions ought not to be agitated.'"[55]

A fifth argument made by the Anti-Federalists was that, in order for a government to be legitimately created, it must first preserve the peoples' "'essential natural rights,'" to use "Brutus'" terms.[56] Furthermore, to answer the common Federalist argument, a popular government needs a Bill of Rights in order to protect these rights of the minority from usurpation by the majority.[57]

In any event, it was said, there was a need for a Bill of Rights simply because there were so few checks provided against federal encroachment on individual rights in the Constitution, despite the new government's vast powers and the limitations it imposed on popular government.[58]

My observation about these Anti-Federalist reasons for a Bill of Rights is that they suggest the need for rights to be enumerated if they are to be protected. To allow any rights to remain unenumerated would seem to leave them open to being "lost by construction." Nevertheless, there is nothing in the quotes above which states that there are no rights which men have which are not enumerated. The last reference from "Brutus," however, makes it clear that they believed that all the *essential* rights had to be enumerated. (And from this, we can reasonably conclude -- my survey below of the earlier sources of rights affirms this -- that they *were* enumerated.) The fact that Madison proposed what became the Ninth Amendment and Congress went on to vote for it, having deferred to Anti-Federalist sentiment on the question of the Bill of Rights, is, of course, the strongest statement that the backers of the Bill of Rights believed that there were other rights which were not enumerated.

The important question, however, is whether they believed that these unenumerated rights *already* existed. The emphasis on natural rights in the Declaration of Independence -- written by the preeminent Anti-Federalist, Jefferson -- suggests that they did. After all, men were "endowed by their Creator" with these rights.[59] Apart from this natural rights philosophy, our survey of the sources of Anglo-American rights shows us that new specific rights were won after struggles in the political arena. Either men got kings to make concessions after political and military conflicts or Parliament passed a statute establishing some new right. Rights were not just fashioned by the courts where they had previously not been known. This all suggests that in the political thought of the Framers' time, natural rights were viewed as always existing and the specific political rights which gave meaning and application to them were created by political -- not judicial -- actions. Thus, nothing stopped a legislature from creating new specific rights, but we get no sense of the courts having the authority to do so.

Sir Edward Coke's writings confirm the points I have made in the above paragraphs. In the words of Professor Corwin, he saw the Magna Carta -- the product of a *political* struggle -- as "the great muniment of English liberties."[60] Coke says that the Magna Carta -- which he emphasized is a "statute"(i.e., something affirmed by subsequent enactment by the legislative body, the Parliament) -- is "'the fountain of all the fundamental laws of the realm.'"[61] It was thus Parliament which created the rights of Englishmen, not courts. The suggestion that this was the proper manner of doing things for Coke is seen not only in his exhortation of the *statute* of Magna Carta as the fundamental law -- which even Parliament cannot contravene with other statutes -- but in the distinction he draws between Parliament and a court. According to Edward S. Corwin, he classifies Parliament "as primarily a *court*, albeit a court which may make new law *as well as declare the old*."[62] (The implication is that a law court could do only the latter.)

Moreover, the statements made by those involved in the debate over a Bill of Rights and by members of the First Congress (i.e., the First House) give a strong sense of rights as pre-existing. (The emphasized words that follow make this point.) The Federalist James

Wilson argued against a Bill of Rights by saying that it was unnecessary to stipulate that "'we should enjoy those privileges of which *we are not divested.*'"[63] Another Federalist took the same view, saying that "'[*m*]*en in full possession and enjoyment of all their natural rights*, cannot lose them but in two ways, either from their own consent, or from tyranny.'"[64] The "Federal Farmer," in calling for a Bill of Rights, admitted that it could not add anything to men's natural rights.[65] He stated that "'[*w*]*e do not by declarations change the nature of things, or create new truths...*'"[66] In a letter to Jefferson, Madison had written that a Bill of Rights would be valuable because "[t]he political truths declared in that solemn manner acquire by degrees the character of fundamental maxims of free Government..."[67] His use of the word "truths" suggests that the rights to be referred to have been always existing.

Statements from the members of the First Congress indicate the same view. Madison says that a Bill of Rights will "expressly *declare* the great rights of mankind."[68] The term "declare" -- which means "to make known clearly; to announce officially; proclaim; to state emphatically; to manifest; reveal; show; and to make due statement of"[69] -- makes clear the idea that the rights in question already were existing. He also refers to bills of rights needing to agree with "the common ideas of liberty."[70] He also speaks of "rights expressly *stipulated* for in the constitution by the *declaration* of rights."[71] (To "stipulate" means to arrange expressly.)[72] Representative Jackson's first speech against a Bill of Rights expresses in numerous places this same idea of rights already existing.[73] Representative Sherman also refers to the amendments being "a *declaration* of rights" and says that "the people are secure in them, whether we *declare* them or not."[74]

The impression given in all these statements that I have cited is that the Framers and their contemporaries understood that man's rights (i.e., their essential, natural rights) already existed; they only needed to be declared in the appropriate manner. The statements give no indication of a belief that essential rights can change or that new ones can be fashioned to meet new perceived needs. Indeed, this would seem compatible with the Framers'views about natural rights.

Can the Courts Create New Rights?

Even if the Framers *did* believe that essential rights could change or be added to by men, did they believe that it would be appropriate for the judiciary to be the institution to do this? I have already shown from Coke that the English said "no" to this. We can get a sense of how the Framers viewed this from two famous early documents, Federalist 78 and the Supreme Court's opinion in *Marbury v. Madison*.

In Federalist 78, Hamilton makes it clear that the courts must strictly adhere to the Constitution in making their judgments. It is the courts' job to make sure that the Constitution -- the "fundamental law" -- takes precedence over and is not violated by any other subsequent law: "...that which has the superior obligation and validity ought...to be preferred...in other words, the Constitution ought to be preferred to the statute, the intention of the people to the intention of their agents."[75] He says that "this conclusion... [does not] suppose a superiority of the judicial to the legislative power. It only supposes that the power of the people is superior to both..."[76] He further declares that "[i]t can be of no weight to say that the courts, on the pretence of a repugnancy, may substitute their own pleasure to the constitutional intentions of the legislature"[77] and "[t]o avoid an arbitrary discretion in the courts, it is indispensable that they should be bound down by strict rules and precedents."[78]

These references clearly tell us that the Framers intended that the courts be bound to acting according to the provisions of the Constitution -- which includes the Bill of Rights -- and that they were to have no legislative power. Hamilton's statements are, of course, subject to some interpretation, but taken on their face -- and coupled with the admonition that judges be strictly bound to precedent -- they would seem to preclude the courts' inventing any rights that are not found in the Constitution or its natural rights and common law background.[79]

Both Federalist 78 and *Marbury v. Madison*, the

case that established judicial review, suggest that the fact of the courts' being bound to act according to the Constitution means that they must adhere quite strictly to its written provisions. This further precludes the possibility that the Framers and their early progeny could have viewed the courts as having the power to create new rights. The words I emphasize in the following quotes support my contention. Federalist 78 says that it is the courts' duty "to declare all acts contrary to the *manifest tenor* of the Constitution void."[80] In declaring the Supreme Court's authority to declare acts of Congress unconstitutional, Chief Justice John Marshall said this in his opinion for the Court in *Marbury:*

> Those, then, who controvert the principle, that the constitution is to be considered, in court, as a paramount law, are reduced to the necessity of maintaining that courts must close their eyes on the constitution, and see only the law. This doctrine would subvert the very foundation of all *written constitutions*. It would declare that an act which, according to the principles and theory of our government, is entirely void, is yet, in practice completely obligatory. It would declare, that if the legislature shall do what is *expressly forbidden*, such act, notwithstanding the *express provision*, is in reality effectual. It would be giving to the legislature a practical and real omnipotence, with the same breath which professes to restrict their powers within narrow limits. *That it thus reduces to nothing, what we have deemed to be the greatest improvement on political institutions, a written constitution*, would, of itself, be sufficient, in America, where written constitutions have been viewed with so much reverence, for rejecting the constitution.[81]

Conclusions

The political thought of the Framers' time held that unenumerated rights do exist above and beyond those which are stated in the Bill of Rights. This was believed even by the Anti-Federalist promoters of the Bill of Rights. These unenumerated rights seem to have been viewed as always existing in nature, and only had to be discovered and enunciated by man; no new "natural" rights could be created by men and none could be taken away. A consideration of the early American view of the judicial power indicates that the courts had no authority to create such "new" fundamental rights -- if we are to equate fundamental rights with natural rights -- nor to legislate generally.

The meaning of all this is, of course, that the Supreme Court acted improperly in *Griswold* and *Wade/Bolton* if the right of privacy -- as applied to reproductive activities -- was not present in our natural law and common law tradition. (I previously demonstrated that the right to abortion *per se* was not part of our common law tradition as claimed by the Court in *Wade*.) The remainder of this Chapter will inquire into whether the right of privacy itself was part of this tradition or whether it was understood historically to be a natural right. It will also consider whether this right, if it was understood to exist in some way, was seen as applying to reproductive matters.

Which Are Our "Fundamental" Rights and Was the Right of Privacy Among Them?

The English Common Law

The American notion of rights had its beginnings,

of course, in England. As historian Robert Allen Rutland of the University of Virginia has written:

> ...the American Revolution had its seeds in the Puritan Revolt of English forebears, with the avowed purpose of giving citizens the freedoms won a century earlier in the mother country.
>
> ...Among their other accomplishments, the managers of the American Revolution were well-read in English constitutional history, and they therefore knew the historical background of their desired rights.[82]

Roscoe Pound, a famous American jurist and legal scholar, agreed that the American colonists adopted the rights of Englishmen. The Continental Congress' Declaration of Rights of 1774 "claims the rights secured by royal charters and the benefit of the common law." Pound shows that the language of the 1774 Declaration clearly goes back to the Magna Carta, the Petition of Right of 1627, and the English Bill of Rights of 1688.[83] We should, then, go back to these documents to begin our search for the rights that the Framers viewed as essential.[84]

The Magna Carta established several categories of rights which formed the basis for English law. The first of these was freedom of the Church to operate without undue state interference. King John promised that "the English church shall be free, and shall have her rights entire, and her liberties inviolate."[85] Another -- comprising a large part of the document -- were various rights of private property. One of these rights was that property cannot be taken arbitrarily without making a fair payment. Some elementary guarantees of due process were also set out, such as those providing that "[n]o freeman shall be arrested, or detained in prison, or deprived of his freehold, or outlawed, or banished, or in any way molested...unless by the lawful judgment of his peers and by the law of the land" and promising that anyone "dispossessed or removed..., without legal judgment of his peers, from his lands, castles, franchises, or from his right" shall have these restored.[86] Clearly, trial by a jury of one's peers was viewed as fundamental even at this early time.

Other provisions were present which guaranteed

fairness in the administration of justice, such as those prohibiting that anything "be given or taken for a writ of inquisition of life or limbs" and pledging that only persons who "know the law of the realm and mean to observe it well" be appointed as constables, sheriffs, and the like.[87] There was also a provision that the punishment given to freemen should be in accordance with the gravity of their offenses. Other provisions guaranteed the free movement of merchants and all law-abiding subjects to and from the realm.

In 1642, Coke spelled out the rights of Englishmen from the Magna Carta in his "Commentary on the Magna Carta" from his *Second Institute*. Most of these involved the requirements of due process of law. He said that no man should be deprived of his liberty -- "because the liberty of a man's person is more precious to him, than all the rest that follow" -- or property or be declared an outlaw or exiled, except by due process of law.[88] He specified the occasions in which noblemen had to be given trials by their peers and those in which a jury trial of any twelve men was acceptable. He emphasized the right of the accused to have his trial conducted fairly and to have no evidence put forth except in his presence. Coke also said that due process requires "indictment or presentment of good and lawfull men." He also states that all these procedural guarantees, while written down in the Magna Carta, are "but declaratory of the old law of England."[89]

Coke also emphasized that "No man [is] to be arrested, or imprisoned contrary to the forme of the great charter" (i.e., without a warrant, except in certain cases) and the importance of *habeas corpus*.[90]

Coke thus seems to see the central rights of Englishmen as involving the various protections of due process.

The Petition of Right also emphasized that due process had to be guaranteed. It claimed the continued applicability of the Magna Carta and various other statutes protecting civil liberties. It also mentioned a few other rights that have not been stated up to now. One was the requirement that subjects "not be compelled to contribute to any tax, tallage, aid or other charge not set by common consent in Parliament."[91] Another was the quartering of troops in private homes without the consent of the owners. A third provided that "none be called to make answer, or take such oath, or to give attendance, or be confined, or otherwise molested or disquieted concerning the same, or for refusal thereof.[92] This refers, in part, to a right to be protected against self-incrimination.

The English Bill of Rights of 1688 set out the following constitutional guarantees, many of which are familiar to us:

> 1. That the pretended power of suspending of laws, or the execution of laws, by regal authority, without consent of parliament, is illegal.
>
> 2. That the pretended power of dispensing with laws, or the execution of laws, by regal authority, as it hath been assumed and exercised of late, is illegal.
>
> 3. That the commission for erecting the late court of commissioners for ecclesiastical causes, and all other commissions and courts of like nature are illegal and pernicious.
>
> 4. That levying money for or to the use of the crown, by pretence of prerogative, without grant of parliament, for longer time, or in other manner than the same is or shall be granted, is illegal.
>
> 5. That it is the right of the subjects to petition the King, and all commitments and prosecutions for such petitioning are illegal.
>
> 6. That the raising or keeping a standing army within the kingdom in time of peace, unless it be with consent of parliament, is against law.
>
> 7. That the subjects which are protestants, may have arms for their defence suitable to their conditions, and as allowed by law.
>
> 8. That election of members of parliament ought to be free.

> 9. That the freedom of speech, and debates or proceedings in parliament, ought not to be impeached or questioned in any court or place out of parliament.
>
> 10. That excessive bail ought not to be required, nor excessive fines imposed; nor cruel and unusual punishments inflicted.
>
> 11. That jurors ought to be duly impanelled and returned, and jurors which pass upon men in trials for high treason ought to be freeholders.
>
> 12. That all grants and promises of fines and forfeitures of particular persons before conviction, are illegal and void.
>
> 13. And that for redress of all grievances, and for the amending, strengthening, and preserving of the laws, parliaments ought to be held frequently.
>
> And they do claim, demand, and insist upon all and singular the premisses, as their undoubted rights and liberties; and that no declarations, judgments, doings or proceedings, to the prejudice of the people in any of the said premisses, ought in any wise to be drawn hereafter into consequence or example.[93]

Finally, let us turn to Blackstone. In his *Commentaries*, Blackstone speaks of many classes of persons (which term includes not only natural persons, but also artificial ones, i.e., corporations) who have rights. The only one of these that concerns us for our purposes is natural persons or individuals. He tells us that the "rights of the people [individuals] of England" may be divided into three "principal or primary articles"; the right of personal security, the right of personal liberty, and the right of private property. (I mentioned this in Chapter Three.)[94]

According to Blackstone, "[t]he right of personal security consists in a person's legal and uninterrupted enjoyment of his life, his limbs, his body, his health, and his reputation."[95] It is because of this right's protecting the "enjoyment of life," which for Blackstone "begins in contemplation of law as soon as an infant is able to stir in the mother's womb," that he opposes abortion.[96] He explains two other interesting points about what this right provides in law. He says the law not only protects a man's life and members, but "furnishes him with every thing necessary for their support." He contends that "there is no man so indigent or wretched, but he may demand a supply sufficient for all the necessities of life from the more opulent part of the community." This is not, however, a right found in nature, but is created "by means of several statutes enacted for the relief of the poor."[97] He says that the security of a man's reputation or good name -- to which he is entitled "by reason of natural justice" -- requires the law to protect him from "the arts of detraction and slander."[98]

For Blackstone, personal liberty is next to personal security as the greatest of the rights of individuals. He explains, in brief, what is included in "personal liberty";

> [It] consists in the power of loco-motion, of changing situation, or moving one's person to whatever place one's own inclination may direct, without imprisonment or restraint, unless by due course of law.[99]

Citing the Magna Carta and other statutes, he tells us that this right of personal liberty includes the right of trial by a jury of one's peers, imprisonment only after a "legal indictment, or the process of the common law," detainment only for probable cause and the right to answer the charges against him, the right of *habeas corpus*, and the protection against the imposition of unreasonable bail. He adds that "[a] natural and regular consequence of this personal liberty is, that every Englishman may claim a right to abide in his own country so long as he pleases; and not be driven from it unless by the sentence of the law" (i.e., it precludes arbitrary banishment).[100]

As far as the right of property is concerned, Blackstone states that it consists in "the free use, enjoyment, and disposal of all...acquisitions, without any control or diminution, save only by the laws of the land."[101] He sanctions the power of the legislature to take private property, but only when exercised cautiously and when a reasonable payment is made.

For Blackstone, in addition to primary rights, there are certain subordinate rights. These included both certain rights of Parliament and limited sovereign power in the King, as well as certain additional individual rights. The latter included the following: to apply to courts for a redress of injuries or that "no freeman shall be...put out of the protection and benefit of the laws, but according to the law of the land" (i.e., roughly speaking, "equal protection.")[102] the "right of petitioning the king, or either house of parliament, for the redress of grievances";[103] and the right of the subject to keep and bear arms.

Now, let us turn to the major documents and statements of rights in the American colonies up to the time of the Bill of Rights. The first that should be pointed to is the Virginia Declaration of Rights of January 12, 1776. This document put forth a number of individual rights, beginning, most broadly, with the inherent and unalienable rights to "the enjoyment of life and liberty, with the means of acquiring and possessing property, and pursuing and obtaining happiness and safety."[104] It stated the following specific civil rights: free elections; the right of suffrage for males who have "sufficient evidence of permanent common interest with and attachment to, the community"; the right not to be taxed or deprived of their property for public uses without their consent; a right of jury trial which, besides embodying the guarantees of the English documents already mentioned, requires that the trial be "speedy" and "by an impartial jury of his vicinage"; protection against self-incrimination; the right not to be deprived of liberty except by the law of the land; a protection against excessive bail and fines and cruel and unusual punishments; a prohibition against general warrants; trial by jury in civil suits; freedom of the press; a prohibition of standing armies and subordination of the military to civilian control; and free exercise of religion.[105]

The Early State Constitutions and Bills of Rights

A substantial number of rights were stated in the colonial and state bills of rights which preceded the federal Bill of Rights. (The ones which came *after* it have generally followed it as the model.) Even some rights which appeared in fewer than half of the bills of rights were considered important enough to find their way into the federal Bill of Rights and later state constitutions. For example, the federal Bill adopted the guarantees against double jeopardy and being held for an infamous crime without indictment or presentment of a grand jury. The body of the U.S. Constitution contained Massachusetts' and Maryland's provision against bills of attainder, the New Hampshire and Pennsylvania provisions that private property was not to be taken for public use without compensation, and Pennsylvania's guarantee of the right to emigrate to another state (which was included in the privileges and immunities clause of the U.S. Constitution). Of the other rights found in fewer than half of the state documents, New Hampshire and Massachusetts guaranteed impartial judges while Maryland guaranteed the independence of judges. These notions were manifested in the federal Constitution in the form of the provision that the salaries of federal judges shall not be diminished during their term. The federal Bill of Rights adopted New Hampshire's and Massachusetts' provision barring the quartering of soldiers in private homes in time of peace. Maryland and North Carolina, following Coke's *Second Institute*, forbade monopolies. South Carolina, New York, and Delaware provided the common law guarantees to their citizens. New Hampshire required penalties to be proportional to the offense.[106]

All of the colonial and early state bills of rights guaranteed the right of a jury trial, freedom of the press, and that the accused be informed of the charge against him and be confronted with the witnesses against him. The protection of life, liberty, and property was the next most frequent guarantee, appearing in the bills of rights in New Hampshire, Massachusetts, Pennsylvania, Maryland, Virginia, and North Carolina and in the first constitutions of Connecticut, South

Carolina, and Georgia. (Virginia stipulated only life and liberty and New Hampshire and Massachusetts divided these three guarantees into different articles.) Georgia provided the right to *habeas corpus* as a specific guarantee of liberty.[107]

Five state bills of rights -- in New Hampshire, Massachusetts, Pennsylvania, Maryland, and Virginia -- and the constitution of New Jersey required that the accused have witnesses in his behalf. General warrants were forbidden in the bills in New Hampshire, Massachusetts, Maryland, Virginia, and North Carolina. This, of course, found its way into the federal Bill. Five states granted the right to be protected against self-incrimination. Cruel and unusual punishments were forbidden in New Hampshire, Massachusetts, Maryland, Virginia (as mentioned) and North Carolina. Five states also prohibited the exaction of excessive bail. All these provisions were put in the federal Bill.[108]

New Hampshire, Massachusetts, Maryland, Virginia, and North Carolina provided that laws were not to be suspended. All these except Virginia forbade *ex post facto* laws. The body of the federal Constitution also prohibited state legislatures from passing *ex post facto* laws. These same four states provided (in the words of the Magna Carta) that justice was not to be sold, denied, or delayed.[109]

New Hampshire, Pennsylvania, Virginia (as noted), and Maryland provided that the military was to be in "strict subordination to the civil power," New Hampshire adding "at all times." South Carolina put a similar provision in its constitution of 1778. New Hampshire, Massachusetts, Maryland, and North Carolina provided also against levies, taxes, or imposts except by authority of the legislature.[110]

Three bills of rights -- in New Hampshire, Pennsylvania, and Maryland -- guaranteed counsel to accused persons. New Hampshire, Massachusetts, and Maryland, as well as the Virginia Bill of Rights as already stated, also provided for trials in the vicinage, which is generally regarded as included in the guarantee of a jury trial. Unreasonable searches and seizures were banned by New Hampshire, Massachusetts, and Pennsylvania and, of course, were also prohibited by the federal Bill. The right to bear arms, which in some fashion was put into the Second Amendment, was guaranteed in Massachusetts, Pennsylvania, and North Carolina.[111]

The Views of the Framers

The next place we shall briefly look for some indication of which rights the early Americans believed to be fundamental or essential is in the statements of the Framers. Because my space is limited, I shall confine myself to a brief consideration of the debates at the 1787 Constitutional Convention and in the House of Representatives in the First Congress which proposed the Bill of Rights (there is little record of the debate in the Senate, which at that time regularly met in executive session). As part of the latter, I shall also consider the opinion of our major constitutional philosopher James Madison, who presented the resolutions for the Bill of Rights in the first House. I shall likewise glance at the writing of our other eminent Founding Father, Thomas Jefferson, to discern what he believed the essential rights to be.[112]

The references to individual civil righs during the debates at the Constitutional Convention are not numerous, but there are enough to give us an insight into the rights the Framers believed to be essential. The rights most frequently mentioned are those of trial by jury and *habeas corpus*. Both of these are provided for in the body of the Constitution. During the course of the proceedings, various speakers mentioned other rights they were concerned to protect. The freedom of the press was emphasized three times,[113] the prohibition of religious tests as a qualification for holding public office was mentioned and adopted,[114] the prohibitions on bills of attainder and *ex post facto* laws were mentioned and eventually put into the Constitution despite Mason's attempt to have them removed,[115] the protection against troops being quartered in a person's home without consent -- which eventually became the Third Amendment -- was proposed,[116] and the Committee on Style and Arrangement also proposed immunity from capitation taxes and taxes on goods one exports to another state (these both found their way in some form into the Constitution). These, then, are the rights which were mentioned at the Convention. They are probably not an exhaustive list, since the state delegations, apparently motivated by the argument that the states' bills of rights were sufficient to protect the citizenry, unanimously voted down a motion to convene a committee to prepare a federal bill of rights. They apparently believed that all the important rights were set out in these state bills of rights. We get the suggestion, because they are mentioned (some repeatedly) and because some are put into the body of the Constitution, that these are the rights uppermost in the Framers' minds, and thus the ones they regarded as the most important.

Now let us turn to Madison and the First Congress. Madison, after having previously downplayed the importance of a written Bill of Rights,[117] presented the proposal for it in the First House in order to respond to the concerns of Americans who were still skeptical of the new Constitution.[118] Most of Madison's proposed provisions were enacted as the Bill of Rights, but it *is* worth mentioning the ones not enacted so that we can see all the rights he believed to be essential. The rights he included in his first proposed amendment were "the enjoyment of life and liberty...[and] the right of acquiring and using property, and generally of pursuing and obtaining happiness and safety."[119] Others were the "full and equal rights of conscience"[120] and the right of a "person religiously scrupulous of bearing arms" not to "be compelled to render military service in person."[121]

Madison also suggested that certain rights are preeminent: "the great rights, the trial by jury, freedom of the press, or liberty of conscience" (i.e., freedom of religious worship and belief).[122] At another part of the debate, he reemphasized this by saying the following:

> Have the people not been told that the rights of conscience, the freedom of speech, the liberty of the press, and trial by jury were in jeopardy, that they ought not to adopt the constitution until those important rights were secured to them?[123]

Throughout the rest of the House debate, mention is made by other Representatives of specific rights.

The fact that they singled them out in such a manner suggests that they attached particular importance to them, even though they approved an entire Bill of Rights. One representative made specific reference to the Magna Carta and the *habeas corpus* act in discussing the rights of Englishmen, suggesting the great importance of the rights provided for in them.[124] Another, after mentioning these two documents said that, while the constitution of Britain is what the Parliament wills, "there are rights granted to the subject that cannot be resumed" (the context suggests that these rights are in those documents).[125] Another indicates the emphasis placed on "the rights of conscience, and a free exercise of the rights of religion."[126] One other Representative spoke of freedom of speech and assembly as being "self-evident."[127] The one mentioned first above echoes the importance of the right of assembly.[128]

Finally, what does Thomas Jefferson say? We can get an indication of what he believed the most important individual rights to be from his first inaugural address. In it, he singled out the rights of freedom of religion, freedom of the press, freedom of person under the protection of *habeas corpus*, and trial by juries impartially selected, along with a number of rules about how to govern a republic, that he says are "principles [which] form the bright constellation which has gone before us."[129] Another place where he lists what seem to be basic rights is a letter he wrote to Madison on December 20, 1787, wherein he commented on the proposed Constitution. He said that a bill of rights should be included which clearly provides for freedom of speech and the press and "trials by jury in all matters of fact triable by the laws of the land, and not by the laws of nations," as well as "protection against standing armies, restriction of monopolies, [and] the eternal and unremitting force of the *habeas corpus* laws."[130]

In examining these sources of American rights we can see that the most essential -- as judged from the frequency that they are mentioned by different sources over time -- are the following: trial by jury, protection of private property from arbitrary government seizure, the various other protections of due process as they relate to the procedural guarantees a person has when accused of a crime, *habeas corpus*, freedom of religion, freedom of the press, freedom of speech, punishments and fines to fit the offense and protection from cruel and unusual punishments, and the right not to have troops quartered in one's home without his consent. The other rights mentioned can be judged to be of secondary importance.

When we look at both the body of the Constitution and the Bill of Rights, we see that almost all the rights mentioned in the various sources I have examined are enumerated. Bennett B. Patterson in his book *The Forgotten Ninth Amendment* contends that there are other rights which have not been enumerated. Most of the examples he gives us, however, are rights which either are enumerated -- he simply contends that the Ninth Amendment applies them to the states -- or are included within the scope of the enumerated rights.[131]

This inquiry into the background of our Constitution has shown one basic point: that, accepting the argument that there *are* fundamental rights which are not enumerated, the right of privacy can still not be considered "fundamental" on the basis of its having appeared among the rights protected by this constitutional background.[132]

The Notion of Privacy in History and the Development of the Right of Privacy in American Law

Even though the right of privacy appears not to have been viewed as an essential right or a right at all in early America, this does not mean that there was no concern about safeguarding individual privacy or that some notion of a right of privacy did not develop later in American law. This is what I shall inquire into in this final Section.

The Notion of a "Right of Privacy" in English and American History

Some notion of what might lossely be called a legal "right" of privacy has existed since the first centuries after Christ. It found its first expression in Jewish law, where it related to the privacy of one's home.[133] It was also present in Roman law, where it pertained to an injury to honor.[134] By the nineteenth century, it was found in the legal codes of such countries as Germany, Switzerland, and France.[135] There is no evidence that the right extended in any of these cases to the reproductive realm, however. I mention its early expressions in England below. There is no acknowledgment of it by such major modern English legal and political thinkers as Blackstone, Locke, and Hobbes.[136]

We see evidence of a conception of privacy rights in colonial America in the protection afforded by the law for the sanctity of the home and the mails. Colonial New England, as seen in the study done by historian David H. Flaherty, is a good example. Flaherty reveals that the Rhode Island Code of 1647 "forbade 'forcible Entry and Detainer,' except that an officer of the law could break open a house under stringent conditions."[137] That Code made "[t]he act of entering a dwelling house at night [i.e., burglary] sufficient cause for serious punishment," which included whippings, brandings, death, banishment, the stocks, and heavy fines.[138] Massachusetts law permitted a man who owned his own house to "'count it unreasonably injurious that another who had no authoritie thereto should intrude and enter his house without his, the owners, consent'" and to kill the intruder.[139]

In the 1760s, court cases over writs of assistance provided a forum for the strong assertion of this notion of privacy of the home. These writs granted customs officials the power to search private homes for smuggled goods without specific warrants. James Otis, in his court argument against these general warrants, emphasized the importance of the privacy of the home in the colonial mind: "'Now one of the most essential branches of English liberty, is the freedom of one's house. A man's house is his castle...This writ, if it should be declared legal, would totally annihilate this privilege.'"[140]

This right of privacy of the home was indeed an outgrowth of the English common law precept of "a man's house is his castle." As Flaherty says, "[t]he connection between a strong sense of private property and privacy was apparent."[141] It was this notion of privacy which found its way into the Constitution in the form of the Fourth Amendment.

Flaherty also points to the existence in colonial New England of the other constitutionally-enumerated expression of the right of privacy which is referred to in Justice Douglas' *Griswold* opinion and the *Griswold* Appellants' brief: the privilege against self-incrimination.[142] I merely note this without further discussion.

The other major area in which colonial law protected privacy was the mails. Flaherty explains the position taken of seventeenth century New England law below:

> Despite the casualness of delivery, there seems to have been little premeditated and malicious perusal of other people's mail, except perhaps on the part of colonial authorities. At least the infrequency of colonial complaints about such interference suggests that the privacy of the mails was fairly secure. No court cases were found in which persons were specifically indicted for opening someone's mail, but the courts revealed their attitude on several related occasions. In 1639 a court fined John Kitchen of Boston "for shewing books which hee was commanded to bring to the Governor, and forbidden to shew them to any other." In 1668 a Plymouth resident succeeded in having the court admonish three persons "for opening a certaine box in his house, wherin were his writings." Both the secretary and the governor of Massachusetts had harsh words for Samuel Sewall in 1709 when he tried to read several letters on the secretary's desk during a Council meeting. *The*

> *School of Good Manners,* representative of the colonial attitude, instructed: "Touch not, nor look upon the Books or Writings of any one, unless the Owner invite or desire thee... Come not near when another reads a Letter or any other Paper."[143]

As the mail service improved in the eighteenth century, the colonists -- and people in the Mother Country -- became more concerned about the privacy of the mails. For example, the British Post Office Act of 1710 contained the following provision:

> "No Person or Persons shall presume wittingly, willingly, or knowingly, to open, detain, or delay, or cause, procure, permit, or suffer to be opened, detained, or delayed, any Letter or Letters, Packet or Packets."[144]

When Benjamin Franklin was postmaster general for the colonies from 1753 until the Revolution, he required everyone who worked for the postal service to take the following oath:

> "I...do swear, That I will not wittingly, willingly, or knowingly open...or cause, procure, permit, or suffer to be opened ...any Letter or Letters...which shall come into my Hands, Power, or Custody, by Reason of my Employment...; except...by an express Warrant in Writing under the Hand of one of the principal Secretaries of State for that purpose."[145]

To show the extent to which the privacy of the mails came to be revered in the colonies, we might look to a letter written to John Jay by his friend Robert Troup, during the Revolution when the mails expectedly deteriorated:

> "To the disgrace of Human Nature, it has become common Practice to betray the Confidence we repose in each other, either by opening Letters, or not sending them to the Persons to whom they are directed. I have seen so many Instances of such Behaviour that I am determined to use more Caution hereafter."[146]

There was also during the eighteenth century one famous English court case on the right of privacy, *Pope v. Curl* (1741). This also involved the privacy of personal correspondence. Curl, a bookseller, acquired some personal letters to and from various English literary figures, including Alexander Pope and Jonathan Swift, and published them without their consent. Pope sought to have the book removed from the market and to have further similar action by Curl enjoined. The court granted Pope his injunction, saying that a book of personal letters was prohibited from publication, under a 1710 English statute, the same as a book of learned work.[147]

Thus the privacy of persons in different activities was protected by the law before and around the framing of the Constitution. The question to be considered now is whether it was protected as it applied to matters of individual morality, which is the claim made by the appellants, and accepted by the Court, in *Griswold* and *Wade/Bolton*.

Flaherty states that, in spite of the surprisingly strong colonial emphasis on protecting privacy, the statute books were full of laws regulating individual morality. In fact, he says that "[t]he enforcement of the moral law [grounded, he explains in the Decalogue] became one of the primary obligations of colonial governments."[148] Among the offenses typically punished in colonial New England were vagrancy, "'excessive and common drunkenness,'" public drunkenness, tobacco abuse, keeping a disorderly house (i.e., prostitution), cursing and swearing, adultery, and fornication.[149] Puritan New England was not the only place where the law regulated and prescribed moral conduct. Flaherty says "[t]here is hardly a specified moral offense in New England that did not have its counterpart in the criminal code of Virginia in the seventeenth century."[150] Other colonies had similar morals legislation. In fact, the colonies in the seventeenth century had many more laws dealing with offenses against morality than those against the state, religion, the person, or property. New England and New York were particularly noted for the severity of their punishment, making adultery, bestiality, sodomy, and rape *capital* offenses.[151] In the eighteenth century -- the Framers' time -- these statutes remained on the books, although the number of prosecutions for some offenses declined. Flaherty says that, to some degree, the thinking about using the criminal law to enforce morality changed in the eighteenth century.[152] There was, however, no question about the authority of the state to enact laws in this area.

Later on in American history, the Supreme Court acknowledged this authority of the states as part of their "police power" and also of Congress to legislate in the morals area when interstate commerce is involved. In *Champion v. Ames* (1903),[153] in which the constitutionality of a Congressional statute making illegal the sending of lottery tickets in interstate commerce was adjudicated, the Court said the following:

> As a State may, for the purpose of guarding the morals of its own people, forbid all sale of lottery tickets within its limits, so Congress, for the purpose of guarding the people of the United States against the "widespread pestilence of lotteries" and to protect the commerce which concerns all the States, may prohibit the carrying of lottery tickets from one State to another.[154]

Whatever protection the law gave to privacy in the Framers' time was not construed as prohibiting or limiting the state's power to legislate on individual morals, and this understanding continued for most of American history. Not only is there no evidence that the Framers' conceived of the right of privacy as an essential right but also, even though the law of their time afforded some protections to privacy, they and their contemporaries did not view these as extending to sexual and reproductive activities or as barring the state from legislating on matters of morality.[155]

The Pre-*Griswold* Legal Notion of the Right of Privacy

The Supreme Court's first recognition of the right of privacy occurred in two late nineteenth century cases, *Boyd v. U.S.* (1886) and *Union Pacific Railway Co. v. Botsford* (1891).[156] In the *Boyd* case, the Court declared unconstitutional a federal statute which required the defendant in a revenue case to produce in court his private books, invoices and papers or else have the government's allegations taken as confessed. The Court held that the statute violated both the Fourth and Fifth Amendments. It said the former was violated even though there was no actual entry upon premises and a search; a compulsory production of one's papers and effects is within the spirit and meaning of the Amendment. The Court said the Fifth Amendment was violated because requiring papers to be produced to be used in evidence against a defendant is equivalent to compelling him to testify against himself. The right of privacy was, in some sense, involved because the statute required the production of private papers and self-incrimination has traditionally been thought of as compelling one to divulge his private thoughts.

It was in the *Botsford* opinion, which involved whether a court could order a plaintiff in a tort case to submit to a surgical examination, that the Supreme Court made its first reference, as mentioned, to a right of privacy, *per se*. I stated that the *Wade* Court and the pro-abortionists both cite this as a precedent for their position. The words of the *Botsford* opinion that they view as most pertinent are as follows:

> No right is held more sacred, or is more carefully guarded, by the common law, than the right of every individual to the possession and control of his own person, free from all restraint or interference of others, unless by clear and unquestionable authority of law.[157]

As I pointed out in Chapter Three, in spite of the strong endorsement of the rights appertaining to the body in this passage, the Court stated that these rights did not take precedence over the unborn child's right to life.

For the most part, the right of privacy has developed in tort, not constitutional law. (Its expressions in constitutional law, at least before *Griswold*, related mostly to search and seizure and criminal procedure, as the cases cited in *Wade* indicate. These did not *expressly* involve a right of privacy, however.) The genesis of the actual right of privacy in American law is generally considered to be an 1890 article in the

Harvard Law Review (Vol. 4) by two young Boston lawyers, Samuel D. Warren and Louis D. Brandeis.[158] The latter, of course, would one day become the eminent Supreme Court Justice.

The following paragraphs from the beginning of their article state why the right of privacy began to evolve in common law courts:

> ...the common law, in its eternal youth grows to meet the demands of society...in very early times, the law gave a remedy only for physical interference with life and property ...Gradually the scope of...legal rights broadened...and now the right to life has come to mean the right to enjoy life -- the right to be let alone; the right to liberty secures the exercise of extensive civil privileges; and the term "property" has grown to comprise every form of possession -- intangible, as well as tangible...[159]
>
> Recent inventions and business methods call attention to the next step which must be taken for the protection of the person, and for securing...the right "to be let alone." Instantaneous photographs and newspaper enterprise have invaded the sacred precincts of private and domestic life; and numerous mechanical devices threaten to make good the prediction that "what is whispered in the closet shall be proclaimed from the house-tops."[160]

The matters, then, which Warren and Brandeis were concerned about extending the legal protection of privacy to were scurrilous and gossipy journalism about individuals' private lives, the unauthorized use of photographs of persons, and the intrusions then starting to occur from eavesdropping devices and the like. They sought to have a new tort action created which could go beyond the protection of material interests -- which are protected by libel and slander actions -- to "spiritual" ones, by which they mean the "injury of feelings" or "mental suffering."[161] They proposed to call this new action the right of privacy. They saw this as being able to protect "the more general right to the immunity of the person -- the right to one's personality."[162]

Over the three-quarters of a century from the Warren-Brandeis article until the mid-1960s, the recognition of a tort action for right of privacy -- as approximately conceived of by Warren and Brandeis -- accelerated in state courts. In 1964, the late Dean William Prosser wrote that what had emerged was "not one tort, but a complex of four."[163] He continues:

> The law of privacy comprises four distinct kinds of invasion of four different interests of the plaintiff, which are tied together by the common name, but otherwise have almost nothing in common except that each represents an interference with the right of the plaintiff "to be let alone."[164]

It is these four categories of tort actions, which shall now be discussed briefly, that comprised most of the law on the right of privacy on the eve of the *Griswold* decision.

The first of these is the action for intrusion. Prosser tells us that it involves the following:

> ...intrusion upon the plaintiff's physical solitude or seclusion, as by invading his home or other quarters, or an illegal search of his shopping bag in a store. The principle has, extended to eavesdropping upon private conversations by means of wire tapping and microphones...[it has] be[en] applied to peering into the windows of a home, as well as persistent and unwanted telephone calls.[165]

The second privacy tort permits a cause of action for publicity of a highly objectionable kind, even if it is true and there would be no action for defamation. For there to be a cause of action, there must be a public disclosure of private facts. A private disclosure or public facts will not do.[166]

The third type of cause of action for privacy involves publicity which places the plaintiff in a false light in the public eye. One form in which it occasionally appears is that of publicity attributing to the plaintiff some opinion or utterance, such as spurious books or articles. Another form in which it frequently appears is using the plaintiff's picture to illustrate a publication with which he has no real connection, with the implication that such a connection exists. Yet another form is the inclusion of the plaintiff's name, photograph, or fingerprints in some public listing of convicted criminals, when he has not been convicted of any crime.[167]

The final privacy tort consists of the appropriation, for the defendant's benefit or advantage, of the plaintiff's name or likeness.[168]

The right of privacy, then, as it had developed in American law in the years before *Griswold*, applied to the following: physical intrusions into one's home or possessions, mechanical intrusions for the purpose of electronic "snooping," objectionable or false publicity, and unauthorized use of his name. This development seems to have been along the lines called for by Warren and Brandeis. Thus, the Court in *Griswold* made a quantum leap by applying it to marital and sexual activities.

Before *Griswold*, the Supreme Court twice considered constitutional challenges to the Connecticut contraceptive statute. In these cases, *Tileston v. Ullman* (1943)[169] and *Poe v. Ullman* (1961),[170] the Court did not reach the merits of the claims of alleged violations of constitutional rights, but made its decisions on procedural grounds. In *Tileston*, the Court contended that a physician had no standing to assert constitutional arguments on behalf of his patients -- whose lives he claimed would be endangered if he could not prescribe contraceptives for them -- because his *own* Fourteenth Amendment rights to liberty and property were not threatened. In *Poe*, the Court said that a physician could not challenge the statute because it was almost never enforced, and so there was no justiciable controversy. In *Griswold*, the standing and justiciability problems were eliminated, at least as to challenging that part of the statute that punished the distributors of contraceptives as accessories. Nevertheless, if the right of privacy were such a fundamental right, why did the Court not just go ahead and strike down the statute in the two previous cases, in spite of the procedural problems? The Court has held that where fundamental rights are involved, it will circumvent procedural limitations and decide the merits.[171] Moreover, the *Griswold* Court was not reluctant to shed these limitations to strike down the usage part of the statute, even though there had been no prosecutions under that. In short, one is led to think that the right of privacy -- particularly as it relates to the sexual and marital arena -- became "fundamental" when the Court denominated it as such.

Conclusion

It is to be concluded that there are rights which are not enumerated in our Constitution and, if they are part of our legal tradition, may be relied upon by the Supreme Court to decide cases. There is no evidence that the unenumerated right of privacy was viewed by this tradition as an essential (i.e., "fundamental") right, as claimed by the Court. A legally-protectable notion of privacy *did* exist, but was never understood as applying to sexual or reproductive needs. Thus, the Court lacked a constitutional or legal foundation for applying the right of privacy as it did in *Griswold* and *Wade/Bolton*.[172]

Chapter Six

The Arguments and the Evidence Presented to the Supreme Court, Part II: The Alleged Justifications for Abortion and the Health Consequences for the Woman

This inquiry into the alleged justifications for abortion and its health consequences for women focuses on the following pro-abortion briefs in *Wade* and *Bolton:* the *Wade* brief and its supplemental brief and the brief of the Planned Parenthood Association of America/American Association of Planned Parenthood Physicians and its supplemental brief. These have been chosen because they treat the matters of justifications and consequences more extensively than the other briefs and give us a thorough picture of the pro-abortion thinking about them.

Although these arguments are medical and sociological rather than legal, the lawyers writing the briefs obviously believed that they would help to convince the Court, since considerable attention is devoted to them. That the Court chose to discuss these questions at some length in the opinions, suggests that they were probably correct. Briefs with arguments like these are in the tradition of the "Brandeis brief" (Louis Brandeis introduced the practice of using extra-legal arguments, comprised of sociological, economic, etc. evidence in his cases.) "Brandeis briefs" have been used with particular frequency in the past generation since the *Brown v. Board of Education*[1] case in civil rights and other major public law litigation.

I should make two points. The first is that in critically examining the justification for and medical consequences of abortion, I am going over ground that has been worked many times before. A thorough treatment of the briefs and the subject of abortion generally requires this. Second, as is apparent from looking at the footnotes to this Chapter, most of the medical and other literature on justifications for abortion appeared before the 1973 decisions. This could mean that the Court chose to ignore the large amount of critical material on justifications that existed -- much was presented to it -- or was simply not convinced by it. Most of the literature on medical and other consequences followed the decisions. A scanning of the anti-abortion briefs in *Wade* and *Bolton* shows that not much material about this was presented to the Court. The fact that this began to appear after 1973 and more frequently in foreign than U.S. medical journals probably reflects the fact that it was only then, after a number of years of experience with legalized abortion and the better records that were made possible by it that its consequences for the woman became apparent.

Part One—The Alleged Justifications for Abortion

The Life and Physical Health of the Mother

Since these are usually the first reasons given to support or justify abortion, and the ones for which the most compelling case can be made, I shall start with these, even though they are not spoken about directly in the two briefs I am studying. The PPFA brief[2] does have a section on "The Dangerous Effects on Life and Health of Restrictive Abortion Laws," but this discusses exclusively the purported dangers to women of illegal abortions, which shall be taken up later. It also has a section that argues anti-abortion statutes violate a woman's right to life and health. This, however, is directed at establishing the legal argument that the fundamental rights to life and liberty are applicable to the woman in abortion. The reason why the briefs do not make an argument about protecting the physical and mental health of the mother is, I believe, simply because they are seeking to have the broader right of abortion on request (for any reason) established. The *Wade* and *Bolton* opinions, as I have stated, do mention physical and mental health reasons for abortion.

Various Diseases as Necessitating Abortion

Let me first consider the alleged physical health justifications. The answer to this point is nicely summed up by the following quote from a physician who has been prominent in the abortion debate: "Medical science has made truly amazing advances over the last thirty years. As a result, it is now *extremely rare* for any pregnancy to be so hazardous to the life of the mother as to necessitate abortion."[3] As we look at various diseases which often have been thought to threaten the life of the pregnant woman, we can understand why this is so. We shall see that the physical health justifications for abortion (the medical term would be "indications," which means those conditions which seem to warrant a certain medical procedure)[4] are today virtually non-existent.

Cancer - Dr. Kenneth R. Niswander, Chairman of the Department of Obstetrics and Gynecology at the University of California - Davis Medical School and a strong pro-abortionist who was President of ACOG at the time it filed its briefs in *Wade* and *Bolton*, wrote the following around the time the Supreme Court first considered these cases:

> Malignancy is occasionally an indication for legal abortion. There is little convincing evidence, however, that pregnancy in any way adversely affects the outcome of neo-plastic disease. Even with cancers known to be endocrine dependent, such as cancer of the breast, the survival seems unaffected by pregnancy interruption.[5]

The same can be said about the cancers of the vital body

fluids, leukemia and Hodgkin's disease. After surveying the medical literature up to that time and reporting on one of his case studies, a physician wrote in 1958: "Pregnancy does not appear to have an adverse effect upon chronic [granulocytic] leukemia [CGL]."[6,7] Two other physicians, writing twenty-one years later after much additional data was compiled, concur with this and point out that the disease can be successfully treated by chemotherapy without danger to either mother or child.[8] (They also state that CGL is rare, with fewer than 150 cases reported in English.)[9] The effect of pregnancy on acute leukemia appears to be the same. Another physician writing in 1958 says that while such a disease in pregnant women is rare, when it occurs "pregnancy does not essentially alter the course of acute leukemia, fatal uterine hemorrhage being rare" and "[i]nterruption of pregnancy is of no benefit and *may hasten the death of the mother*."[10] A 1962 study on pregnant Hodgkin's disease patients "fail[ed] to demonstrate any adverse effect of pregnancy on either the course or longevity of patients with Hodgkin's disease."[11]

Other Blood Diseases -

1) *Anemia* - The *amici curiae* brief submitted by 305 physicians, professors, and fellows of ACOG in the 1980 *Williams v. Zbaraz* case,[12] which involved the question of whether the states had to fund "medically-necessary" abortions under Medicaid, stated that this disease is not an indication for abortion. It cited one article which spelled out the treatments which exist for it: "Anemia in pregnancy is most often caused by iron deficiency...[it] may be treated successfully with oral or parenteral medication. Folic acid deficiency, more common than previously thought...[may be] treated with oral or parenteral folic acid with great success."[13]

2) *Sickle Cell Anemia* - Dr. Bernard N. Nathanson, the one-time vigorous advocate of legalized abortion turned anti-abortion activist who I mentioned earlier, has written that sickle cell anemia is risky to the mother's life and is an indication for abortion.[14] Other physicians, such as those who filed the brief in *Williams* above, disagree.[15] The risk to both the mother and the unborn child seems to vary with the type of sickle cell anemia.[16] Various means of treatment for the mother exist.[17] One study of 72 pregnant sickle

cell patients at the Chicago Lying-In Hospital showed only one maternal death and that was in a patient with massive bilateral pneumonia.[18]

3) *Idiopathic Thrombocytopenic Purpura (ITP)*[19] - According to one expert, "pregnancy *per se* neither routinely nor commonly aggravates ITP."[20] In a British study of 21 pregnant patients with ITP, no maternal deaths were reported.[21] This condition is generally treatable in pregnant women with steroids and, in severe situations, with spleenectomy.[22] ITP thus appears not to be an indication for abortion.

4) *Von Willebrand's Disease*[23] - A review of cases reported in English led three experts to conclude the following:

> ...most...[pregnant] women [with von Willebrand's] tolerate labor and delivery well. Complications often can be avoided by performing coagulation studies throughout pregnancy and observing these and other precautions for either vaginal or cesarean section delivery.[24]

These experts say nothing about abortion and the above leads one to conclude -- the 305 physicians who filed the *amici* brief in *Williams* concur -- that von Willebrand's disease is not an indication for abortion.

Cardiovascular Disease -

1) *Cardiac Disease Generally* - A number of prominent physicians have written that cardiovascular disease no longer poses a serious threat to the life of the pregnant woman. Niswander says the following:

> Cardiovascular disease...has long been known to increase the risk of maternal death during pregnancy. Yet "recent research" has shown that nearly every cardiac patient can be completed successfully with little risk of maternal death.[25]

Writing as early as 1960, these doctors at New York City's famous Mount Sinai Hospital stated that "[t]here is no evidence at present that after delivery life expectancy is decreased in pregnant women with cardiac disease."[26] In their clinic at Mount Sinai, they also recorded only one death of a patient with heart disease during her pregnancy and she was an "urgent admission" who died of congestive heart failure.[27]

In 1979, another expert wrote that "[t]he burden of pregnancy on the woman with heart disease is only temporary. There is no evidence that pregnancy affects the natural history of the disease."[28]

Let us now consider the effect of pregnancy on women with a few specific cardiovascular disorders.

2) *Hypertension* - One expert writes the following about this disorder:

> With the present availability of effective hypertensive drugs there is no reason that blood pressure in each instance cannot be brought to normal. Their proper utilization depends upon the cooperation between the obstetrician and an internist with experience in the treatment of hypertension.[29]

Others say that there are instances when hypertension could be an indication for pregnancy, although they are uncommon. Obstetrician-gynecologist David G. Decker says that while "hypertension is rarely uncontrollable" nowadays the question of abortion might be raised when the woman has "severe pulmonary hypertension."[30] Another expert says, however, that "all severe forms of pregnancy-induced hypertension should be preventable."[31] Dr. Nathanson says that medical science still has not advanced to the point where hypertension is in all cases unthreatening to the life of the pregnant woman.[32] There thus appears to be division within the medical profession about whether hypertension can threaten a pregnant woman's life because of her pregnancy. We might conclude that it could, but this would be highly uncommon.

3) *Other Disorders - Thrombophlebitis* - Nathanson states that this disease, even if of the deep-vein type, can be successfully treated even in a pregnant woman.[33] *Varicose veins*- The aforementioned *amicus curiae* brief in the *Williams* case contends that "...varicose veins are not an indication for pregnancy termination."[34] A number of treatments are available for a pregnant woman with this affliction and surgery is not

even required.[35] *Aneurysm*- Dr. Decker tells us that an aneurysm is not an indication for abortion,[36] but Nathanson says that a woman who has suffered a blood clot or embolism (a clot that breaks off from its site) and later becomes pregnant could face a risk.[37]

Renal Disease - Both Decker and Nathanson agree that renal disease (i.e., afflictions of the kidney) could be an indication for abortion.[38] Nathanson says that while kidney transplants or dialysis could be employed as alternatives, they are risky in themselves.[39] The intervening defendant-appellant physicians in *Williams* state that renal disease in pregnancy is treatable in most cases, but acknowledge that it could be an indication for abortion when the woman's life is in danger.[40]

Diabetes Mellitus - Nathanson states that "there is no firm evidence that pregnancy in and of itself shortens the diabetic mother's life span, so it probably is not an indication [for abortion]."[41] Writing in the same year as Nathanson (1979), Dr. Steven G. Galbe, an expert on diabetes in pregnancy, writes the following:

> During the past ten years, important advances have been made in caring for the pregnant woman with diabetes mellitus. *Maternal mortality has been all but eliminated and maternal morbidity has been reduced significantly.*[42]

Neurologic Disease - Dr. Niswander writes the following on this:

> Neurologic disease is an occasional indication for abortion. The patient with multiple sclerosis, for example, sometimes is, indeed, made worse by pregnancy. The effect of pregnancy in this instance is unpredictable, however, and the condition of some patients actually improves. The effect of pregnancy on epilepsy is equally uncertain and pregnancy itself does not increase the risk of death for the pregnant woman.[43]

Tuberculosis - Dr. Niswander tells us that this disease, which "accounts for nearly all of the pulmonary conditions thought to indicate therapeutic abortion," is really rarely a justification for it in light of the "advance of drug therapy."[44]

Obesity - Dr. Nathanson says that this disease, using 250 (or, some obstetricians say 300) pounds as a "guideline," produces "a higher mortality rate in pregnancy because it is difficult to treat the patient, delivery is more problematic, and other medical problems result." He speaks merely of an "increased threat"; it is by no means definite that a woman could lose her life.[45] Clearly, a sweeping generalization that abortion should be undertaken for this condition is not being advocated by Nathanson.

Toxemia of Pregnancy[46] - What I said above about being able to eliminate hypertension in pregnancy applies to this affliction. One physician says that if the proper steps are taken to control blood pressure during pregnancy, toxemia deaths could be all but eliminated. He says that studies have shown that "if the fetus is alive when the patient is seen with eclampsia [convulsions which can result from a severe case of toxemia], with the use of their specific regimens a fetal salvage rate of 90 per cent and maternal mortality rate of 0 per cent can be expected."[47] It thus seems that this is not really an indication for abortion.

Systemic Lupus Erythemstosus (SLE)[48] - Two experts say this in response to the question of whether SLE is an indication for abortion:

> There have been a number of serious, sometimes fatal, exacerbations of SLE following abortion. It may be less risky for the woman to carry to term than to have an abortion.[49]

Placenta Previa and Abruptio Placenta[50] - The 305 *Williams amici* physicians say that these are not indications for abortion.[51] The medical literature explains various other methods of treatment.[52]

Drug Addiction - The 305 *Williams amici* physicians say the following about this:

> In ten studies of pregnancy in women either addicted to narcotics or being treated for narcotics addiction (e.g., via methadone and/or

> withdrawal) no evidence indicates that pregnancy has an adverse effect upon the disease, nor is there any indication of increased maternal mortality due to pregnancy complicated by addiction or treatment. Quite the contrary, these statistics show a maternal mortality of virtually *zero* and indicate that pregnancy may exert a *beneficial effect* on maternal health by encouraging women to enter and remain part of addiction programs both pre- and post-partum [i.e., before and after delivery]. Although these studies revealed increased maternal complications, there is significant evidence that these complications resulted from pregnancy as opposed to drug addiction.[53]

Conclusion

I have not reviewed all diseases which are claimed to be indications for abortion, but only the most commonly mentioned ones. What can be concluded is that there are few conditions which are actually worsened by pregnancy. Since there are many other means of treatment available for these, abortion would seem to be indicated only on those rare occasions when the woman's life is actually threatened by continuing the pregnancy. These situations appear not to have been entirely eliminated yet.

I should point out what one Buffalo, New York physician knowledgeable about abortion, Dr. Thomas A. O'Connor, has said about the physical health reasons for abortion. He said it is difficult to make a general statement about any particular disease; whether the disease could be fatal to a woman will depend on the circumstances involved.[54] For example, a woman who suffers a severe crisis during one of the above diseases when she is living in an isolated area a hundred miles from a physician or medical facilities may have her life threatened by continuing her pregnancy. A woman living in a metropolitan area five minutes from a large hospital would not. According to Dr. O'Connor, "There is no medical indication for which abortion is the only alternative to be offered the woman. There are no absolute indications for it."[55]

The Mental Health of the Mother

Now, let us consider whether abortion is ever indicated to safeguard the mental health of the mother. Dr. Fred E. Mecklenburg contends flatly that "[t]here are no known psychiatric diseases which can be cured by abortion. In addition, there are none which can be predictably improved by abortion."[56] Rhodesian psychiatrist W. Murdoch has stated that "[m]any psychiatrists on both sides of the argument say there are no psychiatric grounds for termination."[57] The Lane Commission, which studied abortion in Britain, concluded the following in 1974:

> Most women who unexpectedly become pregnant suffer some form of emotional reaction such as anxiety, depression, distress or anger. In only a few instances does the response amount to mental illness. Where mental disturbance is marked, however, some disturbance was present to some degree before the pregnancy.[58]

The Commission also said this:

> Therapeutic abortion has little influence, for good or ill, upon the course of an existing serious mental illness...[59]

Two other British experts stated that when mental disorder begins during pregnancy, it either ends at some point during it or persists until after it for awhile, depending upon the point in pregnancy when it starts, and is unaffected by abortion.[60]

Let us consider what medical experts say about the effect of pregnancy on specific mental disorders. Dr. Lawrence C. Kolb's 1977 (latest) edition of his standard textbook of psychiatry for medical students states that "[p]sychotic illness in association with pregnancy is rare."[61] In a previous edition, he wrote the following:

> Experience does not show that pregnancy and birth of the child influence adversely the course of schizophrenias, manic-depressive illnesses, or the majority of the psychoneuroses...Even women who have a postpartum psychotic reaction often go through later pregnancies without ego disorganization.[62,63]

Writing as early as 1957, Dr. William Sargent, then President of the Section of Psychiatry of the Royal Society of Medicine said that "[m]ental deficiency, psychopathic personality and established mental illness are not, in themselves, indications."[64]

It is often argued that if a woman is likely, or threatens, to commit suicide because of an unwanted pregnancy, abortion should be performed. A major problem with this as a basis for abortion is that it is virtually impossible to ascertain whether or not a woman is suicidal.[65] There also has been some disagreement among authorities about how prevalent suicide actually is among pregnant women.[66] The balance of the evidence, on the basis of suicide studies conducted, is that it is *less* frequent than among normal women. Three important studies can be pointed to particularly. The Minnesota Maternal Mortality Committee reported only fourteen suicides associated with pregnancy in the State of Minnesota in well over 1.5 million live births between 1950 and 1966.[67] Dr. B. Lindbert, in Sweden, studied 304 patients whose requests for therapeutic abortion were refused. Sixty-two indicated that they would commit suicide if their request was refused, but not one actually did.[68] Drs. Allan J. Rosenberg and Emmanuel Silver found in a study of three counties in northern California that the number of suicides of pregnant women was roughly 1/6 that of nonpregnant women of the same age group.[69] They also reported from their association with other experts investigating the same question in New York City "that proportionately fewer pregnant women commit suicide than those who are not pregnant."[70]

Drs. Rosenberg and Silver suggest the following reason as to why the suicide rate among pregnant women is so low.

> Perhaps psychologic and instinctive factors

> manifest themselves in greater maternal protectiveness. On the other hand, there may be effective mechanisms of increased social protectiveness and support [for pregnant women].[71]

It has been said that women will "deliberately attempt to manipulate" the psychiatrist and use suicide threats as a means of getting the psychiatrist to refer them for abortions.[72]

Mecklenburg points out that where abortion has been permitted for mental health reasons the result has been great abuse. The number of abortions drastically increases and mental health is used as a rationale for many abortions even though it is not often really involved.[73]

Mental health is probably not an indication for abortion, and, at any rate, the strongest argument that could be mustered in its behalf is that, within the psychiatric profession, there has been great disagreement about it. Dr. Sargent, whom I cited above, wrote that "[t]he post-war literature shows but little general agreement on the [psychiatric] indications for and the therapeutic effectiveness of abortion."[74]

The Social Welfare and Eugenic Justifications for Abortion

Rape and Incest

Rape and incest, like physical and mental health, are not addressed by the briefs I am considering probably because the appellants and *amici* were seeking not just to have these exceptions to the legal prohibition carved out, but to have the prohibition struck down entirely. (Recall that the Georgia statute, which was being challenged, permitted abortion to preserve the mother's life and physical and mental health, when it is likely that the child would be born with grave defects, and when the pregnancy resulted from rape or incest.) Nevertheless, these are usually put forth as situations in which abortion should be permitted, so I believe that they require some discussion. They must be considered on these different levels: the seriousness of the problem (i.e., how frequent pregnancy due to rape and incest occurs), whether abortion actually aids the woman on whose account it is performed, and the philosophical and moral matter of whether the unborn child should be destroyed because his life is due to one of these.

RAPE

INCIDENCE OF PREGNANCY DUE TO RAPE

The first point that should be made is that the incidence of rape is not as great as is sometimes thought. One survey of female undergraduates discovered that "[t]he general tendency...was...to overestimate the incidence."[75] One writer points to this study as suggesting that "[f]ear...has contributed to an exaggeration of the frequency of rape."[76] I might just speculate that this has occurred because of the increased public attention given to rape in recent years and the raising of the emotional pitch about it by feminist and anti-rape groups.

A number of studies have shown that pregnancy resulting from rape is very uncommon. One, looking at 2190 victims, reported pregnancy in only 0.6 percent.[77] Barbara M. Sims, who once served as an Assistant District Attorney in Erie County, New York (Buffalo and vicinity) wrote in 1969 that the District Attorney's Office in her county "contain[ed] no reported complaints of pregnancy from forcible rape or incest for the past thirty years."[78] In a study of 117 rape victims in Oklahoma City over a one-year period, there were no pregnancies reported.[79] The Cook County, Illinois (which includes Chicago), States Attorney's Office could not recall a single instance of pregnancy in about nine years of prosecuting for rape.[80] St. Paul, Minnesota did not report a single pregnancy from rape in over ten years.[81]

One obstetrician-gynecologist says that "for a victim raped on the day she ovulates, there is only a 10 percent chance of resulting conception" and that "there is only a 4 percent chance of conception if rape occurs at any other time in the menstrual cycle."[82] One other well-known expert states that the "probability of conception resulting from a single unprotected coitus would...appear to lie between 1 in 50 and 1 in 25."[83]

There are a number of medical reasons why pregnancy so seldom results from rape. First of all, a completed act of intercourse does not occur in most rapes.[84] (The law generally requires only penetration, not ejaculation, for rape to have been held to have occurred.) In one study of 500 rape victims, spermatozoa were identified in the vaginal secretions of only 61 percent.[85] In another study, clinical evidence for the presence of sperm was found in only 32 of 69 cases.[86]

Secondly, there is a higher rate of sexual dysfunction in sexual assaults than in intercourse under normal conditions.[87] The latter study concluded that "convicted [rape] offenders' physiologic reactions during rape reveal an impressively high rate of erective and ejaculatory dysfunction at some point during the sexual assault."[88] Also, rapists are often infertile at the time of the assault because of other aberrant sexual behavior, such as excessive masturbation.[89]

Third, it is unlikely with a normal 28-day menstrual cycle that the assault will occur on the one or two days of the month on which the woman would be the most fertile and thus the most subject to becoming pregnant under the conditions.[90]

Fourth, even if a woman is due to ovulate on the day of the assault, the emotional trauma of the rape is likely to prevent her from doing so.[91]

Finally, one can point to a number of other reasons why pregnancy will not occur. These include the woman's being sterile, having previously had a hysterectomy, being past menopause or before menarche, or using contraceptive pills or devices at the time.[92]

Dr. Mecklenburg suggests that by letting abortion be the solution for the pregnant rape victim, we are actually ignoring her real problems. The real solution would be for communities to provide more emergency service for the victim immediately after rape (which would insure that conception would not result) and medical and psychiatric assistance after that.[93] He points to a study which shows that, for the most part, this has not been done.[94]

Mecklenburg also points to abuses which could occur or have occurred when abortion has been permitted for rape which are similar to those resulting from the mental health exception. One is simply that it is difficult to establish that rape actually has occurred. He cites one British expert on this point who says the following:

> "It is easy for a woman to allege that she has been raped, and frequently the story of circumstances is fabricated by a 'victim' in order to account for facts which would otherwise be awkward to explain."[95]

He gives the example of Colorado's legalization of abortion for rape in 1967 to show the abuse. 4.1 percent of all abortions in Colorado during the years 1967 through 1971 were recorded as being performed for rape (290 of 7,015). The further statistic which leads Mecklenburg to doubt the claim that many (or any) of these pregnancies actually occurred from rape is that during the same period of time in Colorado, no one was convicted of, or even charged with the crime of rape.[96]

MORAL CONSIDERATIONS

Lastly, one must consider whether abortion for rape -- and the same applies to incest, which I take up briefly next -- is just for the unborn child. Our entire criminal law works on the principle that only the perpetrator shall be punished for a crime. The common law has also forbade the killing of an innocent person under any circumstances, even when necessary to achieve a just end or when it may be necessary to save yet another innocent life. The unborn child, conceived as a result of rape, is not the perpetrator of the crime. It is thus inconsistent with our law that he should be punished for his father's crime. It is similarly inconsistent to hold the view that the unborn child's life is normally to be protected, but that rape and incest are to be exceptions. Because the life taken is an innocent one, abortion here cannot be any more morally justified than abortion performed just because the mother does not want the inconvenience of a child.

One might argue that it is unfair to subject the woman to the anguish of having to carry and then bear and care for a child that resulted from an intercourse she not only did not want, but was forced upon her in a brutal fashion. I do not doubt that, in the small number of instances when pregnancy occurs, this does involve much anguish. The solution, however, to get back to Mecklenburg's earlier point, is not to destroy the innocent new life, but to provide more assistance to the woman. She should first be assisted right after the rape to get medical attention so she can have any semen removed from her uterus so as to prevent pregnancy. Secondly, when the woman has become pregnant, efforts must be made to give her medical and professional help in dealing with the emotional trauma she may face. Psychological studies have shown that, when given the proper support, most pregnant rape victims progressively change their attitudes about their unborn child from something repulsive to someone who is innocent and uniquely worthwhile.[97] Finally, help should be given her to make it as easy as possible for her to give up her baby for adoption, if she desires. Dealing with the woman pregnant from rape, then, can be an opportunity for us -- both as individuals and as a society -- to develop true understanding and charity. Is it not better to try to develop these virtues than to countenance an ethic of destruction as the solution?

INCEST

INCIDENCE OF PREGNANCY DUE TO INCEST

Unlike rape, pregnancy from incest has often been reported as being more common. Psychiatrist George E. Maloof cites a number of studies which show this in his article in *The Psychological Aspects of Abortion*. For example, one study found that 11 percent of girls became pregnant from incest.[98] Another study of German court cases showed an 18 percent rate.[99] A Brooklyn study came to a figure between these.[100]

On the other hand, Maloof points out that a number of rape treatment programs in the United States have reported much lower rates. One in Minneapolis has seen a 1 percent rate, another in Santa Clara County, California likewise, and one in Washington State no pregnancies. I also mentioned above that there were no pregnancies from incest, according to the records of the District Attorney's Office, in Buffalo, New York for over thirty years.[101] Maloof explains why this discrepancy exists. The treatment program figures, he says, can be trusted to be valid because the counselors in them are very familiar with their clients and would know if pregnancy occurs. The formal studies may be cases which have not been treated and in which the incest may have progressed further than the average case in the treatment programs. Further, he tells us that pregnancy is often a desperate measure taken by the young girl to end the incest and has probably been utilized more in the past -- the studies are older than the treatment program reports -- "when the community was less sensitive to reacting to a possible incest situation and when treatment programs which allow families to work together were not available."[102]

Whatever the rate of pregnancy from incest, we can safely say that it is higher than that for rape.

What are the reasons put forth for permitting abortion when pregnancy *does* occur? One is that permitting the pregnancy to continue is to invite psychological problems for the mother, who is often very young. Another is that it is unfair to require her to bear -- and then perhaps be expected to care for -- a baby who may have resulted from an act of intercourse with a relative as close as her father. This is an ugly situation, but it is made even worse by the fact that she is probably emotionally and financially unprepared for motherhood. Finally, it is sometimes argued, it is unfair to the child to bring him into the world because, as the product of a sexual union of two persons very closely related, he runs a risk of having genetically-based health problems.

THE ALLEGED DANGERS OF PREGNANCY TO THE MENTAL HEALTH OF THE TEENAGE GIRL

On the question of psychological harm to the girl, Maloof says that "there are no specific studies of the effects of incestuous pregnancies on the women who carry to term." How can it be considered as a psychiatric indication for abortion?[103] Maloof thus argues the following:

> The psychiatric basis for terminating the life of the unborn baby incestuously con-

> ceived has absolutely no scientific merit and derives from a blind adherence to a legal formulation espoused by abortion promoters, now including organized psychiatry.[104]

Maloof contends that aborting an incestuous pregnancy may actually be *promoting*, instead of stopping, mental illness. He says the following:

> ...we are promoting mental illness by not allowing the girl to accept the consequences of her own acts. The illness is shared by all who would deny the life of the child conceived by the incestuous act. Accepting the pregnancy can be the first step to accepting the incest and making the changes to alter the family pattern so that it can be more productive rather than withholding and destructive.[105]

He mentions a number of further specific psychological consequences that experts believe aborting the incestuously-conceived child can have on the girl. I shall speak about these in Part Two of this Chapter, "The Physical, Psychological, and Fertility Consequences of Induced Abortion for Women."

What must also be emphasized is that incest reflects very serious problems within the family, which will not go away -- nor will the hurts be repaired -- with abortion.[106] Incest demands treatment, not abortion. As two Canadian experts have written:

> With proper management, the outcome of incest may not always be as traumatic as was previously believed inevitable. In considering incest as basically a family pathology, and treating it as such, there is evidence that there may be gain for all concerned when the family co-operates in treatment, and where this is not possible, less damage for those members who have involved themselves.[107]

THE ALLEGED DANGERS OF PREGNANCY TO THE PHYSICAL HEALTH OF THE TEENAGE GIRL

The evidence indicates that pregnancy, when given

proper medical management, is no riskier for a teenage girl than for a woman in her twenties. A Los Angeles study established that "pregnancy in the young adolescent presents no more significant material risk than that in the older age group."[108] They also reported that the Cesarean section rate -- associated with some problem or maternal disorder in pregnancy -- was actually only one-half as frequent as in their older control group (women 21 and older). Premature births *were* more common among the younger group, but perinatal mortality (death of the unborn child due to natural causes) was "extremely low."[109] A study of Chicago Board of Health clinics of pregnant adolescent women ages 11 to 15 concluded that "exclusive of the variables involved, such as social and emotional factors," the girls studied "who receive[d] adequate maternal care...[were] not at high obstetric risk."[110] A New York City physician concurs: "Pregnancy in a very young teenager (12-16 years) does not appear to be *inherently* high risk."[111] A study in Louisiana concludes the following:

> Under optimal conditions, the medical risk of the child and mother does not differ appreciably from that of the population as a whole but the availability of such optional conditions is rare because the early teenage mother is generally poor, black and medically and nutritionally unsophisticated.[112]

The Louisiana study adds that "the provision of high quality antenatal supervision contributes markedly to the reduction of morbidity and deaths in the mother and child alike."[113]

What we can conclude from the studies and opinions cited is that, *per se*, there is no physical threat presented to the adolescent female by pregnancy. There may be a greater possibility of abnormality or death in the child or of premature birth. The health of both mother and unborn child largely depend on prenatal care. This would suggest that if there is concern about the physical well-being of the girl pregnant from incest or otherwise, the solution is to provide better prenatal care opportunities, not an abortion.[114]

OTHER CONSIDERATIONS

As to the injustice to the girl required to continue her incestuous pregnancy to term, I must go back to what I said about rape. The unborn child has done no wrong. He has not committed the immoral and criminal incestuous act, so why must he pay the penalty of his life for it?

Again, our understanding and charity are tested. We must try to understand the unfortunate situation of families plagued by incest and the girl who has a child from it. We must see to it that our communities -- and, when called upon, we as individuals -- provide support and treatment for these families. We should provide the possibility for adoption, if this will be best for the girl. We should not confuse true with false compassion, however. We should not permit either the girl or the male relative to escape responsibility for what they have done,[115] especially when to do so would perpetrate the greater evil of destroying innocent human life. We will do nothing for either the individuals concerned or for the good of the community by pretending that the former are not responsible moral agents and refusing to acknowledge that they have done wrong.

As to the likelihood of deformities or other eugenic problems in the offspring as an indication for abortion, I shall speak about this further in the next Sub-Section. All I shall say here is that while there is some limited scientific evidence which shows that the products of incestuous unions tend to be of less than average intelligence, Maloof indicates that it is far from conclusive.[116] If it *is* true, however, does it justify abortion?

The Potential Deformity of the Unborn Child

This supposed justification for abortion was discussed only by the PPFA brief.[117] Again, the appellants in both cases were seeking a right to abortion on request in all circumstances, not just particular ones like this.

One of the reasons why the pressure to legalize at least some abortions mounted in the 1960s, as stated in Chapter One, was the substantial public attention focused on the children born in that decade with birth defects due to their mothers taking the tranquilizer thalidomide during pregnancy and, in other cases, to their contracting rubella (German measles) during pregnancy.[118] The first question I shall consider is exactly how great the incidence and risks of birth defects is.

THE OCCURRENCE AND FREQUENCY OF BIRTH DEFECTS

As an essential prelude to answering this question, we must know how birth defects occur. Mecklenburg states the following about this:

> A child can be born deformed (mentally or physically) as the result of an anamoly in his genetic material (either inherited or occurring during the process of conception), an accident which occurs during pregnancy and while still in the womb (e.g., German measles or drug ingestion), or because of some event which occurs during the birth process (e.g., premature delivery, anoxia or trauma).[119,120]

Only the first two causes he mentions are pertinent to the abortion question, but they do not account for most birth defects. He tells us further that "the leading cause of mental and motor retardation in the United States is prematurity,"[121] which, of course, the availability of abortion cannot remedy.

CONGENITAL DEFECTS

Now, let us look at the incidence of the first of these causes above. Mecklenburg states that "[t]here are several hundred disorders which occur as the result of a single 'abnormal' gene inherited from one parent, or from a related pair of 'abnormal' genes."[122] He says that these include Huntington's Chorea, osteogenesis imperfecta, Marfan's syndrome, achondroplasia, phenylketonuria, the Duchenne type of muscular dystrophy, and the hemolytic anemia due to glucose-6-phosphate dehydrogenase (G6PD) deficiency.[123] He explains further that "[t]here can also occur chromosomal abnormalities, which are present from the moment of conception. Down's anomaly (Mongolism) is an example."[124] Overall -- that is, including all three categories of causes of which defects Mecklenburg speaks --, in the United States and Western Europe major malformations are estimated at 1 to 3 percent of all live births; minor malformations are 2 to 4 percent of all live births.[125] Those that are clearly caused by genetic factors, such as those we are speaking about here, make up 20 to 25 percent of the total.[126] There are about 20,000 babies in this group who are born every year in the United States with defects due to chromosomal causes.[127] This is about 2 percent of all live-born infants.[128] 10 percent of these babies with chromosomal abnormalities are born to women over 40.[129]

What we can conclude from this is that birth defects generally are not common and those caused by genetic factors are *very* uncommon. It is also interesting to note from the above that -- contrary to what the media says -- it is even uncommon in older pregnant women. Mecklenburg tells us that Down's anomaly -- the genetic affliction popularly associated most with births to older women -- occurs in only 1 in 600 to 700 live births.[130]

As far as birth defects due to diseases contracted by the mother during pregnancy and drug ingestion by the mother, we can say the following about incidence. There are a number of studies on malformations due to rubella. Fifteen studies were reported on by Drs. Josef Warkany and Harold Kalter in 1961. These studies disclosed that congenital malformations or defects were found in 16.9 percent of the more than 400 live births examined.[131] These studies also showed that when rubella was contracted earlier in the gestation period, the incidence of birth defects was greater, but still nowhere near some exaggerated claims that are often made.[132] The birth defect rate was 23.4 percent when contracted in the first month, 21.3 when in the second, and 10.4 when in the third.[133] An Australian study reported in 1965 revealed that the incidence for the first thirteen weeks of pregnancy of congenital defects from rubella was 21.4 percent.[134] Another source tells us that in the 1964 American rubella epidemic, "about 10 percent of women with clinically recognized rubella gave birth to infants with the rubella syndrome [i.e., deformities and conditions caused by the rubella]."[135] These figures, all told, make it clear that of the children born to mothers who contract rubella in the first trimester -- the time at which it presents medical danger to the child *in utero* -- 80 to 90 percent will be perfectly normal.

The evidence also shows that most women are not susceptible to rubella because of childhood infection and other reasons. One expert writes that "[s]erological studies have shown that between 80 and 90 percent of women of childbearing age living in urban areas possess neutralizing antibodies to rubella virus."[136] Further, as Mecklenburg states, "with the advent of susceptibility testing and the subsequent vaccination of young girls lacking immunity, the elimination of rubella as a factor in birth defects is just around the corner."[137]

DRUG-INDUCED DEFECTS

Tragedies like the thalidomide affair are always possible, but Mecklenburg argues that they are now much less likely.[138] The thalidomide tragedy led to mandatory progeny study requirements by the Food and Drug Administration (FDA) before drug marketing. The result, according to one expert cited by Mecklenburg, is that it is unlikely that a drug with such a teratogenic capability as thalidomide could ever pass these new requirements.[139] The increased public insistence in recent years that the FDA exercise stricter scrutiny over such substances would seem to confirm this view.

LSD is another powerful drug that has often been mentioned as being a cause of birth defects in children born of mothers who have used it. As Mecklenburg points out, however, it is not entirely certain that LSD does this.[140] He points to an article done in the early 1970s -- the most extensive review of the research on this subject so far -- which concludes the following:

> In a study of human pregnancies, those exposed to illicit LSD had an elevated rate of spontaneous abortions. There is no reported instance of a malformed child born [alive]

> to a woman who ingested pure LSD [i.e., the type used in laboratory experimentation on volunteer subjects]; there are...cases of malformation associated with exposure to illicit LSD [i.e., the type bought illegally by drug abusers on the street]...Given, however, the high frequency of unexplained "spontaneous" birth defects, the rare occurrence of malformed infants born to women who used illicit LSD may be coincidental...From our own work and from a review of the literature, we believe that pure LSD ingested in moderate doses does not damage chromosomes *in vivo*, does not cause detectable genetic damage, and is not a teratogen or carcinogen in man.[141]

A later comprehensive review of the research on LSD overall basically confirms this, but points to some studies which have suggested or concluded otherwise. It also points to some specific birth defects that have been reported, but does not state whether they resulted in women using pure or illicit LSD.[142] The point is, however, that while illicit LSD may be a cause of birth defects in a limited number of cases, the jury is still out on the extent of its teratogenic effect.

THE PROBLEMS OF DETECTING GENETIC DEFECTS

A woman who has decided to have an abortion can never be certain that she has not consented to the destruction of a perfectly normal child, until it is too late. One expert has pointed out that never is the risk for a child to be born abnormal greater than 50 percent in any pregnancy[143] -- and we have seen that it is statistically, for all pregnancies taken together, much less. As Mecklenburg puts it, this means that "the chances are *at least* 50 percent for the child to be normal and that to advocate abortion when these factors arise would allow the destruction of many more normal children than abnormal."[144]

Many congenital anomalies can be treated or even corrected. Treatment even exists for some of the most serious.[145] Even Mongoloid children can be trained to develop the potentials they *do* have and lead successful lives.[146] In the case of children damaged by rubella, most suffer defects that can either be cured or corrected.[147]

Finally, in order to even provide abortions for the reason of deformity of the unborn child, the defect must first be detected. The major techniques which are used to do this are fetoscopy, ultrasound, X-rays, and amniocentesis.[148] Let us briefly consider the nature, accuracy, and risks of each of these procedures.

1) *Fetoscopy* - This is direct visualization of the unborn child. It is done by making a small puncture in the woman's abdomen and inserting a solid or fiberoptic system into the uterine cavity to observe the unborn child.[149] The position of the child and the placenta and the difficulty of getting the miniscule equipment in the proper place limit the technique's effectiveness, at least at this stage of its development. Apparently, most of the promise of fetoscopy is in the future after it has been better perfected.[150] Fetoscopy can cause complications both for the unborn child and the mother. The child can be lacerated by the puncture and it is uncertain what the effect of such an intense light source is on him. There have been reports of spontaneous abortions after fetoscopy. The woman, meanwhile, may experience bleeding, scarring, infection, and/or emotional disturbance.[151]

2) *Ultrasound* - This technique involves the use of mechanical radiant energy with a frequency greater than 20,000 cycles per second in the uterus. It is quite safe for both mother and child, but is limited for the most part to detecting disorders (primarily genetic diseases) associated with skull formation or insufficient bone mineralization.[152]

3) *X-Rays* - By nineteen or twenty weeks' gestation -- sometimes as early as seventeen -- the bones have calcified enough that an X-ray picture of the unborn child can be taken. Two methods of contrast radiography that incorporate dye into the amniotic fluid are now being used to delineate the fetal outline. These are amniography, which involves the use of a water-soluble dye to opacify the amniotic fluid, and fetography, which is carried out by injecting an oil-soluble dye into the amniotic fluid which tends to adhere to the vernix caseosa. The injecting of radio-opaque contrast media into the amniotic fluid can result in the detect-

ing of certain soft tissue abnormalities. All these radiographic procedures present the common risks of ionizing radiation on the developing unborn child and *his* progeny. The contrast media present additional risks which are the same as those of amniocentesis below. It is not known if all the risks of the media techniques have yet been determined.[153]

4) *Amniocentesis* - This is the means of detection of defects which has received the most public notice and is, in fact, the primary one used. It involves the insertion of a needle into the uterus and a drawing of some of the amniotic fluid. The cells in the fluid are then studied. Amniocentesis is used particularly to detect chromosomal-based defects, like Mongolism, and defects resulting from enzyme deficiencies. A 1971 study of the National Institute of Child Health and Development (NICHD) at the National Institutes of Health determined that the accuracy rate of amniocentesis in detecting Mongolism and predicting the gender of the child was 99.4 percent.[154] In that same year, however, Dr. Hymie Gordon, the chief geneticist at the Mayo Clinic, said in testimony before a legislative subcommittee of the Minnesota State Legislature that there have been many reported cases of errors, some of which led to the aborting of perfectly normal children.[155] Many fluid taps are unsuccessful and must be repeated because of poor cell growth, failure to obtain an adequate amount of fluid, or inconclusive results. Maternal cells can contaminate the amniotic cells when the needle is being inserted or removed and can cause a misdiagnosis. Also, interpretation can be difficult because of the lack of development of some enzyme systems early in prenatal life or the fact that polyploidy[156] -- a cause of some congenital abnormalities -- is sometimes found in normal amnion.[157]

The gravity of the risk presented by amniocentesis is a matter of some dispute. The NICHD study showed that there was no significant increase in the number of prenatal deaths when amniocentesis was undertaken. There was also no significant increase reported in the frequency of congenital malformations, neonatal problems, or development at one year of age. Complications to the mothers were minor.[158] A study of the Medical Research Council Working Party on Amniocentesis in Britain, however, came to different conclusions. The percentage of prenatal deaths was more than doubled when amniocentesis was done and there seemed to be a similar increase in some abnormalities in infants who were born alive, such as respiratory difficulties upon birth and major orthopedic postural deformities. The mothers also showed an increased incidence of other complications later in the pregnancy, such as abruptio placenta, premature rupture of the membranes, and postpartum hemmorrhage.[159]

Although the extent of the risk is in question, it is clear that there is *some* risk involved to both the unborn child -- because of the possibility of his body being punctured or lacerated -- and the mother -- because of the possibility of infection.[160]

The point of this brief consideration of the methods of detection of prenatal defects is that they are limited in the types of disorders they can detect, can be inaccurate, and can cause complications, to at least some degree, for both unborn child and mother.

What must also be mentioned about abortion to eliminate deformed children is simply that it has not worked. Mecklenburg points to the case of Sweden where this question has been studied. Even though malformation is one of the specific reasons upon which a request for abortion can be granted, the number of children born each year with defects remains the same.[161]

Most importantly, the evidence is that defective persons believe that their lives are *supremely* valuable. No study, for example, has found that handicapped persons are more likely than nonhandicapped persons to want to be killed or to commit suicide. A study by the late Dr. Andre Hellegers of the Kennedy Institute for Bioethics and Human Reproduction at Georgetown University of 200 consecutive suicides at the Baltimore Morgue revealed that none had been committed by people with congenital anomolies.[162]

Contraceptive Failure

One of the justifications in both the *Wade* and

PPFA briefs for abortion legalization was the frequent unavailability and failure of contraception. I shall consider this now.

THE ARGUMENTS AND VIEWS EXPRESSED IN THE BRIEFS

The PPFA brief, not surprisingly, presents the more lengthy and detailed argument on this point, although its essence is the same in both briefs. Contraception is said to be unavailable to many persons in the U.S. and, even when available, is sometimes ineffective and causes medical complications. On the question of availability the briefs quote authorities which give certain figures for the number of individuals who are in need of "family planning services," but not receiving them.[163] One of the authorities places the figure at "4.3 million women."[164] Another says it is "about 5 million medically indigent women."[165] Neither brief shows how these figures were arrived at nor makes clear that they are not just extrapolations of questionable reliability. An example of how statements are made which appear to firmly establish the brief's point but which, on closer consideration, really prove very little is seen in the same passage where the first figure above is presented. It is stated that "[family planning s]ervices continue to be concentrated in relatively few populous counties..."[166] Upon reflection, we see that this does not necessarily mean that most people are not receiving family planning services because most people in the U.S. *live* in relatively few populous counties.

Both briefs lament the plight of "medically indigent" -- i.e., poverty level -- women, who, according to one, "have an average annual fertility rate 53 percent higher than the nonpoor."[167] Neither, however, gives any indication of learning from poverty-level women themselves whether they believe this situation to be so lamentable or whether they do not perhaps wish to have a larger number of children than do non-poverty level couples.

In the *Wade* brief, a further example of a misleading citation -- actually, it is *glaringly* misleading -- of authority creates an exaggerated impression of the unavailability of contraception. The brief states that "[o]nly a few short years ago, a review of texts used in medical schools revealed that '[t]wo thirds of the texts

(25 texts) contained either no mention of contraception or only isolated reference to it with no complete discussion.'"[168] The authority quoted from is the noted biostatistician and human fertility expert, Dr. Christopher Tietze, a vigorous advocate of contraceptive family planning.[169] In the article he is quoted from, we see that the study cited, although appearing in a 1966 issue of the *Journal of the American Medical Association*, was actually done in 1964. This is a full seven years before the brief is filed before the Supreme Court. This is a significant lapse of time, particularly when one considers that the intervening years were ones of literal upheaval in sexual mores in America and of the establishment of contraceptive use as a constitutional right for married persons. Second, and more important, the article makes clear that the teaching of "fertility regulation" in American medical schools was not as uncommon even in 1964 as the quote suggests. The Tietze study actually was of 91 medical schools in the U.S. and Canada, 78 of which were non-Catholic medical schools in the U.S. and four of which were Catholic ones in both countries. Of the 78 U.S. non-Catholic ones -- the most pertinent group in this discussion -- a full 71 had the teaching of "fertility regulation" as "a part of their regular curricula."[170] One other "expected to include it soon," three more had it on an elective basis, and of the three which did not have it at all, two were in states which had legislation severely restricting its teaching. As far as the textbooks are concerned, none was any more recent than 1963 and eight were pre-1961. (This is significant when one considers that medical textbooks are put out in new editions every few years.) Furthermore, the researchers do not say what they mean by "isolated reference" and "no complete discussion" and do not state how many broke down into these categories and "no mention." Also, the discussion in the article about the texts appears in the section on "Roman Catholic Medical Schools." It is not entirely clear that the texts in question are the ones used in most of the medical schools studied (i.e., the non-Catholic ones).

The fact that the *Wade* and PPFA briefs devote entire sections to discussing the shortcomings of contraception indicates a belief about how human beings should deal with their sexual faculties. For example, the PPFA brief says that "[t]he chief disadvantage of both of the rhythm methods [of pregnancy regulation] is that '*oppor-*

tunity for coitus is greatly reduced'" and that "[b]oth techniques [calendar and temperature]...*obviously require that the couple be highly motivated and disciplined*, since careful records must be kept and *periods of abstinence observed*."[171] Summing up its discussion about the effectiveness of all methods of birth regulation, the PPFA brief states this: "The failure rates are...much higher when the *use*-effectiveness is considered, and this too varies with the techniques...*as well as with the motivation and education of the people using them*.[172] The *Wade* brief puts down "abstention and rhythm" as "not seriously regarded by the medical profession in this century."[173] (It gives no indication of being aware of advances in natural family planning which have rendered rhythm obsolete.)

Procreation obviously is not seen as the primary purpose of sex. Indeed, it does not seem to be a purpose at all. The major concern of the briefs seems to be the *avoidance* of babies. Another passage in the *Wade* brief -- that "'[In] the period 1960 to 1965 there were 4.7 million births that could have been prevented by 'perfect contraception'" -- betrays an almost obsessive view about this.[174] Sex is to be separated from procreation.

The passages on abstention, rhythm, and the "failure rates" express the view that people should really not be expected to be disciplined in sexual matters. The need for the individual to develop the virtue of chastity and for the married couple to practice periodic continence is not recognized. The briefs thus betray a view of human nature which holds that the individual cannot reach high standards of virtue by developing good moral habits. Since he cannot exercise an "inner" control over his passions, he must have every opportunity to exert an "outer" control over the consequences of these passions. The best that can be said about the briefs from a moral standpoint is that they undersell man's abilities as a moral agent, the worst that can be said is that they espouse a "free and easy" view about sex.

The first quote above from the PPFA brief makes the further erroneous judgment that coitus or sexual intercourse is the only way a couple can show their love for each other. Again, common experience disproves this.

The briefs' obliviousness to the need for virtue and self-discipline and their emphasis on contraceptive techniques to avoid conception and medically safe abortion to avoid birth indicates the view that sex is essentially a scientific problem. The aim seems to be the use of more and more science and technology to gain greater "outer" control over the powerful force of sex. The ultimate goal seems to be an air-tight guarantee that having sex will *not* produce babies (i.e., "'perfect contraception'").

THE RELATIONSHIP BETWEEN ABORTION AND CONTRACEPTION

There was already literature on this question before *Wade* and *Bolton*. Population expert Abdel Omran of the University of North Carolina had written the following:

> "Many studies from various countries indicate that women who have experienced one or more induced abortions have a proclivity to continue this method of birth control even when effective contraceptives become available."[175]

Dr. Arthur Dyck, Professor of Population Ethics at Harvard, echoes this:

> In countries where contraceptives are widely used, permissive abortion policies exact an immediate price. They lead to the neglect of careful contraception.[176]

We can see this borne out in specific case studies, such as those in England in the first years of its liberalized abortion law. Of 249 induced abortion cases personally attended to by one British physician in the late 1960s, 30 percent normally used no birth control and 48 percent used none on the occasion of the conception which led to the abortion. A study of women who obtained legal abortions under the new law through the Birmingham Pregnancy Advisory Service showed that 45.8 percent normally used no birth control and 73.5 percent used none at the time of the conception.[177] Of the first 300 women given abortions through the London Pregnancy Advisory Service after the new law went into effect, 42 percent said that they normally used no method of birth control and 70 percent used none at the time of the conception.[178] The experience in Japan has been the same. Japan had one of the earliest permissive abortion laws. Half the Japanese women who have abortions admit that they did not even try to prevent conception.[179] The same result occurred in Eastern Europe, which had a permissive abortion policy.[180]

American studies have been mixed in their results about the relationship between abortion and contraceptive use. They have shown that women who have more than one abortion are actually more likely to use contraceptives than those who have had only one.[181] They have also shown, however, that most women -- this is especially true of adolescent girls -- who have had only one abortion did not use contraception prior to it.[182] They have also shown that a sizable number of both groups of women do not use contraception.[183] This suggests that in the U.S., abortion, to at least some degree, has come to be viewed as essentially a means of contraception.

The above studies and authorities raise doubts about the briefs' claim that abortion is needed because contraceptives are unavailable. They indicate that women will have abortions even when they have contraceptives -- and, presumably, effective ones in light of the dates of most of the studies. Part of the reason why was given by the Honorary Medical Secretary of the London Service mentioned above in connection with one of the studies. She said that 60 percent of the women aborted were single and that "[m]any an intelligent young unmarried woman has admitted that she viewed taking oral contraceptives as a degree of commitment she was not prepared for."[184] Thus, abortion is perhaps viewed as an easier way to "solve the problem" than contraception. The tendency of women to turn to abortion, when available, instead of contraception is possibly seen by the increasing rate of abortion recidivism in the United States. The recidivism rate has increased as abortion has become more widely available and accepted. Tietze reports that repeaters went from 0 percent in 1967-1969 to 23 percent in 1976 in the U.S. and that the figures increased steadily during this period. The increase paralleled the increase in total abortions and the number of first-time abortions.[185] The experience abroad, where abortion has generally been available longer, has been the same. There has been a wide variance in recidivism rates in European studies -- as there was in the early American studies --, ranging from 12 to 42.3 percent. Some Asian nations have reported rates as high as 52 percent. All this data led one review article to conclude that "[t]here seems to be little doubt about the positive relationship between the recidivism rate and the length of time a woman has been exposed to abortion practices."[186] In light of this, is there truth to the briefs' claim that an important reason legalized abortion is needed is because the poor have less access to contraceptives than the more affluent? Perhaps, but when women do have such access many tend not to use them when abortion is available.

The strongest testimony to the substitution of abortion for contraception may have come recently when the pro-abortion movement itself conceded that this was happening. One reason given by the Alan Guttmacher Institute, PPFA's research arm, for the increasing U.S. abortion rate is women's disenchantment -- because of the health risks involved -- with the birth control pill and the intrauterine device (IUD).[187]

The Alleged Benefits for Society of Abortion

Is Legalized Abortion Necessary to End Legal Abortions which Present Grave Health Risks to the Woman?

THE NUMBER OF ILLEGAL ABORTIONS

Both the *Wade* and the PPFA briefs present estimates about the number of illegal abortions supposedly performed each year in the U.S. before the *Wade* and *Bolton* decisions. The *Wade* brief says there were between 200,000 and one million; the PPFA brief says "about one million."[188] The PPFA brief also gives estimates of the number of women who died each year because of complications of illegal abortions. It says that at one time (it cites a 1964 source on this) before a change "of several factors including the advent of antibiotics," 5,000 to 10,000 women died each year. For the more recent pre-*Wade/Bolton* years, 500 to 1,000 is the "more reliable national estimate."[189]

The number of illegal abortions given in the *Wade* brief is problematical. If the brief cannot narrow the gap between the possible outer limits of illegal abortions any more than 800,000, we have to suspect that the figure is unreliable. Actually, this is practically admitted by the brief in a footnote which says that "[s]ecret induced abortions are inherently incapable of quantification." It assures us that "[n]evertheless, one can be certain that the number is very high" and gives us several sources to check for estimates.[190]

Commentators have attacked the validity of high figures like these. John M. Finnis, Fellow and Praelector in Jurisprudence at the University College at Oxford University, explains how they were based on unreliable extrapolations:

> ...the great majority of commentators in recent American law journals [circa 1970] accept that 1,200,000 is a plausible estimate of the number of abortions *per annum* in the United States. But on examination it appears that this figure is based on a study published in 1934 -- according to which it may be assumed that there is one illegal abortion for every 3.55 live births. And this latter figure is an extrapolation from the case histories of 10,000 women who attended the Margaret Sanger birth control clinic in New York City between 1925 and 1929! Another widely accepted figure ...is 600,000 *per annum* -- this by extrapolation from the case histories of the women who volunteered information in Kinsey's famous study of female sexuality (a group which included a negligible proportion of blacks and Catholics, and which was unrepresentative even of urban white women).[191]

Finnis could have added that the results of these

studies might have been skewed by the Hawthorne effect. This says that persons who are being questioned in a survey may be motivated to give responses which conform to what they perceive to be the position of the questioner, even if it requires their compromising their beliefs to some degree. This would certainly seem to have been possible in the above cases because neither Mrs. Sanger nor Dr. Kinsey was a dispassionate student of this subject. Both were viewed as opening the way for changed social attitudes about sex.

Professor Dyck quotes the above Finnis passage and then goes further:

> One should not assume that the lower limit of 200,000 is a sacred figure...the study done in Indianapolis in 1941-42, involving married, white Protestant couples [showed that] 1.9 percent of their pregnancies ended in illegal abortions. If we were to extrapolate this figure and apply it to the United States for the year 1940, it would have meant that there were 48,000 illegal abortions in the United States in that year. If we were to increase this number by 50 percent to allow for population growth up to the year 1969, we would be estimating the number of illegal abortions per year in the United States as roughly 72,000.[192]

In a recent elaborate statistical study, Barbara J. Syska, Thomas W. Hilgers, M.D., and Dennis O'Hare came to this conclusion:

> A reasonable estimate for the actual number of criminal abortions per year in the prelegalization era [pre-1967] would be from a low of 39,000 (1950) to a high of 210,000 (1961) and a mean of 98,000 per year.[193]

It thus appears that there are good reasons to dispute the accuracy of the figures presented in the briefs. Not only was the 1,000,000 figure probably too high, but so may have been the 200,000 one.

MATERNAL MORTALITY FROM ILLEGAL ABORTIONS

The next question to consider is the validity of the figures appearing in the PPFA brief about maternal mortality due to illegal abortions. Noonan and Louisell write that the reporting system has been good enough to insure "some exactness" in the statistics on this over the years. They say that these statistics reveal that approximately 250 women died each year as a result of abortions in the U.S. [194] They cite figures from the former U.S. Department of Health, Education, and Welfare which showed a death rate of 0.1 percent per one hundred thousand abortions in the period from 1962 to 1967. Two representative years they point to, according to statistics from the National Center for Health Statistics, were 1965 and 1966, in which 235 and 189 deaths, respectively, from all forms of induced abortion (i.e., both legal and illegal) occurred.[195]

Remember that women sometimes die of disorders which are complications of abortion, but are not recorded as such. This, along with the fact that a small number of deaths may go unreported, suggests that the figures Noonan and Louisell cite may be somewhat low. Dr. Tietze, who is strongly pro-abortion, said that these figures should be slightly increased but called figures in the thousands "unmitigated nonsense"[196] and would have estimated the number at somewhere under 1,000.[197] It appears, then, that the updated statistics of the PPFA brief were at least close to being accurate, but still were a bit high. The figures cited by Noonan and Louisell are probably a bit low, but the number of deaths in actuality was probably considerably less than 1,000 and possibly even less than 500, the low range of the PPFA estimate. It must be realized then even 500 is double or more than double the number of deaths reported. Accuracy has been thought to be fairly high in reporting on this matter over the years and such a wide difference would seem unlikely.

THE EFFECT OF LEGALIZATION ON THE RATE OF ILLEGAL ABORTIONS

What has been the actual effect of legalized abortion in the U.S. and elsewhere on the illegal abortion rate? There was evidence before *Wade* and *Bolton* that legalizing abortion would not eliminate illegal abortions, or in some cases, even reduce them. For example, after the first two years of a liberalized abortion law in Britain, the Royal College of Obstetricians and Gynaecologists stated, on the basis of results from a questionnaire sent to obstetricians-gynecologists employed in the Natioanl Health Service in England and Wales, the following:

> "The figures...indicat[e]...that despite a sharp rise in the number of...therapeutic [legal] abortions from 1968 to 1969, there was not unfortunately a significant change in the number of cases of spontaneous [illegal] abortions requiring admission to hospital.[198]

Dr. Tietze, meanwhile, had written that legalization probably did not reduce the incidence of illegal abortion in the Scandinavian countries.[199] It was estimated that in Japan, which legalized abortion in 1948, that 1,000,000 illegal abortions continued to be performed each year.[200] In the U.S.S.R., which relegalized abortion in 1955 and was thought to have an abortion rate of 5,000,000 per year by 1959, illegal abortions continued.[201] Another study showed that while legalization decreased the number of illegal abortions in Yugoslavia, they continued to take place.[202]

The Syska-Hilgers-O'Hare study addressed the question of the effect of legalized abortion on illegal abortion in the U.S. from 1967, when abortion laws first began to be liberalized, to 1977. These are their findings:

> It would appear that the legal abortion policy in the United States has resulted in a modest decrease in the number of criminal abortions. This decrease began in 1971 and 1972 and continued until 1974 [just a year after *Wade* and *Bolton* opened the door to abortion everywhere in the U.S.], at which time a plateau was reached. For 1974 through 1977, there has been no noticeable reduction in spite of a continued increase in the number of legal abortions.[203]

They tell us further that the decline in criminal abortions did not begin until the legal abortion ratio (the number of legal abortions per 1,000 live births) reached 160 and did not reach its plateau until the abortion ratio was 250. No further reduction in criminal abortion has occurred even though the legal abortion ratio soared to 325 in 1977. Expressed another way, these figures mean that widely available and legal abortion has reduced illegal abortion, but only up to a certain point. (The estimated reduction in the number of criminal abortions is 53,000.) If we think back to the estimations of illegal abortions from the authorities cited, we see that this does not eliminate illegal abortions. What *has* happened is that *legal* abortions have skyrocketed. While 53,000 illegal abortions have been eliminated, 970,000 legal abortions have "replaced" them. This is a ratio of 18 legal abortions performed for every one illegal abortion eliminated. This is as high as an eleven-fold increase in the number of total abortions from the prelegalization era.[204] This directly contradicts the claim of the PPFA supplemental brief that "only 25 percent of legal abortions replace live births. Most of the others probably replace illegal abortions."[205]

Why, one might ask, do criminal abortions continue when legal abortion is so widely available? One reason might be that many poor women who want abortions cannot afford legal ones, so they get cheaper illegal ones. Figures from the U.S. Government about the effect of the Hyde Amendment -- which cut off federal funds for most Medicaid abortions -- on the procurement of abortions cast doubt upon the likelihood of this, however.[206] Moreover, a number of states -- including some of the most populous ones -- still pay for abortions for the poor.[207] The Willkes explain possible reasons which would seem to be present no matter how liberal the laws become. One might be a wife whose husband wants another child, but she does not. She fears he might find out if she gets an abortion in a hospital or clinic, which are regularly operating establishments and keep records (although they are confidential). Another is a married woman whose husband has been away and in the meantime becomes pregnant by another man. Again, she does not want her husband ever to find out. A third is a prominent citizen whose teenage daughter becomes pregnant. He may have enemies who could somehow find out that she had a legal abortion and the result could be scandal. A fourth is a poor woman who wants to avoid the time and incomprehensible red-tape she would have to go through at the public hospital or clinic.[208] And one could think of a thousand more scenarios.

THE EFFECT OF LEGALIZATION ON ABORTION MORTALITY

In the meantime what has been the effect of legalization on the maternal mortality rate from abortion? This is investigated in a recent statistical study by Hilgers and O'Hare. Using data gathered from the National Center for Health Statistics, they state that since legalization there has been an abrupt drop in the relative incidence of abortion-related maternal deaths due to *illegal* abortion (tracing the period 1970 to 1976), but that these deaths have *not* been completely eliminated. The *relative frequency* of abortion-related maternal deaths due to illegal abortions, however, (keeping in mind that there are somewhat fewer illegal abortions) has shown an *increase*.[209] This is not surprising since most illegal abortions before legalization were performed by physicians, who had some degree of competence.[210] When abortion was legalized many of these abortionists began to work for legitimate clinics and hospitals. The result is possibly that now when women seek illegal abortions, they indeed are performed by incompetent, unscrupulous persons or by the women themselves.

Hilgers and O'Hare also show that there was already a downward trend in the maternal mortality rate before legalization, and legalization had no effect on it. They further establish that maternal deaths from illegal abortions have been decreasing, but have been replaced, almost one for one, by deaths due to legal abortion. (This means that if in a particular year deaths due to illegal abortion decline by 3, there will be perhaps 3 deaths due to legal abortions.) The result is that over a period extending through the past thirty years (ranging from a time of tight restriction to a wide-open abortion policy), there has been no significant change in the *relative frequency* of abortion-related maternal deaths due to induced abortion in the U.S.[211]

We might ask why liberalization has not reduced the abortion mortality rate. I might speculate, without any further statistics or other evidence to support my position, that it is simply because there are so many more abortions (as was shown in the Syska, Hilgers, and O'Hare study). When there are more procedures done which are to some degree risky, there will be more deaths. When so many women are demanding abortion -- some clinics treat them in almost assembly-line fashion -- and human frailty being what it is, there is greater haste and more carelessness on the part of medical personnel. Among some physicians and clinics doing abortions a nonchalant, perhaps even disdainful attitude, has developed toward patients. Some unethical physicians may be more concerned with the economic benefits they gain than with their patients' needs.[212] This kind of attitude cannot help but to translate itself into a lack of concern with the quality of care given to patients.

The final point that the Hilgers-O'Hare study addresses is the relative safety of abortion as compared to childbirth. Recall that the Supreme Court accepted the argument that abortion, until the end of the first trimester, "may" result in a lower mortality rate for women than "normal childbirth."[213] Both the *Wade* brief and the PPFA supplemental brief make this same claim.[214] The former cites the abortion mortality figures for the nation as a whole (10.3 per 100,000 procedures), for New York City for approximately the first year of legalized abortion (5.3 per 100,000), for one of the Iron Curtain countries, Hungary (1.2 per 100,000), and the figure for mortality caused by childbirth for the U.S. (28.0 per 100,000). In comparing the first and last figures, the brief says that abortions in the U.S. are 2.7 times safer than childbirth.[215] The PPFA supplemental brief cites the figures from New York State for the last half of 1971. It says that during this period the abortion death rate "dropped to 3.7 per 100,000" which was "less than half the death rate associated with live delivery."[216]

The figures used from New York City (and, we should say, New York State since most of its abortions were done in the City) are open to question. Writing in 1972, Hilgers said that the early New York City data of the type in the briefs was not reliable. It was incomplete, there was inadequate or no follow-up of abortion patients in many cases (especially those who were from outside of the state and city,58.8 percent of the total in the first year), and some deaths were discounted because of the unsubstantiated claim that they were not performed "under legal auspices."[217] Many deaths are often not noted as the result of legal abortions; the cause of death will be recorded as the specific disorder which was actually a complication of abortion.

Statistics from Eastern European countries, such as Hungary, are also questionable. They may be inaccurate, first, because of censorship and distortion from Communist governments. They may also be inaccurate because of generally poorer record-keeping procedures than in the West. Hilgers writes that some Eastern Eureopean spokesmen have admitted that abortion complications are underreported because patients treated outside hospitals are seldom included in hospital statistics.[218]

The Eastern European statistics are shown to be even more ostensibly questionable when compared with statistics from the West on both abortion and childbirth-related mortality. Hilgers shows that for a period of several years in the 1960s to 1970, all the European countires and American states included in a sample study had abortion mortality rates which exceeded their childbirth maternal mortality rate. Only the Eastern European countries sampled had maternal mortality rates due to childbirth which exceeded their abortion mortality rates. This disparity existed even though a few of the Western countries had had a longer experience with induced abortion and would thus be expected to have a lower mortality rate. It was present also despite the acknowledged lesser degree of medical sophistication and lack of adequate medical facilities. This would suggest that not only the childbirth-related mortality rates (which were the highest of any political entity sampled), but the abortion-related ones also would be higher.[219]

Hilgers discounts the explanation given that most Eastern European abortions are done in the safer first trimester. When he compares the first trimester abortion figures of these countries with the Western entities, he finds that the same relationship between the former and the latter exist on abortion versus childbirth-related mortality. Further, when he compared the numbers of induced abortions in Hungary with those in the U.S. in the pre-*Wade/Bolton* period, taking into account the overall population differences of the two countries, he finds that a woman in the former is 2.6 times as likely to die from an abortion than in the latter.[220] When the statistics are looked at from this angle, the low abortion mortality rate in Hungary relative to childbirth as cited in the *Wade* brief -- and with it the overall claim of the greater safety of abortion than childbirth for the woman -- appears very problematical.

Finally, the Hilgers-O'Hare study, using a new formula which adjusts for maternal deaths incident to childbirth which result from spontaneous abortion, ectopic pregnancy, stillbirth, and hydatidiform mole (which are treated differently in most studies), concludes:

> In comparing the relative risk of natural pregnancy versus that of legal abortion, natural pregnancy was found to be safer in both the first and second 20 weeks of pregnancy.[221]

There are limitations of this information in evaluating the statement in the *Wade* opinion, because this study does not break pregnancy into trimesters, nor does it compare the risks of first-trimester abortion with those of childbirth.

CONCLUSIONS

There are serious reasons to challenge the briefs' claim that legalized abortion largely eliminates illegal abortion -- or, in some cases, even substantially reduces it -- or that it eliminates maternal mortality due to abortion (or even maternal mortality due specifically to *illegal* abortion). This is also a valid basis for disputing the claim of both the briefs and the *Wade* opinion that induced abortion is in some sense safer -- in terms of the risk of maternal mortality -- than is childbirth. I shall point to other risks to the woman's physical and mental health -- i.e., the risk of morbidity -- from induced abortion in Part Two of this Chapter.

Is Legalized Abortion Necessary to Cope with Overpopulation?

The PPFA brief argues in one short paragraph that there is an over-population problem. It presents no specific information or statistics to back this up. To prove its views, it says it "need only point to the increasing concern of the United States Government and the governments of many of the states as well as of the United Nations and its constituent members with the threat posed by population increases."[222] The brief gives us only two references in a footnote to support this sweeping claim: President Nixon's *Message on Population* in 1969 and the *Interim Report to the President and the Congress* of the Presidential Commission on Population Growth and the American Future in 1971. It affirms that there are "widely acknowledged dangers of continued increase in population and of the myriad problems presented by unwanted pregnancies."[223] It does not at this point in the brief tell us specifically what these "widely acknowledged dangers" or "Myriad problems" are. It refers us back to the section of the brief which discusses the problems associated with having unwanted children.[224]

IS THERE ACTUALLY A POPULATION CRISIS?

Let us now briefly consider whether we have a "population crisis." Professor Dyck gives us a short statement of what the term has been understood to mean by those making such a claim:

> Population growth is not only linked to many kinds of social problems but is also depicted as a threat to human survival. And so one speaks of a population crisis. If population growth threatens human survival, then measures to curtail such growth would obviously be urgent.[225]

Contrary to the brief's claim, there has been a fairly steady downward trend in the percentage of net increase in U.S. population since 1960.[226] Economist and population expert Colin Clark wrote in 1976 that our population growth hovered near replacement level, which is 2.2 children per family.[227] This means, according to one of the common definitions of the term, that the U.S. is near, or at, zero population growth.[228] What appears to be a problem of overpopulation really is an uneven distribution of population in the country. Most of our population is concentrated in a relatively small number of urban areas.[229] Even with this seven of the ten largest U.S. cities *lost* population in the 1960s.[230] The population density of the U.S. overall is considerably less than most countries in Asia and Europe.[231]

In the world at large, the annual percentage rate of population growth has been declining since the latter half of the 1960s, both in the developed and underdeveloped nations.[232] Some European nations are actually experiencing a decline in population.[233]

As far as the effect of population growth on various social problems is concerned, consider what Professor Dyck has to say:

> Our conclusion...with respect to the relationship between population growth and threats to the human species, such as environmental deterioration, starvation, and poverty, is that none of these dangers, however imminent, ensue directly from present population growth rates. Concern over space and the use of space in a finite world, another genuine concern, is again something that is not solved simply by decreasing numbers.[234]

There is also no proven relationship between population density and the conditions antecedent to rapid population growth and social unrest or revolution.[235]

Let us consider the area of food. Since the 1961-65 period, world food production has increased 43 percent, while population has increased only a bit more than half as fast.[236] In the years between 1961-63 and 1976-77, world grain production increased by nearly 60 percent. In the U.S., it increased by about 50 percent. Even in underdeveloped nations, grain production increased by about 65 percent, substantially faster than the population grew.[237] Even India, often mentioned as the example of a country struggling because of overpopulation, has had a surplus of food in the last few years and is now reasonably self-sufficient in this regard.[238] Further, only a third of the world's agricultural land and a sixth of the arable land is now in use and if we fertilize we will even have more usable land.[239]

There is actually no danger of *running out* of natural resources and water. No mineral resource (including oil) is on the verge of being depleted and no prediction in recent years to this effect has proved correct. It may, however, be more difficult and costly to extract some of these minerals.[240]

It is often said that overpopulation means less economic development. Population expert Colin Clark strongly disputes this. His studies show that developing courtries with the highest rates of population growth actually have, on the average, a higher rate of growth per product head than the countries with low rates of population growth.[241] Economist Julian L. Simon concurs.[242] According to his studies based on a model which takes different demographic factors into account, economies subjected to faster population growth achieve both higher output per capita and higher per-worker income than economies with slower population growth.[243] This applies for both developed and developing economies.

Why, then, have so many "authorities" been saying there is a population problem and why have their claims been so readily accepted? One writer says that population data and projections are typically "guesswork." The forecasting is based on a minimal amount of data and the footnotes accompanying it often admit that full data is unobtainable.[244]

The present-day insistence that there is a population crisis has been referred to as "the prevailing Malthusian wisdom."[245] Fredric Wertham explains why this "wisdom" is incorrect:

> For Malthus and the neo-Malthusians, overpopulation means overcopulation. But a surplus population is never absolute. It is always relative to other factors of production, distribution and social organization. It is relative also in respect to

> occupation, sex, and age...There are definite socio-economic conditions that explain why at certain times and in certain places there are too many people.[246]

Clark expresses agreement on this last point: "...the world's problems...in the coming century...will be political, not economic or environmental...This hysterical clamour about population growth...effectively distracts attention from the political questions..."[247]

Two other problems with this "neo-Malthusian" view is that it underestimates natural resources and the enormous potential of modern scientific knowledge, particularly in agriculture, which can be brought to bear on food and production problems, etc.[248]

Also, population growth is not inevitable or constant, as is widely assumed. Simon says that historically it has adjusted to "productive conditions," with increased income and the urbanization it brings about substantially affecting it.[249] Simon also points to a number of reasons why population growth promotes economic growth and says that population growth, in the long run, produces better economic performance for a nation.[250]

IS ABORTION NEEDED TO STOP OVERPOPULATION?

Even if there were a population crisis, would abortion be the remedy for it? I have already addressed this question, to some extent, in what I said about the effect of easily available abortion on contraceptive use. This would perhaps indicate that the answer is no. Simon's conclusion that population growth has not been steady and that social forces have, to some extent, resulted in its self-regulation would also suggest not. Dyck, writing before the *Wade* and *Bolton* decisions, says the following:

> The decline in birth rates in the United States is being recorded not only in states that have permissive abortion laws but also in states that have restrictive laws...The relation of abortion policies to fertility behavior...is not self-evident: it bears strict scrutiny...Moreover, there are very few studies of the effects of abortion

policy upon birth rates.[251]

On the other hand, easily available abortion appears to have succeeded in limiting population in such Eastern European countries as Rumania and the U.S.S.R.[252] In both those countries, abortion policy has been changed depending on the governments' determination about what the national needs were. The question we should ask before accepting abortion as a solution to whatever population problems exist is what our purpose in shaping policy should be. Should it be the needs of the community alone, without regard to the matter of the dignity of human life, that are to be determinative? Do we really want our government(s) to make decisions about population policy?

Will Legalized Abortion Solve the Problem of "Unwanted" Children?

The third of the alleged benefits of abortion for society is that it will eliminate the problem of unwanted children. The PPFA brief speaks at length about abortion being needed for this purpose. We will have to see whether the connection between abortion, unwantedness, and child abuse runs in the way the brief contends.

THE ARGUMENTS OF THE PPFA BRIEF

The brief begins its section on "The Facts About Unwanted Births" by quoting the President's Commission on Population Growth and the American Future again which claims the following: "one-third of the married couples who did not intend to have any more children already had at least one unwanted child" and "[i]n the period 1960-65 nearly 20 percent of all live births were reported as unwanted by their parents."[253] The statistics may be true, but what is their significance?

The brief does not say what the term "unwanted" was understood to mean by the Commission or by the parents who gave this information.[254] The brief offers no precise explanation of the term, but just refers to alleged manifestations and consequences of "unwantedness." Its opening quotes from the Commission speak about an entirely different facet of the problem, which is illegitimacy. Taken one way -- which may have been the way many or most of the parents mentioned took it --, most children are probably "unwanted." A couple typically does not undertake a *specific* act of sexual intercourse intending to conceive a child. In short, the statistics presented by the brief from the Commission on this point *sound* overpowering, but they do not necessarily tell us much of anything.

The next statement made by the brief is the following:

> It is obvious that unwanted births occurring in marriage frequently result in physical and mental harm to the mother, economic and social hardships to the existing family and often lead to the abuse and neglect of the children.[255]

The brief follows this with its discussion of the problems of illegitimacy. It says that "[i]llegitimacy rates are high in the United States and are increasing."[256] It says that "one-third of all first-born children in the United States in the years 1964 to 1966 were conceived out of wedlock."[257] It then suggests that the numbers are really higher than this official figure. Then, it reveals the plight of the unmarried pregnant woman:

> ...[she] is faced with a number of alternatives, many of which depend on her economic status. In some instances a hastily arranged marriage will take place...Such forced marriages often between immature young people frequently lead to divorce. If the pregnant woman does not marry, she may seek an abortion.[258]

Restricted abortion in some states and lack of funds may mean that a woman "may try to abort herself or may turn to the unskilled quack abortionist and serious injury or even death may result from either course."[259]

The brief then ranges over the many consequences -- social, economic, and health -- of illegitimate birth for the mother and the child, including an "increase in child abuse and neglect."[260] It cites a well-known

Swedish study which concluded that "unwanted" children suffered, among other things, the following problems to a greater degree:

> "They were...registered more often in psychiatric services, and a few more of them than control subjects received psychiatric care. They were more often registered for antisocial and criminal behavior, and slightly more often for drunken misconduct, and they got public assistance more often than the control subjects. A few more of them were educationally sub-normal..."[261]

This section of the brief, again, has great rhetorical effect. Its structure is odd, in that it jumps from discussing "unwanted" births to married couples, to the problems -- for both mother and children -- of illegitimacy, and concludes with a study showing "unwanted" children -- it does not specify if they are mostly the products of marital unions or not -- have a host of problems. Perhaps this section is just poorly drafted, but possibly the brief-writers wanted it to be this way. Perhaps they believed that the Court would have greater empathy for the plight of the teenage girl who in her immaturity made a terrible mistake than for a married couple who could not plan their family responsibly. This may have been their intention, but the brief-writers themselves see these two things as essentially the same. Unwanted children, whether within wedlock or not, represent a problem of sex and reproduction that has not yet been subject to sufficient control by science to yield the most desirable results. Abortion, like contraception, is the scientific means chosen to accomplish this.

A CRITIQUE OF THE ARGUMENTS

With that, consider again the same specific passages from the brief and see precisely what they do and do *not* prove. The passage dealing with the alternatives available to the unwed mother is well constructed to make the reader believe that the mother is in an unbearable dilemma. Restrictive abortion laws are characterized as giving her no way out without suffering enormous personal consequences. In reality, however, the kind of either/or alternative that the brief refers to does not exist. The brief neglects to say that many, if not most, marriages which result from these circumstances *are* lasting. The brief creates great emotional effect by speaking of "forced" marriages, but few women or girls are probably truly compelled by parents or anyone else to marry. If they are, both civil and church law recognizes this as a ready grounds for annulment. The brief also ignores the existence of many programs and homes for unwed mothers and the readily available opportunity to adopt a child out or put him in the state's care. The statistic of one-third of conceptions occurring out of wedlock is also emotionally stirring, but misleading and completely uninformative by itself. This is because many of these women marry after the conception.

The passage also gives the impression that young women were turning to illegal abortions in vast numbers and suffering serious health consequences and death. We have seen, however, that illegal abortions were nowhere near as numerous as claimed. Also, most of these illegal abortions were not performed on the poor, single young woman the brief speaks of, but rather on more affluent, married women.[262]

All of the claims of harm to both mother and child by unwanted and/or illegitimate births heighten the rhetorical effect of the section, but can be challenged on substantive grounds. First, the brief gives the impression that there is a necessary connection between illegitimacy and health and other problems resulting in the mother and the illegitimate child. The one source it cites to prove this -- a study done in Buffalo, New York -- does not say this.[263] Further, it seems to view these problems as resulting primarily from the age of the mothers. (Apparently, most in the study were teenagers.) The other source it cites acknowledges that "many" of the problems in cases of illegitimate births result from a failure to obtain adequate prenatal care.[264] Since no clear connection is made between illegitimacy and health problems, the brief's statement that "because of the frequency with which illegitimate births occur to adolescents, there is a direct relationship between early childbearing and the risks of particular diseases in offspring and the risk of maternal death" is just rhetoric.[265]

I showed, however, in my discussion of incest as a justification for abortion, that a number of studies have shown that there is no greater risk to either mother or child generally when pregnancy occurs in adolescence. The risk is contingent, primarily, on the extent of pre-natal care the mother receives, as the brief's source indicated.

The brief's focus in its section on "unwanted" children manifests only the abortion advocates' perspective on children and sexual morality. Women and parents generally are seen as victimized by an "unwanted" child. Children are viewed as an unwelcome burden. The concern is with preventing the undesired consequences of sexual intercourse; the way to do this is to get rid of these "consequences."

THE RELATIONSHIP BETWEEN UNWANTED BIRTHS AND LATER CHILD PROBLEMS AND ABUSE

There are serious difficulties with each of the sources given by the brief to establish the connection between unwanted births and later child problems and abuse. Dr. Myre Sim, Professor of Psychiatry at the University of Ottawa, has commented on the Swedish study cited in the brief, conducted by Mssrs. Forssmann and Thuwe, which involved a comparison of Swedish women who had made requests for abortion but had them refused, with women who had not requested an abortion. The children of each were followed up for twenty years -- the study using the fact of the request for abortion as the indication of "unwantedness" -- with the conclusions that I quoted above resulting. Sim says, however, that the study was unreliable because the researchers did not control for social class. This was important, he said, because where an abortion was granted after the woman's appearance before one of the Swedish medical boards, it was generally the more educated and articulate who were successful at persuading the board, whereas women of lesser intelligence and education were not. Refused abortion tended to be biased against women in lower social classes. Thus, Sim contends, the study was more truly a comparison of the typical handicaps of lower class children with children of mothers who did not want abortions, than it was between the latter and women generally who wanted abortions.[266] In effect, the group in society that was beset with the most serious social problems was being compared to one that was relatively free of them. The result could not help but be skewed.

The two other sources cited by the brief are David G. Gil's 1970 book *Violence Against Children* and the *Interim Report of the President's Commission on Population Growth*. Neither cites any studies to back up this claim.[267] Gil asserts on the third from last page of his book that "unwanted and rejected children...are known to be frequently victims of severe physical abuse and even infanticide."[268] He also proposes family planning programs and abortion as a solution.[269] None of the studies which he reports on in the book, however, establish -- or even inquire into -- any connection between either unwantedness and abuse or the likelihood that easily available abortion will eliminate or reduce the problem of unwanted and abused children. Again, we have authorities cited by the brief which do not establish what it claims they do.

Other authorities have strongly disputed the claim that it is "unwanted" children who typically become the victims of abuse. One frequently quoted study by Dr. E. F. Lenoski of the University of Southern California Medical School discovered that over 90 percent of the battered children studied had been "wanted" pregnancies.[270] Another showed that only a small percentage of abusive mothers had considered abortion when they were carrying the child they later abused. Only a fifth were "displeased" by the pregnancy, although close to half had "reservations" about it. (The significance of this last point is questionable, however, since over one-third of the control -- non-abusive -- mothers in the study also said this.)[271] Other writers have maintained that the frequency of abuse is higher among adopted children -- who, by definition, were "wanted" by their parents -- than unadopted.[272] The factors causing child abuse cited most frequently by researchers are not "unwantedness," but parents' lack of social support from family, friends, and community, hostility to them by society, based on a disapproved sexual and social pattern of existence, and -- most commonly -- their having been abused and neglected themselves when they were children.[273]

Does aborting unwanted children solve the problem of child abuse? According to Dr. Philip G. Ney, a British Columbia psychiatrist, there is "no convincing evidence" that liberalized abortion has reduced the rate of child abuse "or, similarly, that restrictive abortion resulted in frequent child abuse.[274] Dr. Selwyn M.

Smith, a psychiatrist of the University of Ottawa, states that abortion will produce a reduction in unwanted births only if the motivation for limiting family size already exists.[275]

The easy availability of abortion has not reduced child abuse, and the statistics confirm this view. Dr. Smith indicates that it is difficult to know for sure how much child abuse there is.[276] The National Center on Child Abuse and Neglect (NCCAN) *estimates* that a million children per year are abused or neglected. Of these, it estimates that 250,000 per year are physically abused. Sociologist Richard Gelles, writing seven years after *Wade* and *Bolton*, believes that these figures underestimate the true level of abuse.[277] Dr. Vincent Fontana, Medical Director of New York Foundling Hospital Center for Parent and Child Development, and Dennis J. Besharov, Director of NCCAN, writing in 1979, point out that there has been "[a] continued annual increase" in child abuse reports in New York City. There was, for example, an increase of over 3,900 cases between 1974 and 1975. They say that "[c]hild abuse and neglect has become a widespread, violent, childrearing pattern which is becoming more entrenched in our population."[278]

One of the reasons for these higher child abuse figures is probably that more cases are being reported. Nevertheless, while we cannot be certain of it, child abuse seems to be increasing. In any event, it remains a serious problem. There is no sign that the new abortion liberty is alleviating it.

Furthermore, Dr. Ney writes that, far from ending child abuse, legalized abortion may actually be promoting it:

> Abortion not only increases the rates of child battering at present, it will increase the tendency to batter and abort in succeeding generations. Abortion, producing guilt both in the mother and in the children who survive, increases the probability of displaced hostility, which results in so many battered, murdered children. More importantly, by interrupting the formation of the delicate mechanism which promotes mother-infant bonding, it puts at risk millions of babies who are not aborted...Evidence indi-

> cates that, once implemented, abortion changes attitudes toward infants, such that birth rates do not increase, even when the abortion law is tightened.[279]

While the brief does not say this in so many words, the implication of the passages referred to is clear: "Unwantedness" is undesirable for both mother (or parents) and child and abortion is in the best interests of both. What I have said casts much doubt on this. In most cases, abortion will provide only a remedy for a woman's immediate problem, not for her long-run and deeper ones. It is absurd to say that abortion is in the interest of the child. It is not difficult to reason that no problem or condition of existence that one is confronted with in life is worse than having his life snuffed out even before he is able to see the light of day. As it is, "unwantedness" may not even be one of the worst conditions. It goes without saying that a great many persons have gone on from degradation, rejection, and unhappiness in childhood to have satisfactory adult lives during which they accomplished much and contributed much to their fellow men.

It is even more absurd to talk, as some pro-abortionists do, of the unborn child having a right of non-existence. One cannot place a value on life, and reason cannot fathom the notion of rights appertaining to non-existence. The very notion of "rights" is contingent both on existence and reason. It cannot be understood or applicable -- in specific areas of activity -- unless there are existing, rational individuals.

There is, of course, no basis for saying that an unborn child would choose to be destroyed instead of "unwanted." Self-preservation is the basic motivation of every human being. This was dramatically demonstrated earlier when I said that persons with congenital anomolies -- conditions which are worse than being "unwanted" and, in any event, we can presume that some of them were not entirely "wanted" by their parents when they first saw their deformities -- are apparently much less likely to commit suicide than "normal" persons.

Part Two—The Physical, Psychological and Fertility Consequences of Induced Abortion for the Woman

The *Wade* brief in its discussion of the early New York City experience with maternal mortality from legalized abortion quotes the City's Health Administrator as saying that "'the safety record is improving'" and that "'[c]omplications are decreasing steadily in both early and later abortions.'"[280] (The specifics given about New York City, however, all pertain to mortality.) The brief continues: "abortion is...without clinically significant psychiatric sequellae" and cites a number of studies to back this up.[281] The PPFA brief makes just the general statement that "[a]bortion is an accepted and safe medical procedure."[282] It refers to specific afflictions -- specifically "severe infection" and "subsequent infertility and pelvic disease" -- only in connection with illegal abortion.[283]

Is there evidence of adverse physical, psychological (or psychiatric), and fertility effects of legal abortion short of mortality for women? It must be recognized that knowledge about many such effects may not have been available at the time the *Wade* and *Bolton* cases were being argued and may only have come to light since then.

One article has suggested that the American medical literature has been reluctant to admit the adverse effects of legalized abortion, at least as they relate to subsequent fertility and perinatal problems.[284] My examination of the number of articles under the heading "Induced Abortion -- Adverse Effects" from 1975 through 1982 in *Cumulated Index Medicus* shows that 96 appeared in foreign and international medical journals and 65 in American. This may suggest that less attention has been paid to the overall problem of complications here than abroad.[285]

An evaluation of the claims of the safety of legally induced abortion in the opinion and briefs can be made by looking at a sample of the scholarly articles on the subject written in the last few years.

The Physical Health Consequences

The physical complications of legal induced abortion are contingent on a number of factors: the point in pregnancy at which an abortion is performed; the method of abortion used;[286] and the age of the mother, with younger women pregnant for the first time having more complications.[287] An article by World Health Organization research physician Karin G. B. Edstrom reviewing the literature concluded that "the range of complications reported by different authors varies markedly, as do their definitions of complications.[288]

The complication rate in abortion invariably increases with increasing gestational age in weeks.[289] The dilation and curretage (D. & C.) and suction curretage (or uterine aspiration) methods, which are used in the first trimester, have low complication rates, although how low has varied with different studies.[290] The method frequently used in the second trimester, the intrauterine instillation of hypertonic saline solution, has had high complication rates overseas and has been abandoned there. It is thought, however, that it was often used without adequate safeguards and is still used in the U.S.[291] In fact, the Supreme Court has said that states may not constitutionally bar its use.[292] The methods of abortion which have the highest complication rates are hysterotomy and hysterectomy.[293] There are a number of other methods which are used in certain countries -- but not in the U.S. -- which also have a very high complication rate.[294]

A number of specific afflictions are known to result from legal abortions. One study at a Missouri abortion clinic showed the most common complication to be incomplete evacuation of the uterus (i.e., some fetal tissue was left behind.) The symptoms resulting were bleeding -- sometimes severe -- and cramps.[295] Other problems which sometimes accompany first-trimester abortions are infection (with accompanying fever), perforation of the uterus (which is treated by surgery or lesser treatment, but occasionally requires a hysterectomy), cervical trauma (which accompanies uterine perforation), and trauma to the uterine myometrium.[296]

In second-trimester abortions, bleeding and infection are much more common. The saline injection method results in many cases in intravasal injection of the solution. Accidental transfusion of the saline into the veins, intravasal haemolysis, and changes in blood volume have also been known to occur.[297] Also, the placenta, which is fully formed by this time, may not successfully be removed in an abortion and will have to be retrieved in a subsequent operation.[298]

The hysterotomy and hysterectomy methods carry with them the possibility of serious complications, comparable to Caesarean section operations.

Abortion complications sometimes require major repair surgery and blood transfusions. In their study, Tietze and Lewit point also to a full range of other complications which have occurred, ranging from very mild ones to very severe ones (such as pulmonary embolism, thrombophlebitis, and convulsions). There are also sometimes complications from anesthesia administered in abortions.[299]

In addition, there are later complications. Edstrom writes that "[n]o gynaecologist who has performed an induced abortion ever tries to deny that it can give rise to early or late complications."[300] She says, however, that "we still have very little knowledge of the types of sequela that may or may not occur." She mentions Rh immunization, possible menstrual disorders (though this is very uncertain), future fertility and perinatal problems, and future psychiatric and emotional problems as possibilities.[301] Another writer mentions chronic and latent inflammatory conditions of the genital organs.[302] A recent New Zealand study of 309 women who had had first trimester abortions from three to nine months before (using the uterine aspiration method) found that they had a "low complication rate," even while concluding that "[i]t appears that...there is a definite morbidity following abortion."[303]

What about the rate of frequency of maternal complications from induced abortion? In the Tietze-Lewit

Joint Program for the Study of Abortion (JPSA) study of 72,988 legal abortions performed from July 1, 1970 to June 30, 1971, the *minimum estimate* of the total physical complication rate was 9.6 per 100 abortions and the maximum 13.1 per 100.[304] We can turn to another study of the physical complications of legal induced abortions in Hungary. The study showed that the rate for three types of immediate post-abortion complications combined -- performation, hemorrhage, and fever -- was 25.8 per 1,000 abortions. The rate for the largest city, Budapest, was 41.6 per 1,000. More than 60 percent of the women undergoing abortions in Budapest took one to three days sick leave from work due to the complications. Another 10 percent took eight or more days sick leave.[305]

Other studies in the 1970s -- including the most recent ones that have been published -- produced a similar range of complication rates. The results of another JPSA study (the Tietze-Dawson study) were published in 1973 and showed that 6.1 percent of women without pre-existing disease reported complications after uterine aspiration abortions. 1.1 percent had major complications (i.e., those requiring surgery or blood transfusions or which caused illness or sustained fever).[306] The Ljubljana Abortion Study of 1971-73, published by the National Institutes of Health, showed that a whopping 29.5 percent of women had complications requiring treatment after first trimester abortions done by the same method.[307] In the New Zealand study mentioned above, only 6.7 percent of women reported complications (which the researchers specified as "significant pain, bleeding or fever"). Only 2.6 percent required hospital care for them.[308]

A connection between abortion (both spontaneous and induced) -- when had before a woman's first full-term pregnancy -- and breast cancer also has been suggested. A California study of Caucasian women under age 33 showed an increased risk of such cancer among those who had had a first-trimester abortion before the later pregnancy (but not in those who had had post-first-trimester abortions or pregnancies before an abortion). The research team speculated that this may be due to changes in breast cells and hormone levels occurring during a woman's first full-term pregnancy.[309] A British study, involving more than four times the number of women, disputed this, but admitted that "more data will...be needed...before any firm conclusion can be reached."[310]

The information above shows that immediate physical consequences occur in a minority of cases, but it is not clear exactly how large the minority is. There is also the possibility of later physical complications, but this is now just being investigated. The point is that no one can say that legalizing abortion eliminates its danger.

The Psychiatric, Psychological, and Emotional Consequences

The *Wade* brief cited several sources who claimed that abortion does not have serious psychological side-effects for women. Other experts, however, disagree with this. There appears to be some indication that women who have current mental illness, or are vulnerable to it, run the greater risk of psychological or psychiatric damage from abortions.[311]

Drs. Myre Sim and Robert Neisser -- the latter is Medical Director of Neve On Government Hospital in Israel -- acknowledge that post-abortion psychoses may not occur as frequently as those following childbirth, but say that for this susceptible group of women it may be much higher.[312] They emphasize, however, that it is not exclusively they who can suffer such damage and believe that the frequency of post-abortion psychosis is really higher than previously reported.[313] Their studies in Birmingham, England and Israel reported on the treatment of a number of women with post-abortive psychoses and said that the indications are that it is not "uncommon" in Israel.[314] Another study, by Milwaukee psychiatrist Monte Harris Liebman and Jolie Siebold Zimmer, of 70 women who contacted Milwaukee's Pregnancy Aftermath Hotline revealed that 58 had experienced varied psychological and emotional reactions to their abortions. These were both immediate and long-term and "threatened the woman's view of herself, her relationships, and her future as well as her emotional stability and well being, and...impaired her ability to cope effectively with the present."[315] One interview study of 95 women in Boston showed that women experience both positive and negative emotional responses to abortion. The predominant responses are happiness and relief, but are often combined with mild to moderate feelings of guilt, regret, and depression.[316] Another study based on experiences in psychotherapy indicates that deep pain and bereavement coupled with feelings of love for the unborn are sometimes experienced.[317]

British psychiatrist Bryan D. Lask did a prospective study of 44 women interviewed six months after their abortions. While his results have been cited as giving a boost to the claim that psychiatric complications after abortion are not a serious problem, they show that they *do* occur. He found that the psychiatric outcome was "favourable" for 68 percent (30) of the women and "unfavourable" for 32 percent (14) and that the "psychiatric status" of 89 percent (39) was improved or unchanged and only 16 percent (7) regretted their abortions. He concludes about this latter group that the adverse effects of a majority were caused by what he terms "the patient's environment," which includes her relationship with her partner, age, history of psychiatric illness, etc.[318]

It is useless to say that negative psychiatric sequellae do not result from the abortion itself, but from "environment." Those environmental factors are going to be present to at least some extent in virtually all cases. Further, Lask limits his study to short-term consequences. He says nothing about long-term ones. He thus could be understating the problem of adverse effects.

Other psychiatrists dispute Lask's and other studies' similar findings. Drs. Jean G. Spaulding and Jesse O. Cavenar, Jr. write that women *do* have emotional disturbances after "therapeutic" abortions, and that these are not caused by "environmental factors."[319] Cavenar, Allan A. Maltbie, M.D., and John L. Sullivan, M.D. report on cases of theirs in which severe psychiatric disorders were triggered, at least in part, by abortions on women who had no previous psychiatric problems. They also note the possibility that abortion will have a "profound emotional effect" on other members of the woman's family.[320]

Another psychological complication of abortion is functional sexual disorders. One study of 200 women examined after abortion showed that more than 30 percent held lower or negative attitudes towards sexuality. Those who were more disturbed emotionally did not improve as much as those with lesser disturbances.[321] In another study of 60 women who had had abortions, 13 percent who had had no prior psychological problems said they had mild or serious signs of frigidity, 5 percent said they had even more serious disturbances.[322] In a third study of 570 women, 62 percent said they had no changes in their sexual life, but 32 percent noticed a deterioration.[323]

A recent article raised another possible psychological consequence of induced abortion: a prepensity to suicide. It studied just two adolescent girls who had attempted suicide. Both had had abortions and indications of preexisting emotional problems. Since there were only two girls considered, it was not a systematic study, and their ages make them unrepresentative of most aborted women. Also, their personal situations and psychological histories made a direct cause-and-effect relationship between their abortions and suicide attempts impossible, but the psychologist writing the article seems to suggest the connection and cautions the pediatrician to be alert for adolescents in such situations who have a "high risk for self-destructiveness."[324]

Fertility and Subsequent Perinatal Consequences

The main area in which research on the long-term consequences of induced abortion has focused on the woman's later fertility and problems associated with the birth of subsequent ("wanted") children. Drs. Leslie Iffy, Garry Frisoli, and Antal Jakobovits review a number of studies from Hungary, Great Britain, Czechoslovakia, the Netherlands, Norway, Israel and other countries which show greater numbers -- often substantially greater -- of subsequent spontaneous abortions and premature births in women who have had induced abortions.[325] A Hungarian study showed that the incidence of placenta previa and premature separation of the placenta was increased in women who had had induced abortions and that there might be a connection between this and Rh isoimmunization and low birth weights in subsequent children.[326]

Until recently, the American studies had shown the opposite results. They had found no statistically significant connection between induced abortion and the above subsequent perinatal problems,[327] with the exception of one which showed a slight reduction in average birth-weight.[328] Drs. Iffy, Frisoli, and Jakobovits are inclined to downgrade these studies because they deal with only a small number of cases.[329] Probably the American experience with widely available abortion has not been long enough to do the extensive kinds of studies that are needed. They do cite two early studies -- each of which has serious sampling problems, as well -- which show some of the same connections as have been discerned abroad.[330] One Boston study that was reported in 1980 in the *Journal of the American Medical Association* established a direct relationship between induced abortion and subsequent pregnancy loss in women who had had *more than* one abortion. It found no such relationship for women who had had only one abortion, however.[331]

Two recently reported American studies *have* shown the relationship between induced abortion and some of the subsequent perinatal problems pointed to by the European studies. A California study conducted between 1976 and 1978 found a small but statistically significant connection between previous induced abortion and fetal/neonatal deaths in subsequent pregnancies, even when such other important variables as marital status, economic status, use of contraception, and smoking were controlled. It did not find a similar connection between previous induced abortion and subsequent spontaneous abortion. (The researchers, however, admit that their disagreement with some European studies on this latter point may be due to a difference in the way they defined "spontaneous abortion.") They also did not find evidence of reduced birth weights in later children when the above factors were controlled.[332]

A retrospective study done at Vanderbilt University Hospital compared the rates of placenta previa in women who gave birth at the hospital in the 1972 to 1974 period to women who gave birth there in the period from July 1, 1979 to June 30, 1980. A threefold increase in its incidence occurred in the latter period over the former, from one in 318 deliveries (0.3 percent) to one in 109 deliveries (0.9 percent). The frequency of placenta previa in these groups was highest in one-way maternal transports (3.3 percent) and women who had had a prior induced first trimester abortion (3.8 percent). After correcting for the maternal transports, the researchers found that the women who had been previously aborted had a frequency of placenta previa of 2.1 percent and the remainder had an incidence rate close to 0.3 percent. They concluded that prior induced first trimester abortion is "a highly significant risk factor for the development of placenta previa," probably because both the D. and C. and suction aspiration methods of abortion may damage the endometrium.[333]

There is also some evidence -- although the literature is limited -- that abortion can lead to a subsequent failure to conceive at all. Some older studies from overseas seem to have established a link between *repeat* abortions and sterility.[334] In other foreign studies, sterility has been reported following even single abortions. In Sweden, 2 to 5 percent of women were found to be sterile and in Czechoslovakia 1.3 to 7.4 percent have been found to be sterile in reports by different authors.[335] In a Polish study reported in 1981 of a group of 52 women hospitalized 10 to 15 years before for an abortion of their first pregnancy, 6 (8.6 percent) failed to conceive for three to nine years. Three finally did conceive after four to six years of treatment, although only two carried the pregnancies to term.[336]

It is not yet certain that abortion leads to subsequent fertility and perinatal problems, but a large number of studies from countries overseas with longer histories of legal, easily available abortion than the U.S. indicate that such is the case. The most recent American studies are showing such a possible link also.

Chapter Conclusion

Abortion, in light of medical advances, can hardly be said to be necessary to save the mother's life. There appear to be no diseases which, *per se*, indicate that continued pregnancy will kill or shorten the life of a woman. Other factors may pose such a threat in these cases, but alternative treatments to abortion are available. Abortion is probably not necessary to safeguard a woman's mental health or, at least, there is no agreement within psychiatry that it is. The problem of potential deformity of the unborn child is not as great percentage-wise as is sometimes thought and many deformities or disorders from birth can be effectively treated. Abortion for this reason is not really "therapeutic" for the child, but as much a question of convenience for the woman or couple as induced abortion for other non-medical reasons is. Pregnancy in cases of rape is not very prevalent; it is somewhat more prevalent from incest. In each case, however, there are other solutions and, with incest, abortion may permit more serious problems to be ignored. Rape and incest, like child deformity, demand solutions which involve personal and social compassion and commitment.

On the justifications for abortion addressed specifically by the briefs considered, there is frequent use of misleading citations, questionable statistics and assertions, and unproven points. Some of the points made by the briefs *were* well founded. Some, however, were not and virtually all were put forth as settled fact when, in fact, there really was much doubt about them.

Moreover, even though the level of physical health consequences of abortion for the woman is relatively low and the existence of psychological and fertility (and perinatal) consequences not definitely established, I have presented enough evidence to show that the impression of great safety left ty the *Wade* opinion and the briefs is unjustified. Adverse effects from legalized abortion *do* occur and some women *do* die from them.

CHAPTER CONCLUSION

All in all, I conclude that the arguments about the justifications for and consequences of induced abortion presented by the briefs were weak. They did present such an overwhelming claim of the need for legalized abortion, however, that they perhaps influenced the Supreme Court.

Chapter Seven

An Inquiry into the Unborn Child's Humanity and the Presence of a Soul

Introduction

In this Chapter, the case is made for the humanity of the unborn child. This is done by putting forth three types of arguments, which correspond with the three Sections of this Chapter. These concern the physical attributes of the unborn child, the question of whether he has a human -- i.e., rational -- soul, and various arguments built on common sense, common knowledge, and the common usage of words.

The consideration of the physical structures is an understandable approach to the question of humanity, and is the one most frequently turned to by anti-abortionists. Most of the biological facts that will be presented were put before the Supreme Court in briefs in *Wade* and *Bolton*. The matter of the soul, however, has generally not entered into the abortion debate, except when it has been conducted along strictly religious lines. I believe it can be used as an approach to the issue, even though it was not raised in the briefs, for the following reasons.

Physical structures can give us only a partial understanding of man. This is because, first, some force must be present to animate the sum total of the structures, otherwise we do not have a live man and, second, account must be taken of the fact that man is a rational creature and his rationality can be explained only partly by his physical structures. Man is commonly thought of as different from other physical creatures because he has an intellect and a free will and this difference has traditionally been explained by the notion of the "soul." This understanding of the individual soul is confirmed by a recent edition of *Webster's Third International Dictionary*, which defines the term "soul" as follows:

> The immaterial essence or substance, animating principle, or actuating cause of life or of the individual life; The psychical or spiritual principle in general shared by or embodied in individual human beings or all beings having a rational and spiritual nature.[1]

In line with my intention stated in the Introduction to this book, I shall not pursue this discussion of the soul along religious lines, which is the context within which it is generally considered nowadays. I shall rely instead on the thinking of Aristotle which, I believe, can supply a proper basis for helping to resolve the abortion question.

Aristotle's work presents probably the most comprehensive treatment in Western thought, outside of a religious context, of the nature of man. His works treat the physical, psychological, social, ethical, and spiritual (i.e., that relating to the soul) sides of man. He studies man, as he does all things, by considering what he is by nature, without relying on revealed truths. He is a uniquely suitable source for this discussion also because he is one of the few writers ever who, outside of a religious context, made a major inquiry into the question of what is the soul. His *De Anima* ("On the Soul") is probably the major non-religious treatment of the subject in Western history.

My consideration of the commonsensical, etc. arguments shall begin with and consist of a refutation of the arguments put forth in the major pro-abortion briefs in *Wade* and *Bolton* against the possibility of the unborn child being human.

The Biological Facts about Life in the Womb

The biological facts about the development of the unborn child are *hard facts*, not opinion. There is very little, if any, dispute among authorities about whether the information put forth in this Section regarding physical development is accurate (presuming, of course, normal development). The disputes arise about what we are to conclude from it.

I cite seven authors in this Section: Geraldine Lux Flanagan, Bart T. Heffernan, M.D., Professor Germain Grisez, Professor John T. Noonan, Jr., the late A. William Liley, M.D., M. Krieger, and E. Blechschmidt, M.D. My main sources are Flanagan's little book *The First Nine Months of Life* and Heffernan's article "The Early Biography of Everyman" in *Abortion and Social Justice*. Heffernan, Grisez, Noonan (as mentioned) and Liley are or were involved in anti-abortion efforts. As far as I am aware, the others are not. I do not believe, however, that this is any reason to doubt the accuracy of what they say.

The nonconclusory statements are accepted fact. The authors cite standard medical textbooks such as Patten's *Human Embryology* and *Williams' Obstetrics* and other books and articles by authorities in making them. What Noonan writes about pain and the unborn is less well-established, but he relies on research done by experts. I have used these particular sources instead of medical texts and the like directly because they are much easier to understand for the layman.

Fertilization

The odyssey of a human life begins with the fertilization of the female ovum by the male sperm. M. Krieger, one of the scientific authorities cited by the Senate Subcommittee on Separation of Powers in its re-

report on the Human Life Bill, says the following:

> "In this first pairing [of sperm and ovum], the spermatozoon has contributed its 23 chromosomes, and the oocyte has contributed its 23 chromosomes, thus re-establishing the necessary total of 46 chromosomes. The result is the conception of a unique individual, unlike any that has been born before and unlike any that will ever be born again."[2]

Flanagan tells us that the most fundamental characteristics of the new human being are determined at this point of fertilization. When the nucleus of the father's sperm reaches the nucleus of the mother's egg, these two lie side by side as their content -- genes -- come together. In this short half hour, innumerable traits of the new individual are established. These include the common feature of the human species and such individual trademarks as gender; eye, skin, and hair color; configuration of face and body; the tendency to be tall or short, fat or thin; proneness to certain diseases; and the tendency to acquire certain qualities of temperament and intelligence.[3]

It should be pointed out that there is not really a *moment* of fertilization or conception, as is sometimes thought. Fertilization occurs in stages, but, as Germain Grisez states in his comprehensive work on abortion, there is a "continuity of the process as one stage flows smoothly into the next."[4] The first stage occurs when the sperm reaches the surface of the ovum. The ovum reacts by surrounding the sperm and aiding its entry into it so it can reach the nucleus. Chemical changes occur in the ovum as it prepares for unification of the two nuclei and resists entry by any other sperm cells. This first stage is called "activation."[5]

The second stage is when the two nuclei actually unite and bring together the two sets of chromosomes. The resulting fertilized ovum is called a "zygote" by biologists.[6] This is the name of the first of four stages in the development of the child from fertilization to birth. The others, in order, are embryo, fetus, and upon birth, infant.

The First Two Weeks

Within a week of fertilization, the first two cells of the new person increase to more than a hundred cells. For the first three or four days of the first week the cluster of cells drifts slowly down the tube that leads to the womb. On about the fourth day it arrives there, drifts about for another few days, then becomes attached to the inner lining of the uterus after about a week. It will remain there until birth.[7]

Development occurs in the zygote from the time of fertilization until implantation. First, after fertilization the initial cell division occurs. Also, the zygote grows and differentiation of bodily parts already occurs. Grisez reports on the work of a team of researchers who studied a number of human zygotes who were removed from women as an incident of surgical procedures performed on them. They discovered definite differences in development and cellular differentiation among the zygotes which ranged in age from thirty-six hours to four and one-half days old.[8] Development of various body parts thus is underway before implantation as it is afterwards.

The appearance of a human being only four days after fertilization is already distinctly human. The cluster of cells at that point superficially resembles the earliest cells of all creatures: invertebrates, fish, foul, and mammals. Upon microscopic examination, however, these human cells differ from the cells of other animals in small details. Even the sex of the individual can be determined by microscope at this stage. This all should be kept in mind. I shall refer back to it later in this Chapter when discussing an important point from one of the briefs.

The implantation and pre-implantation stages are important as far as twinning is concerned. In inquiring into the question of the humanity of the unborn child, twinning is an important consideration only in the case of identical twins. (I shall discuss this later in this Section.) Identical twins are quite uncommon, actually. Twinning *per se* is uncommon, but *identical* twins comprise only one-fourth of all twin births.[9] Identical twins occur when one fertilized ovum or zygote apparently splits into two, after which each of the two parts (which are now two separate zygotes) grows independently in the very same manner toward full development and maturity just like the normal single zygote.[10]

This split apparently does not always occur at the same stage of development. It may occur after implantation, but probably occurs at some point between fertilization and implantation. Since most identical twins have separate amnions and this membrane begins to form at or just after implantation, there is probably a duality present even before splitting occurs and, in any event, certainly before implantation.[11] Even if there is only one amnion, duality may still be established before splitting, whenever this occurs, because the splitting may arise from a peculiarity of blastula formation that brings about two foci on a conjoined embryonic disk.[12] Regardless of this, there appears to be a genetic factor involved in identical twinning -- i.e., not every zygote is capable of developing spontaneously into identical twins -- which suggests either that a duality is already present or that identical twins may really develop by a form of parthenogenesis, or non-sexual reproduction, from a pre-existing "parent" which is the original zygote before division.[13] It should be stressed, however, that scientists are divided on the question of how twinning occurs and this latter point is only a theory. I shall return to these points about twinning later in this Chapter.

The Third and Fourth Weeks

By seventeen days blood cells are formed and by eighteen days there is a primitive heart. This embryonic heart, according to Heffernan, "begins as a simple tube, [and] starts irregular pulsations at twenty-four days which, in about one more week, smooths into a rhythmic contraction and expansion" (but see below).[14] He further cites studies which have shown that electrocardiograms (ECG) taken on a 7½-week-old embryo "present the existence of a functionally complete cardiac system and the possible existence of a myroneural or hormonal regulatory system [and] [a]ll the classic elements of the adult ECG were seen."[15] Another study he cites, done in France, "observed occasional contractions of the heart" in a *two week old* embryo and also obtained the classical elements of an adult ECG tracing on a five-week-old embryo.[16]

By thirty days, even though the heart is still

developing there is already a functioning, closed vascular system. The heartbeat at five and half weeks is essentially similar to that of an adult. The heart is "functionally complete and normal by seven weeks," although the energy output is only about twenty percent that of adults. The child *in utero* and his mother do not exchange blood because there is such a complete vascular system from such an early point.[17]

Substantial development of the brain and nervous system occurs from the eighteenth day. This is necessary because the nervous system integrates the action of all the other systems. By the end of the twentieth day the foundation of the child's brain, spinal cord, and entire nervous system will have been established. By the sixth week, this system will have developed so well that it is controlling movements of the baby's muscles, even though the woman may not be aware that she is pregnant. At thirty days the primary brain is seen. By the thirty-third day the cerebral cortex, the part of the central nervous system which governs motor activity as well as intellect, may be seen.[18]

During the first month, other organs are also developing, as is the face. There are simple kidneys, a liver, a digestive tract, and a primitive umbilical cord. The body also has a head with rudimentary eyes, ears, and mouth, even though it is only the size of half a pea. By the end of the first month a whole embryo is formed.[19]

Around the twenty-sixth day, tiny buds that are the beginning of arms appear at the sides of the body. The leg buds appear about two days later. This slower development of the legs relative to the arms continues until the baby is two years old.[20]

One point that should be made clear is that the unborn child does not develop structures *in anticipation of life* which do not begin actual functioning until birth. As the late Dr. A. William Liley, who did much original research on fetal development and came to be known as the "Father of Fetology," said, "[a]ll the evidence shows that, for whatever structure or system we care to nominate, development of structure and development of function go hand in hand."[21]

As we shall see later, the appearance of the one-month-old human embryo motivates some to liken it to other creatures. It appears to have a tail, has ridges along the sides of the head that suggest gill slits, and has arm and leg buds that do not look like human arms and legs. Flanagan notes that it is sometimes said that the human embryo "recapitulates the [supposed] evolutionary history of man," resembling first a fish and then later perhaps a monkey before becoming a baby. *This is not true.*

The alleged gills are never gills and what appears to be a tail is not a tail. The apparent tail encloses the early spinal cord, which, anticipating the complex human nervous system, is temporarily longer than the remainder of the body. It will eventually become the tip of the adult spine, called the coccyx. What appear to be gills are really five folds of tissue that pile up at the base of the head to provide raw material for the chin, cheeks, jaw, and for the external ear. A human embryo superficially looks like a fish or monkey embryo because all embryos grow from one-celled eggs and are made, step by step, out of the building blocks of cells. Nature's repertory of basic structures is limited, and the same forms appear in all the primary units of building blocks. The gills in fish develop out of similar folds of tissue as the jaw of man. The tail of a monkey grows out of the same stub that becomes the human coccyx.[22] The essential difference is that a human embryo will never become a monkey nor a monkey embryo a human being. I shall return to the above facts in Section IV when considering the briefs.

Two more things should be said about the unborn child in the first month. The first concerns his nutrition. Even though his growth is determined by his own make-up, his nourishment comes entirely from his mother. There is only a primitive umbilical cord at this stage, but the food is gathered by rootlike tufts around the capsule that surrounds the embryo and channelled to it by means of this primitive umbilical cord.[23] The other thing to mention is his size. Heffernan says that he is "ten thousand times larger than the fertilized egg" at the end of the first month and "has completed the period of relatively greatest size increase and the greatest physical change of a lifetime," *having gone from one cell to millions of cells.*[24]

By the beginning of the second month, Heffernan

tells us, "the unborn child, small as it is, looks distinctly human" even though "at this time the child's mother may still not be aware that she is pregnant."[25] The brain is already working like an adult brain and sends out impulses that coordinate the functioning of other organs. Reflex responses -- the first movements of the unborn child -- can be present at forty-two days. Brain waves have been detected at forty-three days. The other major organs are working. The heart has been beating for perhaps two weeks and now does so with increasing strength. The stomach produces digestive juices. The liver manufactures blood cells and the kidneys are extracting uric acid from the child's blood (i.e., waste products are being removed from his system).[26]

The muculo-skeletal system undergoes considerable development. The skeletal system is entirely developed by the end of six weeks. (This marks the end of the embryonic stage; after this the unborn child is called a "fetus.") In the sixth to seventh week, nerves and muscles work together for the first time. The area of the lips is the first to become sensitive to touch and if it were gently stroked, the unborn child would respond by bending the upper body to one side and making a quick backward motion with his arms. This is a response involving the entire body (called "total pattern response"). Localized reactions, such as swallowing, begin in the third month.[27] The skeleton is not comprised of bone yet; the first bone cells do not appear until the end of the embryonic period. Until then it is made up of cartilage.[28] The first actual fetal movement -- what traditionally was called "quickening" -- first occurs at six weeks, although the mother will not yet feel it.

The Second Month

The limbs and the face further develop in the first half of the second month. While on the thirteenth day, the arm buds are tiny rounded knobs, on the thirty-first they become subdivided into hand, arm, and shoulder regions. On the thirty-third day, the fingers begin to develop. On this same day, the eyes become dark for the first time because pigment has just formed in the retina. The widely separated nostrils begin to form into the nose and upper jaw. On the thirty-seventh day, the nose becomes apparent. The two nostrils have moved closer to each other and a nose is fully formed with two separated air passages. Also on this day, the internal hearing apparatus of the ear nears completion. The eyelids begin to form as ridges around the rims of the eyes. One week later, they are large enough to cover almost the entire eyeball. On this day -- the forty-fourth -- the unborn child has both an upper and lower jaw, a mouth with lips, a beginning tongue, and the initial buds for the twenty milk teeth embedded in the gum ridges.[29] By seven weeks, the ears are formed and may resemble a specific family pattern. The lines in the hands and the fingerprints start to form by the eighth week.[30]

Professor Noonan, in a review article citing several medical sources, concludes that another phenomenon associated with human beings is also present in the unborn child by late in the second month: the ability to feel pain.[31] I shall not go into an explanation of the bio-chemical test to determine if it is present, but researchers have been able to infer from the child's appearance after abortions, various biological facts about brain development, and the ability to experience sensation at this and later stages of pregnancy that he must be able to feel pain. Addressing the matter of the child's experiencing pain during abortion, Noonan says this: "...we may conclude that as soon as a pain mechanism is present in the fetus -- possibly as early as *day 56* -- the methods [of abortion] used will cause pain. The pain is more substantial and lasts longer the later the abortion is. It is most severe and lasts the longest when the method is saline poisoning."[32]

The Third Month

One word can be used to characterize fetal development in the third month: movement. I have already mentioned that the nerves and muscles start working and localized actions begin in that month. The baby begins to be quite active, though he is smaller than a goose egg and weighs only one ounce. By the end of the month, he can kick his legs, turn his feet, curl and fan his toes, make a fist, move his thumb, bend his wrist, turn his head, squint, frown, open his mouth and press his lips tightly together. He cannot yet purse his lips for sucking, but he can, and frequently does, swallow.[33] All this is happening even though the mother will seldom yet feel her baby since his newly-formed muscles are still quite weak.[34]

By the beginning of the third month the baby moves spontaneously, for the first time, without being touched. Sometimes, his whole body swings back and forth for a few moments. By eight and one half weeks, the eyelids and palms of the hands become sensitive to touch. If the eyelid were to be stroked, the baby squints. If the palm of the hand is touched, the fingers tighten into a partial fist. In two more weeks he will be able to close his fingers better, but only at twenty-three weeks will he be able to grip firmly. In the sixth and tenth weeks, if his forehead is touched, he might turn his head away and pucker up his brow and frown. By that time, he also has full use of his arms and can bend his elbow and wrist. His entire body also becomes sensitive to touch with the exception of the sides, back, and top of the head. The back and top of the head will remain totally insensitive until after birth, which is perhaps nature's way of protecting the head in birth.[35] By the ninth week, the unborn child is also sucking his thumb.[36]

In the twelfth week, he is able to move his thumb in opposition to his fingers, swallow, and pull up his upper lip.[37]

In addition to movement, there is further development in the unborn child's organ functioning and appearance. The taste buds and salivary glands develop, as do the digestive glands in the stomach. When the baby swallows amniotic fluid, he utilizes its contents. He also starts to urinate.[38]

The unborn child may even start to breathe in the third month. He brings the amniotic fluid around him in and out of his primitive lungs. Flanagan tells us that this activity "may be essential to the proper formation of the lungs' air sacs." She also explains that he does not drown from the amniotic fluid because he does not get air by his lungs but rather through his umbilical cord before birth.[39] It is because there is no air in the amniotic sac that he cannot make sounds, even though his vocal cords become completed in this month.[40]

Also in the third month, the eyes, previously far apart, move closer together. The eyelids close over the eyes. The face looks more definitely human. The unborn child's facial expressions may already resemble those of his parents. Primitive eggs and sperm are formed, depending on the gender of the child.[41] One expert tells us that "'the organization of...[the child's] psychosomatic self is now well under way.'"[42]

The Fourth Month

If "movement" was the key word for the third month, "growth" is for the fourth. In the fourth month, the unborn child's weight increases six times and he grows to one-half his height at birth.[43] He receives the food and oxygen he needs for this growth from his mother through the placenta. By means of the placenta, the child also is able to have wastes removed from his body.[44] Even though he heavily depends on his mother, his body functions as a closed system. It is *his* heart which is making his blood circulate and the placenta, which is now known to belong to *him*, which performs most of his other vital functions at this stage.[45] Mother and baby have separate blood and her blood never directly enters the umbilical cord.[46] The child's biological functions are thus independent of his mother.

The Fifth Month

By the end of the fifth month, the child is one foot long and weighs about one pound. Fine baby hair begins to grow on his eyebrows and on his head and slight eyelashes appear. Most of the skeleton hardens and his muscles become stronger.[47] Hard nails form on the nail beds of the fingers and a little later on the toes. In the eighth month the fingernails will reach the tips of the fingers. Girls and boys both develop pale pink nipples and also underlying mammary glands which contain milk ducts.[48]

It is in this fifth month that the mother is likely to first feel the child's movements. She may even perceive his hiccoughing which is caused by his swallowing of amniotic fluid. The heartbeat is so strong that the doctor can hear it with his stethoscope. The child also sleeps and wakes and he sleeps in a favorite position. He may be aroused from sleep by external vibrations, such as the turning on of a loud tap on a tub when his mother takes a bath. He hears and *recognizes* his mother's voice at some point before birth and even the mother's emotional distress can be communicated to him.[49] I shall say more about this later.

It is at the end of the fifth month that we begin to speak about the notion of "viability," the chances the baby has of surviving outside of the womb if prematurely born. Viability is now down to about twenty weeks -- the end of the fifth month. In previous times -- before the advent of intensive neo-natal care units in hospitals -- it was much later. As it is now, the child's survival chances are much higher if he is born between twenty-four and twenty-eight weeks, but survival is *possible* at twenty. It has been estimated that ten percent of the children born between twenty and twenty-four weeks will survive. There have been documented cases of children surviving at twenty-three, twenty-two, twenty-one, and even one at twenty weeks, who all turned out to be normal and healthy.[50] What is more, the future will likely see the time of viability go back even further into the pregnancy. Viability is not a static notion. Such developments as the invention of an artificial placenta -- which is expected soon -- could set viability at ten or twelve weeks or earlier.[51]

The Sixth Month

In the sixth month, the unborn child begins to accumulate a little fat under his skin. His permanent teeth come in, high in his gums behind the milk teeth. Now his lips can open and he may open and close his eyes and look up, down, and sideways. He develops such a strong grip that he will soon be able to support his weight by holding on to a rod with one hand, as seen by experiments. He can also maintain regular breathing for some twenty-four hours if born prematurely.[52]

The Seventh Month

In the seventh month -- recall that abortion is still legal at this point according to what the Supreme Court said in *Bolton* -- the hair on the child's head may grow long.[53] He now looks very much like a newborn baby. It is not necessary to say anything more about the last trimester; let me just make a few points about the biological basis for saying that the unborn child is a separate organism from his mother.

I have already pointed to different biological facts during the development of the unborn child which

which establish that he is a separate biological organism. On the *cellular* and *metabolic* levels, a strong case can be made for the unborn child's individuality and independence from the very point of fertilization. Even before implantation, the fertilized ovum engages in the process of cell division or mitosis.[54] The division does not result in a replication of just the same cells, but begins the differentiation and specificity of the bodily parts.

West German physician and anatomy professor E. Blechschmidt of the University of Gottingen says the following about the individuality and independence of the fertilized ovum:

> ...today we know that each developmental stage of the human being is demonstrably a characteristically human one. Already, on the basis of the well-known chromosomes of the human ova, the specificity of a human germ can no longer be doubted...It may be considered today a fundamental law of human octogenesis that not only human specificity but also the individual specificity of each human being remains preserved from fertilization to death, and that only the appearance of the individual being changes in the course of its octogenesis.
>
> What we term the octogenesis of a human being begins with fertilization because the fertilized ovum is already a form of man. Indeed, it is already active because, seen in its minute dimensions, it constitutes a momentary picture of organized processes...While the unicellular ovum divides, or tather subdivides, a characteristic multicellular condition occurs. All the organs of the developing organism are differentiation products of each unique human ovum. Its specificity is a prerequisite for the later individuality of the human embryo, of the child, and of the adult.[55]

I believe that this fairly detailed statement about the biological development of the unborn child has been worthwhile not only because it provides the material for me to refer back to in the next two Sections, especially Section III, but also because it provides the unknowledgeable reader with a clear understanding of what the organism in the womb that we are talking about is like.

Does the Unborn Child Have a Human Soul?

The account of the biological facts about the unborn child in the previous Section makes a compelling argument by itself for his humanity. In this Section, I consider another side of the issue of humanity: whether the unborn child has a soul. I shall state the pertinent aspects of Aristotle's thinking about the soul -- as found primarily in his *De Anima* -- and, as I go along, shall refer back to the biological facts stated and present additional information about the intellectual and psychological development of the unborn child. I shall seek to determine whether this modern knowledge applied to Aristotle's thinking would indicate that the unborn child has a human soul. Even though, as Chapter Nine makes clear, it is unnecessary to establish that the unborn child has a human soul to morally oppose abortion, doing so is a strong argument against it.

The Existence of the Soul and Why it is Essential for Life

The first question that must be confronted before beginning this discussion is: Why is this inquiry pertinent at all? How do we know that any such thing as a "soul" actually exists? Common sense suggests to us that it does. We know that matter alone cannot cause something to live because not everything that is material (i.e., made up of atoms and the same chemical elements that everything else is made up of) is not "alive." Matter is not made alive by additional matter. This is seen clearly by the fact that non-living matter is constantly being made alive by being taken into living cells; before coming into the cell, it was potentially alive, and in the cell it becomes actually alive even though nothing is added to it.[56]

Man has not been able to actually "create" living matter. Even with *in vitro* fertilization men do not create a new man. The new man comes into existence only when the matter necessary for reproduction -- the human sperm and human ovum -- has been taken from a previously living man and woman. *In vitro* fertilization is nothing more than the uniting of sperm and ovum in an environment other than the Fallopian tube; it is not an alternative *means* of creating a new man. Something inexplicable happens when a human sperm and ovum unite which permits the transmission of the life-giving principle into a new biological organism, regardless of where the uniting occurs.

The transformation of inanimate to animate matter is explained by viewing all matter as potentially living. To become living is to have this potency actualized. The fact that there is a real difference between being alive and not being alive (i.e., between potency and act) indicates that there is a real difference between a living being and its matter. It is not just its matter; it is something more.[57]

What Aristotle Says about the Soul of the Unborn Child

What Aristotle says about the soul generally indicates, in light of the biological facts in the previous Section, that the unborn child surely is "living" (i.e., has a soul of some type):

> ...what has soul in it differs from what has not in that the former displays life. Now this word has more than one sense, and provided any one alone of these is found in a thing we say that thing is living. Living, that is, may mean thinking or perception or local movement and rest, or movement in the sense of nutrition, decay and growth.[58]

Aristotle specifically *did* address the question of when the unborn child received a soul. In his work *History of Animals*, he stated that this occurred -- that the unborn child became "animated" -- at forty days into the gestation period for the male and eighty days for the female.[59] (The Court noted this in a footnote in the *Wade* opinion.)[60] He no doubt came to this conclusion about ensoulment on the basis of the biology of his day. He did not have the knowledge about intrauterine life which I stated in the previous Section; this has only recently become available. Possibly because of his biological understanding, he permitted abortion up to the forty and eighty day points mentioned above. He even favored exposing post-partum infants. In any event, one clearly cannot claim that he opposed all abortion. The question I am seeking to answer, then, is this: Can it reasonably be argued in light of Aristotle's thinking about the soul, that, if he had had modern biological knowledge, he would have concluded that the unborn child has a distinctively human soul? Can Aristotle's theory give us any basis for arguing against abortion?

Aristotle says the following about the ensoulment of the unborn child in *Generation of Animals:*

> ...nobody would put down the unfertilized embryo as soulless or in every sense bereft of life (since both the semen and the embryo of an animal have every bit as much life as a plant), and it is productive up to a certain point. That then they possess the nutritive soul is plain...
>
> As they develop they also acquire the sensitive soul in virtue of which an animal is an animal...an animal does not become at the same time an animal and a man or a horse or any other particular animal. For the end is developed last, and the peculiar character of the species is the end of the generation in each individual...When and how and whence is a share in reason acquired by those animals that participate in this principle? It is plain that the semen and the unfertilized embryo [he presumably means the unfertilized ovum], while still separate from each other, must be assumed to have the nutritive soul potentially, but not actually, except that (like those unfertilized embryos that are separated from the mother) it absorbs nourish-

> ment and performs the function of the nutritive soul...And it is clear that we must be guided by this in speaking of the sensitive and the rational soul. For all three kinds of soul, not only the nutritive, must be possessed potentially before they are possessed in actuality.[61]

Aristotle, then, has a notion of the soul existing both potentially and actually. He has a three-fold notion of "soul": nutritive, sensitive, and rational. The nutritive soul is possessed by all plants and animals (i.e., by any creature that provides nutrition for itself). The sensitive soul is present in most animals and the rational soul is found in "man and possibly another order like man or superior to him" (what Judeo-Christian thought identifies as the angelic).[62] I shall be speaking more about the characteristics of each type of soul shortly. What is clear from this passage is that Aristotle believes the unborn child to have at least a nutritive soul. He appears also to believe -- relying, again, on his limited biological knowledge -- that the unborn child, at every stage in his development, has *potentially* a sensitive and a rational soul. By saying that "the end is developed last," he indicates that he believes that a creature gradually moves toward what it is fully to become. The child, even after birth, does not fully possess a rational soul. Clearly, this is so in some sense. A human being does not reach what we might call his "prime" -- the point at which he is physically and mentally his strongest -- until some time in early adulthood. I believe that a strong case can be made, however, that all three of Aristotle's types of soul can be found in the unborn child from the beginning, even though the full human capacities which they make possible are not realized until different points in gestation, infancy, and even adulthood.

Aristotle says that it is at the point of animation -- when there is some sign of life in the unborn child -- that the three types of soul change from potential to actual.[63] It is also at this point that he believes the child "begins to resolve into distinct parts."[64] Aristotle's error can easily be seen from what I have said. I mentioned that it is as early as the eighteenth day when the first bodily part appears: a rudimentary heart. Using Aristotle's reasoning here, it would seem that all three types of soul would thus be present at least by this time. He seems concerned about distinctiveness. I showed in my biological description, which was underscored by the passage from Blechschmidt, that the unborn child is separate, distinct, and unique -- both in his genetic make-up and in the progress of his development -- from fertilization. I also presented scientific evidence which shows that there is a differentiation in the development of embryos from the earliest point. It is reasonable to argue that if Aristotle had known this, he may have concluded that all three types of soul are possessed *at fertilization*.

We get a further indication that Aristotle would have believed the latter had he had correct biological knowledge when we consider the following. He says that "[a]n embryo is...complete when it is either male or female, in the case of those animals that possess this distinction."[65] It seems logical to infer that since he believes that it is at the point of animation when the unborn child "begins to resolve into distinct parts," it is then that he believes that sex is determined. Thus, animation and sexual differentiation are contiguous and either -- both -- are indicative of complete ensoulment. We know now, as mentioned, that sex is determined at fertilization -- Aristotle did not know about chromosomes -- and, also, that animation begins then since it is clear that life is present from that point because the zygote is already growing and developing.

On the basis of just this much, without even getting into his main work on the soul, we can see that Aristotle's thinking gives us a basis for arguing that all three types of souls are possessed by the unborn child from fertilization. I shall now turn to *De Anima* to show why I believe it permits us to make the same argument.

Does the Unborn Child Have a Nutritive Soul?

Let us first consider Aristotle's definition of "soul":

> ...the body is the subject or matter, not

> what is attributed to it. Hence the soul must be a substance in the sense of the form of a natural body having life potentially within it. But substance is actuality, and thus soul is the actuality of a body...If, then, we have to give a general formula applicable to all kinds of soul, we must describe it as the first grade of actuality of a natural organized body.[66]

and

> The soul is the cause or source of the living body. The terms cause and source have many senses. But the soul is the cause of its body alike in all three senses which we explicitly recognize. It is (a) the source or origin of movement, it is (b) the end, it is (c) the essence of the whole living body...in everything the essence is identical with the ground of its being, and here, in the case of living things, their being is to live, and of their being and their living the soul in them is the cause or source...It is manifest that the soul is also the final cause of its body.[67]

The passage immediately above gives us an indication that the unborn child has a soul of some type. Since Aristotle says that the soul is the origin of movement, and the child's first movements occur at forty-two days, a soul must be present by then. Clearly, it would be present *after* this point in pregnancy because movements become more complex and forceful and by the third month or later the mother will finally feel them.

The growth, development, bodily functions, nutrition and reaction to stimuli all suggest that the unborn child is "living." (Aristotle tells us that "by life we mean self-nutrition and growth -- with its correlative decay.")[68] Aristotle says in this passage that "the soul...is the cause or source of living." He also states that "change of quality and change of quantity are also due to the soul."[69] This is what occurs in growth and development. This gives us a further basis for arguing that the unborn child has a soul from the first.

Now, let us consider what Aristotle says about the characteristics of each of the three types of soul and which creatures possess which one. He states the following:

> ...the psychic powers...we have mentioned are the nutritive, the appetitive, the sensory, the locomotive, and the power of thinking. Plants have none but the first, the nutritive, while another order of living things has this *plus* the sensory. If any order of living things has the sensory, it must also have the appetitive; for appetite is the genus of which desire, passion and wish are the species; now all animals have one sense at least, viz. touch, and whatever has a sense has the capacity for pleasure and pain...desire is just appetition of what is pleasant. Further, all animals have the sense for food (for touch is the sense for food); the food of living things consists of what is dry, moist, hot, cold, and these are the quantities appended by touch...[70]

Also, as already mentioned, the only creatures possessing the thinking faculty -- i.e., mind -- are man and an order above him.[71] He says that "[t]hose which possess calculation have all the other powers above mentioned, while the converse does not hold."[72]

The "power of self-nutrition...is obvious in plants...it is the only psychic power they possess."[73] Plants have a nutritive soul. "Since nothing except what is alive can be fed, what is fed is the besouled body and just because it has soul in it." Similarly, I believe that the unborn child has a nutritive soul because from the beginning he is taking nutrition, first by means of a primitive then a well-developed umbilical cord. His digestive organs begin to develop in the first month and, recalling Liley's statement, all his developing structures are used from the start. The fact that the unborn child must receive his nourishment from his mother does not alter the fact that he has a nutritive soul. Most creatures must get their food from outside of themselves no matter how well developed they are.

Does the Unborn Child Have a Sensitive Soul?

Next, let us speak more about the sensitive soul and determine whether the unborn child has it. The sign of the sensitive soul is, simply, the presence of the senses, primarily the sense of touch. Aristotle says that "some classes of animals have all the senses, some only certain of them, others only one, the most indispensable, touch."[75] He states that "nothing except what has soul in it is capable of sensation."[76] Besides touch, he gives particular emphasis to the characteristic of voice. He explains that "[v]oice is the sound made by an animal, and that with a special organ," that it "is a sound *with a meaning*," and that "nothing that is without soul utters voice."[77]

Now, we shall consider the unborn child in light of the above. I mentioned that by the sixth or seventh week, the unborn child begins to become sensitive to touch. By perhaps the fifty-sixth day -- the eighth week -- he is able even to feel pain. By the tenth week, most of the body is sensitive to touch. By the fifth month, he is as responsive to touch as any normal one-year-old.[78] I believe that this indicates that, with respect to Aristotle's theory, the unborn child exhibits the primary sense and thus possesses a sensitive soul from a quite early state of pregnancy (close to the point at which he believed animation occurred for males).

I mentioned that by the fifth month -- abortion is still almost completely unrestricted at this point -- he possesses another of the senses, hearing. I shall say more about intrauterine hearing in connection with learning shortly.

Lastly on the matter of the senses, the unborn child can be said in some sense to possess voice. As early as the third month, as stated, his vocal cords are completely formed. The only reason he perhaps does not cry or make other sounds with them is that there is no air in the amniotic sac. Crying has actually been heard when experiments have been conducted in which some of the amniotic fluid has been replaced by air.[79] I shall state something further here which, while not directly to Aristotle's point, is still somewhat pertinent. By his eighth week, the unborn child engages in a rudimentary form of communication. It is a sort of body language, through which he communicates his likes and dislikes with well-placed jerks and kicks.[80]

Another sense which the unborn child possesses from an early stage is taste. From the third month on, the unborn child drinks amniotic fluid from the sac. When the fluid has been artificially sweetened in experiments, he drinks more. When it has been given an unpleasant taste, he drinks less.[81]

As Aristotle states in the one passage above, creatures who have sensory powers also have the appetitive one. He explains the reason for this in the following passage:

> ...whatever has a sense has the capacity for pleasure and pain and therefore has pleasant and painful objects present to it, and whereever these are present there is desire, for desire is just appetition of what is pleasant.[82]

What I have already said indicates that the unborn child, from very early, has the appetitive power. The very fact that he takes nutrition *may* suggest appetition in some sense. It is more clearly seen in the fact that he "communicates" likes and dislikes -- this suggests that he finds some things to be pleasant and some unpleasant (I shall speak more about this) --, apparently experiences pain, and spits out amniotic fluid if he does not like its taste.

Aristotle mentions other physical activities which indicate the presence of the sensitive soul. These include sleeping and waking[83] and breathing.[84] The unborn child does these also. I mentioned that by the fifth month, he sleeps and wakes. (He even sleeps in a favored position, another sign of appetition.) I also stated that he starts breathing motions in the third month.

The existence of a heart also indicates the presence of a sensitive soul for Aristotle. He believed that the soul resided in the heart[85] and said that it occupied the most honorable position in the body.[86] We now know that he confused its functioning to some extent with that of the brain since he said it caused movement,[87] breathing,[88] sensation,[89] and warmth.[90]

The unborn child seems to have a sensitive soul almost immediately. By eighteen days there is a primitive heart in the unborn child that begins to beat irregularly at twenty-four days, and there are indications that some kind of cardiac organ exists even before this because heart contractions have been detected at two weeks.

It might be objected that this is not a valid conclusion because Aristotle was incorrect in his understanding of the heart's function in the body and, after all, I am attempting to show that Aristotle's theory proves the presence of a soul in the unborn child in light of *modern* biology.

This objection can be answered. First, the heart retains its importance in Aristotle's theory even when modern biology is applied to it because of his belief that the soul resides in it. Modern biology does not affect this notion at all. It is still valid to conclude, with respect to Aristotle, that the unborn child has a soul from the point at which he first has a heart. Second, even though the heart is not responsible or primarily responsible for the activities and characteristics mentioned above, it does play a key part in an important one. This is body warmth. While this is regulated by the brain, the heart and vascular system to a great degree create it because the circulation of blood keeps the body warm. The circulatory system is present and functioning by the end of one month. The heart and blood cells appear in the second or third week and the whole system quickly follows, pumping blood throughout the tiny body. Additional heat is generated by the digestive activity, which appears to begin in the second month because it is then that the stomach begins to secrete digestive juices. Actually, the body would seem to be warm even before this occurs, probably from the point of fertilization. This is because there is cellular activity from then and this generates heat. The presence of warmth is significant because Aristotle regards it as an indicator of the existence of the soul. He mentions this when discussing digestion, but he appears to make the general point that a body's warmth -- however caused -- is a sign of a soul.[91]

I believe, then, that a reasonable argument can be made that the unborn child, according to Aristotle's scheme, has a sensitive soul. He has it at least from a very early point in gestation and the latter point about warmth indicates that it might even be from fertilization.

Does the Unborn Child Have a Rational Soul?

Now, we come to the question of whether the unborn child has a rational soul. This is, of course, the key question because if answered affirmatively, it means that the unborn child, for Aristotle, is without doubt human.

I have said that the ability of a creature to think is the sign of his having the rational soul. Let us first consider what Aristotle says about the thinking activity. He explains that some form of mental activity occurs in all animals, but only one animal, man, *thinks*:

> ...perceiving and practical thinking are not identical...the former is universal in the animal world, the latter is found in only a small division of it...speculative thinking is also distinct from perceiving -- I mean that in which we find rightness and wrongness -- rightness in prudence, knowledge, true opinion, wrongness in their opposite; for perception of the special sense is always free from error, and is found in all animals, while it is possible to think falsely as well as truly, and thought is found only where there is discourse of reason as well as sensibility. For imagination is different from either perceiving or discursive thinking, though it is not found without sensation, or judgement without it. That this activity is not the same kind of thinking as judgement is obvious...
>
> Thinking is different from perceiving and is held to be in part imagination, in part judgement...[92]

and

> The soul of animals is characterized by two faculties...the faculty of discrimination which is the work of thought and sense, and...the faculty of originating local movement...
>
> These two at all events appear to be sources of movement: appetite and mind (if one may venture to regard imagination as a kind of thinking; for many men follow their imaginations contrary to knowledge, and in all animals other than man there is no thinking or calculation but only imagination.[93]

What Aristotle means from the above is as follows. Animals are capable of certain activities which we might tend to think of as intellectually-based. These include perception, discrimination, and imagination. Actually, these are part of the animal's instinct. This is what I believe he means by the "special sense [that] is always free from error." Man is above this because he can engage in speculative thinking. That is, he can speculate and form opinions which will be either right or wrong (i.e., he can be calculative). This requires more than the above faculties which all or some other animals have. It requires reason.

Further, Aristotle believes that some other animals besides man have memory -- which he says "belongs to the faculty of intelligence only incidentally," --[94] but only man possesses recollection.[95] The latter is different from memory in that it involves not merely recall, but recall at will.[96] This requires reasoning.[97] This ability of recollection is found in that part of the soul called the understanding or mind which men possess but animals do not.[98] Also, since "dreaming..results from imagination, and belongs to the primary organ of sensibility,"[99] it would seem that animals as well as man partake in them.

In now discussing whether the unborn child has the mental abilities which, according to Aristotle, would indicate a rational soul, I shall rely primarily on information in a recent book by psychiatrist Thomas Verny. In this book, Verny presents his conclusions from years of practice and summarizes current knowledge about the mental abilities and psychological development of the unborn child. (It is worth noting at the outset that Verny is for legalized abortion.)[100]

There is evidence to show that the unborn child possesses the faculties Aristotle mentions above, which man shares with some animals, except for imagination. There is probably no way of discerning the possession of the latter in the unborn child. Perception and discrimination are related -- the former involves the latter because when engaging in the former "the soul discriminates and is cognizant of something which *is*."[101] This faculty can simply be described as a creature's knowing what to do in a particular circumstance, recognizing different circumstances and distinguishing between other creatures. Some examples of the unborn child's doing this follow.

It is thought that as early as at three months, he has rudimentary emotional responses -- such as vague feelings of discomfort -- to maternal emotional reactions to him.[102] Later in the pregnancy, as Verny tells us, "[h]e can sense and react not only to large, undifferentiated emotions such as love and hate, but also to more shaded complex states like ambivalence and ambiguity."[103] I mentioned that he hears by the fifth month. Verny says further that even though he cannot understand his mother's words, he does pick up her tone and will respond emotionally to it. He tells us that, "soft, soothing talk makes him feel loved and wanted."[104] From four or five months, he responds very discriminatingly to different sounds and melodies.[105] Further, he has consciousness, although it is not as deep or complex as an adult's. He is aware of things about him to some degree and even, as what I have just said indicates, of fairly subtle emotional nuances.[106] Some researchers believe that he may have some kind of consciousness even from the first hours after conception.[107]

Evidence is mounting that the unborn child also has a functioning memory. Verny tells us that the unconscious memory of hearing his mother's hearbeat while he is in the womb is thought to be the reason why a baby is comforted when held to someone's chest or made sleepy by the constant ticking of a clock. It may also be the reason why adults working in an office are typically not distracted by the sound of typewriters or an air conditioner.[108]

In his book, Verny relates an experience from

the psychiatric practice of Dr. Paul Bick, a pioneer in the use of hypnotherapy. Bick treated a man who had been having severe anxiety attacks accompanied by hot flushes. Bick used hypnosis to get the man to recall events from his time in his mother's womb. The man calmly related various incidents that occurred month-by-month. When he reached the seventh month, he began to act panicky. He felt very hot and afraid. Bick judged that something which happened at that point was the reason for his present anxiety problem. He later found out that the patient's mother had attempted to abort him in her seventh month of pregnancy by taking hot baths.[109]

Verny states that Bick's experience is common. Psychiatrists and psychologists who bring patients back to the point of birth and pre-birth by means of drugs, hypnosis, free association or other means frequently report recollections from them that "appear to go back *even as far as conception*." He says that the following is not an untypical recollection:

> "I am a sphere, a ball, a balloon, I am hollow, I have no arms, no legs, no teeth, I don't feel myself to have front or back, up or down. I float, I fly, I spin. Sensations come from everywhere. It is as though I am a sperical eye."

Verny has concluded, upon examining such recollections, that they often correspond to events in the early stages of pregnancy.[110]

The above appears to show that the unborn child has a memory -- that is, information about his existence gets stored away in his developing brain and often can be retrieved, when special efforts are made years later. The example of remembering the maternal heartbeat could indicate a memory capability that many animals, in addition to man, might have. The recollection of Dr. Bick's patient and Verny's example above, however, suggest that the unborn child has a distinctly human memory capacity, as I shall explain momentarily.

Verny's thinking is supported by others in the psychological and psychiatric communities. Psychologist Andrew Feldman says that "[f]ollowing the lead of Francis Mott, Otto Rank, Nandor Fodor, R. D. Laing, and

Stanislav Grof, it must be postulated that myths, fairy tales, legends, dreams, visions, and hallucinations can be expressions of vivid memories of certain *pre-* or peri-natal experiences."[111]

I thus have shown that the unborn child has at least the characteristics of higher animals. The information put forth so far could be construed to indicate even that he has those of a human, though more will now be presented which more conclusively indicates this. Further, the last two examples above indicate that he has such "higher animal" characteristics *from fertilization.*

Let me begin my exploration of the question of whether the unborn child has the intellectual faculties which suggest distinct humanness -- and the presence of a rational soul -- by returning to these last two passages. Verny uses the term "recollections" in the one, and Aristotle believes that recollection is a uniquely human faculty. I do not know if Verny is using this term as Aristotle would; I am sure he was not even aware of Aristotle's distinction between memory and recollection. Nevertheless, what he describes, I believe, is an example of Aristotle's notion of recollection. Although the methods used in the cases mentioned are extraordinary ways of stimulating recall, they still bring forth what is essentially *willful* recall. The methods, with the possible exception of drug therapy, do not *compel* recall; the patient is just made more able to willfully remember things which lurk in the depths of his mind. Moreover, no one would expect an animal to be able to recall specific things which happened to him if he were under such treatment. These are treatments for humans to help stimulate the human memory. Animals also do not remember specific events as humans do; some will just recall general notions, such as some creature or some situation being bad for them -- i.e., causing them pain -- and so should be avoided.

Even though the power of recollection is not exercised until after birth -- probably long after it -- we can still say, I believe, that the unborn child possesses it. This is because, even though he may not recollect previous intrauterine experiences when still in the womb, the faculty is at least potentially present. Indeed, in a sense it is active from the beginning because the memories are continuously being stored up to be recalled one day.

The fact that the unborn child's consciousness, as mentioned, grows more and more complex as he develops suggests that the higher, distinctively human intellectual faculties come into play at some point before his birth. I have treated such "core" feelings -- to use Verny's term -- as love and hate as something that even higher animals can feel.[112] I believe that this is correct because it is our experience that some animals express, in some sense, affection, rage, and the like. A strong case can nevertheless be made that, in the strict sense, such feelings or emotions are only experienced by humans. Thus, what I have already said can possibly indicate the presence of a rational soul from an early point in gestation. Let me go on to make these additional points, however.

First, an unborn child learns behavior in the womb. Verny tells us of an experiment in which researchers taught unborn babies to respond to a vibrating sensation by kicking. (This is what behavioral psychologists call a conditioned or learned response.) They were exposed to a vibration immediately after a loud noise was made near their mothers. After enough exposures, the association between vibration and kicking would become so automatic in the babies' minds that they would kick even when the vibration was used without the noise.[113] Verny does not state the point in pregnancy at which this experiment was undertaken, but presumably it was in the third trimester.

Verny also explains that human personality begins to be shaped by the learning which occurs *in utero*. As he puts it, "[o]ur likes and dislikes, fears and phobias --...all the distinct behaviors that make us uniquely ourselves -- are, in part, the product of conditioned learning...the womb is where this...begins."[114]

Verny explains how a mother's anxiety can affect the unborn child, and how later feelings of anger and depression can have their beginnings *in utero*. The child becomes excited and sets up various primitive defense mechanisms against the anxiety, such as kicking and squirming. The experience of anxiety and what to do about it slowly become more sophisticated. "What began as a blunt, displeasing feeling...becomes an emotion, acquires a source (his mother), prompts his thoughts about that source's intentions toward him, forces him to conjure up ways of dealing with those intentions, and creates a string of memories that can be referred to later."[115]

The unborn child develops the emotion of anger in a similar way. The child learns something about cause and effect -- e.g., a position his mother assumes causes him discomfort and thus angers him -- and this is "a precursor of human thought." Verny tells us that some types of depression are also learned in the womb. If a mother withdraws love and support from her unborn child this plunges him into a depression.[116]

Verny also believes that what psychologists call the "ego" -- the person as thinking, feeling, and willing, and distinguishing himself from the selves of others and from objects of his thought[117] -- begins to function in the second trimester. This is because by that time, the unborn child's nervous system is capable of transmitting sensations to his higher brain centers.[118]

The above information from Verny signifies that the unborn child -- according to learned opinion -- shares human emotions, human states of mind, human mental activity, and human personality to at least some extent by the beginning of the second trimester. This is further evidence that he has the rational soul, at least by then.

Verny makes some further observations about the unborn child's mental abilities. A catastrophic stress in the third or fourth month may alter an unborn child's neurological development, but until about the sixth month its effect on him is largely physical. Stress does not have much cognitive content until then because his brain is not mature enough to translate maternal messages into emotion. A complex emotion requires tone and definition in the higher centers of the brain. For this to be present, a child must be able to perceive a feeling, make sense out of it, and create an appropriate response. The transformation of a sensation into an emotion requires a perceptive process. This, in turn, requires an ability to do some complex mental calculations at the cerebral cortex level, which is not present in the child until the sixth month.[119]

One can reasonably argue that the above indicates that the unborn child possesses from his sixth month the power that Aristotle says is characteristic only of humans, calculation. It also indicates that he possesses cognitive powers -- relating to knowing[120] -- from a much earlier point. Verny says that "little cognitive content" -- meaning there is at least some -- is present from the third month, or perhaps even before. This cognitive ability may be something which is shared with higher animals because it involves, essentially, knowing and perception.[121] I believe that Verny, however, sees it as a human faculty. The quotes below from Franz also suggest that this is so. This means that distinctively human mental activities are present possibly from the second month.

Dr. Dominick Purpura is another authority cited by Verny. Purpura is editor of the highly regarded journal *Brain Research* and head of the study section on the brain of the National Institutes of Health. He says that in the period from the twenty-eighth to the thirty-second weeks, the unborn child's neural circuits are just as advanced as a newborn's. It is also about this time that the cerebral cortex matures enough to support substantial consciousness.[122] The cerebral cortex is, in Verny's words, "the highest most complex part of the brain -- the part most distinctly human."[123] Possibly the reason why the human-like mental activities I have mentioned occur well before this time is that the cerebral cortex *begins* to form much, much sooner. I mentioned in the previous Section that it is present by the thirty-third *day* of pregnancy. Recall, in fact, that brain waves have been detected at forty-three days.

Wanda Franz, Associate Professor of Child Development and Family Relations at West Virginia University, gives us some impressive facts about the cognitive development of the unborn child which present further evidence of his rational development. Cognitive development involves development of the ability to engage in a wide variety of human actions which may involve, for example, mental processes, physical coordination, or both.[129] Those who study this subject say that even the simplest actions require an integration of the activities of many component mental and physical structures of the body. Franz points to the theory of Jean Piaget, which contends that cognitive development evolves in an organized and predictable pattern from an organism's interaction with its environment. He points to the nervous system as the source of increasingly complex cognitive development. The more complex this system is in an organism, the greater the potential for more and more complex cognitive development.[125]

Franz points to the implications of Piaget's theory for understanding the cognitive development of the unborn. She tells us that no new biological structures which make this development possible "can appear full-blown out of nothing. Every structure must be based on earlier ones; the earlier ones determine the form which the later ones must take."[126] We see some examples of cognitive development in unborn children in the thumb-sucking I mentioned before and in his grasping reflex action. Research has shown that "the early differentiation and rapid growth of the nervous system supporting...[these] reflex[es]" is responsible for them.[127] I have pointed to the early point when reflex action first is present; Franz says that research on spontaneously aborted fetuses has verified it at six weeks.[128]

This leads Franz to conclude that "from the earliest period of human development, the organization of the structures of cognitive functioning is already laid down." It is when the reflex action begins that the unborn child can be said to be reacting to environmental input so that the cognitive structures can emerge. In other words as soon as the requisite biological structures appear, "even in rudimentary form, the organism begins assimilating environmental stimulation. This leads to accommodation of new structures, which are then coordinated and integrated to form a fully developed scheme."[129]

Franz's conclusions are significant because they indicate that the unborn child, from a very early point in pregnancy, acquires the rudimentary ability to do things which are almost uniquely human. For example, few animals -- only humans and the higher primates -- suck their thumbs or are able to grasp onto things. The grasping reflex which is present at birth is presaged by these early fetal reflex actions. This grasping reflex is the rudiment of the high level of manipulative skill[130] -- which involves an integration of physical and mental abilities -- which only humans can acquire. These indications of cognitive development are thus, in part, indications of rational faculties and thus of a rational soul.

Even though the evidence of cognitive development is seen no earlier than nine weeks into the pregnancy -- when thumb sucking begins --, Franz argues that its origin really must be at the start of gestation. This is because each level of development is directly dependent on the earlier level for the form it takes. She argues that the entire life of a human being is continuously evolving from conception. No one level of functioning is superior to any other, since each one depends on and evolves out of lower, less functional forms, and is the basis for the next higher form.[131]

Finally, Blechschmidt's interpretation of the unborn child's development seems to sum up my belief that if Aristotle had had access to modern biology, he would have put aside his view that the tripartite soul is not present from the start, but develops successively. One wonders if he was not thinking specifically of Aristotle when he wrote the following:

> ...a human being does not *become* a human being but rather *is* such from the instant of its fertilization. During the entire ontogenesis, no single break can be demonstrated, either in the sense of a leap from the lifeless to the live, or of a transition from the vegetative to the instinctive or to characteristically human behavior. It may be considered today a fundamental law of human octogenesis that not only human specificity but also the individual specificity of each human being remains preserved from fertilization to death, and that only the appearance of the individual being changes in the course of its octogenesis.[132]

By applying our modern knowledge of intrauterine life to Aristotle's thinking about the unborn child, we can reasonably argue that he has a rational soul, and hence is human, from fertilization. By applying modern biology and psychology to Aristotle's notion of the tripartite soul in *De Anima*, we can say *conclusively* that the unborn child has the nutritive soul from fertilization; almost conclusively that he possesses the sensitive soul from very early in gestation -- probably in the first month -- and quite likely from fertilization; and conclusively that he possesses the rational soul in the eighth and ninth months, almost certainly from the start of the sixth month, and a strong argument can be built that he has it from fertilization.

The Views About the Unborn Child's Humanity in the Pro-Abortion Briefs and Other Common Pro-Abortion Arguments and Some Responses

In the final Section of this Chapter, I shall turn back to the pro-abortion briefs to examine statements they make about the unborn child's humanity. I shall also consider the other usual pro-abortion arguments, not mentioned in the briefs, on this subject. After I state each, I shall answer it with reference to the material I have set out in this Chapter, commonsensical reasoning, common human experience, and common language.

The pro-abortion briefs being considered do not, for the most part, speak about the unborn child's humanity. PPFA, in both its main and supplemental briefs, says that this question is either "religious" or "philosophical" ("metaphysical") in nature.[133] It says that science is incapable of providing an answer to it.[134] In accordance with this, it says that a "culturally and religiously pluralistic society" cannot be permitted to resolve this[135] and quotes biologist Garrett Hardin -- who, as we shall see shortly, is also quoted prominently in another brief -- as saying "'whether the fetus is or is not a human being is a matter of definition, not fact; and we can define it any way we wish.'"[136] The PPFA supplemental brief also says the following:

> That our society has chosen to define human life as beginning at birth is sufficiently indicated by our method of calculating age.[137]

Let us turn now to the *Wade* brief. This brief

addresses the question of humanity more directly. The brief first tries to lump spontaneous and induced abortion together. It argues that "[t]he procedure of *induced* abortion differs from *spontaneous* abortion not in the result, nor in the underlying reason for the abortion but primarily in its being conscious and volitional."[138] It goes on to quote one expert as follows:

> "If spontaneous abortion did not occur, life as we know it would be impossible...If all the abnormal embryos that were conceived survived, then 1 in 10 to 1 in 5 of the population would be abnormal and most of the defects would be gross and incapacitating."[139]

This leads the brief-writers to make this jolting conclusion:

> No law requires that a patient week or a physician provide treatment to prevent *spontaneous* abortion. Neither nature nor the law values an embryo which the patient's biochemical system rejects.[140]

The brief then launches into a biological discussion of the unborn child. It quotes a few prominent medical authorities. One says the following:

> "...during...[the] early stages, the development of all mammals is fundamentally the same... The illustrations of sections of 5-mm human embryos are quite applicable, for example, to similarly located sections of 5-mm pig embryos. The basic plan of early body structure is amazingly similar."[141]

Another is quoted as saying that the 5-mm embryo has "'a conspicuous tail.'"[142] A third says that "'[f]or the first week of development the human embryo is invisible to the naked eye.'"[143]

The brief concedes the following:

> Scientific studies in embryology have greatly expanded our understanding of the process of fertilization and development of the fetus and studies relating to the basic elements of life have shown that life is not only present in the

> in the fertilized egg, sperm and ova but that each cell contains elements which could conceivably constitute the beginning of a new human organism.[144]

It explains away the importance of these for abortion, however, by saying that "[s]uch studies are significant to science but only confuse the problem of defining human life."[145] The brief purports to abandon biology as being able to provide sufficient information to decide about abortion and then promptly turns to a biologist, Garrett Hardin, in order to make its argument. As we can see, the essential points made by Hardin are not biological, but statements about the worth he places on the unborn child:

> "When a fetus is destroyed, has something valuable been destroyed? The fetus has the potentiality of becoming a human being. Therefore, is not the fetus of equal value? This question must be answered.
>
> It can be answered, but not briefly. What does the embryo receive from its parents that might be of value? There are only three possibilities: substance, energy and information. As for the substance, it is not remarkable: merely the sort of thing one might find *in any piece of meat, human or animal*, and there is very little of it -- only one and a half micrograms, which is about half of a billionth of an ounce. The energy content of this tiny amount of material is likewise negligible. As the zygote develops into an embryo, both its substance and energy content increase (at the expense of the mother): but this is not a very important matter -- *even an adult from this standpoint is only a hundred and fifty pounds of meat!*
>
> Clearly, the humanly significant thing that is contributed to the zygote by the parents is the information that 'tells' the fertilized egg how to develop into a human being called "DNA"... *The DNA constitutes the information needed to produce a valuable human being. The question is: is this information precious? I have argued elsewhere that it is not...*"[146]

The brief also uses two quotes to summarize its view about the value of human life and unborn human life in particular. One is the Hardin quote mentioned above as also being in the PPFA supplemental brief (which is a continuation of the above quotation) and the other is from the dissenting opinion of Judge Fred J. Cassibry in *Rosen v. Louisiana State Board of Medical Examiners*,[147] one of the lower court decisions which preceded *Wade* and *Bolton*: "'...[the] meaning of the term 'human life' is a relative one which depends on the purpose for which the term is being defined.'"[148]

With this quote from Hardin, the brief, taking the view that by undercutting the importance of biology it has already put to rest the question of whether the fetus is human, makes an argument about why it should not be protected as even "potential life." The first part of this argument is spelled out in the following quote:

> ...science only leads to a worse quandry for obviously if one goes far enough back along the continuum of human development one encounters the existence of submicroscopic double-helix molecules which have human life potential.[149]

What the brief-writers are saying here is that according to the theory of evolution (in the grander, more all-inclusive sense of the term), all future, as yet non-existing human life can be said to be "potential" since it evolved initially from simple molecules. It, in effect, says, in light of this, that if we consider the fetus as worthy of protection because of its "potential" for life, we reduce the term "potential" to meaninglessness.

The second and third parts of its response to the "potential life" argument attempt to show that potential life should not be protected in this area when it is not protected in others. These other areas it identifies are the "potential" lives not being protected when legislative decisions are made "to cut appropriations from slum clearance, for medical facilities, for food subsidies or in the cases of the following: a declaration of war; a court's refusal to consider the habeas corpus petition of a condemned man" and forbidding abortions which could result in the pregnant woman dying.[150] (Even if one were to concede that the unborn child is or may be only "potential life" and could accept this use of semantics in this area, he would realize that the brief is definitely mistaken -- in light of the way it views the meaning of human lives or human beings throughout -- to consider these other areas as involving "potential" lives; they involve "actual" born and grown human beings.) The brief claims that it is appropriate that these other decisions be left to the "representative process," but the "decision on abortion" demands "exactly the opposite." In arguing that the woman alone must have the "right to choose," the brief twice refers to her as the "host" of her unborn child.[151]

In the passages from the briefs quoted above, we are able to observe a number of the common pro-abortion arguments regarding the unborn child's humanity. I shall point to these arguments roughly in the order that I have considered the quotes and answer them and, after this, shall go on to mention and answer the other common arguments.

First, let me consider the argument from the PPFA briefs that the humanity of the unborn child is not a question for science but for religion and philosophy. This argument is correct in one sense, but not in the way that I believe the brief intends. Let me first explain the level on which it is incorrect.

I believe that the brief is implicitly interchanging two questions: "What is life?" and "What is the value of life and what obligations do we owe to it?" These questions are really separate and distinct and cannot be interchanged. The first of these questions can substantially be answered by common observation and/or by science. We initially learn what a human being is through our senses as well, of course, as our awareness of ourselves. We learn that a human being is a human being because of how he looks and sounds and what we observe he is capable of doing (e.g., solving a problem after thinking about it, operating a complex machine, communicating with others through language). We get this information by means of our senses. We then store it in our minds and we verify that the creatures we subsequently perceive by means of these same senses are human beings by referring to this original information. Thus, our basic knowledge about what is human life is acquired through the senses.

In those cases in which our senses are too limited to enable us to gain a sufficient amount of knowledge and to subsequently verify whether something conforms to this knowledge or whether this knowledge can explain it for us, we must rely on scientific techniques. These techniques have been developed, one might say, to enhance the limited powers of our senses. For example, modern science has enabled us to "see" the unborn child as he develops in the womb. It has enabled us to acquire the knowledge about him that I related in Section II, so that we are aware that he carries out the basic bodily activities of an adult human being. The microscopic techniques of modern science have enabled us to observe, as mentioned in Section II, that even the earliest human embryos have structures which are distinctly human. Science, in the latter case, does not supplement human observation as much as it corrects its shortcomings. Simple observation -- with the assistance of some magnification -- might lead one to conclude that the unborn child at his earliest stages is not human because he does not *look* human. Scientific devices have enabled us to get a "closer look," so we can see the human characteristics that the eye misses. Thus, simple observation and science *can* truly permit us to know what a human being is, at least according to his physical characteristics.

I believe that the argument of the PPFA briefs would concede the above -- that is, would acknowledge the basic biological facts and perhaps even conclude from them that life is present, -- but would say that it does not necessarily indicate that life *should be protected*. That is why I say that the briefs confuse the questions of the definition of life and its value. As I have shown, science can substantially answer the question of what life *is*, but only philosophy and/or religion can tell us about its value and what obligations are owed to it.

On the other hand, science cannot answer the question of what life is *entirely* or even provide the most *fundamental* answer, however, The question is indeed metaphysical, epistemological, and theological in essence. This is because any creature actually has life *not* because of its physical characteristics and structures -- whether observable by the naked eye or scientific devices -- but because of its having a soul, as I have said. A human being has *human* life because he possesses a rational soul. The matter of the soul is the appropriate subject for philosophical or theological inquiry because it involves the spiritual realm. The natural or physical sciences cannot deal with this realm; no science except theology and philosophy can do this. Humanness is also defined by what the unique and proper ends of the human being are. This is also made known to us only through philosophy -- i.e., epistomology -- and religion. Thus, while the PPFA argument is too eager to dismiss the importance of science in answering the question of what life is and is incorrect in saying flatly that this is not a question for science, it is correct in that *most fundamentally* it is not a scientific but a philosophical and religious question.

As I mentioned, however, I do not believe that the briefs mean this on the level I have just described. I say this because for us to find out about the human soul or human ends, one must acknowledge that there is a true philosophy -- i.e., that there are certain truths grounded in nature -- or that there are certain common religious truths based on Divine revelation. The PPFA briefs clearly do not indicate such an acknowledgement. They rather view both philosophy and religion as a smorgasbord, with people able to pick and choose what beliefs they wish to hold without regard to nature or revelation or, if we are to judge from the entire argument of the briefs, very little more than individual desires. In fact, I believe that the brief-writers make this argument about what life is as being a philosophical or religious matter for the very reason that they have this smorgasbord view. Because the prevailing view is that there is no true -- i.e., systematic -- philosophy nor true, universal religious principles, they know that these disciplines probably cannot sufficiently answer the question of what human life is (and, because of this, themselves turn to science to answer such questions). The brief-writers have thus successfully created a "catch-22" situation which plays right into their hands on the abortion issue.

The briefs' quotations from Hardin and Judge Cassibry about the definition of life being open reflect a shockingly relativistic view which, if accepted as an ethic, would cheapen all human life. If the definition of human life depends on the purpose for which it is being defined, why can we not say that other groups (e.g., the mentally retarded, elderly, poor, persons with green eyes) should not be "defined" out of existence? Moreover, who is to do the defining and for whose purposes is it to be done? If the advocates of this position were willing to come to the state (as represented by the Supreme Court) to get it to establish that the one group -- unborn children -- is outside the definition of "human," would they, or others of similar thinking, hesitate to use its powers, if they could, to exclude others from it for some reason? The position they take thus leaves open the door for the ultimate decision about who shall be permitted to live and who shall not to the state. It is not difficult to see how such a view undermines any true basis for human dignity.

Let me further respond to the views of Garrett Hardin. First, consider his statement about the unborn child having the "potentiality" of becoming human. The biological facts cast doubt on this "potentiality" argument. Numerous parts of the human body -- even, to some degree, the brain -- are functioning from a very early point in pregnancy. The analysis of the soul with reference to Aristotle also helps defeat this argument by showing that a strong case can be made for the unborn child's having a distinctively human soul. We might also recall Blechschmidt's statement that no point in pregnancy can be pointed to as showing that the unborn child progresses from one type of creature who is not genuinely alive to another who is. Blechschmidt was, in effect, restating the conclusion of the participants at the international conference in Washington, D.C. in 1967, mentioned in Chapter One.

A human being has the same genetic traits at fertilization as he does at any later point in his life. Nothing is added to what he is except nutrition, time, and oxygen, which simply cause him to grow. A human being does not *come* from a fertilized egg, he once *was* a fertilized egg. He does not come from an embryo or fetus, he once was one. These terms are nothing more than stages of human development. A human progresses from fertilization through the following general states of life: zygote, embryo, fetus, infant, adolescent, adult. (We can further break adult down into young adult, middle-age, old-age.) Pro-abortionists sometimes speak of the unborn child being a "blueprint" for a human being, but a blueprint is a plan for a structure; it does not become the structure. This requires bricks, mortar, and other materials. A human being, however, *does* develop from a fertilized ovum. A blueprint and a building are things of a different nature. A fertilized human ovum and a post-partum human baby are of the same nature. We can, therefore, perhaps identify one of the underlying philosophical problems of the pro-abortion position: a confused notion of the natures of things. This is particularly disturbing because if the things in their nature which make human beings distinctively human are not acknowledged, the basis for defending human dignity is undermined.

Further, the unborn child cannot be said to be a "potential" human being in the sense of his not being animated. As I have shown, he lives and carries out all the functions normally associated with life -- growing, taking nutrition, giving off wastes, etc. -- from the time of fertilization. Because he is growing and developing from the first, differentiation in development of bodily parts and functions is apparent from the first. He is never just "there," fully developed but without life, as was thought by some in an earlier era.

The claim that the unborn child is somehow "not human" or only "potentially human" is puzzling in light of our common sense understanding that the offspring of human parents can be nothing but human.

Looked at in another light, if we take the full meaning of the term "potentiality," almost every person can be said to have failed to measure up to his potential. A very young child could not be said to be "fully" developed. He cannot talk or think in the manner of an older child and his body has not yet developed the strength to deal with various physical afflictions. Actually, most of us have potential abilities, talents, etc., that we have not developed or, possibly, that we do not even know we have. I doubt that Garrett Hardin, Judge Cassibry, and the brief-writers would be willing to say that we forfeit our right to live because we are only "potential" human beings in such circumstances. Yet, this points up the kind of logical dilemma they create.

Niagara University philosophy professor Dennis Bonnette has written that the argument that the unborn child is only *potentially* human is based upon an erroneous notion of potency and the nature of primary and secondary acts performed by individuals. The human being's *primary* act is to live. He engages in various *secondary* acts, such as growing, sensing, thinking, speaking, socializing, etc. A human being lives from fertilization (i.e., engages in his primary act), but the powers or potencies for the secondary acts are progressively actualized as his life goes on. The progressive development of the structures, organ systems, etc. in the unborn child's body represent such an unfolding of secondary acts in an organism whose actual life has been present from fertilization (this is another way of expressing what Blechschmidt said) and upon whose primary and continuous act of living all secondary activity depends. The secondary acts are distinct from the primary act; they may be intermittent or some potentialities may not become acts at all, but human life is continuous. To use Bonnette's examples, we may cease to walk or talk or think and yet still be living, as when we are asleep or comatose.[152]

Let us concede for a moment (for purpose of argument) that the unborn child is only potentially human. Why would it necessarily follow, as Hardin and the *Wade* brief both assert, that the law should not protect him (or it)? If the law is concerned with maintaining a strong sanctity of life ethic in order to avoid social turmoil, why should it not be allowed to prohibit or restrict abortion if it is believed that it contributes to the weakening of this? I point out elsewhere that there is evidence that widespread legalized abortion has led to a devaluation of life in other areas. Furthermore, if the law is permitted to protect other living creatures whose natures will never permit them to become human -- such as with cruelty to animal laws which protect dogs and cats and environmental laws which protect, say, snail darters -- why sould it not be permitted to protect the "potential life" of the unborn child who clearly will "become" human? And if human beings are something distinctively valuable, why should "potential" members of that species -- who will very shortly be "actual" members -- not be given the same or almost the same protection as "actual" members?

Hardin, of course, responds to this latter point by simply asserting that human beings are not distinctively valuable. This is seen in his reference to them -- both unborn children *and* adults -- as "meat." His standard of an organism's value seems to depend on little more than the quantity of matter that it possesses.

(Even the "information" of which he speaks depends on a material substance, DNA. I suspect that he would also consider the intellectual powers of the adult human being as falling into the category of "information." These too, in his thinking, would ultimately be based in a strictly material substance, the brain.) The unborn child is for him the most lacking in value because he has the least matter. (I do not know if Mr. Hardin is skinny or fat, as I do not know if he would consider himself "valuable" on the grounds of his having much substance. Presumably, he would consider himself "valuable" because he has much insightful "information," of the caliber he provides about the unborn child.)

I need hardly mention that Hardin's theory expresses an extreme and vulgar materialism, and it leaves little basis for asserting human beings have a unique dignity. It is, in fact, patently *de*humanizing. The fact that the *Wade* brief chooses to use this quote of Hardin's -- and use it prominently -- is a further indication of the extremely materialistic view it espouses.

There are three other specific resonses to Hardin. The first is that his abrupt dismissal of the "value" of the information contained in DNA is entirely out of order. It is this "information" which is needed to make a human being a human being, instead of a dog or horse. Secondly, in his eagerness to reduce human beings to just conglomerates of matter, he ignores the whole notion that Aristotle had of the soul (which was the reason for my discussion of it). The soul is the life-giving part of the human being. Hardin does not tell us how substance, energy, and information can come together to make a living human being. He does not explain why, if a human being is nothing more than these, scientists in a laboratory cannot create a human being when they just put together the inanimate matter which makes up the human body and add energy to it.[153]

Also on this "potentiality" point, the *Wade* brief's reference to evolution from simple molecules deserves a brief comment. I shall not dwell on the question of evolution, but shall just make these two additional points:

First, the theory of evolution of man from lower species all the way back to one-celled organisms is exactly that -- a *theory*. It is not a *law* of science as the brief seems to imply. Secondly, the grand, all-inclusive theory of evolution referred to (in which one species is held to emerge from another and the highest species come from lower ones) -- to be distinguished from the theory of evolution which says that the characteristics of a particular species "evolve" according to changes in its habitat or environment -- has serious gaps in the scientific evidence supporting it.[154] The brief should thus not be so smug about making an argument which takes it for granted.

The final point of this "potentiality" argument is the *Wade* brief's statement about other areas where "potential life" is not protected by the state. The first of these -- the state's cutting appropriations for slum clearance, etc. -- cannot be equated to abortion because it involves no certain taking of human life, as abortion does. In fact, the very nature of the action is different from abortion because not only the latter's result, but its objective, is to destroy life. (Again, we perhaps see the confusion of natures, this time involving the different natures of different actions.) As it is, refusing to provide a government subsidy for food or medicine does not necessarily mean that people will go without these and thereby die. It may only mean that they will have to find other ways of paying for them or, possibly nothing more than that they will have to purchase them out of a general welfare grant instead of one earmarked for these specific provisions. Also, actions such as slum clearance -- as opposed to providing food or medicine -- may have little to do with preserving human existence. Slum clearance may be undertaken purely for aesthetic reasons and have no other effect.

Two other examples pointed to are a declaration of war and a refusal to grant a reprieve to a man condemned to death. Neither of these compare to abortion because they do not involve the taking of *innocent* human life. A declaration of war will institute hostilities between combatants and the lives that will be taken by individual soldiers will be to repel an aggressor who will kill them if they do not kill first. This would be killing in self-defense. Men are condemned to death usually because they, without justification and with deliberation, have taken the life of another. Taking the unborn child's life cannot be justified on these grounds because he has committed no such act.

The brief's argument about the likelihood of the woman dying because she is not permitted to have an abortion has essentially been addressed in Chapter Six and shall not be gone into again here. I will speak more about possible exceptions to a prohibition of abortion in Chapter Nine.

Let us now turn to the points about spontaneous abortion and biology made by the *Wade* brief. Most of what it says about spontaneous abortion involves poorly reasoned *ethical judgments*, not biology. It seems to make light of the difference between induced and spontaneous abortion of the one being volitional and the other not. It both fails to recognize the importance of this difference and to understand the role that nature plays. It says that were it not for spontaneous abortion there would be so many defective people alive that "life as we know it would be impossible." *Nature* intervenes, however, to end the life of the seriously deformed embryo in the same way as it intervened to cause the defects in the first place. Similarly, *nature* ends human life after so many years of existence because human bodies simply cannot go on any longer. To attempt to justify induced abortion by means of comparing it to the "benefits" of spontaneous abortion is like saying that because nature regulates population by bringing life to a normal end after so many years, men should feel free to try to regulate it by exterminating so many people every so often. The point is that the difference between something volitional and something which happens naturally is substantial. Further, most of the induced abortions are not performed because the child would be born grossly deformed but because the woman simply does not want him or believes that he will be inconvenient or disruptive of her life.

The brief really creates a straw-man when it compares induced and spontaneous abortion. This is because it ignores the biological fact that few of the embryos spontaneously aborted -- because of gross defects -- could ever develop further. They are aborted in a (generally) early stage of development for the very fact that they are defective. They could not live longer and hope to be born, even as defective persons. To talk about a scenario where a large part of the population might be defective for this reason is thus absurd. To somehow suggest that were it not for nature's intervention we would have a population of defectives -- and to suggest that it could somehow be otherwise in most of these cases -- is to misunderstand the very fact of what nature *is*. That is, nature establishes what is "the nature of things" and the fact of so many spontaneous abortions is part of "the nature of things." Induced abortion cannot be equated with spontaneous abortion because, by definition, what is done naturally cannot be said to be done by deliberation. Nature has its own designs, which are frequently beyond our understanding or control. Man, however, carries out acts according to his own free will which have moral consequences.

Next, let us consider the biological points made by the *Wade* brief. It says that there is a similarity of physical appearance between the human embryo and animal embryos. This appears in a different part of the brief than the Hardin quote discussed, but in light of the obvious attempt to use the Hardin quote to establish the non-humanity of the unborn child, I am inclined to think that the purpose of drawing this comparison is the same. The similarity of appearance between the human being at the early embryonic stage and other mammals or fish is superficial, as I have explained. In any event, we can hardly be influenced in making our judgment about the unborn child's humanity by such a superficial consideration as his rapidly changing bodily shape when we know that he contains the human DNA which can make him nothing but a human being.

The latter also refutes the attempt of the brief to make the unborn child seem insignificant because he is so small (i.e., "invisible to the naked eye" in the first week). This is actually a common pro-abortion argument. One might respond by saying that if size is to be a criterion of whether someone is human or not, then a lot of persons could be excluded. For example, a two-year-old is much smaller than an adult, so should he be said not to be human? What about a midget? What is to be the cut-off point of size to "qualify" one to be human? Five-two? Five-feet? Four-eleven? The commonsensical problems encountered by this argument are enormous.

The argument that the unborn child is not human because he does not *look* human on the surface raises other questions which create a commonsensical dilemma. What *precisely* does a human being look like? A severely retarded person may not look human, nor may a quadriplegic, nor may a person with severely distorted facial features. Many people once said that blacks, because of their color and features, were somewhat less than human. Does this mean that all these groups of persons should have to forfeit their right to live? Such a conclusion follows logically from this principle of the pro-abortionists.

A final biological point in the *Wade* brief that should be commented on is its reference to the woman carrying the unborn child as his "host." The unborn child is essentially a self-contained organism. He *does* depend on his mother for nutrition -- as does a young post-partum child --, but his vital functions are controlled by himself. So, he does not sap the resources of his mother as much as the brief implies. Secondly, this use of the term "host" is biologically and linguistically incorrect. For one organism to be a "host," the other must be considered a "parasite." It is from this biological context that the brief seems to get the term. A parasite in the animal world, however, is always of a different species than the host. Clearly, this is not the case with the unborn child and his mother.[155] As emphasized above, the offspring of human parents is human (i.e., of the same species).

Aristotle's thinking in *De Anima* concurs with this. He says that it belongs to a thing existing perfect in its kind to beget another like itself. In the case of the human species, of course, this means two physically capable adults seeking to produce a new human being. They do not beget anything which is not like themselves.[156]

Professor Bonnette makes a noteworthy observation in light of recent events. He says that any lingering doubt about whether the unborn child is a living organism, separate from his mother, from the moment of fertilization vanished with the birth of the first "test-tube" baby (i.e., baby conceived *in vitro*). Since *non*-living tissue would never be able to grow into a living baby just by implanting it in a womb, the embryo must already be *actually* alive as a separate, self-contained organism.[157]

I shall mention one other point from the briefs before closing with a consideration of the other pro-abortion arguments. This is the statement that the unborn child cannot be considered human because "our society has chosen to define human life as beginning at birth." This, of course, is an argument purely from convention; it does not seek to go beyond this to get at the nature of things. Just because a convention or custom has developed as a result of long-term practice, it does not mean that it is desirable or reflects the nature of a thing. Some civilizations have had utterly heinous customs. For example, the Aztecs periodically made scores of human sacrifices and the pre-Christianized natives of the Hawaiian Islands made brother-sister incest a practice. We thus cannot depend on a convention to necessarily explain something for us. As far as the customs of dating a person's age goes, it should be pointed out that another culture, the Chinese, has for centuries dated a person's age from conception.[158] So, if we are to consider nothing other than conventions as being important, we cannot say -- as the brief does -- that our society's convention on this point is any more correct than that of the Chinese.

Convention cannot provide an answer to our question of whether the unborn child is human. This is something, as has been shown, that is primarily within the province of biology and, secondarily, of philosophy.

Nevertheless, considering the conventions of different societies can be valuable on the subject of abortion, because they can answer for us another question: What respect has been given to the life of the unborn child? We can get some insight into this by looking at such questions as when age is dated from, whether a burial is given to spontaneously aborted unborns, etc. We can get an insight into a society's moral norms and, more importantly, into those which are in accord with the nature of man generally by examining the conventions of various peoples. This is what Aristotle did. It is also how C. S. Lewis derived the principles about marriage and respect for offspring that I spoke about in Chapter Four. One must be careful, however, to consider the full range of such conventions, not just some of them. We must also consider what the reason is behind a particular convention, and try to discern how a people viewed and understood it.

With reference to the unborn child, we must acknowledge, for example, that he commonly is not given a funeral ceremony when he is spontaneously aborted. This means that he is accorded less than the dignity that would be shown a born human being in the important matter of death. This *could* be a sign that he has not been regarded typically as a human being. We must consider other customs as well, however -- particularly ones relating to religious groups in a society because these are the groups most closely identified with providing ceremonies and the like for the dead. For example, we could point to the fact that various Christian denominations afford a certain respect for unborn children who are spontaneously aborted, by means of providing them with a proper burial, etc.[159] As far as the laws and customs of nations generally have been concerned, I pointed out in Chapter Three that many nations in pre-Christian times -- both the Jewish and pagan -- had respect and even reverence for the unborn child. Throughout Christian times until only very recently and even in non-Christian societies, abortion has been morally rebuked and often legally punished. I am not surveying the customs of various cultures as they relate to the unborn child; the only point I wish to make here is that one must look at a great number of customs in a society and then in different societies -- instead of just one or a few which the *Wade* brief and some pro-abortion commentators do -- before concluding that a society's customs are such and such and that a certain moral position on abortion is thus indicated.

Now let me move on to these other common pro-abortion arguments:

1) The embryo/fetus is just a mass of tissue and an appendage of the woman's body. The claim about his being just a mass of tissue reflects, again, a confusion about the different nature of different things. He *is* a mass of tissue, but he is unlike any other mass in a person's body because he has differentiated specialized body parts, carries out functions which other tissues do not, and he alone will develop into a full-grown human being. Also, unlike those other tissues he has a soul.

An objection might be made on this latter point: there are other masses of tissue sometimes found in the human body which have certain characteristics of human persons, but clearly are not human. The first of these is called a tertatoma. This is a tumor which includes various types of tissue which are put together without much order. This type of tumor may contain certain human characteristics. For example, it may have some hair, some skin, some teeth, some muscle, even fingers with nails growing. It had been thought that tumors like these were embryos whose development had gone radically awry. Further evidence, however, has strongly suggested that these growths are simply tumors, made up of material from the person's own body. It is thought that they do not at all develop from zygotes, but from stray cells that possibly were misplaced in the course of the woman's own early development and which retain a capacity for growth and differentiation which is like that of embryonic formative tissue.[160]

The point is that tertatomas may contain certain limited human characteristics, but they will not develop, even under ideal conditions, into a fetus, and ultimately into a post-partum infant. This is because they are of a different nature than a human embryo: they are just part of the one person's bodily tissue, whereas an embryo is an entirely different person.

Another type of creature is the fetus which has not developed properly in the head region. One such condition is called anencephaly, in which a fetus is delivered -- prematurely -- who lacks the top of the head and has little brain tissue. This has occurred because the neural tube failed to close, the brain could not develop properly, and the amniotic fluid destroyed what nerve cells did develop. The child dies shortly after his umbilical cord is cut.

A third type of creature that can be spoken of here is the one which results from the imperfect separation of identical twins. Often one perfectly formed twin will have part of another who failed to form properly attached to him in some way. Often, the imperfectly formed one will not have a head. (If there are two heads, the situation of one twin and *part* of another does not prevail. Two brains mean that there are two persons and what exists in such a case are Siamese twins.)

In the case of "anencephalic monsters," we may or may not be dealing with human beings. In the case of imperfectly formed identical twins, as just noted, there are not two human beings if one is missing a head. Grisez states in his book there are two ways that we may view the "anencephalic monster," depending on when their abnormality originates. The first way, when the abnormality or the genetic certainty of it is present from conception, is to view the organism as human in its conception, but incapable of developing beyond a few hours, a few days, or a few weeks. Grisez says that in such cases, especially if the specifically human genetic pattern is greatly transformed, we may not consider the conceptus a human individual.[161] The same would certainly seem to be the case with the imperfectly formed identical twin who has no head.

The other way Grisez says we might view the anencephalic is as we would view an individual whose head is blown off by a gun shot. Such a person is human and remains such until he dies. The anencephalic embryo originated as a human and developed normally up to the point when the neural tube failed to close and this led to degenerative changes. He thus must be viewed as a human being, albeit a damaged one, whose abnormality will cause his death shortly after birth, like the gunshot wounded person will die a short while after his wound.[162]

Various lesser abnormalities which are accompanied by at least some human development must also be considered, according to Grisez, as damaged human individuals.[163]

Thus, it is true that not everything which comes from the womb is human and some things are indeed just masses of tissue. It must be remembered, however, that these are "hard cases," and cannot be compared to the vast majority of unborn children who are developing normally when they are aborted and are certainly not just a mass of tissue.

2) (This point is related to *#1*) *The embryo/fetus is incontrovertibly dependent on the woman because it cannot live outside of her body.* I have acknowledged that the unborn child must depend on his mother for nutrition and protection, but the same is true of any young child. We would probably even be correct in stating that it is difficult for most children to remain alive for very long without a parent or guardian to provide for them until they are adolescents. Indeed, in the kind of interdependent society we live in, most of us must rely on a large number of other people -- farmers, wholesalers, retailers, transporters, etc. -- to get the very food we need to sustain ourselves. So, virtually no one today is truly *independent*.

3) The embryo/fetus cannot be a human being because it does not have a soul. (This argument might be posed by the pro-abortionist who does not share the extreme materialism of a Garrett Hardin.) I have, of course, already answered this point in my analysis of Aristotle.

4) Granted, the embryo/fetus is a human being, but is not a person. I basically addressed this point in my consideration of the briefs' argument that the definition of "human being" is a philosophical and not scientific question. There is simply no basis for asserting a dichotomy between "human being" and "person." It is our common understanding that "human being" and "natural person" are synonymous. It is true that since *Wade* and *Bolton*, the unborn child is not considered a legal "person," at least with respect to the right of life. (Recall that the Supreme Court left open the question of whether he is "human.") There was one other decision in the Court's history when it made a dichotomy between legal person and natural person, with the result that a certain group of natural persons were stripped of their legal rights. The decision was *Dred Scott v. Sandford*[164] and the group was blacks.

The remaining pro-abortion arguments relate to the question of when during the course of pregnancy the unborn child becomes "human":

5) The unborn child cannot be human at least until it is past the point at which twinning occurs because until then it cannot be certain that there will be a unique human individual. First of all, I mentioned how uncommon twinning is, so for this reason alone we should be wary of allowing it to be the basis for our judgment about something as critical as the unborn child's humanity. Secondly, I explained how duality is established even before an actual split of cells occurs. Moreover, the fact that the zygote may split would not take away the fact of the humanity of the one organism before it became two. As Grisez points out, "The zygote, whether it will become a single or a double embryo, is genetically distinct from its parents as soon as it is formed."[165]

6) The unborn child cannot be considered human until the point of implantation in the uterine wall. Dr. Bernard Nathanson, despite his recent anti-abortion views, has made this argument. He premises it on the following points: the existence of the other types of non-human entities that result from the union of sperm and ovum; the large amount of "pregnancy wastage" (i.e., fertilized ova that do not implant) that occurs; and a third, curious argument that he expresses as follows:

> Alpha [his name for the unborn child] establishes its presence to the rest of us by transmitting its own signals -- by producing hormones -- approximately one week after fertilization and as soon as it burrows into the alien terrain of the uterine wall. The HCG is discovered by the mother, doctor, and society when it enters the mother's blood and urine and is picked up via the use of immunological techniques...Before the connection is made, alpha is a free mass of tissue floating in the tube or uterine cavity, connected only by the code of its chromosomes with the entity it will become. It has the genetic structure but is incomplete, lacking the essential element that produces life: an interface with the human community and communication of the fact that it is there.[166]

Nathanson's position both fails to account for the biological facts and gets him into a commonsensical dilemma. First, he essentially seems to consider the pre-implantation unborn child to be a "potential" human being, despite the fact that he denies that he is like a "blueprint."[167] He thus leaves himself open to all of the criticisms made above of the "potentiality" position. He also fails to account for the simple fact that, as has been shown, he is *living* from fertilization and that development and physical differentiation are already occurring. Moreover, if the ability to communicate one's presence to others is to be used as the criterion of his being a member of the human community, a couple of troublesome scenarios can emerge.

First, consider a person who lives alone with no means of communication in an isolated desert area. Would the Defense Department be justified in taking over all the land around him and begin conducting missile tests there without even searching to see if the land was occupied, when the result will be that he is likely to be blown up? Secondly, consider the case of a mute, paralyzed person who is abandoned in an old house earmarked for destruction as part of an urban renewal project. Is the state justified in just letting the boom fly, crushing the house and everything in it to rubble without even checking inside to see if anyone is there? It is clear that the ability to communicate one's existence is not synonymous with the *fact* of one's existence.

Nathanson's point about non-human entities resulting from the union of sperm and ovum has already been addressed.

As for "pregnancy wastage," it is considerable. Estimates of the percentage of fertilized ova that naturally die *before birth* range from twenty to fifty. Of these, it is estimated that about thirty percent die before implantation.[168] This is a large number, but does not establish the non-humanity of the unborn child. All it really shows is that there is a mortality rate of, if we are to accept the accuracy of these figures, fifteen percent within roughly the first week of life (the period from fertilization to implantation). In any event, to say that this much natural "pregnancy wastage" can somehow be seen as a justification for destroying the unborn child before implantation is like the *Wade* brief's confusing spontaneous and induced abortion. Acts which occur naturally and those which are purposely undertaken are, in their nature, different.

Finally, Nathanson says that although he believes that the evidence best indicates that life begins at implantation -- a position with which I do not agree -- he acknowledges that it may in the not-too-distant future disclose that life begins even earlier. ("There is an inexorable march backward into gestation. We may someday learn of neurological activity at an earlier stage, or that a particular number of cells in the earliest days before implantation is the beginning of the brain. Definitions will easily be outdated, and we cannot allow ourselves to be trapped in today's transient date.")[169] If Nathanson is so certain that discoveries may soon be made that will move the moment of life closer to fertilization, he should give it the benefit of the doubt. Again, I say that if one is uncertain, he must err on the side of life.

7) Life cannot be considered to begin in the unborn child until brain wave activity begins. This is because our recent, clearer understanding of when life ends indicates that it is at the point when such activity ceases. Although I shall not go into this, the first point that must be made is that the medical community is by no means united on this understanding about when life ends. Secondly, it does not necessarily follow that the brain wave criterion can be applied to show the beginning of life just because it can show the end of life. This would seem to be indicated especially by the fact that heart activity appears to precede the beginning of brain wave activity in the unborn child, whereas brain wave activity often continues after the end of heart activity in a person near death. It does not then seem that the brain plays the same function at the beginning of life as it plays at the end. Using brain wave activity as the standard of death was intended to be a way of insuring that the person not be given up for dead just because his heart stops, when the continued functioning of the most vital organ, the brain, could well bring about revival. It would be ironic to rely on a standard which was meant to give the benefit of the doubt to the presence of life in making judgments about death to preclude the possibility of life at the human organism's beginning.

The crucial question here is potentiality. Even if the unborn child has no brain activity at all in his earliest stages, he can go in only one direction if his development is normal: toward very shortly having brain activity. A person whose brain activity has completely stopped at the end of life has no chance of getting it back -- barring some yet to be devised extraordinary life sustenance or restoration system. The potentiality then, is clearly there for the unborn child, but not for the person who dies.

8) (The final argument is related to *#7*.) *There can be no life until a person has consciousness or awareness of himself and his surroundings.* (This, of course, depends on a certain amount of brain development.) The first response to this is that, as I have shown, the unborn child appears to have consciousness in some sense -- of, for example, maternal emotions directed toward him -- from sometime in the first trimester. Some, as mentioned, believe it is from fertilization and the apparent memory of events from early pregnancy gives credence to this. The second response is, if we are to make consciousness the criterion of life, we could consider a comatose or a mentally incompetent person expendable. We could even justify the destruction of a person who has momentarily lost consciousness by fainting or a person who is asleep.

It must be concluded that the facts about the physical and mental development of the unborn child, Aristotle's thinking about the rational soul in the light of these facts, and various arguments based on common sense and logical reasoning, taken together, provide a compelling case for the humanity -- actual and not just potential -- of the unborn child.

Chapter Eight

Rights, Politics, Morality, and Science: The Thought Behind the Abortion Controversy

In this Chapter, the political, legal, and philosophical theory espoused in the *Wade* and *Bolton* opinions and in the pro-abortion position generally shall be considered. The first two Sections shall focus on the notion of liberty and rights presented. The remaining Sections shall contrast the pro- and anti-abortion positions on the relationship of the medical community to the political order and, more broadly, of science, morality, and politics.

Natural Rights, Positivism, and the Utilitarian Ethic

Liberty and Positivism in the Pro-Abortion Argument

The *Wade* and *Bolton* opinions and the pro-abortion

*As previously noted (see Chapter Three, footnote 102), I use the term "positivism" to mean the theory which affirms the validity of human law provided only that it be duly enacted.

briefs endorse a broad view of liberty. Both the opinions and the *Wade* brief, as has been stated, assert that one of the constitutional bases for the right of privacy and right to abortion is the liberty provision of the Fourteenth Amendment. By almost anyone's reckoning, this goes well beyond the traditional understanding of liberty in our constitutional law. "Liberty" was understood to mean freedom of movement and freedom from arbitrary restraint, freedom to exercise the specific guarantees of the First Amendment -- speech, press, assembly, and religion --, the right to participate as a citizen in the activities of the government, and the freedom to carry on certain economic activities, such as making contracts.

Two of the concurring Justices in *Wade* and *Bolton*, Stewart and Douglas, address the liberty question more directly than the Court does. Stewart cites several cases which present the notion of liberty as broad and changeable. He quotes Justice Frankfurter as saying that "'Great concepts like...liberty...were purposely left to gather meaning from experience. For they relate to the whole domain of social and economic fact...'"[1] Stewart deduces that liberty is violated by anti-abortion statutes simply because the woman's interests "are of a far greater degree of significance and personal intimacy" than some of the activities that the Court had previously held to be constitutionally protected.[2]

Justice Douglas quotes another Supreme Court opinion in saying "'Without doubt, [liberty] denotes not merely freedom from bodily restraint...[recounts a number of specific rights] and generally to enjoy those privileges long recognized as essential to the orderly pursuit of happiness by free men.'"[3] This is open-ended and, recalling Douglas' catalogue of liberties guaranteed by the Fourteenth Amendment (see Chapter Two), may include rights not clearly indicated by the language of the Constitution.

The liberty interest, as indicated in Chapter Four, also is viewed by the *Wade* brief as extending well beyond its traditional applications. The brief says it includes "the right of individuals to seek and receive health care unhindered by arbitrary state restraint, the right of married couples and of women to privacy and autonomy in control of reproduction; and the right of physicians to practice medicine according to the highest professional standards."[14]

In both the *Wade* opinion and *Wade* brief and in the line of precedents they cite, the right or reproductive privacy put forth is an expression of this expansive notion of liberty.

This view of liberty indicates a few points about the political thought behind the pro-abortion position. First, it seems that for it liberty is the basic, overriding principle. It is so important that it takes precedence over another basic principle of civilized nations: the sanctity and necessity of protecting innocent human life. Other writers have also pointed out how this stress on liberty in modern liberal nations is often permitted to supersede elevating or civilizing norms.[5]

We can appreciate how extreme the Court's and the pro-abortion movement's view of reproductive liberty or freedom is when we see that they will not permit it to be limited even by marital or family considerations. In *Planned Parenthood of Central Missouri v. Danforth* in 1976,[6] the Court held that neither a minor female's parents nor a woman's husband can stop her from having an abortion.

This view of liberty reflects an ever more extreme understanding in modern liberal thought of the individual as being prior to and antagonistic to the political order. As political scientist Walter Berns has pointed out: "The doctrine of liberty *against* government is...central to the liberal creed."[7] This is, of course, contrary to the understanding of the classical Greeks who saw the polis as essential to instilling virtue in man: this was necessary to lead him to a life in which he achieves the higher things of which his nature makes him capable. Most importantly, the polis made the highest of the virtues, justice, possible. As Berns also states, however, the early modern thinkers who laid the basis for America's political thought and order did not themselves take the view that the individual was radically separated from government nor that the latter had no role in elevating or civilizing man.[8] This point shall be developed in Chapter Nine. The contemporary liberal is really not consistent in his suspicion of government, however.[9] While he believes that the individual is to be protected from state interference in the exercise of his civil (and, recently, sexual) liberties, he does not say the same about his economic liberties. In fact, he believes that state activity in the latter realm is decidedly *good*.

Commentators have stated that promoting liberty is the primary preoccupation of modern liberal thought. Berns writes that it "assume[s] the identity of justice and freedom, and regard[s] freedom as a quasi-natural right."[10] It is considered to be "the highest good, the quality that distinguishes good regimes from bad regimes, the goal toward which man has always struggled and has succeeded in reaching only relatively late in his history."[11]

Fordham University political science professor Francis Canavan sees both liberty and equality as being the primary principles of the liberal state, but indicates that it is liberty which is central: "The right to pursue one's own happiness is freedom, equality is the guarantee of the same right to everyone."[12] Canavan explains how everything is subordinated to freedom:

> Under the liberal regime, morality, art, philosophy, all views of the goals of human life, all conceptions of human excellence, all become matters of private, not public judgment. The public goal, which is the purpose of the political order, is limited to the maintenance of equality in freedom.[13]

What this emphasis on liberty means, of course, is that the state must structure its laws primarily to promote it and to make sure that everyone can equally exercise it. Obstacles to it (such as restrictions on abortion) must be removed from the law. The only qualification is that liberty cannot be exercised if the result is the curtailment of others' liberty. It is this conception of liberty which is implicit in the Court's thinking in *Wade* and *Bolton*.

Further, we have already seen how Canavan's conception of the relationship between liberty and equality manifests itself in the abortion issue. In the drive to legalize abortion, it was argued that if abortions were not legally available to all only the rich could get them (by going to the more expensive private hospitals that would provide them, by going abroad, etc.). After legalization, it was seen in the demand that government fund abortions for poor women because otherwise they would not be able to take advantage of this new right.

We can easily see how this notion of liberty leads to the promotion of a utilitarian ethic. The only thing the state is permitted -- indeed, required -- to do, is to create the conditions for as full an exercise of individual liberty -- at least in the civil liberties area -- as possible. It cannot, by and large, restrict individuals as to the ends they are to pursue with that liberty. This would involve the state's deciding what is good and promoting it, which liberalism forbids. As Berns puts it, "*The one inexpiable sin [according to liberalism] is for government to get into the business of distinguishing good from evil.*"[14]

Thus, the state must accept as equally good any activities that individuals choose to engage in. It is not permitted even to do something as basic as protect innocent human life if this challenges the preeminence of liberty. Government, according to contemporary liberalism, must not even place a value on the life within a woman's womb. It must let this value be relative to her wishes and, if she decides to place no value on it, the state must acknowledge and protect her liberty to dispose of it. This, of course, is a utilitarian ethic.

The duty that liberalism imposes on the state to protect liberty in the extreme causes it, ironically, to abandon the other duty that liberalism insists on, neutrality, and to embrace a certain moral position. This is what Canavan, speaking of the state's lifting restrictions against both abortion and non-marital sexual conduct, says:

> It [the state] abandons the previous judgment that human life and marriage are worthy in themselves of the recognition and protection of the law, and replaces it with the equally public judgment that they are merely subjective goods whose only value in the eyes of the law is the value attached to them by the individuals immediately concerned.[15]

In other words, when the state takes a morally neutral position it really adopts the utilitarian ethic of which

I have been speaking.

The view of law as basically man-made (judge-made) -- which was discussed in Chapter Two in reference to "balancing" -- is seen in the arguments presented in the *Wade* brief (which were largely accepted by the Court). The right of privacy is held to be a right only on the basis of previous Supreme Court decisions. This right is held to extend to abortion because of these previous decisions (especially *Griswold* and *Eisenstadt*) and lower court decisions. Lower court decisions and the Court's and brief-writers' understanding of history (which supposedly showed that abortion practices in most of the nineteenth century were relatively free) are the grounds for establishing that the unborn child is not a "person" under the Constitution. The Court also turns to decisions and commentaries in other areas of the law to apparently prove that the law generally has never viewed unborn children as "persons" in the full sense. We see further evidence of it in the Court's and brief's contention that now that medical science has eliminated the health hazard to the woman from abortion, the procedure must be legalized (i.e., when technology changes the law must change) and in the reference to other disciplines to determine when life begins.

Further evidence of this positivist view is the reliance of the Court and brief-writers on changing attitudes -- especially of important professional organizations -- and circumstances as a reason for changing the law.[16]

By bringing the above viewpoint to the *Wade* and *Bolton* cases, the Court did not appear to consider seriously the possibility that the anti-abortion laws and the attitudes that fostered them were grounded in the unchanging nature of man and in such permanent, widely-shared principles as the importance of protecting innocent human life. The relativism of both this positivistic jurisprudence and the utilitarian ethic makes it easy to see why the two go together.[17]

Further, there is a connection between the positivistic notion of law embodied in the *Wade* and *Bolton* decisions and the view that the Court takes of its power and of the judicial activity. It was pointed out in Chapter Two that both the dissenting Justices accused the Court of legislating. A number of constitutional scholars also have said this and have generally argued that the Court exceeded its powers and enunciated a right which did not have a firm constitutional basis. The views of these scholars will not be explored here, since this would take one far afield and could comprise a chapter by itself. I shall just quote one of these whose observations are representative of the others, Professor Archibald Cox of Harvard Law School and Watergate fame:

> My criticism of *Roe v. Wade* is that the Court failed to establish the legitimacy of the decision by articulating a precept of sufficient abstractness to lift the ruling above the level of a political judgment based upon the evidence currently available from the medical, physical, and social sciences...Constitutional rights ought not to be created under the due process clause unless they can be stated in principles sufficiently absolute to give them roots throughout the community over significant periods of time, and to lift them above the level of the pragmatic political judgments of a particular time and place.[18]

How did the Court succeed at making two such sweeping decisions as *Wade* and *Bolton* -- striking down virtually all the states' abortion laws -- with such weak constitutional grounds? Probably, it is because of the widespread acceptance, at least among those in the legal and political arenas, of the positivist view of law and of the Supreme Court as a legitimate maker of law. If law is seen essentially as something propounded by the state and Supreme Court decrees as "the law of the land," to use the familiar phrase, then there is no higher law than that of the Court. The law and the Constitution become synonymous with what the Court says they are. There is no reason for surprise then, when the Court acts without restraint or without basing its decisions firmly on constitutional principles.

Is the Pro-Abortion Position Based on Natural Rights?

Some might quarrel with my assertion that these decisions are an expression of positivist legal philosophy. They would say that they represent an appeal to fundamental principles of justice -- some version of the natural law, if you will -- in order to strike down positive law which is contrary to them. The problem with this argument is that no source for these principles of justice -- as Cox states -- is pointed to.

We have seen that American constitutional history and the common law tradition cannot be the source for the right to abortion. Again, all the briefs and the Court rely on for their notion of reproductive privacy are recent Supreme Court precedents. Neither the Court nor the briefs gives an indication of appealing to Divine Revelation. This would have been turned to as the source for principles of morality and justice in an earlier time. The source cannot be classical natural right -- the classical-Medieval natural law tradition -- because this saw the individual as being subject to a transcendent moral order which restricted his personal activities. The Court's decision was squarely a reflection of an expansive notion of individual freedom and personal privacy.

Moreover, this natural law tradition sees man as being bound to act according to his human nature which directed him to seek the good or eternal salvation, which was his ultimate end. Several writers have made it clear how this tradition, particularly in its Judeo-Christian form, holds abortion to be a moral evil.[19] Moreover, as Professor Harold O. J. Brown has said, abortion cannot be considered to be according to the natural law just because it is *done* by people -- i.e., "natural" in the sense that it is something that people can do or even do commonly -- because they also perform other actions which we clearly regard as wrong and deserving of legal reprobation, such as murder.[20]

Finally, the source that might be referred to is

the natural rights thinking of the Declaration of Independence and of the philosophical progenitor of the American political order, John Locke. If this were the source, it would have to be by implication since neither the Court nor any of the pro-abortion briefs -- nor the pro-abortion literature generally -- alludes to the Declaration or Locke or "natural rights" by name.[21]

One critic of the pro-abortion position, Georgetown University political science professor George W. Carey, believes that its philosophical roots are ultimately found in this Hobbesian-Lockean theory of natural rights. He says that the notion of the state of nature which is part of this theory is crucial to understanding the pro-abortion and similar contemporary movements. People are said to relate to each other as autonomous individuals in a state of nature and are not subordinate to any transcendental law or order not of their own making. The state exists only because of the consent of individuals and becomes "the chief repositor of reason" and the only source of law. It "build[s] itself on the lowest common denominator of the interests and values" of these individuals and its chief function is to "provide for [their] material gratification." He calls this a "crude utilitarianism."[22]

While the current thinking, as reflected in the pro-abortion movement, shares certain notions with the Lockean view which prevailed at our nation's founding -- such as an emphasis on individual rights instead of obligations and the state as the primary source of law -- and may have its initial philosophical roots in Hobbes and Locke, I believe that Carey too readily sees it as an outgrowth of this. The natural rights view of Locke underwent a transformation or was displaced by another perspective before it reached the present era. Canavan makes a similar point when writing about the *Danforth* decision, mentioned above, which he says transferred the *political* thinking (i.e., concerning man's relationship to the state) of Hobbes and Locke -- in the form of the social contract theory -- into the realm of marriage and the family.[23]

What I state in Chapter Nine about Locke emphasizing the need for sexual virtue points to one important way in which this contemporary "natural rights" thinking -- what hereinafter will be called simply "rights thinking" -- differs from Locke's views. Part of the material gratification that the state seeks to make possible for individuals in this new thinking is the gratification of sexual desires (which necessitates legalizing abortion). The fact that Locke holds that the state legitimately can be concerned about sexual virtue means that he does not view this to be a private matter, as the Court and the pro-abortion movement indicate, by means of their views on abortion, it is. This alone means that Locke cannot be appealed to readily to support the pro-abortion position.

Let us consider the matter of the state of nature. Carey may be correct in saying that the radically autonomous view of the individual observed in contemporary thought is like the view of Locke's state of nature. It is clear from his words below that this notion of Locke's can apply to men within a political community as well as in some pre-political state, if this ever existed. Locke's words make it clear, however, that American political society could not be said to be in a state of nature. He says that "[m]en...without a common Superior on Earth, with Authority to judge between them, is *properly the State of Nature*"[24] and that "[t]hose who are united into one Body and have a common establish'd Law and Judicature to appeal to...*are in Civil Society* one with another..."[25] America has functioning political institutions which play this role of "Superior" and so is not in a Lockean state of nature. Indeed, the abortion issue reached its present state of controversy *precisely because* one of these institutions, the Supreme Court, tried to resolve it in the manner it did.

Another writer has argued that the Lockean understanding of natural rights diverges sharply with that present in the contemporary "rights" theory, as expressed in pro-abortion thinking. Northern Illinois University political science professor Gary D. Glenn contends that the argument for abortion on demand is at odds with the Lockean notion of inalienable rights which is at the basis of the American political order.[26] Glenn explains his position as follows.

Locke's notion of inalienable rights prohibits both the political society from violating or taking away an individual's inalienable rights and the individual himself from giving them away. This is why, for example, Locke forbids suicide.[27] Glenn says that it is because Locke denies the individual the power to take his own life that he denies him the unlimited right to consent. *Inalienable rights thus require limited rights or power in both individuals and government.*[28]

For Locke, life and liberty are intimately connected. He says the following:

> ...he who attempts to get another Man into his Absolute Power, does thereby *put himself into a State of War* with him; It being to be understood as a Declaration of a Design upon his Life...He that in the State of Nature, *would take away the Freedom,* that belongs to any one in that State, must necessarily be supposed to have a design to take away every thing else, that *Freedom* being the Foundation of all the rest...[29]

Thus, as Glenn points out, "[t]he inalienability of freedom rests on the inalienability of the right to life."[30]

Locke does not equate this inalienable right to freedom or liberty with license.[31] It is because Locke wishes to preserve the inalienability of liberty that he insists upon this. It then follows that any claimed right which is actually more of the nature of license and will tend to alienate liberty is unacceptable under the Lockean scheme. Glenn claims that the right to abortion on demand is such a right.

The essence of the argument as stated in the pro-abortion briefs and accepted by the Court is that the decision to abort is one which must be made by the woman in consultation with her physician because abortion is something which pertains to her alone. The meaning of the decision in practical terms -- even though the Court expressly rejected the notion in theory[32] -- is that the woman is acknowledged as having a virtual right, at least in the matter of reproduction, to do with her body as she sees fit. Glenn says that this right to do with one's body as one pleases justifies the alienation of liberty and, so, the right to abortion on demand which flows from it also alienates liberty. He explains why this is so:

> In one has an unlimited right to do with one's body as one sees fit, then one cannot at the same time also have inalienable rights which

> limit...what one can do with it. Therefore the woman's right over her own body argument denies the distinction between inalienable freedom and license by denying the logical assumption on which it is based. That assumption is that we do not have the right to alienate our inalienable rights...The propounding of an "absolute arbitrary power" over oneself replaces the unalienable right of freedom with the evidently alienable right of license.[33]

The right to abortion on demand, *per se*, may not have the effect of alienating inalienable rights. This right, however, does not stand alone. It is asserted as being part of the right of privacy, which, as has been explained, is part of the liberty interest of the individual. This realm of liberty pertains in this case to bodily integrity. Thus, what is being spoken about at the most fundamental level when we talk about the right to abortion on demand is the right of the individual to do with his body what he desires. Thus, it is appropriate, as Glenn argues, to judge this latter right as being the real one at issue in abortion. Because this latter right by definition means that the individual can alienate his right to life -- by suicide -- and his right to liberty -- by, for example, selling himself into slavery --, it is contrary to Lockean principles.*

Glenn says that the part of the liberal tradition of which the right to abortion on demand is a legitimate outgrowth, is utilitarianism. It might also be derived from Marxist and existentialist thought.[34] The pro-abortion position then, if the above analysis is correct, is not readily derivable from the Lockean-classical lib-

---

*It might be argued that the Court really *does* reject this right of the individual to control his own body, *per se,* as noted. *Wade* and *Bolton* then, would be said to do nothing more than widen the right of the individual woman to control her reproductive faculty by abortion, contraception, etc. The problem with this is that neither the Court nor the pro-abortion movement gives a basis for the law's treating the reproductive faculty differently from the rest of the body. On the contrary, it is argued in Chapter Nine that the common good is substantially affected by individual sexual and reproductive activity and, as such, the state has an interest in legislating about it.

eral position which the parchment American Republic is based on. Glenn explains that the logic of the classical liberal-inalienable rights thinking is opposed to the utilitarian liberal-unlimited consent position:

> ...if I had an absolutely arbitrary power to kill myself or to enslave myself to another man...then I could consent it away to the government. Then that man or government could kill or enslave me and allege it was with my consent. Locke thought the chances for freedom were better if it were firmly established that government may not justify killing or enslaving its citizens on the ground that it did so with their consent.[35]

Thus, I return to the point that motivated this consideration of Locke: *Wade* and *Bolton* cannot be seen as representing an appeal to principles of morality and justice which are based on the natural rights thinking of Locke and the Declaration of Independence.[36]

A New Basis for Rights: The Individual Will

Canavan explains what, in the final analysis, the source of rights is for the new "rights" thinking:

> Today as our faith in natural rights or...in the Creator, wanes [both are acknowledged in the Declaration of Independence], the rights of the individual are identified more and more with his desires. The individual, it is assumed, has a right to do what he wants and to live as he pleases, provided only that he does not harm others. Respect for the dignity of the individual...means respect for the right to follow his own will (which may be nothing more than his desires).[37]

If we take Canavan's and Carey's descriptions together, we see how the contemporary rights thinking embodies the utilitarian ethic. People are viewed as having something like an inherent "right" to satisfy their desires, particularly for material gratification. Those desires can be for anything that the individual believes will give him the greatest pleasure or benefit, or cause him the least burden, so long as no physical or psychic harm is done to anyone else. It is not for the state to judge how good or evil any of his desires are; its primary responsibility is to protect these desires by legitimating them and affording them the status of legal rights. In some casee -- as in abortion funding for the poor -- it will be called upon to provide the means to permit its citizens to successfully exercise these "rights." The courts, particularly the federal courts, are turned to because it is their unique function to legitimate law and declare rights. They are also turned to because the organizations pushing this new notion of rights, such as the ACLU and PPFA, know that they offer them the greatest opportunity for success. This is because the courts have proven to be more open to their view than legislatures, and are more immune to pressures from opposing organizations. It is also because it is acceptable now for the courts to legislate.

"Material gratification" means, broadly, bodily satisfactions. Sex is an important part of these and much of the new rights thinking has pertained to sexual activities. (This emphasis on sex is probably due to the influence of Freudianism, cultural trends, etc., but a precise determination is too extensive a job for this study.) Since this thinking is concerned about protecting rights which are, for the most part, grounded merely in individual desires, and because its utilitarian ethic involves maximizing benefits and minimizing burdens, it is easy to understand why legalized abortion on demand occupies so prominent a place on its agenda. Sexual pleasure is seen as a "benefit" that the individual has a right to seek while, at the same time, he (more accurately, she) has a right to avoid the "burdens" which may follow from that, babies. The unborn child is not viewed as having any rights or dignity probably because he, ostensibly, does not yet have any desires and is unable to exert his will.

Canavan writes that behind the new rights thinking "lies a doubt whether there is any ascertainable human nature or any objectively valid norms of human conduct derived from that nature."[38] There is no definite human nature because this mode of thought does not acknowledge the existence of a transcendent moral order in which man participates. Because of this, man is seen as having no particular ends that he by nature seeks. He does not have a basis for ordering his conduct in accordance with what Canavan calls his "truly human potentialities."[39] Human nature is like an empty wine bottle that man may pour anything into he wishes. He believes he can manipulate himself and do as he pleases without ever having to worry about moral consequences. Thus, he may seek to freely satisfy any of his desires which he wishes, no matter how base. He need not even feel concerned about determining which desires are base and which lofty and then establishing a heirarchy of morals. Consequently, law has as its purpose primarily the protection of the individual's putative rights to satisfy these desires and is obliged not to make the judgment that any of them is not worth protection. Since there is no transcendent moral order, law is ultimately nothing more than the reflection of human will -- despite appeals to "rights" which are said to be more basic than the existing positive law -- which can be changed as that will dictates. Man does not believe that moral consequences will ensue from violating his nature, so he structures his law to make sure that legal consequences also will not follow. This is seen clearly in the abortion cases. Abortion is not seen as a violation of a natural scheme of things or else this consideration is not believed to be important, so the Court removes the legal injunction against it.

Canavan states that this conception of human nature rests ultimately on a nominalistic metaphysics.[40] He says the following about this:

> In this philosophy, reality is its elements, organized in patterns produced by the blind operation of natural forces or imposed by conscious human choice. Missing is the notion of natural wholes with their own natural forms that transcend and are more real than the elements they organize; there is nothing in natural entities that commands respect and imposes moral norms.[41]

It is easy to understand how the notion of a transcendent moral order or natural law does not have a place in this view. There can be no natural essences -- such as moral norms -- which exist apart from man.

The passage above leads one to think of what

Richard M. Weaver believed was the basis of modern political thought. Indeed, he saw it as responsible for *all* modern Western thought. This was what he called the "fateful doctrine of nominalism." This doctrine "denies that universals have a real existence" and so "universal terms [become] mere names serving our convenience."[42] He goes on to tell us the significance of this:

> This issue ultimately involved is whether there is a source of truth higher than, and independend of, man; and the answer to the question is decisive for one's view of nature and the destiny of human-kind...The denial of everything transcending experience means inevitably -- though ways are found to hedge on this -- the denial of truth. With the denial of objective truth there is no escape from the relativism of "man the measure of all things."[43]

While I am aware that much more analysis -- going well beyond the scope of this work -- is required to fill in the philosophical gaps and show the clear connection between the philosophical transformation Weaver describes and the thought expressed in the decisions, it is nevertheless true that the denial of higher moral norms derives from this earlier rejection of universals. And that is what the Court demonstrated.

The Pro- and Anti-Abortion Views on the Relationship of the Medical Community to the Political Order

In this and the final Section of Chapter Eight, I inquire into the role that science has played in the abortion issue. In Chapter One, I described the important part that one group in the scientific community -- the medical profession -- played in the effort for abortion law liberalization and, after awhile, in the anti-abortion movement. The legal treatment of abortion almost by definition involves the medical profession. So, I first consider the general perspective of the pro- and anti-abortion positions about the relationship of the medical community and the political order. Secondly, I look at the broader philosophical view of each of these positions about how science should influence human activities and morality.

The Pro-Abortion Position

Purdue University political science professor Joseph Haberer's book, *Politics and the Community of Science*,[44] contains some useful reference points for considering the role of the medical profession. Including physicians among the members of scientific community, he says:

> ...the pressures and influence scientists can exert upon the polity because of the strategic and central placement of their work cannot lightly be dismissed.[45]

We can expect that the influence of the scientific community will be greatest in those areas in which its members are directly involved. Thus, medical organizations will speak up and try to shape public policy about abortion because many of their members were or could have a part in it. The fact that obstetrician-gynecologists and psychiatrists are most likely to have a part in it may explain the fact that, as stated in Chapter One, they were the most outspoken for abortion. Moreover, the medical community seems to have sensed that it was *likely* to be politically influential on abortion. Many of its members actively worked for, and its largest and most prestigious organizations passed resolutions calling for, legal reform. The Supreme Court clearly made the views of the American medical community an important consideration in its decisions. Haberer's thesis above, then, seems to be confirmed as regards abortion policy.

The very fact of the medical community's substantial activity in the abortion issue, apart from its influence on it, demonstrates the validity of another of Haberer's observations:

> If it were ever possible to think of

> science as truly divorced from politics, events and developments of the last few decades have made such a view untenable. The rapid growth of its institutions has brought not only heightened internal politicalization...but also an intensified involvement with the political order itself.[46]

Starting with Glanville Williams, the legal inspiration of the pro-abortion movement, there is a tendency to view abortion as almost exclusively a medical question. The theme is sounded repeatedly that the law should withdraw from it, and leave abortion to the "scientific expert," the physician. At first, of course, the call was for the law to withdraw partially, later, it was totally. Also later, as contemporary feminism began to influence the debate, the prerogative of deciding was not seen as just exclusively the physician's but the woman's and her physician's. This, of course, was accepted by the Supreme Court.

The Court and the concurring Justices in *Wade* and *Bolton* demonstrate a high regard for the physician. Justice Blackmun refers to the decisions as "vindicat[ing] the right of the physician to administer medical treatment."[47] Justice Douglas is concerned that anti-abortion statutes result in "a total destruction of the right of privacy between physician and patient" and he wants to protect "the right to place reliance on the physician of one's choice."[48] Justice Blackmun says that "we trust that most physicians are 'good' -- will have sympathy and understanding for the pregnant patient..."[49] Chief Justice Burger is confident that "the vast majority of physicians observe the standards of their profession."[50] He does not consider that the moral standards of the profession may be low.

To Glanville Williams, freedom of physicians to perform abortions was necessary for scientific progress. The New York Academy of Medicine, the 1968 Hot Springs conference, *The New York Times* and *Time* magazine, it will be recalled, all affirmed that the laws were harmful because physicians were not given enough latitude to make judgments about a matter essentially in their province. *Time* perhaps enunciated the perspective behind this claim better than the others when it said that medical science should be put in the place of law and "archaic and hypocritical concepts" (i.e., morals).[51]

The *Wade*, PPFA, and ACOG briefs all make the claim that the laws infringed upon the rights of the physician. All of them make their primary argument on the fact that the laws did not permit the physician to exercise his "right" to make sound medical judgments.[52] The other major point is that the laws set up a conflict between the physician and the woman. It is argued that he will refuse to perform an abortion even if in his medical judgment the woman "needs" it, because of his fear of punishment.[53]

The briefs also echo what I stated was the appeal of *The New York Times* and the New York Academy of Medicine for legal change: abortion is accepted as a valid medical procedure by the medical community.[54] The latter argued that because most physicians (the New York Academy added also most of the public) wanted the laws changed, they should be.

The fact that the pro-abortion movement was so willing to take this issue out of the moral and political realms and place it squarely in the medical one -- where it was to be decided about by a physician according to *medical* criteria -- shows an incredible willingness to defer to the physician's judgment. Medical science is thus, in a sense, actually being permitted not only to have its conclusions deferred to, but also *to frame the very issues involved.* The fact that the collective opinion of the medical community about the laws was viewed as one of the prime reasons for changing them shows another dimension of this deference: the willingness to allow that community's thinking to actually shape the laws. This confirms another Haberer thesis, at least as it relates to the view of some in our political society (i.e., those in the pro-abortion movement and the judges and other public officials who agree with them).

> So pervasive is the vocabulary of science today that men increasingly look to it and to the scientist not only to answer their perplexities, but also to state them, to tell them what the questions are. For modern man looks not to the Church or the State...but to Science and the scientist for answers to his besetting problems. It may well be that

> science is becoming the leading institution of society...The leading institution's values and patterns of conduct are pre-eminent and pervasive.[55]

I shall not try to determine if science is *the* leading institution in America. The important point is that one part of the community of science, the medical community, was very influential on abortion.

The Anti-Abortion Position

It is clear from looking at a number of the anti-abortion briefs, as well as many anti-abortion publications, that science is relied on heavily to make the case for the humanity of the unborn child and to show the medical complications of abortion for the mother. The most extensive medical and biological arguments among the briefs are in the *amicus curiae* brief for "Certain Physicians, Professors and Fellows of the American College of Obstetricians and Gynecologists."

Pro-abortionists, curiously, use science for the latter purpose also, but in the context of showing the danger of illegal abortions. They also use science, as we have been able to see from their briefs, in order to show the medical safety of legal abortion and the shortcomings of contraceptives, so as to provide a rationale for abortion as a back-up. The pro-abortionists do not use science in refuting the claim of the unborn child's humanity, but, as can be seen in the *Wade* brief, rely on legal interpretations, social norms, and personal judgments about the value of life. They do not in the briefs directly refute the anti-abortion claims of medical complications but just cite numerous statistics showing the relative safety of legal abortion.

Consideration of a few of the anti-abortion briefs, as well as the very fact that the anti-abortion movement's primary goal is to make abortion illegal again, presents a clear picture of what this movement believes should be the relationship of the medical practioner to the political order and law. The NRLC's brief says that abortion laws infringe upon neither the physician's right to free speech nor his right to give medical advice. They prohibit "criminal acts."[56] Far from being willing to turn moral decisions over to physicians, LIFE's brief expresses a clear distrust of their ability to exercise such a power rightly when it says that they used the limited California statute and *Vuitch* ruling to create virtual abortion on demand.[57] The brief for Women for the Unborn, et al., squarely rejected the notion that abortion, except so-called "therapeutic" abortion, is essentially a medical matter because it does not really involve medical questions.[58] Implicitly rejected was the view that the medical community is the place for moral issues to be resolved.

I conclude that the anti-abortion movement, as seen by the briefs, does not believe that the making of public policy on abortion should be taken from the political realm and put in the hands of the medical community. It believes that it is proper for the law to regulate and even prohibit what physicians can do here. It does not see fit to take moral judgment-making out of the province of law and politics and put it into the medical.

Science, Morality, and Politics

The Nature of the Problem

Before considering how both the pro- and anti-abortion sides view science in its relationship to sex and human reproduction, pertinent statements by a few contemporary writers should be considered.

C. S. Lewis, a generation ago, stressed the objective of modern science, which was first enunciated by Francis Bacon: "'Man's Conquest of Nature.'"[59] In other words, man seeks, through science, to gain control of the natural conditions affecting his life. As Bacon, its major early philosopher, put it, the aim of modern science was "to relieve man's estate."

Besides this emphasis on its practical applications in order to help man to better control his life, modern science has exhibited certain other characteristics. One is a tendency, grounded in Bacon, to be somewhat suspicious of the political and to look for scientific solutions to problems. This has manifested itself, *inter alia*, in the contemporary attempt to let administrative and managerial principles replace politics as a basis for governing. Baconian science created sentiments for a state in which, as Haberer puts it, "public problems have disappeared and only technical-scientific problems remain," with the result that the "community is endowed with the permanent solution of its political problems at its very founding."[60] The citizenry need not participate in public decisions, but just leave them to scientific experts.

This tendency is reflected in the Court's and the pro-abortion movement's view about the relationship between the medical community and the political order. It denies that abortion is either a political or moral question and believes it should be left to the woman and the representative of the scientific community, the physician -- even though he is not necessarily trained in either ethics or politics -- to decide according to medical criteria. That is, abortion is primarily a *scientific* question. (It is not *exclusively* seen as such because the woman's prerogative is also involved. In reality, however, the physician and his supporting cast are perhaps in the preeminent position because they exercise a great amount of influence over the woman by the advice, counseling, etc., that they give her.) The desire of modern science to remove decisions from the public forum is also, of course, reflected here by the pro-abortionists' turning to the courts. It cannot be said that a permanent solution to abortion or other problems was sought at America's Founding, but the pro-abortionists do like to view the issue as "resolved" in a similar manner by the Supreme Court's decisions, without any further need for public discussion.

A second characteristic of modern science has been its optimistic view of the future. It has seen progress in a humane direction as being virtually inevitable, at least until fairly recent times. Both Lewis and Haberer point to this view and argue that it is unmerited.[61] I shall consider if the pro- and anti-abortion movements share this view later.

A third characteristic of modern science, which is probably linked up with its zeal to move everything into the scientific realm, is pointed to by Lewis,

Haberer, and Weaver. It is, as Lewis puts it, the tendency of the scientist to exhibit a "pronounced disinterest in first-order philosophical questions" and only a "superficial awareness of the social implications of his work."[62] According to Weaver, this is an outgrowth of the nominalism which colors modern thought generally. He says that "[t]he question of what the world was made for now becomes meaningless because it presupposes something prior to nature in the order of existents...[what] interests the new man...[is] explanations of how the world works."[63]

Haberer and Lewis say the result of this is that modern science has created technologies which threaten rather than enhance human well-being. Haberer says, "It is almost as if the very Nature which Bacon and Descartes sought to conquer, has turned upon those who attempted to dominate and master her."[64]

Lewis speaks of the area under discussion, human reproduction, and calls it the "final stage" in man's attempt to conquer nature.[65] Actually, he says, it will really be nature which has finally conquered man. For if man, "by eugenics, by pre-natal conditioning, and by an education and propaganda based on a perfect applied psychology," believes that he "has obtained full control over himself," he will really find that the control that is exerted is that of a few men over all the rest.[66] The most frightful aspect is that the masters of this awesome reproductive technology who determine the direction of all future generations will have rejected the "Natural Philosophy" -- i.e., natural moral order, natural law, or what Lewis calls the "Tao" -- and allowed themselves to be governed by their "natural," irrational impulses. These are the desire for power, wealth, and self-aggrandizement. We shall ask below whether the roots of this futuristic scenario are not present in the pro-abortionists' perspective.

What Haberer and Lewis say is that modern science has been fooling itself in trying to believe that it can hope to operate in an amoral context (i.e., that it can disregard the "Tao"). It is no doubt because of this belief that it has had such an optimistic view of progress and has believed that all questions can be turned into purely "scientific" ones. Christopher Derrick, the English writer and pupil of C. S. Lewis, also addressing the matter of sexual morality and human reproduction, makes the point that scientific knowledge is not sufficient to provide guidance in these areas:

> Science, strictly so-called, has told us a great deal about the universe; and for this, one can properly be grateful. But there are notorious dangers in the consequent power. Moreover, the scientific method is specialized and selective: it deals only with those aspects of reality that are amenable to one particular kind of intellectual treatment. Using scientific weapons, the armies of the intellect advance deep into the universe but on a narrow front: to either side of them, territories lie which they can never occupy... At the imaginative level at least, strictly scientific ways of knowing the universe may need to be supplemented.[67]

What all of these writers are saying is that this supplementary knowledge must come in the form of the "Tao." As Hans Jonas says, "benevolence" does not automatically emerge from modern scientific theory.[68]

Lewis says clearly that modern science has sought to do essentially the same thing that the older tradition emphasizing the "Tao" sought to do: help man to gain control of himself to make his life more liveable. Modern science, however, seeks to do it in a radically different way. Lewis says this:

> There is something which unites magic and applied [modern] science while separating both from the 'wisdom' of earlier ages. For the wise men of old the cardinal problem had been how to conform the soul to reality, and the solution had been knowledge, self-discipline, and virtue. For magic and applied science alike the problem is how to subdue reality to the wishes of men: the solution is a technique; and both, in the practice of this technique, are ready to do things hitherto regarded as disgusting and impious...[69]

One might say that the older tradition sought to transform man from within whereas modern science seeks to give man the power to transform the world outside of him in accordance with his inner desires, whatever they may be.

Moreover, Leon Kass, a physician teaching in the Department of Community Social Thought at the University of Chicago, suggests that modern science is not just morally neutral, as the writers above make clear. It has a certain dynamic which may actually entice man, with his weak human nature, to use it wrongly:

> ...modern science is guided overall by an ethical -- if prideful -- intention: a lifting up of downtrodden humanity, a reversal of the curses laid upon Adam and Eve, and, ultimately, a restoration of the tree of life, *by means of* the tree of knowledge. Never mind the question how a science invincibly ignorant of and in principle skeptical about standards of better and worse can *know* how to do *good* for mankind. The new humanitarians simply point to the seemingly self-evident truth that life becomes better as it becomes less poor, nasty, brutish, and short.[70]

There is one further aspect of this problem of modern science and ethics which these writers address, suggested most clearly so far by Lewis. This is that modern science has tended to push reality aside and to substitute abstractions for it. It has substituted theorizing for prudence and a sense of awe. Derrick and Kass see this particularly in the area of sex and reproduction. Derrick says this:

> ...we need to remember that Venus [sex] is a great and powerful goddess. Even at the level of mere self-preservation and self-interest, she needs to be approached with a certain respect, a certain nervousness, a certain awe. Her mysteries are holy and archaic and creative and bloodstained, concerned with the roots of life.[71]

Kass, in an article on *in vitro* fertilization research, argues that the human blastocyst in the petri dish should be viewed with awe and reverence simply because of its human origin and its capacity to grown into an adult human being. He accordingly calls for restraint and prudence in our approach to this new technology. He indicates his pessimism, however: "...it is hard to speak about restraint in a culture that seems to venerate very little above man's own attempt to master all."[72]

Lewis tells us that losing awe and respect for what is distinctly human in order to gain this greater scientific control may bring the following consequences:

> ...if man chooses to treat himself as raw material, raw material he will be: not raw material to be manipulated, as he fondly imagined, by himself, but by mere appetite, that is, mere Nature, in the person of his dehumanized Conditioners.[73]

We can think back to some of the characterizations made of the unborn child by the pro-abortion briefs and, particularly, by Professor Garrett Hardin in Chapter Seven and we can see that they were not far from viewing him as exactly that: raw material. This seems to have come precisely from pushing biological reality about the unborn aside.

These dangers that science poses to humanity lead Kass to suggest, reluctantly, that the common good requires that potentially dangerous technologies be controlled in some way by the state.

What these authors say, in sum, is that man has been trying to use modern science to gain as complete a control over his life as possible. It is a control over the circumstances he is in, however, not over his inner passions. In order to get this former kind of control, he has put aside the moral restraints of the "Tao." The result has been -- and will be even more dramatically and convincingly so as he progresses toward his goal of complete control -- that he has made his lot worse.

Haberer tells us that Bacon identified science with progress.[74] This may be the reason why he "was not keenly aware that scientific theory and practice might be two-edged" and have serious philosophical and social consequences.[75] He did have *some* awareness of this, however. Haberer points to one passage from the *New Atlantis* -- Bacon's work which spells out most clearly his thinking about science and its relationship to politics -- which shows this. In this passage, the scientist-governors (of Bensalem, the "New Atlantis") express the need to keep some scientific discoveries secret and even propose that they take an oath to preserve secrecy.[76]

This passage is characteristic of the "extraordinary prudence" that political science professor J. Weinberger of Michigan State University says that Bacon exhibited in his writings about science and the political order.[77] He points specifically to the *New Atlantis* as expressing this prudence:

> The new [Baconian] science suggests the possibility in...reality of what would, before...be possible only in speech or imagination. The new Atlantis promises to all men what most men desire, but...the *New Atlantis* shows that the perfection of science contains possible grotesque extremes that may threaten the felicity of some or even most men. The extraordinary restraint of the sheeplike Bensalemites is necessary for the conquests of science. But if the promises of science encourages and opens the way for human conquest, it does nothing to restrain the horizons of those men who are by nature conquerers.[78]

The "conquerers" are, of course, the same men as Lewis' "Conditioners."

Bacon scholar Howard B. White says that Bacon "tried to construct defenses against the misuse of scientific power." His faith in science was not "naive or unconscious," but it was a faith nonetheless, and according to White, it "rest[ed] on a radical revision of political philosophy." It was radical because it was utopian; that is, a kind of political optimism was an "essential ingredient" of it.[79]

We can conclude that Bacon shared the thinking of the contemporary promoters of science to the extent of being supremely optimistic about it, viewing it as an essentially amoral enterprise, and, by and large, not considering its threatening aspects and social implications. He clearly differed from them, however, in maintaining a certain awe about the possibilities it presented, and believing that it had to be approached with a certain prudence.

This Sub-Section suggests the following questions to be considered as part of my inquiry in the next two Sub-Sections: How does the pro-abortion position view science in relation to the "Tao." or the natural moral order? Is it permitted to replace them? Is the desire of the pro-abortion position to view abortion as essentially a "medical" (i.e., scientific) problem an avoidance of the larger philosophical questions mentioned above? Does the frequent pro-abortion claim that legalized abortion is needed to improve the "quality of life" represent the same kind of extreme optimism about science as seen above? Is there a strong stress in the pro-abortion position on "control," as I have discussed the notion? Is modern scientific abstractionism seen in the pro-abortion analysis? Is there a loss of a sense of awe about human life in this anlysis? Is there a sufficient stress on prudence? How does the anti-abortion position contrast with the pro-abortion one on these points?

The Pro-Abortion Position: Science, Morality, and Politics

Now, it is time to look again at the opinions and pro-abortion briefs, and at a few additional pro-abortion writings, particularly materials from PPFA, to see how they address the problems above.

Betty Sarvis and Hyman Rodman say the following about the pro-abortion perspective in their book, *The Abortion Controversy:*

> The future envisioned by the pro-abortionists... [sees] [p]ersonal choice in contraception and abortion [which] heralds an age of positive control over fertility and ultimately the "Century of the Wanted Child."[80]
>
> The pro-abortion argument...provides reassurance that people can and will use technology to create a better world. In a complex society filled with remote and uncontrollable forces,

> the promise of total and individual control over an important part of life appeals to many.[81]

Carey makes some of the same points about the "new rights" thinking that have been stated:

> Science figures predominantly in this process for two reasons. First, science is the area which is presumably value free; where, unlike the moral realm, findings, holdings, and the like are free from subjectivism. Thus science provides an objective yardstick in an otherwise relativistic world. Second, insofar as material gratification is the principal end of the state, scientific techniques can be of use.[82]

In the above passages, the authors indicate that the pro-abortion and "new rights" perspectives stress two important themes that have been discussed: "control" and the optimism associated with modern science.

I have already made reference to points from the briefs which show the "control" theme. One was in Chapter Six, where I mentioned the *Wade* brief's saying that millions of births could have been prevented by a "'perfect contraceptive.'" This and the strong emphasis on the problem of contraceptive failure and the need for more effective contraceptives implies that complete control over reproduction is the objective. The fact that artificial contraceptives and safe abortions -- the "fruits" of scientific and technological advancement -- are proposed presents the notion that this perfect control is to be achieved through modern science.

The *Wade* brief is very emphatic elsewhere about the importance of "control" over the reproductive faculties:

> Without the ability to *control* their reproductive capacity, women and couples are largely unable to *control* determinative aspects of their lives and marriages.[83]

In the briefs, this notion of scientifically-based control is mixed up with the constitutional and legal notion of "rights" throughout. Right after the sentence above, the *Wade* brief says the following:

> If the concept of "fundamental" rights means anything, it must surely include the right to determine when and under what circumstances to have children.[84]

The *Wade* brief expresses another dimension of the notion of "control" when it quotes the 1891 *Union Pacific v. Botsford* case as holding that the individual's right to control his own person is the preeminent right. The PPFA brief says that "the right to abortion must be viewed as a corollary of the right to control fertility."[85]

The "control" idea provides something of a bridge between two important aspects of the abortion question -- science and rights. The legal notion of the right to control one's body (i.e., the freedom to make decisions relative to it) is expanded to include the right to control the reproductive activity of that body, when science has afforded the means to do this.

The methods of fertility regulation which require the most discipline -- i.e., the greatest development of virtue -- in the individual, abstention and rhythm, are dismissed by the PPFA brief just for that reason. They demand too much of the individual. We can see this view expressed even more directly in PPFA's *amicus curiae* brief in the *Eisenstadt* case, in which it quotes approvingly from the U.S. Court of Appeals opinion in the case:

> "To say that contraceptives are immoral as such, and are forbidden to unmarried persons *who will nevertheless persist in having intercourse*, means that such persons must risk for themselves an unwanted pregnancy, for the child, illegitimacy, and for society, a possible obligation of support."[86]

The kind of control, then, that is being sought is that accomplished from without, by the individual's use of what science has provided, not that accomplished from within, which Lewis said is what the older tradition tried to promote. In short, science replaces virtue.

This point can be concluded by asking if the kind of "control" that the pro-abortionists had hoped for has come about. The indications are that it has not, and science, as Lewis and the others thought, has proven to be an unfit substitute for the "Tao." This is seen not only in the apparent medical consequences of abortion for women and in the increased rates of child abuse (both discussed in Chapter Six), but also in the soaring illegitimacy rate.[87] These are the very problems that we were told legal abortion would "control." Not only has this not been borne out, but the "anti-life" ethic created by legalization has possibly been responsible for an increased push for, and growing acceptance of, euthanasia and infanticide.[88]

I stated in Chapter Six the confidence that the pro-abortion briefs express about legalized abortion finally ending the problem of "unwanted" children and being medically safe for women. In Chapter One, we saw the belief expressed by PPFA and others in the pro-abortion movement that legalized and easily available abortion was needed to enhance our quality of life and that human "progress" would occur if only the whole matter were left to medical science. The notion of "quality of life" was put forth there in a societal context, but in Chapter Four we saw it asserted also on the individual level by the *Wade* brief's concern about furthering the individual's "well-being." All of this, when considered in light of what I have just said about science being the chosen vehicle of the pro-abortion movement demonstrates the kind of optimism that Haberer and Lewis speak about.

A clear and concise statement of the pro-abortion movement's optimism is found in PPFA's statement of purpose from its Certificate of Incorporation which appears in the "Statement of Interest" as *amicus*-intervenor in its *Eisenstadt* brief:

> "To undertake, support and promote investigation and *scientific research* touching upon and embracing the sociological, biological, medical and economic aspects of marriage, procreation, maternal health and *family betterment*, and to collect, circulate, evaluate and disseminate information concerning said subjects of investigation *and scientific research and matters related thereto*."[89]

The thoroughness of this confidence is seen even more starkly in a 1963 PPFA brochure:

> Planned Parenthood applies the profound philosophy of "Reverence for Life" by placing the creation of life under the guidance of man's ethics and intellect [i.e., through science].[90]

I might propose that a force which has helped to promote so much confidence in the ability of science to "control" sex and reproduction to man's advantage is modern liberalism. Kass points out that "modern science ...found a political home and able defenders in modern, liberal regimes."[91] Liberalism has long been a supporter of the advancement of science. Indeed, the optimism about human progress which has characterized modern liberalism is probably due, at least in part, to its embracing of science. Other strains of liberal thinking are seen in the briefs and in PPFA documents, such as the strong emphasis on individual freedom and the confidence in education being able to correct human problems.[92] Just as American liberalism had previously supported the birth control movement, with its similar emphasis on science to conquer sex, now it supported the pro-abortion movement.[93] The pro-abortionists' basic optimism about science, then, was fueled by a two-pronged source -- the community of medical science and the liberal community.

The pro-abortion position exemplifies modern scientific abstractionism, and this is shown by the passages in the *Wade* brief discussing the humanity of the unborn child, and by the suggestion that the unborn child has no "value."[94] He is essentially equated with an animal.[95] In one place it is with a pig embryo.[96] There is a stunning certainty expressed about the *non*-humanity of the unborn child:

> Neither the medical profession nor state health authorities treat spontaneous or induced abortions prior to 20 weeks of development as events which *in any way are comparable to the loss of human life*.[97]

This is abstraction not only because the brief does not discuss or answer the extensive biological evidence, but also because it does not even see fit to consider what history and long-time custom have taught about respecting the unborn child.

Even if the brief *could* build a strong scientific case against the unborn child's humanity until at least some point in the pregnancy, its eagerness to explain away even his "value" shows a chilling absence -- recalling Kass -- of a sense of awe at least of what he might *become*. There is no evidence of a *respect* for human life and of distinctiveness, except when the narrow, largely artificial issue of the woman's life being threatened is raised. The discussion of sex and reproduction, generally, in this and the other pro-abortion briefs, is devoid of a sense of the awe which these human faculties have long been held. The great power and mystery of these are lost.

The pro-abortionists in *Wade* and *Bolton*, in their insistence upon establishing a new fundamental right of abortion, case prudence aside. First, they disregard history and custom about the unborn child. Secondly, it is seen in their readiness to "go for broke" and wipe away virtually all legal restraints with one fell swoop. They ignored what eliminating the abortion laws -- and doing so abruptly -- might do to the efforts of the law to protect human life in other ways, to the moral norms about sex held by the public, and to the stability of the family. As I pointed out at the beginning of Chapter Four, they seemed hardly to concern themselves with the deep respect for the latter which has been held by virtually all traditions throughout history. Indeed, their obliviousness to this was demonstrated even more pointedly when they successfully sought to isolate the woman's abortion decision from the veto of even her husband or parents in the *Danforth* decision. A year or two before the pro-abortion movement had shifted its objective to repeal, one of its medical leaders, Dr. Alan F. Guttmacher, recognized the importance of taking a prudent approach: "Today, complete abortion license would do great violence to the beliefs and sentiments of most Americans...I am therefore reluctant to advocate it in the face of all the bitter dissension...[it] would create."[98] Dr. Guttmacher and the pro-abortion movement soon changed their minds. The Supreme Court joined them in their imprudence.

To close this discussion of the pro-abortion movement and modern scientific abstractionism, let us consider this one other passage from Lewis:

> ...[We have witnessed] the use of the abstraction Man. Not that the word Man is necessarily a pure abstraction. In the *Tao* itself, as long as we remain within it, we find the concrete reality in which to participate is to be truly human: the real common will and common reason of humanity...While we speak within the *Tao* we can speak of Man having power over himself in a sense truly analogous to an individual's self-control. But the moment we step outside and regard the *Tao* as a mere subjective product, this possibility has disappeared. What is now common to all men is a mere abstract universal.[99]

Lewis' view is justified by the *Wade* brief. The brief makes the judgment that "[n]either nature nor the law values an embryo which the patient's bio-chemical system rejects."[100] In a passage quoted above, it states that abortions are not treated by "the medical profession...[or] state health authorities" as "*in any way...comparable to the loss of human life*." In both cases, the brief refers to human authorities and man-made law as the basis for judging the most fundamental of questions: what human life is. The "Tao" implicitly is treated, in Lewis' language, as a "mere subjective product," determined by apparently nothing more than human opinion. (The brief mentions "nature" in the one passage, but does not tell us what it is and seems to permit man-made "law" to carry the same weight.) Further, the ethic of self-control which Lewis points to above -- which is the heart of the "Tao" -- is treated by the PPFA brief as unworkable or unrealistic.

The new rights thinking generally, by its nature, bears out Lewis' view, since it views rights as being based essentially on individual will. It reflects the philosophical viewpoint of nominalism, which contends that there is no moral order which transcends man.

I mentioned above Weaver's stating that this nominalism stands behind modern science. It is not surprising, then, that science is important to the new rights thinking.

Since contemporary man has difficulty believing in non-scientific truth (i.e., in any reality which is not verifiable by the senses through the scientific method), he tends to view anything non-scientific as mere opinion, and hence subjective. Science is seen as the only source of certainty, so he turns to it even to make his moral judgments for him. Without any other guiding truth, he does not want to make such judgments himself and, indeed, does not even believe himself capable of making them. It is not surprising, then, that the Court and the pro-abortion movement has been so eager to turn the essentially moral question of abortion over to scientific experts.[101]

Finally, let us return to the point about the pro-abortion movement's letting the medical community preempt moral and political decision-making. I showed in my account of the pro-abortion history that there was a tendency to believe that the "scientific expert" -- the physician -- is the one who can make the best choice; it was seen at "progress" to turn abortion exclusively into a medical question.

The pro-abortion position, however, is actually contradictory on this point. On the one hand, it claims that abortion must be viewed as a medical question, and that restrictive laws violate physicians' rights. On the other, it admits that these same physicians cannot find their way out of the supposed moral dilemma that the restrictive laws created for them, and have allowed their self-interest to get in the way of their giving the best advice to their pregnant patients.[102]

This emphasis on turning over more decision-making authority to physicians, as representatives of the scientific community, is not really a willingness to let scientific knowledge be the basis for decisions. This is evident from the fact that the pro-abortionists' analysis of the humanity of the unborn child is really quite *unscientific*. Indeed, this point is admitted when the *Wade* brief says that "science only leads to a worse quandary" in resolving the question of humanity.[103] What we really see is a kind of *scientism*. It is a willingness to accept the *"philosophy"* of modern science -- broadly understood -- at the disposal of the individual to use as he wishes, without the constraint of the "Tao" and with the aid only of scientific and technical experts. What happens is that scientific knowledge is used or disregarded according to whether it promotes the end of this "philosophy": human betterment and happiness. The political activity is relevant in this way of thinking primarily as a means of initially isolating and subsequently protecting the isolation of the delivery of these scientific "benefits" from political pressure or regulation (i.e., by legislative or judicial action which shields it by a "right of privacy" or some similar legal construct).

Since the woman's freedom is part of the pro-abortion concern, legalized abortion may not, in and of itself, result in the shaping of Lewis-type "controllers." What might result from it in the future, however, is another matter.

The acceptance of the abortion ethic is an erosion of the belief in the sanctity of offspring and the family (which is part of the "Tao"). Once this is accomplished, what is to prevent our moving, at some point when the commitment to individual freedom lessens, to compulsory abortion according to the determination of technocrats and scientific professionals? There are population and family planning experts who have already spoken in terms of putting contraceptive agents in the water and food supplies[104] and compulsory sterilization was carried out in "democratic" India during its 1975-76 "state of emergency." Indeed, the new rights thinking has laid the groundwork for such compulsory action by the prominent place it gives to the state (i.e., it must necessarily rely on the state to give legal legitimacy to the will-based rights it claims and to compel their recognition by the political society) and by its subverting the Lockean notion of the inalienability of rights.

The Anti-Abortion Position: Science, Morality, and Politics

We can come to an initial, tentative judgment about the anti-abortion movement's thinking about the relationship between science, morality, and politics on the basis of a few facts. First, the very fact that the movement seeks to prohibit virtually all abortions by law -- and thus to limit the physician's decision-making -- tells us quite a bit about this. The religious motivation of many movement members also makes clear their belief that abortion is primarily a moral question. The fact that they rely heavily on scientific information suggests that they believe that science has a rightful role in helping to shape public policy. The NRLC brief clearly suggests that medicine should "lead" the law on abortion.[105] It seems, however, to recognize the primacy of the law and sees science as just helping to inform it. It states that "the common law has not been impervious to the findings of modern science in changing and adjusting its concepts and rules regarding the legal rights possessed by a child in the womb."[106] (Note that it is the *lawmakers* who make the decision to follow science.)

Different briefs emphasize different aspects of the issue: medical, biological, legal, constitutional, historical, and moral.[107] Nevertheless, the moral issue is made preeminent. The language of the NRLC brief makes this apparent:

> ...a state has a compelling interest in protecting human life from unjustified destruction by abortion...a state's important and compelling interest in protecting human life, in the form of a live fetus, justifies it in prohibiting abortions that destroy such a life without demonstration of the strongest justification...[108]

In another place the brief indicates that physicians are not the proper ones to turn the issue of abortion, *carte blanche*, over to:

> The legitimacy of an abortion operation is more than merely a medical decision: it involves legal, moral, ethical, philosophical, theological, sociological, and psychological considerations. These realities cannot be brushed aside merely by calling the problem "medical." Moreover, the primary training and function of physicians is to diagnose and heal, not to adjudicate. And if war is too important to be entrusted solely to the generals, the ultimate issues of life and death are too important to be entrusted solely to the surgeons.[109]

Also, the main objective of the anti-abortion movement since the *Wade* and *Bolton* decisions -- as well as the argument of one of the briefs in the cases -- that constitutional protection should be given to the lives of the unborn, gives an indication of the role they believe politics should play.[110] These demonstrate the same desire that the pro-abortionists have: to permanently -- after an initial political decision of a constitutional nature -- remove abortion from the political arena. Whether this is a reflection, in some sense, of the tendency of modern *scientism* to turn all questions into scientific ones is uncertain. Our constitutional order definitely intends that some matters be removed from politics. If the anti-abortionists are just thinking of this, then their argument is grounded more squarely in constitutional law than Baconian science. It is easier to believe that the argument is essentially legal or constitutional because the right to life -- and, more specifically, the right to life of the unborn child -- has a foundation in our legal history.

On the other hand, the anti-abortionists use *science* to argue that the unborn child is a person and thus should receive constitutional protection. They also seem to let science supersede constitutional history when they argue that the Fourteenth Amendment intended that the unborn child come within its reach -- because, after all, he is scientifically a "person" -- even though this intention of its Drafters is not certain.

A new thinking grounded in science is permitted by the pro-abortionists to replace the "Tao." The *amicus curiae* brief filed by the University of Texas law professor Joseph P. Witherspoon, Jr. for the Texas Association of (Catholic) Diocesan Attorneys indicates that this is not so for the anti-abortion movement. The brief makes a statement of the molding of natural law philosophy and modern science, arguing that scientific knowledge simply has reaffirmed what the natural law has taught on the matter of the unborn child's humanity. It says that St. Thomas Aquinas -- the author of what is probably the most comprehensive and systematic treatise ever on the natural law, *Summa Theologica* -- put forth the "classic definition" of "person": "'the individual substance of a rational nature.'"[111] By individual substance," it says he means "that the person has an existence that is peculiar to itself and different and distinct from the existence of anything else." By "rational nature," he means, with reference to the human being, "the cognitive and appetitive rational powers of man."[112] The brief then proceeds to state the biological knowledge about the unborn child which it concludes affirms this.

The appeal to the "Tao" while also calling for adjudication in accordance with modern scientific knowledge is also seen in LIFE's brief. The brief called the push for legalized abortion an undermining of "'[t]he traditional western ethic [which] has always placed great emphasis on the intrinsic worth and equal value of every human life regardless of its stage or condition.'"[113] It argues for the humanity of the unborn child under a section heading which reads as follows: "The Protection Of The Right to Life Should Be Based On Current Medical Knowledge (Which Indicates That A 10-Ounce Child Can Survive), Not Medical Knowledge Hundreds of Years Old."[114]

A few prominent anti-abortion writers indicate how the anti-abortion position varies from the pro-abortionists' on other points. They address not only the abortion issue, but the other "life" issues as well and the larger questions of which it is part.[115] Professor Charles E. Rice, for example, echoes C. S. Lewis' fears and shows how these various "life" issues prompt them:

> Science has given the modern state the tools with which to play God. At one end of the scale, the statists are reaching for the power to determine who shall die and when. Abortion and euthanasia, both reduced to an exact science, are examples of this power used to dispose of the inconvenient innocent. At the other end of the scale, contraception, sterilization, and artificial insemination offer the statists, for the first time in history, the chance to decide who shall be born and what physical characteristics they shall have. The eugenics engineers literally can play God. And they apparently have every intention of doing so.[116]

Princeton University theology professor Paul Ramsey states that Lewis and Aldous Huxley -- the author of *Brave New World* -- were "prescient" in what they saw as the eventual effects of biotechnology. He is concerned with the writing of one of the men who engineered the world's first "test-tube" baby, who accepts genetic manipulation as a "remedy" to the numerical imbalance of the sexes and to create chimeras and who looks forward to the time when "[s]cientist-kings will manage everything." Ramsey finds "ominous" the "calim that scientists have the 'right' to exercise their professional activities *to the limit that is tolerated by society*...as lay attitudes *struggle to catch up* with what scientists can do."[117]

Francis Canavan raised these questions about the new biotechnology: "What are the permissible goals which public policy may promote through genetic engineering and related technologies? What means, if any, should law bar as not worthy of man?" He says that answering questions like these is made difficult by the very stress of pro-abortionists on individual freedom: "We repeat endlessly that we believe in the sanctity of the individual human being. But we find it difficult to explain what there is about human beings that makes each and every one of them the object of such veneration. One reason for the difficulty...is, curiously, our very individualism."[118]

As the belief has taken hold that there is no such thing as a distinctively human nature, the notion of "natural rights" -- which was seen as something attaching to man because of the very fact of this human nature -- has passed on and nothing more than the will and desires of individuals replaces it.[119] It follows that if there is no distinctively human nature -- that man can be viewed or molded any which way -- there cannot be a moral order natural to man. All morality is subjectivized.

Canavan believes that "[u]ltimately one must fear that even individual consent will cease to be regarded as a prerequisite for genetic engineering."[120] (This is the same possibility I raised above as happening just with abortion.) The fact that there has been such a pronounced shift in our understanding of the basis of rights and human nature makes this occurrence possible and even probable. The following passage is relevant for both abortion and genetic engineering:

> The consent of the individual who is to be improved or even "created" by the engineering can hardly be asked because he either does not yet exist or exists at a very early stage of development. The consent of his parents hardly matters, and may not be obtainable, if they are mere anonymous donors of sperm and ova.[121]

He goes on then to explain how the "controllers" Lewis warns against could take over:

> ...since liberal emphasis on individual will as the substance of human rights will have destroyed all other criteria of judgment, the scientists and authorities will have no standard but their own wills by which to judge what kind of human beings they want to produce [since they have rejected the "Tao" as their guide]. Liberal individualism will then have proved to be the ultimate enemy of the sanctity and integrity of the individual.[122]

Canavan registers a certain sense of the awe about human life that is absent in the pro-abortion briefs. In the writers just cited there is a concern that the overpowering new technology of life be approached prudently. There is no evidence of the optimism about the scientific future or the smug certainty that the scientific community is the best judge of what "progress" is that is seen in some of the pro-abortion writing.

Both Ramsey and Dr. Bernard Nathanson express the same views that the anti-abortion briefs do about ethical constraints on the scientific community. Ramsey speaks critically of the view that "science does not operate within the ethics of a wider human community" and that "a scientific ethics, or whatever *can* be done, ...should shape our public philosophy."[123]

Nathanson, testifying before the Senate Judiciary Committee's Subcommittee on Separation of Powers about the Human Life Bill in 1981, said the following:

> Physicians are healers who function not in a moral vacuum but within a codified set of socially acceptable rules called ethics. Medical ethics are only a specific application

of the universal norms of moral behavior.[124]

The anti-abortion movement is prudent in its approach to science. It does not want the new technologies which made abortion medically "safe" to be used, and it is concerned about other new technologies -- e.g., genetic screening and genetic engineering -- being developed which are likely to be used in a manner not fitting the dignity of life. The anti-abortion movement's approach to politics, however, has not always been so prudent. At times, it has engaged in public demonstrations, confrontations with public officials, and acts of civil disobedience (e.g., "sit-ins" at abortion clinics) which have hurt its cause more than helped it. Its members have made embarrassing statements to the press. It has tended to push legislative solutions so sweeping as to have little chance for approval, and which ignore the practical problems of enforcement. Too many of its members are oblivious to the political problem of approaching a public issue in such a manner as to take account of political constraints and realities, while at the same time safeguarding the basic principles of the regime. (This is the "principle-expediency problem" discussed in Chapter Nine and Appendix A.) The movement has also at times shown its lack of political prudence by too readily trusting and supporting politicians uncommitted to the anti-abortion cause.

In conclusion, the anti-abortionists tend to let the scientific realm take precedence over the political, as when discussing whether the unborn child is a "person" to be protected by law. They are also, at times, not concerned enough with the political virtue of prudence, and in these ways, are similar to the pro-abortionists. All in all, however, they sharply diverge from the latter on every other point regarding contemporary thinking about science.

In conclusion I have shown that extreme views of liberty underlie the pro-abortion position, and that these views lead to a utilitarian ethic, which in turn leads to a view that the law is valid only if it issues from the state. Such a perspective is at odds with the natural rights philosophy our Republic is based on.

A further conclusion is that a pro-abortion view,

in contrast to anti-abortion view, demonstrates a substantial optimism about scientific progress and seeks to convert the ethical question in abortion to simply a scientific one. Its optimism about science betrays a troubled lack of prudence about its dangers.

Chapter Nine

A Basis for the Proscription of Abortion in Liberal Democratic and Religiously Pluralistic America

A Just Resolution of the Abortion Question: A Preview of the Chapter

In this final Chapter, I shall propose a different resolution of the abortion question which accords with the facts about abortion that have been stated and takes account of America's unique political circumstances.

It is possible that classical thought can provide a resolution, or at least a framework, to solve the abortion problem. Aristotle and the Stoics are good sources to turn to because their ethical and political thought is built around what is intrinsically good or right by nature. It does not fall into the contradiction utilitarianism does by saying no action is any better or any more just than any other.

Both Aristotelian and Stoic thought assert that there is a standard for judging what is right or wrong everywhere and in all cases. The difference between them is subtle, but important. Professor Jaffa states that for Aristotle "[w]hat is best in itself is always and everywhere the same, but what is right or just in any particular case depends upon the particular circumstances...[w]hat is just...is what is fitting here and now."[1] For the Stoics, there is a much clearer sense of there being, specifically, a higher *law.* In his *Republic* (or *Commonwealth*), the later Stoic Marcus Tullius Cicero states that "'[t]here is a true law, right reason in accord with nature; it is of universal application, unchanging and everlasting...There is one law...binding at all times upon all peoples.'"[2] This higher law clearly has the marks of law as being something which "'commands what ought to be done and forbids the opposite.'"[3] It is "'right reason applied to command and prohibition.'"[4] No such notion of a higher law with specific rules and prohibitions is found in Aristotle. As political science professor James E. Holton of Lewis and Clark University says in his discussion of Cicero, in any situation this law's "standards remain, even though their complete realization, given the nature of man and the nature of political society, is extremely unlikely."[5] The standards of right and wrong are for Aristotle and the Stoics both found in nature. Aristotle believes that the standards are supposed to be just an ideal against which to measure actual conduct. They do not define whether an action is actually just or right; this is done by the standards of the particular regime that the individual lives in. The Stoics, on the other hand, *do* define the rightness or wrongness of an action by reference to the standards in nature -- they are meant to be actually applied, in and of themselves, to human conduct --, but they recognize that individuals will not live up to them entirely and that the extent to which they do depends partly on the political regime they are in. Both approaches thus emphasize the importance of political prudence on the legislator's part in enacting laws which will "temper the demands of pure justice and pure reason...so that they become compatible with the requirements of civil society."[6]

I shall build much of my ethical argument against abortion on Aristotle, but shall explain why he does not provide a completely satisfactory basis for dealing with it in light of the facts surrounding abortion. Aristotelian thought needs to be supplemented in certain ways by Stoic thought. Since each philosophy stresses the importance of political prudence and neither is founded on religious doctrine, they also provide the basis for a politically realistic resolution of the question in our religiously pluralistic political society.

There is another purpose I have in mind in turning to classical thought. This is simply that it is a good source to turn to for an alternate articulation of the questions of political philosophy that stand behind the abortion problem. This is the same alternate articulation that political scientist Walter Berns sought when considering the problem of obscenity and pornography: instead of accepting the liberal formulation of the issue as one involving a question of freedom, we should assert that the primary concern is virtue.[7] The proper question for us to ask is how will a particular public policy contribute to making individuals good, instead of how will it preserve or promote individual freedom. In doing this, we are moving away from the understanding of modern political thought (from, say, the time of Hobbes) that freedom is the central political principle to the view of pre-moderns like Aristotle and the Stoics that virtue, not freedom, was the central principle.[8] As Berns puts it, for the moderns "the problem of making men virtuous and *deserving* of freedom is completely ignored."[9] Their attention to virtue is needed because it must be doubted if, in any real sense, government can ignore virtue and structure its laws just for the purpose of maximizing freedom when people have to live together in civil society. This is not to say that individual freedom or liberty should not be a concern of the policymaker, but just that it should not be the preeminent concern.

Even if Aristotle and the Stoics can be shown to provide a basis for the proscription of abortion, an important question remains which is suggested by the above. Since the United States is a nation founded with reference to modern political thought with its strong emphasis on freedom, how can government restrict freedom in the name of virtue? I deal with this problem at length in Section IV. As an introduction, however, we might consider what the following two contemporary commentators say about this. Rutgers University political science professor Benjamin R. Barber tells us that the American Republic was based, in part, on "classical republicanism." a notion which stretched from Plato's *Reputlic* through the early modern political philosophers.

He says that the principles embodied in it -- concern for a government of excellence, a citizen body of virtue, a public order grounded in fundamental law, and a community of moderation -- were widely shared by all the social and political groups which had a hand in the American Founding.[10]

The late political scientist Martin Diamond states that while the United States is not a regime in the sense that the ancient Greek polis was (a political association *preeminently* concerned with the formation of character), it was not intended by the Framers to abandon the pursuit of virtue and excellence. He puts it this way:

> ...the American political order rises respectably high enough above the vulgar level of mere self-interest in the direction of virtue--if not to the highest reaches of the ancient perspective, still toward positive human decencies or excellences.[11]

These commentators state that America's Founders did not ignore the importance of virtue in our Republic or cease to be concerned that there be some means for promoting it among the citizenry. We shall discuss the role that they intended government and the law to have in doing this. I do not intend to put the matter of freedom aside, but by placing the focus on virtue instead of on freedom, I simply seek to give virtue its due as the Framers and the political philosophers who inspired them would have on a matter such as abortion.

Other questions are dealt with in this Chapter. One will seek to address the problem of the relationship of science and the political order, considered in Chapter Eight. This is important because, by Aristotle's reckoning, the creation of a just political order -- and if we are to make virtue the central concern we must be primarily concerned about justice because it is the main political virtue[12] -- depends upon the right ordering not only of the citizens themselves but of their activities as well. This includes the arts and sciences that they are to engage in, as Aristotle emphasizes in his *Nicomachean Ethics*. I shall turn to this discussion of his as a basis for proposing a political response to the abortion problem.

Another question I shall address is the role that religion can and actually must play in justly resolving the abortion issue. I shall explain first why it is needed to shape individual beliefs about abortion so as to insure that a legal prohibition will work. Secondly, I shall show how there are important principles, of a religious nature, which are part of our political tradition and which are at stake in abortion. I shall explain how they can be invoked -- and have been by a contemporary American statesman -- to encourage acceptance of new anti-abortion legislation.

The final point that shall be considered in this Chapter concerns the importance of legislators employing political prudence in the fashioning of a resolution to the issue.

After the Epilogue of this book, there shall follow two appendices which shall state my thinking about the constitutional basis for federal legislation and executive action against abortion and shall contain a specific legislative proposal.

With that, let me begin my discussion of how classical thought can give us a guide to determining the morality of abortion.

The Argument Against the Morality and Legality of Abortion from the Perspective of Classical Thought

Aristotle's Ethical Thought

THE FOCUS ON THE PROPER ENDS

THE END OF THE SEXUAL FACULTY

What I shall do in the first four Sub-Sections of

this Section is to examine the teaching of the *Nicomachean Ethics* and to try to determine whether, in light of our other knowledge and understanding about human sexual relationships, it might be possible to come to a conclusion about the rightness or wrongness of abortion on the basis of it. Aristotle does not address the morality of abortion at any length, saying only that it should not be permitted after "sense and life" have begun in the unborn child, which he believed was forty days for the male and eighty days for the female. These following passages from the *Nicomachean Ethics* state Aristotle's thinking about the end for man which I shall then go on to apply to the abortion question:

> For just as the goodness and performance of a flute player, a sculptor, or any kind of expert, and generally of anyone who fulfills some function or performs some action, are thought to reside in his proper function, so the goodness and performance of man would seem to reside in whatever is his proper function. Is it then possible that while a carpenter and a shoemaker have their own proper functions and spheres of action, man as man has none, but was left by nature a good-for-nothing without a function? Should we not assume that just as the eye, the hand, the foot, and in general each part of the body clearly has its own proper function, so man too has some function over and above the functions of his parts?[13]

Aristotle, then, believes that man as man must have an end toward which he works, as does all of his bodily activities. He tells us what this end is in the following passage:

> The proper function of man...consists in an activity of the soul in conformity with a rational principle or, at least, not without it. In speaking of the proper function of a given individual we mean that it is the same in kind as the function of an individual who sets high standards for himself...if we take the proper function of man to be a certain kind of life, and if this kind of life is an activity of the soul and consists in actions performed in conjunction with the rational element, and

> if a man of high standards is he who performs these actions well and properly, and if a function is well performed when it is performed in accordance with the excellence appropriate to it; we reach the conclusion that the good of man is an activity of the soul in conformity with excellence or virtue...[14]

Aristotle's statement at the end of man as man forms the basis for most of my discussion in this Chapter. In the first part of my discussion, however, the view of his which is pertinent is that each bodily activity of man has a proper end. The activity or function which shall be spoken about is the sexual one. In developing this argument, I shall rely on his thought, common understanding, and points that I have made earlier in this book.

First, abortion is contrary to the end of pregnancy, as we can judge from common sense. The end of pregnancy is obviously the birth of a new child. This is seen simply in the fact that the child *in utero* is constantly growing and developing and that, if all proceeds normally, he will emerge from the womb in nine months' time. That this is the end is also seen in the fact that when a couple wants a new, live child they undertake a pregnancy. It is also seen in the fact that people do not conceive new life for the predetermined purpose of destroying it. We would be repulsed by such a notion.

Second, abortion is contrary to the primary end of the sexual faculty: procreation. In order to show this, I shall first have to show that procreation is indeed the primary purpose of this faculty.

The first reason that I can point to in order to demonstrate this is simple biology. That procreation is supposed to occur from sexual intercourse is seen in the simple fact that babies result from it. There can be little doubt that *a* purpose of sexual intercourse is procreation. Granted that, why should it be said that procreation is the *primary* purpose of it? It is true that there are other purposes of intercourse: the deepening of love between a husband and wife and an outlet to remedy concupiscence, for example. The biological facts, however, show that nature has ordained that procreation be the primary function. This is because if an act of intercourse is undertaken during the woman's monthly fertile period, there will be an ovum present and the man always transmits semen -- with sperm in it -- in a completed act of intercourse.[15] The "stuff" of life is present and pregnancy -- i.e., "new man" -- thus can occur. The fact that it may not occur or that it will not occur if the woman is not in the fertile part of her cycle does not defeat the claim that procreation is the primary purpose or end of the sexual faculty or even of the act. It just means that nature has provided a means to permit couples to regulate their fertility. They still possess the sexual faculty and, if they are normal, they will still have the capacity for childbearing when the fertile period returns. Undertaking sexual intercourse outside of the fertile period or when a couple is permanently sterile can be done without their acting contrary to the primary end because, again, nature has provided this built-in regulatory mechanism in the woman and because there are the other or secondary purposes of the sexual faculty which I mentioned that they may seek to further. The fact that a couple or the woman alone if she has an abortion is able to frustrate the primary purpose at will does not mean that the purpose is not valid. People are *capable of* doing all sorts of actions which are undesirable, contrary to common norms, or even heinous. This does not mean they are normal or a legitimate purpose of the human faculties used to carry them out.

Also, the very fact that in order to prevent conception from occurring people have to utilize some means of birth regulation when undertaking sexual intercourse is an emplicit statement of the primacy of the end of procreation for the sexual function.

Further, the *sole* means that nature has provided for propagation of the race is sexual intercourse. There is no other natural way.[16] If something other than procreation were the primary natural purpose of intercourse, nature -- considering human weakness and inclination to selfishness -- would end up frustrating this only means it has provided for this. This would, in effect, be contradictory.

The usual alternative proposed as the primary purpose of the sexual faculty is pleasure. The problem with this can be inferred from what I have already said. I shall explain Aristotle's thinking about this later in connection with my discussion of chastity in his ethical scheme. I will just say at this point that Aristotle did not see sexual pleasure as being an end in itself. Loyola College philosophy professor Thomas J. Higgins explains to us the proper role of pleasure in both an Aristotelian and a natural law type of ethics which stresses the ends of human faculties. Pleasure would be considered a "delectable good." Such a good, Higgins says, "is desirable inasmuch as it is the satisfaction consequent to the attainment of perfective good." We recall the passage above of Aristotle's as we consider Higgins' saying that "[n]othing so perfects a faculty as attainment of its natural end; this end attained is the perfection of the faculty."[17]

Higgins goes on to explain how a faculty is distorted and evil results:

> ...to set a faculty in motion, to enjoy its pleasure, and to allow the action to proceed to its natural term--that is the orderly use of the faculty. However, to set a faculty in motion, to enjoy its delectable good, and then so to distort the act that its natural end is made impossible--this is always evil because it is deprivation of a good which ought to be present, namely, the possibility of issuing in its natural and.[18]

The above shows that the pleasure of the sexual act or any act -- as I shall go on to say in my consideration of Aristotle on this -- is not wrong; it is a good. A couple may undertake a particular act of sexual intercourse for the purpose of seeking pleasure and, in this scheme, this is not wrong. Indeed, this is probably the reason that couples undertake most such specific acts, just as a person almost all the time will eat for the pleasure of satisfying his appetite with some tasty delicacy. The evil occurs when this pleasure is allowed itself to become the end of an act, to the point that it subverts the primary end of the faculty. Abortion clearly subverts the end of the sexual faculty -- procreation -- because it destroys the newly conceived child. Human or not, he represents the fulfillment of the procreative function.[19]

THE ENDS OF THE FAMILY

Next, abortion subverts the family and the family's chief end: the procreation and rearing of children. We can see the importance of the family and the esteem within which children have been held in virtually all societies from what I said in Chapter Four. This, as C. S. Lewis from whom I derived the examples of this states, indicates that respect for family and childbearing are commanded by the "Tao."

In both his *Politics* and his *Nicomachean Ethics*, Aristotle indicates that the family is ordained by nature. In Book I of the *Politics* he tells us that "[t]he first form of association naturally instituted for the satisfaction of daily recurrent needs is...the family."[20] Also in the *Politics*, he criticizes Plato's scheme for community of wives and children. He points to the problems it would result in, such as the parents neglecting their duties to the children because they believe others will take care of them, the increase of crimes and contention among persons, and the weakening of the spirit of fraternity among a people which will result in greater civil unrest within the political community.[21]

In Book Eight of his *Nicomachean Ethics*, where he speaks of friendship, he shows the essentiality of the family. He says that the "many kinds of friendship among kinsmen...all seem to depend upon parental friendship." He further says the following:

> The friendship between man and wife seems to be inherent in us by nature. For man is by nature more inclined to live in couples than to live as a social and political being, inasmuch as the household is earlier and more indispensable than the state, and to the extent that procreation is a bond more universal to all living things (than living in a state) ...But human beings live together not merely for procreation, but to secure the needs of life...Children are regarded as the bond that holds them [the marital partners] together, and that is why childless marriages break up more easily.[22]

In the above, Aristotle indicates that the "household" -- the family -- is a more fundamental association even than the polis and that one of its essential purposes is the procreation of children.[23] Professor Jaffa explains further that for Aristotle the "highest function of the family, like that of the *polis*, is the formation of character." (The family cannot, however, do this to the fullest extent necessary, so the polis is then needed.)[24] This means that the other important function of the family is the *rearing* of children. The procreation and rearing of children, then, are for Aristotle the primary purposes of the family. The above passage also explains what children "give" in return to their parents: their presence helps their parents' marriage stay together.

Higgins tells us that only "a permanent union of man and woman...can fittingly realize nature's purpose regarding the propagation and rearing of human beings." "Casual, temporary unions" cannot do this because typically "their purpose is not offspring but self-gratification" and "are not apt to provide for the proper rearing of children." In sum, "[s]ince the task of raising children is so onerous, only parents, definitely known and permanently united, can exercise that care without which the suitable physical, intellectual, and moral development of the child is impossible."[25]

I speak mostly in the next Sub-Section about an implied emphasis on chastity in Aristotle's thought and how a failure to be chaste can harm the individual. Since I have just spoken about the need for a permanent union of man and woman to insure that the proper end of the family will be achieved, it is appropriate that I speak here of the harm to the family and the unlikelihood of attaining this end that can result if persons do not practice chastity.

We can point to the harms to the family which are likely to occur if one becomes involved in many casual sexual unions before marriage and if an ethic of fornication becomes widely accepted. First, when a person who has led the life of a fornicator finally does marry and start a family, the family will possibly suffer the effects of a lessened attitude of responsibility which has become ingrained in him or her. Fornication, by its very nature, implies an evasion of responsibility; it is sex without the assumption of responsibility that the proper use of sex brings with it. Marriage, and particularly childrearing, however, demand a great amount of responsibility. Moreover, why should the person who has had so many sexual partners before marriage suddenly settle down and be faithful to only one after marriage? The possibility of adultery is greater in such a circumstance and, with it, destructive implications for the family.

Also, if fornication became morally acceptable and widely practiced, the effect might also be -- with or without the availability of legalized abortion to buttress it -- that people will desire marriage less. It would logically follow that family life would no longer be held in such a positive light.

The possibility of harm to married life and the family is presented even in the case of someone who has sexual relations before marriage only with the person he or she ultimately marries. Such relations may retard the development of a couple's later marital love. One writer explains this:

> A successful marriage demands...an intellectual, emotional, spiritual, cultural union as well as a physical one. Physical union is normally the easiest to obtain, and ideally should be the last to come. The other unions take time, effort, patience to develop. The physical beautifully expresses them and can deepen and sustain them. But a too quick entrance of the physical union into courtship can retard the birth and growth of those more subtle, but more stable and permanent unions.[26]

I have thus shown the essentiality of marriage and the family in Aristotle's thought and in the natural scheme of things and the harms that a disregard for chastity can have for the family. Now we must ask this question: How does abortion threaten the family and its proper ends of the procreation and rearing of children? One part of the answer is obvious and is synonymous with what was said before about it frustrating the end of the sexual faculty: it subverts the procreative end of marriage (and, in turn, the end of rearing) because the child is destroyed. Secondly, as was seen in many of the pro-abortion arguments discussed in Chapter Five and most vividly in the "unwantedness" one, abortion is undertaken essentially for the convenience of the woman or parents and subverts the basic good of mankind, existence. Thirdly, the fact that a woman can go and procure an abortion without notifying or securing the agreement of her husband makes likely serious discord within marriage, which could result in its dissolution. Even if the law required that a woman obtain her husband's permission -- it has been stated that the Supreme Court has held such a requirement to be unconstitutional --, the availability of easy and legal abortion means that she could easily evade it. Fourthly, the availability of abortion could motivate many young couples not to enter the marital and familial state. They might choose this because it is easier, responsibilities are fewer, and it can more readily be broken off. Abortion is one more enticement to this for weak persons because they know that they can safely live this way without the risk of being saddled with an unwanted pregnancy. Even though abortion is also available for married couples, they might reason that it would be more difficult for them to decice to do it within the confines of marriage than in a non-permanent union. Fifthly, as was alluded to in Chapter Five when discussing the connection between abortion and "unwantedness," legal abortion will soon lead to the acceptance of an "abortion ethic" -- our experience in the U.S. so far seems to confirm this -- which will result in an antipathetic or at least less positive attitude toward children. Such an attitude cannot help but to harm the institution of the family which people have always associated, in some sense, with children. Finally, the availability of abortion may lead more married couples to choose to be childless with the result, thinking of the passage above from Aristotle, that more marriages will break up.

What I have said in these preceding two Sub-Sections about procreation being the primary end of sexual intercourse and the proper end of the family being the procreation, rearing, and education of children does not mean that a couple may not limit the number of children they have. Indeed, a couple *must* do this when genuine and grave needs -- of a physical, emotional, or economic nature -- indicate it. For some couples, a large number of children may be too great of a strain on them individually or on their marital relationship. It is important, however, that the natural ends of both the sexual faculty and of marriage and the family not be violated by the couple. It is only reasonable to believe that pursuing the ends which are natural to us will cause us to live happy and well-balanced lives.

Because of these proper ends, one must be skeptical of the claim that a couple's marriage will do better without any children at all. I am inclined to think that the problem with a couple who thinks this is not with their ability to rear a child, but with their perspective about children and family life.

THE END FOR MAN: HAPPINESS DERIVING FROM THE VIRTUOUS LIFE

What I have said up to now shows that abortion is contrary to the ends of the sexual faculty and of the family in the Aristotelian understanding. Now I will show why it is also against the scheme of virtue in Aristotle's ethical thought.

Let me first summarize the major points of this ethical scheme. Aristotle tells us that moral virtue is formed by habit, in contrast to intellectual virtue which is formed by learning. For example, we become self-controlled by practicing self-control and courageous by performing courageous acts. The foundations of all virtue are in the soul. He says that "[b]y human virtue we do not mean the excellence of the body, but that of the soul."[27] The human soul has rational and irrational elements (some of this will be recalled from Chapter Seven). The irrational element has two parts: the vegetative, which is common to all living things and is responsible for nurturing and growth and has no share in reason at all, and the other which aristotle says "is the seat of the appetites and of desire in general and partakes of reason insofar as it complies with ...[it] and accepts its leadership."[28] What the moral virtues -- the focal point of my attention -- are seems self-evident for Aristotle. He says simply that "praiseworthy" characteristics are what we call virtues."[29] He lists the moral virtues in Books III and IV of the *Nicomachean Ethics*. There are three virtues concerned with the right attitude one should have toward the three emotions of fear, pleasure, and anger: self-control (the *fundamental* virtue), courage, and gentleness. There are three concerned with man's right attitude toward his practical activity in society (concerning money and honor): generosity, magnificence, and high-mindedness or self-respect. There are three concerned with man's social relationships and his attitude toward himself: friendliness, wittiness, and truthfulness. There are also two mid-points of feeling (not exactly virtues):

modesty and righteous indignation.[30] Justice is the chief political or social virtue for Aristotle. It concerns man's political and economic relationships.

Virtue depends on the "mean" being maintained in the object. (Virtue is not "found" in the mean; the mean is the object of virtue.) That is, one must avoid both an excess and a deficiency of a certain way of behaving if he is to develop the respective virtue. He tells us, however, that "[n]ot every action nor every emotion admits of a mean."[31] Some actions and emotions are simply bad, no matter to what degree they are done. He lists as examples of these spite, shamelessness, envy, adultery, theft, and murder.[32] He also says that pleasure -- which I speak of further below -- and pain are the test of virtue: "pleasure...makes us do base actions and pain...prevents us from doing noble actions" and "virtue...makes us act in the best way in matters involving pleasure and pain, and...vice does the opposite."[33]

Let us consider what Aristotle considers the end for man to be. This end, of course, is a good -- the *highest* good -- for man, since it represents his perfection. Aristotle tells us that "the highest good is some sort of pleasure" because it must result from an activity which is the most *desirable* of all activities.[34] That is, it is desirable in and of itself, not for the sake of something else.[35] Only happiness falls into this category; it is thus "the end or goal of human (aspirations)."[36]

What is the "happy life" for Aristotle? It is "a life in conformity with virtue...which involves effort and is not spent in amusement."[37] He goes on to say what the happiest life is:

> Now, if happiness is activity in conformity with virtue, it is to be expected that it should conform with the highest virtue, and that is the virtue of the best part of us ...it is the activity of this part (when operating) in conformity with the excellence or virtue proper to it that will be complete happiness.[38]

Put another way, it is man's end "to become immortal as far as that is possible and to do our utmost to live in accordance with what is highest in us."[39]

To move this in the direction that will lead us back to abortion, it must be asked whether this happiness which is the highest end of man can result from the pleasures of the body (specifically sexual pleasure) and whether pursuing this pleasure in any manner one chooses -- and to eliminate anything that gets in the way of this, like pregnancy by means of abortion -- is in accordance with virtue and conducive to man's achieving complete happiness.

The first question can be quickly answered. Aristotle tells us that "[t]he pleasures of thought...are superior to the pleasures of the senses."[40] The latter, of course, includes sex. He contends that "the activity of the divinity which surpasses all others in bliss must be a contemplative activity, and the human activity which is most closely akin to it is, therefore, most conducive to happiness."[41] The greatest happiness, then, is achieved through contemplation, not bodily pleasure.

Now, is sexual activity compatible with the achievement of this happiness of contemplation, according to Aristotle? The realm of virtue which includes sexual activity is separate from the one which includes the contemplative activity. The former is in the realm of practical or moral virtue and the latter in that of intellective virtue. The two realms are connected, however. The development of intellective virtues depends upon the prior acquisition of the practical virtues. The moral virtue of self-control is key because man must control his tendency to self-indulgence before he can take any further steps toward becoming fully human. Further, both realms are involved in our activity of choosing. Both reason from the intellective realm and desire -- which is based on emotions and thus is in the part of the affective element of the soul which we seek to control by the moral virtues -- are involved in choice, but reason is the most important. This is because before we can choose, we must rely on our reason to tell us what the right course of action is. Thus, the moral virtues which relate to sexual activity are important because all moral virtues help to lead one to the intellective virtues which will bring him to the highest happiness. The proper control of the sexual faculty would seem to be especially important because it is one of the prime areas in which self-indulgence can occur and thus frustrate the beginning efforts at virtue.

It is no doubt for this reason, in the final analysis, that Aristotle admonishes us about the possible dangers of the bodily pleasures and the right use of them. He says this:

> Now, excess is possible in the case of the goods of the body, and it is the pursuit of excess, but not the pursuit of necessary pleasures, that makes a man bad. For all men get some kind of enjoyment from good food, wine, and sexual relations, but not everyone enjoys these things in the proper way.[42]

There is, then, for Aristotle proper and improper sexual conduct. The question is: which sexual conduct is improper? Another way of asking this is, to use Aristotle's phrase, when are sexual pleasures pursued "to excess and contrary to right reason"?[43] Aristotle provides us with a two-pronged answer for this, which I can relate forthwith to the abortion question. First, if it or the other bodily pleasures "are harmful, it is bad."[44] The second answer is found in the following passage from the *Nicomachean Ethics*:

> Those pleasures...which complete the activities of a perfect or complete and supremely happy man, regardless of whether these activities are one or several, can be called in the true sense the pleasures proper to man.[45]

Let me start my discussion on this point with this second answer. According to the above passage, the pleasures which go along with those activities which bring a man to his proper end are good pleasures. It follows that pleasures which fail to do this are bad pleasures. If the pleasures can be morally evaluated on the basis of whether they bring a man to his proper end, can they also be so evaluated on the basis of whether they bring the *faculties* of a man to their proper end? I believe that the answer is yes, according to what Aristotle says about the whole being prior to the parts of it when he speaks about the polis and its individual members in the *Politics*. There, he says that "[a]ll things derive their essential character from their function and their capacity". which, he is indicating, is determined by what they are part of.[46] The individual, then, takes his character from the polis of which he is part. Similarly, the human faculties take their character from the man of which they are part. It thus follows, to answer our question, that pleasures can be determined to be good or bad on the basis of whether they bring a faculty to its proper end (i.e., perfect it). The pleasure of sexual intercourse is not good if it is enjoyed without permitting the procreative end of the sexual faculty to be carried out. Abortion, as I have already explained, prevents this from being done; it permits the pleasure of intercourse to be enjoyed without regard to the end. It is thus a wrong act. We can here see how both Aristotle's notion of the ends and his ethics come together -- his ethics is based squarely on his understanding of man's end.

Also, what is suggested here is that any sexual pleasure which is divorced from the procreative end of the sexual faculty -- i.e., this would almost certainly mean, for the reasons I previously indicated, sex outside of marriage -- is wrong. Thus, we see one basis for an Aristotelian notion of chastity.

Now, let me return to the point about harmfulness which, I believe, will provide us with our second basis for such a notion as well as a further rationale for rejecting abortion -- in the case of a pregnancy resulting from sexual activity outside of the marital union -- under Aristotle's ethical scheme. What needs to be done is to show that harm will result -- to both the individual and others -- when one seeks the pleasures of sex outside the context of marriage. It is really not necessary for me to show the harmfulness of adultery because Aristotle, as mentioned, condemns it as evil *per se*, apparently considering its harms self-evident. (He thus shares the judgment historically made by a wide variety of societies, as I indicated in Chapter Four.) The question, then, is how is fornication or premarital sexual activity harmful and thus to be avoided?

I have already explained how sex outside of the marital union -- since it is not primarily aimed at procreation -- is "harmful" or disruptive of the human sexual faculty. How is it harmful to the whole person? First, there is the danger of actual physical harm. There is always the danger of venereal disease, which is not a problem in marriage because states have required physical examinations, blood tests, and the like before granting marriage licenses. In addition to this, there is increasing evidence that sex with several partners can result in many other diseases, including cancer.[47] Even if sex occurs with only one partner outside of marriage, emotional harm can result. As psychiatrist Max Levin writes, "The physician...speaks from the standpoint of health, which includes emotional health. From this standpoint I submit that the desirable ideal is premarital chastity."[48] It is easy to see why this is so when one considers that the sexual act -- except perhaps for a hardened prostitute -- is not only a physical activity, but involves the person's psychological and emotional make-up as well. People become emotionally involved with each other as a result of their sexual experiences. When they break their relationship off after sharing the greatest possible intimacy, they will most likely experience a negative psychological or emotional reaction. It may be fairly mild for most -- although even this can disrupt their lives --, but for some it will be traumatic. The result can be deep suspicion and even hatred for the opposite sex that may make successful adjustment in marriage someday difficult. In some cases, their non-marital sexual experiences could result in unhappy and unsatisfying sexual experiences in marriage.[49] Further, the individual may be disturbed by guilt from what he is doing.

Thus, I conclude that sexual relations outside of the marital union presents the possibility of harming the individual. It is thus not in accord with Aristotle's ethical thinking which requires that the mean be sought. What I believe I have shown overall is that the pleasures attendant to this type of sexual activity are not "good" pleasures for man. It is thus reasonable to infer the desirability of chastity -- i.e., refraining from pre-marital or extramarital sexual activity -- in Aristotle's ethics.

It follows that any scheme of ethics that promotes chastity would have to oppose abortion. This is simply because the availability of abortion makes it easier for weak men and women to violate the norm of chastity. Women may feel freer to have non-marital sexual relations because they know that abortion will be available to eliminate any resulting pregnancies. Men similarly know that the availability of abortion releases them from responsibilities that would come from fathering a child out of wedlock. Moreover, I have explained why abortion can harm the family. There are thus reasons, grounded in Aristotle, to oppose abortion for both unmarried and married women.

Why, it must be asked, would Aristotle support abortion in some circumstances -- as mentioned in Chapter Three -- if the case can be made that it is contrary to his ethical thinking? This is a point that will be taken up shortly.

WHY ABORTION SHOULD BE LEGISLATED AGAINST IN ARISTOTLE'S SCHEME

THE ROLE OF THE LAWS IN PROMOTING VIRTUE FOR THE INDIVIDUAL

Now that I have shown abortion to be contrary both to Aristotle's ethics and its basis in the nature of man, it remains for me to explain why it should be restricted or prohibited by law. One reason is that, according to Aristotle's thinking, the state must help the individual to become virtuous. Professor Jaffa says that for Aristotle the highest function of the state, like the family, is the shaping of character. The political order must bring this activity to its conclusion after it has been started by the family because the latter is limited in its ability to accomplish it.[50] Aristotle says the following about the state's role:

> Lawgivers make citizens good by inculcating (good) habits in them, and this is the aim of every lawgiver; if he does not succeed in doing that, his legislation is a failure.[51]

and

> To obtain the right training for virtue from youth up is difficult, unless one has been brought up under the right laws. To live a life of self-control and tenacity is not pleasant for most people, especially for the young. Therefore, their upbringing and pursuits must be regulated by laws...But it is perhaps not enough that they receive the right upbringing and attention only in their youth. Since they must carry on these pursuits and cultivate them by habit when they

> have grown up, we probably need laws for this, too, and for the whole of life in general. For most people are swayed rather by compulsion than argument, and by punishments rather than by (a sense of) what is noble.[52]

When we think back to what I said in Chapter Six about how legalization has caused the total number of abortions to skyrocket, we can see that there appears to be truth to what Aristotle says about the threat of punishment being needed to make people act rightly.

It would be appropriate, then, under Aristotle's thinking, to promote his notion of chastity and the proper use of man's faculties which make virtue possible by legislating against abortion because, as I have shown, it is contrary to these. The last sentence in the passage immediately above explains why it would be especially fitting to enact criminal legislation against it with penalties.

ABORTION IS CONTRARY TO THE COMMON GOOD

I have set down the promotion of individual morality as one reason for the state to legislate against abortion. Another is suggested by what I discussed in Chapter Seven: to protect innocent human beings. Surely Aristotle regarded the protection of its citizens to be an important rationale for legislation by the state. A third basis for anti-abortion legislation is to promote the common good, which is a central responsibility of the state. I have already stated in this book ways in which easily available and widely resorted to abortion harms the common good. One way is that it possibly limits population growth which, as I stated in Chapter Six, is a benefit and even a necessity to a nation. It robs the state of citizens -- both those destroyed by the procedure and those never conceived because of the infertility that results in aborted women -- who could contribute to its well-being. Another way is that, due to the damage to their health that sometimes results (as discussed in Chapter Six), it deprives the community of the full services of at least some women who have had abortions. A third way is that, as has already been stated, abortion harms the family. Let me say more about this now in light of the important role that Aristotle sees the family as playing in a political society.

Aristotle says that the family is the basis for the state which emerged from it. I have already made reference to this. A number of families united to form a village -- which was at first something like an extended family -- then several villages united to form a single, largely self-sufficient political community or the state.[53]

Next, Aristotle tells us of the functions the family plays vis-a-vis the state. I have already mentioned his stating that if there is a breakdown of the family institution, there will be civil unrest. In addition to this, he tells us that such crimes as assault and homicide will increase.[54] Civil relations will thus become more tense and community life less bearable. Does this not seem borne out in our times by the increase in juvenile delinquency and drug abuse with its attendant crime resulting from family breakdown?[55]

The family for Aristotle, then, as Professor Jaffa states, "lays a foundation of restraints upon behavior which is then extended to members of different families, and finally to civic morality."[56] In other words, the family begins the education of good citizens. The state obviously has an interest in protecting it.

Finally, the family appears to play an important role for Aristotle in the development of the art of acquisition in individuals. He tells us that "there is a natural art of acquisition which has to be practiced by managers of households and statesmen."[57] The two are not identical, but are related.[58] The family, it can be inferred, can serve as something of a training ground for this: a husband-father who eventually will become a statesman will get practice at it by running his household before he assumes the reins of state. A son who might one day go on to be a statesman will get his initial education about this by watching his father. This translates itself today into the importance of the family in providing much of the practical education for life that a person needs.

The family is thus important to the state, so the state can protect it by law from various threats, including abortion. One might ask, however, if abortion should not be permitted or even encouraged by the state, according to this reasoning, in those cases when it might "help" the family. One such case that might be put forth is incest. I showed in Chapter Six, however, that abortion in this case really will not help a family and, in fact, might further damage it. Another case might be adultery. Accepting that adultery is capable of causing serious harm to a marriage and family, would it not be better to eliminate the product of such an activity, possibly before the other party in the marriage learns about it? My response to this is twofold. First, as I have already said, the availability of abortion would actually make adulterous activity easier. Second, destroying the child who results from adultery will not solve the problems in a marriage that may have given rise to it. Indeed, as Dr. Bernard Nathanson says, the child of an adulterous union may actually help the married couple to achieve reconciliation, if they want this. He may serve not just as a reminder of a past misdeed, but more importantly of the offended party to forgive what has happened and of the couple to start anew.[59] Another possible way that some might say abortion can help the family is to eliminate deformed children. I shall address this in the next Sub-Section.

A fourth way legalized and frequently resorted to abortion harms the common good is that it holds out the prospect of damaging our social fabric and lessening our sense of civility. It was pointed out earlier that our abortion policy may be leading us to both an "anti-life" and anti-child ethic. Infanticide, euthanasia, and child abuse were mentioned as examples of this. This may not be an easy phenomenon to measure by means of social science methodology. It may be next to impossible to show that a particular case of infanticide resulted from the widespread abortion ethic. It is rather, that our social milieu -- all of the beliefs, attitudes, and notions of right and wrong that permeate the society we are part of -- creates a certain mind-set in us that sooner or later influences our behavior. Even people whose immediate environment largely isolates them from the currents of the larger society and inculcates contrary ideas in them are hard-pressed to avoid being influenced to at least some degree. Kenyon College political scientist Harry Clor expresses this as follows with regard to the obscenity question, which I believe is related to abortion on this point:

> People are influenced by what they think others believe and particularly by what they think are the common standards of

> the community. There are few individuals among us whose basic beliefs are the result of their own reasoning and whose moral opinions do not require the support of some stable public opinion. The free circulation of obscenity can, in time, lead many to the conclusion that there is nothing wrong with the values implicit in it -- since their open promulgation is tolerated by the public. They will come to the conclusion that public standards have changed -- or that there are no public standards. Private standards are hard put to withstand the effects of such an opinion.[60]

The community as a whole, then, is a moral educator and the law is one of the major means by which it does its educating. Harvard sociologist James Q. Wilson has pointed to race and sex discrimination as public policies which "are based in part precisely on the presumed educative force of law."[61] Professor Clor contends that in the area of race the Supreme Court's decisions have indeed "had significant effects upon moral attitudes, values, and beliefs."[62]

When one looks at the apparently substantial increase in the absolute number of abortions which has occurred since *Wade/Bolton*, he gets the sense that our public morality about this question has been at least partially shaped by these decisions. They would seem to have contributed to the development of the anti-life and anti-child ethics. It thus seems likely that if the law on abortion is now changed back, it will encourage a restoration of our previous moral opposition.

The final reason that, according to Aristotle's thinking, concern for common good would justify the state's legislating against abortion is that the common good permits the state to legislate about the medical art. There are two reasons why this may be done. The first is that the ends of the arts and sciences -- Aristotle says that every art or applied science (*techne*) and every pure or theoretical science (*episteme*) aims at some good (i.e., each has an end)[63] -- are subsumed under the overarching end of politics, "the most sovereign and most comprehensive master science."[64] Aristotle expresses this point as follows:

> Since this science uses the rest of the sciences, and since, moreover, it legislates what people are to do and what they are not to do, its end seems to embrace the ends of the other sciences.[65]

The second reason why the state may legislate about the medical art explains further why politics is the "master science." As I have stated, Aristotle believes that one of the prime purposes of the state is to help man achieve his proper end. As just mentioned, the arts and sciences, like all things and all activities of man and man himself, have a proper end. While the large number of these means that the number of ends (i.e., "goods") is large,[66] there is one highest good. The highest good *in general* is synonymous with the highest good for man because he is the highest of earthly creatures. As mentioned earlier, it consists in the happiness that comes from leading a life of virtue. The reason that this highest good of man is important to the common good of the state is that "the end of politics is the good for man."[67] In other words, the good is the same for both man and the state, even though the state's good -- it would be more correct to say the *community's* good or the *common* good -- takes precedence.

Man's end is achieved largely through his actions. The arts and sciences are included among these, so if this end -- and correspondingly the community's end -- is to be achieved, the arts and sciences must be properly controlled or regulated by the state. In other words, the right ordering of the state depends not only on the right ordering of its citizens, but also on the right ordering of their activities.

The way that the activities of man, such as the arts and sciences, can be properly ordered to insure that they help bring man to his proper end is that they be made to achieve *their* proper ends. This is a subject for legislation. As Aristotle writes, politics "determines which sciences ought to exist in states, what kind of sciences each group of citizens must learn, and what degree of proficiency each must attain."[68]

The above, and particularly this latter quote, can be understood as applying to abortion in the following way. The science which is involved most directly in abortion is medicine. Aristotle says that "of medicine the end is health."[69] The state may legislate about abortion as part of its aim of making sure that medicine achieves this end. What has been said in this book indicates that abortion may stand in the way of it because it very possibly results in a lessening of the health of the women who undergo it and definitely results in the destruction of the health -- and life -- of the unborn child. Thus, the state could legislate against abortion. By saying that the state may determine which sciences should exist, etc., Aristotle gives a further basis for anti-abortion legislation. The "science" of abortion methodology might be said to be a "branch" of the art of medicine. The state may rightfully determine whether this "science" should be permitted to exist and whether anyone may legally practice it (i.e., whether abortionists should be permitted to flourish) or learn it (e.g., whether medical schools may teach abortion techniques to their students). If it does permit abortionists to practice, it may determine what level of skill they should have to demonstrate.

Moreover, abortion, as I have already shown, is contrary to man's proper end and, in light of the above, it would seem that the state should not permit one of the sciences to bring it about.

Thus, in accordance with the views expressed by C. S. Lewis, *et al.* in Chapter Eight -- against the pro-abortion thinking --, Aristotle believes that the state may -- actually, *must* -- legislate on matters involving the sciences. He makes a further point to explain why this must be so in the following passage:

> Each man can judge competently the things he knows, and of these he is a good judge. Accordingly, a good judge in each particular field is one who has been trained in it, and a good judge in general, a man who has received an all-round schooling.[70]

Aristotle says that only those who are trained in a particular area can properly judge about it. We can infer from this that Aristotle would emphatically disagree with the implicit pro-abortion view that physicians, who seldom have an extensive or deep training in moral philosophy, should be left to decide an essentially moral question like abortion. (Indeed, in light of the decline of the liberal arts and the way legal education is --

i.e., emphasizing a mechanical study of court cases and legal rules --, Aristotle might even dispute the competence of law judges to decide an issue like this.) Moreover, neither present-day physicians nor judges might succeed in meeting another of his requirements for judging moral questions: a proper moral education (i.e., shaping of personal morality). He says that "to be a competent student of what is right and just, and of politics generally, one must first have received a proper upbringing in moral conduct."[71]

Thus, Aristotle's ethical thinking calls for the state to legislate to bring about the proper ordering of the arts and sciences. The question remains, however, as to whether Aristotle's view about this is embodied in the basic principles of our political society. I shall address this shortly, along with the question about whether our political society may properly legislate to promote virtue which is tied up with legislating on the arts and sciences.

In summary, I have shown in this Sub-Section various ways in which the common good is threatened by abortion, so as to be a basis for the state to legislate against it.

RESOLVING THE PROBLEMS OF USING ARISTOTLE'S THOUGHT AS A BASIS FOR LEGISLATING AGAINST ABORTION

THE OBJECTIONS THAT CAN BE RAISED AND POSSIBLE ANSWERS TO THEM

Undoubtedly, if Aristotle had had modern biological knowledge about unborn human life, he -- in light of what he says in the passage quoted in Chapter Three about permitting miscarriage to be induced only before sense and life have begun in the child -- likely would have disapproved of abortion from the beginning of pregnancy. What I argued in Chapter Seven about the soul makes this contention even more plausible. An important objection remains, however. In that same passage in Chapter Three of this book, Aristotle makes it clear that he would *require* that children born deformed be permitted to die. (It is indicated by the sentence following the one in which he says this that this would be done by exposure.) How can Aristotle, one must ask, provide a basis for legislating against abortion when he favors infanticide? (The difference between abortion and infanticide is generally understood to be that the former is the taking of a child's life before birth and the latter is the taking afterwards.) Moreover, Aristotle's apparent penchant for the less extreme course of action, which shall be discussed further shortly, makes one think that if he had known of amniocentesis he would have favored that it be used to detect deformities and, if any were found, to take the child's life when still in the womb. What this means is that Aristotle could not be used to justify an absolute ban on abortion because he would favor it in cases of deformity. (Although he does not address this, one wonders if he would not also call for it when the child has been conceived as a result of rape or incest or perhaps from any intercourse out of wedlock. He might say that if such a child were viewed as an outcast by the particular state he was born in, this would be a sort of social "deformity" and it would be justified to abort or expose him. I am more inclined to think, however, that he would not support this. I believe he would simply tell us in the passage in question that he favored this, if he really did. Also, such circumstances are of the nature of a "social" -- as opposed to eugenic -- justification for abortion or infanticide and he specifically rejects one other social justification in the passage: keeping the population down.)

I believe that I can provide a few explanations which can overcome the apparent dilemma. As I explain, however, they are possibly not satisfactory. It is for this reason that I turn to the thought of the Stoics for additional support.

Let me attempt to answer this infanticide objection. First, I believe that Aristotle might not have supported infanticide of deformed newborns if he had had the modern biological knowledge which would have altered his thinking about ensoulment. Actually, although Aristotle did not permit abortion after the time he believed that life and sense were present, he did not believe (as mentioned) that then or even after birth the child had a rational soul in the full sense. He believed that after this point the unborn child merely has a *potential* rational soul. This is due to his view that the soul develops to its full state over time.[72] He may have been willing to permit his destruction because he did not think him fully human. It is almost certain that Aristotle would have been much more reluctant about agreeing to the putting to death of a deformed adult, who somehow escaped exposure as an infant, merely because he was deformed. This is apparently because an adult *does* have a completely developed soul. Thus, it would seem reasonable to conclude that if Aristotle had realized that his "developing soul" notion were erroneous -- which is indicated by my discussion in Chapter Seven -- he would not have permitted infanticide of deformed newborns (and, in turn, would not permit their abortion if their defects were discovered before birth).

I must admit that my response above is not an air-tight argument. Any discussion of the soul is always at least somewhat speculative. Even a Christian writer like St. Thomas Aquinas who had Revelation and Church doctrine to guide him could provide only inconclusive answers about many aspects of the soul. Even if one is uncertain about the presence of a rational soul -- which is the indication of humanity -- it is only sensible that the benefit of the doubt must be given, however.

Since ensoulment is uncertain, it follows that a further basis should be sought for responding to the infanticide objection. This can perhaps be found in Aristotle's thinking about the virtues, which has been the subject of much of the discussion so far in this Chapter. It was mentioned that two of the virtues that Aristotle points to are courage and generosity. It would seem that by choosing to rear a deformed child, parents could give themselves the opportunity to further develop these virtues, at least as we are accustomed to thinking about them. Since the end for the individual and the state is the good that comes from virtue, it would seem that the state should thus want to encourage deformed children to be reared instead of requiring their destruction. Certainly, it takes a great deal of courage to accept a tragic situation and to face the almost certain challenges, pitfalls, and discouragements that will come with rearing a deformed child, especially a severely deformed or defective one. Clearly this also requires great generosity. Parents will be required to give such a child more time, attention, and perhaps love than a normal child. They will probably also incur a greater financial burden. Moreover, such a child, depending on the type of deformity, may never be able to accomplish the kinds of things in life that would make his parents proud of him. Again, depending on the type of deformity, much sacrifice is involved.

The problem with this explanation is that Aristotle did not have the same understanding of these virtues that we commonly have today. Our view has been shaped by the Judeo-Christian perspective. What Aristotle meant by "courage" was essentially physical courage (i.e., the courage exhibited by a soldier in battle).[73] Our notion of courage tends to be broader: we believe that it includes moral, as well as physical courage. It is moral courage which is the kind required for keeping and rearing a deformed child. Similarly, "generosity" does not mean for Aristotle quite the same thing as our notion of charity. His notion of generosity relates basically to the giving and taking of money and is oriented to achieving the mean in each of these.[74] This difference in his and our usual thinking about such virtues as courage and generosity is due to his image of the "great-souled man" (i.e., the man who has achieved great heights of virtue). Although he is what we would understand as a good and decent man, he is primarily characterized by the fact that he does all things (except those which I mentioned earlier are not subject to this standard) with a sense of proportion (i.e., he maintains the mean).[75] The notion of compassion, which comes to us today from the Christian perspective, is not present. It is this quality which transforms the virtues of courage and generosity from the way he understood them to the way we understand them today.

Moreover, Aristotle's very notion of virtue actually *contributes* to the shaping of the view that deformed children should not be reared. This is because in order to achieve his proper end, man must become virtuous -- according to Aristotle's conception of virtue. The deformed child can hardly measure up to this, however, so he would not be considered capable of a truly worthwhile life. For instance, how can a deformed child ever show physical courage in battle?

(One point that should be noted parenthetically is that Aristotle's notion of the virtue of courage could provide a rationale for not permitting abortion in such other "hard cases" as the pregnancy threatening the life or health of the mother. This is because the courage required of the woman in those cases is most like the physical courage of the soldier in battle.)

There is perhaps another reason why Aristotle supported the destruction of deformed children. He shared the ancient Greek bias for perfection. Greek art and sculpture demonstrates this bias: the Greeks were, in some sense, offended by a human body which appeared to be less than perfectly structured. The deformed child, of course, falls into this category. If one objects that as a philosopher, Aristotle would have risen above such common prejudices I can only point to the example of Socrates. In Plato's *Phaedo*, after drinking the poison and laying down, Socrates covers his face.[76] He apparently does this because he does not want his friends to see the expressions of pain and torment on his face as the poison takes effect. He is perhaps motivated by this Greek bias for perfection: a pained look on the face distorts the perfection of the body. Moreover, even if one were to concede that Aristotle was not himself taken with this particular Greek bias, he calls for exposure of deformed newborns perhaps because he knows that his countrymen are and the prudent legislator must take account of such prejudices.

Another argument that can be made to answer the infanticide dilemma is that the people of Aristotle's time -- whether this was actually his belief or he was just taking cognizance of Greek prejudices about this is not pertinent -- had superstitious beliefs about deformed children. They also did not have the modern medical achievements which have made the correction or mitigation of many of their defects possible and made it more likely that they can lead useful and productive lives. Such advancements have made it easier to understand why deformed children are born and what the possibilities for their lives are. Because we now know they can make contributions to the society they live in, Aristotle's concern for the common good would be an argument *against* destroying them.

There is yet another reason why Aristotle might not favor destroying the deformed unborn or newborn. I mentioned above that he seems to prefer less extreme measures to accomplish the objective he has in mind of a population without deformed persons. We can judge this from the passage cited in Chapter Three in which he favors abortion before sense and life are supposedly present instead of infanticide in order to regulate the population. I mentioned in Chapter Three that this suggests a prudence about the use of infanticide, as his limiting of abortion to the period before sense and life are present suggests it about abortion. This prudence indicates his sense that infanticide and possibly abortion really are terrible things. He prefers abortion to infanticide for population control because it is not quite so terrible, one might say. Had the problem of deformed children been routinely dealt with in his time by abortion instead of infanticide -- as would have been possible to at least some extent if they would have then had amniocentesis and the other techniques discussed in Chapter Six --, Aristotle perhaps would have sought to have employed sterilization, contraception, or natural family planning methods as "less terrible" options. Since he says the law *should* prohibit the rearing of deformed children, he perhaps would today call for something like the law in Scandinavian countries which mandates the sterilization of couples that are revealed by genetic screening to be likely to have defective babies.

The problem with this latter argument, of course, is that it provides only an essentially utilitarian instead of a philosophical basis for answering the infanticide point. If abortion or infanticide were to prove the only feasible means of stopping the birth of deformed children, Aristotle would desire that they be used. Here, as with Aristotle's view of the virtues, there is a shortfall.

Overall, Aristotle's ethical thought gives us a "hard" basis for morally opposing and legislating against abortion generally, but only a "soft" basis for legislating against it in some cases, such as deformity. As has been said, however, the research in this book indicates that abortion is unjustified and should be outlawed in *all* cases. A "hard" rationale for prohibiting it even in the case of likely or certain deformity of the child can be found in the thought of the ancient Stoics.

STOIC THOUGHT AS A SUPPLEMENT TO ARISTOTLE

Since I have built the bulk of my ethical argument against abortion on Aristotle's thought, I shall not discourse on the Stoics at length. I shall just speak briefly about the few aspects of their thought that will be relied on to supplement Aristotle's thought so as to provide a basis for the moral and legal rejection of abortion in the case of deformity. I should first acknowledge that there were many different views among the ancient Stoics and that the thinking of the earlier Stoics diverged from that of the later ones, as did that of the ones who were in Greece and the ones in Rome. On the points I am concerned about, however, there appears to have been substantial agreement.

The first and most important of these points is the Stoic notion of charity or a type of compassion toward our fellow men. Ludwig Edelstein, whom I previously cited in another context, tells us the following about this notion. Particularly among the later Stoics, there was an emphasis on the virtue of philanthropy, or *humanitas*. This philanthropy was understood to be a "'proficiency and benevolence towards all men without distinction.'"[77] The Stoics believed that a man, for instance, has an obligation to save another man who is attacked by wild beasts or threatened by fire. The Stoics, Edelstein says, "insist on charity as a virtue. To feed the hungry and to clothe the naked is also a Stoic virtue."[78] He contends the following:

> Those who unlike Lactantius considered Seneca, Musonius, and Epictetus [prominent Stoics] to have been Christians by nature if not by revelation were more nearly right than he was. The identity of ethical standards is indeed striking. The love of our fellow men, that is, "love thy neighbor"..."what shall it profit a man to gain the whole world and lose his own soul"...are in spirit Stoic and sometimes even in word.[79]

Another commentator tells us that the Stoics "were not hard-hearted, but they grounded the impulse to help and save, not upon pity, but upon the tie of a common humanity, the knowledge of the rights and duties in which all men share."[80] Edelstein echoes this, saying that the Stoics believed that "man is a social being who can perfect himself only within the community of man and not just the community of citizens either" (the latter would be Aristotle's position). Social obligations for the Stoic took precedence over individual ones.[81] Charity was emphasized; men had a duty to help those who were in need.[82]

The Stoic notion of charity or compassion for one's fellow men, then, was based on the belief in the brotherhood of all men. Seneca writes that nature implanted in all men a mutual love.[83] Cicero and Epictetus also emphasized this brotherhood in their writings.[84]

What is more, the high standard of virtue was not something to be held simply as an ideal -- like the standards of right and wrong as they exist in nature for Aristotle -- but was realizable here and now by any man who followed the dictates of reason.[85] (As indicated earlier, however, they did not believe that this would be most men.)

This view of charity also affected the Stoic thinking about the relationship of parents to their children and masters to slaves. Children were seen as having rights which their parents had to respect, especially their rights to educate themselves and choose their own way of life. Slavery was viewed as the *subordination* of slave to master, not the *possession* of the slave by him. The latter was to be regarded as an evil. As human beings, free men and slaves are equals.[86]

The fact that the Stoics emphasized that helping the less well off and showing charity to all without discrimination -- practicing compassion -- is expected of men and is required if they are to become virtuous would suggest that the life of a deformed child should be spared. Certainly, their notion of social ethics would seem to preclude laws *requiring* infanticide because the community would want to encourage and not discourage charitable conduct by men which sustains the community. Second, the very fact of the Stoic belief in brotherhood would seem to reject the practice of destroying or letting these children die since they share in this brotherhood of men. (I consider a problem with this view in light of the Stoic thinking about when life begins below.) And thirdly, this practice would seem incompatible with the Stoic view of children and slaves mentioned above. The Stoics apparently did not speak of the right to life of children, but they did speak of lesser rights (as stated). It follows logically that the most basic right, the right to life, would have to be respected if the other rights are to follow. Further, since the notion of a man actually possessing another man was repudiated even in the case of slaves -- slaves were held to be lower than children in the ancient world --, it would seem that the Stoics would not accept children being "possessed" by their parents, so that the latter could actually discard or destroy them if they wished.

The obvious objection that can be raised to my reliance on the Stoics is simply that they supported abortion themselves. In his monograph on the Hippocratic Oath which was cited by the Supreme Court in *Wade*, Edelstein says that the Stoics believed that the animation of the child began at the moment of birth. He concludes that for them, then, "abortion must have been permissible throughout pregnancy."[87] There is reason to believe, however, that at least many of the Stoics were not supportive of abortion. In this book, reasons apart from animation or ensoulment have been given as to why abortion should be opposed. The Stoics apparently also saw other reasons. It was mentioned that the Stoic Musonius Rufus spoke against abortion. He also appears to have opposed infanticide since he condemned the refusal of some married couples to let more than their first-born live, although this may have been less on moral grounds than because he believed a large family is more powerful.[88] It was also mentioned in Chapter Three that Seneca indicated that he believed abortion to be wrong by praising his mother for not having had one. Cicero similarly suggests that abortion is immoral by complaining in one of his letters to Atticus about an abortion committed by Tertulla, wife of Cassius and sister of Brutus. In the same letter, however, he says that he wanted to see the destruction of the detested offspring of Caesar by an abortion of Cleopatra.[89] Also in his dialogue *Laws*, one of the characters, Quintus, referred to the power of the tribunes of plebeians having been "quickly killed, as the Twelve Tablets [tablets on which were engraved the most important practices and rules which governed Roman life] direct that terribly deformed infants shall be killed."[90] The context does not necessarily express approval of the practice and, in any event, the same problems of discerning the writer's views when the dialogic mode is used are present, as I showed with Plato. These apply equally to Cicero. Galen, mentioned in Chapter Three, was also a Stoic. It will be recalled that he valiantly defended the Hippocratic tradition, including its injunction against abortion, at a time when medicine shared in the general depravity of the time.

Thus, while there is some inconsistency in what the Stoics say about abortion, it cannot be simply said that they endorsed it; and in fact, on balance, they appear to have disagreed with it. I believe that, all in all, my analysis of their thought is valid.

Stoic thought, then, could provide a philosophical basis for the rejection of all abortion. I believe, in any event, that it gives us a rationale to reject the putting to death of deformed children, which is difficult to infer from Aristotle.

Our own legal background provides a further reason for not allowing abortion to be justified by legislation, even when the mother's life is threatened. This is the fact that our common law tradition has never permitted, on the basis of its principle of necessity, the killing of an innocent non-aggressor to save the life of another person (even if the other is also innocent).[91] That the unborn child is not an aggressor is seen by Rice University philosophy professor Baruch Brody's philosophical analysis of this question. He says that in such cases the unborn child fits only one of the three conditions he sets up to justify killing an aggressor: he presents a *danger* to the mother. He does not fit the other conditions. The first is that of *attempt*. He has neither beliefs or intentions to kill or harm his mother. The other is that of *action*. The unborn child has performed no action that threatens his mother.[92]

Another aspect of Stoic thought mentioned in connection with Cicero in the Introduction to this Chapter should be discussed. The Stoics had a notion of a universally applicable law found in nature and discerned by human reason which is not present in Aristotle. This is an important supplement to Aristotle for my purposes because (recalling that the actual standard of justice to be employed depends for Aristotle on the particular regime) it provides an answer to the argument that a prohibition of abortion is not indicated by the kind of political order we have in the U.S. (Actually, I do not believe that Aristotelian thought needs any supplementing on this point, as should be apparent from the next Section, as well as from the fact that abortion was prohibited in all or virtually all cases for the first 175 years of American history. These laws were not considered "unrealistic" or, as Justice Rehnquist asserted, contrary to fundamental rights until the abortion reform movement started in the 1960s.)

A more important reason why this Stoic notion of natural *law*, as opposed to natural *right*, is valuable for my analysis is that, as mentioned, it provides specific mandates and prohibitions. It is thus more conducive to serving as a basis for the outright and sweeping prohibition of abortion than is Aristotelian thought, which is not characterized by a natural law notion.

In summation, Aristotle's ethical thought, when supplemented by ancient Stoic thought as indicated, gives us a sound basis for regarding abortion as immoral and proscribable in all cases.

The Compatibility of the Aristotelian-Stoic Formula with the American Republican Tradition

My discussion of Aristotelian and Stoic thought cannot automatically be said to be a basis for legislating against abortion in America. Washington is not Athens or Rome and the 1980s A.D. are not the fourth or first century B.C. or the first century A.D. I have already acknowledged that the United States of America was established as a different type of political community than was the Greek polis or the Roman Republic and Empire. What remains to be shown is that legislating to promote individual virtue and to channel, limit, and prohibit the various arts and sciences for the sake of that virtue is in agreement with the traditions of the American Republic. There is little doubt that government in America can legislate for the common good, which, as I have shown, is a sufficient basis by itself for legislation against abortion. Can it, however, act in these other ways when its authority vis-a-vis the individual is expressly limited? I begin by making it clear that the Founders of our Republic consciously rejected the idea of this being a nation like the ancient polis in which the shaping of individual character was a primary and overriding purpose of government.[93] Nevertheless, as stated in the first Section of this Chapter, the Founders did not ignore the necessity of a virtuous citizenry. In this Section, it will be explained at more length why the promotion of virtue by our laws, specifically in the sexual realm, is not incompatible with our traditional political principles. This will be done by looking at various statements of the major thinkers who either played a part in the shaping of our founding thought -- John Locke, Baron de Montesquieu, and Thomas Jefferson -- or acted as a commentator about it and our way of life -- Alexis de Tocqueville -- to determine what view they had on this matter of virtue.

First, what did these writers say about the place of virtue generally in a republic? I shall begin with Montesquieu, who is one of the most important figures behind our early political thought. Locke and Montesquieu are generally believed to have had a substantial influence on early American thought. Montesquieu says the following about the need of virtue in a nation with a popular government like ours:

> ...it is clear that in a monarchy, where he who commands the execution of the laws generally thinks himself above them, there is less need of virtue than in a popular government, where the person entrusted with the execution of the laws is sensible of his being subject to their direction.[94]

He goes on to explain why virtue is so badly needed in this type of regime:

> When virtue is banished, ambition invades the minds of those who are disposed to receive it, and avarice possesses the whole community... they were free while under the restraint of laws, but they would fain now be free to act against law...The members of the commonwealth not on the public spoils, and its strength is only the power of a few, and the license of many.[95]

Locke also believes in the importance of education for virtue in order to shape a solid citizenry. Much of his teaching about this is presented in his work entitled *Some Thoughts Concerning Education*. The connection between virtue and good citizenship can only be discerned by looking at many passages throughout this work and then only indirectly and inferentially, so it would take us too far afield to go into it. Kenyon College political scientist Robert H. Horwitz says that this essay showed that Locke believed that a strong political order could not be maintained only by means of the "individual pursuit of self-interest narrowly understood."[96] It would also require that there be a virtuous gentry -- the virtue would be different from classical or Christian virtue, but would be virtue nonetheless --, which would have been formed by Locke's educational proposals.[97]

For Thomas Jefferson, a virtuous group of individuals -- a "natural aristoi" -- was needed to govern a nation.[98] He believed in the republican form of government because it was the one best suited for selecting this "natural aristoi" by means of free election by a well-educated citizenry. Jefferson was no "democrat" in the sense of wanting the mass of people to govern. This is because few had this high level of virtue. It was because the "natural aristoi" had such virtue that they would govern for the sake of the people instead of themselves.[99]

Tocqueville echoes Montesquieu about the dangers that confront a democratic people which is not concerned about seeking virtue:

> If the members of a community, as they become more equal, become more ignorant and coarse, it is difficult to foresee to what pitch of stupid excesses their egotism may lead them; and no one can foretell into what disgrace and wretchedness they would plunge themselves, lest they should have to sacrifice something of their own well-being to the prosperity of their fellow-creatures.[100]

Tocqueville explains how he understands the role of virtue and the form it takes in the American context in the following quotes:

> In the United States hardly anybody talks of the beauty of virtue; but they maintain that virtue is useful, and prove it every day. The American moralists do not profess that

> men ought to sacrifice themselves for their fellow-creatures because it is noble to make such sacrifices; but they boldly aver that such sacrifices are as necessary to him who imposes them upon himself as to him for whose sake they are made.[101]

and, spelling out this notion of virtue further:

> The doctrine of interest rightly understood is not, then, new, but amongst the Americans of our time it finds universal acceptance; it has become popular there; you may trace it at the bottom of all their actions, you will remark it in all they say. It is as often to be met with on the lips of the poor man as of the rich. In Europe the principle of interest is much grosser than it is in America, but at the same time it is less common, and especially it is less avowed; amongst us, men still constantly feign great abnegation which they no longer feel. The Americans, on the contrary, are fond of explaining almost all the actions of their lives by the principle of interest rightly understood; they show with complacency how an enlightened regard for themselves constantly prompts them to assist each other, and inclines them willingly to sacrifice a portion of their time and property to the welfare of the State.
>
> The principle of interest rightly understood is not a lofty one, but it is clear and sure. It does not aim at mighty objects, but it attains without excessive exertion all those at which it aims. As it lies within the reach of all capacities, everyone can without difficulty apprehend and retain it. By its admirable conformity to human weaknesses, it easily obtains great dominion; nor is that dominion precarious, since the principle checks one personal interest by another, and uses, to direct the passions, the very same instrument which excites them.[102]

He further tells us the virtuous behavior that the doctrine of self-interest properly understood brings about in people:

> The principle of interest rightly understood

> produces no great acts of self-sacrifice, but it suggests daily small acts of self-denial. By itself it cannot suffice to make a man virtuous, but it disciplines a number of citizens in habits of regularity, temperance, moderation, foresight, self-command; and, if it does not lead men straight to virtue by the will, it gradually draws them in that direction by their habits.[103]

Writing as "Publius" in Federalists 10 and 51, Madison enunciated the doctrine of self-interest properly understood which Tocqueville later observed. He was concerned about the problem of faction and sought to solve it, in Professor Diamond's words, "not by trying to make opinion more disinterestedly virtuous but by reducing it to a safe reflection of diverse interests." He was "following the general tendency of modern political thought to solve the problems of politics by reducing the scope of politics."[104] It was mentioned that our Founders did not turn their backs on the classical emphasis on politics and virtue. What Madison sought to do, as my quote from Diamond earlier in the Chapter states, was simply to aim the sights a little lower in the public realm. The political order would not try to promote the highest levels of human excellence, but it would not abandon efforts to promote it to some degree. The area in which Madison was most concerned about faction and about lowering the expectations of men -- i.e., permitting some release of their passions -- was the economic. Some sense of virtue would still be working here, however. The passion that would be unleashed would not be avarice, but acquisitiveness. While both are rooted in the (possibly) inordinate desire for material things, there is a difference. Avarice does not require the cultivation of any virtues necessary to its being satisfied. Satisfying acquisitiveness, however, requires such "bourgeois" virtues as venturesomeness, hard work, and the ability to still immediate desires for long-term goals.[105] It also requires the cultivation of virtues to govern one's relations with others. For example, honesty in one's commercial associations with others is needed. Venturesomeness -- the need to invest to get returns -- is akin to the classical virtue of liberality. Some sense of justice must be developed because the acquisitive man must accommodate himself to others' interests in a society where acquisitiveness rules widely.[106] Thus, Tocqueville's doctrine of self-interest properly understood took hold.

This brings us back to our issue. What has just been said shows that our political tradition lowered the expectations of men's acquisition of virtue in the economic realm. It did not intend that such expectations would be lowered in the realm of sexual conduct and family life, as some today seem to believe. The insistence that there are fundamental rights to abortion and consensual sexual activity of any sort which deserve to be protected by law is a reflection of such a confused belief about the American political and constitutional background. The thinkers we have considered believed that sexual virtue was important and had to be maintained and promoted by the political society.

Jefferson, for example, quoted a passage from Theognis in a letter to John Adams which said that "'we do not commix for the sake of pleasure, but for the procreation of the race. For the powers, the organs and the desires for coition have not been given by God to man for the sake of pleasure, but for the procreation of the race.'" He referred to this as a "moral" motive and said that the perpetuation of the race comes about more typically by the "unhallowed impulse" of the "*oestrum* implanted in the constitution of both sexes."[107]

Tocqueville points to the strong emphasis that was placed on sexual virtue in the America he visited:

> In America all those vices which tend to impair the purity of morals, and to destroy the conjugal tie, are treated with a degree of severity which is unknown in the rest of the world. At first sight this seems strangely at variance with the tolerance shown there on other subjects, and one is surprised to meet with a morality so relaxed and so austere amongst the selfsame people.[108]

The prevalence of laws strictly regulating sexual misconduct earlier in American history, which was pointed to in Chapter Five, gives some evidence of what he says.

Locke and Montesquieu also included sexual virtue within the general realm of virtue. First, in his *Some Thoughts Concerning Education*, Locke instructs the parent or educator of a young man to "[t]each him to get a mastery over his inclinations, and submit his appetite to reason. This being obtained, and by a constant practice settled into habit, the hardest part of the task is over."[109] (Locke was no doubt aware that one of the strongest appetites in a young man is the sexual.) Next, in his *First Treatise on Government* Locke implicitly condemns adultery, incest, and sodomy.[110] In his *Second Treatise*, he says that conjugal society "consist[s] chiefly in such a Communion and Right in one anothers Bodies, as is necessary to support its chief End, Procreation." He sounds like Aristotle in adding this about "conjugal society":

> ...it draws with it mutual Support, and Assistance, and a Communion of Interest too, as necessary not only to unite their Care, and Affection, but also necessary to their common Off-spring, who have a Right to be nourished and maintained by them, till they are able to provide for themselves.[111]

The conjugal society is a "Compact, where procreation and Education are secured, and Inheritance taken care for."[112] Locke, then appears to have believed the primary purpose of the family to be what Aristotle thought: the procreation, rearing, and education of children. He may have sought in the *Second Treatise* to present a rationale for the release of the acquisitive passion and for an overthrow of the divine right of kings, but there is no evidence that he wanted to liberate the sexual passion or propose revolutionary change in the family.

Montesquieu makes a number of references to the sexual virtues in *The Spirit of the Laws* and he ties them in with his political theory. At one place, he says that "[t]here are rules of modesty observed by almost every nation in the world" and calls "absurd" any attempt to violate these when punishing crimes. He gives examples of how sexual modesty was violated in this manner in ancient and Oriental states.[113] At another place, he speaks of countries of "the East" where polygamy is practiced. In some cases, all the wives and the children from each wife live in the same house. When this is the case, he says that all the wives should be separated from all the male children who are not their own, all the male children should be separated from all the female ones, and each wife should, in effect, be permitted to have her own small household.

This is all so that "each [wife] derives all that relates to the practice of morality, chastity, reserve, silence, peace, dependence, respect, and love" and so each has "a single and entire attachment to her family."[114] It sounds odd when being stated in reference to a polygamous situation, but Montesquieu is defending the sexual virtues and the well-being of the family. He also speaks of the role that the laws should play in a polygamy-tolerant society: "the more a family ceases to be united" and "the greater the diversity of interests," the more the laws should act to bring it closer together. At a third place, he says the following:

> All nations are equally agreed in fixing contempt and ignominy on the incontinence of women. Nature has dictated this to all... To individuals she has granted a long succession of years to attend to their preservation: but to continue the species, she has granted only a moment.
>
> It is then far from being true that to be incontinent is to follow the laws of nature; on the contrary, it is a violation of these laws, which can be observed only by behaving with modesty and discretion...
>
> When, therefore, the physical power of certain climates violates the natural law of the two sexes, and that of intelligent beings, it belongs to the legislature to make civil laws, with a view to opposing the nature of the climate and reestablishing the primitive laws.[115]

Thus, Montesquieu clearly endorses virtue in the realm of sex and family life and believes that the civil laws have a definite place in helping to insure it. In one other place, he emphasizes the importance of individual virtue for the political order when he says the following (we can see that he apparently includes sexual virtue in this):

> Virtue in a republic is a most simple thing; it is a love of the republic...The love of our country is conducive to a purity of morals, and the latter is again conducive to the former. The less we are able to satisfy our private passion, the more we abandon ourselves to

those of a general nature.[116]

The importance of my showing the concern of these thinkers with sexual virtue is that it shows that on this matter our tradition did not essentially diverge from Aristotle's view. The Aristotelian scheme for promoting such virtue that I laid out, then, can appropriately be applied to American political society.

Even, however, if the philosophy behind our Founding had intended to permit man's passions to be released and self-interest to rule in the sexual realm as it did in the economic realm, abortion -- and possibly also other types of sexual misconduct -- would still be undesirable for the individual. This is because, as I have shown previously, it is actually *contrary* to his self-interest in its truest sense. The state also could still legislate against it in such circumstances, in order to both protect the individual's best interests and to preserve the common good, which has been shown that abortion is contrary to.

The final point for me to establish in this Section is that a republic like ours should actually be permitted to legislate the virtue that it finds to be important. Diamond tells us that once America's founding principles were set down which established the framework of the system of economic self-interest, the government did not have to thereafter superintend the formation of character in that area. The "bourgeois" virtues flowed naturally, as did the republican virtues of the citizen -- independence, initiative, a capacity for cooperation, and patriotism.[117] Besides this, Diamond tells us, the "Founders seem simply to have taken for granted that the *full range* of the higher human virtues would have suitable opportunity to flourish, so to speak privately." They believed that these "would develop from religion, education, family upbringing, and simply out of the natural yearnings of human nature."[118]

What I said in Chapter Five, however, makes clear that the Founders and those who succeeded them as leaders of our governments for most of our history believed that law has a role in shaping *sexual* virtues in the individual, or at least in maintaining certain social norms of sexual conduct. (These two motives are virtually inseparable because, as Clor indicated, the former must be acted upon -- if the individual is not actually made "moral," at least certain actions of his must not be tolerated -- if the latter is to be accomplished.) My discussion in Chapter Five establishes that it has long been believed in this country that one of the major ways in which this is to be done -- just about the only way our political institutions have done it -- is by the prohibitions and punishments spelled out in our criminal law. We seem to have followed the basic thinking of Montesquieu mentioned above on this.

It is reasonable to conclude, then, that our political order can properly legislate against abortion not only because it wants to protect the unborn child who it believes is human or to safeguard the common good which can be endangered by the harm to family life, etc., but to promote sexual virtue in the individual. It is especially justified in doing this because the latter affects the civilizing standards of the community.

As a final point, let us take up the matter of the arts and sciences. This can be troublesome because America has always been proud of the fact that it permits freedom of scientific inquiry. Jefferson believed that science gave support to the goal of equality among men, so it could be used as a counterwright to revealed religion which, in his view, opposed such equality.[119] Our Republic has encouraged and supported science, financially and otherwise, since its early days.[120] Would a prohibition of abortion not be contrary to these traditions, since it constrains the activities of the medical profession which is part of the scientific community?

The answer is *emphatically no*. This point was answered briefly in Chapter Four. The state already regulates medicine and all learned and many other professions by various means, including the criminal law. Their liberty, like that of others, is not and never has been absolute. Abortion procedures by their nature do not involve scientific inquiry. They are an application of science, and such applications have always been the subject of state legislation. Moreover, it would be conceded by most people raising this objection to abortion laws that the state can restrict even scientific *inquiry* to some degree, as when it sets down regulations for experimentation with human subjects.

One indication that the Framers believed that the

arts and sciences should serve the interest of the common good, if not of virtue, is found in a letter Jefferson wrote to John Adams: "And *if* science produces no better fruits than tyranny, murder, rapine and destitution of national morality, I would rather wish our country to be ignorant, honest and estimable as our neighboring savages are."[121]

The Importance of Religion in the Abortion Question

The Shaping of the Individual's Beliefs About Abortion

Abortion has often wrongly been considered primarily a religious issue. This is due, in part, to the attempts of some pro-abortion advocates to promote it as such in order to further their cause (see Chapter One). It is due *primarily*, however, to the fact that it is a moral question which all major religious denominations have a teaching about and because religion, especially in America, always has been viewed as a major, if not *the* major, shaper of morality in the populace. As George Washington said in his Farewell Address, "'... let us with caution indulge the supposition that morality can be maintained without religion. Whatever may be conceded to the influence of refined education on minds of peculiar structure, reason and experience both forbid us to expect that national morality can prevail in exclusion of religious principle.'"[122] The reliance on religion to do this has become increasingly important in twentieth century America, as the political order has been forced to retreat more and more from the responsibility of shaping good character by its laws. Even if the state is permitted to legislate against abortion, it is still essential that religious denominations teach its immorality if new laws are to be effective.

The above suggests one of the ways in which

religion is important for the political order in the abortion question. It is needed to shape the morality of the individuals who live in the political order. No law can be universally or even substantially effective if it is not backed up by a moral sanction. Making abortion illegal again will serve as an instructive moral force in itself. As I have pointed out, however, there is a limit to which a political order like ours can use law to make individuals moral or to shape character. To do this with anything approaching sweeping results would mean an enforcement effort which would threaten our legitimate constitutional liberties and severely tax our national resources. Even if new anti-abortion laws are effectively and constitutionally enforced, the facts of human nature, the nature of abortion, and the acclimation of the American people to years of abortional freedom will guarantee that there still be abortions -- many of them. The wrongness of the act has to be impressed upon women who might consider having abortions, physicians who would agree to do them, and the public generally that might be inclined to simply accept them as a way of life. The importance of virtue in sexual matters generally must be promoted. The churches and synagogues will be needed to do this. It is they that will be primarily responsible for shaping a new moral consensus that will ultimately decide how successful new laws are. Tocqueville echoes Washington above about the importance of religion and explains how the loss of this can ultimately harm a people, especially a free people:

> When the religion of a people is destroyed, doubt gets hold of the highest portions of the intellect, and half paralyzes all the rest of its powers. Every man accustoms himself to entertain none but confused and changing notions on the subjects most interesting to his fellow-creatures and himself. His opinions are ill-defended and easily abandoned: and, despairing of ever resolving by himself the hardest problems of the destiny of man, he ignobly submits to think no more about them. Such a condition cannot but enervate the soul, relax the springs of the will, and prepare a people for servitude. Nor does it only happen, in such a case, that they allow their freedom to be wrested from them; they frequently themselves surrender it.[123]

He goes on to say the following about the importance of the role of religion in the American democracy:

> Religion is much more necessary in the republic which they set forth in glowing colors than in the monarchy which they attack; and it is more needed in democratic republics than in any others. How is it possible that society should escape destruction if the moral tie be not strengthened in proportion as the political tie is relaxed? and what can be done with a people which is its own master, if it be not submissive to the Divinity?[124]

and

> Thus, whilst the law permits the Americans do do what they please, religion prevents them from conceiving, and forbids them to commit, what is rash or unjust.[125]

Although new laws rigorously enforced will reduce the number of abortions and can help to shape a new ethic of respecting life, it is because of this fact that religion will ultimately have to play such an important role that the scourge of abortion will probably not substantially disappear from our national landscape soon. (Again because of the nature of abortion, we should not ever expect to see abortion disappear completely as slavery did after it was made a violation of our fundamental law. The law was required to sustain American slavery; it was a creature of the law. Abortion is not.) Most American religious denominations officially accept abortion under at least some circumstances and many have been active promoters of the abortion liberty, as was stated in Chapter One.

Classical thought has been used in this book as the basis for opposition to abortion, but I do not believe that this can be a guide for very many people. I have written uppermost for the legislator, the political scientist, and the moral philosopher, with the hope of giving each of them a means for approaching this question, in each of their particular roles, in a way which is appropriate to the American situation. They are (this would apply even to most legislators) liberally educated in at least some sense and are likely to understand and appreciate the reasoning of an Aristotle, *et al*. Most citizens are not in this category, however. Moral beliefs and behavior are shaped for them by their particular religious upbringing and religious creed -- or lack of them. The likely lack of support by most religious denominations is thus going to be a significant factor in the success of new anti-abortion laws. It is one good reason for legislators to proceed prudently.

Abortion and American Political Religion

Political regliion is defined as the use of religious beliefs in order to foster support for political principles or institutions. This does not necessarily imply a utilitarian approach to religion, for the political principles that underlie a regime may be based on religious principles, and religion thus helps to insure that these political principles will be carried out. This is the case with the United States.

We can see evidence of the latter in a few of the statements of prominent American statesmen of the past. Jefferson, despite his being author of the Bill for Establishing Religious Freedom and rejecting most of the traditional theological doctrines of Christianity, wrote the following about the possible undermining of American liberty by slavery:

> "And can the liberties of a nation be thought secure when we have removed their only firm basis, a conviction in the minds of the people that these liberties are of the gift of God? That they are not to be violated but with his wrath? Indeed I tremble for my country when I reflect that God is just..."[126]

Washington wrote the following in his Farewell Address:

> "Of all the dispositions and habits which lead to political prosperity, religion and morality are indispensable supports. In vain would that man claim the tribute of patriotism who should labor to subvert these great pillars of human happiness, these firmest props of the duties of men and citizens."[127]

University of Dallas political scientist Glen E. Thurow also gives many examples of Lincoln's invocation of God as being behind American political principles and events in his *Abraham Lincoln and American Political Religion*. We shall turn to these shortly.

To the above, we must of course add one of the fundamental documents of our political order, the Declaration of Independence, which speaks of the "Laws of Nature and of Nature's God" and of men being "endowed by their Creator with certain unalienable Rights." The Declaration thus invokes both the Judeo-Christian conception of God and some notion of natural law. Likewise, the above statesmen and, as we shall soon see, Lincoln, invoke (as seen in their use of present tense verbs) the Judeo-Christian conception of a God who is active in human affairs.

In Chapter Four, I spoke of the sanctity of marriage and the reverence and duties owed to offspring as being upheld by the Judeo-Christian tradition, as well as by other traditions (thereby indicating that these are principles ordained by the natural order -- the "Laws of Nature"). Since the Judeo-Christian God and the "Laws of Nature" stand behind our political tradition, these principles are part of it. The presence of these principles in our tradition is seen further by what I said earlier about sexual and family life virtues being emphasized in the thinking of the political philosophers who most influenced us, Locke and Montesquieu. Another passage from Locke's *Second Treatise*, which was not quoted before, particularly points up the duties to offspring:

> ...*Adam* and *Eve*, and after them all *Parents* were by the Law of Nature, *under an obligation to preserve, nourish, and educate the Children*, they had begotten, not as their own Workmanship, but the Workmanship of their own Maker, the Almighty, to whom they were to be accountable for them.[128]

Thus, while our laws do not say in so many words that the "sanctity" of young life and of the family are to be protected, this is implicitly contained in many of them as a guiding principle grounded in our most basic traditions. These traditions are shaped by our religious and philosophical background and have been sustained by our religious beliefs. This is because religious beliefs are the means by which people respect principles like the two mentioned. If these hallowed principles are weakened, even in one area, they are then subject to being weakened in others (as the connection between abortion and child abuse, infanticide, and euthanasia show). Then, the laws which embody these principles and the tradition of which they are a part will be threatened. So, we can see an example of what Washington meant about religion being essential to "political prosperity" and what Jefferson meant by such an important part of our tradition as our liberties being undermined when the people no longer believe that they are from God.

The latter suggests a specific consequence of abortion for our political order. A principle such as the sanctity of life translates itself most fundamentally into our political order in the form of the right to life stated in the Declaration. Any weakening of this principle may result in a compromising of this right which will strike at the very foundation of the political order whose purpose, in common with that of all governments according to the Declaration, is to secure natural rights such as this.

Let us consider various specific points on which political religion can and has been invoked as a means of helping to resolve the abortion question. Most of this discussion shall focus on an important speech by Senator Jesse Helms, one of the major Congressional foes of legalized abortion. I shall draw parallels between this and a number of points that Thurow makes in his book on how Lincoln used political religion in connection with slavery.

Senator Helms' speech was made in August, 1982, when he introduced his comprehensive Human Life Bill (the "Super Helms" Bill) in the Senate as an amendment to the Debt Limit Bill. The attempt to show the religious dimension of American politics and to invoke religion in its relation to our political traditions is unmistakable.

Helms begins by saying the following:

> There has been a longstanding tradition in Anglo-American jurisprudence and in Western

> civilization generally that the protection of innocent human life is a preeminent value. On Jan. 22nd, 1973 the Supreme Court made a radical break with that tradition [in *Wade* and *Bolton*].[129]

Helms speaks of another sacred, cherished principle, the sanctity of innocent human life, and indicates the specific way it is given recognition in our jurisprudence and way of life generally: by affording it legal protection. He goes on to say that he is specifically concerned about two important principles: the sanctity of marriage and family life and the respect owed to offspring.

> I believe that we all would admit that our most precious gift in America...is the gift--and mystery--of children. Can we ever overestimate the immense value of American children?[130]

Further on, he says the following:

> Abortion is, tragically, not really about freedom of choice or reproductive rights. I wish it were. It is, instead, about children. It is about which children will live and which will not.[131]

and

> Even when it is called "termination of pregnancy," we naturally recoil from the thought of a mother and an abortionist destroying an unborn child.[132]

Like Lincoln, Washington, and Jefferson, Helms contends that belief in God stands at the base of the American political order and takes an active part in its on-going affairs. He says that "[t]he United States has been given many great gifts."[133] God, obviously, is the giver. He also speaks of the words of the Declaration, saying that "[t]he wisdom of the 'Laws of Nature and of Nature's God,' as Thomas Jefferson put it, is lost on ...[certain] legal scholars and their disciples in government."[134]

The quotation I presented from Jefferson above -- Professor Thurow tells us that Lincoln stated the same -- expresses the view that our nation ultimately is going to be judged by God if we do not do what is just.[135] This same idea comes across in Helms' speech. He disputes the argument that God's law as a basis for human law is unconstitutional. (This is an argument sometimes made by pro-abortionists.) He says that "[t]o do otherwise -- to ignore God's revelation in human history -- would be to reject the only sure foundation we have on Earth." He also says that men cut off from God and relying only on their own authority is "a fearful prospect which has always produced fearful consequences."[136]

In his Second Inaugural Address, Lincoln points to the possibility that the War Between the States is a punishment inflicted by God which will continue until reparation for our offense of practicing and tolerating slavery has been made:

> If we shall suppose that American Slavery is one of those offences which, in the providence of God, must needs come, but which, having continued through His appointed time, He now wills to remove, and that He gives both North and South, this terrible war, as the woe due to those by whom the offence came, shall we discern therein any departures from those divine attributes which the believers in a Living God always ascribe to Him?[137]

Helms also paints a picture of serious consequences to America by our permitting an evil like abortion, which is so contrary to the law of God which stands behind the nation, to take place. He says this:

> The fact of 10 million abortions since 1973 has created an unmistakable void in our land. We are missing our own children. Where there would have been laughter, there is silence. Where there would have been tears, there are no eyes to cry. Where there would have been love for the now living, there is nothing.[138]

He makes this further statement about consequences following from abortion:

> Legal positivism and its rejection of God's authority are alien to traditional Anglo-American jurisprudence, and they are destructive of American society. I say that it is time to return to our heritage and return to God and His Law as the basis for our own.[139]

In the above quotations, Helms makes clear the gravity of the offense that abortion gives to God. Where the Civil War was the punishment inflicted by God for slavery, the loss of the spirit that the aborted children would have given to America and of the promise they held out for its future is our punishment for abortion. Both Helms' statement about "fearful consequences" and the last passage above suggest that if we do not change our national policy even more foreboding things could be in store for us.

Helms does not spell out what these further consequences might be. He does, however, give us a basis for speculating as to what they could be. He says that "[t]o my mind, every single abortion is an incalculable blow to the moral order ordained by Almighty God." One is led to think of some of the consequences pointed to earlier in this book, such as the rise of the "anti-life" ethic and the weakening of family life. The health damage to women and infertility also come to mind as manifestations in the physical realm of harm to the natural moral order.

Helms further says the following: "The plague of legalized abortion has inflicted, I am afraid, a moral wound to the American ceremony of innocence."[140] The latter part of this sentence is taken from a poem by William Butler Yeats. This makes one think of consequences accruing to our political order from abortion. The idea of a people suffering a *moral* wound and of their losing innocence suggests a loss of goodness and an ensuing loss of belief in themselves. A people in this state may lose faith in their (republican) institutions and perhaps be less willing to resist an external aggressor or be ready to join extremist, anti-republican movements.

Lincoln closes his Second Inaugural with the following words:

> With malice towards none; with charity for all; with firmness in the right, as God gives us to see the right, let us strive on to finish the work we are in; to bind up the nation's wounds; to care for him who shall have borne the battle, and for his widow, and his orphan--to do all which may achieve and cherish a just, and a lasting peace, among ourselves,

> and with all nations.[141]

Thurow tells us that Lincoln's aim in the Second Inaugural, with the war clearly nearing its close and a Union victory at hand, was to encourage a new attitude in the citizenry which would gain support for his policies for reunification. This had to be done by getting them to put aside the enmity of the war, but at the same time acknowledge that the injustice of slavery, which the entire nation was responsible for, had been paid for by the suffering of the war.[142]

Helms makes a similar call for reconciliation after the injustice of legalized abortion has been ended:

> Let us turn away from the corruption of *Roe v. Wade*, but let us do so in a spirit of forgiveness and reconciliation. The abortion matter in the United States has caused much acrimony and hard feelings over these last 9 years. It is indeed an emotional subject. Many fine people with the best of intentions have been deceived by the rhetoric of "freedom of choice." But let us all, both as individuals and as Americans, make a resolute commitment to forgive each other for the errors which have been made. "To err is human, to forgive divine," according to the familiar counsel of Alexander Pope. The Divine in this case will lead us out of the abortion tragedy, and He will surely provide the means for national healing as well...[143]

For Helms, respect for God's law demands that abortion be outlawed again, but this will not end the great divisiveness and strife the issue has caused. He is appealing to us to be forgiving, as our Judeo-Christian religious beliefs require, so that a national healing will come about. He tells us that if only we will do this, God will help in this healing.

A successful appeal to political religion to support the resolution of the abortion question that is herein proposed can help overcome the ambivalence to abortion of many because, even while we may be a less religious people now than in the past, we still tend to view our political institutions and traditions in a "religious" way. That is, we see them, in some sense, as sacred and as the basis for greatness and strength. An aspect of our political religion that Lincoln spoke of that may be especially worth appealing to in order to insure the effectiveness of new anti-abortion legislation is the reverence we traditionally have given to our laws.

Prudence and Principle in Resolving the Abortion Issue

I have already stated that many American religious denominations are not teaching that abortion is wrong and do not support laws against it. This requires that legislators approach the matter prudently. The very magnitude of the abortion problem further dictates this. In the U.S. today, over 1.5 million abortions are performed annually.[144] It is the most frequently done surgical procedure.[145] Abortion clinics are prospering and most of the medical profession and much of the public seems to accept the liberty the Supreme Court created. All of this commonly prompts the argument that if abortion is again prohibited by law, the law will be widely defied and probably not enforced. This seems to present the deeper problem that political authority will be threatened.

Two passages from Edmund Burke indicate the dangers of ignoring the need for political prudence and suggest the approach that the true statesman will take to serious political problems, such as this one. Speaking of a group in England that shared the views of the French revolutionaries, he said the following:

> They despise experience as the wisdom of unlettered men; and as for the rest, they have wrought under-ground a mine that will blow up at one grand explosion all examples of antiquity, all precedents...They have "the rights of men." Against these there can be no prescription... these admit no temperament, and no compromise: any thing withheld from their full demand is so much of fraud and injustice.[146]

He says that the statesman's approach, by contrast, is

like this:

> A man full of warm speculative benevolence may wish his society otherwise constituted than he finds it; but a good patriot, and a true politician, always considers how he shall make the most of the existing materials of his country. A disposition to preserve, and an ability to improve, taken together, would be my standard of a statesman.[147]

Burke, of course, is reacting to an extreme position; he is speaking against revolutionaries. Although the *Wade* and *Bolton* decisions were hardly a society-changing revolution in the sense that the French Revolution was, his general point -- that prudence must guide public decision-making -- is applicable here.

It has been said that it is a great misfortune for our political order that abortion ever became a political issue in the first place. One argument holds that the incessant political struggle that we have witnessed about it has heightened political and social conflict. In effect, we are now in something like a Hobbesian state of nature on this issue. This means that the sovereign must intervene to resolve it. The danger of this, however, is that the sovereign may not decide on the basis of what is right, but on which side has the most votes and many on the losing side will not accept the resolution. For example, if abortion should be prohibited by law once again, many physicians and women will not abide by it because they will consider it "tyrannical." The result will be that political authority will be undermined.[148]

This argument is flawed for the following reasons. First, abortion *is* an appropriate matter for the sovereign to decide because how it is resolved can profoundly affect the common good. Also, it is the sovereign's responsibility to protect its citizens, and it must legislate on abortion to protect two groups of its citizens: women -- whose personhood nobody doubts -- and unborn children -- whose personhood is strongly indicated by the evidence. Secondly, the Supreme Court has already tried to provide the sovereign's resolution of the matter. If the resolution is incorrect, the only way to rectify it is by further political action by the sovereign. Thirdly, this argument overstates the threat to political authority that prohibition would present. Professor Rice argues that anti-abortion laws *can* be effectively enforced.[149] Dr. Nathanson, who should know from first-hand experience, said that "there was general social compliance under the pre-1973 abortion laws."[150] Nathanson also indicates that the medical profession is rather conservative.[151] It is not given to breaking laws with impunity. Also, of course, the likelihood of unenforceability is a weak argument against a particular type of law because many laws -- including those that are universally accepted as necessary -- are difficult to enforce and frequently circumvented. Moreover, the charge of "tyranny" is likely to have a hollow ring to it. This is because our legal background clearly shows that a prohibition in no way would be tyrannical and it really would be right -- regardless of how many votes it commands -- for the variety of reasons stated already. (Actually, as argued in Chapter One, it is the Supreme Court that is the more appropriate target of charges of having made a "political" decision. This is because it responded to the segment of political society that has the "most votes" as far as influencing the Court on social questions is concerned.)

Abortion is, of course, a very devisive national issue about which passions run high on both sides. The most difficult aspect of it is that it is not the kind of issue that lends itself to substantive compromise. This is because of the more fundamental problem involved: the clash of two competing world views. This goes well beyond abortion and was addressed only in a limited way in Chapter Eight and in scattered references elsewhere. One is, in some sense, led to think again of the American slavery controversy as a comparison. This involved two opposing views about such questions as liberty, the relations between the races, and the nature of man, or at least of some men. Politcially, the opportunities for compromise ran out and substantial numbers of people became polarized in the years just before the Civil War on the question of the extension of slavery into the Western territories. A deadlock developed because both North and South realized that its outcome would ultimately determine the future of the entire institution of slavery in the U.S.[152]

In 1860, of course, there was a total breakdown of the political consensus between North and South, with violence and bloodshed being the result. This kind of breakdown of the *political* consensus is very unlikely on abortion, even minus the violence. There is no sectional cleavage, with one section perceiving a threat to an essential aspect of its way of life with the abortion issue as there was with slavery. Further, although abortion has touched many more Americans than slavery did,[153] it has not and is very unlikely to bring many of those it has touched into the active political arena on the pro-abortion side.[154] This is because most women who have had abortions view it as a personal matter, not a political one. Most probably view it as something they are glad is behind them and many regret it. Few even are eager to tell many others about it. Many people give their ideological support to legalized abortion, but it is an intense or high priority issue for few of them. It does not *directly* affect the great majority of people -- despite the large number of abortions that have occurred -- in the same way as does, say, the state of the economy. (Slavery, by contrast, concerned most of the politically active strata in the ante-bellum South.) The number of persons who are pro-abortion activists or who have a financial stake in continuing abortion is relatively small.[155] Moreover, abortion is not the single, overriding issue even for most of the latter.[156]

Even if there would not be a breakdown of political consensus due to abortion, the breakdown of agreement about what public policy on it should be and of the moral consensus that this disagreement reflects would continue.[157] There will be a problem of enforcement, as has been indicated: it may be difficult both to stop violations of the law and to motivate prosecutors to file charges against the violators. There will probably be a rash of acts of civil disobedience directed against the laws which, even if they do not involve too many people, will receive favorable treatment in a sympathetic media. In short, to return to the argument pointed to above, there will be *some* authority problem. The matter must thus be dealt with according to the Burkean type of prudence mentioned. Those who wish to outlaw abortion must not in their struggle to vindicate an important right "admit no temperament, and no compromise" or believe that if "any thing is withheld from...[their] full demand" being satisfied immediately it is no good. They cannot engage in the abstractionism that the pro-abortion movement does. They have to recognize that an abortion mentality has taken root in this country and runs wide and that it can be reversed only gradually. They should take their cue from Burke to bring about improvement according to what is politically possible in light of "the existing materials of...[our] country." They must do it this way because no other way provides the greatest possibility for ultimate, complete success. In sum, they must compromise, but their compromise cannot be a substantive one. I have already said that we must prohibit abortion *entirely*. The compromise must be in the *approach*.

It is perhaps wise that we turn back to Lincoln on this point. Legislators and others who wish to enact new laws against abortion must be concerned about what the late legal scholar Alexander M. Bickel called the "Lincolnian tension between principle and expediency."[158] Bickel, taking his cue from Professor Jaffa, gleaned this notion from the dispute between Abraham Lincoln and Stephen A. Douglas in their historic 1858 debates. Both men were opposed to slavery and were concerned about its potential for splitting the Union apart. They realized that compromises had to be forged. Lincoln was willing, out of necessity, to accept slavery in the Southern States where it already existed. He believed that gradually the institution might die out. Already, efforts were being made before the Civil War to free the black slaves through manumission and colonization in Liberia. He could tolerate this much of a compromise *in application* of the bedrock principle of the Declaration of Independence that "all men are created equal" (i.e., that, as Bickel puts it, "all men, black or white, are equal in the right to own themselves."[159]) What he could not accept was the compromise of this principle itself. This is why he opposed the *Dred Scott* decision, which meant that, as a matter of our fundamental law, blacks could not share in this principle. It is also why he opposed the compromise that Douglas championed: "squatter sovereignty." This would have permitted settlers in the new western territories to decide by popular vote whether or not slavery would be established within their boundaries. This was also a compromise of the principle itself, for to permit the freedom of some men to depend upon a vote by other men meant that not all were really created equal.

While Lincoln understood that practical difficulties precluded the sudden abolition of slavery, he insisted that the goal of its eventual abolition -- and, thereby, the full realization of the principle of the Declaration -- had to be maintained, if only in theory. This maintenance, as Bickel puts it, had "vast educational value, [and] as such it exerted its crucial influence on the tendency of prudential policy."[160]

The Lincolnian tension between principle and expediency," then, refers to the difficult task the statesman has of making the political compromises which are necessary to maintain stability and keep support for the state and respect for its authority intact, while at the same time not allowing its fundamental principles *qua* principles to be eroded even when they are not being carried out sufficiently in practice.

This point suggests another parallel, although not a precise one, between abortion and slavery. Like slavery, what is at stake in abortion is one and possibly two fundamental constitutional principles: the right to life, which is enunciated in the Declaration of Independence, and the same principle of "all men are created equal" that was present in the slavery question. The latter is pertinent because all men cannot be considered equal if the law permits some of them to destroy others.

Also like slavery, abortion is bitterly divisive. Slavery would not die easily because it was too deeply rooted as an institution in a large part of the country. It became virtually impossible to deal with in the political arena because no more compromises could be struck after awhile. Abortion, especially since the 1973 Supreme Court decisions, has become widely accepted and used. It also will not be easily eliminated and it is very unlikely that both sides can be satisfactorily accommodated. In both cases, conflicting notions of rights clashed. Political authority was subverted when the slaveowners saw the North's threatening their right to own slaves. Political authority may be threatened in our issue if physicians and militant women defy an attempt by the law to take away their abortion "rights." In both cases also, the situation reached a more serious point after the Supreme Court tried to remove it from the political arena and resolve it itself.

So, the fact that abortion involves many of the same political aspects that slavery does makes us see that the principle-expediency problem is also involved in it. The fact that it is different in important ways, however, must make us aware of the need to address this problem differently than Lincoln proposed for slavery. One of these differences is seen simply in the fact that the existence of slavery was squarely the result of law. When the law permitting slavery was abolished, it could no longer exist. Abortion, however, will continue to some degree whether it is legal or not. It is a matter that the state of the law, while having definite impact on it, is not able to affect so completely. The opportunity for defiance of the law is thus greater and the role of the law as a moral educator much greater. Although, as has been said, if strictly enforced the law will stop many abortions, its long-term effects in wearing down the abortion mentality may be more important.

On the other hand, as has been emphasized throughout this Chapter, abortion is also a legal question and the law on it can more easily be changed, from the political perspective, than could the law on slavery had the Civil War not intervened, as can be seen from Lincoln's thinking about it. Because we maintained the legal situation that the anti-abortion movement seeks for most of our history and only recently changed it -- this was the opposite of slavery -- and because such a change will not have the devastating political consequences that the threat of abolition had, there is a greater likelihood of delegalizing abortion sooner than might have been the case with slavery. Moreover, it was *legal* developments -- changing the laws prohibiting abortion -- which precipitated the current political crisis and law will have to undo it. What must occur is that the law must be made to affirm the basic principles that are at stake; it will then be able to begin its educational efforts. Only more gradually -- but with a persistent commitment to this course of action and without too great of a time lapse --, the criminal law must be made to conform to the principle, thereby insuring that it will be carried out to a much greater degree in practice. This will take our expediency problem into account.

What this means, however, is that there *cannot* be at any time, even as an interim measure, legislation enacted which will compromise the fundamental principles that are at stake. This means that a "states' rights" constitutional amendment and a proposal like the Hatch Amendment (explained in the notes to Chapter One) -- the so-called "legislators' rights" approach -- are unacceptable. Since they permit fundamental rights to be voted on, even though by the peoples' representatives and not by the people themselves, they are subject to the same criticism that "squatter sovereignty" was. They would obliterate the fundamental principles of the equality of men and the right to life. These principles would surrender their true meaning because a whole class of persons -- unborn children -- would be excluded from them *in principle*. This would especially be so because the enactments which establish this would be constitutional amendments which are part of our fundamental law (i.e., they set down the principles for the political order).[161] This, of course, would undercut both the long-range legal *and* educational aims of the anti-abortion effort. It would be difficult to argue for laws recriminalizing abortion in order to protect the unborn child when you have conceded that the basic principles of the political order do not apply to him. This would also make more difficult the even more long-range aim of using the law to educate about the fundamental immorality of abortion and the essential personhood of the unborn child so as to end the actual *practice* of abortion as much as possible. These proposals seem sensible to many people now because they promise saving some unborn children's lives in the face of the present pro-abortion climate. They will be disastrously counterproductive in the end, however. In short, such proposals must be rejected because they are so concerned about expediency -- i.e., getting the most that the current political situation will permit -- that they lose sight of the importance of principle.

A final point that prudence dictates is that there be an understanding that when the mother's life is clearly at stake, and perhaps even when it is virtually certain that continuing a pregnancy would cause grievous and permanent physical injury to her, the law against abortion should not be enforced. This should be so even though, for the reasons I have stated, the law should not specifically *permit* it in these cases. As Cicero believed, the law cannot demand too much of those under it. The absolute proscription against taking innocent human life must be preserved in principle, although human nature indicates that some leeway will have to be given in practice. How will we avoid the problem of the original and the ALI-type statutes which supposedly placed physicians in "catch-22" situations with the law when trying to exercise their best clinical judgment?

This will require good and judicious law enforcement officials in the same way that good legislators are required.

In Appendices A and B, the type of legislative proposal is stated which exhibits the understanding of the principle-expediency problem generally that Lincoln had and deals with it in accordance with the ideas set out above.

Chapter Conclusion

This Chapter has covered many important questions, each one of which has followed from the ones before it. All in all, they provide both a strong ethical basis for opposing all abortion and a strong basis for and reasonable approach to legislating against it in America. I have argued that Aristotle's ethical thinking can be construed to be against most abortions and ancient Stoic thought to oppose those that Aristotle would not. There is thus a sound argument that can be made from classical, non-religious thought for the complete prohibition of abortion. It has been shown how this thought can be the basis for such legislation in our political order because our tradition permits government to legislate to promote virtue. This is in addition to the fact that it could prohibit abortion in order to preserve the common good -- which virtually no one doubts is a grounds for legislation -- which is damaged by abortion. This prohibition can be accomplished in a politically prudent manner.

Epilogue

There are no certain justifications for abortion and a good many reasons to be against it. Admittedly, human reason does not make it *certain* either that the unborn child is human or that abortion diverts the individual from his end of seeking virtue or that it harms the social fabric. The arguments for these points, however, are strong; about the unborn child's humanity they are overwhelming. Indeed, the basic weakness of the pro-abortion position is seen in the fact that virtually no one defending it actually will say that abortion is a good thing. As Senator Helms said, "Abortion makes us all a little weak-kneed."[1]

That abortion should be illegal is seen by the fact that since it has become legalized, it has become widespread and the harms associated with it have become more evident. Law is needed for social control, the promoting of individual virtue, and the preserving of public morality. The legalization of abortion has contributed in some way to the erosion of all these. Justice dictates the opposite solution to the abortion question. Law is necessary to build a culture based on justice, which is needed to at least some degree to make individuals just. To have such a culture, we must forbid abortion by law.

For whatever reasons, the Supreme Court chose not to fully weigh the evidence about the justifications for abortion or its likely consequences. Nor did it seriously consider its proper institutional role and limitations when it boldly took it upon itself to resolve this issue. The result has been that our political institutions are paralyzed as far as being able to address a national problem of growing seriousness.

What I have written makes apparent that abortion poses a threat both to cherished traditions of Western Civilization, which our people from the beginning clearly acknowledged, and to important principles of our political order itself: the right to life and the Lockean notion of natural rights generally, representative government as the means for dealing with crucial public issues, the common law tradition, and a citizen body of virtue. Abortion is thus a profoundly *political* question for America, despite the naive or opportunistic statements of some, such as Senator Lowell Weicker of Connecticut in his 1982 filibuster against the Human Life Bill, that it does not belong in the political forum.

There is another sense, besides that mentioned in Chapter Nine, in which abortion is "a moral wound to the American ceremony of innocence." We have, as a people, believed ourselves to be committed to the truth. It is true that we have thought too highly of ourselves in this regard. After all, we are a nation built on modern principles, embodying the philosophical errors present in the modern mind-set. We are, nevertheless, justified to at least some extent in believing this. This is because we are the inheritors of a religious tradition which set before man the highest moral principles and carried him to the greatest heights of civility ever, a legal tradition which has contained conflict by the rule of law and rendered justice better than most others, and a political tradition whose institutional arrangements are of the nature of a mixed regime -- one of the "good" regimes of the classics -- and which has a proven record of preserving liberty, stability and the common good at the same time. The acceptance of abortion demands that one simply ignore the truth, or at least what the limited human intellect can best determine to be the truth. This book has determined precisely what the truth on many aspects of the abortion question is and, thereby, showed the *untruth* of the pro-abortion arguments. Can a people which sees itself as believers in the truth not help to become disheartened and disillusioned when it is asked to accept a national abortion policy so thoroughly grounded in untruth?

The large number of pro-abortion claims refuted herein give us a sense of how fallacies, misconceptions, misinterpretations, and ignorance helped to shape an important American public policy. My belief is that most of these were not deliberate -- although what Dr. Nathanson says about NARAL's anti-Catholic propaganda campaign makes clear that *some* were --, but were the logical result of the perspective of many people. They were swept along by views and sentiments about freedom, equality, compassion, the quality of life, etc. which fashioned a perspective which made them almost instinctively accept some arguments and reject others. Each of the various types of organizations which sought to change the anti-abortion laws emphasized certain of these concerns more than others, but by 1973 almost all were united in what the new policy should be. They showed much political strength in moving legislators to act. Their greatest impact, however, was in spreading this perspective throughout our political society and finally to most of the Justices of the Supreme Court. Could one doubt, after reading this study, that the Court, as a result, readily accepted these fallacies, etc.?

The abortion issue has fostered new political alliances and brought people into the political arena -- largely on the anti-abortion side -- who were not there before. Abortion has resulted in unexpected challenges to the reigning or previously ascendant political and social movements of our time. The vast majority of Americans, of course, have not taken any part in the abortion issue, but it has no doubt motivated even many of them to doubt the wisdom of these movements. This is because abortion has exposed their ugliest sides, as well as some of the basic untruths which are embodied in them. Liberalism, for example, by its strong support for legalized abortion, has shown itself willing to defend the most horrendous of practices in the name of "freedom" and has made its claim of being "compassionate" sound hollow. Feminism has shown that its lofty aim of "equality" includes, as an essential component, the right of a woman to destroy her offspring. The population control and "family planning" movements have displayed a crude utilitarianism which holds that the "good life" for families and society requires the expendability of the innocent unborn. Secularized religion has shown itself willing to surrender the most fundamental moral tenet of the Judeo-Christian tradition: the sacredness of innocent human life.

It is partly because of such unaccustomed opposition that the activists in these movements have worked with incredible vigor and intensity to preserve the abortion freedom. They have a suspicion that if this "advance" is reversed others may be also. I believe, however, that their primary motivation is something else, although they may not be conscious of it. It is implicit in their mind-set. They have inherited the modern obsession with the sovereignty of the individual. Earlier modern men, however, were wiser about human nature. They understood that there had to be limitations to that sovereignty if men were not to harm themselves and their political society. When they removed one set of restraints, such as a state religion or the overriding role of the state in shaping character, they substituted another, such as new institutional arrangements, "private" religion, family, and social attitudes. Further, the early moderns, as was showed to some extent, did not believe that people could or should repudiate the age-old beliefs about sex and family as the pro-abortionists do.

Hannah Arendt writes that modern man previously rejected religion and tradition and more recently came to reject authority.[2] I would add that -- as perhaps was made apparent in my discussion of science -- he now wants to reject nature. Sex and family are tied up with all four of these, but in the final analysis they are governed by nature. Contraception could give man a substantial amount of control over his reproductive life, but abortion was needed to make it complete. Abortion thus has an important part to play in this attempt to become free of the constraints of nature, which is the last frontier of human "liberation."

This leads me back to C. S. Lewis, with whose words this book closes. Speaking about man's attempt to conquer nature without any attention to the "Tao," Lewis says this:

> We have been trying, like Lear, to have it both ways: to lay down our human preroga-

tive and yet at the same time retain it. It is impossible. Either we are rational spirit obliged for ever to obey the absolute values of the *Tao*, or else we are mere nature to be kneaded and cut into new shapes for the pleasures of masters who must, by hypothesis, have no motive but their own 'natural' impulses. Only the *Tao* provides a common human law of action which can overreach rules and ruled alike. A dogmatic belief in objective value is necessary to the very idea of a rule which is not tyranny or an obedience which is not slavery.[3]

Appendix A
The Constitutional Basis and Guidelines for Federal Legislation Against Abortion

The method for overturning the *Roe v. Wade* and *Doe v. Bolton* decisions that most frequently is proposed is a constitutional amendment. This is undesirable for the following reasons. First, to "amend" something, in common usage, means to change it. As has been shown, the Constitution already guarantees the right to life to unborn children. There is no need to amend it to provide for this. Second, because of this fact that an amendment *changes* the Constitution, it would be an admission that *Wade* and *Bolton* were correct. More broadly, it would express implicitly the view that the Constitution is what the Court says it is. Such a position, if widely accepted, could undermine our constitutional order. The Framers, as expressed by Hamilton in Federalist 78, intended -- and the continuation of our republican form of government requires -- that the Court, like all of our governors, be subject to the Constitution. Third, since the regulation, restriction, and/or prohibition of abortion is a national policy question, the use of an amendment will be a blow to Congress' position as the principal maker of national policy. Amendments have been used as the vehicle for making national policy, and there is no constitutional prohibition on such a use.[1] The effect of an amendment, however, is to shift a matter from the political arena to the judicial. The Court then becomes the policymaker because it is charged with interpreting the amendment. Because of this *de facto* transfer of policymaking power to the Court, an amendment against abortion could result in no solution at all.[2] The Court may read exceptions into an amendment -- even the "Paramount" one which would seem to have the effect of banning all abortions -- to permit abortions in some cases. The preferred solution, then, is a Congressional statute.

What is the constitutional basis for Congressional legislation against abortion? There are several possibilities. One which is being tried is seen in the Human Life Bill, an idea originally put forth by attorney Stephen H. Galebach. It uses Congress' authority to enforce the provisions of the Fourteenth Amendment -- pursuant to Section 5 of the Amendment -- to restore legal personhood to unborn children and thus guarantee their right to life.[3] In order to do this, the bill declares that Congress has found "that the life of each human being begins at conception."[4]

The Human Life Bill approach is acceptable, but it is not necessary to rely on the Fourteenth Amendment. There are other bases for Congressional action. The one I prefer is simply to premise the statute on Congress' inherent power to make national policy. This is recognized by Article I, Section 8 of the Constitution which states that "Congress shall have Power...to provide for the...general Welfare of the United States" and that it may do this and carry out its other powers and all the powers of the national government by means of "all Laws which shall be necessary and proper." I have shown how individual virtue relates to the common good ("general welfare" is just another term for common good). Thus, the promotion of virtue is as legitimate an object of national legislation as it is state or local. This means that it is appropriate for Congress to legislate against abortion out of a consideration for individual virtue. It also can do so because abortion harms the common good. The famous constitutional decision of *McCulloch v. Maryland*[5] affirms, at least indirectly, the existence of this power to make national policy and holds that it is broad:

> ...the government of the Union, though limited in its powers, is supreme within its sphere of action. This would seem to result, necessarily, from its nature. It

> is the government of all, its powers are delegated by all; it represents all, and acts for all.[6]
>
> To have prescribed the means by which government should, in all future time, execute its powers would have been to change, entirely, the character of the instrument [the Constitution], and give it the properties of a legal code.[7]
>
> We admit, as all must admit, that the powers of the government are limited, and that its limits are not to be transcended. But we think the sound construction of the constitution must allow to the national legislature that discretion, with respect to the means by which the powers it confers are to be carried into execution, which will enable that body to perform the high duties assigned to it, in the manner most beneficial to the people.[8]

A third basis for Congressional abortion legislation is the commerce power. Article I, Section 8 gives Congress the power to regulate interstate and foreign commerce. This provision has resulted in a number of federal court decisions which have asserted the existence of a national police power (i.e., the power of Congress to close the channels of interstate commerce to goods and transactions determined by it to be harmful to the health, morals, safety, or welfare of the nation).[9] Thus, federal law now prohibits or regulates a broad range of activities.[10] The Supreme Court has permitted Congress to move into more and more areas of activity, particularly since the New Deal.[11] Congress could base a legal prohibition of abortion on the commerce power for a number of reasons: the abortion facilities in a particular locale are available to women who travel interstate; at least some of the instruments or other items used in abortion procedures -- or the materials they are made from -- are shipped interstate; and the physicians and their supporting personnel who man abortion facilities, in many cases, will have received their training in other states. If one thinks that these considerations are not sufficient to place the abortion activity "in interstate commerce", he should consider the Supreme Court's decisions in *Katzenbach v.*

McClung[12] and *Maryland v. Wirtz*.[13] In *McClung*, the Court held that a restaurant located on a state highway, eleven blocks from an interstate highway and somewhat farther from railroad and bus stations, which got 46 percent of its food from a local supplier who had procured it out of state, was engaged in interstate commerce to enough of a degree for it to be covered by the 1964 Civil Rights Act (which was premised on the commerce power). In *Wirtz*, it sustained Congress' extension of the provisions of the Fair Labor Standards Act (also based on the commerce power) to hospitals, nursing homes, and educational institutions (both public and private). Its reasons were that these institutions are major users of goods brought in from other states and job actions by their employees would interrupt the flow of these goods across state lines.[14]

Even though the Court has officially sanctioned the exercise of police power by Congress on the basis of the commerce clause, the clear stretching of the notion of "commerce" has meant that it has, *de facto*, recognized the existence of an independent national police power. This is, implicitly, an acknowledgement of Congress' inherent national policymaking power.

The final possible basis for national legislation is the Article I, Section 8 provision which gives Congress the authority "[t]o define and punish...Offenses against the Law of Nations." I believe that "Law of Nations" does not mean simply the obligations established by the agreement of various nations (i.e., what we today call "international law"). It also refers to a notion of natural law. (The term "law of nations" is the English translation of "jus gentium", which was used by such thinkers as Cicero and St. Thomas Aquinas to mean the common rules and norms which were found in the laws of all nations.)[15] It is true that the notion of "law of nations" had undergone a change in Hugo Grotius' time before the writing of the Constitution. It came to be regarded as meaning something similar to the present notion of "international law" above. It was for the first time viewed as being based on will and not just on what is discerned by reason as representing the rational and social nature of man, as had been the case.[16] The break with the previous idea of the "law of nations" was not total, however. As was made clear in Chapter Nine, the Framers intended that, to some extent, this idea be embodied in the Constitution. Thus, Congress could declare that abortion is contrary to the "jus gentium" -- as is definitely indicated by my discussion in this book and particularly in Chapter Nine -- and prohibit and punish it on those grounds.

Moreover, even the newer notion of the "law of nations" could be viewed as permitting such Congressional legislation. The Grotian theory did not reject natural law. It simply regarded the "law of nations" as being separate from it. Nevertheless, this "law of nations" might, in substance, be closely related to the natural law, especially when nations decide to give force to natural law principles.[17] Thus, Congress could enact the opposition of the natural law to abortion into positive law.

Even if one were to view the notion of "law of nations" as meaning nothing more than the law of international agreements and customary international law, it would still afford Congress a basis for legislating against abortion. Congress can decide to give the force of law to the provisions of an international agreement, such as the American Convention on Human Rights of 1969 -- which the U.S. has not yet become a party to --, which specifically protects the right to life of the unborn child.

What should be the substance of federal anti-abortion legislation? It may take the approach of the Human Life Bill, establishing the personhood of the unborn child in order to determine that he is entitled to the constitutional protection of his right to life. This does not require that Congress actually declare that human life begins at fertilization. Legal personhood has, of course, been conferred on entirely man-made entities, such as corporations, so there is no obstacle to Congress' conferring it on the child *in utero*.

A second approach that Congress could take would be to simply declare that it is adopting a national policy against abortion. It can declare in the preamble to the statute that it premises this on the compelling public interest to protect human life or potential human life. Its power to do this is not contingent on its making a finding that the child *in utero* actually is "human" because the government has an equally compelling public interest to protect "actual human life" and "potential human life." This is so because, regardless of what one thinks about whether the unborn child is *actually* human, no one doubts that he is at least potentially so and that he will indeed become actually so if all progresses normally. Indeed, Congress may assert a compelling public interest against abortion even without at all getting into the matter of actual *or* potential human life. It can simply make a finding that abortion seriously harms the common good in other ways. Congress thus has the authority to legislate here as much as it had the authority to protect the snail darter as an endangered animal species.

I believe, however, that a statute which finds that the unborn child is a *biological* person from fertilization, as the Human Life Bill before its final version in the U.S. Senate did, is preferable. As has been shown, the evidence for this is overwhelming. Such a statute would then serve an educational function for the public which could help to wear down the "anti-life" mentality. The proposed bill in Appendix B makes this finding of biological personhood.

The Human Life Bill approach of not specifically prohibiting abortion is correct. The statute should just establish the new national anti-abortion policy and give to the states and Congress the authority to enact further legislation to effectuate it. It thus gives the states time to enact specific prohibitions against abortion, with the understanding that if they do not Congress will.

This proposal, then, addresses the principle-expediency problem spoken of in Chapter Nine. Its purpose is to put forth -- actually, to reassert, since, as has been stated, they are already part of our constitutional law -- the constitutional and moral principles involved in abortion. While thus acknowledging the "principle" part of the equation, it also takes account of the "expediency" part by recognizing, in its withholding of an actual legal prohibition, that attitudes will have to change before such a prohibition can be put in place and effectively enforced. The educative value of the statute itself, supplemented by continued and even accelerated educational efforts by the anti-abortion movement, will make it easier for the states to adopt prohibitory statutes and will also result, I believe, in a reduction of the number of abortions, legal and illegal.

It seems to me that these ensuing state prohibitory statutes -- or a federal statute -- will have to be of the criminal sort. This is because, as Aristotle states (mentioned in Chapter Nine), the threat of punishment is needed for most people to get them to comply and to teach morality. Moreover, also as mentioned, the only means our tradition has given to the state to promote morality has been through the criminal law. Also, it does not seem that there is any other way of sustaining a complete or almost complete prohibition of abortion. The states could *supplement* the criminal law with such measures as a permanent, mandatory license revocation of physician-abortionists and civil court orders, subject to contempt proceedings, to compel hospitals to stop performing abortions. Over time, these could perhaps be relied on more than the criminal law.

New state criminal abortion statutes are almost certain to contain exceptions at first, as the early Hyde Amendments did. Some states are likely to have more sweeping statutes at the beginning than other states. An initial approach that the states could take would be to exploit the leeway for restrictions mentioned in Chapter Two that *Doe v. Bolton* seems to leave them. With sustained pressure on state legislatures by the pro-life movement and the development of new attitudes respecting life these will be eliminated in time. It will be much easier to tighten these exceptions when written into statutes than when in a constitutional amendment. If the states delay too long in acting or do not enact strong enough laws Congress can enact nationwide prohibitions.

Is there any reason to adopt a constitutional amendment at all? An amendment may be appropriate at some point in the future -- after abortion has generally been recriminalized and the "anti-life" ethic has eroded substantially -- which expressly guarantees constitutional protection to the right to life of all innocent human beings, from fertilization to natural death (thereby addressing related issues such as euthanasia and infanticide). Again, this is already protected by our Constitution, but the amendment would serve a declaratory role like the first ten amendments. Such an amendment would *expressly* recognize as part of our fundamental national law that which implicitly already exists. The fact that it will come in the future, after the statute has long since been in place, will mean that it has not been used as the vehicle for reversing the policy established by the Court. Practically speaking, however, such an amendment is not politically possible now.

There are other subsidiary steps Congress can take to attack abortion while the states proceed to reenact criminal statutes. It can use its commerce power to prohibit the sending of items used in abortion procedures and of all materials addressed to independent abortion facilities in interstate commerce. It can also use this power to prohibit the making of interstate advertising arrangements for abortion facilities. It can also cut off all federal funds for medical schools which teach abortion techniques, as was attempted with the Hatfield bill in 1982. Another action would be for Congress to cut off Hill-Burton Act funds for hospitals which permit their facilities to be used for abortions.

The important question that all of this raises, of course, is this: Is Congress not infringing on the Court's rightful powers in enacting a statute which reverses the rule of *Wade* and *Bolton*? The answer to this is flatly *no*. It has been shown in this book that these decisions were without a basis in the Constitution. In fact, what I said about Blackstone and the Fourteenth Amendment indicates that they were a *violation* because they stopped the states from protecting the unborn child's right to life which the Constitution guarantees. They violate it also by ignoring the separation of powers. It cannot be disputed that *Wade* and *Bolton* created a new national policy on abortion. As has been said, however, the Constitution places national policymaking power in Congress, not the Court. The Court, of course, tried to justify its policymaking in these cases as being an exercise of its authority to interpret the Constitution. What has been shown, however, clearly demonstrates this to have been a subterfuge. As regards Congressional policymaking, the Court's role is essentially limited to stopping or restricting the effectuation of a policy by the executive. It is not free to remove any particular subject matter from the realm of Congressional policymaking. Whenever it acts on the effectuation, it is bound to do so strictly within the context of a legitimate case and controversy. (On this latter point, *Wade* and *Bolton* might fail because in neither case was there a completed prosecution under the states' statutes and, in fact, there was no likelihood that the women plaintiffs Roe and Doe or any woman seeking an abortion would be prosecuted. Moreover, it appears that neither plaintiff was even pregnant when the trial courts reached their judgments.)

Assuming, however, that *Wade* and *Bolton* were valid cases and controversies, we are led to the next point. This is that although the Court's judgments in these cases are valid and binding on the particular parties that were before it -- for Congress to attempt to reverse these would truly be an infringement on judicial power --, the constitutional rules they enunciate are not final. Professor Edward S. Corwin speaks about this idea of "finality" (which was picked up by Senator Helms in the speech referred to in Chapter Nine):

> ...while the [Supreme] Court can and must decide *cases* according to its own independent view of the *Constitution*, it does not in so doing fix the Constitution for an indefinite future.[18]

Corwin turns to Lincoln to explain the meaning of this for the other branches of the government. Lincoln believed that an interpretation of the Constitution by the Court for the purpose of deciding a case, besides being binding on the parties, was entitled to "very high respect" from the other branches. Nevertheless, he went on to state the following:

> "The candid citizen must confess that if the policy of the Government upon vital questions affecting the whole people is to be irrevocably fixed by decisions of the Supreme Court, the instant they are made in ordinary litigation between parties in personal actions, the people will have ceased to be their own rulers, having to that extent practically resigned their Government into the hands of that eminent tribunal. Nor is there in this any assault upon the Court or the judges. It is a duty from which they may not shrink to decide cases properly brought before them, and it is no fault of theirs if others seek to turn their decisions to political purposes."[19]

Corwin concludes the following from this:

> The idea...that a pronouncement of unconstitutionality by the Court fixes the *meaning of the Constitution* as against the national legislative power, though an inescapable inference from the Hamiltonian, *juristic* conception of judicial review, has never assumed a sufficiently authoritative shape to put it beyond the reach of important challenge.[20]

Corwin means that national policymaking, as I have emphasized, is in the hands of Congress and as political exigencies occur, it can enact new policies even if they are not in accord with the Court's interpretations of the Constitution. The Court's decisions are not "final" in the sense that they stop Congress from doing this. When the Court makes such an interpretation it does so only if it is necessary in the adjudication of a particular case. Congress must be guided by these interpretations and must even give them great weight, but it is still free to go ahead and make the policies it deems appropriate.[21] Indeed, the concept of popular government demands that it be free to carry out its policymaking function without encumbrance.

In the above passage from Corwin, the "Hamiltonian" of "juristic" conception of judicial review is seen in Federalist 78. Hamilton seems to state there that the courts act on the *legislative* power when they void statutes.[22] This is also the notion expressed by Coke's dictum in *Dr. Bonham's Case*.[23] This is today commonly understood to be what occurs. Corwin says, however, that this conception has not triumphed. Other modern authorities, in essence, also agree. These include Justice Sutherland in his opinion for the Supreme Court in *Adkins v. Children's Hospital*,[24] Professor Emeritus W. Howard Mann of the law school at the State University of New York at Buffalo, and Professor Raoul Berger of Harvard Law School to whom I turn now.

Berger believes that Corwin is incorrect in that the latter does not seem to be willing to clearly concede that the Supreme Court is the "final interpreter of the Constitution."[25] Nevertheless, he does accept Corwin's idea that Congress may make public policy in an area even if in doing so it acts against a previous decision of the Court. He sympathetically quotes Professor Henry M. Hart, Jr., who says the following:

> "The political branches...retain at all times the crucial ability to force the Court to reexamine in new contexts the validity of the constitutional positions it has previously taken."[26]

Berger goes on to explain how his notion of "finality" differs from Corwin's:

> Reinterpretation [of the Constitution][27] by the other branches may be justified...not because those branches are free to depart from "respect," but as a response to exigencies that no longer may be denied...The "bonds" of a judicial construction can then be relaxed by a preliminary legislative interpretation because circumstances demand that the Court be enabled "to reexamine in new contexts the validity of constitutional positions [it] has previously taken." Judicious reinterpretation by the other branches does not, in this light, mark a deviation from "respect" but rather constitutes a necessary part of the constitutional machinery whereby the Court is better enabled to fulfill its own continuing function.[28]

Berger's position, then, differs from Corwin's in that he is not as willing to see judicial review as something which just acts on individual cases and does not restrict legislative power *per se*. Both men seem to view Congress' perceived need to exercise its legislative or national policymaking function as the rationale for its acting against judicial precedent. Berger, however, believes that Congress cannot legitimately do this as a means of overturning the decision, but in order to compel the Court to reexamine it.

This "finality" argument can be related to abortion in that Congress may create a new public policy about it -- taking the place of the one fashioned by the Court -- because of errors in the Court's understanding of it (e.g., its apparent inattention to the facts which indicate that the unborn child is human) or a need to respond to problems caused by legalization which suggest that it was not desirable (e.g., the threat to the physical and mental health of women from abortion and the harm to the common good caused by the erosion of the "sanctity of life" ethic).

Are there historical precedents for Congressional resistance to the Supreme Court? There have been several instances of the political branches standing up to the Court. Berkeley law professor Jesse H. Choper tells us that "Supreme Court abrogations of majority-sponsored activities have been the primary source of retaliation, real and seriously threatened, by the national political branches...against the federal judiciary."[29] We are all familiar with the major instances of presidential refusal to carry out judicial mandates: Jackson's refusal to block the Cherokee removal from Georgia[30] and Lincoln's refusal to acknowledge the writ of *habeas corpus* issued in *Ex parte Merryman*.[31] The most frequently used Congressional tactic to resist the Supreme Court has been the threat of curtailing its jurisdiction. Professor Choper points out that in the nineteenth century seventeen attempts were made to do this, although only one, involving the Court's review of Congressional Reconstruction policy after the Civil War, was successful.[32] In this century, there have been attempts to curtail the Supreme Court's jurisdiction over internal security cases in the 1950s, reapportionment decisions in the 1960s, and public school desegregation in the 1970s.[33]

More to the point of my proposal, Congress has attempted to circumvent or override Supreme Court mandates with simple legislation on a number of occasions. One occurred in 1868 when the House of Representatives, fearing that the Court would strike down its entire Reconstruction policy, passed a bill prohibiting the Court from declaring any act of Congress unconstitutional without a vote of two-thirds of the Justices. The Senate did not go along, however, possibly because it believed that more than two-thirds of the Justices would vote against Reconstruction.[34] In this century, there have been similar attempts although they have not always been direct. One involved Congressional child labor legislation before the New Deal. Congress tried a different legislative approach to this after the Court had struck down the previous one not long before. The Court, however, invalidated the second one also.[35] (Congress finally succeeded in legislating against child labor during the New Deal era of the next decade after the Court's personnel and positions on social and economic legislation had changed.) Another was the Omnibus Crime Control and Safe Streets Act of 1968,[36] which was aimed, to some extent, at modifying the Supreme Court's *Miranda v. Arizona*[37] (involving confessions given by criminal suspects who had not been informed of their rights by the police) and *U.S. v. Wade*[38] (extending the right of counsel to suspects placed in police lineups) rulings. Another was the Education Act Amendments of 1974 which addressed the federal courts' use of busing to achieve school desegregation. Others -- involving Congress, but not actually legislation -- occurred in 1947, when a House committee formally recommended -- the full House narrowly voted not to go along -- that no funds be appropriated for the purpose of carrying out the Court's mandate in *U.S. v. Lovett*[39] (requiring the government to pay the salaries of federal employees who a committee had found engaged in "subversive activity") and in 1975 when the Senate directed the comptroller general to reject a subpoena from a U.S. *district* court in Florida that was trying former U.S. Senator Edward J. Gurney for bribery and perjury.[40] Finally, there was the Congressional legislation in the 1960s and 1970s on civil rights and voting rights -- which Galebach used as his basis for proposing the Human Life Bill -- which extended the protections of the three Civil War amendments beyond the Court's interpretation and even altered that interpretation (and was upheld by the Court).[41]

I used the term "resistance," but, strictly speaking, not all of the above were examples of Congress *resisting* the Court. Many were simply cases of Congress carrying out its legitimate policymaking function, even though this put it in opposition to the Court. The Court had gone beyond *its* rightful powers by trying to infringe upon that function. My proposal also involves, as mentioned, policymaking and so also does not constitute "resistance" (which implies intruding into the Court's proper domain).

If the Court's rightful prerogatives are not to be infringed upon at all, however, it will have to be permitted to review the proposed statute (barring, that is, legislation removing the subject matter from the Court's jurisdiction, which is within Congress' authority). Can we be certain that the Court will uphold the statute? No, we cannot be. We can rely, however, on the historical fact that the Court at times has reversed itself. Sometimes it has almost literally overturned prior decisions, as in such matters as racial segregation, child labor (as indicated), and school flag saluting requirements. This has generally occurred, however, only after a substantial period of time had elapsed after the original case and the Court's personnel had drastically changed (the flag salute cases were an exception). More typically, the Court will go in a different direction by modifying or distinguishing a prior decision or decisions. This has occurred even when the lapse of time between cases is not too great. A good example was the *Dennis v. U.S.* and *Yates v. U.S.* decisions in the 1950s, which involved Smith Act prosecutions of members of the U.S. Communist Party. It is this latter type of "overturn" which is the more likely possibility on abortion (e.g., permitting *some* restrictions on abortion), at least until there is a greater change in the complexion of the Court. The fact that a statute such as the one proposed is a federal instead of a state one might make a difference. The Court historically has granted greater leeway to Congress than state legislatures. (The willingness to defer to Congress in the abortion area may have been seen by the 1980 Hyde Amendment decision, *Harris v. MacRae.*[42]) Perhaps another factor is that the statute would not be a criminal one and will not penalize anyone. (The state criminal statutes passed pursuant to it might have a harder time clearing the Court.)

I believe, however, that the likelihood of a federal statute being upheld is going to depend most of all on how determined Congress is to make a policy against abortion *despite* the Court. If Congress makes this determination clear and, in effect, challenges the Court, the Court may permit the statute to stand. This is so, particularly, because of the fact that most of the Justices presently on the Court are not ideologues, and may swing. The Court historically has backed down when faced with a determined political majority, spearheaded by the other branches -- although it has often taken time.[43] My analysis of the public opinion on abortion in Chapter One shows that most Americans do not support *Wade* and *Bolton*. This opposition for the most part has not asserted itself, although the Court may be aware of it from recent election results. The task for the anti-abortion movement is clear: it must galvanize this opposition and motivate members of Congress to overcome their customary reluctance to challenge the Court.

What if the Court should invalidate the statute? The answer is that Congress should simply reenact it with an even more insistent statement in the preamble that it is within Congress' policymaking authority to do so. Again, this would not be an intrusion into the Court's prerogatives, but a rightful assertion of Congress'. I am not suggesting that such a Congressional challenge to the Court be undertaken frequently or for insignificant reasons. It is justified only when the Court has rendered a clearly unconstitutional decision or grossly and manifestly exceeded its rightful powers. Otherwise, the Court would be seriously weakened.

If the Court should repeatedly refuse to uphold Congressional anti-abortion legislation -- which is unlikely -- Congress should consider further measures which are within the province of its powers. It can, for example, make use of its appropriation power. It cannot constitutionally cut the salaries of sitting Justices, nor should it imperil the judicial branch by freezing all of its funds. What it *can* do is to sharply reduce its appropriation for operating expenses and the hiring of law clerks, secretaries, and other personnel. It should also consider impeaching recalcitrant individual Justices, as Professor Berger has recommended.[44] I have mentioned that Congress can withdraw jurisdiction over the subject matter from the Court, though this could be counterproductive because abortion would then be dealt with by the highest state courts where the results, in many cases, are likely to be equally unconstitutional and undesirable.

Another alternative available would be for Congress simply to expressly exercise the function of constitutional interpretation, correcting the Court's misinterpretation in *Wade* and *Bolton* and give it the power of law. This should only be done, however, if the situation were to become dire because it definitely would be entering into the Court's province. The Framers appear to have reserved constitutional interpretation and judicial review of statutes for the courts,[45] but the departmental right of constitutional construction that was discussed -- although rejected -- early in our Republic stands as precedent for such an action.[46]

Invalidation of the statute or not, I favor at least one constitutional change that could go a long way toward curbing judicial excesses. There should be a set term of appointment for each federal judgeship. Congressman Henry Hyde introduced a proposed constitutional amendment that would set Supreme Court appointments at fifteen years. This is a desirable length for every level of the federal courts. It should also be added that no individual should be eligible for reappointment to the same level of court. This would be a term long enough to protect judicial independence, but also short enough to dispel a judge's notion that he has absolute or near absolute power.[47]

Appendix B
A Model Federal Anti-Abortion Statute

A BILL

To establish as a policy of the United States of America that the lives of unborn children shall be given legal protection and that human abortion procedures shall be prohibited by law.

SHORT TITLE

Section 1. This Bill may be cited as the "Federal Anti-Abortion Policy Bill."

PREAMBLE

Section 1. The Congress has authority to enact the foregoing policy on the basis of the following:
(a) Its inherent power to make public policy for the United States, as recognized in Article I, Section 8 of the Constitution and by numerous judicial decisions;

(b) Its power, under Article I, Section 8 of the Constitution to regulate commerce among the several states; (c) Its power, under Section 5 of the Fourteenth Amendment to the Constitution, to enforce by appropriate legislation, the provisions of such Amendment; and (d) Its power, pursuant to Article I, Section 8 of the Constitution, to define and punish offenses against the Law of Nations.

Section 2. The Congress finds that the general welfare of the United States is seriously harmed by our present *de facto* policy of legalized abortion in the following ways: (a) Since both the best scientific and metaphysical-ethical evidence indicates that unborn children are *human persons*, the United States is not protecting this group of its citizens as the general welfare -- which is concerned both with the good of individuals, as well as the whole nation -- requires; (b) The nation is suffering a substantial loss of productive citizens, many of whom would make important contributions to its welfare; (c) Since our constitutional and legal background granted protection to the right to life and other lesser rights of unborn children, to continue to deny that protection at present is to disregard that tradition and to allow a precedent to stand which could provide a basis for the undermining of other rights of other groups of citizens; (d) Scientific, demographic, sociological, and psychological evidence indicates that there is no likelihood that abortion provides clear benefits for either the nation, its parts, or individuals; (e) Scientific and psychological evidence indicates that abortion can result in harm, sometimes serious, to the physical, mental, and reproductive health of women and to physical harm to subsequent offspring, and that such harm has become a greater and more widespread public health problem during the period of our present *de facto* policy, with the result of a temporary or in some cases permanent loss of productive citizens to the nation; (f) It has given rise to a professional abortion industry whose practices threaten the rights, health, and well-being of pregnant women and the nation and its various communities by violating or circumventing its laws on such matters as the disposal of unborn children's bodies; (g) It has led to a devaluation of other innocent human life, such as the elderly and handicapped post-partum children; (h) It has placed the United States in opposition to the position of important international agreements, such as the American Convention on Human Rights, which harms our prestige in the international community; and (i) It has undermined, to some degree, the long-prevalent norms of sexual morality among our people and, as a result, has made the development of sexual morality in individuals more difficult, which has in turn made more difficult the development of the civic virtue our nation needs.[1,2]

DEFINITIONS

Section 1. The following definitions of terms used in the text of this Bill shall apply:

(a) "Unborn children" means all human beings from fertilization until live birth.

(b) "Person" means an individual human being or natural person.

(c) "Establishment" means any corporation, partnership, proprietorship, government body, organization, association, or other cooperative activity involving two or more persons, whether established for a temporary or indefinite period of time.

(d) "Abortion" and "abortion procedures" means all surgical and other means undertaken with the intention to interrupt or end a human pregnancy, except for the purpose of saving the life of the unborn child or children.

(e) "Performance" means the carrying out of surgical or other medical procedures with the intention of causing abortion.

(f) "Procurement" means the carrying out of any activities with the intention of arranging, assisting in, causing to be brought about, counseling, facilitating, or providing abortion procedures.

(g) "Prohibit" means the forbidding by law of the performance or procurement of all abortion procedures, except as otherwise provided by this Bill.

(h) "Nation" means the United States of America.

(i) "Parts" (of the nation) and "communities" means all political subdivisions and geographical areas within the United States.

(j) "Policy" means the duly enacted legislation of the Congress of the United States which has the force of law, pursuant to which the Congress may enact criminal and/or civil penalties.

(k) "Federal" means a policy or legislation of the national government of the United States, duly enacted by the Congress, to apply to the several States, the District of Columbia, all Territories and Commonwealths of the United States, and all other lands under the direct or indirect control or trusteeship of the United States, or about whose affairs the Congress has the authority to legislate.

(l) "Public" means operated by, sustained by, or related or associated to an organ of government.

(m) "Commercial" means operating for the purpose of acquiring a profit.

(n) "Non-profit" means not operating for the purpose of acquiring a profit. This includes charitable, philanthropic, service, educational, political, and all other establishments that do not operate for profit.

(o) "Fertilization" means the point at which the nucleus of the human sperm unites with the nucleus of the human ovum.

(p) "Implement" means the carrying out or putting into effect of the policy herein established.

FEDERAL POLICY ON ABORTION

Section 1. It shall be the policy of the United States to prohibit the performance and procurement of abortion procedures. This policy shall apply to all persons and establishments, whether public, private, non-profit, or commercial, which are engaged in the performance or procurement of abortion procedures, or operating, in whole or in part, for this purpose.

Section 2. It shall be the policy of the United States to prohibit the production, disbursement, interstate or foreign transport, and promotion of equipment, materials, or drugs which have as their sole and primary purpose the performance and procurement of abortion procedures.

Section 3. The right to life, as provided in our constitutional and legal background and the Fifth and Fourteenth Amendments to the Constitution, shall apply to all persons, including unborn children, from the moment of fertilization.

Section 4. The right to life shall not be deprived an unborn child or children under any circumstances or by any person(s) or establishment(s). Unborn children are entitled to have their lives protected by law to the same extent as other persons. Provided that, nothing in this Bill shall prohibit the setting up of different categories of criminal or civil offenses or different or lesser punishments or liability for the taking, assisting in the taking, or aiding, abetting, or counseling of the taking, of unborn and post-partum persons.

AUTHORITY TO LEGISLATE RESPECTING ABORTION

Section 1. The Congress and the several States shall have the power to enact all laws, both criminal and civil, for the purpose of implementing or enforcing the provisions of this Bill, notwithstanding any existing legislation or judicial decisions, whether federal, state, territorial, or local.

SEPARABILITY

Section 1. If any provision of this Bill once enacted, or the application of such provision to any person, establishment, or circumstance, shall be held invalid, the remainder of it, or the application of such provision to persons, establishments, or circumstances other than those as to which it is held invalid, shall not be affected thereby.

Notes

NOTE FOR INTRODUCTION

1. Jaffa, Harry V., *Thomism and Aristotelianism: A Study of the Commentary by Thomas Aquinas on the Nicomachean Ethics* (Chicago: U. of Chicago Press, 1952), p. 193. (Hereinafter cited as "Jaffa I.") His quotation is from Winston Churchill's address at the Mid-century Convocation of the Massachusetts Institute of Technology as printed in *The New York Times*, April 1, 1949.

CHAPTER ONE NOTES

1. Noonan, John T., Jr., *A Private Choice: Abortion in America in the Seventies* (New York: The Free Press, 1979), p. 1. (Hereinafter cited as "Noonan II.")

2. I use the term "liberalizing" to mean changing the very restrictive statutes many of which dated to the last century to permit abortion for limited reasons. I use the term "reform" -- e.g., I refer to the "reform statutes" -- in the same way. This is to be distinguished from "legalization"

or outright repeal of the statutes to permit abortion for any reason until some point in pregnancy, usually at or near the end of the second trimester.

3. (New York: Vanguard Press, 1933).

4. Brennan, William, *Medical Holocausts: Exterminative Medicine in Nazi Germany and Contemporary America* (Houston: Nordland, 1980), pp. 81-83.

5. Grisez, Germain, *Abortion: the Myths, the Realities, and the Arguments* (New York: Corpus Books, 1970, 1972), p. 226.

6. (St. Louis: C. V. Mosby, 1936).

7. Taussig, pp. 29-30, cited in Brennan, p. 83.

8. *Ibid.*, p. 396 cited in Brennan, p. 84.

9. *Ibid.*, p. 422, cited in Brennan, p. 84.

10. *The Abortion Problem:* Proceedings of the conference held under the auspices of the National Committee on Maternal Health (Baltimore: Williams & Wilkins, 1944).

11. Calderone, Mary Steichen, M.D., ed., *Abortion in the United States*. A Conference Sponsored by the Planned Parenthood Federation of America, Inc. at Arden House and The New York Academy of Medicine (New York: Hoeber-Harper, 1958), pp. 6-7. Calderone cites Taylor writing in *The Abortion Problem*.

12. K.D. Whitehead has shown that far from being viewed as eliminating the need for abortion, contemporary promoters of sex education have viewed sex education as a necessary complement to legalized abortion in order to permit the former, as well as their vision of the ideal sexually free society, to gain widespread moral acceptance. He also points out that the most ardent pro-abortion activitists have often been the main advocates of sex education. See Whitehead, K. D., *Agenda for the "Sexual Revolution": Abortion, Contraception, Sex Education and Related Evils* (Chicago: Franciscan Herald Press, 1981), pp. 59-64.

13. SIECUS has been one of the main developers and promoters of classroom sex education in this country. Upon reading on about the conclusions and recommendations of the conference, the point that Whitehead makes above (note 12) may thus seem

to the reader to be borne out in the person of Dr. Calderone even though he does not mention her as an example.

14. Calderone, p. 181.

15. *Ibid.*, pp. 182-183.

16. *Ibid.*, pp. 183-184.

17. (New York: Julian Press, 1954).

18. (New York: Alfred A. Knopf, 1957).

19. Gebhard, Paul H. *et al.*, *Pregnancy, Birth and Abortion* (New York: Harper, 1958). These authors finished the book for Kinsey after his death.

20. Schwartz, Michael C., personal correspondence, June 8, 1981. Mr. Schwartz is Director of Public Affairs for the Milwaukee-based Catholic League for Religious and Civil Rights and has written on abortion and related questions.

21. Williams, pp. 218-219.

22. *Ibid.*, p. 222.

23. *Ibid.*, pp. 222-223.

24. *Roe v. Wade*, 410 U.S. 113, 164.

25. Williams, p. 223.

26. *Ibid.*, p. 225.

27. *Ibid.*, p. 33.

28. The ACLU did not file its own brief in the cases. Professor Norman Dorsen of New York University Law School, one of the ACLU's top constitutional lawyers, is listed on the appellant's brief in the *Wade* case (i.e., those challenging the Texas abortion statute) as "Of Counsel." Professor Dorsen informed me that he was "on the *Wade* case" and that "[t]he main ACLU involvement" in both *Wade* and *Bolton* "was in the nature of general advice." He also wrote me that *Bolton* was argued before the Supreme Court by Margie Pitts Hames, then a leader of the Georgia Civil Liberties Union (the ACLU's affiliate for that state, wherein the *Bolton* case arose) and soon

thereafter a member of the ACLU National Board. On the appellants' brief in *Bolton* were two lawyers from the ACLU Southern Regional Office. (Information gotten from correspondence with Professor Dorsen, March 2, 1982.)

29. The full list of organizations whose names appear on briefs in the cases is as follows:

Against the laws:

American Association of Planned Parenthood Physicians
American Association of University Women
American Civil Liberties Union (joined *Bolton* appellants' brief)
American College of Obstetricians and Gynecologists
American Ethical Union
American Friends Service Committee
American Humanist Association
American Jewish Congress
American Medical Women's Association
American Psychiatric Association
American Public Health Association
Board of Christian Social Concerns of the United Methodist Church
California Committee to Legalize Abortion
Episcopal Diocese of New York
National Abortion Action Coalition
National Legal Program on Health Problems of the Poor
National Organization for Women
National Organization for Women, South Bay (Calif.) Chapter
National Welfare Rights Organization
National Women's Conference of the American Ethical Union
New Women Lawyers
New York Academy of Medicine
Planned Parenthood Federation of America
Planned Parenthood of Atlanta (PPFA affiliate--joined *Bolton* appellants' brief)
Professional Women's Caucus
State Communities Aid Association
Union of American Hebrew Congregations
Unitarian Universalist Association
Unitarian Universalist Women's Federation
United Church of Christ
Women's Alliance of the First Unitarian Church of Dallas
Women's Health and Abortion Project, Inc.
Young Women's Christian Association, National Board
Zero Population Growth, Inc.

For the laws:

Americans United for Life
Celebrate Life
Columbiettes, New York State Council
League for Infants, Fetuses, and the Elderly (LIFE)
Minnesota Citizens Concerned for Life
National Right to Life Committee
Texas Association of Diocesian Attorneys
Women Concerned for the Unborn Child
Women for the Unborn

Briefs were also filed or joined by the appellants, the states whose laws were under attack, several other states, and a number of individuals.

30. Major works emphasizing this are: Bentley, Arthur F., *The Process of Government* (Chicago: Univ. of Chicago Press, 1908); Key, V. O., Jr., *Politics, Parties, and Pressure Groups* (N.Y.: Thomas Y. Crowell, 1947); and Truman, David B., *The Governmental Process: Political Interests and Public Opinion* (N.Y.: Alfred A. Knopf, 1951).

31. Tocqueville, Alexis de, *Democracy in America*, Vol. Two, Second Book. Tr. by Henry Reeve. Rev. ed. (N.Y. & London: Cooperative Publication Society, 1900), p. 115.

32. *Ibid.*, Vol. One, pp. 191-192.

33. I use the term "moral" in this paragraph loosely to refer to people being motivated to act on the issue because they believe that their position is just. Whether it actually is in accord with natural justice is another matter. I am also aware of the fact that some of the groups or members of the groups which sought to have the statutes declared unconstitutional may not have been motivated primarily by "moral" concerns. For example, some obstetrician-gynecologists stood to gain economically from legalized abortion.

34. Tocqueville, Vol. One, p. 192.

35. *Ibid.*, Vol. Two, Second Book, p. 118.

36. Even prior to the liberalization of any of the laws in the 1960s, many hospitals had boards which had to approve requests for abortions which were sought under the then very restrictive exception clause in the state statutes. The early literature is full of claims that the boards often went beyond the specific exception provisions.

37. Finkbine, Sherri, "The Lesser of Two Evils," in Guttmacher, Alan, M.D., ed., *The Case for Legalized Abortion Now* (Berkeley, Calif: Diablo Press, 1967), pp. 16-23. (Hereinafter cited as "Guttmacher II.")

38. See various issues of the *Times* between July 30 and August 30, 1962.

39. See *Time*, August 3, 1962, p. 30 and *Newsweek*, August 6, 1962, p. 52.

40. Lader, Lawrence, *Abortion* (Indianapolis: Bobbs-Merrill, 1966), p. 13. (Hereinafter referred to as "Lader I.")

41. *The New York Times*, May 23, 1962, p. 35, col. 5.

42. Grisez, pp. 350-351, quoting the statement as cited in "The Churches Speak," 1 *Trends* (1967), p. 16.

43. *Model Penal Code*. Philadelphia: American Law Institute, 1962, pp. 189-190, cited in Sarvis, Betty & Rodman, Hyman, *The Abortion Controversy* (N.Y.: Columbia U. Press, 1973), p. 43.

44. *The New York Times*, April 30, 1962, p. 55, col. 3.

45. Lader I, pp. 146-147. In 1961, a reform bill went through the New Hampshire legislature, but was vetoed by the governor. The California reform bill was also pushed for awhile that year in the legislature. In New York, a bill modifying the law passed the legislature during the Dewey administration, but Governor Dewey vetoed it. (See Lader I, p. 145.)

46. Sarvis and Rodman, p. 6.

47. *The New York Times*, Dec. 14, 1964, p. 48, col. 5.

48. Nathanson, Bernard N., M.D. (with Richard N. Ostling), *Aborting America* (Garden City, N.Y.: Doubleday), p. 30; *Time*, Sept. 17, 1965, p. 82.

49. Lader I, p. 148.

50. Nathanson, pp. 30-31; *Time*, Sept. 17, 1965, p. 82.

51. *The New York Times*, Nov. 19, 1965, p. 15, col. 3.

52. Lader I, p. 169.

53. Dorsen, Norman, ACLU "Campaign for Choice" membership appeal letter, *circa* 1978, p. 3.

54. *Western Reserve Law Review,* No. 2 (Dec. 1965). It was later expanded and republished as a book, *Abortion and the Law,* edited by David T. Smith (Cleveland: Case Western Reserve Univ. Press, 1967).

55. See Williams, George Hunston, "The Sacred Condominium", in Noonan, John T., Jr., ed., *The Morality of Abortion: Legal and Historical Perspectives* (Cambridge, Mass.: Harvard U. Press, 1970), p. 146, f.n. 2. (Hereinafter cited as "Noonan I.")

56. Lader I, p. 145.

57. *The New York Times,* Jan. 31, 1965, p. 73, col. 6.

58. *Ibid.,* Oct. 26, 1965, p. 37, col. 4.

59. *Ibid.,* June 22, 1965, p. 42, col. 4.

60. *Ibid.,* Feb. 13, 1965, p. 20, col. 2.

61. *Ibid.,* April 7, 1965, p. 42, col. 2.

62. *Ibid.,* December 8, 1965, p. 46, col. 1

63. *Ibid.,* Feb. 13, 1965, p. 20, col. 2.

64. *Ibid.,* The editorial said that "Catholics...are chiefly but not exclusively the opponents of a more flexible law." It also misstates the Catholic position by indicating that the Church permits "abortion" if it results from life-saving medical treatment given to the mother. Actually this is not "abortion" as we commonly understand the term. Catholic teaching permits the mother to receive medical treatment even if the unborn child will die as a result; it does not permit the life of the child ever to be taken directly and deliberately. Neither the life of the mother nor the child is to take precedence.

65. *The Times* stated that "[a]n estimated 1.2 million women have abortions in the course of a year--one estimate is that the total will reach 1.5 million this year [1965]--yet only 18,000 are performed by qualified surgeons in accordance with medically accepted standards...the consensus is that nearly 10,000

women die each year as the result of such operations." (*Times* editorial, Dec. 8, 1965, p. 46, col. 1). During the course of my research, I was amazed at how many writers accepted these figures, without question, as established fact.

66. *The New York Times,* April 7, 1965 and Dec. 8, 1965 editorials.

67. *Ibid.,* Dec. 8, 1965 editorial.

68. *Ibid.,* Mar. 31, 1966, p. 13, col. 4.

69. *Ibid.,* July 20, 1966, p. 83, col. 4.

70. *Ibid.,* Dec. 6, 1966, p. 52, col. 2.

71. *Ibid.,* Dec. 13, 1966, p. 52, col. 2.

72. *Ibid.,*

73. Lader I, p. 147.

74. *The New York Times,* Oct. 11, 1966, p. 35, col. 6.

75. *Ibid.,* Oct. 25, 1966, p. 29, col. 1.

76. *Ibid.,* May 6, 1966, p. 31, col. 4.

77. *Ibid.,* Nov. 6, 1966, p. 87, col. 5.

78. (N.Y.: Pocket Books, 1966.)

79. Von Damm, Helene, ed., *Sincerely, Ronald Reagan* (Ottawa, Ill.: Green Hill, 1976), pp. 92-93.

80. 35 *Modern Medicine,* No. 9 (April 24, 1967), pp. 12-13.

81. *The New York Times,* Apr. 30, 1967, p. 82, col. 6.

82. *Ibid.,* Feb. 4, 1967, p. 24, col. 2.

83. Guttmacher, Alan F., M.D. "Abortion--Yesterday, Today, and Tomorrow," in Guttmacher I, pp. 12-13.

84. *The New York Times,* Apr. 13, 1967, p. 15, col. 1.

85. *Ibid.,* May 19, 1967, p. 23, col. 1, quoting the Medical Committee's statement.

86. Willke, Dr. & Mrs. J. C., *Handbook on Abortion* (Cincinnati: Hayes, 1971, 1975. Reprinted by Life Cycle Books, Toronto), p. 9, quoting the Conference's statement. The proceedings of the Conference were published in 1968 under the title *The Terrible Choice: The Abortion Dilemma* (N.Y.: Bantam).

87. *The New York Times,* Feb. 25, 1967, p. 1, col. 1, quoting the statement.

88. *Ibid.,* p. 30, col. 2; continuation of the article on p. 1, quoting both the Bishop's pastoral letter and the Protestant-Jewish statement.

89. *Ibid.,* May 22, 1967, p. 1, col. 2.

90. *Ibid.,* p. 36, col. 3, continuation of article from p. 1, quoting the clergymen's statement. The Service initially included clergymen from Methodist, Presbyterian, Unitarian, Congregational, Episcopal, Reformed, Baptist, and Jewish Denominations.

91. *Ibid.,* May 10, 1967, p. 22, col. 1 and Jan. 31, 1967, p. 25, col. 3.

92. *Ibid.,* May 21, 1967, p. 82, col. 4.

93. Nathanson, p. 300.

94. *Time,* Oct. 13, 1967, p. 33.

95. *Ibid.,* p. 32.

96. *Ibid.,* pp. 32-33.

97. *The New York Times,* May 10, 1968, p. 21, col. 7.

98. Grisez, p. 259, citing an APHA mimeograph "Abortion," Nov. 1968.

99. *The New York Times,* Nov. 14, 1968, p. 50, col. 2.

100. Grisez, p. 259.

101. *The New York Times,* Apr. 2, 1968, p. 58, col. 4.

102. *Ibid.,* Apr. 2, 1968, p. 10, col. 1. The Commission proposed that abortion be legalized if a pregnancy threatened the life

of the mother or impaired her physical or mental health, or if the child would be born abnormal, or if the pregnancy were the result of rape or incest, or if the mother were under age 16 and unmarried.

103. *Ibid.*, Jan. 11, 1968, p. 36, col. 1 and Feb. 10, 1968, p. 32, col. 1.

104. *Ibid.*, Jan. 11, 1968, p. 36, col. 1.

105. See Hall, Robert E., M.D., ed., *Abortion in a Changing World*, 2 vols. (N.Y.: Columbia U. Press, 1970). This is the proceedings of the conference.

106. *The New York Times*, Nov. 24, 1968, p. 77, col. 1.

107. Lader, Lawrence, *Abortion II: Making the Revolution* (Boston: Beacon, 1973), pp. 81-82. (Hereinafter referred to as "Lader II.")

108. Means, Cyril C. Jr., "The Law of New York Concerning and the Status of the Foetus, 1664-1968: A Case of Cessation of Constitutionality," 14 *New York Law Forum* 411 (1968). (Hereinafter cited as "Means I.")

109. (Dayton, O.: Pflaum, 1968).

110. 71 Cal. 2d 954, 458 P. 2d 194. The decision did not involve the liberalized 1967 California statute, which remained in effect.

111. 305 F. Supp. 1032 (D.D.C., 1969).

112. *The New York Times*, Oct. 1, 1969, p. 55, col. 3.

113. *Ibid.*, Nov. 12, 1969, p. 30, col. 1. None of the four states the ACLU targeted were among the two from which the *Wade* and *Bolton* cases came. Note 28 above states what the ACLU's involvement in those cases was.

114. Group for Advancement of Psychiatry, *The Right to Abortion: A Psychiatric View* (N.Y.: Chas. Scribner's Sons, 1969), p. 49.

115. *Ibid.*, p. 10.

116. 37 *Modern Medicine*, No. 22 (Nov. 3, 1969), p. 19.

117. Raymond J. Adamek, professor of sociology at Kent State University, came to this conclusion after analyzing the responses to variously-worded questions about abortion in major national surveys. See Adamek, "Abortion and Public Opinion in the United States," article done for and published by National Right to Life Educational Trust Fund, p. 2. One particularly striking example he points to is the drastically different responses received from the same persons on a question about a Human Life Amendment in a *New York Times*/CBS News Poll which was reported in the *Times* on Aug. 18, 1980, p. 1:

	Should Be	*Shouldn't Be*
1. "Do you think there should be an amendment to the Constitution prohibiting abortions, or shouldn't there be such an amendment?"	29%	67%
2. "Do you believe there should be an amendment to the Constitution protecting the life of the unborn child, or shouldn't there be such an amendment?"	50%	39%

118. *The New York Times*, Nov. 25, 1969, p. 51, col. 3.

119. *Ibid.*, Nov. 15, 1969, p. 26, col. 8.

120. Lader II, p. 82.

121. NARAL changed its name after the Supreme Court's *Wade* and *Bolton* decisions to the National Abortion Rights Action League.

122. Nathanson, pp. 32-33, 51-53.

123. My source for this list is *Proposed Revisions of the Abortion Law*. Report of the Joint Legislative Committee (New York Legislature) on the Problems of Public Health, Medicare, Medicaid and Compulsory Health and Hospital Insurance, 1969, p. 91.

124. (N.Y.: Macmillan, 1969).

125. (Chicago: U. of Chicago Press, 1969).

126. (Garden City, N.Y.: Doubleday, 1969). (Hereinafter cited as "Rice I.")

127. (Garden City, N.Y.: Doubleday (Image Books), 1969).

128. Reiterman, Carl, ed., *Abortion and the Unwanted Child* (N.Y.: Springer, 1969).

129. *Proposed Revisions of the Abortion Law,* p. 9.

130. See *The New York Times* for these dates: Feb. 7, 1969, p. 26, col. 6; Feb. 21, 1969, p. 46, col. 3; Feb. 12, 1969, p. 79, col. 4; and Feb. 22, 1969, p. 35, col. 1.

131. *Ibid.,* Mar. 3, 1969, p. 40, col. 2.

132. *Ibid.,* Feb. 25, 1969, p. 46, col. 2, quoting the committee's statement.

133. *Ibid.,* Feb. 13, 1969, p. 28, col. 1.

134. Interview with Mrs. Helen Green, former president of the New York State Right to Life Committee, Mar. 4, 1982, in person. Mrs. Greene was an early lobbyist in the New York State Legislature against changing the law.

135. *New Yorker,* Feb. 22, 1969, p. 28. My source for the information about NOW's decision to support legalized abortion is Freeman, Jo, *The Politics of Women's Liberation: A Case of an Emerging Social Movement and Its Relation to the Policy Process* (N.Y.: David McKay, 1975), pp. 80-81.

136. *The New York Times,* April 12, 1970, p. 47, quoting Rockefeller.

137. *Proposed Revision of the Abortion Law,* pp. 5-8. The Committee report made the same proposals for liberalization as the Governor's 1968 Commission did, with the following exceptions: abortion should be permitted if there is medical evidence of a substantial risk that the fetus, if born, would be so grossly malformed or would have such other serious physical or mental abnormalities as to be permanently incapable of caring for himself, or if pregnancy occurred while the woman was declared to be a mentally disabled or incompetent person as defined by the state's mental hygiene law, or if the pregnancy occurred in a girl under 15 and unmarried.

138. See the following editions of *The New York Times:* May 3,

1969, p. 34, col. 1; May 8, 1969, p. 28, col. 1; and May 30, 1969, p. 26, col. 2.

139. *Ibid.*, May 8, 1969 and May 30, 1969.

140. *Ibid.*, May 30, 1969.

141. Grisez, p. 342, quoting Ginsberg where indicated.

142. *The New York Times*, May 3, 1969, p. 34, col. 1.

143. Lader II, pp. 123-124.

144. *The New York Times*, Oct. 28, 1970, p. 33, col. 6. The quoted terms are from the Church convention's statement.

145. *Ibid.*, June 19, 1971, p. 28, col. 1.

146. *Ibid.*, July 11, 1970, p. 15, col. 2.

147. *Ibid.*, Aug. 19, 1970, p. 43, col. 1.

148. *Ibid.*, June 26, 1970, p. 1, col. 1.

149. *Doe v. Bolton*, 319 F. Supp. 1048 (N.D. Ga.), which, of course, then went to the Supreme Court, and *Babbitz v. McCann*, 310 F. Supp. 293 (E.D. Wis.).

150. *Rosen v. Louisiana State Board of Medical Examiners*, 318 F. Supp. 1217 (E.D. La.) and *Steinberg v. Brown*, 321 F. Supp. 741 (N.D. Ohio).

151. Sarvis & Rodman, p. 47.

152. Grisez and Noonan I, cited above.

153. Callahan, Daniel, *Abortion: Law, Choice and Morality* (N.Y.: Macmillan, 1970).

154. Lader II, pp. 122-148.

155. Greene interview; interview with Mr. Edward Golden, first president of both the New York State and National Right to Life Committees, Mar. 16, 1982, by telephone.

156. Golden interview.

157. Golden interview; Greene interview.

158. Lader II, pp. 125-134.

159. *The New York Times*, Feb. 4, 1970, p. 42, col. 2 and Mar. 3, 1970, p. 40, col. 2.

160. *Ibid.*, Feb 4, 1970, p. 42, col. 2.

161. Lader II, pp. 142-146.

162. The Florida decision was *State v. Barquet*, 262 So.2d 431 (1972). The referenda states were Michigan (61 percent against legalization) and North Dakota (77 percent against). (Noonan II, at p. 34.)

163. *Abele v. Markle*, 342 F.Supp. 800(D.Conn.1972).

164. *Doe v. Scott*, 321 F.Supp. 1385(N.D.Ill.1971).

165. *Poe v. Menghini*, 339 F.Supp. 986(D.Kan.1972).

166. *YWCA v. Kugler*, 342 F.Supp. 1048(D.N.J.1972).

167. *State v. Barquet*, cited above, note 162.

168. *Crossen v. Attorney General*, 344 F.Supp. 587(E.D.Ky.1972).

169. *Corkey v. Edwards*, 322 F.Supp. 1248(W.D.N.C.1971).

170. *Doe v. Rampton* (1971). I could find no opinion reported for this case. It appears to have been a state trial court case from the fact that the *Wade* opinion gives no citation, but simply says "(Utah 1971), appeal docketed, No. 71-5666." (*Wade* at 155.)

171. *Spears v. State*, 257 So.2d 876 (1972).

172. *State v. Munson*, 86 S.D. 663,201 N.W.2d 123 (1972).

173. *Cheney v. State*, 285 N.E.2d 265 (1972).

174. *U.S. v. Vuitch*, 402 U.S. 62 (1971).

175. 402 U.S. 62,72.

176. *The New York Times*, Feb. 8, 1972, p. 37, col. 2.

177. PPFA, "What Some Organizations Have Said in Support of Legal Abortion...," mimeograph, 1976.

178. *The New York Times*, June 30, 1971, p. 42, col. 1; Apr. 27, 1972, p. 16, col. 2; and May 25, 1972, p. 11, col. 1,

respectively.

179. *Ibid.*, June 3, 1971, p. 43, col. 1.

180. *Ibid.*, May 9, 1971, p. 8, col. 1.

181. *Ibid.*, Sept. 12, 1971, Sec. I, p. 48, col. 1.

182. *Ibid.*, Oct. 15, 1971, p. 53, col. 1.

183. *Ibid.*, Aug. 18, 1972, p. 36, col. 2.

184. *National Right to Life News*, Feb. 1974, p. 9, citing *Playboy*, Jan. 1974.

185. Collegeville, Minn.: Human Life Center, St. John's University, 1971.

186. (N.Y.: Sheed & Ward).

187. (N.Y.: McGraw-Hill, 1971).

188. Means, Cyril C., "The Phoenix of Abortional Freedom: Is a Penumbral or Ninth-Amendment Right About to Arise From the Nineteenth-Century Legislative Ashes of a Fourteenth-Century Common-Law Liberty," 17 *New York Law Forum* 335 (1971). (Hereinafter cited as "Means II.") The first Means article (Means I) was cited for the Court in the following briefs: the *Bolton* appellants'; the National Legal Program on Health Problems et al.; and New Women Lawyers. Means II was cited in the *Wade* appellants' brief. Further, it is mentioned in the oral argument of the *Wade* case that a copy of Means II was submitted to the Court. (See *Roe v. Wade* oral argument (Dec. 13, 1971) in Kurland, Philip B. & Casper, Gerhard, eds., 75 *Landmark Briefs and Arguments of the Supreme Court of the United States: Constitutional Law 1*. University Publications of America, 1975, p. 788.)

189. Nathanson, pp. 155-156.

190. *Newsweek*, May 22, 1972, p. 32.

191. *The New York Times*, May 2, 1972, p. 32, col. 4; Golden interview.

192. Greene interview; Golden interview.

193. Golden interview.

194. *The New York Times*, Mar. 14, 1972, p. 1, col. 1, continued on p. 62, col. 1.

195. For data on the greater group participation of the better educated and more affluent, see, Wright, Charles R. & Hyman, Herbert, "Voluntary Memberships of American Adults: Evidence from National Sample Surveys," in Salisbury, Robert H., ed., *Interest Group Politics in America* (N.Y.: Harper & Row, 1970), pp. 77-79. (Reprinted from 23 *Amer. Socio. Rev.*, No. 2 (June 1958).) David B. Truman, among others, has discussed the tendency of active minorities to take charge of organizations. (See Truman, pp. 139-155.) James Q. Wilson discusses the prominent role played by staffs in organizations. He says, significantly for our purposes, that the staff can often have the effect of giving an organization a politically and socially liberal orientation. He cites one study of the National Council of Churches--which is comprised of many of the Protestant church bodies which pushed for abortion law change--in which the staff was found to have had precisely this effect. (See Wilson, James Q., *Political Organizations* (N.Y.: Basic Books, 1973), pp. 225-232. The study he cites is from Pratt, Henry J., *The Liberalization of American Protestantism* (Detroit: Wayne St. Univ. Press, 1972), Chapter 13. The main groups on the pro-abortion side that have been mentioned which had economically and educationally diverse memberships were religious bodies. The prominent role of staff in the National Council of Churches may suggest a similar prominence (along with another educated and affluent group, clergy) within the governing structures of these bodies, especially one like the New York State Council of Churches which is an affiliate of the National Council.

196. 35 *Modern Medicine*, No. 9 (Apr. 24, 1967), p. 12.

197. Crowley, Ralph M., M.D. & Laidlaw, Robert W., M.D., "Psychiatric Opinion Regarding Abortion: Preliminary Report of a Survey," 124 *Amer. Jour. of Psychiatry* (1967), p. 146. The survey was conducted in Dec. 1965 by the Association for the Study of Abortion which sent questionnaires to the total membership of the American Psychiatric Association (12,974 psychiatrists in the U.S. and 794 abroad). The figures I have cited are just for those in the U.S. Some questions could perhaps be raised about how accurately the survey represented the views of the entire domestic A.P.A. membership since only 40.6 percent of it returned completed questionnaires. The A.P.A., however, obviously thought the results to be fairly representative because it was willing to have

them presented in its official journal.

198. 37 *Modern Medicine*, p. 19. The precise figures were 79.5 percent and 71.7 percent, respectively.

199. Brennan, p. 124.

200. 37 *Modern Medicine*, p. 19. The precise figures were 41.4 percent ("unqualified") and 50.6 percent ("total" - "unqualified" and "with qualifications" together) respectively.

201. Eliot, Johan W., M.D. et al., "The Obstetrician's View," in Hall, ed., p. 91. The figure was 89.4 percent for heads of these departments in private non-Catholic hospitals and 98.3 percent for those in public hospitals. This suggests that ACOG's most *influential* members--we can reasonably presume that most were ACOG members--were strongly pro-abortion.

202. Unless there was a further shift toward the pro-abortion position by obstetrician-gynecologists between 1969 and 1970, we could say, on the basis of these surveys, that the only one of these three associations that arguably was not representing most of its members in calling for outright repeal was ACOG.

203. An interesting aside which perhaps helps to put this medical opinion in a larger context is seen in Brennan's recounting the results of a survey conducted in the late 1960s by Dr. Robert H. Williams of the University of Washington Medical School. He sent questionnaires to the full membership (344) of the Association of Professors of Medicine and the Association of American Physicians. He received 333 (97 percent) back. They showed that 87 percent of the respondents supported passive euthanasia (i.e., withholding necessary care from a dying patient in order to expedite his death) and that 80 percent admitted having done this. (Brennan, p. 127, citing Williams, "Our Role in the Generation, Modification, and Termination of Life," in 124 *Archives of Internal Medicine* (1969), pp. 229-233.)

204. Levene, Howard I., M.D. & Rigney, Francis J., M.D., "Law, Preventive Psychiatry, and Therapeutic Abortion," 151 *Jour. of Nerv. and Mental Disorders* (1970), p. 51.

205. *Ibid*.

206. Sarvis & Rodman, pp. 107-112.

207. Marder, Leon, M.D., et al., "Psychosocial Aspects of Therapeutic Abortion," 63 *Southern Med. Jour.* (1970), p. 659.

208. Sarvis & Rodman, p. 108.

209. *Ibid.*, p. 121.

210. The source for these polls is Blake, Judith, "Abortion and Public Opinion: The 1960-1970 Decade," 171 *Science* 540-549 (1971). (Hereinafter cited as "Blake I.") Figures are rounded off to the nearest half-percent.

211. The source for the 1969 and 1972 polls is *Gallup Opinion Index*, Reports No. 54 (Dec. 1969), p. 19, and No. 87 (Sept. 1972), pp. 13-15.

212. Blake, Judith, "The Supreme Court Abortion Decisions and Public Opinion in the United States," IV *The Human Life Review*, No. 1 (Winter 1978), pp. 67-68. Originally published in *Population and Development Review*, Vol. 3, (Nos. 1 & 2, March and June, 1977). (Hereinafter cited as "Blake II.")

213. *Ibid.*, p. 71.

214. Professor Blake concurs with this conclusion on the basis of her review of the survey data. See Blake II, p. 66.

215. See Noonan II, pp. 33-46; O'Meara, Joseph, "Abortion: The Court Decides a Non-Case," I *The Human Life Review*, No. 4 (Fall 1975), p. 17; and Stanmeyer, William A., "Governing the Judiciary," in McGuigan, Patrick B. & Rader, Randall R., *A Blueprint for Judicial Reform* Wash., D.C.: Free Congress Education and Research Fdn., Inc., 1981), p. 49. These commentators' assessment, as well as my argument in this Sub-Section, gain support from the *Connecticut Mutual Life Report on American Values in the 80's: The Impact of Belief*. This report, based on wide-ranging surveys of the views of both the general public and top individuals in various leadership groups, documented the gap between the thinking of these two groups on a large number of issues. The leaders--from business, education, government, law and justice, military, news media, religion, science, and voluntary associations--had sharply divergent views from the public on the "moral issues," including abortion, homosexuality, premarital sex, cohabitation, and pornography. The general public was much more likely than the leaders to find these "morally wrong." The "law and justice" group of leaders--which includes judges and lawyers--was even less likely to find these activities "moral-

ly wrong." On abortion, 65 percent of the public believed it "morally wrong," as compared to 36 percent of all leaders and 25 percent of the leaders in the "law and justice" group. When we consider these views in light of the Supreme Court decisions in these and related areas, we can see that the Court's views have most clearly coincided with those of the leadership group and especially of the activist lawyers who have brought the cases before them. That is, it has responded affirmatively to the beliefs of these groups by reshaping the law in these areas in accord--at least to some degree--with the latter's preferences. (Source for statistics above: McGuigan, Patrick B. & Rader, Randall, R., "Judicial Oligarchy: Have the People Ceased to be Their Own Rulers?" in McGuigan & Rader, pp. 361-363. They cite the *Connecticut Mutual Life Report*.)

216. See United Methodist Church resolution on "Responsible Parenthood" (1972) and United Presbyterian Church, U.S.A. resolution "Freedom of Choice in Problem Pregnancies," May, 1972.

217. See, for example, the statements of the following: the New York Council of Churches, as quoted in *The New York Times*, Feb. 7, 1969, p. 26, col. 6; the Council of the Episcopal Diocese of New York, as quoted in the *Times*, Feb. 22, 1969, p. 35, col. 1; Resolution passed by the American Baptist Convention, as quoted in the *Times*, June 6, 1968, p. 58, col. 4.

218. I am not referring, of course, to the forms of contraception which are really forms of very early abortion, such as the IUD and many birth control pills.

219. See the discussion of Tocqueville's thinking about this in Chapter Nine.

220. See Noonan II, pp. 53-54; Grisez, pp. 347-348; and Greeley, Andrew M., "*An Ugly Little Secret: Anti-Catholicism in North America* (Kansas City, Kan.: Sheed, Andrews, and McMeel, 1977), pp. 22-25, 108-109.

221. For a discussion of the evolution of the contemporary feminist movement, see Freeman, pp. 44-70 and Hole, Judith & Levine, Ellen, *Rebirth of Feminism* (N.Y.: Quadrangle, 1971), pp. 109-122.

222. For example, it was during the Nixon administration that Congress, responding to President Nixon's initiatives,

passed a sweeping family planning act which put the federal government prominently into this area. The family planning bureaucracies in Washington--the Department of Health, Education and Welfare and the Office of Economic Opportunity--had a strong commitment to family planning and tried to outdo each other in doling out federal funds and grants. Congress also passed legislation--vetoed by Nixon--which would have established government-supported day-care centers for the children of welfare mothers. (See Littlewood, Thomas B., *The Politics of Population Control* (Notre Dame, Ind.: U. of Notre Dame Press, 1977) pp. 55, 95, 139.) It was also, of course, during the Nixon years that the Equal Rights Amendment was proposed by Congress.

223. Hitchcock, James, "Catholics and Liberals," II *The Human Life Review*, No. 4 (Fall 1976), pp. 109-110. (Hereinafter cited as "Hitchcock I.")

224. Schwartz, Michael, personal correspondence, June 8, 1981.

225. See, for example, Grisez, p. 432; Marx, p. 15; Rice I, p. 32; Willke, p. 187.

226. PPFA pamphlet "Plan Your Children for Health and Happiness" (1962).

227. Mrs. Sanger was, with Frederick Blossom, the founder of the American Birth Control League, in 1921. It became the preeminent birth control organization in the U.S. She also organized the Clinical Research Bureau--a center for the medical study of contraception--in 1923. In the 1930s, Sanger left the League and turned her attention to the National Committee for Federal Legislation on Birth Control, a lobbying organization. In 1938, the League and her Clinical Research Bureau merged into the Birth Control Federation of America. In 1942, this organization changed its name to the Planned Parenthood Federation of America. (Gordon, Linda, *Woman's Body, Woman's Right: A Social History of Birth Control in America* (N.Y.: Grossman, 1976), pp. 263, 291, 326, 329, 341.) So, Sanger can legitimately be called the true founder of PPFA. She also started the International Planned Parenthood Federation (IPPF). (Gordon, p. 397).

228. Noonan II, p. 36; Nathanson, p. 32. For her own words on the subject--which characterized her position for most of her career--see Sanger, Margaret, *My Fight for Birth Control* (N.Y.: Farrar & Rinehart, 1931), p. 133.

229. Gordon, p. 382.

230. Noonan II, p. 37, quoting Majima, Kan, "Induced Abortion Is No Longer a Crime in Japan," in Third International Conference on Planned Parenthood, *Report of the Proceedings* (Bombay, India: Family Planning Association of India, 1952), p. 156, and Harnsen, Hans, "The Medical Evil of Abortion," ed., p. 153.

231. Noonan II, quoting Klinger, Andras, "Rapporteur's Summary: The World-Wide Problem of Abortion," *Proceedings of the Eighth International Conference of the International Planned Parenthood Federation* (London: IPPF, 1967), p. 153.

232. PPFA mimeograph, "The Facts Speak for Planned Parenthood" (1954), p. 3.

233. Grisez, p. 58, quoting Guttmacher, "Discussion" in Muramatsu, Minoru & Harper, Paul A., eds., *Population Dynamics: International Action and Training Programs* (Baltimore: Johns Hopkins U. Press, 1965) p. 175.

234. PPFA in *Cosmopolitan* (March 1965), quoted in Right to Life of Greater Cincinnati, "News Letter" (July 1973).

235. Voting Summary on "Objectives" set out in "A Proposal for a 1971/76 Plan for the Planned Parenthood Federation." The full tabulation for the "objective" dealing with abortion is as follows:

"Objective" voted on: "To play a leading role in the rapid acceptance of abortion as a medical back-up in the event of contraceptive failure, and to help provide safe, legal and inexpensive abortion services to every woman who needs and wants one."

Service or Activity	Current Priority	Number of Votes (No. of Affiliates) (Priority Should Be) Higher (Closer to 1)	As Proposed	Lower (Closer to 10)
Objective #4-Abortion	3	50	142	20
P1 Public Policy	6	78	123	11
P2 Information, Referral, Monitoring	3	45	156	11

	Current Priority	Higher (Closer to 1)	As Proposed	Lower (Closer to 10)
P3 Direct Services				
a) affiliates	4	47	151	14
b) PP-WP (national office)	4	38	163	11

236. Guttmacher, Alan F., M.D., *Birth Control and Love: The Complete Guide to Contraception and Fertility* (N.Y.: MacMillan, 1961), p. 12. ("Guttmacher I.")

237. Guttmacher, Alan F., M.D., "Symposium: Law, Morality, and Abortion," 22 *Rutgers L. R.* 436 (1968). ("Guttmacher III.")

238. Noonan II, pp. 37-38.

239. Golden interview; Nathanson, p. 70.

240. Nathanson, p. 70.

241. Gordon, p. 223.

242. Drogin, Elasah, *Margaret Sanger: Father of Modern Society* (Coarsegold, Calif.: CUL Publications, 1979, 1980), p. 69.

243. 381 U.S. 479 (1965). This decision invalidated a state statute which forbade married couples from using birth control devices and forbade disbursing them to such couples.

244. 405 U.S. 438 (1972). This decision struck down a Massachusetts statute which prohibited the disbursement of contraceptives to unmarried persons.

245. See brief for appellants in *Griswold*. To be precise, there was not an argument about contraceptive failure, but about the alleged unreliability or harmfulness of the non-artificial methods: abstinence, rhythm, and withdrawal.

246. See PPFA brief in *Eisenstadt*, pp. 20-25.

247. "The Facts Speak for Planned Parenthood," p.4.

248. *Ibid.*, p. 1.

249. *Ibid.*, p. 3.

250. *Ibid.*, p. 9.

251. *Ibid.*, p. 4.

252. Emerson, Haven, M.D., "What May Health Departments Do to Further Improve the Quality of Life?--the Whether or Not and When of Pregnancy," mimeograph (N.Y.: Birth Control Federation of America, Inc., 1939), p. 4. (Emphasis is mine.)

253. *Ibid.*, p. 8.

254. *Ibid.*, p. 6.

255. There is a ring of eugenist sentiment in the passages from the 1954 publication that I have quoted. Linda Gordon writes that "eugenists had been among the earliest of the nonradicals to support birth control" and that they "had a great influence not only on Sanger but on the whole birth-control movement," at least in its earlier years. (Gordon, pp. 273-274).

256. Truman, p. 511.

257. For an examination of the anti-abortion movement since *Wade* and *Bolton*, wee Putka, John S., "The Supreme Court and Abortion: The Socio-Political Impact of Judicial Activism." Unpublished Ph.D. dissertation, U. of Cincinnati, 1979, Chapter Six.

258. Shapiro, Fred C., "'Right to Life' Has a Message for New York State Legislators," *The New York Times Magazine*, Aug. 20, 1972, p. 34.

259. Greene interview.

260. New York State Right to Life Committee, Inc. *Convention '79* program, p. 6.

261. Greene interview.

262. Golden, Edward, "Evolution of Right to Life as a National Movement," in *National Right to Life News* (Feb. 1974), p. 12.

263. Greene interview. The word in quotation marks is hers.

264. *Ibid*.

265. Phone conversation with Mrs. Barbara Willke, Jan. 18, 1982.

266. Corresp.-J. C. Willke, Dec. 7, 1983. Book cited in note 86.

267. *National Right to Life News* (April-May 1974), p. 11.

268. MCCL mimeograph, "MCCL History."

269. *Ibid.,* The resolution was not a memorial to Congress to convene a constitutional convention to propose an amendment. A movement to have a convention called for this purpose ("Con-Call") has been underway for some years.

270. *Ibid.*

271. Shapiro, p. 34.

272. *Ibid.*

273. Greene interview.

274. Shapiro, pp. 38-39.

275. *The New York Times,* Apr. 17, 1972, p. 27, col. 3 and Apr. 18, 1972, p. 43, col. 1.

276. Shapiro, p. 34.

277. *Ibid.*

278. Golden interview.

279. Greene interview.

280. *Ibid.*

281. Greene and Golden interviews.

282. Golden interview.

283. *Time,* (March 29, 1971), p. 73.

284. *The New York Times,* June 28, 1972, p. 21, col. 1.

285. See *Byrn v. New York City Health and Hospitals Association,* 31 N.Y.2d 194, 286 N.E.2d 887 (1972).

286. *Time,* (March 29, 1971), pp. 71, 73. The case was *Doe v. Scott,* supra.

287. Greene interview.

288. *Chicago Tribune,* July 6, 1980, reprinted in AUL fund-raising letter, 1980. The Legal Defense Fund is the legal arm of AUL.

289. Greene interview.

290. Greene interview; Shapiro, p. 42.

291. *Time,* (March 29, 1971), pp. 71-73.

292. Tocqueville, Vol. One, p. 192.

293. Golden interview.

294. The Hatch Amendment would specifically overturn the *Wade* and *Bolton* decisions and give authority to both the states and to Congress to legislate against abortion, although it would not require them to do so. One of the main points of controversy within the anti-abortion movement over the Amendment has been this "legislative option" and the fact that it accords no constitutional protection to the unborn child. Most in the movement who have supported it have seen it only as the first step, with a "Human Life Amendment" which *does* guarantee such protection to follow.

295. Putka, p. 219.

296. See Shapiro.

297. *Ibid.,* p. 43.

298. *Ibid.,* pp. 42-43.

299. Golden and Greene interviews.

300. Golden interview.

301. Greene interview.

302. Putka, p. 239, citing his interview with Archbishop Joseph L. Bernadin on July 22, 1977.

303. McHugh, Rev. Msgr. James T., "The Moral Principles and Methodology of the Statements of the National Conference of Catholic Bishops of the United States on Respect for Life and Abortion 1968-1978" (unpublished Ph.D. dissertation, 1979), p. 51,

quoting Confidential Minutes, NCCB Administrative Committee, Nov. 14, 1975.

304. *Ibid.*, p. 35, quoting NCCB, *Statement on Abortion* from USCC - *Documentation on the Right to Life and Abortion,* Vol. I, pp. 65-67.

305. *Ibid.*, p. 48, referring to the testimony.

306. Greene interview.

307. Surveys have been somewhat mixed about the percentage of the population that would actually make a candidate's stand on abortion the decisive factor in judging about whether to vote for him and about whether most such people are on the anti-abortion side. What is clear, in any event, is that there is a small but hard core minority of voters who will oppose any candidate who might have to deal with the issue who favors legalized abortion. (See Rees, Grover III, "Confessions of a One-Issue Voter," V *The Human Life Review,* No. 3 (Summer 1979), pp. 30-41 and Jaffe, Frederick S., Lindheim, Barbara L., & Lee, Philip R., *Abortion Politics: Private Morality and Public Policy* (N.Y.: McGraw-Hill, 1981), pp. 100, 107-108.

CHAPTER TWO NOTES

1. *Roe v. Wade,* 314 F.Supp. 1217.

2. *Doe v. Bolton,* 319 F.Supp. 1048.

3. *Roe v. Wade,* 410 U.S. 113, 116.

4. *Ibid.*

5. A declaratory judgment simply declares the rights of the parties or expresses the opinion of the court on a question of law, without ordering anything to be done. An injunction is a prohibition writ issued by a court forbidding the party to whom it is directed to do some act which he is threatening or attempting to do or to restrain him from continuing some act. (*Black's Law Dictionary*. Fourth ed. St. Paul, Minn.: West, 1968, pp. 497, 923.)

6. The names "Roe" and "Doe" are, of course, pseudonyms. The

plaintiffs in abortion cases typically use such pseudonyms.

7. *Wade,* at 121, 128.

8. *Ibid.,* at 132, quoting Edelstein, L., *The Hippocratic Oath* (1943), p. 64.

9. *Wade,* at 135.

10. *Ibid.,* at 141-142, quoting 12 *Transactions of the Amer. Med. Assn.,* pp. 73-78 (1859) and 22 *Transactions of the Amer. Med. Assn.,* p. 258 (1871).

11. *Ibid.,* at 143-144, citing *Proceedings of the AMA House of Delegates,* p. 220 (June 1970).

12. *Wade,* at 153.

13. *Ibid.,* at 154.

14. *Ibid.,* at 157.

15. *Ibid.,* at 160-161.

16. *Ibid.,* at 162.

17. *Ibid.,* at 162-163.

18. *Ibid.,* at 163.

19. It should be pointed out that there appears to be an inconsistency in the Court's holding here. On one hand, it says that after and *only after* the first trimester the state can impose regulations regarding the qualifications of the person performing abortions. This would seem to suggest that the state could not even require the person to be a licensed physician. On the other hand, it says that prior to the end of the first trimester the decision about whether to abort is a matter for the woman and her physician. It is not clear if in saying this the Court implies that the state can require first trimester abortions to be performed by licensed physicians or whether it just expects that this will be the case because of actual practice. From this, it would seem that the decision leaves in limbo the question of whether the state could prohibit do-it-yourself abortive drugs which are now being developed.

    In Part XI, where the Court summarizes its holding, it says that the state "may define the term 'physician'...to mean only a physician currently licensed by the State, and may proscribe any abortion by a person who is not a physician as so defined." This is a clear statement, but it is uncertain as to whether it applies to the entire pregnancy or only a part of it. In light of the ambiguity in Part X, this point remains uncertain.

20. *Wade,* at 163-164.

21. In a subsequent decision, *Connecticut v. Manillo,* 423 U.S. 9 (1975), the Supreme Court affirmed that a state may prohibit abortions by non-physicians.

22. *Wade,* at 165, 166.

23. *Wade* (J. Stewart, concurring), at 169.

24. 405 U.S. 438 (1972).

25. *Wade* (J. Stewart, concurring), at 169-170.

26. *Ibid.,* at 170.

27. *Wade* (J. Rehnquist, dissenting), at 172.

28. *Ibid.,* at 174.

29. *Ibid.*

30. *Bolton,* at 183-184, citing the statute. The wording of the statute gave no indication of permitting abortion when the pregnancy is due to incest. The Court, however, notes that in oral argument the State said that "rape" in the statute included incest. (*Bolton* at 183, f.n. 5).

31. 402 U.S. 62 (1971).

32. *Bolton,* at 192.

33. This interpretation is warranted because the Court says that the *Wade* and *Bolton* opinions "are to be read together" (*Wade,* at 165). The Court's definition of "health" in *Bolton* thus explains what it means by its "life and health" exception after viability (the third trimester), mentioned earlier.

34. *Bolton,* at 199.

35. *Ibid.,* (C. J. Burger, concurring), at 207-208.

36. *Ibid.*, at 208.

37. *Ibid.*, (J. Douglas, concurring), at 210.

38. See *ibid.*, pp. 209-215. "Substantive due process" is the limitation on the *substance* of legislation, state or federal, permitted by the Fifth and Fourteenth Amendments. (Lockhart, William B., et al., *Constitutional Law: Cases, Comments, Questions*. Fourth Ed. St. Paul, Minn.: West, 1975, p. 506.) It differs from "procedural due process" which requires only that the government guarantee that certain judicial or quasi-judicial procedures be made available to the individual to defend himself when the government seeks to deprive him of life, liberty, or property.

39. *Bolton* (J. Douglas, concurring), at 214.

40. *Ibid.*, at 215, quoting the District Court's opinion in *Bolton*, 319 F.Supp. 1048, 1056.

41. *Ibid.*, (J. White, concurring), at 222.

42. *Wade*, at 116.

43. The transcript of the oral reargument in *Wade*--the case was argued twice before the Court, in 1971 and 1972--,gives further evidence that the Court sees abortion, and specifically the humanity of the unborn child, as essentially a medical question. "The Court"--Justices asking questions of the lawyers arguing the case are not identified--pressed Robert C. Flowers, Assistant Attorney General of Texas, for *medical* testimony to support the state's claim that human life begins at conception. (See *Roe v. Wade* oral reargument (Oct. 11, 1972) in Kurland & Casper, *op. cit.* (Chap. One), pp. 825-827.

44. What the Court says specifically is that if personhood within the meaning of the Fourteenth Amendment--i.e., "legal personhood"--were established, the appellants' case "collapses." (The Court notes that even the appellants, *per* their counsel Mrs. Sarah R. Weddington, conceded on oral reargument that their case would collapse if such personhood were established. See *Roe v. Wade* oral reargument (Oct. 11, 1972) in Kurland & Casper, pp. 816-817.) In saying this, however, the Court makes reference to the appellee and some anti-abortion *amici* presenting biological "facts of fetal development." This suggests that the appellant's case would also collapse if actual--i.e., biological personhood-- were established. The

Court, I believe, really means that the *humanity* of the unborn child is the decisive point. I thus believe that my conclusion in the text is correct. (See *Wade*, at 156.)

45. *Wade*, at 129.

46. *Ibid.*, at 155. Emphasis is mine.

47. *Ibid.*, at 153.

48. I made reference to what the appellant said in oral reargument above (note 44). The Court also makes reference to the appellee's (Texas) conceding in reargument that no decision could be found which held the unborn child to be a "person" under the Fourteenth Amendment. (Kurland & Casper, p. 819.) It is pointed out in Chapter Three that there actually was such a decision.

49. *Wade*, at 160.

50. *Ibid.*, at 161.

51. *Ibid.*, at 162.

52. *Ibid.*, at 163.

53. 381 U.S. 479 (1965). What is interesting about this is that Justice Stewart joined Justice Hugo L. Black's dissenting opinion in *Griswold* in which Black specifically condemns the Court's resurrection of the doctrine of substantive due process in that case. (See 381 U.S. 479, 507.)

54. 405 U.S. 438 (1972).

55. *Pierce v. Society of Sisters*, 268 U.S. 510 (1925).

56. *Meyer v. Nebraska*, 262 U.S. 510 (1925).

57. *Wade* (J. Stewart, concurring), at 170.

58. *Ibid.*

59. *Ibid.*, at 170-171.

60. *Ibid.*, (J. Rehnquist, dissenting), at 174, quoting *Snyder v. Massachusetts*, 291 U.S. 97, 105 (1934).

61. *Bolton*, at 191.

62. *Ibid.,* (C. J. Burger, concurring), at 207.

63. *Ibid.,* at 208.

64. *Ibid.,* (J. Douglas, concurring), at 220.

65. *Ibid.,* at 211, 213.

66. *Ibid.,* (J. White, dissenting), at 221.

67. Sobran, M.J (Joseph), "Abortion: Rhetoric and Cultural War," I *The Human Life Review,* No. 1 (Winter 1975), p. 92. As is already obvious, I use the term "unborn child" throughout this book. I do so because I do not wish to bias the discussion in the manner indicated. I also do so because of the convincing case made for his humanity in Chapter Seven, and because, even if one wants to quibble about his humanity, the term "unborn child" makes it clear that we are talking in any event about the offspring of a human being. Its use also focuses attention on the fact that there is indeed a moral issue in abortion, which involves whether innocent human life in any form should be destroyed.

68. Mall, David, "Stalemate of Rhetoric and Philosophy," in Hilgers, Thomas W. and Horan, Dennis J. (*Op. cit.,* Chap. 1), p. 204.

69. *Ibid.,* pp. 204-205.

70. *Ibid.,* p. 205.

71. Neuhaus, Richard, *In Defense of People: Ecology and the Seduction of Radicalism* (N.Y.: Macmillan, 1971), p. 194. Neuhaus is a Lutheran minister.

72. *Wade,* at 140, text and footnote, quoting Clark, Tom C., "Religion, Morality, and Abortion: A Constitutional Appraisal," in 2 *Loyola U. (L.A.) L.R.,* 1, 11.

73. *Ibid.,* at 147, footnote. The proposed legislation was approved by the ABA House of Delegates in February 1972. It is worth noting that this "enlightening Prefatory Note" includes a statement which refuses to propose prohibitions against sanctions imposed upon medical personnel who refuse to take part in abortion procedures for religious or similar reasons. (See *Wade,* at 148, footnote.)

74. *Bolton* (J. Douglas, concurring), at 216. Emphasis is mine.

75. *Wade,* at 153.

76. *Bolton,* at 197.

77. *Wade,* at 159.

78. *Bolton,* at 196.

79. *Ibid.,* at 191.

80. *Ibid.,* at 192.

81. *Ibid.,* at 197.

82. See *Wade,* at 140-141 and 153.

83. *Wade* (J. Stewart, concurring) at 170.

84. *Bolton* (J. Douglas, concurring), at 211.

85. *Wade,* at 163.

86. Cramton, Roger C., "The Ordinary Religion of the Law School Classroom," in VII *The Christian Lawyer,* No. 2 (Spring 1978), p. 18.

87. *Wade,* at 162.

88. I do not profess here to be able to read the Justices' minds. The Court does make clear, however, that the question of when a life begins is "difficult" and that "the judiciary...is not in a position to speculate as to the answer." (*Wade,* at 159.) Moreover, the very fact that it says it "need not resolve (*Wade,* at 159) such a paramount question and makes its decision after the detailed explicit consideration of only other factors can lead one to reasonably conclude that my assessment is correct.

89. *Wade,* at 163.

90. The argument I make in Chapter Seven strongly disputes the Court's contention, in effect, that life does not begin until viability. I dispute it on both biological and philosophical grounds. One might wonder if by showing there that the biological evidence is against the Court, I do not contradict my contention in this Chapter that the Court relies primarily on medical knowledge in its opinions. I think not because, as will become apparent after Chapters Six, Seven, and Eight,

I believe that, to the extent that the Court deferred to medicine, it was not to "hard" biological and medical facts, but to the views of the medical community about when "meaningful" life begins and about the value of prenatal life and about the pregnant woman's interests being more important than the child's.

91. *Wade*, at 131, 160.

92. *Ibid.*

93. *Ibid.*, at 161.

CHAPTER THREE NOTES

1. *Wade*, at 129.

2. *Ibid.*, at 130.

3. Brown, Harold, O. J., "What the Supreme Court Didn't Know: Ancient and Early Christian Views on Abortion," in I *The Human Life Review*, No. 2 (Spring 1975), p. 6.

4. Brown expresses this relationship between infanticide and abortion. Eugene Quay also mentions this relationship. He states that as ancient Rome got away from the practice of exposing newborn infants, the number of abortions increased. See Quay, "Justifiable Abortion--Medical and Legal Foundations," 49 *Georgetown Law Review* 395, 420 (1961), Part Two.

5. Brown, p. 6 and Quay, p. 399.

6. Brown, p. 7 and Quay, p. 400.

7. Quay indicates that the code of Tiglath-Pilesar probably descended from that of Hammurabi. He informs us that the Babylonians and Assyrians were kindred peoples and intermarried and that there was "an unbroken tradition which carried over when the rule of the Near East passed from the South [Babylon] to the North [Assyria]" (p. 400).

8. Brown, PP. 7-8.

9. Quay, p. 401.

10. *Ibid.*, pp. 402-403.

11. *Ibid.*, pp. 401-402, citing the hymn from 2 *The Cambridge Ancient History* 118 (1924 ed.).

12. *Ibid.*, p. 402, citing Needham, Joseph, *History of Embryology* 9 (1st ed., 1934).

13. *Ibid.*, pp. 403-405.

14. Connery, John, *Abortion: The Development of the Roman Catholic Perspective* (Chicago: Loyola Univ. Press, 1977), pp. 8, 21.

15. *Ibid.*, pp. 11-12.

16. *Ibid.*, p. 14.

17. *Ibid.*, p. 17.

18. See Quay, pp. 406, 422 and Noonan, John T. Jr., "An Almost Absolute Value in History," in Noonan I (*op. cit.*, Chap. One), p. 3. (This article hereinafter is cited as "Noonan in Noonan I.") The Court cites both of these sources on this point. Both indicate that the practice was known, but only Noonan says that it was common in *both* civilizations. (See Noonan in Noonan I, p. 61) Quay says that it was "common among the well to do of all classes" in Rome (p. 422), but that it was infanticide, not abortion, which seems to have been more common in Greece. (See pp. 406-409). In fact, he says that the Spartans did not permit abortion because they would never take the risk of losing what might be a perfect male child (pp. 406-407). The Court, in its footnotes, makes reference to these works of both Quay and Noonan I.

19. The Court gives the following as its source for this: Edelstein, Ludwig, "The Hippocratic Oath" (1943), p. 10. This appeared in *Supplements to the Bulletin of the History of Medicine*, No. 1, ed. by Harry E. Sigerist (Baltimore: Johns Hopkins U. Press, 1943). (Hereinafter cited as "Edelstein I.")

20. This source is Castiglioni, Arturo, *A History of Medicine*, Tr. by: E. B. Krumbhaar, 2nd ed., rev. (N.Y.: Alfred A. Knopf, 1958), p. 227.

21. Noonan in Noonan I, p. 5, quoting Soranus, *Gynecology*, edited by J. Ilberg, in 4 *Corpus Medicorum Graecorum*, I. 19. 60,

London & Berlin, 1927.

22. Noonan in Noonan I, p. 7, footnote.

23. Brown, p. 12, citing Henriot, Eugene, *Moeurs juridiques et judicaires de l'ancienne Rome,* Vol. II (Paris: Didot, 1865), p. 173.

24. *Ibid.,* citing Dolger, Franz Joseph, "Das Lebensrecht des ungeborenen Kindes und die Fruchtabtreibury in der Bewertung der heidnischen und christlichen Antike," in Dolger, *Antike und Christentum,* Vol. IV (Munster: Aschendorff, 1934), p. 14.

25. *Wade,* at 131.

26. Plato, *The Republic,* Book V, 461C, in Warmington, Eric H. and Rouse, Philip G., eds., *Great Dialogues of Plato.* Tr. by W.H.D. Rouse (N.Y.: The New American Library, Inc.), p. 259.

27. Noonan in Noonan I, p. 5.

28. The rationale for this is explained by note 18 above where it is stated that infanticide was a much more common practice among the Greeks than abortion.

29. Plato, *The Republic,* Book V 461A-B, in Warmington & Rouse, p. 259.

30. *Ibid.,* 460C, p. 258.

31. Pangle, Thomas L., "Interpretative Essay," in *The Laws of Plato* (Pangle ed.), (N.Y.: Basic Books, 1980), p. 376.

32. Bloom, Allan "Interpretive Essay," in *The Republic of Plato* (Bloom ed.), (N.Y.: Basic Books, 1968), p. 386.

33. *Ibid.,* pp. 386-387.

34. *Ibid.,* p. 388.

35. I should acknowledge that Professor Bloom's translation of *The Republic* seems to support the Court's conclusion better. Bloom translates the relevant passage at 461C as follows:

> ...and all this only after they have been told to be especially careful never to let even a

> a single foetus see the light of day, if one should be conceived, and if one should force its way, to deal with it on the understanding that there's to be no rearing for such a child. (Bloom, p. 140)

This indicates that Plato is proposing abortion to eliminate the unborn child who will upset the city's optimum population level. What I said about the "city in speech" and Plato's purpose in advocating what he does still holds, however.

36. A reference is made here to Aristotle's *Politics*, viii, 16, 1335b, 20-27, which shall be discussed shortly.

37. Plato, *Laws*, Book V, 740D *The Dialogues of Plato*, tr. by Benjamin Jowett (Chicago: Encyclopedia Britannica, 1952), p. 693.

38. *The Politics of Aristotle*, vii 15, 1335b 24-25, Ed. and tr. by Ernest Barker (N.Y.: Oxford Univ. Press, 1972), p. 327.

39. Noonan in Noonan I, p. 5.

40. Brown, p. 11, citing Dolger, p. 10, footnote. This information about the attitude of Lycurgus and Solon is found in a text written by Galen.

41. Castiglioni, Arturo, p. 227.

42. Brown, p. 14.

43. Noonan in Noonan I, p. 6, footnote.

44. Brown, p. 11.

45. Noonan in Noonan I, p. 6, footnote 10 cites Plutarch on Romulus in his *Lives* where he states that Romulus' original laws for Rome permitted a husband to divorce his wife for "pharmakeia" toward the children. Noonan explains that this probably means the use of contraceptive or abortifacient drugs to prevent birth.

46. My source for the text of the Oath is Edelstein I. Another translation of this part of the Oath is found in Castiglioni, at p. 154: "I will give no deadly medicine to anyone if asked, nor suggest any such counsel; and in like manner I will not give to a woman a pessary to produce abortion.

47. *Wade*, at 131-132.

48. *Ibid.*, at 132, quoting Edelstein I, p. 63.

49. *Wade*, at 132.

50. Brown, p. 13.

51. *Ibid.*

52. *Ibid.*

53. *Ibid.*, p. 13, quoting Edelstein I, p. 64.

54. Brown, pp. 13-14.

55. Galen, "Adhortatio ad artes addiscendas," cited from Temkin, Owsei, *Galenism: Rise and Decline of a Medical Philosophy* (Ithaca, N.Y. & London: Cornell Univ. Press, 1973), p. 27.

56. Temkin, p. 63.

57. *Ibid.*, p. 35.

58. Robinson, Victor, *The Story of Medicine* (N.Y.: Albert & Chas. Boni, 1931), p. 100.

59. The text of this case is taken from the translation by Means II (*op. cit.*, Chap. One). All footnotes have been omitted from the quotes of these and the following law review articles. See the articles for the citations.

60. Destro, pp. 1269-1270.

61. Byrn, Robert M., "An American Tragedy: The Supreme Court on Abortion," in 41 *Fordham Law Review* 807, 817-818 (1973). I should point out that in his article Means states that both the King's Bench and the Common Bench were convening at York in 1327. The former was there because King Edward III had gone there because of an impending threat of invasion by the Scots. The Common Bench was also transferred there that term from London because the King believed it would bring more people to that part of the country so there would be more to defend against the invasion. Means says that that explains Chief Justice Herle's physical presence, but--unlike Byrn--he says he cannot explain Herle's intervention in the case.

62. *Ibid.*, p. 818.

63. The text of this case is also from the Means' translation in 17 *New York Law Forum* 335, 339. It was quoted in Byrn, p. 818.

64. Byrn, pp. 818-819.

65. See Means II, pp. 340-343.

66. Means II, p. 340, cited in Destro, p. 1271.

67. Destro, p. 1271.

68. *Ibid.* The full text of the pertinent passage in Stanford (*Les Plus del Coron* (1557), Book I, c. 13, "What Things are Required to Constitute Homicide") as quoted by Means II at 340-341, with brief references interspersed (by Means), is as follows:

> It is required that the thing killed be *in rerum natura*. And for this reason if a man killed a child in the womb of its mother: this is not a felony, neither shallhe forfeit anything, and this is so for two reasons: First, because the thing killed has no baptismal name; Second, because it is difficult to judge whether he killed it or not, that is, whether the child died of this battery of its mother or through another cause. Thus it appears in the [*Abortionist's Case* (1348). And see *The Twinslayer's Case* (1327)] a stronger case [*sic*]: if a man beats a woman in an advanced stage of pregnancy who was carrying twins, so that afterwards one of the children died at once and the other was born and given a name in baptism, and two days afterward through the injury he had received he died, and the opinion was, as previously stated, that this was not a felony, etc. [Stanford here gives an alternative citation to *The Twinslayer's Case*, and then reverts to *The Abortionist's Case.]* But it it seems that this reason, that he had no baptismal name, is of no force, for you shall see [here, Stanford cites an infanticide case decided in 1314-15] that there was a presentment "That a certain woman whilst walking opposite a chapel gave birth to a son, and immediately she cut his throat and threw him in a pond of stagnant water and fled: on that account she shall be

> summoned by writ of *exigent* and shall be outlawed"; for this was homicide inasmuch as the thing was *in rerum natura* before being killed: thus this [infanticide] case is in no wise like those above mentioned where the child is killed in the womb of its mother, etc. Which case Bracton affirmed as law in his division of homicide, above mentioned [in a previous chapter in Stanford's treatise] saying as follows: "If there by anyone who strikes a pregnant woman or gives her a poison whereby he causes an abortion, if the foetus be already formed or animated, and especially if it be animated, he commits homicide." But the contrary of this seems to be the law as above stated.

69. See National Right to Life Committee brief in *Wade* and *Bolton*, pp. 26, 28. Prof. Byrn was one of the lawyers on this brief.

70. Bracton, Henri de, 2 *On the Laws and Customs of England,* Thorne, Samuel E., translator and revisor (Cambridge, Mass.: Beklnap Press of Harvard Univ. Press, 1968), p. 341.

71. 2 *Fleta* 60-61 (Bk. I). Selden Society ed., 1955.

72. Coke, Edward, *Third Institute* 50 (1644).

73. *Oxford English Dictionary,* Vol. VI (Oxford: Clarendon Press, 1961 ed.), p. 523.

74. *Ibid.*

75. Blackstone, William, I *Commentaries on the Laws of England* 129-130 (Bk. I) (Philadelphia: Childs & Peterson, 1859). Pages 129-130 are the original pages in Blackstone; the passage appears on p. 100 in the edition used. Blackstone includes a footnote in which he says the following:

> The distinction between murder and manslaughter, or felonious homicide, in the time of Bracton, was in a great degree nominal. [Recall that Bracton regarded abortion as homicide.] The punishment of both was the same; for murder as well as manslaughter, by the common law, had the benefit of clergy.

76. Storing, Herbert J., "William Blackstone," in Strauss, Leo & Cropsey, Joseph, *History of Political Philosophy* (2nd ed.)

(Chicago: Rand-McNally, 1972). The quote within the quote is taken by him from Blackstone, I *Commentaries* San Francisco: Bancroft-Whitney, 1890), pp. 123-124. (This is the edition of the *Commentaries* cited by Storing.) (This piece hereinafter will be referred to as "Storing I.")

77. Stephen, James Fitzjames, I *A History of the Criminal Law of England* (N.Y.: Burt Franklin, 1964), p. 54.

78. *Ibid.*, Vol. II, p. 398. Stephen also traces the English law on abortion back to Roman law which he says similarly--at least according to what Coke and Blackstone say about the English common law of abortion--treated abortion as a criminal offense, but not as homicide. This is noteworthy for two reasons. First, it means that English common law from its beginning treated abortion as a crime and did not recognize it as a liberty. Stephen suggests that the treatment of abortion in the common law as less than homicide derives from the way the Romans treated it. (This does not explain, however, why the earliest English commentators, Bracton and Fleta, treated it as homicide.) Second, it is further proof that abortion was legally rebuked in ancient Rome. (See Stephen, Vol. I, pp. 24-25.)

79. The case is cited from Means II, p. 343.

80. Means II, p. 343.

81. Byrn, p. 820.

82. Means II, p. 346. The *Third Institute* was published nine years before the publication of *Sims's Case in Gouldsborough's Reports*, according to Means. This, of course, is really not relevant because if Coke was Attorney General at the time of the case--and especially if he was involved in it, as Means implies--he presumably knew of its disposition and the reasoning of the court.

83. Means II, p. 346.

84. Byrn, p. 820.

85. Means II, p. 347.

86. Hale, Sir Matthew, *History of the Pleas of the Crown* (1736), p. 433, cited in Means II, p. 349. Hale lived from 1609 to 1676; the book was posthumously published. The emphasis apparently is Hale's .

87. Hale, unnumbered first page, cited in Means II, p. 350. Again, the emphasis appears to be Hale's.

88. Putka, *op. cit.* (Chap. One), pp. 92-93.

89. *Ibid.,* p. 93. I should add as an aside that the present-day American understanding of a rigid "wall of separation" between church and state is not a correct reading of our Constitution and cannot stand up under historical scrutiny, but that is another subject.

I have tried to show, for the most part, that abortion was rebuked at common law, even while it may not have been punished often by the criminal law for practical reasons. Destro presents another perspective on this question by saying that, in looking back at the common law to determine whether there is a constitutional right to abortion, the important question to ask is not whether it was always punished by the common law, but how the common law about it evolved. He says, as we shall go on to see further in this Chapter, that the willingness by both the common law and statutory law to punish abortion grew over time. This reflected, simply, a greater ability to deal with the problems of proof as science came to understand more and more about fetal development. Destro says that to the extent that Coke may have changed the law--he says that his refusal to recognize *The Twinslayer's Case* and *The Abortionist's Case* as precedent in the last lines of the passage from the *Third Institute* that I quoted is evidence of this (and he thereby concedes part of Means' argument about Coke)--,it was in order to bring it "into step with the times," as was the traditional practice of the common law judge. (See Destro, pp. 1271-1273.)

90. Horan, Dennis J. & Marzen, Thomas J., "Abortion and Midwifery: A Footnote in Legal History," in Hilgers, Thomas, M.D.; Horan, Dennis J.; & Mall, David, eds., *New Perspectives on Human Abortion* (Frederick, Md.: University Publications of America (Aletheia), 1981), p. 199.

91. See Means I, *op. cit.* (Chap. One), p. 419.

92. Horan & Marzen, p. 200.

93. *Ibid.*

94. *Ibid.*, pp. 200-201.

95. Means II, p. 336.

96. See Kelsey, Knowlton H., "The Ninth Amendment of the Federal Constitution," in 11 *Indiana L.J.* 309, 321 (1936); Patterson, Bennett B., *The Forgotten Ninth Amendment* (Indianapolis: Bolk-Merrill, 1955), p. 55; Rogge, O. John, "Unenumerated Rights," in 47 *California L.R.* 787, 799-804 (1959); and Redlich, Norman, "Are There 'Certain Rights...Retained by the People'?" in 37 *New York Univ. L.R.* 787, 795 (1962). These preceded the first recognition that the Supreme Court gave to the possibility of the right of privacy being inherent in the Ninth Amendment in *Griswold v. Connecticut*, 381 U.S. 479 (1965). (Justice Douglas' opinion for the Court mentioned the Ninth Amendment as one basis for the decision, but Justice Goldberg, in his concurring opinion, gave it even greater emphasis.)

97. See cite above.

98. Kelsey, p. 313.

99. *Ibid.*, pp. 313-314.

100. Blackstone, *Commentaries*, Book I, pp. 129-145, cited in Kelsey, p. 314. Kelsey also states that Chancellor Kent added a fourth heading which he said was the specific and characteristic contribution of American law: Religious Freedom.

101. Corwin, Edward S., "The 'Higher Law' Background of American Constitutional Law," 42 *Harvard L.R.* 149, 405 (1928). Hereinafter cited as "Corwin I.") Corwin was a famous constitutional scholar.

102. I have adopted Professor Rice's following definition for the term "positivism" when using it in this book: the theory which affirms the validity of human law provided only that it be duly enacted. (Rice, Charles E., *Beyond Abortion: The Theory of Practice of the Secular State*. Chicago: Franciscan Herald Press, 1979, p. 8. Hereinafter cited as "Rice III.") Positivism is intimately connected with utilitarianism because both essentially reject the idea that there are any binding moral principles or norms--i.e., those grounded in nature or God--above those decided on by the individual or the "community" (i.e., the sum total of individuals within a given area). The utilitarian view of morality necessitates a position of positivism because when there is no higher standard of morality there can be no "higher law." The relationship between the utilitarian notion of morality and positivism is discussed further in Chapter Eight in the specific context of the abortion issue.

103. Storing I, p. 600, quoting I *Commentaries*, p. 52.

104. *Ibid.*, p. 598.

105. *Ibid.*, p. 595.

106. *Ibid.*, p. 598, quoting I *Commentaries*, p. 193.

107. *Ibid.*, p. 600, quoting I *Commentaries*, p. 52. Emphasis is mine.

108. *Ibid.*, quoting I *Commentaries*, pp. 125-126. Emphasis is mine.

109. *Ibid.*, quoting I *Commentaries*, pp. 125-126. Emphasis is mine.

110. See Byrn and estro articles cited above. See also: Rice, Charles E., "The Dred Scott Case of the Twentieth Century," in 10 *Houston L.R.* 1059 (1973). (Hereinafter cited as "Rice II.")

111. Byrn, p. 816.

112. 43 Geo. 3, c. 58. The provisions against abortion were actually part of a more sweeping bill which dealt with "several offences of the most criminal nature," including also assault with intent to commit murder and arson. Its proper title was Lord Ellenborough's Maiming and Wounding Bill. (See 36 *The Parliamentary History of England," from the Earliest Period to the Year 1803* (London: Thomas C. Hansard, 1820), pp. 1245-1247.

113. Means II, pp. 357-358.

114. Byrn, p. 824, footnote. He cites Percival, Thomas, *Medical Ethics* (Leake ed., 1927), pp. 134-135.

115. *Wade*, at 136.

116. *Wade*, at 136-137. Quotations are from the 1929 Infant Life (Preservation) Act, 19 & 20 Geo. 5 c. 34.

117. I checked the debates for the pertinent years in *The Parliamentary Debates: Forming a Continuation of the Work Entitled "The Parliamentary History of England," from the Earliest Period to the Year 1803*, 2nd Series (London: Hansard, 1820).

118. *Wade*, at 139.

119. See *Wade*, at 151-152.

120. See Quay, Appendix I, pp. 447-520 for a compilation of the state statutory provisions.

121. See Means II, pp. 376-392.

122. *Wade,* at 148.

123. *Ibid.,* p. 149.

124. 27 N.J.L. 112.

125. 125 Me. 48.

126. 2 N.J. 443, 67 A.2d 141.

127. *Watson v. State,* 9 Tex. App. 237 (1880); *Moore v. State,* 37 Tex. Cr. R. 552, 40 S.W. 287 (1897); *Shaw v. State,* 73 Tex. Cr. R. 337, 165 S.W. 930 (1914); *Fondren v. State,* 74 Tex. Cr. R. 552, 169 S.W. 411 (1914); *Gray v. State,* 77 Tex. Cr. R. 221, 178 S.W. 337 (1915).

128. N.J.L., at 114. Emphasis is the court's.

129. 33 Me., at 55.

130. *Ibid.,* at 58. The prosecutibility of the woman may have had a basis at common law, as indicated in my discussion of Fleta.

131. *Ibid.,*at 57. Emphasis is the court's.

132. *Ibid.,* at 56

133. 2 N.J., at 451.

134. *Ibid.,* at 450.

135. *Ibid.,* at 451.

136. 43 N.J.L. 86.

137. 21 N.J. 249, 121 A.2d 490.

138. Byrn, pp. 854-855. His quote in the passage is from *State v. Farnam,* 82 Ore. 111, 217 (1916).

139. Gorby, John D., "The 'Right' to an Abortion, the Scope of Fourteenth Amendment 'Personhood,' and the Supreme Court's

Birth Requirement," in *Southern Illinois Univ. Law Journal* 1979, 1, 16-17. The decisions, in addition to *State v. Gedlicke* and *State v. Siciliano,* already mentioned, are the following: *Trent v. State,* 15 Ala. App. 485, 73 So. 834 (1916), *cert. denied,* 198 Ala. 695, 73 So. 1002 (1917); *State v. Miller,* 90 Kan. 230, 133 P. 878 (1913); *Dougherty v. People,* 1 Colo. 514 (1872); *Nash v. Meyer,* 54 Idaho 283, 31 P.2d 273 (1934); *State v. Alcorn,* 7 Idaho 599, 64 P. 1014 (1901); *State v. Watson,* 30 Kan. 281, 1 P. 770 (1883); *Joy v. Brown,* 173 Kan. 833, 252 P.2d 889 (1933); *State v. Tippie,* 89 Ohio St. 35, 105 N.E. 75 (1913); *Bowlan v. Lunsford,* 176 Okla. 115, 54 P.2d 666 (1936); *State v. Ausplund,* 86 Ore. 121, 167 P. 1019 (1917); *State v. Howard,* 32 Vt. 380 (1859); *Anderson v. Commonwealth,* 190 Va. 665, 58 S.E.2d 72 (1950); and *State v. Cox,* 197 Wash. 67, 84 P.2d 357 (1938). Gorby states further that the following decisions *implied* that the protection of the child was at least *one* of the purposes of the respective states' statutes: *Smith v. State* (the Maine case discussed in the text; Gorby thus agrees with my reading of it); *Worthington v. State,* 92 Md. 222, 48 A. 355 (1901); *People v. Sessions,* 58 Mich. 594, 26 N.W. 291 (1886); *Montgomery v. State,* 80 Ind. 338 (1881); *Edwards v. State,* 79 Neb. 251, 112 N.W. 611 (1907); *Bennet v. Hymers,* 101 N.H. 483, 147 A.2d 108 (1958); *Mills v. Commonwealth,* 13 Pa. St. 630 (1850); and *State v. Crook,* 16 Utah 212, 51 P. 1091 (1898).

140. Putka, p. 109.

141. Haagensen, C. & Lloyd, W., *A Hundred Years of Medicine,* 1943, p. 12, cited in Putka, p. 109.

142. Putka, p. 109.

143. *Ibid.*

144. *Ibid.*, p. 106.

145. *Ibid.*, pp. 106-107.

146. *Ibid.*, p. 107. Putka makes reference to the following authorities as the basis for his assertions in this passage: Churchill, F., *The Theory and Practice of Midwifery* (4th ed., 1860); Hodge, H., *The Principles and Practice of Obstetrics* (1864); Tucker, D., *Elements of the Principles and Practice of Midwifery* (1848); Velpeau, A., *A Complete Treatise on Midwifery* 4th American ed., (1852); Wharton, F. & Stille, M., *A Treatise on Medical Jurisprudence* (2nd ed., 1860); Denman, Thomas, *An Introduction to the Practice of Midwifery* (1802);

and Rigby, Edward, *A System of Midwifery* (1841). The first quotation within the passage quoted from Putka is from Wharton & Stille, p. 49; the second, from Denman, pp. 96-97; and the third from Velpeau, p. 530. See Putka, p. 290, for the precise pages of these works he referred to otherwise as the source of his statements. He finds these sources and the information from them in Ernest, Alan, "The Evidence in *Roe v. Wade*," a brief filed with the U.S. Supreme Court for a motion to the Court to reconsider *Wade* and *Bolton*.

147. Means I, p. 436, quoted in Putka, p. 96.

148. Means I, p. 436, footnote 59, quoted in Putka, p. 96.

149. *Wade*, at 162.

150. *Ibid.*, at 161-162.

151. Louisell and Noonan say that the reason for this was 1) the difficulty of proving causation in view of the then deficient state of medical knowledge; and 2) the reliance by courts upon the statement of Justice Holmes in *Dietrich v. Northampton*, 138 Mass. 14, 17 (1889), that "the unborn child was a part of the mother at the time of the injury." (Louisell, David W. & Noonan, John T., Jr., "Constitutional Balance," in Noonan I, pp. 226-227.) This seems anomalous in light of what I said earlier about how the law in the nineteenth century was moving more and more in the direction of recognizing the unborn child at every stage of his development as a distinct human being. Perhaps this position is explained by Holmes' further statement in the case that "'any damage to it [the unborn child] which was not too remote to be recovered for at all was recoverable by...[the mother].'" (*Dietrich*, at 17, cited in "Note, The Law and the Unborn Child: The Legal and Logical Inconsistencies," in 46 *Notre Dame Lawyer* 349, 355. Hereinafter cited as "Note.") This suggests that the courts may not have deemed a legal action on behalf of the child as necessary because an action was already available to the mother. Also, since the legal changes recognizing the new biological facts about fetal development came only gradually over the course of the nineteenth century, it is possible that the court in *Dietrich* was not even by 1884 aware of the new information or of the changes that were taking place in statute law and in common law in other courts in other areas of the law. Or perhaps it just reflects the greater slowness with which courts historically have reacted to changes as compared to legislatures.

152. This entire passage is cited from Louisell & Noonan in Noonan I, pp. 226-228.

153. Byrn, p. 843. This note article, fully cited in 151 above, is signed by William J. Maledon. Hereinafter, I shall cite it merely as "Note."

154. The citation for the *Allaire v. St. Luke's Hospital* is 184 Ill. 359, 56 N.E. 638 (1900). The *Boggs* opinion, part of which is quoted, is in 184 Ill., at 368.

155. 65 F. Supp. 138.

156. *Ibid.*, at 140, cited in "Note," p. 356.

157. *Ibid.*, at 143, cited in "Note," p. 356.

158. "Note," pp. 356-357.

159. The lists of cases by jurisdiction holding that the unborn child may recover for injuries and that the viability requirement was rejected is found in "Note," pp. 356-358 (footnotes 59, 60, and 67 of the article).

160. "Note," p. 359. See footnote 76 on p. 359 for the list of states.

161. Prosser, William, *The Law of Torts* (4th ed.) (St. Paul, Minn: West, 1971), pp. 904-906.

162. "Note," p. 360.

163. *Ibid.*, p. 351.

164. Blackstone, *Commentaries*, p. 130, cited in "Note," p. 351.

165. Louisell & Noonan in Noonan I, p. 220, citing for the first example *Doe dem. Clarke v. Clarke*, 2H. Bl. 399, 166 Eng. Rep. 617 (C.P. 1795) and, for the second example, *Trower v. Butts*, 1 Sim. & Stu. 181, 57 Eng. Rep. 72 (Ch. 1823).

166. The Rule Against Perpetuities is a common law rule, still applied, which holds that no contingent interest is good unless it must vest in someone (i.e., the title to the interest becomes definitely fixed in a person) no later than twenty-one years after some life in existence at the creation of the interest. (Gifis, Steven H., *Law Dictionary*. Woodbury, N.Y.: Barron's 1975, p. 184.)

167. *Ibid.*, p. 221, citing *Thellusson v. Woodford,* 4 Ves. 227, 31 Eng. Rep. 117 (Ch. 1798).

168. *Ibid.*, citing *Hall v. Hancock,* 32 Mass. (15 Pick.) 255 (1834); *Barnett v. Pinkston,* 238 Ala. 327, 191 So. 371 (1939); *Cowles v. Cowles,* 56 Conn. 240, 13A. 414 (1887); and *McLain v. Howald,* 120 Mich. 274, 79 N.W. 182 (1899).

169. *Ibid.*, p. 222, citing *Industrial Trust Co. v. Wilson,* 61 R.I. 169, 200A. 467 (1938).

170. 175 Misc. 1022, 1024, 26 N.Y.S. 2d 140, 143 (Sur. Ct., 1941), quoted from Louisell and Noonan in Noonan I, p. 222.

171. Louisell & Noonan in Noonan I, p. 222.

172. *Wagner v. Gardner,* 413 F.2d 267.

173. 98 Colo. 133, 53 P.2d 1189.

174. Cited in Grisez, pp. 373-374.

175. 38 Cal. App. 2d 122, 100 P.2d 806.

176. Cited in Grisez, p. 374.

177. Since *Wade* and *Bolton*, the trend in courts of allowing greater opportunities for recovery by the unborn in tort law has continued. Indeed, since 1973 courts have begun to recognize causes of action for injuries suffered to children *in utero* because of *preconception* acts. See Robertson, Horace B., Jr., "Toward Rational Boundaries of Tort Liability for Injury to the Unborn: Prenatal Injuries, Preconception Injuries and Wrongful Life," 1978 *Duke L.J.* 1401-1457. Robertson dislikes the judicial trends and says that recovery should be limited to infants subsequently born alive (p. 1434). I have found no evidence of a change in the law regarding the property rights of the unborn child. This appears to be an area of the law long since settled.

178. Ash, John, *The New and Complete Dictionary of the English Language,* Vol. II (London: Edward & Charles Dilly in the Poultry, 1775), cited in Putka, p. 33.

179. Barclay, James, *A Complete and Universal English Dictionary* (London: Geo. Virtue, Ivy Lanc., 1841), cited in *Ibid.*

180. Ash, Vol. I, cited in *Ibid.*

181. Barclay, cited in *Ibid.*

182. Ash, Vol. I, cited in *Ibid.*, p. 34.

183. Grimshaw, William, *An Etymological Dictionary of the English Language* (Philadelphia: Grigg, Elliot & Co., 1848), p. 96, cited in *Ibid.*

184. Corwin I, p. 405.

185. *The Complete Works of Edward Livingston on Criminal Jurisprudence*, Vol. I (New York: National Prison Assn. of the U.S.A., 1873) pp. vii-viii, cited in Putka, p. 53.

186. Berg, A., ed., *The Writings of Thomas Jefferson*, Vol. 16 (1907), p. 113, cited in Putka, p. 53.

187. U.S. Constitution, Art. I, Sec. 9, Cl.8 and Art. II, Sec. 1, Cl.2. Clause 3 refers to a "person" again in the context of being a candidate for President.

188. *Wade* (J. Rehnquist, dissenting), at 174-175.

189. *Ibid.*, at 177.

190. Putka, p. 56, citing the Ernest brief mentioned in note 146 above, at 67. The five states were North Carolina, South Carolina, Nebraska, Tennessee, and Rhode Island.

191. Witherspoon, Joseph P., Testimony beofre the House Subcommittee on Civil and Constitutional Rights of the House Committee on the Judiciary, Ninety-Fourth Congress, Second Session, 1976, cited in Congressional Record, March 3, 1976, p. 5108. The Subcommittee was conducting hearings on a constitutional amendment to guarantee a right to life to the unborn.

192. Putka, p. 53.

193. *Transactions of the American Medical Association*, 1859, Vol. XII, p. 75, cited in Witherspoon, *ibid.*, p. 5107.

194. The provision is from 12 Stat. 19 (1860), cited in Witherspoon, *ibid.*, p. 5108.

195. 14 Stat. 13 (1866).

196. Witherspoon, *ibid.*, p. 5108

197. *Ibid.*

198. *Ibid.*

199. Storer, Horatio R. and Heard, Franklin F., *Criminal Abortion: Its Nature, Its Evidence, & Its Law* (Boston: Little, Brown & Co., 1868), pp. 28-29, 79, cited in Witherspoon, Joseph P., "Impact of the Abortion Decisions Upon the Father's Role," written material submitted as part of the author's testimony before the Subcommittee on Constitutional Amendments of the Senate Committee on the Judiciary, Ninety-Fourth Congress, First Session, 1976. This Subcommittee was conducting hearings on a proposed "Human Life Amendment" to the Constitution. The proceedings of the hearings were published under the title of *Abortion,* in four parts. This quote and Witherspoon's full testimony appears in Part IV, p. 551. Note the quote's saying that physicians had arrived at a "unanimous opinion" about the child's being alive from conception. It is curious that while the medical profession had arrived at agreement on this point in the last century, voices from within the medical profession today (as witnessed by the hearings on the proposed Human Life Bill before Senator John P. East's Subcommittee on Separation of Powers in the summer of 1981), with the benefit of the even greater knowledge of fetal development gained in the twentieth century (see Chapter Seven), can claim that it is not so.

200. Noonan II, *op. cit.* (Chap. One), p. 6.

201. *Congressional Glove,* Thirty-Seventh Cong., Second Sess. (April 11, 1862), pp. 1638, 1640, cited in Witherspoon, prepared testimony, in *Abortion IV*, p. 527.

202. Rep. C. A. Newcomb (Rep. of Mo.), in *Congressional Globe,* Fortieth Cong., Second Sess. (March 21, 1868), App. p. 303, cited in *ibid.,* p. 528, 553.

203. Witherspoon, *Ibid.,* p. 553.

204. *Ibid.,* p. 528.

205. *Ibid.,* p. 526.

206. *Sincerely, Ronald Reagan, op. cit.* (Chap. One), p. 93.

207. 116 U.S. 616 (1886).

208. 116 U.S., at 635, cited in Witherspoon, Joseph P., Brief in

Wade filed on behalf of the Texas Association of Diocesan Attorneys, p. 12. Emphasis is mine.

209. *Wade,* at 157. Texas' statement is found in Kurland & Casper, eds. *op. cit.* (Chap. Two), p. 819.

210. 321 F. Supp. 741. Putka points out this case.

211. 321 F. Supp., at 746.

212. 405 U.S. 438 (1972).

213. *Union Pacific R.R. Co. v. Botsford,* 141 U.S. 250 (1891).

214. *Boyd v. U.S.,* 116 U.S. 616 (1886) and *Terry v. Ohio,* 392 U.S. 1 (1968).

215. *Olmstead v. U.S.,* 277 U.S. 438 (1928) and *Katz v. U.S.,* 389 U.S. 347 (1967).

216. *Stanley v. Georgia,* 394 U.S. 557 (1969).

217. *Meyer v. Nebraska,* 262 U.S. 390 (1923) and *Pierce v. Society of Sisters,* 268 U.S. 510 (1925).

218. *Skinner v. Oklahoma,* 316 U.S. 158 (1942).

219. *Prince v. Massachusetts,* 321 U.S. 158 (1944).

220. *Loving v. Virginia,* 388 U.S. 1 (1967).

221. *Griswold v. Connecticut,* 381 U.S. 479 (1965) and *Eisenstadt.*

222. *State v. Munson,* 201 N.W. 2d 123, 126 (So. Dak., 1972).

223. O'Meara, *op. cit.* (Chap. One), pp. 18-19.

224. *Griswold,* at 482, 486.

225. Noonan II, p. 21.

226. *Botsford,* at 253. The Court stated further that in civil matters such a writ was permitted at common law only for the purpose of protecting "the rightful succession to the property of a deceased person against the fraudulent claims of bastards, when a widow was suspected to feign herself with child in order to produce a supposititious heir to the estate, in which case the heir or devisee might have this writ

to examine whether she was with child or not, and, if she was, to keep her under proper restraint till delivered."

227. Gorby, p. 19, footnote 95.

228. *Ibid.*, p. 19.

229. *Parens patriae,* literally "parent of the country," refers traditionally to the role of the state as sovereign and guardian of persons under legal disability. (See *Black's Law Dictionary,* Fifth ed. (St. Paul, Minn.: West, 1979), p. 1003.)

230. 67 N.J. Supp. 517, 171 A.2d 140 (Juv. Ct., 1961).

231. 42 N.J. 421, 201 A.2d 537, *cert. denied,* 377 U.S. 985 (1964).

232. 331 F.2d 1000 (C.A., D.C.), *cert. denied,* 377 U.S. 978 (1964).

233. See, for example, Justice Douglas' opinion for the Court in *Saia v. New York,* 334 U.S. 558, 562 (1945).

234. The parents in these cases refused transfusions either for the mother or the child for religious reasons.

235. 49 N.J. 22, 227 A.2d 689.

236. 227 A.2d 689, 693.

CHAPTER FOUR NOTES

1. The *Wade* appellants also submitted a short supplemental brief prior to the reargument of the cases before the Court which I shall also make reference to.

2. The *Bolton* appellants and PPFA also filed both main and supplemental briefs. NLPHPP filed roughly identical briefs *amicus curiae* in both *Wade* and *Bolton*.

3. A class action is a lawsuit brought by representative member(s) of a large group of persons on behalf of all members of the group. (Gifis, Steven H., *Law Dictionary* (Woodbury, N.Y.: Barron's Educational Series, Inc.), p. 33.)

4. Hughes said the following to Douglas: "'Justice Douglas, you must remember one thing. At the constitutional level where we work, 90 percent of any decision is emotional. The rational part of us supplies the reasons for supporting our predilections.'" Douglas said that it was "'shattering'" to hear this, but "'over the years [it] turned out to be true.'" (See Mauro, Robert L., "Reflections on Choosing Supreme Court Justices," in *The Wanderer*, July 2, 1981, p. 8.)

5. *Wade* brief, p. 12.

6. *Ibid.*, p. 30.

7. *Ibid.*, p. 94.

8. Brief for appellants in *Roe v. Wade* (*Wade* brief), p. 99.

9. *Maynard v. Hill*, 125 U.S. 190, 211 (1888), cited in *Wade* brief, p. 99.

10. *Skinner v. Oklahoma*, 316 U.S. 535, 541 (1942), cited in *Wade* brief, p. 99.

11. *Wade* brief, p. 100.

12. *Ibid.*, p. 92.

13. *Loving v. Virginia*, 388 U.S. 1 (1967).

14. *Meyer v. Nebraska*, 262 U.S. 390 (1923) and *Pierce v. Society of Sisters*, 268 U.S. 510 (1925).

15. *Skinner v. Oklahoma*, *infra*.

16. 321 F. Supp. 1385 (N.D., Ill., 1971).

17. *Wade* opinion, at 152-153.

18. *Wade* brief, p. 103. Emphasis is mine.

19. *Ibid*. Again, emphasis is mine. The term "sovereignty," I believe, justifies my conclusion that the brief is making an extreme statement of individual liberty. "Sovereignty" implies total independence.

20. The initial round of briefs in the cases was filed in 1971. *Eisenstadt*, of course, was decided in 1972.

21. *Wade* brief, p. 102.

22. *Ibid.*, p. 106.

23. *Ibid.*, p. 99, quoting 381 U.S., at 486.

24. Genesis 2:24, *The Holy Bible,* Douay ed., 1941.

25. Genesis 9:1, *Ibid.*

26. Jeremias, Joachim, *New Testament Theology* (N.Y.: Charles Scribner's Sons), pp. 224-225.

27. *Ibid.*, p. 227.

28. Lewis, C. S., *The Abolition of Man* (N.Y.: Collier Bks., 1962), pp. 107-109. Originally published by Macmillan, 1947.

29. *Wade* brief, p. 104.

30. Professor Francis Canavan points out that the Court, rather soon after *Wade* and *Bolton*, more clearly and directly asserted this primacy of the individual over the marital union --to the point of almost endorsing the currently fashionable view of marriage as merely a contract--in the *Planned Parenthood of Central Missouri v. Danforth* case, 428 U.S. 52 (1976). In that case, the Court held that a state cannot require that a married woman get her husband's consent and a minor girl her parent's consent before an abortion is performed. Canavan likened this view of marriage to the social contract theory of the state in politics. Just as the social contract theory believed that man is not a social or political animal by nature and that civil society is created only by the consent of individuals, so marriage has no given nature nor rights and obligations except those which the individuals contracting it wish to give it. Marriage is seen as something which essentially cannot bind the parties in it to anything which they believe infringes on their individual freedom. (See Canavan, Francis, "The Theory of the Danforth Case," in II *Human Life Review* , No. 4 (Fall 1976), p. 5.)

31. 141 U.S. 250, 251, cited in *Wade* brief, p. 103.

32. *Wade* brief, p. 102.

33. *Ibid.*, p. 105.

34. *Ibid.*, p. 106.

35. *Ibid.* A curious point about this comment is the way it likens the human being to a machine made possible by modern technology. The human being seems to be understood in the same way that a machine would be, in terms of a function he performs. I should also point out that the *Wade* appellants in oral reargument reemphasized the almost hostile attitude toward children and pregnancy seen in their brief. Mrs. Sarah Weddington, in trying to justify the federal courts taking up this case, stated that "the women who continue to be forced through pregnancy have certainly gone through something that is irreparable...It is certainly 'great'; and it is certainly 'immediate.'" She also said that "there is great, immediate, irreparable injury..." (*Roe v. Wade* oral argument (Dec. 13, 1971) in Kurland and Casper, *op. cit.* (Chap. Two), pp. 811, 812.)

36. Clark, *op. cit.* (Chap. Two), p. 9.

37, *Wade* brief, p. 97.

38. 197 U.S. 11.

39. *McCollum v. Mayfield,* 130 F. Supp. 112 (N.D. Calif., 1955); *Coleman v. Johnson,* 247 F.2d 273 (7th Cir., 1957); *Edwards v. Duncan,* 355 F.2d 993 (4th Cir., 1966); *Tolbert v. Eyman,* 434 F.2d 625 (9th Cir., 1970).

40. *Wyatt v. Stickney,* 325 F. Supp 781 (M.D. Ala., 1971).

41. *EDF v. Hoerner Waldorf,* 1 E.R. 1960 (D. Mont., 1970).

42. *Chrisman v. Sisters of St. Joseph of Newark,* Cir. No. 70-430 (D. Ore., July 22, 1971).

43. ACOG brief, p. 12.

44. *Wade* brief, p. 95.

45. *Ibid.*

46. 197 U.S., at 27.

47. *Ibid.*, at 38.

48. ACOG brief, p. 12.

49. *Wade* brief, p. 111.

50. *Ibid.*, pp. 111-112.

51. *Wade* brief, p. 98.

52. *Ibid.*, p. 95.

53. *Ibid.*, p. 98, quoting the statute.

54. Attorney Stephen H. Galebach, however, emphasizes that in a number of decisions in recent years, involving the Fourteenth and Fifteenth Amendments, the Court has accepted Congressional attempts to interpret provisions of these amendments by statute--i.e., which have had the result of creating new rights--even when at variance with its previous opinions. See Galebach--"A Human Life Statute," in VII *The Human Life Review,* No. 1 (Winter 1981), pp. 5-33.

55. *Wade* brief, p. 97. Emphasis is mine.

56. *Ibid.*, p. 104.

57. Guttmacher, Alan, "Abortion--Yesterday, Today and Tomorrow," in Guttmacher I, *op. cit.* (Chap. One), p. 1, cited in National Legal Program on Health Problems of the Poor Brief in *Bolton,* p. 24.

58. Mandy, Arthur J., "Reflections of a Gynecologist," in Rosen, Harold, ed., *Abortion in America,* p. 288, cited in *Ibid.*, p. 26.

59. NLPHPP brief in *Bolton,* p. 33.

60. *Yick Wo v. Hopkins,* 118 U.S. 356, 373-74 (1886), cited in *Ibid.*

61. Lockhart, William B., et al., *Cases and Materials on Constitutional Rights and Liberties,* Fourth ed. (St. Paul, Minn.: West, 1975), p. 894. The first quote within the quote is from *McDonald v. Board of Election Commissioners of Chicago,* 394 U.S. 802, 807 (1969).

62. 396 U.S. 246.

63. 383 U.S., at 668.

64. 402 U.S. 137.

65. 411 U.S. 1.

66. 411 U.S., at 29.

67. 109 U.S. 3.

68. *Ibid.*, at 11.

69. Lockhart, William B., et al., *Constitutional Law: Cases--Comments--Questions*, Fourth ed. (St. Paul, Minnl: West, 1975) p. 1385.

70. *Smith v. Allwright*, 321 U.S. 649 (1944).

71. *Burton v. Wilmington Parking Authority*, 365 U.S. 715 (1961).

72. *Shelley v. Kraemer*, 334 U.S. 1 (1948).

73. The Court's action in *Panama Refining Company v. Ryan*, 293 U.S. 388 (1935), *Schechter Poultry Corp. v. U.S.*, 295 U.S. 495 (1935), and *Carter v. Carter Coal Co.*, 298 U.S. 238 (1936), which still stand as precedents, indicates that this would be how the case would be decided.

74. 118 U.S., at 373.

75. NLPHPP brief in *Bolton*, pp. 28-29. The quote within the quote is from Packer, Herbert L., *The Limits of the Criminal Sanction* (Stanford, Calif.: Stanford U. Press, 1968), p. 344.

76. NLPHPP brief in *Bolton*, p. 23. The brief quotes Bumpass, Larry L. & Westoff, Charles F., "The Perfect 'Contraceptive' Population," 169 *Science* 1177, 1179 (1970).

77. NLPHPP brief in *Bolton*, p. 23.

78. *Ibid*.

79. The nationwide Gallup Polls taken on the question of approval for legalized abortion back up my claim. In the Gallup Polls of June 1975, December 1977, February 1979, July 1980, July 1981, and June 1983, non-whites were shown as opposing legalized abortion to a significantly greater extent than whites. The way the question was asked differed in these Polls. In June 1975, Dec. 1977, and Feb. 1979, non-whites were found to oppose abortion for all reasons asked about and in all three trimesters of pregnancy to a significantly greater extent than whites. In 1980 and 1981, questions about specific reasons and different trimesters were not

asked, but a higher percentage--significantly higher in most categories of responses--of non-whites than whites still opposed legalized abortion. The November 1969 Gallup Poll was the only one to show that a higher percentage of non-whites than whites favored legalized abortion, but an identical percentage of whites and non-whites opposed it.

In the 1983 Poll, the most recent, this trend was continued, although less dramatically. By 83 percent to 69 percent, whites outran non-whites in believing that abortion should be legal under "any" or "only certain" circumstances. Non-whites were ahead of whites by 26 to 15 percent in believing that it should be illegal in all circumstances. Similarly, more whites than non-whites (by 52 to 44 percent) "favored" and more non-whites than whites "opposed" the Supreme Court's 1973 rulings, which were erroneously stated to have held that "a woman may go to a doctor to end a pregnancy at any time during the first three months of pregnancy" (a more conservative position than the Court actually took).

(An interesting inconsistency seems to appear in a Gallup Poll taken in September 1982 which asked about support for a federal ban on the financing of abortions. By 46 to 30 percent whites favored such a ban to a greater extent than non-whites, and by a 70 to 54 percent margin non-whites outran whites in opposing it. This result stands in sharp contrast to the rest of the trend in these poll results. I do not know the reason for it, but it may not have to do with views about abortion *per se*.)

As far as the poor are concerned, these Gallup Polls and the one taken in September 1972 (which did not include a breakdown according to race) showed that the percentage of persons with incomes of under $5,000 per year who opposed legalized abortion was higher--generally, significantly higher --than the percentages which opposed it in the highest income groups. This applied for most of the specific reasons and different trimesters asked about in certain of the Polls. The greatest opposition to abortion among different income groups was registered consistently by those with incomes of below $3,000.

The findings of the March 1976 Gallup Poll showed that a significantly higher percentage of non-whites than whites supported a constitutional amendment to prohibit abortion except when the mother's life is in danger. The Poll also showed that the highest percentage of support for such an amendment was in the two lowest income groups ($3,000-4,999 and under $3,000). (Source: Gallup, George H., *The Gallup Poll*. Various years from 1969 to 1981. Two different editions published by Scholarly Resources, Inc. of Wilmington, Del. and Random House of New York, N.Y. The source for the

1982 and 1983 Poll results was *The Gallup Poll Report*. Nov. 1982/Report No. 206 and Aug. 1983/Report No. 215. Princeton, N.J.: The Gallup Poll (Princeton Opinion Press).)

Further evidence of black oppostion to abortion prior to the *Wade* and *Bolton* decisions is reported by black social worker Erma Clardy Craven. She points to studies conducted by the Bowman Gray Medical School on poverty-level blacks which showed that 79% of 776 poverty-level black females, 86% of 500 of their partners, and 70% of low-income black females were found "not in favor of abortion under any circumstances." When another 990 urban black females were studied, 77% were found to be opposed to abortion under any circumstances, and this opposition was found to be manifest in their actions of actually carrying their children to term. When black males under 30 were studied, 88% of them were found to be opposed to abortions as a form of birth control. (See Craven, Erma Clardy, "Abortion, Poverty and Black Genocide: Gifts to the Poor?" in Hilgers & Horan, *op. cit.* (Chap. One), p. 239. The sources for the figures she cites are on p. 241.)

80. NLPHPP brief in *Bolton*, p. 23.

81. *Ibid.*, p. 34.

82. *Wade* brief, p. 117.

83. *Ibid.*, p. 118.

84. Also joining New Women Lawyers in this brief were the Women's Health and Abortion Project, Inc. and the National Abortion Action Coalition.

85. New Women Lawyers *amicus curiae* brief, pp. 46-47.

86. *Ibid.*, p. 46.

87. I was informed by the ACLU National Office in New York City that the organization's state affiliates in New Jersey, Pennsylvania, and Wisconsin--I was told that state affiliates are "part of the ACLU"--were involved in cases which challenged such statutes. I believe it is fair for me to bring this up to show how shallow and even deceptive this statement in the brief is because, even though the brief was not drafted by the ACLU and this statement may not have been put in by its lawyers, it did work on behalf of the appellants and one of its top constitutional lawyers, Professor Norman Dorsen is listed on the brief as "Of Counsel." (See Chapter One

Notes, note 28.) We must presume that Dorsen and the other ACLU lawyers read and approved the brief before its submission.

88. Ryan, Kenneth J., "Humane Abortion Laws and the Health Needs of Society," in 17 *Western Reserve L.R.* 424, 432 (1965).

89. It should be pointed out that one of the developers of the oral contraceptive also disagrees with Dr. Ryan on this point. Dr. Minchuch Chang has said that, "I personally feel the pill has rather spoiled young people...It's made them more permissive...But people will abuse anything." (Cited in *Christchurch* (New Zealand) *Press,* Dec. 6, 1981.) His last sentence touches the problem of people using a new technology without moral guidance, which I shall explore in Chapter Eight.

90. NWL brief, p. 46.

91. See Blake II, *op. cit.* (Chap. One), pp. 64-81.

92. Tribe, Laurence H., *American Constitutional Law* (Mineola, N.Y.: Foundation Press, 1978), pp. 710, 712. Emphasis is his.

93. *Wade* brief, p. 126 cited in *Connally v. General Construction Co.,* 269 U.S. 385, 391 (1926).

94. In oral argument, the *Wade* appellants made the odd contention that the difference between *Vuitch* and their case was--despite the fact that they raise the vagueness argument in the brief--that the Texas statute had been held by the Texas Court of Criminal Appeals to be "more definite than the D.C. law." They also said that the latter permitted the physician to exercise his medical judgment more fully than the former. (*Roe v. Wade* oral argument (Dec. 13, 1971) in Kurland & Casper, *op. cit.* (Chap. Two), p. 783.)

95. Texas Penal Code, Articles 1191-1194, 1196, cited in *Wade* opinion, at 117-118, f.n. 1.

CHAPTER FIVE NOTES

1. *Griswold v. Connecticut,* 381 U.S. 479, 483, quoting from *NAACP v. Alabama,* 357 U.S. 449, 462 (1958).

2. *Griswold,* at 485.

3. *Ibid.*, at 486.

4. *Ibid.* (J. Goldberg, concurring), at 486.

5. *Ibid.*, at 493.

6. *Ibid.*, quoting from *Powell v. Alabama,* 287 U.S. 45, 67 (1932).

7. *Ibid.*, at 494, quoting from *Olmstead v. U.S.*, 277 U.S. 438, 478 (1928).

8. *Griswold* (J. Goldberg, concurring), at 499.

9. *Ibid.*, at 498.

10. *Ibid.*, at 496.

11. *Ibid.* (J. Black, dissenting), at 519.

12. *Ibid.*

13. *Ibid.*, at 522.

14. *Ibid.*, at 525, quoting *Calder v. Bull* (J. Iredell's opinion), 3 Dall. 386, 399 (1798).

15. 3 Dall. 386.

16. *Ibid.*, at 387-388. Emphasis is mine.*

17. 3 Dall. 386, 399.

18. 16 Wall. 36, 55.

19. *Ibid.*, at 76.

20. *Ibid.*, (J. Field, dissenting), at 77. Emphasis is mine.

---

*Wherever I indicate that the "emphasis is mine" in the quotations from the opinions in this Section, I have made the emphasis in order to point out the reference made to some notion of unenumerated rights or natural justice.

21. *Ibid.* (J. Bradley, dissenting), at 119. Emphasis is mine.

22. 198 U.S. 45.

23. *Ibid.*, at 56.

24. *Ibid.* (J. Harlan, dissenting), at 68, 72-73. Emphasis is mine.

25. 110 U.S. 516.

26. *Ibid.* (J. Harlan, dissenting), at 546. Harlan here explains the Court's position.

27. 110 U.S., at 538.

28. *Ibid.* (J. Harlan, dissenting), at 547.

29. *Ibid.*, at 549.

30. 211 U.S. 78.

31. *Ibid.*, at 110.

32. 261 U.S. 525.

33. *Ibid.* (J. Holmes, dissenting), at 568.

34. *Ibid.*, at 570.

35. 316 U.S. 455.

36. *Ibid.*, at 473. Emphasis is mine.

37. *Ibid.*, at 462. Emphasis is mine.

38. *Ibid.* (J. Black, dissenting), at 476-477. Black's quotes are from the Court's opinion. Emphasis is mine.

39. 332 U.S. 46.

40. *Ibid.* (J. Black, dissenting), at 90.

41. *Ibid.* (J. Frankfurter, concurring), at 65, 67-68, quoting *Palko v. Connecticut*, 302 U.S. 319 (1937). Emphasis is mine.

42. 342 U.S. 165.

43. *Ibid.*, at 169, quoting *Malinski v. New York*, 324 U.S. 401,

416-417 (1945). Emphasis is mine.

44. *Ibid*. The first quote is from *Snyder v. Massachusetts*, 291 U.S. 319, 325 (1937).

45. *Ibid.*, at 173.

46. *Ibid*. (J. Black, dissenting), at 175.

47. *Ibid.*, at 175, 176.

48. On the earlier substantive due process cases, specifically, demonstrating the Court's responding to the business community, see the following: Mason, Alpheus T. & Beaney, William M., *American Constitutional Law: Introductory Essays and Selected Cases* (Sixth ed.) (Englewood Cliffs, N.J.: Prentice-Hall 1978), pp. 323-341; Miller, Arthur S., *The Supreme Court and American Capitalism* (N.Y.: Free Press, 1968), and McClosky, Robert G., "Economic Due Process and the Supreme Court: An Exhumation and Reburial," *Supreme Court Review* 1962, p. 34. For a general argument that the Court reflected the views of business in the late nineteenth and early twentieth centuries, see: Mason & Beaney and Miller above and also Pritchett, C. Herman, "Judicial Supremacy from Marshall to Berger," in Harmon, M. Judd, ed., *Essays on the Constitution of the United States* (Port Washington, N.Y.: Kennikat, 1978), p. 103; Swindler, William F., *Court and Constitution in the Twentieth Century*, Vol. 1 (Indianapolis: Bobbs-Merrill, 1969), pp. 18-38.

49. See appellant's brief in *Griswold*, pp. 39-61.

50. 1 Cranch 137 (1803).

51. Storing, Herbert J., *What the Anti-Federalists Were FOR* (Chicago: Univ. of Chicago Press, 1981), p. 64, quoting "Centinel I," p. 25 and "A Confederationist" in *Pennsylvania Herald and General Advertiser*, Oct. 27, 1787. (This book by Storing will hereinafter be cited as "Storing II.")

52. "Letters of Brutus," cited in Storing II, p. 66.

53. Storing II, p. 66.

54. *Ibid.*, pp. 66-67, quoting Agrippa. Agrippa--and Storing--may here be suggesting the independence of the new government from established legal norms and constraints. Article III of the Constitution clearly grants recognition to the common

law by saying that "[t]he judicial Power shall extend to all Cases, in Law and Equity..."

55. *Ibid.*, p. 67, quoting "Federal Republican." In any event, these Federalist arguments lost some force by the very fact that the Constitution already did stipulate a few limitations on federal power *vis-a-vis* the individual (i.e., relating to such matters as the suspension of *habeas corpus*).

56. *Ibid.*, p. 68, quoting "Brutus."

57. *Ibid.*, p. 68.

58. *Ibid.*, p. 69.

59. Declaration of Independence, cited in *Family Almanac* '72 (N.Y.: The New York Times, 1971), p. 11.

60. Corwin, *op. cit.* (Chap. Two), p. 54.

61. Coke, Edward, First Institute, p. 81, cited in *Ibid.*, p. 55.

62. Corwin, p. 55. Emphasis on "court" is Corwin's; the other emphasized words are mine.

63. Storing II, p. 65, quoting Wilson from McMaster, John Back and Stone, Frederich D., eds., *Pennsylvania and the Federal Constitution,* Historical Society of Pa., 1888, pp. 143-144.

64. Storing II, p. 68, quoting "Remarker" in *Boston Independent Chronicle,* Dec. 27, 1787.

65. Storing II, p. 70.

66. *Ibid.*, quoting "Federal Farmer." Emphasis is mine.

67. Madison to Jefferson, Oct. 17, 1788, in Padover, Saul K., ed., *The Complete Madison* (N.Y.: Harper & Bros., 1953), p. 254.

68. "Proceedings in the House of Representatives," May 4, 1789, first first published in *Annals of Congress* (Wash., D.C.: Gales & Seaton, 1934), reprinted in Patterson, Bennett B., *The Forgotten Ninth Amendment* (Indianapolis: Bobbs-Merrill, 1955), pp. 107-110.

69. *The Random House Dictionary of the English Language* (N.Y.: Random House, 1967), p. 375.

70. "Proceedings..." in Patterson, p. 115.

71. *Ibid.*, p. 116. Emphasis is mine.

72. *Random House Dictionary*, p. 1398.

73. See "Proceedings..." in Patterson, pp. 118-119.

74. *Ibid.*, p. 145. Emphasis is mine.

75. Hamilton, Alexander, Federalist 78 in *The Federalist* (Modern Library ed.) (N.Y.: Random House, p. 506.)

76. *Ibid.*

77. *Ibid.*, p. 507.

78. *Ibid.*, p. 510.

79. If we were to accept "Agrippa's" assessment (note 54 above), we might well conclude that the courts would have to stay strictly with the text of the Constitution (including its amendments) and could not even refer to the constitutional or common law background of the document.

80. Federalist 78 in *The Federalist*, p. 505.

81. 1 Cranch, at 178. The Anti-Federalists apparently were even more suspicious of the judiciary than the legislature and, as the "Letters of Brutus," Nos. XI and XV make clear, they believed that the new constitution had given the national judiciary a dangerously great amount of power. This is because they believed the judiciary would act to increase national government power at the expense of the states and would subvert individual rights. In the early years of the new Republic, they actively opposed the actions of the federal courts. It is questionable whether the Anti-Federalists would have opposed the federal courts' acting to *expand* individual rights (i.e., what the Supreme Court in *Griswold* and *Wade/Bolton* claimed to be doing). It is possible they may have opposed even this, since they disapproved of any federal institution accumulating more power. They might have viewed even this as in the long-run working to the *disadvantage* of individuals and the states.

82. Rutland, Robert Allen, *The Birth of the Bill of Rights, 1776-1791* (Chapel Hill, N.C.: Univ. of No. Carol. Press, 1955), p. 3.

83. Pound, Roscoe, *The Development of Constitutional Guarantees of Liberty* (New Haven, Conn.: Yale Univ. Press, 1957), p.75.

84. The Delcaration of 1774 makes reference to what seems to have been regarded as a few of these essential rights when it states the following: "'Whereupon the Deputies so appointed ...do...declare their claim to the legal rights of free natural born subjects, to the common law, to trial by jury, and to assemble peaceably to consider grievances and petition for redress.'" (This passage from the Declaration is quoted from Pound, pp. 75-76.)

85. Magna Carta (McKechnie's Translation), cited in Pound, p. 117.

86. *Ibid.*, pp. 123, 124.

87. *Ibid.*, pp. 122, 124.

88. Coke, Sir Edward, "Commentary on the Magna Carta," in *Second Institute,* England, 1642, cited in Pound, p. 148.

89. *Ibid.*, p. 153.

90. *Ibid.*, p. 158.

91. Petition of Right, 1627, printed in Pickering, *Statutes at Large,* pp. 317-320 cited in Pound, p. 166.

92. *Ibid.*, pp. 168-169.

93. English Bill of Rights, 1688 (Statute I Wm. & Mary, Session 2, Chap. 2), cited in Pound, pp. 181-182.

94. Blackstone, *op. cit.* (Chap. Three), pp. 93-94

95. *Ibid.*, p. 94.

96. *Ibid.*

97. *Ibid.*, p. 95.

98. *Ibid.*, p. 97.

99. *Ibid.*

100. *Ibid.*, p. 99.

101. *Ibid.*, p. 100.

102. *Ibid.*, p. 102.

103. *Ibid.*, p. 103.

104. Virginia Declaration of Rights, Jan. 12, 1776 (9 Hening, Statutes at Large of Virginia, pp. 109-112), cited in Pound, p. 187. This was the first written bill of rights in America.

105. Pound, pp. 187-189.

106. *Ibid.*, pp. 83-84.

107. *Ibid.*, pp. 85-86.

108. *Ibid.*, pp. 86-88.

109. *Ibid.*, p. 88.

110. *Ibid.*, p. 89.

111. *Ibid.*, pp. 89-90.

112. Another fruitful source of information might be the debates of the state conventions which were convened to ratify the Constitution. I believe, however, that considering the provisions of the state bills of rights has given a sufficient insight, for my purposes, into the views prevalent in the various states. As to Jefferson, some might object that he is not really one of the Founding Fathers nor a significant influence on the Bill of Rights because he was neither at the Convention nor in the First Congress. I will stand with Harvey C. Mansfield, Jr., however, who says that "[a]s the author of the Declaration of Independence, Jefferson made himself one of his country's Founders..." (Cited in Mansfield essay on Jefferson in Frisch, Morton J. & Stevens, Richard G., *American Political Thought: The Philosophic Dimension of American Statesmanship* (N.Y.: Charles Scribner's Sons, 1971), p. 23).

113. See C. Pinckney's proposals submitted on August 20, 1727, Pinckney's and Gerry's motion to insert a declaration protecting freedom of the press into the Constitution on September 14 (which was voted down after Sherman said it was unnecessary since Congress' power does not extend to the press), and Pinckney's pamphlet submitted to the Convention on May 28

before it began its work. These appear in Ferrand, Max, ed.--*The Records of the Federal Convention of 1787*, Vol. II, New Haven, Conn.: Yale Univ. Press, 1937, pp. 341, 617.

114. See Pinkney's pamphlet and his August 20 proposals.

115. Mason moved on September 14 to have it removed from the report of the Committee on Style and Arrangement. This was unanimously rejected.

116. See Pinkney's August 20 proposals.

117. See his letter to Jefferson, October 17, 1788, in Padover, ed., p. 253.

118. "Proceedings..." in Patterson, pp. 107-110.

119. *Ibid.*, p. 110.

120. *Ibid.*

121. *Ibid.*, p. 111.

122. *Ibid.*, p. 113.

123. *Ibid.*, p. 178.

124. *Ibid.*, p. 144. This is Representative Jackson's speech. Jackson mentions these documents, along with the statute *De Tollagio non concedendo*, as along with yet *other* acts of Parliament, as forming "the basis of English liberty" (p. 144). While he emphasizes that it is not these documents alone that do this, the fact that he singles them out perhaps indicates that he believes the rights contained therein to be preeminent. In any event, I have discussed the most important of the other statutes he refers to (e.g., the Petition of Right, the English Bill of Rights), so we know whatever other rights he might be speaking of.

125. *Ibid.*, p. 145. This is Representative Sherman speaking.

126. *Ibid.*, p. 161. This is Representative Huntington speaking.

127. *Ibid.*, p. 162. This is Representative Sedgwick speaking.

128. *Ibid.*, p. 167. This is Jackson again.

129. Jefferson, Thomas, "Inauguration Address--March 4, 1801," in

Koch, Adrienne & Peden, William, eds., *The Life and Writings of Thomas Jefferson* (N.Y.: Modern Library, 1944), p. 324.

130. *Ibid.*, p. 437.

131. See Patterson, pp. 51-56. He also mentions certain economic rights which are protected by statute and which one would not be able to infer as being fundamental from a Constitution and a constitutional tradition which has sought to protect primarily political rights. He also mentions the right of privacy, but gives no firmer basis for it than the Court does in *Griswold* or *Wade/Bolton*.

132. The *Griswold* appellants' brief argues, in effect, that the Court should not be deterred from establishing the right of privacy even if there is no explicit basis for it in our constitutional background. (See brief, pp. 79-89.) The problem with this view is that it does not answer the objections of Justice Black and others that if a firm constitutional basis does not have to be put forth by the Court for its decisions, there is no way to check the unjustified exercise of discretion by the Justices. Professor Means, as noted in Chapter Three, apparently does not share the *Griswold* appellants' view. He says that the right to abortion, as part of a right to liberty or privacy, could be considered protected by the Constitution only if it were a common law right in 1791. It has been shown in this Chapter that the right of privacy--as was shown in Chapter Three about the right to abortion--was *not* such a right.

133. Hofstadter, Samuel H., *The Development of the Right of Privacy in New York* (N.Y.: Crosby, 1954), pp. 1-2.

134. *Ibid.*, p. 2.

135. *Ibid.*, pp. 2-3.

136. *Ibid.*, p. 4.

137. Cited in Flaherty, David H., *Privacy in Colonial New England* Charlottesville, Va.: Univ. of Virginia Press, 1972), p. 86. (Hereinafter cited as "Flaherty I.")

138. *Ibid.*, p. 88.

139. *Ibid.*, p. 86, citing Mass. Rec. IV, pt. 1, pp. 388-389.

140. *Ibid.*, p. 87, quoting Otis in Wroth, L. Kinvin & Zobel,

Hiller B., eds., *Legal Papers of John Adams,* Vol. II (Cambridge, Mass.: 1965), p. 125.

141. *Ibid.,* p. 88.

142. *Ibid.,* see pp. 232-241.

143. *Ibid.,* p. 119. See the book for the sources of the quotations.

144. *Ibid.,* p. 120, quoting 9 Anne, cap. X, s. 40.

145. *Ibid.,* p. 121, citing the oath from Labaree, Leonard W., ed., *The Papers of Benjamin Franklin* (New Haven, Ct., 1959), Vol. V, pp. 162-168.

146. *Ibid.,* p. 124, quoting Troup's letter to Jay of July 22, 1777. From Jay Papers, Special Collections, Columbia University.

147. Ernst, Morris L. & Schwartz, Alan U., *The Right To Be Let Alone* (N.Y.: MacMillan, 1962), pp. 5-9.

148. Flaherty, David H., "Law and the Enforcement of Morals in Early America," in Fleming, Donald & Bailyn, Bernard, eds., *Law in American History* (Boston: Little, Brown and Co., 1971), p. 211. (Hereinafter cited as "Flaherty II.")

149. Flaherty I, pp. 179-184, 207.

150. Flaherty II, pp. 212-213.

151. *Ibid.,* p. 213.

152. See Flaherty I, pp. 179-184 and Flaherty II, pp. 246-249.

153. 188 U.S. 321.

154. 188 U.S., at 357.

155. The examples of morals legislation given involve, of course, what some call "victimless crimes" (though it is argued in Chapter Nine that they really *do* have victims). As my discussion about the unborn child's humanity in Chapter Seven makes evident, abortion cannot be considered to be a crime without a victim. I include abortion as a matter involving sexual morality because procreation, of course, occurs as a result of the use of the sexual faculty and the circumstances which led to the procreation usually involve questions of sexual morality. I believe that abortion, however, is more

properly classified as a matter involving the sanctity of innocent human life, like euthanasia and infanticide.

156. 116 U.S. 616 and 141 U.S. 250, respectively.

157. 141 U.S., at 251.

158. The late Dean William L. Prosser explains in an article on the right of privacy in 48 *California L. Rev.* 383 (1960) how the two men happened to write the article. In 1890, Mrs. Samuel D. Warren, a young Boston society woman, was having elaborate social activities regularly in her home. Her husband had only recently given up the practice of law to devote himself to an inherited paper-manufacturing business. Mrs. Warren was an obvious subject of interest for the Boston newspapers, especially the *Saturday Evening Gazette,* "which specialized in 'blue blood' items." They "covered her parties in highly personal and embarrassing detail." In that period of "yellow journalism," "the press had begun to resort to excesses in the way of prying that have become more or less commonplace today." The Warrens were understandably annoyed, especially since "Boston was perhaps, of all the cities in the country, the one in which a lady and a gentleman kept their names and their personal affairs out of the papers." They decided that they had had enough when the newspapers "had a field day" with the wedding of one of their daughters. The result was that Samuel Warren consulted with his recent law partner, Louis D. Brandeis, and the two collaborated on the famous *Harvard Law Review* article.

159. I should point out that the common law has long been understood as something which judges should be able to alter to meet new circumstances which grow out of technological, demographic, etc. changes. The view expressed in the *Griswold* appellants' brief (see pp. 48, 68-69) also is that the Supreme Court should reinterpret the Constitution to respond to changes or perceived changes. The changes referred to there, however, are changes in social and moral attitudes which occur in at least certain segments of the population. This is quite different from the common law notion. First, the latter did not traditionally view morality as changing, so it did not change the law to accommodate changed moral thinking. Second, changing the common law is drastically different from changing the interpretation of a constitutional provision. Common law judges are understood as having the authority to adapt the unwritten law they work with (e.g., they can create new tort actions); the Supreme Court, however, does not have the authority to change the Constitution. Only

the people and/or their representatives do by amendment. Also, a decision of a common law judge may be overturned by the legislature by statute. A constitutional decision of the Supreme Court, at least according to the general understanding, cannot be.

160. Warren, Samuel D. & Brandeis, Louis D., "The Right to Privacy," 4 *Harvard L. Rev.* 193, 193-195 (1890).

161. *Ibid.*, pp. 197-198.

162. *Ibid.*, p. 207.

163. Prosser, *op. cit.* (Chap. Three) (1964 ed.), p. 832.

164. *Ibid.*

165. *Ibid.*, p. 833.

166. *Ibid.*, pp. 834-836.

167. *Ibid.*, pp. 837-838.

168. *Ibid.*, p. 839.

169. 318 U.S. 44.

170. 367 U.S. 497.

171. See, for example, *Barrows v. Jackson*, 346 U.S. 249 (1953); *NAACP v. Alabama*, 357 U.S. 449 (1958); and *Dombrowski v. Pfister*, 380 U.S. 479 (1965).

172. It is possible to view the use of contraceptives by a married couple as something included in the common law's traditional protection of the sanctity of the family. This could, in some sense, be regarded as creating a right of marital privacy, as discussed in *Griswold*. This would not seem to have any application to the disbursers of contraceptives, however, who were the convicted parties in this case.

CHAPTER SIX NOTES

1. 347 U.S. 483 (1954).

2. I refer here to the main PPFA brief. Whenever a reference is made just to the appellants' or PPFA's "brief," what is meant is their or its main brief. The term "supplemental brief" shall be used if it is this brief of either that is being referred to.

3. Mecklenburg, Fred E., M.D. "The Indications for Induced Abortion: A Physician's Perspective," in Hilgers, Thomas W. & Horan, Dennis J. eds., *Abortion and Social Justice, Op. cit.* (Chap. One), p. 38. Dr. Mecklenburg is a Planned Parenthood physician who obviously does not agree with the organization he works for on the subject of abortion. Emphasis is mine.

4. Grisez, *op. cit.* (Chap. One), p. 72.

5. Niswander, Kenneth R., M.D. "Indications and Contraindications, Highlight from the 1971 A.M.A. Meeting," in "Abortion --A Legal Fact" 18 *Audio Digest: Obstetrics and Gynecology* (Aug. 3, 1971), cited in Mecklenburg, p. 39.

6. This is a type of leukemia in which there is excessive proliferation and accumulation of granulocytic blood cells and polymorphonuclear leukocytes. C.f. Isselbacher, Kurt J., M.D., et al., Harrison's *Principles of Internal Medicine* (9th ed.) (N.Y.: McGraw-Hill, 1980), p. 1630.

7. Sheehy, Thomas W., M.D., "An Evaluation of the Effect of Pregnancy on Chronic Granulocytic Leukemia," 75 *Amer. J. of Ob. & Gyn.* 788, 793 (1958). The case Dr. Sheehy considers was at the Walter Reed Army Medical Center in Washington, D.C.

8. Levine, Alexandra M., M.D. & Collea, Joseph V., M.D., "When Pregnancy Complicates Chronic Granulocytic Leukemia," 13 *Contemporary Ob/Gyn,* No. 1 (Jan. 1979), pp. 49-50.

9. *Ibid.,* p. 47.

10. Mulla, N., M.D., "Acute Leukemia and Pregnancy," 75 *Amer. J. of Ob. & Gyn.* 1283, 12, 1285 (1958). Emphasis is mine.

11. Barry, Richard M., M.D., et al., "Influence of Pregnancy on the Course of Hodgkin's Disease," 84 *Amer. J. of Ob. & Gyn.* 445, 451 (1962).

12. 100 S. Ct. 2694 (1980).

13. Kitay, David Z., M.D., "Assessing Anemia in the Pregnant

Patient," 2 *Contemporary Ob/Gyn,* No. 4 (Oct. 1973), p. 24.

14. Nathanson, Bernard N., M.D., *op. cit.* (Chap. One), p. 246.

15. Brief *Amici Curiae* of Certain Physicians, Professors, and Fellows of the American College of Obstetrics and Gynecology in Support of the Appellants in *Williams v. Zbaraz,* p. 5. 305 obstetrician-gynecologists joined the brief.

16. See Horger, Edgar O., III, M.D., "Managing the Patient With Sickle Disease," 2 *Contemporary Ob/Gyn,* No. 2 (Aug. 1973), pp. 55-58 and Fiakpui, Evans Z., M.D. & Moran, Edgar M., M.D., "Pregnancy in the Sickle Hemoglobinopathies, 11 *Jour. of Reproductive Med.,* No. 1 (July 1973), pp. 28-34.

17. See articles mentioned in the brief cited in note 15 above.

18. Evans and Moran, p. 30. The article does not state if this one death was precipitated or caused by the pregnancy.

19. ITP is a disease characterized by a reduction in the blood platelet count. The chronic recurrent form usually occurs in women twenty to forty (i.e., child-bearing age). Its chief sign is purpura (tiny blood vessels bleed into the skin and mucous membranes and cause purplish patches or pin-point hemorrhages). In the chronic form, this bleeding will persist for six months or more. C. f. Isselbacher, et al., pp. 1555-56. Even though the chronic form is most common in women of child-bearing years, it is a 'comparative rarity" that this disease is associated with pregnancy. (See Heys, R. F., M.B., "Steroid Therapy for Idiopathic Thrombocytopenic Purpura During Pregnancy," 28 *Obstetrics and Gynecology,* No. 4 (Oct. 1966), p. 532.)

20. Flessa, Herbert C., M.D., "Hemorrhagic Disorders and Pregnancy," 17 *Clinical Obstetrics and Gynecology,* No. 4 (Dec. 1974), p. 240.

21. Heys, p. 538. He seems, nonetheless, to contend that the threat to pregnant women with ITP who have not previously had a prior splenectomy is "considerable" (p. 538). This was written, however, at a time when steroid therapy was just beginning and seems to be contradicted by what Flessa was noted as saying.

22. Flessa, p. 241.

23. This is an hereditary hemorrhagic disorder characterized by

prolonged bleeding time associated with reduced coagulant activity. C. f. Isselbacher, et al., p. 1562. It is thought to be the most common inherited bleeding disorder in women and is "encountered occasionally" in expectant mothers. C. f. Noller, Kenneth L., M.D., et al., "Managing von Willebrand's Disease During Pregnancy," 4 *Contemporary Ob/Gyn*, No. 2 (Aug. 1974), pp. 107-108.

24. Noller, et al., p. 108.

25. Niswander, cited in Mechlenburg, p. 38.

26. Dack, Simon, M.D., et al., "Heart Disease," in Guttmacher, Alan F. & Rovinsky, Joseph J., eds., *Medical, Surgical, and Gynecological Complications of Pregnancy* (Baltimore: Williams & Wilkins Co., 1960), p. 11. Guttmacher, it will be recalled, was a prominent pro-abortion advocate.

27. *Ibid.*, p. 8.

28. Ueland, Kent, M.D., "What's the Risk When the Cardiac Patient Is Pregnant?" 13 *Contemporary Ob/Gyn*, No. 1 (Jan. 1979), p. 117.

29. Ferris, Thomas F., M.D. in Burrow, Gerald N., M.D. & Ferris, eds., *Medical Complications During Pregnancy* (Philadelphia: W. B. Saunders, 1975), p. 86.

30. Decker, David G., "Medical Indications for Therapeutic Abortion: An Obstetrician's View," 50 *Minnesota Medicine* 29, 31 (1967).

31. Zuspan, Frederick P., "Problems Encountered in the Treatment of Pregnancy-Induced Hypertension," 131 *Amer. J. of Ob. & Gyn*, 594 (1978).

32. Nathanson, p. 246.

33. *Ibid.*

34. *Amici* brief of 305 obstetrician-gynecologists in *Williams*, p, 11.

35. See Cranley, John J., M.D., "Managing Varicose Veins in Pregnancy," 7 *Contemporary Ob/Gyn*, No. 5 (May 1976), pp. 139-144.

36. Decker, p. 31.

37. Nathanson, p. 246.

38. Decker, p. 31; Nathanson, p. 245.

39. Nathanson, p. 245.

40. Brief of Drs. Williams and Diamond in *Williams*, pp. App. 8 and 9, citing Ferris in Ferris & Burrows, p. 34.

41. Nathanson, p. 245.

42. Gabbe, Steven G., M.D., "New Ideas on Managing the Pregnant Diabetic Patient," 13 *Contemporary Ob/Gyn*, No. 109 (Jan. 1979), p. 109. Emphasis is mine.

43. Niswander, cited in Mecklenburg, pp. 38-39.

44. *Ibid.*, cited in Mecklenburg, p. 39.

45. Nathanson, p. 245.

46. This is a disturbance of metabolism which in severe form is accompanied by fever, headache, convulsions called eclampsia, and a rapid rise in blood pressure. C. f. Cooley, Donald G., ed. *Better Homes and Gardens Family Medical Guide* (N.Y.: Better Homes and Gardens Books, 1973), p. 1044.

47. Zuspan, p. 594.

48. SLE is a multisystem disease in which renal (kidney) involvement is extremely common. C. f. Isselbacher, et al., p. 1320.

49. Rothfield, Naomi, M.D. & Chao, Solan, M.D. Interviewed in *Contemporary Ob/Gyn*, "The Effects of SLE on Pregnancy," 10 *Contemporary Ob/Gyn*, No. 1 (July 1977), p. 64.

50. Placenta previa is the condition whereby the placenta becomes implanted over or near the internal os of the cervix. If the cervix were to dilate (or be dilated) too early, severe bleeding could occur. Abruptio placenta is the premature separation of a normally implanted placenta from the uterus. C. f. *Amici* brief of 305 Physicians in *Williams*, p. 6.

51. *Ibid.*

52. See Kitay, David Z., M.D., "Bleeding Disorders in Pregnancy," 7 *Contemporary Ob/Gyn*, No. 1 (Jan. 1976), pp. 87-89 and

Lunan, C. B., M.D., "The Management of Abruptio Placentae," 28 *Ob/Gyn Surgery* 589 (1973).

53. *Amici* brief of 305 physicians in Williams, pp. 5-6. The first emphasis is theirs, the second is mine. See p. 2a of the brief for the citations to the ten studies.

54. Conversation with Thomas A. O'Connor, M.D., Buffalo, New York, anesthesiologist and anti-abortion leader, November 9, 1981.

55. Conversation with Dr. O'Connor, January 9, 1982.

56. Mecklenburg, p. 39.

57. Murdoch, W., "Are There Psychiatric Grounds for Terminating a Pregnancy?" 25 *Cent. Afr. J. Med.*, No. 7 (July 1979), p. 158. This is an address he gave to the annual general meeting of the Society for the Protection of the Unborn Child in Rhodesia (now Zimbabwe), Nov. 17, 1978.

58. *Report of the Committee on the Working of the Abortion Act*, Vol. I (London: HMSO, 1974), p. 53, cited in Drower, Sandra J., & Nash, Eleanor S., "Therapeutic Abortion on Psychiatric Grounds: Part II. The Continuing Debate," 54 *S. Afr. Med. J.*, No. 16 (Oct. 14, 1978), p. 644.

59. *Ibid.* p. 55 of Report, cited in Drower & Nash, p. 645. The views and studies I shall discuss in the Section on "The Consequences of Abortion for the Physical and Mental Health of the Mother" cast doubt upon the one part of this claim that abortion may not have an "ill" effect on a serious mental illness.

60. Tregold, A. F. & Tregold, R. F., *Manual of Psychological Medicine*, 3rd Ed., London, 1957.

61. Kolb, Laurence, M.D., *Modern Clinical Psychiatry*, 9th Ed. (Philadelphia: W. B. Saunders, 1977), p. 180.

62. *Ibid.*, 7th ed., p. 447.

63. Mecklenburg, in his article, cites a number of other prominent psychiatrists who say that "few neurotic or psychotic women are *ever* benefitted by abortion and that the few would be extremely difficult to select." (Mecklenburg, p. 40. The list of authorities he cites is on p. 53.)

64. Sargent, William, "Discussion" The Psychiatric Indications for the Termination of Pregnancy," 50 *Proc. Roy. Soc. Med.* 321 (1957).

65. Asch, S. S., "Mental and Emotional Problems," in Guttmacher, A. F. & Rovinsky, J. J., eds., p. 375, cited in Mecklenburg, p. 40.

66. See Drower & Nash, p. 644.

67. Mecklenburg, p. 40.

68. Lindberg, B., 45 *Svenska Lak--Tidn* 1381 (1948, cited in Mecklenburg, p. 40.

69. Rosenberg, Allan, J., M.D., & Silver, Emmanuel, M.D., "Suicide, Psychiatrists and Therapeutic Abortion," 102 *California Medicine* 407, 409 (June 1965). The age group examined was 16 to 50. There were 3 suicides by pregnant women of the 207 total suicides by women in this age group in a three-year period studied.

70. *Ibid.*

71. Rosenberg and Silver, p. 411.

72. Drower & Nash, p. 644. Dr. Myre Sim of Great Britain, a psychiatrist concurs with this assessment. See Sim, "Abortion and the Psychiatrist," *Br. Med. J.,* Vol. 2 (1963), p. 148. Recall that in Chapter One I also alluded to the sense that psychiatrists had of being manipulated by women to provide justifications for their abortions.

73. Mecklenburg, pp. 40-41. He cites three states as examples: Colorado, Oregon, and California. Before the *Wade/Bolton* decisions, these states had changed their laws to permit abortion for mental health reasons. He says that the result was that, by the time he wrote his article in 1972, 71.5 percent of all abortions in Colorado were performed for this reason, 97 percent in Oregon, and 90 percent in California. (See Mecklenburg, p. 54, for his sources for these figures.) He says that if this many abortions really had to be performed for this reason, it would mean that "in these states serious mental illness [was] 15-20 times greater than serious physical illness in pregnant women and that 25-50 percent of pregnant women are mentally ill." (Mecklenburg, p. 41.)

74. Sargent, p. 321.

75. McGuire, L. S. & Stern, Michael, "Survey of Incidence of Physicians' Attitudes Toward Sexual Assault," 91 *Pub. Hlth. Rep.*, No. 2 (Mar-Apr., 1976), p. 108.

76. Mahkorn, Sandra Kathleen, "Pregnancy and Sexual Assault," in Mall, David & WAtts, Walter F., M.D., *The Psychological Aspects of Abortion* (Wash., D.C.: University Publications of America, 1979), p. 56.

77. Hayman, Charles R., M.D. & Lanza, Charlene, "Sexual Assault in Women and Girls," 109 *Amer. J. of Ob. & Gyn.*, 480-486 (1971).

78. Sims, Barbara M., "A District Attorney Looks at Abortion," 8 *Child and Family* 176, 178 (1969). In the article, Mrs. Sims, described as a strong supporter of both black and women's liberation, says she opposed the attempts which were then underway to reform or repeal New York's criminal abortion law.

79. Everett, Royice B., M.D. & Jimerson, Gordon K., M.D., "The Rape Victim: A Review of 117 Consecutive Cases," 50 *Ob. & Gyn*. 88, 89 (1977).

80. Diamond, Eugene F., M.D. "ISMS Symposium on: Medical Implications of the Current Abortion in Illinois," 131 *Ill. Med. J*. 678 (May 1967). Dr. Diamond appears to have received this information from personal communication with the States Attorney's Office.

81. Mecklenburg, p. 48. He states that this information comes from a personal communication with a C. Bailey of the Sex-Homicide Division of the St. Paul Police Department.

82. Seltzer, Vicki, M.D., "Medical Management of the Rape Victim," 32 *J. Amer. Med. Women's Assn*. 141, 144 (1977). As the authority for this, she cites Weiss, K., "What the Rape Victim Should Know About the Morning-After Pill" (Houston: Advocates for Medical Information). This appears to be a pamphlet.

83. Tietze, Christopher, M.D., "Probability of Pregnancy Resulting from a Single Unprotected Coitus," 11 *Fertility and Sterility* 485, 488 (1960). (Tietze I.")

84. Mecklenburg, p. 49.

85. Dahlke, Miriam B., M.D., et al., "Identification of Semen in

500 Patients Seen Because of Rape," 68 *Amer. J. Clin. Path.* 740, 741 (1977).

86. Groth, A. Nicholas & Burgess, Ann Wolbert, "Sexual Dysfunction During Rape," 297 *N. Eng. J. Med.* 764, 765 (1977).

87. The types of sexual dysfunction usually involved are erective inadequacy (conditional impotence), premature ejaculation, and ejaculatory incompetence. See *ibid.*, pp. 764-765.

88. *Ibid.*, p. 765.

89. Mecklenburg, p. 49.

90. *Ibid.*

91. *Ibid.*

92. Mahkorn, p. 56.

93. Mecklenburg, p. 56.

94. The study he cites was done in the mid-1960s of Washington, D.C. and fourteen county health departments around the country. It revealed the following:

> Only four of the departments reported an organized effort by the police department to take the victim to a hospital or physician for examination and emergency treatment. None of the respondents reported having a formal program for nursing followup, and they also indicated that no specific community efforts were being made to provide medical and psychiatric assistance beyond the emergency service for women and girls.

(Hayman, Charles R., M.D. et al., "A Public Health Program for Sexually Assaulted Females," 82 *Pub. Hlth. Rep.* 497, 502 (1967). My brief perusal of the literature since this time failed to turn up any similar later studies.

95. Barnes, Josephine, "Rape and Other Sexual Offenses," *Br. Med. J.*, Vol 2 (1967), p. 293, cited in Mecklenburg, p. 49.

96. Mecklenburg, pp. 49-50. He cites as his source for these figures a personal communication with Denver attorney J. E. Archibald.

97. See Mahkorn, pp. 67-68.

98. DeFrancis, V., *Protecting the Child Victim of Sex Crimes Committed by Adults: Final Report* (Denver: American Humane Assn., 1969), cited in Maloof, George E., "The Consequences of Incest: Giving and Taking Life," in Mall & Watts, p. 75.

99. Maisch, Herbert, *Incest*. Tr. by Beame, Colin (N.Y.: Stein & Day, 1972), cited in *Ibid*.

100. Tormes, Yvonne M., *Child Victims of Incest* (Denver: American Humane Assn., Children's Division, 1968), cited in *Ibid*.

101. ee Sims, note 78.

102. Maloof, p. 75.

103. *Ibid.*, p. 87.

104. *Ibid.*, pp. 87-88. We saw how correct Maloof's assessment of the psychiatric profession is in Chapter One.

105. *Ibid.*, p. 101.

106. Mecklenburg, p. 50.

107. Kennedy, M. & Cormier, B. M., M.D., "Father-Daughter Incest --Treatment of the Family," 40 *Laval Med*. 946, 949-950 (1969).

108. Briggs, Richard M., M.D., et al., "Pregnancy in the Young Adolescent," 84 *Amer. J. of Ob. & Gyn*. 436, 440 (1962). The teenage girls they studied ranged in age from 12 to 16.

109. *Ibid*.

110. Zackler, Jack, M.S., et al., "The Young Adolescent as an Obstetric Risk," 103 *Amer. J. of Ob. & Gyn*. 305, 311 (1969).

111. Durger, J., M.D., *Fam. Prac. News*, p. 7 (May 1, 1978), cited in Willke, *op. cit*. (Chap. One), p. 44. Emphasis is mine.

112. Dott, Andrew B., M.D. & Fort, Arthur T., M.D. "Medical and Social Factors Affecting Early Teenage Pregnancy: A Literature Review and Summary of the Findings of the Louisiana Infant Mortality Study," 125 *Amer. J. of Ob. & Gyn*. 532, 535 (1976).

113. *Ibid*. Emphasis is mine.

114. Dott and Fort state that "the young teenager uses prenatal

services much less than older women for various cultural and psychological reasons" (*Ibid.*, p. 535). This suggests that communities and families should make more determined efforts to inculcate the importance of prenatal care in pregnancy in girls as they grow up and that communities and the obstetric-gynecological profession should make a greater effort to see to it that pregnant teenagers are sought out and these services provided them.

115. I am referring here, of course, to cases where the male has not forcibly sexually assaulted the girl. The girl then, if she had made clear that she did not want the intercourse, would not be morally culpable or responsible for it.

116. Maloof, p. 87. He makes reference here to "two small studies where less than 50 percent of the[se] offspring were of normal intelligence." These studies, according to his footnotes, are mentioned in Nathan M. Simon's article "Psychological and Emotional Indications for Therapeutic Abortion," in Sloane, R. Bruce, *Abortion: Changing Views and Practice* (N.Y. & London: Greene and Stratton, 1971).

117. PPFA brief, p. 31.

118. Sarvis & Rodman, *op. cit.* (Chap. One), pp. 6-7.

119. Anoxia is an oxygen deficiency in the organs and tissues of the child being born and a disturbance resulting from it. Cooley, p. 885.

120. Mecklenburg, p. 41.

121. *Ibid.*, p. 42, citing Schaeffer, A. J., *Diseases of the Newborn*, 2nd Ed. (Philadelphia: W. B. Saunders Co., 1966), p. 29. A more recent work confirms that this still holds true. See Barden, Tom P. in Behrman, Richard E., M.D., ed., *Neonatal-Perinatal Medicine: Diseases of the Fetus and Infant*. (St. Louis: C. V. Mosby, 1977). p. 49.

122. Mecklenburg, p. 42.

123. *Ibid.* Huntington's Chorea is a disease which combines progressive dementia with bizarre involuntary movements and odd postures. Osteogenesis imperfecta is a group of generalized disorders of connective tissue with clinical manifestations in the skeleton, ear, joints, ligaments, teeth, sclera, and skin. Marfan's syndrome is a generalized disorder of connective tissues of the ocular, cardiovascular, and skeletal

systems. Achondroplasia is a form of dwarfism which results from decrease in the proliferation of cartilage in the growth plate. Phenylketonuria is a disorder characterized by progressive mental retardation and hyperactivity. The Duchenne type is the most common form of muscular dystrophy beginning in infancy and childhood. In G6PD deficiency-induced form of hemolytic anemia, as with related hemolytic anemias, an adequate level of reduced glutathione in the red blood cell cannot be maintained and the patient can suffer repeated hemolytic crises. C. f. Isselbacher, et al., pp. 1993, 532, 534, 1868, 463, and 2060, respectively.

124. Mecklenburg, p. 42.

125. Bloom, Arthur D. & Polin, Richard in Behrman, p. 171. Behrman describes a "major malformation" as one with potentially significant clinical consequences, whereas a "minor malformation" is one which is relatively trivial clinically.

126. *Ibid.*, p. 172.

127. *Ibid.*, p. 174.

128. *Ibid.*, p. 173.

129. *Ibid.*, p. 174.

130. Mecklenburg, p. 42.

131. Warkany, Josef, M.D. & Kalter, Harold, M.D., "Congenital Malformations" 265 *N. Eng. J. Med.* 993, 998 (1961).

132. The Mecklenburg and Warkany-Kalter articles both mention *retrospective* studies of the incidence of defects from rubella which had been done before 1940 and which purported to show a rate of about 75 percent defectiveness when contracted during the first four months of pregnancy. These results, proved erroneous by the later *prospective* studies such as the ones reported on by Warkany and Kalter, nevertheless continued to be cited to the public and raised needless alarm. See Mecklenburg, pp. 45-46 & Warkany-Kalter, p. 998.

133. Warkany & Kalter, p. 999.

134. Pitt, David, M.D. & Keir, E. H., "Results of Rubella in Pregnancy: I," *Med. J. of Australia*, Vol. 2 (1965), p. 647.

135. Isselbacher, et al., p. 796.

136. Banatvala, J. E., M.D. "Laboratory Investigations in the Assessment of Rubella during Pregnancy," *Br. Med. Jour.*, Vol. 1 (1968), p. 561.

137. Mecklengurg, p. 47. I should say that Mecklenburg's optimistic prediction holds true only if all other things are equal. The elimination of rubella, like polio, will not occur in one final event but will be an on-going struggle and will depend on continued efforts to have all girls and young women tested and vaccinated. The point is, of course, that man has a solution available--if he puts his mind down to implementing it--other than abortion.

138. Mecklenburg, p. 45.

139. Diamond, p. 678, cited in Mecklenburg, p. 45.

140. Mecklenburg, p. 45.

141. Dishotsky, Norman I., et al., "LSD and Genetic Damage: Is LSD Chromosome Damaging, Carcinogenic, Mutagenic or Teratogenic? 172 *Science* (April 30, 1971), p. 439.

142. See Sankar, D. V. Siva, *LSD--A Total Study* (Westbury, N.Y.: PJD, 1975), pp. 470-500.

143. Gordon, Hymie, "Genetical, Social and Medical Aspects of Abortion," 42 *S. Afr. Med. J.*, 721, 724 (1968).

144. Mecklenburg, p. 42.

145. Gordon, P. 727.

146. See Buresh, Marjorie Ann, "Mongolism," in Hilgers, Horan, & Mall, *op. cit.* (Chap. Three), pp. 60-68.

147. Mecklenburg, p. 47, citing Rendle-Short, J., "Maternal Rubella: The Practical Management of a Case," in 2 *Lancet* 373 (1964).

148. Monteleone, Patricia L., M.D. & Moraczewski, Albert S., "Medical and Ethical Aspects of the Prenatal Diagnosis of Genetic Disease," in Hilgers, Horan, & Mall, pp. 45-59.

149. *Ibid.*, p. 46.

150. *Ibid.*, p. 47.

151. *Ibid.*, p. 46.

152. *Ibid.*, p. 47.

153. *Ibid.*, p. 48.

154. *Ibid.*, p. 49.

155. Mecklenburg, p. 43, citing Gordon, Hymie, "Genetic Aspects of Abortion." Testimony given before a House subcommittee of the Minnesota State Legislature conducting hearings on abortion reform in March 1971.

156. Polyploidy is the condition in which cells are present which have more than two full sets of homologous chromosomes.

157. Monteleone & Moraczewski, p. 50.

158. Milunsky, Aubrey, "Risk of Amniocentesis for Prenatal Diagnosis," 293 *New England Jour. of Med.* 932 (1975). The point about development at one year of age is corroborated by a Univ. of Colorado study. See Robinson, Jean, et al., "Amniocentesis: Its Impact on Mothers and Infants: A 1-year Follow-Up Study," 8 *Clin. Genetics* 97-106.

159. "The Risk of Amniocentesis." (Editorial) 2 *Lancet* 1287 (1978).

160. Monteleone & Moraczewski, p. 49; Brinsmead, M. W., "Complications of Amniocentesis," 1 *Med. Jour. of Australia* 370 (1976).

161. Mecklenburg, p. 41, citing Swedish statistics and a personal communication with a Swedish embryologist.

162. Binding, Karl & Hoche, lfred, *The Release of the Destruction of Life Devoid of Value*. Comments by Robert L. Sassone. (Santa Ana, Calif.: A Life Quality Paperback, 1975), p. 65. (Originally published by Felix Meiner in Leipzig, Germany in 1921.) The Hellegers study is cited in Sassone's "Comments" section.

163. *Wade* brief, p. 44.

164. *Ibid.*, citing Dryfoos, et al., "Eighteen Months Later: Family Planning Services in the United States, 1969," 3 *Fam. Plan. Perspec.*, No. 2 (Apr. 1971), p. 29.

165. PPFA brief, p. 13, citing U.S. *Senate Report No. 91-1004*, 91st Cong., 2d Sess. (1970) (Labor and Public Welfare Committee), p. 9.

166. *Wade* brief, p. 45, citing Dryfoos, et al. above.

167. PPFA brief, p. 13, citing the U.S. Senate Report above.

168. *Wade* brief, p. 45, citing Tietze, Christopher, M.D., et al., "Teaching of Fertility Regulation in Medical Schools," 196 *Jour. of Amer. Med. Assn.* 20, 23 (1966). (Hereinafter cited as "Tietze II.")

169. Dr. Tietze is a consultant to PPFA and an associate director of the pro-abortion, pro-contraception Population Council. He is also a member of the Association for Voluntary Sterilization. (See Chambers, Claire, *The SIECUS Circle* (Belmont, Mass.: Western Islands, 1977), p. 354) Dr. Mecklenburg calls him "an outspoken pro-abortionist." (Mecklenburg, p. 51)

170. Tietze II, p. 20.

171. PPFA brief, p. 16. The quote within the quote is from Segal & Tietze, "Contraceptive Technology: Current and Prospective Methods," in *Reports on Population/Family Planning*, Report No. 1 (July 1971 ed.), p. 5. Emphasis is mine.

172. PPFA brief, p. 20. Emphasis is mine. I shall not go into the data presented by the briefs about the levels of effectiveness of the various means of family planning. This would involve a scientific and medical study in itself. For the purposes of this Sub-Section, I accept the breifs' claims that contraceptive failures do occur.

173. *Wade* brief, p. 46.

174. *Wade* brief, p. 44, quoting Bumpass & Westoff, *op. cit.* (Chap. Four), p. 1179.

175. Omran, Abdel, "Abortion in the Demographic Transition," in *Rapid Population Growth: Consequences and Policy Implications*, Vol. II, Chap. 13, p. 512, cited in Dyck, Arthur J., "Is Abortion Necessary to Solve Population Problems?" in Hilgers & Horan, p. 168.

176. Dyck, p. 167.

177. Diggory, P. L., "ome Experiences of Therapeutic Abortion," in 1 *Lancet* 873, 875 (1969).

178. Abels, Sara R., Letter to 1 *Lancet* 1051 (1969).

179. 14 *Medical World News*, No. 41 (Nov. 9, 1973), p. 37, quoting Professor T. S. Ueno of Nihon University in Tokyo, who is a Japanese medical authority.

180. Sherlock, Richard, "The Demographic Argument for Liberal Abortion Policies: Analysis of a Pseudo-Issue," in Hilgers, Horan, & Mall, p. 460.

181. See Bracken, Michael B., et al., "Correlates of Repeat Induced Abortion," 40 *Obstetrics and Gynecology* 816 (1972); Daily, Edwin F., M.D., et al., "Repeat Abortions in New York City, 1970-1972," 5 *Family Planning Perspectives* 89 (1973); and Shepard, Mary Jo & Bracken, Michael, "Contraceptive Practices and Repeat Induced Abortion: An Epidemiological Investigation," 11 *Jour. of Bio. Science* 289 (1979).

182. See Bracken, et al,, Shepard & Bracken; and Gispert, Maria, M.D., & Falk, Ruth, "Adolescent Sexual Activity: Contraception and Abortion," 132 *Amer. Jour. of Ob. & Gyn.* 620 (1978).

183. See Bracken, et al., and Shepard & Bracken.

184. Abels, p. 1051.

185. Tietze, Christopher, "Repeat Abortions--Why More?" 10 *Family Planning Perspectives* 286, 287 (1978). (Tietze III.)

186. Gibb, Gerald David & Millard, Richard John, "Research on Repeated Abortion: State of the Field: 1973-1979," in 48 *Psychological Reports* 415, 416-417 (1981).

187. *Buffalo Evening News*, Feb. 23, 1982, p. A-3, col. 2.

188. *Wade* brief, p. 22; PPFA brief, p. 22. In its supplemental brief, PPFA states that there are 200,000 to 1,200,000 illegal abortions annually in the U.S., but also makes a similar admission as the *Wade* brief by saying that "[n]o meaningful figures" are readily available.

189. PPFA brief, p. 23.

190. *Wade* brief, footnote 19, p. 22.

191. Finnis, John M., "Three Schemes of Regulation," in Noonan I, *op. cit.* (Chap. Three), p. 181. Emphasis is his. He also states that the source of the 200,000 to 1,000,000 estimate was the statistics committee "at a 1958 conference called by Planned Parenthood," which he says also believed that there is no way of pinpointing the number any more closely than that. (It is not clear what conference he is referring to, but it may be the 1954 conference I discussed in Chapter One, whose proceedings were published in a book in 1958. Perhaps he has these two dates confused.)

192. Dyck, p. 166. Emphasis is his.

193. Syska, Barbara J., Hilgers, Thomas W., M.D., & O'Hare, Dennis, "An Objective Model for Estimating Criminal Abortions and Its Implications for Public Policy," in Hilgers, Horan, & Mall, p. 178.

194. Louisell, David W. & Noonan, John T., Jr., "Constitutional Balance," in Noonan I, p. 231.

195. *Ibid.*, p. 232, footnote 53. See the footnote for the specific documents they cite from.

196. *The New York Times*, Sept. 7, 1967, p. 38. Noonan notes this quote in his article.

197. Tietze, Christopher, M.D., and Lewit, Sarah, "Abortion," 220 *Scientific American* 21, 23 (1969).

198. "The Abortion Act (1967): Findings of an Inquiry into the First Year's Working of the Act Conducted by the Royal College of Obstetricians and Gynaecologists," in 2 *British Med. Jour.* 529, 532-533 (1970), cited in Willke, p. 106, with slight corrections to their quote made after a check of the text.

199. Tietze, Christopher, M.D., "Abortion in Europe," in 57 *Amer. Jour. of Public Health* 1923, 1927 (1967). ("Tietze IV.")

200. Grisez, p. 254, citing Gebhard, Paul H., et al., *Pregnancy, Birth and Abortion* (N.Y.: John Wiley & Sons, Inc. 1958), p. 219. Grisez says that these authors were sympathetic to legalized abortion.

201. Grisez, p. 200, citing Heer, David M., "Abortion, Contraception, and Population Policy in the Soviet Union," in 2 *Demography* 536 (1965).

202. Jurukovski, J., M.D. & Sukarov, L., M.D., "A Critical Review of Legal Abortion," in 9 *International Jour. of Gynaecology and Obstetrics* iii, 115-116 (1971).

203. Syska, Hilgers, & O'Hare, pp. 178, 180.

204. *Ibid.*, pp. 175, 178, 180.

205. PPFA supplemental brief, p. 10.

206. A report of the U.S. Center for Disease Control on abortion complications for the woman showed that only a small percentage were due to illegal procedures. This seems to indicate that illegal abortion has not been widely turned to by women on Medicaid. "See Center for Disease Control, "Epidemiologic Notes and Reports: Health Effects of Restricting Federal Funds for Abortion--United States," 28 *Morbidity and Mortality* (1979), p. 37. Three prominent pro-abortion writers concur with my interpretation of this report. (See Jaffe, Lind-Heim, & Lee, *op. cit.* (Chap. One), p. 144.)

207. The states which still voluntarily pay for abortions, even in situations not required by the Hyde Amendment, were the following as of 1981: Alaska, Colorado, Hawaii, Maryland, Michigan, New York, North Carolina, Oregon, and Washington. A number of others, including California, Massachusetts, and Pennsylvania, are paying for them under court order. (See Jaffe, Lindheim, & Lee, pp. 188, 198.) One could argue that the reason that more Medicaid women have not turned to illegal abortion is that most of them are in these populous states that still provide funding. There may be some truth to this, although it is not an adequate answer. In the year reported on in note 206 above, the number of *federally* funded abortions dropped from 300,000 to 2,000, but 191,000 Medicaid women received abortions funded by the *states*. This is still a reduction of more than one-third. (Jaffe, Lindheim, & Lee, pp. 188, 198.)

208. Willke, pp. 108-109.

209. Hilgers, Thomas W., M.D. & O'Hare, Dennis, "Abortion Related Maternal Mortality: An In-Depth Analysis," in Hilgers, Horan & Mall, pp. 82, 84.

210. Brennan, *op. cit.* (Chap. One), pp. 59-61. He cites several studies.

211. Hilgers & O'Hare, pp. 84, 90.

212. For evidence of these assertions, see the Chicago *Sun-Times'* three-week-long expose of four Chicago abortion clinics, entitled "The Abortion Profiteers," which began running on November 12, 1978. Reprinted in a "Special Edition" of *National Right to Life News,* Vol. 6, No. 2 (Feb. 1979).

213. *Wade* opinion, 410 U.S., at 163.

214. *Wade* brief, p. 32; PPFA supplemental brief, p. 6.

215. *Wade* brief, p. 33.

216. PPFA supplemental brief, p. 6. The brief further states that "[t]his record, when combined with the decrease in illegal abortions...caused the maternal mortality rate in New York City to drop by two-thirds to a record low in 1971... Maternal deaths due to criminal abortions in New York City in the 1960s ranged from a high of 130 in 1961 to a low of 66 in 1968. This represented 33 maternal deaths due to criminal abortions per 100,000 live births in 1961 and 15 in 1968. In the first 6 months of 1971 only one maternal death due to criminal abortion was reported" (pp. 6-7). These additional figures do not do a great deal to back up the claim in the main PPFA brief that abortion was needed to reduce the number of deaths due to illegal abortions, since they make it clear that there was already a clear downward trend in such deaths. This unwitting admission precisely corresponds with the conclusion of Hilgers and O'Hare.

217. Hilgers, Thomas W., M.D., "The Medical Hazards of Legally Induced Abortion," in Hilgers & Horan, pp. 60-61. The figures on residency are cited by Hilgers from Chase, Gordon, "Gordon Chase Cites Success of First Year of New York's Abortion Law in Twelve-Month Report on 165,000 Abortions." News release, Health Services Administration, The City of New York, June 29, 1971, Appendix C--Place of Residence (%). (Hereinafter cited as "Hilgers in Hilgers & Horan.")

218. Hilgers in Hilgers & Horan, p. 63.

219. *Ibid.*

220. *Ibid.*, pp. 63, 65. The pertinent tables that appear in Hilgers' piece are reproduced here. Much of this information was submitted to the Court in the *amicus curiae* briefs of LIFE and Certain Physicians, et al., of the American College of Obstetrician-Gynecologists.

TABLE ONE (as designated in Hilgers' article): **ABORTION MORTALITY vs MATERNAL MORTALITY**

Country/State	*Year*	*Legal Abortions*	*Deaths*	*Abortion Mortality/ 100,000 Abortions*	*Maternal Mortality/ 100,000 Live Births*
Denmark	1960-66	27,435	9	30	10-20
England and Wales	1968-69	27,331	8	30	Abortion Mortality higher than maternal mortality
Sweden	1960-66	30,600	12	39	14.0
Yugoslavia (Skopje Univ.)	1965-68	18,758	2	10.6	96.5
Hungary	1964-68	939,800	11	1.2	49.7
Oregon	1970	7,196	1	13.9	8.4
Maryland	1968-70	7,664	3	40.5	23.1

(Cited in Hilgers & Horan, p. 62.)

TABLE TWO (as designated in Hilgers' article): **LEGAL ABORTION MORTALITY--FIRST TRIMESTER ONLY***

Country/State	*Year*	*Abortions 1st Trimester*	*Deaths*	*Abortion Mortality/ 100,000 Abortions*	*Maternal Mortality/ 100,000 Live Births*
Denmark	1961-66	8,684	2	23.0	10-20
Yugoslavia (Skopje Univ.)	1965-68	7,833	2	25.5	96.5
Hungary	1964-68	939,800	11	1.2	49.7
Oregon	1970	5,351	1	18.6	8.4

**Breakdown data for England and Wales and Sweden are not available. There were no early abortion deaths in Maryland 1968-70, but a relatively small number (3,900) were performed early.*

TABLE THREE (as designated in Hilgers' article): **ABORTION DEATHS (ALL CAUSES) PER UNIT POPULATION**

Country	*Abortion Deaths 1967 (All Causes)*	*Est. 1967 Population*	*Abortion Deaths/ 100,000 Population*
Hungary	21	10,255,000	2.06
United States	160	197,576,952	0.80

(Cited in Hilgers & Horan, p. 64.)

221. Hilgers & O'Hare, p. 90. See pp. 84-86 for an explanation of their statistical formula.

222. PPFA brief, p. 41.

223. *Ibid.*

224. As to the "widely acknowledged dangers" of increasing population, the brief *may* intend that we consider the listing of such problems given in the two sources it cites right above this, President Nixon's message and the *Interim Report* (even though it does not cite them for *this* point). These sources indicate that the problems include, *inter alia* environmental deterioration, a maldistribution of resources, income, and wealth in the world, the threat of a more contrived and regulated society, the financial burden on government, housing shortages, the danger of serious unemployment, and problems with transportation.

225. Dyck, p. 159.

226. U.S. Bureau of the Census--*Statistical Abstract of the United States: 1980* (101st Ed.) Wash., D.C., 1980, p. 7.

227. Clark, Colin, "Abortion and Population Control," II *The Human Life Review,* No. 3 (Summer 1976), p. 6. (Hereinafter cited as "Clark I.")

228. If births are *equal* to deaths at the present time, population is certain to decline, for the simple reason that births will then only be replacing the much smaller generation born on the average some sixty or seventy years ago. See Clark I, *ibid.*

229. Sassone, Robert L., *Handbook on Population* (4th ed.). Self-published, 1978, p. 117. Sassone is a lawyer, physicist, and computer analyst who is well known for his writing on the population question. In this book, he offers a $1,000 reward to anyone who can prove the validity of any reason why population growth should be limited within the next century. There have been no serious claims.

230. *Ibid.*, p. 116.

231. *Ibid.*, pp. 118-119.

232. *Statistical Abstract of the United States,* 1980, p. 896.

233. Sassone, p. 111.

234. Dyck, p. 164.

235. *Ibid.*, p. 161.

236. Sassone, p. 43.

237. *Ibid.*, p. 45

238. *Ibid.*, pp. 51-52.

239. *Ibid.*, pp. 55-56.

240. *Ibid.*, pp. 66-82.

241. Clark, Colin *Population Growth: The Advantages* (Santa Ana, Calif: A Life Quality Paperback, 1975) p. 85. (Hereinafter cited as "Clark II.")

242. Simon, Julian L., "World Population Growth," in *Atlantic Monthly* (Aug. 1981), p. 73.

243. *Ibid.*, p. 76.

244. Rushdoony, Rousas J., *The Myth of Over-Population*. (Fairfax, Va.: Thoburn Press, 1975), p. 18. He seems to base his claim about population forecasting being "guesswork" on the following document of the U.S. Government: Stanbery, Van Bueren & Hermann, Frank F., *Population Forecasting Methods*, U.S. Dept. of Commerce, Bureau of Pub. Roads, Urban Planning Div., 1964 revision, p. 6. It calls population forecasting "'essentially a matter of judgment.'"

245. Breindel, Eric M. & Eberstadt, Nick, "Paradoxes of Population," in *Commentary* (Aug. 1980), p. 42.

246. Wertham, Fredric, "The Malthus Myth," in 11 *Child and Family*, No. 2 (1972), p. 177. This is an excerpt from Wertham's book *A Sign for Cain--An Exploration of Human Violence* (N.Y.: Macmillan, 1966) Chap. 6, pp. 97-113. Thomas Robert Malthus was an Anglican clergyman and professor of political economy who in 1798 put forth his theory in *An Essay on the Principle of Population*.

247. Clark II, p. 105.

248. Wertham, pp. 183, 184.

249. Simon, pp. 70-71.

250. *Ibid.*, pp. 73, 76. The reasons why population growth promotes economic growth, briefly, are: 1) people make special efforts (with a resulting productivity increase) when they perceive a special need, such as providing better for more children. (E.G., a father may work more overtime to support an additional child.); 2) More population growth means a larger proportion of young people in the work force. This means more productivity because young workers produce more in relation to what they consume than older workers, largely because the latter receive increases in pay (in Western economies, at any rate) regardless of productivity; 3) Population growth creates business opportunities and a changing of facilities. It makes expansion investment and new ventures more attractive, by reducing risk and by increasing total demand. (E.g., if housing is overbuilt, a growing population will take up the slack; 4) More young people working means more job opportunities and more mobility within the labor force. Greater mobility means a more efficient allocation of resources (i.e., the best matching of young people to jobs); 5) Population growth creates "economies of scale." The more people, the larger the market, and therefore the greater need for bigger and more efficient machinery, division of labor, and improved transportation and communication. (See Simon, p. 73.)

251. Dyck, p. 165.

252. See Grisez, pp. 196, 263.

253. Commission on Population Growth and the American Future, *An Interim Report* (1971), p. 21, cited in PPFA brief, p. 24.

254. I examined the *Final Report* of the Commission and could find no precise definition given of "unwantedness." The closest the Commission comes to a definition is its saying that "many ...couples will have children before they want them." (*Population and the American Future: The Report of The Commission on Population Growth and the American Future* (N.Y.: The New American Library (Signet), 1972, p. 163.)

255. PPFA brief, pp. 24-25.

256. *Ibid.*, p. 25.

257. *Ibid.*, p. 26.

258. *Ibid.*

259. *Ibid.*

260. *Ibid.*, p. 27.

261. Forssmann & Thuwe, "One Hundred and Twenty Children Born After Application for Therapeutic Abortion Refused," in Reiterman, Carl, *op. cit.* (Chap. One), p. 143, cited in *Ibid.*, p. 29.

262. See Grisez, p. 53.

263. Anderson, Ursula M., M.D., et al., "The Medical, Social, and Educational Implications of the Increase in Out-of-Wedlock Births," in 56 *Amer. Jour. Pub. Health* 1866 (1966), cited in PPFA brief, p. 27.

264. Bernstein & Herzog, *Health Services for the Unmarried Mother* (Wash., D.C.: U.S. Dept. of HEW (Children's Bureau), 1964), cited in *ibid*.

265. PPFA brief, pp. 27-28

266. Sim, Myre, M.D., "Abortion and Psychiatry," in Hilgers, Horan, & Mall, p. 159.

267. On this point, I checked the Commission's *Final Report*.

268. Gil, David G., *Violence Against Children: Physical Child Abuse in the United States* (Cambridge, Mass.: Harvard U. Press, 1970), p. 146.

269. *Ibid.*

270. Lenoski, E. F., M.D., "Translating Injury Data into Preventive Health Care Services: Physical Child Abuse," unpublished, 1976, cited in Ney, Philip G., M.D., "Infant Abortion and Child Abuse: Cause and Effect," in Mall & Watts, p. 25.

271. Smith, Selwyn M., M.D., *The Battered Child Syndrome* (London: Buttersworth, 1975), pp. 161-162. 12 percent of the abusive mothers in the study considered abortion, as compared to 2 percent of controls. Smith says this difference is "not significant." 20 as opposed to 6 percent, respectively, were "displeased." 49 as opposed to 37 percent, respectively, had "reservations." Thus, a higher percentage of abused than unabused children in Smith's study were in some sense "unwant-

ed," but most apparently were not. Moreover, the statistics regarding "reservations" tell us that some other factors were probably at work besides "unwantedness" which were responsible for the abuse. (Dr. Smith is an associate professor of psychiatry at the Univ. of Ottawa and Head of the Forensic Dept. at Royal Ottawa Hosp.)

272. Schmitt, B. D. & Kempe, C. H., *Child Abuse: Management and Prevention of the Battered Child Syndrome* (Basle: Ciba-Geigy, 1975), cited in Ney, p. 26.

273. See Hunter, Rosemary S., M.D., et al., "Antecedents of Child Abuse and Neglect in Premature Infants: A Prospective Study in a Newborn Intensive Care Unit," in 61 *Pediatrics* 629, 634 (1978); Fontana, Vincent J., M.D. & Besharov, Douglas J., *The Maltreated Child,* 4th ed. (Springfield, Ill.: Chas. C. Thomas, 1979), pp. 12-13, 27; Gelles, Richard, "A Profile of Violence Toward Children in the United States," in Gerbner, George, Ross, Catherine J. & Ziegler, Edward, eds., *Child Abuse: An Agenda for Action* (N.Y.: Oxford U. Press, 1980), pp. 102-103.

274. Ney, p. 25.

275. Smith, p. 205.

276. *Ibid.*

277. Gelles, p. 88.

278. Fontana & Besharov, p. 12.

279. Ney, p. 34. As his authority for the claim made in the last sentence of this quote, he cites Moore-Carver, E. C., "The International Inventory on Information on Induced Abortion," International Institute for the Study of Human Reproduction, Columbia U., 1974.

280. *Wade* brief, p. 32, quoting Chase, Gordon, *op. cit.*, p. 2.

281. *Ibid.*, p. 34.

282. PPFA Brief, p. 10.

283. *Ibid.*, pp. 23, 24.

284. Iffy, Leslie, M.D.; Frisoli, Garry, M.D.; & Jakobovits, Anatal, M.D., "Perinatal Statistics: The Effect International-

ally of Liberalized Abortion," in Hilgers, Horan, & Mall, pp. 122-124. The authors point out that they are "committed enither to pro-abortionist nor to anti-abortionist thinking," p. 92.

285. *Cumulated Index Medicus* is the international index of articles appearing in medical and related journals. In my tabulation, I excluded letters to the editor, but included editorials. I also counted one journal, *The International Journal of Gynaecology and Obstetrics* as a "foreign or international" journal, even though it is published in the U.S. This is because most of its editorial board are from overseas and most of its articles drawn from foreign writers. There were 5 articles from this journal.

286. See Edstrom, Karin G. B., "Early Complications and Late Sequelae of Induced Abortion: A Review of the Literature," in 52 *Bull. of the World Health Organ.* (1975), pp. 123-139.

287. Hilgers, in Hilgers & Horan, p. 70. One major study indicates that the reason for the higher level of complications among young women is simply the fact that they appear to seek abortions later in pregnancy--when the risks are greater --than do women who are older. It is suggested that this is due primarily to inexperience, ignorance, and emotional reasons. See Tietze, Christorpher, M.D. & Lewit, Sarah, "Joint Program for the Study of Abortion (JPSA): Early Medical Complications of Legal Abortion," in 3 *Studies in Family Planning* (No. 6) (June 1972), p. 102.

288. Edstrom, p. 125.

289. *Ibid.*, p. 125.

290. *Ibid.*, p. 125. In a D.& C.,the physician inserts a curette, a loop-shaped steel knife, up into the uterus. Then he cuts the placenta and child into pieces and scrapes them out into a basin. When using the suction method, the physician must first paralyze the cervical muscle ring (womb opening) and then stretch it open. He then inserts a hollow plastic tube with a knife-like edge on the tip, into the uterus. The suction tears the child's body into pieces. Then the physician cuts the deeply rooted placenta from the inner wall of the uterus. The scraps are then sucked out into a bottle. (See Willke, p. 29.)

291. *Ibid.*, p. 126. The saline method involves the insertion of a long needle through the woman's abdominal wall and into

the child's amniotic sac. A concentrated saline (salt) solution is injected into the amniotic fluid. The child breathes and swallows this and is poisoned. It usually takes over an hour for the poisoning to kill the child. The mother will go into labor a day later and deliver a dead baby, though sometimes the babies are born alive. (See Willke, p. 31.)

292. See *Planned Parenthood of Central Missouri v. Danforth,* 428 U.S. 52 (1976).

293. Edstrom, p. 127. A hysterotomy is like a Caesarian section delivery. The woman's abdomen is surgically opened, as is her uterus. The baby is then lifted out and, with the placenta, discarded. (See Willke, p. 31.)

294. See Edstrom, p. 127.

295. Wulff, George J. L., Jr., M. D. & Freiman, S. Michael, "Elective Abortion: Complications Seen in a Free-Standing Clinic," in 49 *Obstetrics and Gynecology* 351, 355 (1977).

296. Edstrom, p.126. "Trauma" is a general term for injury. The uterine myometrium is the muscular wall of the uterus. (Stedman's *Medical Dictionary* (24th ed.) (Baltimore: Williams & Wilkins, 1982), p. 921.

297. Intravasal rejection involves an immune reaction of veins in the woman's body to the entry of some of the saline solution into them. Intravasal haemolysis is the alteration, dissolution, or destruction of red blood cells in such a manner that hemoglobin is liberated into the medium in which the cells are suspended. (*Ibid.*, p. 636.)

298. Brudenall, Michael, "Gynaecological Sequelae of Induced Abortion," 224 *The Practitioner*, 893, 897 (1980).

299. Tietze & Lewit, p. 107.

300. Edstrom, p. 128.

301. *Ibid.*, p. 129.

302. Kotasek, Alfred, "Report from Czechoslovakia: Medical Consequences of Induced Abortion and Its Effect on Subsequent Pregnancy," II *The Human Life Review*, No. 2 (Spring 1976), p. 121.

303. Tietze, C. & Dawson, D., *Induced Abortion: A Factbook*. Re-

ports on Population, Family Planning 14 (1973), cited in Hunton, R. B. & Bates, Deidre, "Medium Term Complications After Termination of Pregnancy," 11 *Aust. & N.Z. Jour. of Ob. & Gyn.*, 99, 102 (1981).

304. Tietze & Lewit, p. 109.

305. Bognar, Zoltan, M.D. & Czeizel, Andrew, M.D., "Mortality and Morbidity Associated with Legal Abortions in Hungary, 1960-1973," 66 *Amer. Jour. of Pub. Health* 568, 572 (1976). The statistics for the entire country appeared in the country's Obstetrical Registers. The figure given for Budapest was compiled from figures gathered by the Budapest City Council and Health Department. The figure for Budapest which appeared in the national government-compiled Obstetrical Register was 31.1 per 1,000. This led the authors to conclude that there was "some underreporting" to the national government. So, it is possible that the true figures for the rest of the country are also somewhat higher.

306. Tietze, C. & Dawson, D., *Induced Abortion: A Factbook*. Reports on Population, Family Planning 14 (1973), cited in Hunton, & Bates, p. 102.

307. Andolsek, L., ed., *The Ljubljana Abortion Study 1971-1973*. Bethesda, Md.: National Institute of Health, 1974, cited in Hunton & Bates, p. 102.

308. Hunton & Bates, p. 102.

309. Pike, M. C., et al., "Oral Contraceptive Use and Early Abortion as Risk Factors for Breast Cancer in Young Women," 43 *British Jour. of Cancer* 72-76 (1981).

310. Vessey, M. P., et al., "Oral Contraceptive Use and Abortion Before First Term Pregnancy in Relation to Breast Cancer Risk," 45 *British Jour. of Cancer*, 327, 328, 331 (1982).

311. See Ewing, J. A. & Rousse, B. A., "Therapeutic Abortion and a Prior Psychiatric History," in 130 *Amer. Jour. of Psychiatry*, 37 (1973) and Sim, Myre, M.D. & Neisser, Robert, M.D., "Post-Abortive Psychoses: A Report from Two Centers," in Mall & Watts, p. 1.

312. Sim & Neisser, p. 2.

313. *Ibid.*, p. 2, 8.

314. *Ibid.*, pp. 3-7.

315. Liebman, Monte Harris, M.D. & Zimmer, Jolie Siebold, "The Psychological Sequelae of Abortion: Fact and Fallacy," in Mall & Watts, p. 137.

316. Adler, Nancy E., "Emotional Responses of Women Following Therapeutic Abortion" 45 *Amer. Jour. of Orthopsychiatry* 446, 453 (1975). She apparently refers to the abortion cases studied as being "therapeutic" because they involved "problem pregnancies." She does not define what she means by "problem pregnancies" and the article suggests that the abortions she studied were simply elective, not for a putative medical reason.

317. Kent, Ian, et al., "Emotional Sequelae of Therapeutic Abortion: A Comparative Study." Paper presented at the annual meeting of the Canadian Psychiatric Association, 1978, cited in Liebman & Zimmer, p. 127.

318. Lask, Bryan, "Short-term Psychiatric Sequelae to Therapeutic Termination of Pregnancy," 126 *British Jour. of Psychiatry* 173, 176 (1975). He does not define "therapeutic."

319. Spaulding, Jean G., M.D. & Cavenar, Jesse O., Jr., M.D., "Psychoses Following Therapeutic Abortion," 135 *Amer. Jour. of Psychiatry* 364 (1978). The cases they describe indicate that their notion of "therapeutic" really includes abortions performed for virtually all reasons, not just allegedly medical ones.

320. Cavenar, Jesse O., Jr., M.D., et al., "Psychiatric Sequelae of Therapeutic Abortions," 39 *North Carolina Medical Journal* 101, 104 (1978).

321. Kotasek, p. 122, citing a 1970 study by Kolarova (no further information given).

322. *Ibid.*, citing a 1970 study by Dlhos, et al, (no further information given).

324. Tisher, Carl L., "Adolescent Suicide Attempts Following Elective Abortion: A Special Case of Anniversary Reaction," 68 *Pediatrics* 670, 671 (1981).

325. Iffy, Frisoli, & Jokobovits in Hilgers, Horan & Mall, pp. 92-127. See the article for their various citations.

326. Bognar & Czeizel, pp. 572-573.

327. See Daling, Janet R. & Emanuel, Irvin, M.D., "Induced Abortion and Subsequent Outcome of Pregnancy in a Series of American Women," 297 *New England Journal of Medicine* 1241 (1977); Harlap, Susan, et al., "A Prospective Study of Spontaneous Fetal Losses After Induced Abortions," 301 *New England Jour. of Medicine* 677 (1979); Kline, Jennie, et al., "Induced Abortion and Spontaneous Abortion: No Connection?" 107 *Amer. Jour. of Epidemiology* 290 (1978); Levin, Ann Aschengrau, et al., "Association of Induced Abortion with Subsequent Pregnancy Loss," 243 *JAMA* 2495 (1980); Schoenbaum, Stephen C., et al., "Outcome of the Delivery Following an Induced or Spontaneous Abortion," 136 *Amer. Jour. of Obstetrics and Gynecology* 19 (1980).

328. See Daling & Emanuel, p. 1243.

329. Iffy, Frisoli, Jakobvits, p. 119.

330. Freeman, Malcolm G., M.D. & Graves, William L., "Risk of Premature Delivery Among Indigent Negro Women Based on Past Reproductive Performance," 34 *Obstetrics and Gynecology* 648 (1969); Chung, C., et al., quoted in an editorial in "Editorial, Five Studies: No Apparent Harmful Effect from Legal Abortion on Subsequent Pregnancies: D & C is Possible Exception," 10 *Family Planning Perspectives* No. 1 (1978), p. 34, both cited in Iffy, Frisoli, & Jakobovits, p. 178. The Freeman-Graves study is not necessarily reliable because the "past reproductive performance" considered appears to include both spontaneous and induced abortions. The Chung, et al. Hawaii study has the same defect as the other American studies are alleged to have of limited time.

331. See Levin, et al.

332. Madore, Carol, et al., "A Study on the Effects of Induced Abortion on Subsequent Pregnancy Outcome," 139 *Amer. Jour. of Obst. & Gyn* 516, 519-520 (1981). The article in which the study is reported suggests that the difference between a "spontaneous abortion" and a "fetal/neonatal death" is the point in pregnancy at which the unborn child dies. It states that "spontaneous abortion" is used to indicate any death occurring at less than 20 weeks (at p. 520).

333. Barrett, Jeffrey M., M.D., et al., "Induced Abortion: A Risk Factor for Placenta Previa," 141 *Amer. Jour. of Obst. & Gyn.* 7690772 (1981). The endometrium is the mucous mem-

brane comprising the inner layer of the uterine wall. *(Steadman's Medical Dictionary* (24th Ed.)), p. 464.

334. Hilgers, in Hilgers & Horan, pp. 73-74, citing Klinger, A., "Demographic Consequences of the Legalization of Induced Abortion in Eastern Europe," 8 *Inter. Jour. of Obstetrics and Gynecology* 680-691 (1970). Hilgers also mentions a number of specific studies. (See Hilgers, pp. 73-74).

335. Kotasek, p. 122, citing *Report of the Swedish Government Commission,* 1971 and the Kohoutek study of 1970.

336. Lembrych, Stanislaw Z., M.D., "Fertility Problems Following an Aborted First Pregnancy," in Hilgers, Horan, & Mall, p. 129. Male sterility was eliminated as a possible factor in these cases.

CHAPTER SEVEN NOTES

1. *Webster's 3rd International Dictionary* (Springfield, Mass.: G. C. Merriam, 1976), p. 2176.

2. *The Wanderer,* Jan. 7, 1982, p. 6.

3. Flanagan, Geraldine Lux, *The First Nine Months of Life* (N.Y.: Simon and Schuster, 1962, 1965), pp. 30-32.

4. Grisez, *op. cit.* (Chap. One), p. 13.

5. *Ibid.*

6. *Ibid.,* pp. 13-14.

7. Flanagan, p. 35.

8. Grisez, pp. 14-16.

9. Patten, Bradley M., *Human Embryology* (3rd ed.) (N.Y.: McGraw-Hill, 1968), p. 159.

10. Willke, *op. cit.* (Chap. One), p. 12.

11. Grisez, P. 25, citing Hamilton, W. J., M.D., et al., *Human Embryology* (erd ed.) (Cambridge, Eng.: W. Heffer & Sons, Ltd., 1962), p. 152.

12. Grisez, p. 25.

13. *Ibid.*, cited in Gedda, Luigi, *Twins in History and Science* (Springfield, Ill.: Chas. C. Thomas, 1961), p. 125; see also Willke, p. 13.

14. Heffernan, Bart T., M.D., in Hilgers & Horan, *op. cit.* (Chap. One), p. 5. See pp. 21-25 of Heffernan for his citations which are to various biological and medical texts and medical articles.

15. *Ibid.*

16. *Ibid.*

17. *Ibid.*, p. 6.

18. *Ibid.*, pp. 5-6.

19. Flanagan, p. 51.

20. *Ibid.*, p. 47.

21. Liley, A. William, M.D., "A Day in the Life of the Fetus," in Hilgers, Horan, and Mall, *op. cit.* (Chap. Three) p. 30.

22. Flanagan, pp. 53-54. Emphasis is mine.

23. Heffernan, p. 6.

24. *Ibid.*

25. *Ibid.*

26. *Ibid.*, p. 7.

27. *Ibid.*

28. Flanagan, p. 72.

29. Heffernan, p. 7.

30. Flanagan, pp. 67, 72.

31. Noonan, John T., Jr., "The Experience of Pain by the Unborn," in Hilgers, Horan, and Mall, pp. 205-216. ("Noonan III.")

32. *Ibid.*, p. 213. Emphasis is mine. The fact of the unborn

experiencing pain during abortion was confirmed by 26 physicians in a letter to President Ronald Reagan in early 1984. They wrote to show their agreement with a public statement he had made that unborn babies suffer "long and agonizing" pain during abortions. See *The Wanderer*, Feb. 23, 1984, p. 1, col. 3.

33. Flanagan, p. 73.

34. *Ibid.*, p. 74.

35. *Ibid.*, pp. 79-81.

36. Liley, p. 34.

37. Flanagan, p. 81.

38. Heffernan, p. 16.

39. Flanagan, pp. 73-74.

40. Heffernan, p. 15.

41. *Ibid.*

42. *Ibid.*, citing Gesell, Arnold, *The Embryology of Behavior* (N.Y.: Harper & Bros., 1945), p. 65.

43. Heffernan, p. 16; Flanagan, p. 87.

44. Flanagan, pp. 87, 92.

45. Flanagan, pp. 89, 93; Heffernan, p. 16.

46. Flanagan, p. 95.

47. Heffernan, p. 16.

48. Flanagan, pp. 100-101.

49. Heffernan, pp. 16-17.

50. *Ibid.*, p. 17; Willke, pp. 22-23. The dates of these babies' births are dated from the first day of the last normal menstrual period.

51. Heffernan, p. 17; Willke, p. 22.

52. Flanagan, pp. 105-106.

53. *Ibid.*, p. 112.

54. Grisez, p. 14.

55. Bleckschmidt, E., M.D., "Human Being from the Very First," in Hilgers, Horan, and Mall, pp. 7-8. Emphasis is his.

56. Gerrity, Benignus, *Nature, Knowledge and God: An Introduction to Thomistic Philosophy*. (Milwaukee: Bruce, 1947), p. 164.

57. *Ibid.*, p. 165.

58. *De Anima*, in McKeon, Richard, ed., *The Basic Works of Aristotle* (N.Y.: Random House, 1941), 413a, p. 557.

59. Aristotle, *History of Animals*, 583b, in Thompson, D'Arcy Wentworth, ed., *The Works of Aristotle*, Vol. IV (Oxford, Eng.: Clarendon, 1910).

60. 410 U.S. 113, 133, f.n. 22.

61. Aristotle, *Generation of Animals*, 736a-736b, in Smith, J. A. & Rose, W. D. eds., *The Works of Aristotle*, Vol. V (Oxford, Eng.: Clarendon, 1912).

62. *De Anima*, in McKeon, Richard, ed., *The Basic Works of Aristotle* (N.Y.: Random House, 1941), 414b, p. 560.

63. *Generation of Animals*, p. 736b.

64. *Ibid.*, p. 583b.

65. *Ibid.*, p. 737b.

66. *De Anima*, 412a, p. 555.

67. *Ibid.*, 415b, pp. 561-562.

68. *Ibid.*, 412a, p. 555.

69. *Ibid.*, 415b, p. 562.

70. *Ibid.*, 414a-414b, p. 559.

71. *Ibid.*, 414b, p. 560.

72. *Ibid.*, 415a, p. 560.

73. *Ibid.*, 413a, p. 557.

74. *Ibid.*, 416b, p. 563.

75. *Ibid.*, 414a, p. 558.

76. *Ibid.*, 415b, p. 562.

77. *Ibid.*, 420b, pp. 572, 573. Emphasis is his.

78. Verny, Thomas, M.D. (with John Kelly), *The Secret Life of the Unborn Child* (N.Y.: Summit, 1981), p. 37. Dr. Verny is a psychiatrist in Toronto who has done much study of the mental and psychological development of the unborn child and the influence of maternal attitudes and emotions on the unborn child.

79. Willke, p. 22.

80. Verny, p. 37.

81. Heffernan, p. 19.

82. *De Anima*, 414b, p. 559.

83. *Ibid.*, 412a, p. 555.

84. *History of Animals*, 482b.

85. *Parts of Animals*, in Smith & Ross, ed. (Vol. IV), 703a,b. This point is at odds with Christian thought which has held that the soul does not reside in any particular place. (See St. Thomas Aquinas, *Summa Theologica*, Vol. One, Pt. 1, Ques. 76, Art. 8 (Westminster, Md.: Christian Classics, 1981), p. 381.)

86. *Parts of Animals*, 665b.

87. *Ibid.*, 703a.

88. *History of Animals*, 482b.

89. *Parts of Animals*, 666a.

90. *Ibid.*, 665b.

91. *De Anima*, 416b, p. 564. His precise words are as follows: "...all food must be capable of being digested, and that

what produces digestion is warmth; that is why everything that has soul in it possesses warmth." I believe that the context indicates that my conclusion that warmth indicates a soul, whether or not there is digestion, is correct. The semi-colon separates the statement about digestion from that about warmth and the soul generally; the latter is essentially a separate sentence. Actually, the wording suggests that Aristotle had the relationship between digestion and warmth the opposite of what it really is. That is, it is digestion which creates warmth. Also, I believe that Aristotle is saying that warmth indicates the presence of a *sensitive* soul, even though he does not specify which type of soul he is referring to. This is because he doubtless knew that plants, which he says have a nutritive soul, are not warm. They also do not digest their "food" in the sense that we commonly understand the term.

92. *De Anima,* 427b, pp. 586-587.

93. *Ibid.,* 432a, 433a, pp. 596, 597.

94. Aristotle, *On Memory and Reminiscence,* in McKeon, ed., 450a, p. 608.

95. *History of Animals,* 488b.

96. *Ibid.*

97. Spicer, E. E., *Aristotle's Conception of the Soul* (London: Univ. of London Press, 1934), p. 93.

98. See *De Anima,* 429a, p. 590.

99. *Ibid.,* p. 94.

100. Verny, p. 197.

101. *De Anima,* 427a, p. 586.

102. Verny, p. 62

103. *Ibid.,* p. 18.

104. *Ibid.,* p. 22.

105. *Ibid.,* p. 21.

106. *Ibid.,* p. 18

107. See Verny, p. 19. He says, however, that this is "a theory, not proven fact."

108. *Ibid.*, p. 38.

109. *Ibid.*, pp. 66-67.

110. *Ibid.*, p. 190. The emphasis in the first quotation is mine.

111. Feldmar, Andrew, "The Embryology of Consciousness: What Is a Normal Pregnancy?" in Mall & Watts, *op. cit.* (Chap. Six), p. 17. Emphasis is mine. See p. 23 of the article for his citation of the works of the men mentioned.

112. Verny, p. 51.

113. *Ibid.*, pp. 19-20.

114. *Ibid.*, p. 20.

115. *Ibid.*, p. 64.

116. *Ibid.*, p. 65.

117. *The Random House Dictionary of the English Language*, Unabridged Edition (N.Y.: Random House), p. 456.

118. Verny, p. 64.

119. *Ibid.*, pp. 61-62

120. *Random House Dictionary*, p. 287.

121. *Ibid.*

122. Purpura, Dominick, M.D., cited by Verny, p. 41.

123. Verny, p. 41.

124. Franz, Wanda, "Fetal Development: A Novel Application of Piaget's Theory of Cognitive Development," in Hilgers, Horan, & Mall, pp. 36-37.

125. *Ibid.*, pp. 40-41.

126. *Ibid.*, p. 41.

127. *Ibid.*, p. 42, citing Anokhin, P. K., *Biology and Neurophysi-*

ology of the Conditioned Reflex and its Role in Adaptive Behavior (Elmsford, N.Y.: Pergamon Press, 1974). Translated from the Russian version, published 1968.

128. Franz, p. 42, citing Humphrey, T., "The Development of Human Fetal Activity and Its Relation to Postnatal Behavior," in 5 *Advances in Child Development and Behavior* (1970, pp. 1-57.)

129. Franz, pp. 42-43.

130. *Ibid.*, p. 42, citing Anokhin.

131. *Ibid.*, p. 43.

132. Blechschmidt, pp. 7-8. Emphasis is his.

133. See PPFA brief, p. 44 and PPFA supplemental brief, p. 29.

134. See PPFA supplemental brief, p. 29.

135. See PPFA brief, p. 44.

136. PPFA supplementql brief, pp. 29-30, quoting Hardin, Garrett, "Abortion or Compulsory Pregnancy?" in 30 *Jour. of Marr. and Family*, No. 2 (May 1968), p. 250.

137. PPFA supplemental brief, p. 30.

138. *Wade* beirf, p. 19. Emphasis is the brief's.

139. *Ibid.*, p. 19, quoting Potts, Malcolm, "The Problem of Abortion" in Ebling, F. J., ed., *Biology and Ethics*, 1969, p. 3. The page citation given in the brief is incorrect. It should really be pp. 77-78.

140. *Wade* brief, p. 20. Emphasis is the brief's.

141. *Ibid.*, p. 21, quoting Patten, p. 5.

142. *Ibid.*, quoting Arey, Leslie Brainerd, *Developmental Anatomy*, 7th ed. (Philadelphia: W. B. Saunders, 1965), p. 98.

143. *Ibid.*, quoting Potts, p. 1.

144. *Ward* brief, p. 121.

145. *Ibid.*

146. *Ibid.*, pp. 121-122, quoting Hardin, p. 250. I should note that the argument "elsewhere" which he refers to is "Blueprints, DNA, and Abortion: A Scientific and Ethical Analysis," in 3 *Medical Opinion and Review*, No. 2 (1967), p. 74. Emphasis is mine in the passages in the text. These emphasized passages may be sufficient to enable the reader to understand and make a judgment about the pro-abortion perspective, without any comment on them.

147. 318 F. Supp. 1217 (E. D. La., 1970).

148. *Ibid.*, at 1236.

149. *Wade* brief, p. 122.

150. *Ibid.*, p. 123.

151. *Ibid.*, p. 124.

152. Bonnette, Dennis, "Hylomorphism, Positivism, and the Question of When Human Life Begins," in 72 *Social Justice Review*, pp. 41, 45 (Mar.-Apr. 1981).

153. It should be noted that scientists do not "make life" when carrying out, say, *in vitro* fertilization. They make use of ova and sperm which come from already-living human beings. Further, the ova and sperm are "alive" themselves and carry the potential for making a new human being when they unite.

154. See Young, R. V., Jr., "An Anatomy of Evolution" (Parts I and II), in *The Wanderer*, Oct. 1 and Oct. 8, 1981 for a good summary of the scientific gaps and problems in the "theory" of evolution. For a more detailed study of evolution, see Hoyle, Fred & Wickramasinghe, Chandra, *Evolution From Space* (N.Y.: Simon & Schuster, 1982).

155. See Grisez, p. 16 and Helgesen, Martin W., Letter to the Edito- of *TLS*, Nov. 20, 1981, p. 1367.

156. See *De Anima*, 415a, p. 561.

157. Bonnette, p. 44.

158. Flanagan, p. 34.

159. My inquiries of clergymen of various denominations revealed the following: The United Methodist Church states that there should be a burial ceremony if a child is born alive, no

matter how long he lives. This is not the case with a stillborn child. The Episcopal Church has no specific formula or rite. The clergyman would probably treat it as a normal Christian burial. The Lutheran Church-Missouri Synod will provide a burial service if desired by the parents. The foregoing is likely to apply for the most part, to children miscarried in the later stages of pregnancy. None of these churches, no doubt due to their particular doctrines on the subject, *require* spontaneously aborted unborn children to be baptized. Apparently, at least some evangelical Protestants also favor burial in such cases. We can judge this from the fact that James Dobson, a Los Angeles psychologist, evangelical author, and radio personality, was one of the most outspoken public figures in calling for a proper burial for the bodies of some 17,000 unborn children found in containers outside a pathology laboratory there in February 1982. (See *Christianity Today*, Sept. 17, 1982, pp. 46, 48.) The Greek Orthodox Church provides a baptism, funeral service, and burial, at least if the parents request them. The Catholic Church stipulates that there be a burial and also a baptism before the child dies or as soon after the death or miscarriage or stillbirth as possible. The Catholic Church also has the traditional doctrine of limbo to explain where the soul of the unbaptized miscarried child goes.

160. Grisez, p. 28, citing Arey, Leslie B., *Developmental Anatomy: A Textbook and Laboratory Manual of Embryology*, 7th ed. (Philadelphia: W. B. Saunders, p. 180, and Willis, R. A., *The Borderland of Embryology and Pathology* (Washington, D.C.: Butterworth, 1962), pp. 458-460.

161. Grisez, p. 30.

162. *Ibid.*, pp. 28-30.

163. *Ibid.*, p. 30.

164. 19 Howard 393 (1857).

165. Grisez, p. 26.

166. Nathanson, *op. cit.* (Chap. One), p. 216.

167. See *ibid.*, p. 214.

168. Grisez, p. 32.

169. Nathanson, p. 217.

CHAPTER EIGHT NOTES

1. *Roe v. Wade* (J. Stewart, concurring), 410 U.S. 113, 169, quoting *National Mutual Ins. Co. v. Tidewater Transfer Co.* (J. Frankfurter, dissenting), 337 U.S. 582, 646 (1949).

2. *Ibid.*, at 170.

3. *Doe v. Bolton* (J. Douglas, concurring), 410 U.S. 179, 214, quoting *Meyer v. Nebraska,* 262 U.S. 390, 399 (1923).

4. *Wade* brief. p. 94.

5. Walter Berns and Harry Clor have stated this in connection with the regulation of obscenity. (See Berns, *Freedom, Virtue, and the First Amendment* (Baton Rouge, Oa.: LSU Press, 1957), and Clor, *Obscenity and Public Morality* (Chicago: U. of Chicago Press, 1969). (Hereinafter cited as "Clor I.")

6. 428 U.S. 52.

7. Berns, p. 157. Emphasis is mine.

8. *Ibid.*, p. 159.

9. *Ibid.*, p. 165.

10. *Ibid.*, p. 28.

11. *Ibid.*, p. 164.

12. Canavan, Francis, "The Dilemma of Liberal Pluralism," in V *The Human Life Review,* No. 3 (Summer 1979), p. 6. (Hereinafter cited as "Canavan III.")

13. *Ibid.*, p. 7.

14. Berns, p. 72. Emphasis is mine.

15. Canavan I, p. 13.

16. See *Wade* opinion, at 141-147 (implicit), 165; *Wade* brief, pp. 23, 98.

17. Professors Noonan and Rice have also called these decisions expressions of a positivist jurisprudence. (See Noonan II,

op. cit. (Chap. One) and Rice II, *op. cit.* (Chap. Three).) Both say that the Court follows the thinking of the most prominent modern exponent of this, Hans Kelsen. Rice writes the following: "Law, in Kelsen's view, is a form into which contents of any kind may be put, according to the prevailing social views...The possibility of natural law is categorically denied by Kelsen" (p. 1066, quoting Bodenheimer, E., *Jurisprudence* (1940), p. 285). This, according to Rice, is seen in *Wade* and *Bolton* for the following reasons. Kelsen's theory sees the "'legal person'" as simply "'the subject of legal duties and legal rights'" (quoting Bodenheimer, p. 93). Kelsen does not believe it necessary for the law to regard all human beings as persons...Thus, there is no ground...for labeling a law as essentially unjust if it excludes from personhood and therefore deprives of the right to live any particular class of humans [as the Supreme Court did unborn children]..." (p. 1066). Kelsen's conception of law essentially echoes that of the eminent American jurist, Justice Oliver Wendell Holmes, Jr. (See footnote 101 below for a brief discussion of Holmes.)

18. Cox, Archibald, *The Role of the Supreme Court in American Government* (London: Oxford U. Press, 1976), pp. 113-114. See also: Bickel, Alexander, *The Morality of Consent* (New Haven, Conn.: Yale U. Press, 1975); Ely, John Hart, "The Wages of Crying Wolf: A Comment on *Roe v. Wade*," in 83 *Yale Law Journal* 920 (1973); Epstein, Richard, "Substantive Due Process by Any Other Name: The Abortion Cases," in *Supreme Court Review* 154 (1973); Wellington, Harry, "Common Law Rules and Constitutional Double Standards," in 83 *Yale Law Journal* 22 (1973); and Noonan II, above.

19. See Noonan, John T., Jr., "Abortion and the Catholic Church: A Summary History," in 12 *Natural Law Forum* (1967), p. 85. (Hereinafter cited as "Noonan IV.") Gerber, Rudy J., "Abortion, Two Opposing Legal Philosophies," in 15 *American Jour. of Jurisprudence* (1970), p. 1; and Grisez, *op. cit.* (Chap. One), pp. 123-155. See also Chapter Three of this book for the traditional Jewish teaching.

20. Brown, Harold O. J., "What Makes the Law the Law?" in V *The Human Life Review,* No. 1 (Winter 1979), p. 78.

21. The briefs generally refer just to "rights" or "fundamental rights."

22. Carey, George W., "Abortion and the American Political Crisis," in III *The Human Life Review,* No. 1 (Winter 1977),

pp. 45-46.

23. Canavan, Francis, "The Theory of the Danforth Case," in II *The Human Life Review,* No. 4 (Fall 1976), pp. 11-13. (Hereinafter cited as "Canavan I.")

24. Locke, John, "The Second Treatise," in *Two Treatises of Government.* (Laslett, Peter, ed.) (N.Y.: Cambridge Univ. Press, 1963), Sec. 19, p. 321. (Hereinafter cited as "Locke II.") Emphasis is Locke's.

25. *Ibid.,* p. 367.

26. I have already stated that Locke's thought stands behind the Declaration of Independence. The Declaration clearly acknowledges the Lockean notion of inalienable rights: "We hold these truths to be self-evident, that all men are created equal, that they are endowed by their creator with certain inalienable rights; that among these are life, liberty & the pursuit of happiness..."

27. Locke's precise words on this point are as follows:

> ...a Man, not having the Power of his own Life, *cannot*, by Compact, or his own Consent, *enslave himself* to any one, nor put himself under the Absolute, Arbitrary Power of another, to take away his Life, when he pleases. No body can give more Power than he has himself; and he that cannot take away his own Life, cannot give another power over it. (Locke II, Sec. 23, p. 325.) (Emphasis is Locke's.)

28. Glenn, Gary E.,"Abortion and Inalienable Rights in Classical Liberalism," in 20 *Amer. Jour. of Jurisprudence* (1975), pp. 68-69.

29. Locke II, Sec. 17, p. 320. (Emphasis is Locke's.)

30. Glenn, p. 72.

31. Locke's precise words on this point are as follows (the first quote pertains to man in the state of nature, the second to man in civil society):

> But though this be a *State of Liberty,* yet it is *not a State of License,* though Man in that State have an uncontrollable Liberty, to dispose of his Person or Possessions, yet he has not Lib-

> erty to destroy himself, or so much as any Creature in his Possession, but where some nobler use, than its bare Preservation calls for it. (Locke II, Sec. 6, p. 311. Emphasis is Locke's)

and

> ...Freedom is not, as we are told, *A Liberty for* every Man to do what he lists: (For who could be free when every other Man's Humour might domineer over him?) But a *Liberty* to dispose, and order, as he lists, his Person, Actions, Possessions, and his whole Property, within the Allowance of those Laws under which he is; and therein not to be subject to the arbitrary Will of another, but freely follow his own. (Locke II, Sec. 57, p. 348. Emphasis is Locke's.)

32. *Wade* opinion, at 154.

33. Glenn, p. 75.

34. *Ibid.*, p. 79.

35. *Ibid.*, p. 80.

36. *Ibid.*, pp. 76-77.

37. Canavan, Francis, "Genetics, Politics and the Image of Man," in IV *The Human Life Review*, No. 2 (Spring 1978), p. 54. (Hereinafter cited as "Canavan II.")

38. *Ibid.*

39. *Ibid.*, p. 59.

40. To be precise, Canavan says that this view of human nature reflects a reductionist and mechanistic conception of nature which in turn rests on a nominalistic metaphysics. In this conception of nature, which took root at the time of Descartes and Kepler, the world is seen as a vast machine. In time this vision came to be applied to man himself and, by the eighteenth century, the human organism came to be regarded as an automatic clock and knowledge of this clockwork was all that is supposedly needed to understand human action. There is no need to consider the possibility that man has any human nature beyond this. Further discussion of this view of nature, however, will take me far afield. The point I

wish to make is that in omitting further discussion, I do not believe that I am distorting or misstating Canavan's point.

41. Canavan II, p. 59. Emphasis is his.

42. Weaver, Richard M., *Ideas Have Consequences* (Chicago: U. of Chicago Press, 1948), p. 3.

43. *Ibid.*, pp. 3-4.

44. Haberer, Joseph, *Politics and the Community of Science* (N.Y.: Van Nostrand Reinhold, 1969).

45. *Ibid.*, p. 5.

46. *Ibid.*, p. 6.

47. *Wade* opinion, at 165.

48. *Bolton* (J. Douglas, concurring), at 219.

49. *Bolton*, at 197.

50. *Bolton* (C. J. Burger, concurring), at 208.

51. *Time*, Oct. 13, 1967, p. 33.

52. See *Wade* brief, pp. 111-112; PPFA brief, p. 37; ACOG brief, p. 10.

53. See *Wade* brief, *ibid.*; PPFA brief, p. 38; ACOG brief, pp. 11, 13-15.

54. See *Wade* brief, p. 98; PPFA brief, p. 10.

55. Haberer, p. 3.

56. NRLC brief, p. 55.

57. LIFE brief, pp. 52-54.

58. Brief of Women for the Unborn, et al., p. 15, footnote 10.

59. Lewis, C. S., *The Abolition of Man* (N.Y.: Collier, 1962), p. 67.

60. Haberer, pp. 46-47.

61. See Lewis, pp. 67, 90-91; Haberer, p. 323.

62. *Ibid.*, p. 324.

63. Weaver, p. 5.

64. Haberer, p. 324.

65. Lewis, p. 72.

66. *Ibid.*

67. Derrick, Christopher, *Honest Love and Human Life* (Hutchinson of London, 1969), p. 105.

68. Jonas, Hans, *The Phenomenon of Life: Toward a Philosophical Biology* (N.Y.: Harper & Row, 1966).

69. Lewis, pp. 87-88.

70. Kass, Leon, M.D., "Patenting Life," in 72 *Commentary*, No. 6 (Dec. 1981), p. 46. Emphasis is his. (Hereinafter cited as "Kass II.")

71. Derrick, p. 106.

72. Kass, Leon, M.D., "'Making Babies' Revisited," in 54 *The Public Interest*, No. 54 (Winter 1979), pp. 39, 59. (Hereinafter cited as "Kass I.")

73. Lewis, p. 84.

74. Haberer, p. 46.

75. *Ibid.*, p. 43.

76. *Ibid.*, p. 44.

77. Weinberger, J., "Science and Rule in Bacon's Utopia: An Introduction to the Reading of the *New Atlantis*," in 70 *Amer. Pol. Sci. Review* (1976), p. 871.

78. *Ibid.*, p. 883.

79. White, Howard B., *Peace Among the Willows: The Political Philosophy of Francis Bacon* (The Hague: Martinus Nyhoff, 1968), p. 5.

80. Sarvis & Rodman, *op. cit.* (Chap. One), p. 24. They take the term "Century of the Wanted Child" from Lader I, *op. cit.* (Chap. One), p. 155.

81. *Ibid.*, p. 25.

82. Carey, p. 46.

83. *Wade* brief, p. 109. Emphasis is mine.

84. *Ibid.*

85. PPFA brief, pp. 10-11.

86. PPFA brief in *Eisenstadt*, p. 27, quoting the Court of Appeals opinion, 429 F.2d 1398, 1401-02 (1st Circuit, 1970). Emphasis is mine.

87. The illegitimacy rate during the era of liberalized/legalized abortion shows a steady increase. In 1965--roughly the beginning of the push for changing the laws--,there were 291,200 births out of wedlock; in 1970, there were 398,700; in 1973, 407,300; in 1975, 447,900; in 1977, 515,700; and in 1978, 543,900. (Source: *Statistical Abstract of the United States: 1980, op. cit.* (Chap. Six), p. 66.

88. Rice points to such a connection between abortion and euthanasia. He cites a survey by sociologist William McCready of the National Opinion Research Center which indicates that acceptance of voluntary euthanasia (the taking of the victim's life with his consent) is increasing among Catholics who "'agree that artificial contraception is permissible'" and who "'favor the legalizing of abortion.'" (Rice III, *op. cit.* (Chap. Three), p. 129, quoting *Our Sunday Visitor* (news ed.), Jan. 9, 1977, p. 2, col. 1.) He further shows the consequences when an anti-life ethic is established in one area by quoting U.S. Supreme Court Justice Robert H. Jackson's forward for the record of the Hadamar trial, one of the Nuremberg trials of Nazi war criminals:

> "A freedom-loving people will find in the records of war crimes trials instruction as to the roads which lead to such a regime and the subtle first steps that must be avoided. Even the Nazis probably would have surprised themselves, and certainly they would have shocked many German people, had they proposed as a single step to establish the kind of extermination institution that the evidence

> shows the Hadamar Hospital became. But the end was not thus reached; it was achieved in easy stages.
>
> To begin with, it involved only the incurably sick, insane and mentally deficient patients of the institution. It was easy to see that they were a substantial burden to society, and life was probably of little comfort to them. It is not difficult to see how, religious scruples apart, a policy of easing such persons out of the world by a completely painless method could appeal to a hardpressed and unsentimental people. But 'euthanasia' taught the art of killing and accustomed those who directed and those who administered the death injections to the taking of human life. Once any scruples and inhibitions about killing were overcome and the custom was established, there followed naturally an indifference as to what lives were taken. Perhaps also those who became involved in any killings are not to be in a good position to decline further requests. If one is convinced that a person should be put out of the way because, from no fault of his own, he has ceased to be a social asset, it is not hard to satisfy the conscience that those who are willful enemies of the prevailing social order have no better right to exist. And so Hadamar drifted from a hospital to a human slaughterhouse." (Rice III, pp. 131-132.)

Other writers have also pointed to the logical connection in theory between abortion and euthanasia and how the promoters of one have also been the promoters of the other. (See Brown, Harold O. J., "The First Amendment and the Question of Justice in Light of the Abortion Issue," in Hilgers, Horan, & Mall, *op. cit.* (Chap. Three), p. 296; Zahn, Gordon, "Abortion and the Corruption of the Mind," *Ibid.*, p. 338; Overduin, Daniel Ch., "The Ethics of Abortion," *Ibid.*, p. 375; de Guerrero, Maria Eugenia C. & Rojas, Oscar I., M.D., "Abortion in Latin America," *Ibid.*, p. 481.)

Also, public opinion surveys and political developments in the wake of the legalization of abortion give us evidence of the connection. In Britain, which had legalized abortion in 1967, the results of a survey by the Voluntary Euthanasia Society--released in January 1979--showed that almost two-thirds of the British public favored voluntary euthanasia. (*Catholic Almanac: 1977*, Huntington, Ind.: *Our Sunday*

Visitor, 1976, p. 65.) In the U.S., as of September 1981, 10 states had enacted so-called "living will" legislation, which provides for the possibility of a written directive by an adult patient authorizing the withholding of extraordinary life-sustaining procedures in cases of terminal illness. Many anti-abortion groups have opposed such legislation as opening the way to the legalization of euthanasia. (McCormick, Richard A., S.J., "Legislation and the Living Will," in *America* (Mar. 12, 1977), p. 210 & McCormick, Richard A., S.J. & Paris, John J., S.J., "Living-Will Legislation, Reconsidered," in *America* (Sept. 5, 1981), p. 87.) In 1973, the same year that the Supreme Court legalized abortion, the Gallup Poll asked people the following question: "When a person has a disease that cannot be cured, do you think doctors should be allowed by law to end the patient's life by some painless means if the patient and his family request it?" A full 53 percent answered "Yes"; only 40 percent said "No." In 1975, the percentages were reversed, but still a full 40 percent said that a person "has the moral right to end his or her life" when afflicted with "a disease that is incurable." 41 percent stated that a person "has the moral right to end his or her life" when "suffering great pain" and having "no hope of improvement." (*The Gallup Poll: Public Opinion 1972-1977*. (Vol. Two), Wilmington, Del.: Scholarly Resources, Inc., pp. 143, 462, 462.)

A similar connection between abortion and infanticide has been pointed to. Professor J. David Bleich of the Benjamin N. Cardozo School of Law reviews the writing of a few prominent defenders of both:

> From the historical perspective, it is not at all surprising that in the aftermath of the 1973 Supreme Court decision in *Roe v. Wade* legalizing abortion, attempts are being made to effect what is tantamount to the legalization of infanticide. Even before *Roe v. Wade,* the prominent situation ethicist, Joseph Fletcher, argued that if the life of a mongoloid baby can be "ended prenatally, why should it not be ended neonatally (i.e., just after birth?)" [Quoting Fletcher]. Dr. James Watson, recipient of a Nobel Prize for the discovery of DNA's double helix...In an article...in the AMA's socio-economic magazine, Prism...writes, "If a child were not declared alive until three days after birth, then all parents could be allowed the choice that only a few are given under the present system [of legalized abortion]." Dr. Francis

> Crick, Dr. Watson's partner in DNA research and the consequent Nobel Prize, has in a similar vein advocated legislation under which newborn babies would not be considered legally alive until they are two days old and certified as healthy by medical examiners. Michael Tooley, professor of philosophy at Stanford University...argues that human babies after birth are no more than kittens and cannot be bearers of rights until they have self-consciousness of themselves as persons. Accordingly, he finds no reason to view with disapprobation the killing of any child within the first two weeks of life. (He cites Tooley, "Abortion and Infanticide," 2 *Philosophy and Public Affairs* 37 (1972).) (Hilgers, et al., pp. 417-418.)

In 1982, much of America was shocked to learn of the "Infant Doe" case, in which the Indiana Supreme Court permitted the parents of a deformed newborn baby to decide to let him die by ordering the attending physician to withhold food from him. In reality, it seems that such episodes have taken place for some time. In a noteworthy speech before the American Academy of Pediatrics in October 1976, Dr. C. Everett Koop, the current U.S. Surgeon General, told his colleagues that "you all know that infanticide is being practiced right *now* in this country..." (Speech reprinted in III *The Human Life Review,* No. 2 (Spring 1977), p. 103.) In the same year that *Wade* and *Bolton* were handed down an important article appeared in the prestigious *New England Journal of Medicine* which documented many cases of infanticide of deformed newborns in one hospital. (See Duff, R. S., M.D. & Campbell, A. G., M.D., "Moral and Ethical Dilemmas in a Special-Care Nursery," 289 *New England J. of Med.* (1973), p. 890.)

Actually, many abortions late in pregnancy are *de facto* cases of infanticide. Almost all babies aborted by hysterotomy are born alive. Many aborted by means of prostaglandins are also. Sometimes, abortions done by the use of saline solution result in live babies. (Willke, *op. cit.* (Chap. One), p. 32.) Some physicians have been tried for murder or manslaughter when such attempted abortions have resulted in live births of children who later died. (See Noonan II, pp. 128-145.)

89. PPFA *amicus curiae* brief in *Eisenstadt,* p. 2. Emphasis is mine.

90. PPFA, "This Is Planned Parenthood--World Population," bro-

chure (1963). This is a reprint of part of a speech by then PP/WP Chairman Donald B. Strauss, "Planned Parenthood and Reverence for Life," Oct. 15, 1963.

91. Kass II, p. 47.

92. In addition to the *Wade/Bolton* briefs, see, for example, PPFA's statement of purpose in its *Eisenstadt* brief; PPFA's mimeograph "The Facts Speak for Planned Parenthood" (1954); and PPFA's mimeograph "Objectives, Activities and Structures in the 1970's."

93. Gordon, *op. cit.* (Chap. One), p. 343.

94. *Wade* brief, pp. 20, 121.

95. *Ibid.*, pp. 21, 122.

96. *Ibid.*, p. 21.

97. *Ibid.* Emphasis is mine.

98. Guttmacher, Alan F., M.D., "Abortion--Yesterday, Today and Tomorrow," in Guttmacher I, *op. cit.* (Chap. One), p. 13.

99. Lewis, p. 86.

100. *Wade* brief, p. 20.

101. I might just repeat that the legal thought behind the pro-abortion position and the *Wade* and *Bolton* opinions possibly has its roots in the thinking of the late, eminent Justice Oliver Wendell Holmes, Jr. His thinking reflected the perspective that Weaver discussed. Holmes was clearly a positivist. He said that what the law depends on is the political judgments made in a political society at a given time, particularly those made by the dominant groups. He believed that morals or ethics should be separated from the law. Law should be "uncolored" by anything outside of it, such as morals. He made it clear that he believed that there is no higher, unchanging moral standard. He put it this way: "Morals deal with the actual internal state of the individual's mind, what he actually intends." Morality, then, is just an attitude that the individual has. Holmes' disbelief in the existence of universals is further seen in his notion of the word "law" as being like any other word in the dictionary--it has many meanings. Consistent with the view of contemporary courts (as seen in the "balancing" activity

which was discussed in Chapter Two), he thus believed that the law must depend on the particular case. He defined it to mean "the prophecies of what the courts will in fact do, and nothing more pretentious..."

In spite of Holmes' desire to separate law and morality, he seemed to reintroduce moral considerations by intimating that when judges make the law it may be with reference to certain social and moral concerns. A judge may be faced with having to resolve a dispute between groups whose desires or values go in opposite directions and will thus have to measure the "relative worth" of their claims. That is, he has to determine the "relative worth of our different social ends" which are what is really at stake; he has to decide what is best for purposes of public policy. So, like the contemporary rights theory, Holmes' view has an inherent contradiction caused by his unwillingness to make moral judgments. Even though no position of any of the competing groups coming before the judge is to be viewed as any better than any other, his decision to accept one or the other alters public policy in the manner the winning groups wants and thus implicitly recognizes that position as superior. (This is so, as in abortion, even if the result of the decision is only to remove the legal prohibitions on a particular activity.) Holmes says that making this kind of moral judgment is acceptable (indeed unavoidable), but it is not really a "moral" judgment (i.e., a choice between right and wrong). This is because it is to be made with reference to science.

Empirical science, for Holmes, permits us to make judgments about moral matters. As he said: "Very likely it may be that with all the help of statistics and every modern appliance can bring us there will never be a commonwealth in which science is everywhere supreme. But it is an ideal, and without ideals what is life worth?" So, Holmes, like the contemporary rights theory that has been discussed, sought to find an objective refuge in a world he viewed as being morally subjective (since he recognized no transcendent moral order). He let science make the moral judgments. Holmes has had a great influence on present-day American jurisprudence and, as my comments suggest, he perhaps inspired the framework of legal philosophy reflected in the abortion opinions. (My source for this discussion of Holmes" thought is White, Morton, *Social Thought in America: The Revolt Against Formalism*. (Boston: Beacon Press, 1957), pp. 59-75, 203-212. (Originally published by Viking Press in 1949.) The quotes from Holmes are taken from his works by White.

102. See PPFA brief, p. 38.

103. *Wade* brief, p. 122.

104. See Ketchel, Melvin M., "Should Birth Control Be Mandatory?" 0 *Med. World News*, No. 42 (Oct. 18, 1968), pp. 68, 70.

105. NRLC brief, p. 21.

106. *Ibid.*, p. 42.

107. The brief of Certain Physicians, et al., stresses biological and medical facts; AUL's and to a larger degree, NRLC's, stress legal and constitutional arguments; that of the Texas Association of Diocesan Attorneys, constitutional and historical ones; and that of Women for the Unborn, some that are most correctly categorized as "moral" ones--despite the fact that the argument of all these briefs is implicitly moral --,such as the following:

> "We realize that the pro-abortionists are often acting out of mercy. They want to save the mother--and occasionally the child--from future suffering. But is that reason sufficient to kill?
>
> "The answer to that depends upon what we are killing. When a dog or a cat is suffering terribly, we kill it out of mercy. When a man or a woman is suffering terribly, we do not kill. Why? Not because we think less of a man than of a cat, but because we think more. We believe that the man has a certain infinite dignity we should respect." (P. 10 of brief.)

108. *Ibid.*, p. 20.

109. *Ibid.*, p. 41.

110. See brief of Texas Association of Diocesan Attorneys. For statements of the anti-abortion movement's position regarding the necessity of providing a constitutional guarantee of the right to life of the unborn child, see *National Right to Life News*, Nov. 1973 (editorial), p. 8, col. 1 and Willke, pp. 161-162.

111. *Amicus curiae* brief of Texas Association of Diocesan Attorneys in *Wade*, p. 64, quoting St. Thomas Aquinas, *Summa Theologica*, Part I, Question XXIX, Article I.

112. *Ibid.*

113. *Amicus curiae* brief of LIFE, pp. 9-10, quoting an editorial in 113 *California Medicine*, No. 3 (Sept. 1970), pp. 67-68.

114. *Ibid.*, p. 11.

115. In the passages cited, these writers may not address abortion specifically, but are all known as writers or spokesmen for the anti-abortion position in the U.S. This fact distinguishes them from the present-day living writers in the first Sub-Section, such as Haberer and Kass. Derrick *is* anti-abortion, but lives in England. This, along with the fact that they address *only* abortion or the other "life" issues in the works referred to, instead of broader questions about modern scientific thought, is why I have chosen to consider them here instead of in the first Sub-Section.

116. Rice I, *op. cit.* (Chap. One), p. 24.

117. Ramsey, Paul, "On *In Vitro* Fertilization," in V *The Human Life Review,* No. 1 (Winter 1979), p. 27. The article is the text of his testimony before the Ethics Advisory Board of the U.S. Dept. of HEW in 1978. Emphasis is his. He makes reference to R. G. Edwards' article "Fertilization of Human Eggs *in Vitro:* Morals, Ethics and the Law," in 49 *The Quarterly Review of Biology,* No. 1 (March 1974), pp. 3-26.

118. Canavan II, p. 53.

119. *Ibid.*, p. 54.

120. *Ibid.*

121. *Ibid.*

122. *Ibid.*, pp. 55-56.

123. Ramsey, p. 27. Emphasis is his.

124. Nathanson, Bernard N., M.D., Testimony, printed in *The Human Life Bill, Hearings Before the Subcommittee on Separation of Powers of the Committee on the Judiciary, United States Senate, 97th Congress, First Session,* p. 1046.

CHAPTER NINE NOTES

1. Jaffa I, *op. cit.* (Intro.), p. 183.

2. Cicero, *The Republic (Commonwealth)*, Bk. III, Chap. 22, cited in Sigmund, Paul E., *Natural Law in Political Thought* (Cambridge, Mass.: Winthrop, 1971), p. 22.

3. Cicero, *The Laws*, Bk. I, Chap. 6, cited in Sigmund, p. 22.

4. *Ibid.*, Bk. I, Chap. 12, cited in *Ibid.*

5. Holton, James E., "Marcus Tullius Cicero," in Strauss & Cropsey, *op. cit.* (Chap. Three), p. 148.

6. *Ibid.*

7. Berns, *op. cit.* (Chap. Eight), p. 228.

8. *Ibid.*

9. *Ibid.*, p. 229. Emphasis is mine.

10. Barber, Benjamin, "The Compromised Republic: Public Purposelessness in America," in Howitz, Robert H., ed., *The Moral Foundations of the American Republic* (Charlottesville, Va.: Univ. of Virginia Press, 1977), pp. 20-21.

11. Diamond, Martin, "Ethics and Politics: The American Way," in Horwitz, p. 63.

12. Berns, p. 228.

13. Aristotle, *Nichomachean Ethics*, Tr. by Martin Ostwald, Library of Liberal Arts (Indianapolis: Bobbs-Merrill, 1962), p. 16, 1097b.

14. *Ibid.*, p. 17.

15. I am aware, of course, that the man could not transmit sperm if he had been sterilized. This, however, would not be a natural disruption of the faculty, but a deliberate one which would be contrary to the end of the faculty in the same way that it will be argued abortion is. If he--or his wife--had been rendered sterile by accident or for medical reasons, their undertaking of sexual intercourse would not be contrary to the natural end of the faculty. This is because they

would be giving of themselves as completely as they could within the bounds of natural limitations of the faculty over which they have no control. They would be carrying out the primary end of the faculty as far as they could. They would not be deliberately frustrating its primary end if they undertook it chiefly to satisfy its secondary ends.

16. I am aware, of course, that pregnancy can occur through artificial insemination or *in vitro* fertilization. These, however, are not "natural" means.

17. Higgins, Thomas J., S.J., *Man as Man: The Science and Art of Ethics.* (Revised Edition) (Milwaukee: Bruce, 1958), p. 395.

18. *Ibid.*

19. I must acknowledge Dr. Raphael T. Waters of the Philosophy Department of Niagara University, Niagara Falls, New York for suggesting this argument to me.

20. *The Politics of Aristotle, op cit.* (Chap. Three), I, ii, Sec. 5, 1252b, p. 4.

21. *Ibid.*, I, iii, Sec. 4, 1261b; I, iv, Secs. 1-10, 1262a-1262b.

22. *Nichomachean Ethics,* p. 239, 1162a.

23. Professor Harry V. Jaffa explains the apparent contradiction between the statement in this passage that "the household is earlier and more indispensable than the state" and the better known passage in Book I of the *Politics* that "the polis is prior in the order of nature to the family and the individual." (I, ii, Sec. 13, 1253a.) He says that Aristotle believes that the household is prior in the order of efficient causality and the polis is prior in the order of final causality. (See Jaffa, Harry V., "Aristotle," in Strauss & Cropsey, *op. cit.* (Chap. Three), p. 77. (Hereinafter cited as "Jaffa II.")

24. *Ibid.*

25. Higgins, p. 360.

26. Champlin, Joseph M., *"Don't You Really Love Me?"* (Notre Dame, Ind.: Ave Maria Press, 1967), p. 111.

27. *Nichomachean Ethics,* p. 29, 1102a.

28. *Ibid.*, p. 31, 1102b.

29. *Ibid.*, p. 32, 1103a.

30. My source for this classification of the virtues is Monarch's handy student study guide for *The Philosophy of Aristotle* by Prof. Barbara Jancar.

31. *Nichomachean Ethics*, p. 44, 1107A.

32. *Ibid.*

33. *Ibid.*, pp. 37-38, 1104b.

34. *Nichomachean Ethics*, p. 208, 1153b.

35. *Ibid.*, p. 286, 1176b.

36. *Ibid.*, 1176a.

37. *Ibid.*, pp. 287-288, 1177a.

38. *Ibid.*, p. 288, 1177a.

39. *Ibid.*, p. 291, 1177b.

40. *Ibid.*, p. 285, 1176a.

41. *Ibid.*, p. 293, 1178b.

42. *Ibid.*, p. 210, 1154a.

43. *Ibid.*, p. 198, 1151a.

44. *Ibid.*, p. 211, 1154b.

45. *Ibid.*, pp. 285-286, 1176a.

46. *The Politics of Aristotle*, I, ii, Sec. 13, 1253a, p. 6.

47. See Millard, Charles E., M.D., "The Case for Chastity," 15 *Child and Family*, No. 3 (1976), p. 244 (VD and its complications); "ACS Report on the Cancer-Related Health Checkup--Cancer of the Cervix," 30 *Ca-C Cancer Journal for Clinicians*, No. 4 (July-Aug. 1980), p. 219 (cervical cancer); *Time*, Aug. 2, 1982, pp. 62-69 (genital herpes).

48. Levin, Max, M.D., "The Meaning of Sex and Marriage: A Lec-

ture to College Students," 34 *Current Medical Digest*, No. 8 (Aug. 1967), pp. 1074-1075.

49. Champlin, p. 115.

50. Jaffa II, p. 77.

51. *Nichomachean Ethics*, p. 34, 1103b.

52. *Ibid.*, 296, 1179b-1180a.

53. *The Politics of Aristotle*, I, ii, Secs. 5-9, 1252b, pp. 4-5.

54. *Ibid.*, II, iv., Secs. 8-10, 1262b, p. 47.

55. The following are a few present-day experts who have pointed to the connection between family problems/breakdown and juvenile delinquency or drug abuse: Walken, Robert N., *Psychology of the Youthful Offender* (end ed.) (Springfield, Ill.: Chas. C. Thomas, 1973), pp. 19-32; Chein, Isidor, et al., *The Road to H: Narcotics, Delinquency, and Social Policy* (N.Y.: Basic Books, 1964), pp. 251-298; and Goldberg, Leonard, "Epidemiology of Drug Abuse in Sweden" in Zarafonetis, Chris J. D., M.D., ed., *Drug Abuse: Proceedings of the International Conference* (Philadelphia: Lea & Febiger, 1972), p. 57. He cites several studies.

56. Jaffa II, p. 84.

57. *The Politics of Aristotle*, I, viii, Sec. 15, 1256b, p. 21.

58. *Ibid.*, I, viii, Sec. 2, 1256a, p. 19.

59. Nathanson book, *op. cit.* (Chap. One), p. 239.

60. Clor I, *op. cit.* (Chap. Eight), p. 170. Elsewhere, Clor gives some examples of ways in which the "new freedom with which sexual matters are treated in the arts and the media has been accompanied by corresponding liberties in sexual behavior." He mentions increases in wife-swapping, "sex clubs," and premarital and extramarital experimentation of various kinds. He does not try to make the elusive cause-and-effect connection here, but simply calims that this "'expression' is *a* significant factor in the shaping of attitudes, values, dispositions, and ultimately conduct." Still, this raises the strong possibility of a connection. (Clor, Harry M., "Obscenity and Freedom of Expression," in Cline, Victor B., ed., *Where Do You Draw the Line? An Ex-*

ploration into Media Violence, Pornography, and Censorship. (Provo, Utah: Brigham Young Univ. Press, 1974), p. 325. (Hereinafter cited as "Clor ii.") Emphasis is mine.

61. Wilson, James Q., "Violence, Pornography, and Social Science," in Cline, p. 306.

62. Clor I, p. 204.

63. *Nichomachean Ethics*, p. 3, 1094a.

64. *Ibid.*, p. 4, 1094a.

65. *Ibid.*, p. 4, 1094b.

66. *Ibid.*, p. 3, 1094a.

67. *Ibid.*, p. 4, 1094b.

68. *Ibid.*, p. 4, 1094a.

69. *Ibid.*, p. 3, 1094a.

70. *Ibid.*, p. 5, 1095a.

71. *Ibid.*, p. 7, 1095b.

72. Aristotle's belief that a child does not have a complete rational soul even *after* birth is suggested by the passage I quoted in Chapter Seven from *Generation of Animals* (736a-736b). It is also indicated from the passage in his *Politics* where he says that "[t]he rule of the freeman over the slave is one kind of rule; that of the male over the female another; that of the grown man over the child another still. It is true that all these persons...possess in common the different parts of the soul; but they possess them in different ways." As to the deliberative faculty specifically... "if children also possess it, it is only in an immature form." (*The Politics of Aristotle*, I, xiii, Sec. 7, 1260a, p. 35.) Another translation speaks of freemen, slaves, women and children possessing the various parts of the soul "in different degrees." (See McKeon, ed., *op. cit.* (Chap. 7), p.1144.)

73. Jancar, p. 162.

74. *Ibid.*, p. 163.

75. *Ibid.*, p. 164.

76. See Plato, "Phaedo," 118, in Warmington & Rouse, *op. cit.* (Chap. Three), p. 521.

77. Edelstein, Ludwig, *The Meaning of Stoicism* (Cambridge, Mass.: Harvard U. Press (Pub. for Oberlin Col.), 1966), p. 90. It is not clear who he is quoting. (Hereinafter cited as "Edelstein II.")

78. *Ibid.*, pp. 90-91.

79. *Ibid.*, p. 91.

80. Hicks, R. D., *Stoic and Epicurean* (N.Y.: Russell & Russell, 1962), p. 146.

81. Edelstein II, p. 72.

82. *Ibid.*, p. 3. The Stoic would not, however, countenance what one commentator calls "weak pity" (i.e., misguided compassion). For example, those who violate the law must receive the punishment which they deserve. (Hicks, p. 148.) This makes one think that Stoic thought might not be too sympathetic toward the woman who becomes pregnant as a result of a freely-chosen act of intercourse, then wants to escape the consequences, whether legal or otherwise, by being permitted to have an abortion.

83. *Ibid.*, p. 90, citing Seneca, *Epis. Mor.* 95, 52.

84. *Ibid.*, citing Cicero, *Laws*, Bk. III, Chap. 63 and Epictetus. He does not make clear which of Epictetus' works he is citing.

85. Hicks, p. 88.

86. Edelstein II, p. 74.

87. Edelstein I, *op. cit.* (Chap. Three), p. 16.

88. Sandbach, F. H., *The Stoics* (London, Eng.: Chatto & Windus, 1975), p. 163.

89. Connery, *op. cit.* (Chap. Three), p. 25.

90. Cicero, *Laws*, Bk. III, Chap. viii, 18, in Cicero, *De Re Publica/De Legibus*. (Tr. by Keyes, Clinton Walker) (London: Wm. Heinemann, Ltd., 1928). Reprinted in 1966, p. 481.

91. Rice I, *op. cit.* (Chap. One), p. 8. It would not be incompatible with this principle of the common law to perform surgical procedures to save the mother's life which would have the indirect and secondary effect of taking the life of the unborn child. Examples would be surgery to end an ectopic pregnancy (when in most cases the child already would be dead by the time the surgery is undertaken) or to remove a cancerous uterus. This is because the intent is not to take the unborn child's life and his death would only occur as an incidental result of such surgery. These types of surgery are not considered abortion procedures; they are governed by the philosophical principle of double or indirect effect. This would be understood by any statute banning abortion.

92. Brody, Baruch, *Abortion and the Sanctity of Human Life: A Philosophical View* (Cambridge, Mass.: MIT Press, 1976), pp. 6-25.

93. In Federalists 10 and 14, Madison makes it clear that the American Republic did not view itself as acknowledging the same overriding purpose of government that the classics did and was not to possess the conditions necessary to the maintenance of an ancient Greek type of polis.

94. Montesquieu, Baron de, *The Spirit of the Laws*. Tr. by Thomas Nugent, Vol. One, Bk. III (N.Y.: Hafner Press, 1949), p. 20.

95. *Ibid.*, p. 21.

96. Horwitz, Robert H., "John Locke and the Preservation of Liberty: A Perennial Problem of Civic Education," in Horwitz, p. 154.

97. *Ibid.*, pp. 154-155.

98. Jefferson, Thomas, Letter to John Adams, Oct. 28, 1813, in Koch, Adrienne & Peden, William, eds., *The Life and Selected Writings of Thomas Jefferson* (N.Y.: Random House (Modern Library ed.), 1944), pp. 632-633.

99. Mansfield, *op. cit.* (Chap. Five), pp. 39-40.

100. Tocqueville, *op. cit.* (Chap. One), Vol. Two, Second Book, p. 132.

101. *Ibid.*, pp. 129-130.

102. *Ibid.*, pp. 130-131.

103. *Ibid.*, p. 131.

104. Diamond, p. 56.

105. *Ibid.*, pp. 63-64

106. *Ibid.*, pp. 64-65.

107. Jefferson, Letter to Adams, Oct. 28, 1812, in Padover, Saul K., compiler, *The Complete Jefferson* (N.Y.: Duell, Sloan & Pearce), pp. 282-283.

108. Tocqueville, Vol. Two, Third Book, p. 248.

109. Locke, John, "Some Thoughts Concerning Education," in Gay, Peter, *John Locke on Education* (N.Y.: Teachers College, Columbia Univ., 1964), p. 164 (Hereinafter cited as "Locke III.")

110. "The First Treatise," in Laslett, *op. cit.* (Chap. Eight), Sec. 59, p. 220. (Hereinafter cited as "Locke I.")

111. Locke II, in Laslett, Sec. 78, p. 362.

112. *Ibid.*, Sec. 81, p. 364.

11e. Montesquieu, Bk. XII, p. 195.

114. *Ibid.*, Bk. XVI, pp. 256-257.

115. *Ibid.*, Bk. XVI, pp. 258-259.

116. *Ibid.*, Bk. V, p. 40.

117. Diamond, pp. 70-71.

118. *Ibid.*, p. 71. Emphasis is mine.

119. Mansfield, p. 29.

120. See Cox, Donald W., *America's New Policy Makers: The Scientists' Rise to Power* (Philadelphia: Chilton, 1964), pp. 3-8 and Penick, James L., Jr., et al., *The Politics of American Science: 1939 to the Present* Rev. ed.) (Cambridge, Mass.: MIT Press, 1972), pp. 1-4.

121. Mansfield, p. 41.

122. Thurow, Glen E., *Abraham Lincoln and American Political Religion* (Albany, N.Y.: State U. of New York Press, 1976), p. 4, quoting Washington's "Farewell Address," from Fitzpatrick, John C., ed., *The Writings of George Washington,* Vol. 35 (Wash., D.C.: Supt. of Documents, 1931-44), p. 229.

123. Tocqueville, Vol. Two, Book One, pp. 22-23.

124. *Ibid.,* Vol. One, p. 312.

125. *Ibid.,* p. 310.

126. Thurow, p. 3, quoting Jefferson, *Notes on the State of Virginia* (N.Y.: Harper & Row, 1964), p. 156.

127. Thurow, p. 3, quoting Washington's "Farewell Address," in Fitzpatrick, p. 229.

128. Locke II, Sec. 56, p. 347. Emphasis is Locke's.

129. Helms, Jesse, Speech in the U.S. Senate, August 1982, reprinted as "God's Authority Vs. Legal Positivism," in *The Wanderer,* Sept. 2, 1982, p. 4.

130. *Ibid.*

131. *Ibid.*

132. *Ibid.*

133. *Ibid.*

134. *Ibid.*

135. Thurow, p. 116.

136. Helms, p. 4.

137. Lincoln, Abraham, "Second Inaugural Address," printed in Thurow, p. 89.

138. Helms, p. 4.

139. *Ibid.*

140. *Ibid.*

141. Lincoln, in Thurow, p. 89.

142. Thurow, p. 106.

143. Helms, in *The Wanderer,* Sept. 2, 1982, p. 7.

144. A survey by the Alan Guttmacher Institute, PPFA's research arm, showed that in 1980 there were approximately 1.55 million legal induced abortions in the U.S. (*Buffalo Evening News,* Feb. 23, 1982, p. A-3, col.2.)

145. Jaffe, Lindheim, & Lee, *op. cit.* (Chap. One), p. 7.

146. Burke, Edmund, *Reflections on the Revolution in France,* Paine, Thomas, *The Rights of Man* (Garden City, N.Y.: Anchor Press/Doubleday, 1973), pp. 70-71.

147. *Ibid.,* p. 172.

148. This argument was made to me by Professor Richard B. Friedman of the Political Science Department at the State University of New York at Buffalo.

149. Rice I, p. 39.

150. Nathanson book, p. 263.

151. *Ibid.,* p. 74.

152. This understanding of the slavery controversy is set out in Dahl, Robert A., *A Preface to Democratic Theory* Chicago: Univ. of Chicago Press, 1956), pp. 39-40, 96-97.

153. Professor William H. Marshner of Christendom College has compared the extent of slavery in pre-Civil War America with that of abortion today. In 1860, there were about 7 million white nuclear families in the U.S., of which fewer than 1.5 million lived in the Deep South. Only about 384,000 Southern and Border State whites owned slaves; it was usually the same families in the long term who were slaveowners. Today, there are about 50 million American families. There were about 10 million legal abortions between 1973 and 1981. Even if it is generously conceded that one-half of these are repeat performances by women who have previously had abortions, it still remains that at least 5 million *different* women have had abortions during this period. This means that there has been an abortion in one American family in ten--and the number increases each year. Thus, abortion is much more prevalent than slavery was. (See Marshner, William H., "The Hatch Amendment: New Hope for a Pro-Life Strategy," in *IDEA Ink,*

Vol. I, No. 1 (1982), p. 3.)

154. Rees, *op. cit.* (Chap. One), pp. 40-41.

155. I am aware, however, that some are very powerful. For example, a number of large drug and surgical equipment companies profit substantially from legalized abortion. So do many of the members of ACOG. I do not believe, though, that these people are prepared to tear our political order apart over abortion.

156. As mentioned in Chapter One, note 321 the surveys have at times yielded mixed results about whether it is the pro- or anti-abortion side that has more persons who regard this issue as so important that it would determine whether they voted for a particular political candidate. (See, again, Jaffe, Lindheim, & Lee, *op. cit.* (Chap. One), p. 100.) By the late 1970s, however, it was clear that most of these were on the anti-abortion side. In 1978, only 7 percent saw abortion as the decisive issue, but three-quarters of these were abortion opponents. (CBS News/*New York Times* Poll, cited in Jaffe, Lindheim, & Lee, pp. 107-108.) In 1979, a surprising 39 percent of respondents to a Louis Harris Survey said that they would vote against a candidate they otherwise agreed with if they disagreed with him on the abortion issue. 53 percent of this group were anti-abortion, 30 percent pro-abortion. (Harris Survey, cited in Jaffe, Lindheim, & Lee, p. 108.) The results of some of the races in the last three Congressional elections (1978, 1980, and 1982)--in which candidates were acknowledged to have won narrowly because they were opposed to abortion--seem to have confirmed this. Jaffe, Lindheim. and Lee, give us further evidence of how the abortion issue is of overriding importance to a greater extent on the anti- than on the pro-abortion side when they tell us that after the 1973 decisions "[t]he diverse organizations of the abortion-rights coalition turned back to their other, primary concerns" (p. 117).

157. Professor James Hitchcock presents a good analysis of the nature of the split in this moral consensus in present American political society in his article "Abortion and the Moral Revolution," in V *The Human Life Review*, No. 2 (Spring 1979), pp. 5-15. (Hereinafter cited as "Hitchcock II.")

158. Bickel, Alexander M., *The Least Dangerous Branch: The Supreme Court at the Bar of Politics* (Indianapolis: Bobbs-Merrill, 1962), p. 68.

159. *Ibid.*, p. 66.

160. *Ibid.*, p. 68.

161. I am aware of the counter-argument to this latter point that such amendments would not really be changing the fundamental law because the Constitution never protected the unborn child. In other words, they would just be restoring the situation that existed prior to *Wade* and *Bolton* when our governments could protect the unborn child's life, if they wished. This is answered by the arguments in Chapter Three, however, where it is showed that at least a respectable argument can be made that the original Constitution, the Fourteenth Amendment, and our Blackstonian tradition intended that the unborn child's right to life be protected.

NOTES TO EPILOGUE

1. *The Wanderer*, Sept. 2, 1982, p. 4.

2. Arendt, Hannah, *Between Past and Future: Eight Exercises in Political Thought* (N.Y.: Viking, 1961), p. 93.

3. Lewis, *op. cit.* (Chap. Eight), pp. 84-85.

APPENDIX A NOTES

1. A "legislating" amendment can be distinguished, say, from one which changes some aspect of the operation of the constitutional mechanisms of our government. For example, an amendment which specifically changed the enumerated powers of Congress or the means of electing Senators would be the latter type. One might argue that a pro-life or human life amendment is not really "legislative"--in spite of the fact that abortion was governed by legislative enactments for most of our history--because the unborn child already has a naturally-endowed right to life. The amendment would just be declaratory of this right. (This is close to the position of the argument I have presented that the Blackstonian tradition already protects such a right.) This, however, would not mean that the amendment would be classified as something other than "legislative" because it would mean that Congress and

the states would be acting to make previously recognized, but unwritten, rights part of our national public policy. This is essentially what happened in the case of the first eight amendments. By recognizing these rights by constitutional amendment, instead of just a statute, Congress and the states stressed that they were *fundamental* national policy. For a defense of the use of amendments to make policy, see Orfield, Lester B., *The Amending of the Federal Constitution* (N.Y.: DaCapo Press, 1971), pp. 103-106.

2. Hamilton seems to preclude a policymaking role for the federal courts in Federalist 78 in *The Federalist, op. cit.* (chap. Five), pp. 506-507. For a good recent argument, grounded in historical scholarship, that the federal courts were to be excluded from policymaking, see Berger, Raoul, *Government by Judiciary: The Transformation of the Fourteenth Amendment* (Cambridge, Mass.: Harvard Univ. Press, 1977), pp. 300-311. (Hereinafter cited as "Berger II.")

3. Galebach gives a thorough discussion of the case law precedents which indicate that Congress has the authority to use the Fourteenth Amendment for this purpose. (See Galebach, *op. cit.* (Chap. Four).)

4. The original version of the bill read that "Congress finds that present scientific evidence indicates a significant likelihood that actual human life exists from conception." The wording of the bill was changed again by Senator Jesse Helms, its Senate sponsor, when it was finally submitted to the Senate for debate in August 1982. It replaced the claim that life begins at conception with wording to the effect that Congress finds that, on the basis of treaties, international bodies, American history, and Senate hearings, the unborn child has a fundamental right to life.

5. 4 Wheat. 316 (1819).

6. *Ibid.*, at 405.

7. *Ibid.*, at 415.

8. *Ibid.*, at 421.

9. Among these were *Champion v. Ames,* 188 U.S. 321 (1903); *Buttfield v. Stranahan,* 192 U.S. 470 (1904); *Hipolite Egg Co. v. U.S.,* 220 U.S. 45 (1911); *Hoke v. U.S.,* 227 U.S. 308 (1913); *Weber v. Freed,* 239 U.S. 325 (1915); and *Brooks v. U.S.,* 267 U.S. 432 (1925.)

10. These include such matters as narcotics, firearms, alcohol, pure food, prostitution, and traffic safety as they relate to interstate commerce. See the United States Code.

11. See, for example, *NLRB v. Jones & Laughlin Steel Corp.*, 301 U.S. 1 (1937) (application of labor relations law to manufacturing company); *Steward Machine Co. v. Davis*, 301 U.S. 548 (1937) (social security legislation); *U.S. v. Darby*, 312 U.S. 100 (1941) (Federal regulation of industry's wages and hours); *Wickard v. Filburn*, 317 U.S. 111 (1942) (regulation of the marketing of agricultural products); *U.S. v. Sullivan* 332 U.S. 689 (1948) (regulation of drug labelling); and *Perez v. U.S.* 402 U.S. 146 (1971) (credit regulation).

12. 379 U.S. 294 (1964).

13. 392 U.S. 183 (1968).

14. Lockhart, Kamisar, & Choper, *op. cit.* (Chap. Four), p. 238.

15. Sigmund, *op. cit.* (Chap. Nine), pp. 24, 42.

16. Cox, Richard H., "Hugo Grotius," in Strauss & Cropsey, *op. cit.* (Chap. Three), pp. 363-364.

17. Sigmund, p. 64.

18. Corwin, Edward S., *Court Over Constitution: A Study of Judicial Review as an Instrument of Popular Government* (Princeton, N.J.: Princeton Univ. Press, 1983), p. 74. (Hereinafter cited as "Corwin II.")

19. *Ibid.*, p. 73, quoting Richardson, James Daniel, ed., *A Compilation of the Messages and Papers of the Presidents, 1789-1897* (Wash., D.C.: U.S. Govt. Printing Office, 1896-1899), Vol. VI, pp. 9-10.

20. Corwin II, p. 82. Emphasis is his.

21. Corwin presents, in a footnote, another quote from Lincoln which explains what the practical meaning of this view of judicial review is for the Congressmen. In one of his debates with Douglas, Lincoln said: "'All I am doing is refusing to obey [the *Dred Scott* decision] as a political rule. If I were in Congress and a vote should come up on a question whether slavery should be prohibited in a new territory, in spite of the *Dred Scott* decision, I should vote that it should.'" (Corwin II, p. 74, c.f. Sparks, Edwin Erle, ed.,

The Lincoln Douglas Debates of 1858 (Lincoln Series, Vol. II) (Springfield, Ill: Ill. St. Hist. Library, 1908), pp. 29-30.

22. See Hamilton, Federalist 78 in *The Federalist*, pp. 505-506.

23. 8 Co. 118a (1610).

24. 261 U.S. 525 (1923). Justice Sutherland says the following (at 544) (emphasis is mine):

> From the authority to ascertain and determine the law in a given case, there necessarily results, in case of conflict, the duty to declare and enforce the rule of the supreme law and reject that of an inferior act of legislation which, transcending the Constitution, is of no effect and binding on no one. This is not the exercise of a substantive power to nullify acts of Congress, for no such substantive power exists. *It is simply a necessary concomitant of the power to hear and dispose of a case or controversy properly before the Court*, to the determination of which must be brought the test and measure of the law.

25. Berger, Raoul, *Congress v. The Supreme Court* (Cambridge, Mass.: Harvard Univ. Press, 1969), p. 188. (Hereinafter cited as "Berger I.")

26. Berger, I, p. 195, quoting Hart, Henry M., Jr., Book Review, "Professor Crosskey and Judicial Review," in 67 *Harvard L. Rev.* 1456 (1954).

27. This is what, in effect, is involved in the Corwin notion of finality when Congress legislates in a manner which is contrary to a Court decision.

28. Berger I, p. 196.

29. Choper, Jesse H., *Judicial Review and the National Political Process: A Functional Reconsideration of the Role of the Supreme Court* (Chicago: Univ. of Chicago Press, 1980), p. 143.

30. Jackson refused to uphold the Supreme Court's mandate in *The Cherokee Nation v. Georgia*, 5 Pet. (30 U.S.) 1 (1831).

31. 17 F. Cas. 144 (C.C.D. Md., 1861).

32. Choper, p. 145. The attempts, both success and unsuccessful, occurred in 1808, 1821, 1822, 1824, 1825, 1826, 1830, 1831, 1832, 1833, 1846, 1858, 1867, 1868, 1871, 1872, and 1882.

33. *Ibid.* I should mention that one response to *Wade* and *Bolton* which has been proposed is that Congress take away the Supreme Court's jurisdiction over abortion cases. In fact, one of the provisions of the Helms-Hyde Human Life Bill removes such jurisdiction from the *lower* federal courts. Professor Raoul Berger has made a convincing case, based on statements made by the Framers and other early commentators, that Congress was not intended to have the authority to do this under the "exceptions" clause of Article III, Section 2. (See Berger I, pp. 285-296.) However, the very frequency with which it has been attempted from fairly early in our history presents a strong contrary argument to this interpretation. So does the fact that the Court, throughout our history, has repeatedly held that its appellate jurisdiction is strictly a matter for Congressional legislation. (See, for example, *Barry v. Mercein,* 46 103 (1847), *Daniels v. Railroad Co.*, 70 U.S. 250 (1865), and *The Francis Wright,* 105 U.S. 381 (1881).) For a good brief review of the important decisions and discussion, see C. Dickerman Williams, "Congress and the Supreme Court," in *National Review* (Feb. 5, 1982), p. 109. My belief is that it should not be used except as a last resort. A solution should be fashioned which does not undercut the prerogatives of any branch of government and which utilizes a particular branch's prerogatives to check excesses of the other branches. This is what my proposal does.

34. Murphy, Walter F., *Congress and the Court: A Case Study in the American Political Process* (Chicago: Univ. of Chicago Press, 1962), p. 38.

35. These decisions were, respectively, *Hammer v. Dagenhart,* 247 U.S. 251 (1918) and *Bailey v. Drexel Furniture Co.,* 259 U.S. 20 (1922). In the first, Congress had tried to forbid the shipment in interstate commerce of the products of child labor. In the second, it had tried to impose a tax on the net profits of companies that employed child labor.

36. 181 U.S.C., Sec. 3501, 3502.

37. 384 U.S. 436 (1966).

38. 388 U.S. 218 (1967).

39. 328 U.S. 303 (1946).

40. My source for all these twentieth century examples of Congressional resistance is Choper, pp. 142-146.

41. Galebach, pp. 10-17.

42. 100 S. Ct. 2671 (1980).

43. See, for example, Dahl, Robert A., "Decision-Making in a Democracy: The Supreme Court as a National Policy-Maker," in 6 *J. of Pub. Law,* No. 2 (Fall 1957), pp. 279-295 and Funston, Richard Y., "The Supreme Court and Critical Elections," in 69 *Amer. Pol. Sci. Rev.,* No. 3 (Sept. 1975), pp. 795-811. It should be emphasized that these writers point to what the Court has done in the face of solid national political consensuses and over long periods of time. Nevertheless, since most of the public has never endorsed the *Wade/Bolton* formula and because Congress would be directing its strong and determined efforts as the national policy-making body against the Court, I believe that the Dahl-Funston analysis is to some degree applicable. I believe that the Court is especially likely to retreat if it sees that the general public and not just the leadership elite can exert muscle on moral issues such as abortion. Also, the recent trend of the Court to defer to Congress holds out hope for a legislative initiative such as this.
   Consider also the "switch in time" of Justice Owen J. Roberts, which resulted in the Court's suddenly sustaining New Deal legislation. It is perhaps the clearest example in this century of the Court deferring to the wishes of the political majority when pressured to do so by one of the other branches.

44. Berger II, p. 414.

45. See Hamilton, Federalist 78 in *The Federalist,* p. 506. See also Corwin, Edward S., *The Doctrine of Judicial Review: Its Legal and Historical Basis* (Gloucester, Mass.: Peter Smith, 1963), pp. 10-17. (Originally published by Princeton U. Press, 1914.) (Hereinafter cited as "Corwin II."); Beard, Charles A., *The Supreme Court and the Constitution* (Englewood Cliffs, N.J.: Prentice-Hall, 1962), pp. 46-79.

46. Corwin II, pp. 54-65. The departmental right of constitutional construction means, roughly, that the three branches of the national government have the equal right when carrying out their particular functions, to authoritatively interpret the Constitution. It was espoused, at one time or another, by such eminent American political figures as Madi-

son and Jackson. (See Corwin, Edward S., *The Doctrine of Judicial Review: Its Legal and Historical Basis* (Gloucester, Mass.: Peter Smith, 1963), pp. 21, 47-48, 58.)

47. The impact that this proposal might have can be understood when it is considered that 46 of the 101 U.S. Supreme Court Justices in our history have sat on the Court for longer than 15 consecutive years.

APPENDIX B NOTES

1. The assertions made in Section 2 of the Preamble should be substantiated by adding footnotes which present the kind of evidence I have set forth in this book.

2. The bill can easily be extended to prohibit euthanasia, infanticide, etc. by including in the Preamble assertions to show why these harm the general welfare--in some cases the assertions will be the same--and by adding phrases in the text to indicate that the right to life applies until the point of natural death, etc.

Index

A

*As is the case in the text, "abortion," when standing alone, refers to induced abortion. The entry for spontaneous abortion or miscarriage appears separately under "abortion, spontaneous."

E

G

H

I

S

T

About the Author

Stephen M. Krason is the Eastern Director of the Intercollegiate Studies Institute in Bryn Mawr, Pennsylvania. He is also a lawyer. He received his B.A. degree from LaSalle College (now LaSalle University), his M.A. and Ph.D. degrees (both in political science) and law degree (J.D.) from the State University of New York at Buffalo. He was a Richard M. Weaver, Christopher Baldy, and SUNY at Buffalo Graduate School Fellow. He has previously published in *Fidelity, Social Justice Review,* and *Reflections*... He and his wife Therese reside in the Philadelphia area.